# ⇾ THE ⇽

# NORTON
# SAMPLER

## NINTH EDITION

ALSO BY THOMAS COOLEY

*Back to the Lake:*
*A Reader and Guide*

*The Norton Guide to Writing*

*Adventures of Huckleberry Finn,*
*A Norton Critical Edition*

*The Ivory Leg in the Ebony Cabinet:*
*Madness, Race, and Gender in Victorian America*

*Educated Lives:*
*The Rise of Modern Autobiography in America*

# THE
# NORTON
# SAMPLER

## SHORT ESSAYS FOR COMPOSITION

### NINE EDITION

NINTH EDITION

# THOMAS COOLEY

THE OHIO STATE UNIVERSITY

W. W. NORTON & COMPANY
NEW YORK · LONDON

W. W. Norton & Company has been independent since its founding in 1923, when William Warder Norton and Mary D. Herter Norton first published lectures delivered at the People's Institute, the adult education division of New York City's Cooper Union. The firm soon expanded its program beyond the Institute, publishing books by celebrated academics from America and abroad. By midcentury, the two major pillars of Norton's publishing program—trade books and college texts—were firmly established. In the 1950s, the Norton family transferred control of the company to its employees, and today—with a staff of four hundred and a comparable number of trade, college, and professional titles published each year—W. W. Norton & Company stands as the largest and oldest publishing house owned wholly by its employees.

---

*Editor:* Sarah Touborg
*Associate Editor:* Ariella Foss
*Project Editor:* Katie Callahan
*Production Manager:* Jane Searle
*Electronic Media Editor:* Erica Wnek
*Assistant Media Editor:* Ava Bramson
*Editorial Assistant:* Madeline Rombes
*Marketing Manager:* Lib Triplett
*Photo Editor:* Stephanie Romeo
*Photo Researcher:* Fay Torresyap
*Permissions Clearing:* Bethany Salminen
*Designer:* JoAnn Metsch
*Composition:* Jouve North America
*Manufacturing:* LSC Communications, Crawfordsville

ISBN: 978-0-393-60291-3

W. W. Norton & Company, Inc., 500 Fifth Avenue, New York, NY 10110
wwnorton.com

W. W. Norton & Company Ltd., 15 Carlisle Street, London W1D 3BS

1  2  3  4  5  6  7  8  9  0

# CONTENTS

The simplicity of the structure gives it its power—power that can be seen at the memorial every day through the tears shed by veterans taking in their fallen brothers' names. Its lack of ornament gives it a solemn feel that facilitates reflection on those we have lost and the sacrifice they made.

Dreamland could fit hundreds of people, and yet, magically, the space around it kept growing and there was always room for more.

"He's mostly silver, but the silver is somehow made up of *all* the colors, if you know what I mean." I stopped. "Do you know what I mean by colors?"

Miss Dennis always wore a variation of one outfit—a dark-colored, flared woolen skirt, a tailored white blouse and a cardigan sweater, usually black, thrown over her shoulders and held together by a little pearl chain.

Can you see her? I can. And the image of her makes me smile. Still.

As alarming as the Gaines-burgers were, their soy meal began to seem like an old friend when the time came to try some *canned* dog foods.

My grandmother's house is like a chambered nautilus; it has many rooms, yet it is not a mansion. Its proportions are small and its design simple. It is a house that has grown organically, according to the needs of its inhabitants. To all of us in the family it is known as *la casa de Mamá*.

*Annotated Example

To say my grandmother loved Elvis would be like describing the ceiling of the Sistine Chapel as a nice little mural.

"The real heroes are the passengers on Flight 93 who were willing to sacrifice themselves," Penney says. "I was just an accidental witness to history."

The summer I was twelve my family went away on a "vacation"—one of my father's half-baked get-to-know-our-country-better, sleep-in-the-van extravaganzas—and when we returned to Jersey, exhausted, battered, we found our front door unlocked.

Even my mother had an empty Tang bottle with a snug orange nylon net over it, a present from one of her fellow schoolteachers. She carried it from the office to the classroom and back again as if our family had also consumed a full bottle.

Most Americans have never had to live with terror. I had had to live with it all my life—the psychological terror of segregation, in which there was a special set of laws governing your movements. You violated them at your peril. . . .

I was with my teacher, and in a while I was going to sit at my desk, with my crayons and pencils and books and classmates all around me, and for the next six hours I was going to enjoy a thoroughly secure, warm and stable world. It was a world I absolutely relied on. Without it, I don't know where I would have gone that morning.

## 9 ✱ PROCESS ANALYSIS

Straightening my hair became a skill. My mother and I moved on from the wand to a flat iron. We learned words like *anti-frizz* and *heat-protectant.* . . . We traded secrets and shampoos.

Halfway through the summer I was cleaning out a cage that contained several pygmy rattlesnakes, a venomous but not deadly species. One coiled closer to my hand than I'd realized, suddenly uncoiled, and struck me on the left index finger.

No. A chicken would probably have had the sense to get out of the way. This boy was already well on the road to becoming a *man*, having learned one of the central ethics of his gender: Experience pain rather than show fear.

To begin, don't write about yourself. I'm not saying you're uninteresting. I realize that your life has been so crazy no one could make this stuff up. But if you want to be a writer, start by writing about other people.

Every culture comes up with tests of a person's ability to get out of a sticky situation. . . . When they slam the [car] trunk, though, you're helpless unless someone finds you. You would think that such a common worry should have a ready fix, and that the secret of getting out of a locked trunk is something we should all know about.

We live in a culture awash in talk about happiness. In one three-month period last year, more than 1,000 books were released on Amazon on that subject. But notice this phenomenon. When people remember the past, they don't only talk about happiness.

### *MATT TREACY | She 375

My mother is not a woman so much as she is a field of energy. Mom is a force, a kind of aura that only takes human form to be that much more intimidating.

### DAVE BARRY | Guys vs. Men 380

And what, exactly, do I mean by "guys"? I don't know. I haven't thought that much about it. One of the major characteristics of guyhood is that we guys don't spend a lot of time pondering our deep innermost feelings. There is a serious question in my mind about whether guys actually *have* deep innermost feelings unless you count, for example, loyalty to the Detroit Tigers. . . .

### TANYA MARIA BARRIENTOS | Se Habla Español 388

The Spanish language was supposedly the glue that held the new Latino community together. But in my case it was what kept me apart. . . . I wanted to call myself Latina, to finally take pride, but it felt like a lie. So I set out to learn the language that people assumed I already knew.

### GEETA KOTHARI | If You Are What You Eat, Then What Am I? 394

I want to eat what the kids at school eat: bologna, hot dogs, salami—foods my parents find repugnant because they contain pork and meat byproducts, crushed bone and hair glued together by chemicals and fat. . . . Indians, of course, do not eat such things.

### JACK HORNER | The Extraordinary Characteristics of Dyslexia 401

What most non-dyslexics don't know about us, besides the fact that we simply process information differently, is that our early failures often give us an important edge as we grow older.

### MIKE ROSE | Blue-Collar Brilliance 405

I couldn't have put it in words when I was growing up, but what I observed in my mother's restaurant defined the world of adults, a place where competence was synonymous with physical work.

*ELISA GONZALES | Family History   428
I briefly wonder if I have always known that I carried with me more than my father's curly hair and dry sense of humor. But this is impossible . . . It is true, though, that I have always feared my father . . .

TIM WENDEL | King, Kennedy, and the Power of Words   433
After King's assassination, riots broke out in more than 100 U.S. cities—the worst destruction since the Civil War. But neither Memphis nor Indianapolis experienced that kind of damage.

MARISSA NUÑEZ | Climbing the Golden Arches   439
Working at McDonald's has taught me a lot. . . . I'd like to have my own business someday, and working at McDonald's is what showed me I could do that.

MYRIAM MÁRQUEZ | Why and When We Speak Spanish in Public   445
Let me explain why we haven't adopted English as our official family language. For me and most of the bilingual people I know, it's a matter of respect for our parents and comfort in our cultural roots.

MOLLY IVINS | Get a Knife, Get a Dog, but Get Rid of Guns   449
In truth, there is no rational argument for guns in this society. This is no longer a frontier nation in which people hunt their own food.

SONIA SOTOMAYOR | My Beloved World   454
There are uses to adversity, and they don't reveal themselves until tested. Whether it's serious illness, financial hardship, or the simple constraint of parents who speak limited English, difficulty can tap unsuspected strengths.

# 14 * CLASSIC ESSAYS AND SPEECHES

JONATHAN SWIFT | A Modest Proposal  542

I have been assured by a very knowing American of my acquaintance in London, that a young healthy child well nursed is at a year old a most delicious, nourishing, and wholesome food, whether stewed, roasted, baked, or boiled. . . .

THOMAS JEFFERSON | The Declaration of Independence  553

We hold these truths to be self-evident, that all men are created equal, that they are endowed by their Creator with certain unalienable Rights, that among these are Life, Liberty and the pursuit of Happiness.

SOJOURNER TRUTH | Ain't I a Woman?  558

If my cup won't hold but a pint, and yours holds a quart, wouldn't you be mean not to let me have my little half measure full?

ABRAHAM LINCOLN | Second Inaugural Address  561

Both parties deprecated war, but one of them would *make* war rather than let the nation survive, and the other would *accept* war rather than let it perish, and the war came.

ZORA NEALE HURSTON | How It Feels to Be Colored Me  565

But I am not tragically colored. There is no great sorrow dammed up in my soul, nor lurking behind my eyes. I do not mind at all.

MARTIN LUTHER KING JR. | I Have a Dream  571

We have also come to this hallowed spot to remind America of the fierce urgency of Now. This is no time to engage in the luxury of cooling off or to take the tranquilizing drug of gradualism. Now is the time to make real the promises of democracy.

## APPENDIX: USING SOURCES IN YOUR WRITING ...............................577

Finding and Evaluating Sources • Incorporating Source Materials into Your Text • Acknowledging Sources and Avoiding Plagiarism • Documentation • MLA In-Text Documentation • MLA List of Works Cited • Sample Research Paper

# CONTENTS BY THEME

## HOME AND FAMILY

## HUMOR AND SATIRE

## LANGUAGE AND IDENTITY

## LIFE AND DEATH

## MEDIA

## MEMORIES OF YOUTH

## MORALITY AND ETHICS

## NATURE AND THE ENVIRONMENT

## OVERCOMING ADVERSITY

## PUBLIC POLICY

## SCIENCE AND TECHNOLOGY

## SCHOOL AND EDUCATION

## STUDENT WRITING

## WRITERS AND WRITING

# PREFACE

❖————◄━━━►————❖

T HE NORTON SAMPLER is a collection of short essays for composition students illustrating the basic rhetorical patterns of description, narration,
example, classification, process analysis, comparison and contrast, definition,
cause and effect, and argument.

Like the cloth samplers of colonial America that young people made in
order to practice their stitches and ABCs, *The Norton Sampler* assumes that
writing is a practical art that can be learned by studying and applying these
basic, familiar patterns. Each chapter of readings focuses on a single pattern
and includes six or so essays organized primarily around that pattern. Each
reading is followed by study questions and writing prompts.

Most of the model essays in the *Sampler* are only a few pages long, and
even the longest can be easily read in one sitting. The essays are not only short
but complete. I have found over the years that even classic essays are often
reprinted with unacknowledged changes—yet as teachers, we cannot credibly
ask students to study beginnings, middles, and endings or the shape of an
argument if those forms and shapes are not the work of the author. Thus I
have taken pains to include complete essays, or, in a few cases (indicated in
the headnotes), complete chapters of books or sections of longer articles.

Though the chapters and essays in *The Norton Sampler* can be taken up in
any order, the first chapter introduces four basic rhetorical patterns of
writing—description, narration, exposition, and argument—and includes an
analysis of E. B. White's classic essay "Once More to the Lake" to show how
one writer combines several patterns to tell a story. This chapter also shows
students how to read and analyze a text, including the selections in this book,
with an eye to using the various patterns in their own writing. Next come a
brand new chapter on the elements of the essay, a chapter on the writing process, and a chapter on writing paragraphs. The rest of the book takes up the

patterns of writing in greater detail. Chapters 5 and 6 are devoted, respectively, to the basic techniques of description and narration. These are followed by six chapters of exposition, ranging from the simpler techniques of exemplification and classification to the more complex strategies of process analysis, comparison, definition, and cause and effect. Then there is an extended chapter on argument, followed by a chapter of classic essays that demonstrate how the rhetorical patterns work in combination. Finally, there is an appendix on research and documentation, and a glossary/index.

## HIGHLIGHTS

- **Short essays—classic and contemporary—by a diverse group of writers.** There are 65 readings in all with 21 titles new to this edition. All selections cover a variety of topics that should spur students' interests, from such recent pieces as Sonia Sotomayor's account of her childhood and Warren Buffett's essay on taxing the super-rich, to old favorites by Zora Neale Hurston and Sojourner Truth.

- **A new chapter on the elements of the essay,** with expanded coverage of topic, thesis, coherence, tone, and style.

- **One student essay in each chapter of readings—four are new.** Essays by student writers are annotated to show how they illustrate the principles discussed in the chapter, and are the length of papers that students will write themselves.

- **Navigation features** make the book especially easy to use. Notes in the margins explicitly link the readings with writing instructions, and a combined glossary/index provides full definitions of key terms and concepts, serving as an easy reference point for students.

- **Help for students whose primary language is not English,** including glosses for unfamiliar terms and expressions, templates to help students get started writing, and grammar tips.

- **Everyday examples** that show how the patterns taught in this book play an important role across media—from book covers and billboards to packaged goods and road signs.

- **Updated coverage of argument,** with one *new* cluster of readings on the effects of recent technologies upon the human mind and heart, and another cluster on the all-pervading influence of big-time sports on college life.

## WHAT'S ONLINE?

- **Ebook.** Searchable, portable, and interactive. The complete textbook for a fraction of the price. The ebook can be viewed on—and synced between—all computers and mobile devices.

- **InQuizitive for Writers.** Practice editing and have fun doing it with InQuizitive. Adaptive exercises work like a game to help students practice the grammar issues that matter.

- **A companion website** with multimodal readings—one for each pattern in the book; reading comprehension and common error quizzes; and worksheets on revising.

- **Coursepack.** Easily add high-quality Norton resources to your online, hybrid, or lecture course—all at no cost. Norton Coursepacks work within your existing learning management system; there's no new system to learn, and access is free and easy. Find reading quizzes, worksheets, documentation guides, model student papers, and more.

- **An instructor's manual** includes brief answers to study questions in the book.

Find it all at **digital.wwnorton.com/sampler9**.

## ACKNOWLEDGMENTS

There are three people above all whom I want to thank for their work and support on this new edition of *The Norton Sampler*: my wife Barbara Cooley, a gifted technical writer, editor, and blogger; Marilyn Moller, editor extraordinaire, who continues to shape an entire generation of composition texts, including this one; and my hands-on editor at Norton, Ariella Foss, who somehow managed to keep me on schedule. Then there are Julia Reidhead and Rebecca Homiski, constant supporters of the book; and all the other people at Norton who have made possible this and earlier editions, including managing editor Marian Johnson; editor Sarah Touborg; Katie Callahan, who project edited the book and made sure every detail—big and small—got the attention it needed; Jane Searle, who is a masterful production manager; Lib Triplett, who helped spread the word about the book; Bethany Salminen, who cleared the permissions; Stephanie Romeo, who edited all photos; and Fay Torresyap who researched the photos. I'm also grateful to Michal Brody for her excellent work on the instructor's notes and quizzes and to JoAnn Metsch for her superb design.

I am also indebted to Richard Bullock of Wright State University for allowing me to draw from his research and experience in the research appendix, and to Gerald Graff and Cathy Birkenstein, whose work inspired the writing templates in this book.

Among the teachers and composition experts across the country who reviewed this edition in progress and gave me advice on the selections and pedagogy, I wish especially to thank Matthew Allen, Purdue University; Lisa Alvarez, Irvine Valley College; Britt Benshetler, Northwest Vista College; Kathleen A. Bombach, El Paso Community College; Suzanne Bravo, Northwest Vista College; Sarah Bruton, Fayetteville Technical Community College; Kate Cottle, Wilmington University; Mary Elizabeth Darling, Lone Star College—Kingwood; Ashley Dawson, College of Staten Island/CUNY; Nancy England, University of Texas—Arlington; Janice Fioravante, The College of Staten Island; Lisa Fitzgerald, Long Beach City College; Jan Geyer, Hudson Valley Community College; Jessy Goodman, San Jose State University; Kenneth E. Harrison, Jr., Webster University; Renee Iweriebor, Hostos Community College; Christine Pipitone-Herron, Raritan Valley Community College; Margaret Nelson Rodriguez, El Paso Community College; Mauricio Rodriguez, El Paso Community College; Avantika Rohatgi, San Jose State University; Stasha Simon, Petoskey High School; Julie Vega, Sul Ross State University; Courtney Huse Wika, Black Hills State University; Maria Zlateva, Boston University.

Many thanks, too, to my colleagues in composition at Ohio State over the years, including the late Edward P. J. Corbett, who influenced a generation of scholars and teachers of writing; to Roy Rosenstein of the American University of Paris; and to Ron and Elizabeth Beckman of Syracuse University.

Thomas Cooley

# THE
# NORTON
# SAMPLER

NINTH EDITION

# ❧1❧

# READING AS A WRITER

Writing is a little like sewing or weaving. The end product is a written text that must be constructed thread by thread using certain basic patterns and strategies that good writers follow all the time in their work. In fact, the root meaning of *text*, like *textile,* is something *woven*—a fabric of words.

As with any practical art, we learn to write by writing. Many of the fundamental patterns and strategies of writing that we all must master if we're to construct tightly woven texts of our own, however, we learn in part by reading the work of other writers. Thus we'll be reading the essays in this book *as writers*, with an eye for what we can learn from them about writing. Coolly and systematically (but maybe with a little passion), we'll pay close attention to how the pieces fit together—and how we can use those same techniques in our own work. In this chapter, we'll start by focusing on a classic American essay about a father and son who go fishing together on a tranquil lake in Maine—E. B. White's "Once More to the Lake" (1941).

Years ago, as a young assistant professor of English and teacher of writing, I rashly fired off a letter to White asking him how he wrote this famous piece—and why. To my astonishment, White not only responded, he said he didn't really know how he wrote anything. (His carefully composed letter appears on page 3.) "The process," White confided, "is probably as mysterious to me as it is to some of your students—if that will make them feel any better." In case it doesn't, this chapter and, indeed, the rest of this book, are for you as a writer looking to polish your own writing skills.

Fortunately, we've come a long way toward demystifying the writing process since the days when White went back to the lake and wrote his masterful account of that experience. We've

Does writing seem mysterious to you? See Chapter 3 for a step-by-step guide to the process.

firmly established, for example, that writing well is closely tied to reading well. Of course, you don't have to read every book or article that was ever written in order to be a good writer, but you do need to read *some* texts closely, with a critical eye as to how they're put together. In this chapter, we'll start with some general strategies for reading as a writer; then we'll turn to specific questions you can use to analyze White's classic essay—and the other essays in this book.

## SOME STRATEGIES FOR READING AS A WRITER

When you read any text, you generally engage in several activities: previewing the text, reading closely and critically, and responding to what you read. Let's take a look at each of these steps.

### Previewing the Text

Before you plunge into a text, take a few moments to survey the territory. Try to get a sense of where the text is going and what you want to focus on. Here are some tips for previewing the readings in this book:

- *Look at the headnote* to learn about the author and the original context—the time, place, and circumstances in which the text was written and published.
- *Think about the title.* What does it reveal about the topic and TONE* of the text? Does it point to a serious argument? Does it poke fun at its subject? Something else?
- *Skim the text for an overview,* noting headings, boldfaced words, and lists.
- *Skim the introduction and conclusion.* What insights do they give you into the purpose and message of the text?
- *Think about your own purpose for reading.* Do you want to obtain information, confirm a fact or opinion, fulfill an assignment? How will your purpose affect what you focus on?

*Words printed in SMALL CAPITALS are defined in the Glossary/Index.

## Letter from E. B. White

I'm not an expert on what goes on under my hood, but I'll try to answer your questions.

When I wrote "Once More to the Lake," I was living year round in this place on the coast of Maine and contributing a monthly department to *Harper's*. I had spent many summers as a boy on Great Pond—one of the Belgrade Lakes. It's only about 75 miles from here and one day I felt an urge to revisit the lake and have a week of freshwater life, which is very different from saltwater. So I went over with my small son and we did some fishing. I simply started with a desire to see again and experience again what I had seen and experienced as a boy. During our stay over there, the "idea of time" naturally insinuated itself into my thoughts, because my son was the age *I* had been in the previous life at the lake, and so I felt a sort of mixed-up identity. I don't recall whether I had the title from the start. Probably not. I don't believe the title had anything to do with the composing process. The "process" is probably every bit as mysterious to me as it is to some of your students—if that will make them feel any better. As for the revising I did, it was probably quite a lot. I always revise the hell out of everything. It's the only way I know how to write. I came up with the "chilling ending" simply because I was describing a bodily sensation of my own. When my son drew on his wet bathing trunks, it was as though I were drawing them on myself. I was old enough to feel the chill of death. I guess.

Sorry I can't be more explicit. Writing, for me, is simply a matter of trying to find out and report what's going on in my head and get it down on paper. I haven't any devices, shortcuts, or tricks.

*January 22, 1984*

# Reading Closely and Critically

Reading a text closely and critically is a little like investigating a crime scene. You look for certain clues; you ask certain questions. Your objective is to determine, as precisely and accurately as you can, both what the text has to say and how it says it. Your primary clues, therefore, are in the text itself—the actual words on the page.

If you've previewed the text, you already have some idea of what it's about. Now is the time to examine it closely. So pull out your pencil and highlighter, and annotate the text as you go along—jot down questions or comments in the margins, underline important points, circle key words, and mark places you may want to come back to. Here are some questions you might ask yourself as you read:

- *What is the writer's main point?* Is it clearly stated in a thesis? If so, where? If the main point is not stated directly, is it clearly implied?

- *What is the writer's primary purpose?* To provide information? Sell a product or service? Argue a point of view? Make us laugh? Tell a story? What's motivated the author to write—is he or she responding to something others have said?

- *Who is the intended audience?* Readers who are familiar with the topic? Those who know little about it? People inclined to agree—or disagree? How can you tell?

- *What is the tone of the text?* Serious? Informal? Inspirational? Strident?

- *How and where does the writer support the main point?* Look for specific details, facts, examples, expert testimony, or other kinds of evidence.

- *Is the evidence sufficient?* Or does it fail to convince you? Are sources clearly identified so that you can tell where the material is coming from?

- *Has the writer fairly represented—and responded to—other points of view?* Has any crucial perspective been left out?

- *What is the larger historical and cultural context?* Who is the author? When was the text written? What ideas or events does it reflect?

## Responding to What You Read

After you have read and reread a text closely, think about and respond to it in writing. Here are a few tips for doing so:

- *Summarize what you've read in your own words.* If you can write a brief, accurate SUMMARY of the main point, you probably have a good grasp of what you've read.

- *Think about and record your own reactions.* Where are you most inclined to accept the writer's ideas? Least inclined? Aren't sure? Indicate specific passages in the text where you think the writer's ideas are particularly well presented, whether you agree with those ideas or not.

- *Consider what you've learned about writing.* Note any techniques that you might want to try in your own writing, such as a strong introduction, cogent use of examples, apt choice of words, or striking use of visuals.

# IDENTIFYING COMMON PATTERNS

Like writing, reading is an active process. Even when you take a thriller to the woods or beach and read just for fun, your brain is busily at work translating the words on the page into mental images and ideas. It's even busier when you read to see what a text has to offer you as a writer. Let's now consider some of the common patterns of writing that we'll be looking for as we explore the texts in this book.

Suppose you went on a camping trip in the mountains. After settling in and doing a little fishing and hiking, you text the following messages to a friend:

- nce hr bt bggy & chly
- ptchd tnt, lnchd cnoe, cght 2 bass
- fsh bggr thn last yr
- vry rlxng, u shld cm

These four text messages—and they're still *texts*, whether composed with a pencil or on a smartphone—are examples, however brief, of four traditional types of writing: description, narration, exposition, and argument. These basic patterns of writing can be defined as follows:

- DESCRIPTION appeals to the reader's senses. Descriptive writing tells what something looks, feels, sounds, smells, or tastes like ("nice here but buggy"). Patterns and methods of description are discussed in Chapter 5.

- NARRATION is storytelling. Narrative writing focuses on events; it tells what happened ("pitched tent, launched canoe, caught two bass"). Patterns and methods of narration are discussed in Chapter 6.

- EXPOSITION is informative writing ("the fish are bigger this year than they were last year"), and it is the form of writing you are likely to use most often. Exposition explains by giving EXAMPLES (Chapter 7); by CLASSIFYING (Chapter 8); by analyzing a PROCESS (Chapter 9); by COMPARING AND CONTRASTING, (Chapter 10); by DEFINING (Chapter 11); and by analyzing CAUSES AND EFFECTS (Chapter 12). Exams, research papers, job applications, sales reports, insurance claims—in fact, almost every kind of practical writing you do over a lifetime, including your last will and testament—will require expository skills.

- ARGUMENT is persuasive writing. It makes a claim and offers evidence that the writer hopes will be sufficient to convince the reader to accept that claim—and perhaps even to act on it ("it's very relaxing here; you should come"). Patterns, methods, and strategies of argument are discussed in detail in Chapter 13.

With these basic patterns of writing in mind, let's read E. B. White's "Once More to the Lake." If we can grasp how White uses these common patterns to create such a fine piece of work, we'll be well on our way to using them in our own writing.

## E. B. WHITE

# ONCE MORE TO THE LAKE

ELWYN BROOKS WHITE (1899–1985) was born in Mount Vernon, New York. After graduating from Cornell University in 1921, he worked as a journalist and advertising copywriter before joining the staff of the *New Yorker* in 1926. He also wrote a regular column for *Harper's*. White's numerous books include the children's classics *Stuart Little* (1945) and *Charlotte's Web* (1952), as well as *The Elements of Style* (1959), a guide to writing that updates the work of his teacher William Strunk. "Once More to the Lake," which originally appeared in *Harper's*, was written in August 1941, just a few months before the United States entered World War II. The lake described here is Great Pond, one of the Belgrade Lakes in Maine. When White returns to the familiar scene, it seems unchanged—at first.

O NE SUMMER, ALONG ABOUT 1904, my father rented a camp on a lake in    1
Maine and took us all there for the month of August. We all got ringworm from some kittens and had to rub Pond's Extract on our arms and legs night and morning, and my father rolled over in a canoe with all his clothes

on; but outside of that the vacation was a success and from then on none of us ever thought there was any place in the world like that lake in Maine. We returned summer after summer—always on August 1 for one month. I have since become a salt-water man, but sometimes in summer there are days when the restlessness of the tides and the fearful cold of the sea water and the incessant wind that blows across the afternoon and into the evening make me wish for the placidity of a lake in the woods. A few weeks ago this feeling got so strong I bought myself a couple of bass hooks and a spinner and returned to the lake where we used to go, for a week's fishing and to revisit old haunts.

I took along my son, who had never had any fresh water up his nose and   2 who had seen lily pads only from train windows. On the journey over to the lake I began to wonder what it would be like. I wondered how the time would have marred this unique, this holy spot—the coves and streams, the hills that the sun set behind, the camps and the paths behind the camps. I was sure that the tarred road would have found it out, and I wondered in what other ways it would be desolated. It is strange how much you can remember about places like that once you allow your mind to return into the grooves that lead back. You remember one thing, and that suddenly reminds you of another thing. I guess I remembered clearest of all the early mornings, when the lake was cool and motionless, remembered how the bedroom smelled of the lumber it was made of and of the wet woods whose scent entered through the screen. The partitions in the camp were thin and did not extend clear to the top of the rooms, and as I was always the first up I would dress softly so as not to wake the others, and sneak out into the sweet outdoors and start out in the canoe, keeping close along the shore in the long shadows of the pines. I remembered being very careful never to rub my paddle against the gunwale for fear of disturbing the stillness of the cathedral.

The lake had never been what you would call a wild lake. There were cot-   3 tages sprinkled around the shores, and it was in farming country although the shores of the lake were quite heavily wooded. Some of the cottages were owned by nearby farmers, and you would live at the shore and eat your meals at the farmhouse. That's what our family did. But although it wasn't wild, it was a fairly large and undisturbed lake and there were places in it that, to a child at least, seemed infinitely remote and primeval.

I was right about the tar: it led to within half a mile of the shore. But   4
when I got back there, with my boy, and we settled into a camp near a farmhouse and into the kind of summertime I had known, I could tell that it was
going to be pretty much the same as it had been before—I knew it, lying in bed
the first morning, smelling the bedroom and hearing the boy sneak quietly out
and go off along the shore in a boat. I began to sustain the illusion that he was
I, and therefore, by simple transposition, that I was my father. This sensation
persisted, kept cropping up all the time we were there. It was not an entirely
new feeling, but in this setting, it grew much stronger. I seemed to be living a
dual existence. I would be in the middle of some simple act, I would be picking
up a bait box or laying down a table fork, or I would be saying something, and
suddenly it would be not I but my father who was saying the words or making
the gesture. It gave me a creepy sensation.

We went fishing the first morning. I felt the same damp moss covering   5
the worms in the bait can, and saw the dragonfly alight on the tip of my rod as
it hovered a few inches from the surface of the water. It was the
arrival of this fly that convinced me beyond any doubt that everything was as it always had been, that the years were a mirage and
that there had been no years. The small waves were the same,

See p. 72 on how concrete physical details can bring abstract ideas down to earth.

chucking the rowboat under the chin as we fished at anchor, and the boat was
the same boat, the same color green and the ribs broken in the same places,
and under the floorboards the same freshwater leavings and débris—the dead
helgrammite,[1] the wisps of moss, the rusty discarded fishhook, the dried blood
from yesterday's catch. We stared silently at the tips of our rods, at the dragonflies that came and went. I lowered the tip of mine into the water, tenta-
tively, pensively dislodging the fly, which darted two feet away, poised, darted
two feet back, and came to rest again a little farther up the rod. There had been
no years between the ducking of this dragonfly and the other one—the one
that was part of memory. I looked at the boy, who was silently watching his
fly, and it was my hands that held his rod, my eyes watching. I felt dizzy and
didn't know which rod I was at the end of.

We caught two bass, hauling them in briskly as though they were mack-   6
erel, pulling them over the side of the boat in a businesslike manner without

1. Larvae of the dobsonfly.

any landing net, and stunning them with a blow on the back of the head. When we got back for a swim before lunch, the lake was exactly where we had left it, the same number of inches from the dock, and there was only the merest suggestion of a breeze. This seemed an utterly enchanted sea, this lake you could leave to its own devices for a few hours and come back to, and find that it had not stirred, this constant and trustworthy body of water. In the shallows, the dark, water-soaked sticks and twigs, smooth and old, were undulating in clusters on the bottom against the clean ribbed sand, and the track of the mussel was plain. A school of minnows swam by, each minnow with its small individual shadow, doubling the attendance, so clear and sharp in the sunlight. Some of the other campers were in swimming, along the shore, one of them with a cake of soap, and the water felt thin and clear and unsubstantial. Over the years there had been this person with the cake of soap, this cultist, and here he was. There had been no years.

Up to the farmhouse to dinner through the teeming, dusty field, the road 7 under our sneakers was only a two-track road. The middle track was missing, the one with the marks of the hooves and the splotches of dried, flaky manure. There had always been three tracks to choose from in choosing which track to walk in; now the choice was narrowed down to two. For a moment I missed terribly the middle alternative. But the way led past the tennis court, and something about the way it lay there in the sun reassured me; the tape had loosened along the backline, the alleys were green with plantains and other weeds, and the net (installed in June and removed in September) sagged in the dry noon, and the whole place steamed with midday heat and hunger and emptiness. There was a choice of pie for dessert, and one was blueberry and one was apple, and the waitresses were the same country girls, there having been no passage of time, only the illusion of it as in a dropped curtain—the waitresses were still fifteen; their hair had been washed, that was the only difference—they had been to the movies and seen the pretty girls with the clean hair.

Summertime, oh, summertime, pattern of life indelible, the fade-proof 8 lake, the woods unshatterable, the pasture with the sweetfern and the juniper forever and ever, summer without end; this was the background, and the life along the shore was the design, the cottages with their innocent and tranquil design, their tiny docks with the flagpole and the American flag floating against tight the white clouds in the blue sky, the little paths over the roots of the trees leading from camp to camp and the paths leading back to the out-houses and the can of lime for sprinkling, and at the souvenir counters at the store the miniature birch-bark canoes and the postcards that showed things looking a little better than they looked. This was the American family at play, escaping the city heat, wondering whether the newcomers in the camp at the head of the cove were "common" or "nice," wondering whether it was true that the people who drove up for Sunday dinner at the farmhouse were turned away because there wasn't enough chicken.

It seemed to me, as I kept remembering all this, that those times and those summers had been infinitely precious and worth saving. There had been jollity and peace and goodness. The arriving (at the beginning of August) had been so big a business in itself, at the railway station the farm wagon drawn up, the first smell of the pine-laden air, the first glimpse of the smiling farmer, and the great importance of the trunks and your father's enormous authority in such matters, and the feel of the wagon under you for the long ten-mile haul, and at the top of the last long hill catching the first view of the lake after eleven months of not seeing this cherished body of water. The shouts and cries of the other campers when they saw you, and the trunks to be unpacked, to give up their rich burden. (Arriving was less exciting nowadays, when you sneaked up in your car and parked it under a tree near the camp and took out the bags and in five minutes it was all over, no fuss, no loud wonderful fuss about trunks.)

See p. 73 on the importance of stating your point.

Peace and goodness and jollity. The only thing that was wrong now, really, was the sound of the place, an unfamiliar nervous sound of the outboard motors. This was the note that jarred, the one thing that would sometimes break the illusion and set the years moving. In those other summertimes all motors were inboard; and when they were at a little distance, the noise they made was a sedative, an ingredient of summer sleep. They were one-cylinder and two-cylinder engines, and some were make-and-break and some were jump-spark, but they all made a sleepy sound across the lake. The one-lungers throbbed and fluttered, and the twin-cylinder ones purred and purred, and that was a quiet sound, too. But now the campers all had outboards. In the daytime, in the hot mornings, these motors made a petulant, irritable sound; at night, in the still evening when the afterglow lit the water, they whined about one's ears like mosquitoes. My boy loved our rented outboard, and his great desire was to achieve single-handed mastery over it, and authority, and he soon learned the trick of choking it a little (but not too much), and the adjustment of the needle valve. Watching him I would remember the things you could do with the old one-cylinder engine with the heavy flywheel, how you could have it eating out of your hand if you got really close to it spiritually. Motorboats in those days didn't have clutches, and you would make a landing by shutting off the motor at the proper time and coasting in with a dead rudder. But there was a way of reversing them, if you learned the trick, by cutting the switch and putting it on again exactly on the final dying revolution of the flywheel, so that it would kick back against compression and begin reversing. Approaching a dock in a strong following breeze, it was difficult to slow up sufficiently by the ordinary coasting method, and if a boy felt he had complete mastery over his motor, he was tempted to keep it running beyond its time and then reverse it a few feet from the dock. It took a cool nerve, because if you threw the switch a twentieth of a second too soon you would catch the flywheel when it still had speed enough to go up past center, and the boat would leap ahead, charging bull-fashion at the dock.

We had a good week at the camp. The bass were biting well and the sun 11 shone endlessly, day after day. We would be tired at night and lie down in the accumulated heat of the little bedrooms after the long hot day and the breeze would stir almost imperceptibly outside and the smell of the swamp drift in through the rusty screens. Sleep would come easily and in the morning the red squirrel would be on the roof, tapping out his gay routine. I kept remembering everything, lying in bed in the mornings—the small steamboat that had a long rounded stern like the lip of a Ubangi, and how quietly she ran on the moonlight sails, when the older boys played their mandolins and the girls sang and we ate doughnuts dipped in sugar, and how sweet the music was on the water in the shining night, and what it had felt like to think about girls then. After breakfast, we would go up to the store and the things were in the same place— the minnows in a bottle, the plugs and spinners disarranged and pawed over by tight the youngsters from the boys' camp, the Fig Newtons and the Beeman's gum. Outside, the road was tarred and cars stood in front of the store. Inside, all was just as it had always been, except there was more Coca-Cola and not so much Moxie[2] and root beer and birch beer and sarsaparilla. We would walk out with the bottle of pop apiece and sometimes the pop would backfire up our noses and hurt. We explored the streams, quietly, where the turtles slid off logs and dug their way into the soft bottom; and we lay on the town wharf and fed worms to the tame bass. Everywhere we went I had trouble making out which was I, the one walking at my side, the one walking in my pants.

One afternoon while we were there at that lake a thunderstorm came up. It was like the revival of an old melodrama that I had seen long ago with childish awe. The second-act climax of the drama of the electrical disturbance over a lake in America has not changed in any important respect. This was the big scene, still the big scene. The whole thing was so familiar, the first feeling of oppression and heat and a general air around camp of not wanting to go very far away. In midafternoon (it was all the same) a curious darkening of the sky, and a lull in everything that had made life tick; and then the way the boats suddenly swung the other way at their moorings with the coming of a breeze out of the new quarter, and the premonitory rumble. Then the kettle drum, then the snare, then the bass drum and cymbals, then crackling light against the dark, and the gods grinning and licking their chops in the hills. Afterward the calm, the rain steadily rustling in the calm lake, the return of light and hope and spirits, and the campers running out in joy and relief to go swimming in the rain, their bright cries perpetuating the deathless joke about how they were getting simply drenched, and the children screaming with delight at the new sensation of bathing in the rain, and the joke about getting drenched linking the generations in a strong indestructible chain. And the comedian who waded in carrying an umbrella.

When the others went swimming, my son said he was going in, too. He pulled his dripping trunks from the line where they had hung all through the shower and wrung them out. Languidly, and with no thought of going in, I watched him, his hard little body, skinny and bare, saw him wince slightly as he pulled up around his vitals the small, soggy, icy garment. As he buckled the swollen belt, suddenly my groin felt the chill of death.

2. Brand name of an old-fashioned soft drink.

## FOR DISCUSSION

1. When and why did E. B. White return with his young son to the lake he himself had visited as a boy?

2. In paragraph 2, is White describing the lake as it was in the past, or as it is in the present time of his essay? How about in paragraphs 4–6? And in paragraph 11? Explain your answers.

3. In addition to the lake, White is also describing "the American family at play" (8). What qualities and attributes does he identify as particularly "American"?

4. Do American families still take summer vacations "at the lake"? How has the pattern of family play—on a lake or elsewhere—changed since White wrote his classic essay? How has it remained the same?

## STRATEGIES AND STRUCTURES

1. In his description of the "primeval" lake, what qualities does White emphasize (3)? Point out particular details in his description that you find particularly effective. What is his main point in citing them?

2. Is White's description of the lake more **OBJECTIVE** or **SUBJECTIVE**? Or both at different times? Explain.

3. What **DOMINANT IMPRESSION** does White's description create? How?

4. When he returned to the lake with his young son, the two of them, says White, went fishing "the first morning" (5). Point out other direct references to time in White's essay. How does he use chronology and the passing of time to organize his entire description?

5. One way in which the lake of his childhood has definitely changed, says White, is in its sounds. What new sounds does he describe? How does he incorporate this change into his description of the lake as a timeless place?

6. How would White's essay be different without the last paragraph, in which he watches his young son get ready to go swimming?

## WORDS AND FIGURES OF SPEECH

1. What's the difference between an "illusion" and a "mirage" (4, 5)? Which is White describing here at times? Explain.

2. When he describes the lake as not only "constant" but "trustworthy" (6), White has **PERSONIFIED** the natural scene. Where else does he use this figure of speech and why?

3. Why does White repeat the word *same* in paragraph 5?

4. As a boy on the lake, White did not want to disturb the "stillness of the cathedral" (2). What are the implications of this phrase? In what ways is White's son depicted as a chip off the old block?

5. How does White's reference to "a dropped curtain" (7) anticipate his description of the storm at the end of his essay?

## FOR WRITING

1. Think back to a memorable family vacation or other outing. What do you recall most clearly about it and why? Make a list of the details—objects, sounds, smells, tastes, colors, textures—that you remember.

2. Using your list of details as a basis, write a few paragraphs describing the vacation or outing and where you went and what you did there. Consider describing how the place has changed since you first visited and how it remains the same.

## HOW E. B. WHITE USES COMMON PATTERNS
## IN "ONCE MORE TO THE LAKE"

E. B. White uses several common patterns of writing in his classic essay. Let's go through the text point by point with some of these patterns in mind.

White begins his essay with a phrase pertaining to time: "One summer, along about 1904." He might as well have written, "Once upon a time," as the opening paragraph takes place long ago and is almost pure narrative. NARRATIVE writing tells about something that happened. White's narrative focuses on a particular occasion "a few weeks ago" when, as an adult, he took his young son to fish for the first time on a freshwater lake in Maine where White himself vacationed when he was a boy (1). What follows is an account of the ordinary events that take place during that brief visit, leading up to a CLIMAX at the end of the week when a storm gathers over the lake, and the writer suddenly feels older as his son puts on his wet bathing suit.

In addition to telling a story, "Once More to the Lake" is a superb piece of DESCRIPTIVE writing. White describes the lake itself as "fairly large and undisturbed" (3). Its shores are "heavily wooded"; and the whole place feels remote, despite some cottages "sprinkled around" the water (3). When White goes fishing the first morning, he pictures the boat in vivid, CONCRETE detail: "the dead helgrammite, the wisps of moss, the rusty discarded fishhook, the dried blood from yesterday's catch" (5). And, of course, there are the dragonflies: "We stared silently at the tips of our rods, at the dragonflies that came and went" (5). The DOMINANT IMPRESSION we get of the lake and its surroundings here is one of tranquility and timelessness—at first.

White is not only narrating a story and describing a place; he is COMPARING AND CONTRASTING his sensations of that place in the present with those of the past. At first, everything seems "pretty much the same as it had been before" (4). The water is still "cool and motionless"; the bedroom still smells "of the lumber it was made of" (2); and the rowboat is "the same boat, the same color green and the ribs broken in the same places" (5). White's comparison shades into contrast, however, as the tranquil scene is interrupted by the "unfamiliar nervous sound of the outboard motors" (10). In the past, White explains, the noise of the motors was peaceful. Now, however, the boats are more powerful and "whine . . . like mosquitoes" in the night (10). At the end of the essay, the peace and calm of the lake are also interrupted by a thunderstorm. Using various SIMILES and METAPHORS, White likens the gathering storm to a scene in a drama: the thunder sounds first like a "kettle drum"; then comes "the snare, then the bass drum and cymbals"; lightning flashes against the dark sky; and, as in a Greek tragedy, "the gods" grin from the hills (12). Why this sudden turn of events in an otherwise peaceful scene from the life of the American family on vacation? Are the gods grinning, perhaps, at the swimmers' sense of security?

White's essay was published just a few months before the United States entered World War II, and in the background lurks his suspicion that the world is about to change forever. By comparing the apparent similarities between his past and present experiences at the lake, White is constructing an ARGUMENT about time and change. As the boy prepares to go swimming in the lake in the rain, White cannot escape the realization that time has actually passed since he last visited the place. As he grows older, and war lies just around the corner, he concludes that the generations are bound not only by "the return of light and hope and spirits" (12) after a storm, but also by the reality of change and "the chill of death" (13). The dream of "summer without end," no matter how warmly inspired by nature and fond memories of childhood, is just that—a dream (8).

White makes his point by weaving together various strands of narrative, description, comparison and contrast, and argument. When you compose a text, let the great writers you have read guide you. In the end, however, you should choose the particular patterns (or perhaps a single pattern) of development that best fit the particular point you have to make—and your singular audience and purpose in writing.

## USING THE STUDY QUESTIONS TO FOCUS YOUR READING

When you interrogate a text as a writer, you need to ask certain general questions about the text; you also need to get down to specifics as soon as you can. To help you focus your reading more clearly, each of the sample essays in the main chapters of this book is followed by a set of questions, with writing prompts about specific details and issues pertaining to that text. These study questions and prompts are the teaching heart of the book; they encourage you to approach each reading in the following ways:

- *For Discussion*. These questions are intended to help you look at the text as an exchange of ideas between a writer and a reader. They prompt you to read in order to understand what the text is saying and to discover your own views on the subject under discussion. In other words, these are questions that will help you to think about what the author is saying and then to consider what you think, and why.

- *Strategies and Structures*. These questions will help you to recognize and understand how the text is constructed—to think about what patterns and techniques the authors have used to organize their ideas and present them to an AUDIENCE, and to imagine how you might use them in your own writing.

- *Words and Figures of Speech*. These questions focus on the language and STYLE of the text. They're designed to help you think about both the literal and figurative meanings of specific words and phrases.

- *For Writing*. These are prompts that will help you get started, in some cases by suggesting topics to write about, and in other instances by asking questions to help you respond to whatever the author of the reading has said.

# ❧2❧

# ELEMENTS OF THE ESSAY:
# TOPIC, THESIS, COHERENCE,
# TONE, AND STYLE

L IKE many other things, an essay is composed of certain fundamental ele-ments. Works of art, for example, have form, line, color, space, and tex-ture; musical compositions are made up of rhythm, pitch, tempo, and volume; and in the field of chemistry, a compound like water ($H_2O$) is a combination of such physical elements as hydrogen and oxygen.

Essays are made up of ideas, and ideas are not substances in the same sense as those that make up chemical compounds. With any essay you write, however, we can speak of both its content (what you have to say) and its form (how you say it). Most essays have an introduction, a body, and a conclusion as part of their basic form. In this chapter, we'll focus on the elements of the essay that will be most important for communicating what you have to say, whether you're telling a story, drawing comparisons, analyzing a process, making an argument, or something else.

There are no simple formulas for writing a good essay. Fortunately, how-ever, the basic elements that you can use to make meaning in an essay are far fewer than the 118 chemical elements in the standard periodic table. In this chapter, we'll boil them down to just five: topic, thesis, coherence, tone, and style.

# TOPIC

Although we often lump the two together, the TOPIC* of an essay is not the same as the SUBJECT. A subject is a broad field of inquiry; a topic is a specific area within that field. For example, if you're writing about the use of drugs in professional baseball, *baseball* is your subject and *the use of drugs in baseball* is your topic. The following subjects, for instance, are too broad to be manageable topics in an essay: education, college sports, science, pets.

A good topic focuses on a particular aspect of your general subject. It is your subject narrowed down to a manageable scope and size for the length of the composition you're writing. The following are more specific areas within general fields and would make more manageable topics for an essay:

- The advantages of attending a community college rather than a university
- The rewards of college sports
- Studying science as a profession
- Choosing a pet

Here's a template that can help you get started as you look for a meaningful topic to write about in an essay:

> ▸ Within the general subject of _____, what I want to write about specifically is _____.

Here's just one way you might fill in the blanks, for example:

> ▸ Within the general subject of <u>higher education</u>, what I want to write about specifically is <u>the advantage of attending a community college</u>.

# THESIS

In any essay you write, your topic is the specific aspect of your subject you plan to focus on. Your THESIS is what you have to say about that topic—the

*Words printed in SMALL CAPITALS are defined in the Glossary/Index.

main point you want to make about it. That point is usually set forth in a thesis statement. Here are some examples taken from essays in this book:

> I believe the community college system to be one of America's uniquely great institutions.
>
> —LIZ ADDISON, "Two Years Are Better Than Four"

> No, college athletics is not *about* the players. College athletics is FOR the players.
>
> —JOE POSNANSKI, "College Athletes Should Not Be Paid"

> Whether it's serious illness, financial hardship, or the simple constraint of parents who speak limited English, difficulty can tap unsuspected strengths.
>
> —SONIA SOTOMAYOR, *My Beloved World*

The following template can help get you started as you figure out the main point you want to make (the thesis) about your topic in an essay:

> ▶ The main point I want to make about _____ is that _____.

You might fill in the blanks like this:

> ▶ The main point I want to make about <u>competitive college sports</u> is that <u>the players should be paid</u>.

Once you've come up with a thesis that makes a particular point about a specific topic, you may need to limit it further by using such qualifiers as *possibly, may be, often, in some cases, for most people, in this situation.* Liz Addison qualifies her thesis about the unique value of community colleges, for example, by saying "I believe" it to be true. The purpose of qualifying a thesis is to make it narrower and, thus, easier to support. Addison's thesis would be pretty strong even if she just said "the community college system is a uniquely great institution"; by qualifying this statement with "in America" and "I believe," however, she defines the scope of her argument more explicitly.

# Where to Position a Thesis Statement

**THESIS STATEMENT AT THE BEGINNING OF THE ESSAY.** A direct statement of your thesis can appear anywhere in your essay. Most often, however, it should come near the beginning and help to set up the rest of what you have to say, as in this example from the opening paragraph of a humorous piece on the English language:

> English is the most widely spoken language in the history of our planet, used in some way by at least one out of every seven human beings around the globe. Half of the world's books are written in English, and the majority of international phone calls are made in English . . .
>
> Nonetheless, it is now time to face the fact that English is a crazy language.
>
> —RICHARD LEDERER, "English Is a Crazy Language"

From this statement in the second paragraph of his essay, Lederer goes on to provide one example after another of linguistic "craziness" to support his claim: "no egg in eggplant, no grape in grapefruit . . . and no ham in hamburger."

**THESIS STATEMENT IN THE BODY OF THE ESSAY.** Building up to a thesis is almost as common a pattern in essay writing as building down from one. Consider the following thesis statement from an essay about the social and psychological effects of computer and video games:

> Those who continue to dismiss games as merely escapist entertainment will find themselves at a major disadvantage in the years ahead, as more gamers start to harness this power for real good. My research over the past decade at the University of California, Berkeley, and the Institute for the Future has shown that games consistently provide us with the four ingredients that make for a happy and meaningful life: satisfying work, real hope for success, strong social connections and the chance to become a part of something bigger than ourselves.
>
> —JANE MCGONIGAL, "Be a Gamer, Save the World"

This thesis statement about the power of computer and video games to do "real good" in the world comes about a third of the way into the body of

McGonigal's essay. To lead up to this statement of the specific benefits of gaming as she sees them, McGonigal first addresses the common claim that games are distractions. In the rest of her essay, she then goes point by point through each of the four benefits that she cites here.

**THESIS STATEMENT AT THE END OF THE ESSAY.** When your thesis statement comes at the end of an essay, it can both sum up what you have to say and also give your reader a satisfying sense of closure. See how a renowned biologist explains, in the last paragraph of his essay, how he became a successful scientist:

> My confessional . . . is intended to illustrate an important principle I've seen unfold in the careers of many successful scientists. It is quite simple: put passion ahead of training.
> —EDWARD O. WILSON, "First Passion, Then Training"

The point of Wilson's story is not simply that he always put passion ahead of training in the pursuit of his own career. As stated in these words from the final paragraph of his narrative, his thesis is that following one's passions is an "important principle" of success in general, at least among scientists.

**IMPLIED THESIS.** In the following passage, by another successful scientist, the message is only implied rather than stated explicitly. The writer, who died in 2015 at age eighty-two, is speaking about a chemical element on his desk:

> Bismuth is element 83. I do not think I will see my 83rd birthday, but I feel there is something hopeful, something encouraging, about having "83" around. Moreover, I have a soft spot for bismuth, a modest gray metal, often unregarded, ignored, even by metal lovers. My feeling as a doctor for the mistreated or marginalized extends into the inorganic world and finds a parallel in my feeling for bismuth.
> —OLIVER SACKS, "My Periodic Table"

Sacks is writing about bismuth most explicitly, but he is also making a larger point about the importance of passion in the pursuit of science and medicine.

Diane Guerrero
concludes her essay
with a thesis that
also proposes a
solution, p. 488.

However you choose to develop your thesis, it's probably always a good idea to restate it at the end of an essay. Sacks himself did this in an essay he wrote at the end of his life when he noted that it "has been an enormous privilege and adventure" to be "a sentient being, a thinking animal, on this beautiful planet" ("My Own Life," 2015).

# COHERENCE

COHERENCE in writing has to mainly do with meaning, with what you have to say. A piece of writing is coherent when every idea in the text is clear—and clearly related to every other idea.

Consider the following example from one student's response to a writing prompt that "the best way for a society to prepare its young people for leadership in government, industry, or other fields is by instilling in them a sense of cooperation, not competition":

> Some may argue that competition is not needed. That those that are meant to be leaders will not become complacent, because they have their own internal drive to lead. If there was no competition, there would be no world records. Michael Phelps may not be a leader of government or industry, but he is certainly educated on the technique of swimming, and a leader in his field. Would he be as good as he is today if there was not competition? Would the leaders of Microsoft have been motivated to create Bing if there was no Google?
>
> —EDUCATIONAL TESTING SERVICE, GRE Practice
> General Test in Analytical Writing

Although the ideas expressed in this passage may be related in the writer's mind, the passage lacks coherence because those ideas are not clearly and explicitly tied together in ways that are immediately evident to a reader.

See how this passage can be edited to make it more coherent.

> Some may argue that competition is not needed *and* that those *of us who* ~~that~~ are meant to be leaders *in any field* will not become complacent,

because ~~they~~ *we* have ~~their~~ *our* own internal drive to lead. If there was no competition, *however,* there would be, *for example,* no world records *in athletics. The Olympic swimmer* Michael Phelps may not be a leader of government or industry, but he is certainly ~~educated on the technique of swimming, and~~ a leader in ~~his field~~ *the pool.* Would he be as good *a swimmer* as he is today if there was not competition *from other world-class swimmers? Or, to take an example from the field of business,* would the leaders of Microsoft have been motivated to create Bing if there was no Google?

This edited version is hardly perfect, but it is more coherent than the original. Simply adding the word *however* in the second sentence, for instance, makes it clear that the example of Michael Phelps is intended to challenge the idea of cooperation, not uphold it. And by indicating that the writer is talking about leadership in "other fields" besides industry and government, the new language helps to justify comparing an athlete with "the leaders of Microsoft."

Adding connecting words and phrases like *because, however,* and *for example* is one of the best ways to make your writing more coherent; but be careful to choose transitions that actually lend unity to your paragraph. Otherwise, your paragraph is just longer and more wordy. (See Chapter 4, for more on tying sentences together into coherent paragraphs and tying paragraphs together into coherent essays.)

> Julio M. Ottino and Gary Saul Morson use "however," "but," and other transition words throughout their essay, p. 258.

## Using Rhetorical Patterns to Make Your Ideas Coherent

You can use any of the rhetorical patterns discussed in this book—description, narrative, example, and so on—to help you achieve coherence in an essay. Here are five examples of how these patterns can help you to tie your ideas together into a coherent whole and to make clear what you have to say:

### Using DESCRIPTION to show how physical characteristics are related

> [The house] rested on its perch like a great blue bird, not a flying sort of bird, more like a nesting hen, but with spread wings."
>
> —JUDITH ORTIZ COFER, "More Room"

One key idea in Ortiz Cofer's essay is that this house is at the center of her family's life. By describing the house as a "great blue bird" and a "nesting hen," Ortiz Cofer gives a unified impression of a home that is a source of sustenance and stability.

## Using NARRATIVE to show how events are related in time

> When the Supreme Court outlawed segregation in the public schools in 1954, I was twenty-one. When Congress passed the Civil Rights Act of 1964, permitting blacks free access to public places, I was thirty-one.
>
> —MARY MEBANE, "The Back of the Bus"

The main point in Mebane's essay is that her personal life is historically important because she was "part of the last generation born into a world of total legal segregation in the Southern United States." Mebane makes that point by linking public events with personal ones in time.

## Using COMPARISON AND CONTRAST to show similarities and differences

> [General Robert E.] Lee was tidewater Virginia, and in his background were family, culture, and tradition. . . . He embodied a way of life that had come down through the age of knighthood and the English country squire. . . . [General Ulysses S.] Grant, the son of a tanner, was everything Lee was not. He had come up the hard way and embodied nothing in particular except the eternal toughness and sinewy fiber of the men who grew up beyond the mountains.
>
> —BRUCE CATTON, "Grant and Lee: A Study in Contrasts"

Catton's main point in his essay is that Grant and Lee were "great Americans" who shaped the course of the nation's history—that is, for all their differences, which Catton outlines point by point in this passage, they were actually "very much alike," as he makes clear elsewhere in the essay.

## Using CAUSE AND EFFECT to explore consequences

> I liked having a job because I was learning how to be a responsible person. I was meeting all kinds of people and learning a lot about them.

I started making friends with my co-workers and getting to know many of the customers on a first-name basis. And I was in charge of my own money for the first time.

—MARISSA NUÑEZ, "Climbing the Golden Arches"

The point of Nuñez's essay is to show how much she learned from working at McDonald's. Starting with that cause, she ties this paragraph together by tracing specific effects—learning to be responsible, meeting all kinds of people, and making friends. Elsewhere in her essay, Nuñez ties her ideas together by using other common rhetorical patterns, such as EXEMPLIFICATION, PROCESS ANALYSIS, and CLASSIFICATION.

### Using ARGUMENT to make logical connections among ideas

. . . I spoke with more than three hundred teens and young adults about their online lives. I saw a generation settle into a new way of dealing with silence from other people: namely, deny that it hurts and put aside your understanding that if you do it to others, it will hurt them as well. . . . This style of relating is part of a larger pattern. You learn to give your parents a pass when they turn to their phones instead of responding to you. You learn to give your friends a pass when they drop in and out of conversations to talk with friends on their phones.

—SHERRY TURKLE, "Romance: Where Are You? Who Are You? Wait, What Just Happened?"

Here, Turkle argues that what she observed in her conversations with teens is related to a greater trend, "a larger pattern" about texting culture. When we text people and they don't text back, after a while we start to do the same to others, and then begin to expect the same behavior from our friends and family.

## TONE AND STYLE

The ideas you express in an essay can be meaningful and logically coherent; yet readers still may not fully understand what you have to say, or accept your conclusions, if your ideas do not reflect a clear and consistent POINT OF VIEW.

The elements of writing that most directly convey your stance toward your topic are TONE and STYLE. Tone may be defined as your attitude toward your subject or audience. Style refers to the kind of language you use to present yourself in a piece of writing. In practice, tone and style are closely intertwined because both are directly affected by your AUDIENCE and PURPOSE in writing.

## Tone

Let's suppose you have an essay due before noon. You've been working on it for days, and you've gotten up at 6:45 a.m. to add the finishing touches. In your neighborhood, local ordinances prohibit excessive noise before 8:00 a.m. As you begin to write, however, a jackhammer starts up outside your window, making it impossible for you to concentrate. Exasperated, you text the following message to a friend:

> Jerks making huge noise outside! Can't write! Grrrrrrrr

In this example, your audience is your friend and your purpose is to express your frustration. Your tone here is one of annoyance, suggesting a certain animosity toward your subject—those who persist in disturbing the peace when you have an assignment to complete. As for your style of writing: it might be called informal and personal (*Jerks, Grrrrrrr*), as befits one aggrieved friend texting another.

Now assume a different audience for your grievances and a different purpose in writing. Logging on to your city's official website, you discover a virtual suggestion box and file the following complaint:

> As a concerned citizen, I would like to report a violation of the city noise ordinance this morning at 7:00 a.m. outside 907 Whitehead Street. While studying for class, I found it impossible to concentrate when, as I sat down to finish an important writing assignment . . .

Writing to a different audience (city officials) with a different purpose in mind (to inform them of a violation of a law) so that they can address the problem, your tone and style have changed considerably. Your tone is now more measured and detached; your style is more formal and impersonal (with terms like *violation* and *ordinance*) in keeping with the role (concerned citizen) that you've adopted in your text.

The range of tones you have to choose from as a writer is virtually limitless—for example, you can sound annoyed and angry, patient and rational, or sympathetic and enthusiastic. Since tone is a reflection of your attitude toward your subject, a useful way to think about the tone you might adopt in an essay is simply to consider whether you want to sound largely positive, neutral, or negative toward your subject and then to choose words to suit your audience and purpose.

> John McWhorter's (p. 490) tone is measured, even as he makes clear what he finds troubling about the name *Redskins*.

In our jackhammer examples, the indignant text to a friend clearly adopts a negative tone toward the noisemakers. The message to city hall, on the other hand, is more neutral in tone. You can probably imagine a written message that would be positive in its attitude toward construction noise and thus more enthusiastic in tone, but that would require a different audience, perhaps the readers of a trade publication for paving companies, and a different purpose, let's say to sell jackhammers or other equipment.

As you look for the right tone to use in an essay, try the following template to help you get started:

> ▶ On the topic of _____, my attitude is _____; my purpose in writing is _____ to an audience of _____. My tone, therefore, should be _____.

You might fill in the blanks this way:

> ▶ On the topic of <u>paying student athletes</u>, my attitude is <u>mixed</u>; my purpose in writing is <u>to argue for more discussion and debate on the subject</u> to an audience of <u>college sports fans</u>. My tone, therefore, should be <u>even-handed</u>.

## Style

As with tone, there are almost as many possible variations in style as there are writers. As in our jackhammer examples, however, a useful way to think about the style you want to adopt in a particular piece of writing is to consider whether you want to come across as formal or informal, personal or

impersonal—or something else. Let's look at two examples from the work of
Ernest Hemingway. In the following passage from his novel *A Farewell to Arms*,
the narrator comes across as impersonal, a detached observer.

> In the late summer of that year we lived in a house in a village that looked
> across the river and the plain to the mountains. In the bed of the river
> there were pebbles and boulders, dry and white in the sun, and the water
> was clear and swiftly moving and blue in the channels. Troops went by
> the house and down the road and the dust they raised powdered the
> leaves of the trees.
>
> —ERNEST HEMINGWAY, *A Farewell to Arms*

Contrast this style of writing with the style in the next passage, which includes
part of a letter that Hemingway wrote for *Esquire* magazine, when the town of
Key West, where he was living at the time, went bankrupt. To deal with this
economic crisis, the authorities introduced tourism as the main industry in
the town and published a tourist guide that included Hemingway's house.

> The house at present occupied by your correspondent is listed as num-
> ber eighteen in a compilation of the forty-eight things for a tourist to see
> in Key West. So there will be no difficulty in a tourist finding it or any
> other of the sights of the city, a map has been prepared by the local . . .
> authorities to be presented to each arriving visitor. Your correspondent
> is a modest and retiring chap with no desire to compete with the Sponge
> Lofts (number 13 of the sights), the Turtle Crawl (number 3 on the map),
> the Ice Factory (number 4), the Tropical Open Air Aquarium containing
> the 627 pound jewfish (number 9), or the Monroe County Courthouse
> (number 14). . . . Yet there your correspondent is at number 18 between
> Johnson's Tropical Grove (number 17) and Lighthouse and Aviaries
> (number 19). This is all very flattering to the easily bloated ego of your
> correspondent but very hard on production.
>
> —ERNEST HEMINGWAY, "The Sights of Whitehead Street:
> A Key West Letter"

In this journalistic passage, Hemingway adopts a writing style that is different
from the celebrated "plain style" of his fiction. In much of Hemingway's
fiction, the language is informal; yet the plain-speaking narrator comes across

as impersonal, a detached observer. In his letter, the style is the reverse. The language of the passage is deferential and formal: "modest and retiring chap"; "your correspondent" (as opposed to "this reporter"); "no desire to compete"; "all very flattering." And the implied author is a self-consciously personable "chap" who claims to have an "easily bloated ego." This difference in style suggests a difference in audience and purpose.

As a famous writer living in a small town, Hemingway may well have felt overwhelmed and annoyed by the hordes of tourists at his door. His purpose in writing here, however, is not to produce great literature or even to register a complaint about a public nuisance that, in this case, has been officially promoted by the authorities. His main purpose is to entertain the knowing and sophisticated readers of *Esquire*, a men's general interest magazine. For this audience, Hemingway the journalist adopts a different style of writing from that of Hemingway the novelist and short story writer.

See Zora Neale Hurston's essay, p. 565, to observe another writer's unique style.

The point of this example, however, is not that you should write like Hemingway or any other particular writer, though imitating the various styles of writers whose work you admire is a good way of developing a style of your own. The point, rather, is that your writing style—how you present yourself through the kind of language you use—will depend not only on who you are but on your audience and your specific purpose in writing.

As you think about the most appropriate writing style to use in an essay, try this template to help you get started:

> ▶ In this essay on _____, I want to present myself as _____; my purpose in writing is _____ to an audience of _____. My style of writing, therefore, should be _____.

Here's one way to fill in the blanks:

> ▶ In this essay on <u>Hemingway's journalism of the 1930s</u>, I want to present myself as <u>an informed reader</u>; my purpose in writing is <u>to explain the novelist's role as a reporter</u> to an audience of <u>my classmates and teacher</u>. My style of writing, therefore, should be <u>formal enough for an academic paper but still fun to read</u>.

# PUTTING IT ALL TOGETHER

Here's a template you can use to check that any essay you write includes all the basic elements outlined in this chapter:

> ▸ Within the general subject of _____, I focus in this essay on the specific TOPIC of _____.
>
> ▸ My THESIS is that ____.
>
> ▸ To present what I have to say as COHERENTLY as I can, I have used the following rhetorical strategies: _____; _____; and _____.
>
> ▸ My general attitude toward this subject is _____; so my TONE, overall, is _____.
>
> ▸ Since I am writing largely to an audience of _____ with the purpose of _____, my STYLE is _____.

Here's one way that Liz Addison might have filled in the blanks:

> ▸ Within the general subject of <u>higher education</u>, I focus in this essay on the specific TOPIC of <u>the advantages of going to a community college</u>.
>
> ▸ My THESIS is that <u>community colleges are often a better choice, particularly economically, than four-year universities</u>.
>
> ▸ To present what I have to say as COHERENTLY as I can, I have used the following rhetorical strategies: <u>my own example; a point-by-point comparison of the two kinds of schools; and logical argument</u>.
>
> ▸ My general attitude toward this subject is <u>very positive</u>; so my TONE, overall, is <u>enthusiastic and encouraging</u>.
>
> ▸ Since I am writing largely to an audience of <u>students and potential students</u> with the purpose of <u>making a recommendation</u>, my STYLE is <u>direct and personal</u>.

If you can't fill in one or more of the blanks, something might be missing.

# ❧ 3 ❧

# THE WRITING PROCESS

U NLIKE flying from Seattle to Hawaii, writing is not a linear process. We plan, we draft, we revise; we plan, we draft, we revise again. In addition, we tend to skip around as we write, perhaps going back and completely rewriting what we've already written before plunging in again. This chapter is about the various stages of the writing process that you will typically go through in order to get from a blank page or screen to a final draft.

## PLANNING

Before you plunge headlong into any writing assignment, think about the nature of the assignment, the length and scope of the text you're supposed to write, and your PURPOSE* and AUDIENCE. To help budget your time, also keep in mind two things in particular: (1) *When the assignment is due.* As soon as you get an assignment, jot down the deadline. And remember that it's hard to write a good paper if you begin the night before it's due. (2) *What kind of research the assignment will require.* For many college papers, the research may take longer than the actual writing. Think about how much and what kind of research you will need to do, and allow plenty of time for it.

*Words printed in SMALL CAPITALS are defined in the Glossary/Index.

## Considering Your Purpose and Audience

We write for many reasons: to organize and clarify our thoughts, express our feelings, remember people and events, solve problems, persuade others to act or believe as we think they should. As you think about *why* you're writing, however, you also need to consider *who* your readers are. The following questions will help you think about your intended purpose and audience:

- *What is your reason for writing?* Do you want to tell readers something they may not know? Entertain them? Change their minds?

- *Who is going to read (or hear) what you say?* Your classmates? Your teacher? Readers of a blog? Your supervisor at work?

- *How much does your audience know about your subject?* If you are writing for a general audience, you may need to provide some background information and explain any terminology that may be unfamiliar.

- *What should you keep in mind about the nature of your audience?* Does the gender of your audience matter? How about their age, level of education, occupation, economic status, or religion? Are they likely to be sympathetic or unsympathetic to your position? Knowing your audience will help you generate ideas and EVIDENCE to both support what you have to say and appeal to that audience.

## Coming Up with a Subject—and Focusing on a Topic

Before you can get very far into the writing process, you will need to come up with a subject and narrow it down to a workable topic. Though we often use the words interchangeably, a SUBJECT, strictly speaking, is a broad field of inquiry, whereas a TOPIC is a specific area within that field. For example, if you are writing a paper on "the health care system in the United States," your teacher will still want to know just what approach you plan to take to that general subject. A good topic focuses in on a specific area of a general subject—such as the *causes* of waste in the health care system, or *why* more Americans need health insurance, or *how* to reform Medicare—that can be adequately covered in the time you have to write about it. (See p. 20 for more examples of how to move from a subject to a topic.)

With many writing assignments, you will be given a specific topic, or choice of topics, as part of the assignment. Make sure you understand just what you are being asked to do. Look for important words like *describe, define, analyze, compare and contrast, evaluate, argue.* Be aware that even short assignments may include more than one of these directives. For example, the same assignment may ask you not only to define Medicare and Medicaid but also to compare the two government programs.

For some assignments, you will have to find a topic, perhaps after meeting with your teacher. Let your instructor know if you're already interested in a particular topic. Ask your instructor for suggestions—and start looking on your own. In each chapter in this book, you'll find ideas for finding a topic and for developing it into an essay by using the basic patterns of writing—DESCRIPTION, NARRATION, EXAMPLE, CLASSIFICATION, PROCESS ANALYSIS, COMPARISON AND CONTRAST, DEFINITION, CAUSE AND EFFECT, and ARGUMENT—that good writers use all the time.

## GENERATING IDEAS

Once you have a topic to write about, where do you look for ideas? Over the years, writing teachers have developed a number of techniques to help writers generate ideas. All of the following techniques may come in handy at various points in the writing process, not just at the outset.

### Freewriting

Simply put pen to paper (or fingers to keyboard) and jot down whatever pops into your head. Here are some tips for freewriting:

1. Write nonstop for five or ten minutes. If nothing comes to mind at first, just write: "Nothing. My mind is blank." Eventually the words *will* come—if you don't stop writing until time runs out.

2. Circle words or ideas that you might want to come back to, but don't stop freewriting. When your time is up, mark any passages that look promising and revisit the words and ideas you circled.

3. Freewrite again, starting with something you marked in the previous session. Do this over and over and over again until you find an idea you want to explore further.

## Keeping Lists

Keeping lists is a good way to generate ideas—and to come up with interesting examples and details. Here are some tips for keeping a list:

- A list can be written anytime and anywhere: on a computer, in a notebook, on a napkin. Always keep a pencil handy.

- If your lists start to get long, group related items into piles, as you would if you were sorting your laundry. Look for relationships not only *within* those piles but *among* them.

## Brainstorming

When you brainstorm, you write down words and ideas in one sitting rather than over time. Here are a few tips for brainstorming:

- If you are brainstorming by yourself, start by jotting down a topic at the top of your page or screen. Then write out a list of every idea, comment, or word that comes to mind.

- Brainstorming is often more effective when you do it collaboratively, with everyone throwing out ideas and one person acting as scribe. If you brainstorm with others, make sure everyone contributes—no one person should monopolize the session.

## Asking Questions

Journalists and other writers ask *who, what, where, when, why,* and *how* to uncover the basic information for a story. Here is how you might use these questions if you were writing an essay about an argument in a parking lot:

- **Who** was involved in the argument? What should I say about my brother (one of the instigators) and his friends? The police officer who investigated? The witnesses?

- ***What*** happened? What did the participants say to one another? What did my brother do after he was struck by one of his friends?

- ***Where*** did the argument occur? How much of the parking lot should I describe? What can I say about it?

- ***When*** did the argument take place? What time did my brother leave the party, and when did he arrive in the parking lot?

- ***Why*** did the argument occur? Did it have anything to do with my brother's girlfriend?

- ***How*** would my brother have reacted if he hadn't been drinking? Should I write about the effects of alcohol on anger management?

## Keeping a Journal

A personal journal can be a great source of raw material for your writing. Often, what you write in a journal today will help you with a piece of writing months or even years later. Here are some pointers for keeping a journal:

- Write as informally as you like, but jot down your observations as close in time to the event as possible.

- The observations in a journal do not have to deal with momentous events; record your everyday thoughts and experiences.

- Make each journal entry as detailed and specific as possible; don't just write, "The weather was awful" or "I went for a walk." Instead, write, "Rained for an hour, followed by hail the size of meatballs" or "Walked from my place to Market St."

## Doing Research

Most academic writing—and especially longer assignments—will require at least some research beyond simply thinking about your topic and deciding what you want to emphasize. Finding out and taking notes on what has already been said on your topic, particularly by experts in the field, is basic to writing about anything much more complicated than how to tie your shoes. (And even there, you can find entire websites devoted to the subject.)

When you do research and writing in any field, you enter into an ongoing "conversation" with others who have preceded you in that same field of inquiry. Quoting, paraphrasing, or otherwise referring to what they have said is common in academic writing, and you'll find copious information on how to do this in the Appendix ("Using Sources in Your Writing"). Whenever you use someone else's work, of course, you need to document your sources scrupulously and accurately, using a standard form of citation. The Appendix, which uses the style of the Modern Language Association (MLA), will help with this, too.

As with any lively conversation, the purpose of doing research is not only to learn what others are saying but to spark ideas of your own. To keep track of those ideas (and your sources), consider keeping a research journal. It can reside in a section of a personal journal or, even better, in a separate research notebook or file on your computer.

## ORGANIZING AND DRAFTING

Once you have an abundance of facts, details, and other raw material, your next job is to organize that material and develop it into a draft. Generally, you will want to report events in chronological order—unless you are tracing the causes of a particular phenomenon or event, in which case you may want to work backward in time. Facts, statistics, personal experience, expert testimony, and other EVIDENCE should usually be presented in the order of their relative importance to your topic. But more than anything else, the order in which you present your ideas on any topic will be determined by exactly what you have to say about it.

### Stating Your Point

Before you actually begin writing, think carefully about the main point you want to make—your THESIS. You may find that your thesis changes as you draft, but starting with a thesis in mind will help you identify the ideas and details you want to include—and the order in which you present them to the reader. Often you'll want to state your thesis in a single sentence as a **THESIS STATEMENT**.

What makes a good thesis statement? First, let's consider what a thesis statement is not. A simple announcement of your topic—"In this paper I will discuss what's wrong with the U.S. health care system"—is not a thesis statement. A good thesis statement not only tells the reader what your topic is, it makes an interesting CLAIM *about* your topic, one that is open to further discussion. That's why statements of fact are not thesis statements, either: "More than thirty million people in the United States have no health insurance." Facts may support your thesis, but the thesis itself should say something about your topic that requires further discussion. For example: "To fix health care in America, we need to develop a single-payer system of health insurance." (For more on coming up with a claim and finding effective evidence, see pp. 465–66.)

A thesis statement like this at the beginning of your essay clarifies your main point—and it helps to set up the rest of the essay. In this case, the reader might expect a definition of a single-payer insurance system, with an analysis of the effects of adopting such a system, and an argument for why those particular effects will provide the needed fix.

## Making an Informal Outline

Making an informal outline can also help you organize and develop your draft. Simply write down your thesis statement, and follow it with the main subpoints you intend to cover. Here is an informal outline that one student in a medical ethics class jotted down for an essay on the U.S. health care system:

> **THESIS**: The costs of health care in America can be contained by paying for medical results rather than medical services.
> —what the current fee-for-services system is
> —problems with the system, such as unnecessary tests, high administrative costs
> —how to reform the system
> —how to pay for the new system

## Using the Patterns Taught in This Book

As you draft, consider using the various MODES OF WRITING to help you think of things to say about your topic. For example:

• Use DESCRIPTION (pp. 67–76) to show what some aspect of your topic looks, sounds, feels, smells, or tastes like: "The pool was the size of a football field. Over the decades, generations of the town grew up at the edge of its crystal-blue water."

—SAM QUINONES, "Dreamland"

• Use NARRATION (pp. 121–30) to tell a story about some aspect of your topic: "I was seven years old the first time I snuck out of the house in the dark."

—LYNDA BARRY, "The Sanctuary of School"

• Use EXAMPLES (pp. 173–82) to give specific instances of your topic: "Every culture comes up with tests of a person's ability to get out of a sticky situation. The English plant mazes. Tropical resorts market those straw finger-grabbers that tighten their grip the harder you pull on them, and Viennese intellectuals gave us the concept of childhood sexuality—figure it out, or remain neurotic for life."

—PHILIP WEISS, "How to Get Out of a Locked Trunk"

• Use CLASSIFICATION (pp. 219–26) to divide various aspects of your topic into categories: "If you make money with money, as some of my super-rich friends do, your [tax] percentage may be a bit lower than mine. But if you earn money from a job, your percentage will surely exceed mine—most likely by a lot."

—WARREN BUFFETT, "Stop Coddling the Super-Rich"

• Use PROCESS ANALYSIS (pp. 271–82) to explain how some aspect of your topic works or is made: "It is quite simple: put passion ahead of training. Feel out in any way you can what you most want to do in science, or technology, or some other science-related profession. Obey that passion as long as it lasts . . . But don't just drift through courses in science hoping that love will come to you."

—EDWARD O. WILSON, "First Passion, Then Training"

- Use COMPARISON AND CONTRAST (pp. 317–26) to point out similarities and differences in various aspects of your topic: "The classroom is a different environment for those who feel comfortable putting themselves forward in a group than it is for those who find the prospect of doing so chastening, or even terrifying."

—DEBORAH TANNEN, "Gender in the Classroom"

- Use DEFINITION (pp. 365–73) to explain what some aspect of your topic is or is not: "Should I explain . . . that I am Guatemalan by birth but *pura gringa* by circumstance?"

—TANYA MARIA BARRIENTOS, "Se Habla Español"

- Use CAUSE AND EFFECT (pp. 417–26) to explain why some aspect of your topic happened or what effects it might have: "There are uses to adversity, and they don't reveal themselves until tested. Whether it's serious illness, financial hardship, or the simple constraint of parents who speak limited English, difficulty can tap unsuspected strengths."

—SONIA SOTOMAYOR, "My Beloved World"

- Use ARGUMENT (pp. 461–74) to make and support your thesis: "[Technology] encourages us to feel that we have infinite choice in romantic partners, a prospect that turns out to be as stressful as it is helpful in finding a mate."

—SHERRY TURKLE, "Romance: Where Are You? Who Are You? Wait, What Just Happened?"

## Templates for Getting Started

The following templates outline ways to use the common patterns of writing, or rhetorical modes, to get started with almost any topic ("X"). Don't take these as formulas where you just have to fill in the blanks; there are no easy formulas for good writing. However, these templates can help you get started with some of the basic moves you'll need to make as you draft:

> ▸ X can be described as having the following characteristics: _____, _____, and _____.
>
> ▸ What has happened to X is _____, _____, and _____.
>
> ▸ Some examples of X are _____, _____, and _____.
>
> ▸ X can be divided into the following categories: _____, _____, and _____.
>
> ▸ The process of X can be broken down into the following steps: _____, _____, and _____.
>
> ▸ X is like Y in that both are _____ and _____; however, X is different from Y in _____ and _____.
>
> ▸ X can be defined as a(n) _____ with the following characteristics: _____ and _____
>
> ▸ X was caused by _____ and _____; the effects of X are _____ and _____.
>
> ▸ What should be done about X is _____, _____, and _____.

## The Three Parts of a Draft

As you construct a draft, think of it as having essentially three parts: a beginning, a middle, and an ending. Each of these parts should be shaped with your potential readers in mind.

Your beginning is the introduction, the first thing the reader sees. It should grab—and hold—the reader's attention. The introduction should also tell the reader exactly what you're writing about and, most of the time, should include a clear statement of your thesis. Occasionally, you may want to build up to your thesis statement, but most of the time it's best to state your thesis right off the bat. (For more on drafting an introduction, see p. 63.)

The middle of your draft is the body, and it may run anywhere from a few paragraphs to many pages. This is the part in which you present your best commentary and **EVIDENCE** in support of your main point. That evidence can include facts and figures, examples, the testimony of experts (usually in the form of citations from sources that you carefully acknowledge), and perhaps your own personal experience. How much evidence will you need?

The amount of evidence you'll need will depend in part on how broad or narrow your thesis is. A broad thesis on how to combat climate change would obviously require more—and more-detailed—evidence than a thesis about the cost of textbooks at a campus bookstore. Ultimately, it is the reader who determines whether or not your evidence is sufficient. So as you draft, ask yourself questions like these about the details you should include:

- *What is the best example I can give to illustrate my main point?* Is one example enough, or should I give several?

- *Of all the facts I could cite, which ones support my thesis best?* What additional facts will the reader expect or need to have?

- *Of everything I've read on my topic, which sources are absolutely indispensable?* What sources were particularly clear or authoritative on the issue? How do I cite my sources appropriately? (For more information on using and citing sources, see the Appendix.)

- *Is my personal experience truly relevant to my point?* Or would I be better off staying out of the picture? Or citing someone whose experience or knowledge is even more compelling than mine?

The ending of your draft is the conclusion, a **SUMMARY** of what you have to say, often by restating the thesis—but with some variation based on the evidence you have just cited. For instance, you can make a recommendation ("more research is needed to show which frequently prescribed medical tests actually work") or explain the larger significance of your topic ("lowering health care costs for individuals will allow more people to be covered without incurring additional outlays"). (For more on drafting a conclusion, see p. 65.)

## Using Visuals

Illustrations such as graphs and charts can be especially effective for presenting or comparing data, and photographs or drawings can help readers "see" things you describe in your written text. For example, if you were writing about the Civil War generals Ulysses S. Grant and Robert E. Lee, you might want to supply your readers with photographs like the ones on pp. 346–47 of the two men in uniform. But remember that visuals should never be mere decoration or clip art. When considering any kind of illustration, here are a few guidelines to follow:

- *Visuals should be relevant to your topic and support your thesis* in some way. In this book, for example, you'll notice that most of the chapters include an illustrated example, such as a sign or cartoon, showing how the pattern of writing discussed in that chapter is used in an everyday writing situation.

- *Any visuals should be appropriate for your audience and purpose.* You might add a detailed medical drawing of a lung to an essay on the effects of smoking directed at respiratory specialists, but not to an essay about smoking aimed at a general audience that wouldn't necessarily need—or want—to see all the details.

- *Refer to any visuals in the text* ("in the diagram below")—and, if necessary, number them so readers can find them ("see fig. 1").

- *Position each visual close to the text it illustrates,* and consider adding a caption explaining the point of the visual.

- *If you use a visual you have not created yourself,* identify the source.

# REVISING

Revising is a process of *re-vision*, of looking again at your draft and fixing problems in content, organization, or both. Sometimes revising requires some major surgery: adding new EVIDENCE, cutting out paragraphs or entire sections, rewriting the beginning, and so on.

Many writers try to revise far too soon. To avoid this pitfall, put aside your draft for a few hours—or better still, for a few days—before revising. Start by reading your draft carefully, and then try to get someone else to look it over—a classmate, a friend, your aunt. Whoever it is, be sure he or she is aware of your intended audience and purpose. Here's what you and the other person should look for:

- **Title.** Does the title pique the reader's interest and accurately indicate the topic of the essay?

- **Thesis.** What is the main point of the essay? Is it clearly stated in a thesis statement? If not, should it be? Is the thesis sufficiently narrow?

- **Audience.** Is there sufficient background information for the intended readers? Are there clear definitions of terms and concepts they might not know? Will they find the topic interesting?

- **Support.** What evidence supports the thesis? Is the evidence convincing and the reasoning logical? Are more facts or specific details needed?

- **Organization.** Is the draft well organized, with a clear beginning, middle, and ending? Does each paragraph contribute to the main point, or are some paragraphs off topic?

- **Patterns of Writing.** What is the main pattern the writer uses to develop the essay? For example, is the draft primarily a NARRATIVE? A DESCRIPTION? An ARGUMENT? Should other patterns be introduced? For instance, would more EXAMPLES or a COMPARISON be beneficial?

- **Sources.** If there is material from other sources, how are those sources incorporated? Are they quoted? Paraphrased? Summarized? Are sources clearly cited following appropriate guidelines for documentation, so readers know whose words or ideas are being used? Do sources effectively support the main point? (For tips on using sources and citing them properly, see the Appendix.)

- **Paragraphs.** Does each paragraph focus on one main idea and, often, state it directly in a clear topic sentence? Do your paragraphs vary in structure, or are they too much alike? Should any long or complex paragraphs be broken into two? Should short paragraphs be combined with other paragraphs, or developed more fully? How well does the draft flow from one paragraph to the next? If any paragraph seems to break the flow, should it be cut—or are transitions needed to help the reader follow the text? (For more help with paragraphs, see Chapter 4.)

- *Sentences.* If all of the sentences are about the same length, should some be varied? A short sentence in the midst of long sentences can provide emphasis. On the other hand, too many short sentences in a row can sound choppy. Some of them might be combined.

- *Visuals.* If the draft includes visuals, are they relevant to the topic and thesis? If there are no visuals, would any of the text be easier to understand if accompanied by a diagram or drawing?

After you analyze your own draft carefully and get some advice from another reader, you may decide to make some fairly drastic changes, such as adding more examples, writing a more effective conclusion, or dropping material that doesn't support your thesis. All such moves are typical of the revision process. In fact, it is not unusual to revise your draft more than once to get it to a near-final form.

## EDITING AND PROOFREADING

When you finish revising your essay, you've blended all the basic ingredients, but you still need to put the icing on the cake. That is, you need to edit and proofread your final draft before presenting it to the reader.

When you edit, you add finishing touches and correct errors in grammar, sentence structure, punctuation, and word choice. When you proofread, you take care of misspellings, typos, problems with margins and format, and other minor blemishes. Here are some tips that can help you check your drafts for some common errors.

### Editing Sentences

#### Check that each sentence expresses a complete thought

Each sentence should have a subject (someone or something) and a verb performing an action or indicating a state of being. (The Civil War started in 1861.)

## Check capitalization and end punctuation

Be sure each sentence begins with a capital letter and ends with a period, a question mark, or an exclamation point.

## Look for sentences that begin with *it* or *there*

Often such sentences are vague or boring, and they are usually easy to edit. For example, if you've written "There is a security guard on duty at every entrance," you could edit it to "A security guard is on duty at every entrance."

## Check for parallelism

All items in a list or series should have parallel grammatical forms—nouns (Lincoln, Grant, Lee), verbs (dedicate, consecrate, hallow), phrases (of the people, by the people, for the people), and so on.

# Editing Words

### There, their

Use *there* to refer to a place or direction, or to introduce a sentence. (Was he there? There was no evidence.) Use *their* as a possessive. (Their plans fell apart.)

### It's, its

Use *it's* to mean "it is." (It's often difficult to apologize.) Use *its* to mean "belonging to it." (Each dog has its own personality.)

### Lie, lay

Use *lie* when you mean "recline." (She's lying down because her back hurts.) Use *lay* when you mean "put" or "place." (Lay the blanket on the bed.)

## Use concrete words

If some of your terms are too ABSTRACT (Lake Michigan is so amazing and incredible), choose more CONCRETE terms (Lake Michigan is so cold and choppy that swimming in it often seems like swimming in the ocean).

### Avoid filler words like *very, quite, really,* and *truly*

You could write that "John Updike was truly a very great novelist," but it's stronger to say, "John Updike was a great novelist."

## Editing Punctuation

### Check for commas after introductory elements in a sentence

▶ After that day, it was as if Miss Dennis and I shared something.
—ALICE STEINBACH, "The Miss Dennis School of Writing"

### Check for commas before *and, but, or, nor, so,* or *yet* in compound sentences

▶ Book sales are down, but creative writing enrollments are booming.
—ALLEGRA GOODMAN, "So, You Want to Be a Writer? Here's How."

### Check for commas in a series

▶ Where you live, where you go to school, your job, your profession, who you interact with, how people interact with you, your treatment in the healthcare and justice system are all affected by your race.
—ROBERT WALD SUSSMAN, "The Myth of Race"

### Put quotation marks at the beginning and end of a quotation

▶ Finally he said, "Once you get to be thirty, you make your own mistakes."
—PHILIP WEISS, "How to Get Out of a Locked Trunk"

▶ "Dogs love real beef," the back of the box proclaimed loudly.
—ANN HODGMAN, "No Wonder They Call Me a Bitch"

## Check your use of apostrophes with possessives

Singular nouns should end in 's, whereas plural nouns should end in s'. The possessive pronouns *hers, his, its, ours, yours,* and *theirs* should not have apostrophes.

> ▶ But to me, my mother's English is perfectly clear, perfectly natural.
>
> —AMY TAN, "Mother Tongue"

> ▶ With these rulings and laws, whites' attitudes towards blacks have also greatly improved.
>
> —ERIC A. WATTS, "The Color of Success"

# Proofreading and Formatting

Proofreading is the only stage in the writing process where you are *not* primarily concerned with meaning. Of course you should correct any substantive errors you find, but your main concern is the surface appearance of your text: misspellings, margins that are too narrow or too wide, unindented paragraphs, and missing page numbers.

It is a good idea to slow down as you proofread. Use a ruler or piece of paper to guide your eye line by line; or read your entire text backward a sentence at a time; or read it aloud word by word. Use a spellchecker, too, but don't rely on it: a spellchecker doesn't know the difference, for example, between *their* and *there* or *human* and *humane.*

Also check the overall format of your document to make sure it follows any specific instructions that you may have been given. If your instructor does not have particular requirements for formatting, here are some guidelines:

**Heading and title.** Put your name, your instructor's name, the name and number of the course, and the date on separate lines in the upper-left-hand corner of your first page. Center your title on the next line, but do not underline it or put it in quotation marks. Double-space the heading and title.

**Typeface and size.** Use ten- or twelve-point type in an easy-to-read typeface, such as Times New Roman, `Courier`, or Palatino.

**Spacing and margins.** Double-space your document. Leave at least one-inch margins on each side and at the top and bottom of your text.

**Paragraph indentation and page numbers.** Indent the first line of each paragraph five spaces. Number your pages consecutively, and include your last name with each page number.

# ✦4✦

## WRITING PARAGRAPHS

T HIS chapter is about writing paragraphs. A paragraph is a group of closely related sentences on the same topic. In any piece of writing longer than a few sentences, paragraphs are necessary to indicate when the discussion shifts from one topic to another. Just because a group of sentences is on the same topic, however, doesn't mean they're all closely related. All of the following sentences, for example, are about snakes:

> There are no snakes in Ireland. Ounce for ounce, the most deadly snake in North America is the coral snake. Snakes are our friends; never kill a snake. North America is teeming with snakes, including four poisonous species. Snakes also eat insects.

Although they make statements about the same topic, these sentences do not form a coherent paragraph because they're not closely related to each other: each one snakes off in a different direction. In a coherent paragraph, all the sentences work together to support the main point.

## SUPPORTING THE MAIN POINT

Suppose the main point we wanted to make in a paragraph about snakes was that, despite their reputation for evil, snakes should be protected. We could still mention snakes in North America, even the deadly coral snake. We could say that snakes eat insects. But the sentence about snakes in Ireland would have to go. Of course, we could introduce additional facts and figures about snakes and snakebites—so long as we made sure that every statement in our paragraph worked together to support the idea of conservation. For example, we might write:

> Snakes do far more good than harm, so the best thing to do if you encounter a snake is to leave it alone. North America is teeming with snakes, including four poisonous species. (Ounce for ounce, the most deadly snake in North America is the coral snake.) The chances of dying from any variety of snakebite, however, are slim—less than 1 in 25,000,000 per year in the United States. Snakes, moreover, contribute to a healthy ecosystem. They help to control the rodent population, and they eat insects. (Far more people die each year from the complications of insect bites than from snakebites.) Snakes are our friends and should be protected. Never kill a snake.

This is a coherent paragraph because every sentence contributes to the main point, which is that snakes should be protected.

## Don't Go Off on a Tangent

Anytime the subject of snakes comes up, it is tempting to recall the legend of Saint Patrick, the patron saint of Ireland who, in the second half of the fifth century, is said to have driven the snakes from the land with his walking stick. Beware, however, of straying too far from the main point of your paragraph, no matter how interesting the digression may be. That is, be careful not to go off on a tangent.

Every sentence in Richard Lederer's essay, p. 200, makes the point that "English Is a Crazy Language."

The term *tangent*, by the way, comes from geometry and refers to a line that touches a circle at only one point—on the periphery, not the center.

And, incidentally, did you know that St. Patrick used a three-leaf clover to explain the Christian doctrine of the Trinity to the Irish people? Which is why shamrocks are associated with St. Patrick's Day. Also, there's another really interesting legend about St. Patrick's walking stick. . . . But we digress.

## Topic Sentences

To help you stay on track in a paragraph, state your main point in a TOPIC SEN-
TENCE* that identifies your subject (snakes) and makes a clear statement about it
("should be protected"). Usually your topic sentence will come at the beginning,
as in this paragraph from an essay about the benefits of working at McDonald's:

> Working at McDonald's has taught me a lot. The most important thing I've
> learned is that you have to start at the bottom and work your way up. I've
> learned to take this seriously—if you're going to run a business, you need
> to know how to do all the other jobs. I also have more patience than ever
> and have learned how to control my emotions. I've learned how to get along
> with all different kinds of people. I'd like to have my own business some-
> day, and working at McDonald's is what showed me I could do that.
>
> —MARISSA NUÑEZ, "Climbing the Golden Arches"

When you put the topic sentence at the beginning of a paragraph like this,
every other sentence in your paragraph should follow from it.

Sometimes you may put your topic sentence at the end of the paragraph.
Then, every other sentence in the paragraph should lead up to the topic sentence. Consider this example from an essay on how to be happy:

> . . . What matters is friends and family, and human relationships: what
> you did for other people, what they did for you. How you helped and
> were helped. Where you cared and were cared for. That's the heart of
> happiness, and all the rest is commercial hustle. Don't buy it. Make the
> world a better place and you make your life worthwhile. Make your life
> worthwhile and you'll be happy. You don't need to buy anything or ask
> anybody for advice. You can just go do it.
>
> —MICHAEL CRICHTON, "Happiness"

All of the statements in this paragraph are about the nature of happiness, leading up to the topic sentence at the end, which tells the reader how to actually
achieve it.

---

*Words printed in SMALL CAPITALS are defined in the Glossary/Index.

Sometimes the main point of a paragraph will be implied from the context, and you won't need to state it explicitly in a topic sentence. This is especially true when you're making a point by telling a story. In both of the following paragraphs from her essay about working at McDonald's, Marissa Nuñez explains how she got the job in the first place:

> Two years ago, while my cousin Susie and I were doing our Christmas shopping on Fourteenth Street, we decided to have lunch at McDonald's.
> "Yo, check it out," Susie said. "They're hiring. Let's give it a try."
> I looked at her and said, "Are you serious?" She gave me this look that made it clear that she was.

Nuñez doesn't have to tell the reader that she is explaining how she came to work for McDonald's because that point is clear. (Also, she later writes that "finally one day the manager came out and said we had the job.")

Topic sentences not only tell your reader what the rest of a paragraph is about; they help, collectively, to tie all your ideas together in support of the main point of your essay. In Nuñez's case, the main point is what she learned about people, business, and herself from working at a fast-food restaurant, as she states clearly at the beginning: "Working at McDonald's has taught me a lot."

To see how topic sentences work collectively to tie an essay together and to support the main point of the essay, read through each paragraph in "Climbing the Golden Arches" (pp. 439–44), and scout out topic sentences like these:

- Before you can officially start working, you have to get trained on every station (7).

- Working at McDonald's does have its down side (11).

- The most obnoxious customer I ever had came in one day when it was really busy (12).

- Sometimes we make up special events to make the job more fun for everyone (14).

Once you've identified a number of the topic sentences in Nuñez's essay, read back through her entire narrative but skip the topic sentences. The takeaway here is that it's still an interesting story; but without the topic sentences, the narrative is less coherent, and the significance of the events is less clear.

## Using Parallel Structures

Most of the topic sentence sentences in Nuñez's essay have basically the same grammatical form: Subject + Verb + Phrase. Parallel structures like this are a good way to help readers see the connections between your sentences and your ideas.

Using parallel structures can help you to link ideas within paragraphs as well as between or among them. Michael Crichton used them in his paragraph about happiness: "Make the world a better place and you make your life worthwhile. Make your life worthwhile and you'll be happy." The similarities in form in these two sentences tie them together in support of the topic sentence to come: "You can just do it."

See how parallel structure is used in "Watching Oprah from Behind the Veil," p. 332.

Parallel structures indicate key elements in a paragraph, or even in an entire essay. They do not, however, tell the reader exactly how those pieces of the puzzle fit together. For this we need transitions.

## Using Transitions

Paragraphs are all about connections. The following words and phrases can help you to make TRANSITIONS that clearly connect one statement to another—within a paragraph and also between paragraphs:

- *When describing place or direction:* across, across from, at, along, away, behind, close, down, distant, far, here, in between, in front of, inside, left, near, next to, north, outside, right, south, there, toward, up

- *When narrating events in time:* at the same time, during, frequently, from time to time, in 2020, in the future, now, never, often, meanwhile, occasionally, soon, then, until, when

- *When giving examples:* for example, for instance, in fact, in particular, namely, specifically, that is

- *When comparing:* also, as, in a similar way, in comparison, like, likewise
- *When contrasting:* although, but, by contrast, however, on the contrary, on the other hand
- *When analyzing cause and effect:* as a result, because, because of, consequently, so, then
- *When using logical reasoning:* accordingly, hence, it follows, therefore, thus, since, so
- *When tracing sequence or continuation:* also, and, after, before, earlier, finally, first, furthermore, in addition, last, later, next
- *When summarizing:* in conclusion, in summary, in the end, consequently, so, therefore, thus, to conclude

Consider how transitional words and phrases like these work together in the following paragraph about a new trend in shopping; the transitions are indicated in **bold**:

> We are awakening to a dollar-store economy. **For years** the dollar store has **not only** made a market out of the leftovers of a global manufacturing system, **but** it has **also** made it appealing—by making it amazingly cheap. **Before** the market meltdown of 2008 **and** the stagnant, jobless recovery that followed, the conventional wisdom about dollar stores— **whether** one of the three big corporate chains (Dollar General, Family Dollar, and Dollar Tree) **or** any of the smaller chains (**like** "99 Cents Only Stores") **or** the world of independents—was that they appeal to only poor people. **And while** it's true that low-wage earners still make up the core of dollar-store customers (42 percent earn $30,000 or less), what has turned this sector into a nearly recession-proof corner of the economy is a new customer base. "What's driving the growth," says James Russo, a vice president with the Nielsen Company, a consumer survey firm, "is affluent households."
>
> —JACK HITT, "The Dollar-Store Economy"

Without transitions, the statements in this paragraph would fall apart like beads on a broken string. Transitions indicate relationships: they help to tie the writer's ideas together—in this case by showing how they are related in time (*for years, before*), by contrast (*not only, but also; whether, or*), and in comparison (*like, and while*).

## DEVELOPING PARAGRAPHS

There are many ways—in addition to supporting a topic sentence and using parallel structures and transitions—to develop coherent paragraphs. In fact, all of the basic patterns of writing discussed in this book work just as well for organizing paragraphs as they do for organizing entire essays. Here are some examples.

### Describing

A common way of developing a paragraph, especially when you're writing about a physical object or place, is to give a detailed DESCRIPTION (Chapter 5) of your subject. When you describe something, you show the reader how it looks, sounds, feels, smells, or tastes, as in the following description of a tarpon that has just been caught by a blind boy; the point of the paragraph is to help the reader (and the boy) to picture the fish:

> Okay. He has all these big scales, like armor all over his body. They're silver too, and when he moves they sparkle. He has a strong body and a large powerful tail. He has big round eyes, bigger than a quarter, and a lower jaw that sticks out past the upper one, and is very tough. His belly is almost white and his back is a gunmetal gray. When he jumped, he came out of the water about six feet, and his scales caught the sun and flashed it all over the place.
>
> —CHEROKEE PAUL MCDONALD, "A View from the Bridge"

Descriptions of physical objects are often organized by the configuration of the object. Here the object is a fish, and the writer develops this descriptive paragraph by moving from one part of the fish to another (scales, tail, eyes, jaw, belly, back), ending up with an overall view of the whole tarpon glinting in the sun.

In "More Room," p. 114, Judith Ortiz Cofer organizes her description around the architecture of her grandmother's house.

## Narrating

One of the oldest and most common ways of developing a paragraph on almost any subject is by narrating a story about it. When you construct a NARRATIVE (Chapter 6), you focus on events: you tell what happened. In the following paragraph, a reporter tells what happened to two fighter pilots on September 11, 2001:

> They screamed over the smoldering Pentagon, heading northwest at more than 400 mph, flying low and scanning the clear horizon. Her commander had time to think about the best place to hit the enemy.
>
> —STEVE HENDRIX, "F-16 Pilot Was Ready
> to Give Her Life on Sept. 11"

Narratives are usually organized by time, presenting events in chronological order. In this narrative, the time is the morning of September 11, 2001, soon after the Pentagon has been hit. Two fighter pilots fly over the burning building; they head northwest, "scanning" the horizon; the commander thinks about "the best place to hit the enemy"—in that order in time.

## Giving Examples

When you use EXAMPLES (Chapter 7) to develop a paragraph, you give specific instances of the point you're making. In the following tongue-in-cheek paragraph, a linguist uses multiple examples to show how "unreliable" the English language can be:

> In this unreliable English tongue, greyhounds aren't always grey (or gray); panda bears and koala bears aren't bears (they're marsupials); a woodchuck is a groundhog, which is not a hog; a horned toad is a lizard; glowworms are fireflies, but fireflies are not flies (they're beetles); ladybugs and lightning bugs are also beetles (and to propagate, a significant proportion of ladybugs must be male); a guinea pig is neither a pig nor from Guinea (it's a South American rodent); and a titmouse is neither mammal nor mammaried.
>
> —RICHARD LEDERER, "English Is a Crazy Language"

Although the language and punctuation of this paragraph are playfully complex, the organization is simple: it is a series, or list, of brief examples in more or less random order.

## Classifying

When you CLASSIFY (Chapter 8), you divide your subject into categories. In the following passage, a writer classifies different kinds of English:

> Fortunately, for reasons I won't get into today, I later decided I should envision a reader for the stories I would write. And the reader I decided upon was my mother, because these were stories about mothers. So with this reader in mind—and in fact she did read my early drafts—I began to write stories using all the Englishes I grew up with: the English I spoke to my mother, which for lack of a better term might be described as "simple"; the English she used with me, which for lack of a better term might be described as "broken"; my translation of her Chinese, which could certainly be described as "watered down"; and what I imagined to be her translation of her Chinese if she could speak in perfect English, her internal language, and for that I sought to preserve the essence, but neither an English nor a Chinese structure. I wanted to capture what language ability tests can never reveal: her intent, her passion, her imagery, the rhythms of her speech and the nature of her thought.
>
> Janet Wu tells another story about mothers and languages on p. 195.
>
> —AMY TAN, "Mother Tongue"

This is a complex paragraph; but the heart of it is the author's classification of her various "Englishes" into four specific types. The opening statements in the paragraph explain how this classification system came about, and the closing statement explains the purpose it serves.

## Analyzing a Process

When you use PROCESS ANALYSIS (Chapter 9) to develop a paragraph, you tell the reader how to do something—or how something works or is made—by breaking the process into steps. In the following paragraph, a young writer explains what she sees as the first steps in learning to be a writer:

> To begin, don't write about yourself. I'm not saying you're uninteresting. I realize that your life has been so crazy no one could make this stuff up. But if you want to be a writer, start by writing about other people. Observe their faces, and the way they wave their hands around. Listen to the way they talk. Replay conversations in your mind—not just the words, but the silences as well. Imagine the lives of others. If you want to be a writer, you need to get over yourself. This is not just an artistic choice; it's a moral choice. A writer attempts to understand others from the inside.
>
> —ALLEGRA GOODMAN, "So, You Want to
> Be a Writer? Here's How."

In a process analysis, the steps of the process are usually presented in the order in which they occur in time. Here the first step ("To begin") is something not to do: "don't write about yourself"; it is followed by five more steps in order: start, observe, listen, replay, imagine. At the end of the paragraph comes the end result of the process: (you will) "understand others from the inside."

## Comparing

With a COMPARISON (Chapter 10) of two or more subjects, you point out their similarities and differences. In the following paragraph, a historian compares two Civil War generals, Ulysses S. Grant and Robert E. Lee:

> So Grant and Lee were in complete contrast, representing two diametrically opposed elements in American life. Grant was the modern man emerging; beyond him, ready to come on the stage, was the great age of steel and machinery, of crowded cities and a restless burgeoning vitality. Lee might have ridden down from the old age of chivalry, lance in hand, silken banner fluttering over his head. Each man was the perfect champion of his cause, drawing both his strengths and his weaknesses from the people he led.
>
> —BRUCE CATTON, "Grant and Lee"

Here the writer examines both of the subjects he is comparing in a single paragraph, moving systematically from the characteristics of one to those of the other.

Often, when comparing or contrasting two subjects, you will focus first on one of them, in one paragraph; and on the other, in another paragraph, as in this comparison of sports and academics at the University of Texas, Austin:

> Football is the most popular spectator sport in the state of Texas without rival. The sport's importance to our heritage is well known and documented.
>
> Vietnamese is the third-most-spoken language in the state of Texas behind English and Spanish. This is a fact that is not well known or documented.
>
> —DAN TREADWAY, "Football vs. Asian Studies"

In this first brief paragraph, the writer focuses on two characteristics of his first subject (college football): (1) its popularity and (2) its importance to Texas's heritage, which is well known. In the second paragraph, the writer focuses on similar characteristics of his second subject (the Vietnamese language): (1) its popularity and (2) how, in contrast to football, its importance to Texas is not well known.

## Defining

A **DEFINITION** (Chapter 11) explains what something is—or is not. According to the author of this paragraph from an essay on the "brilliance" of blue-collar workers, how we define intelligence depends on a number of factors:

> I couldn't have put it in words when I was growing up, but what I observed in my mother's restaurant defined the world of adults, a place where competence was synonymous with physical work. I've since studied the working habits of blue-collar workers and have come to understand how much my mother's kind of work demands of both body and brain. A waitress acquires knowledge and intuition about the ways and

the rhythms of the restaurant business. Waiting on seven to nine tables, each with two to six customers, Rosie devised memory strategies so that she could remember who ordered what. And because she knew the average time it took to prepare different dishes, she could monitor an order that was taking too long at the service station.

—MIKE ROSE, "Blue-Collar Brilliance"

In this paragraph, the writer first presents an overly simplified definition of "competence" among "blue-collar workers" as the ability to do physical labor. He then redefines this key term to include a mental component ("knowledge and intuition"), concluding the paragraph by observing how his mother's work as a waitress demonstrates these defining traits.

A photo of Rosie is on p. 408.

## Analyzing Causes and Effects

One of the most fundamental ways of developing a paragraph is to examine what caused your subject, or what effects it may have (Chapter 12). In the following paragraph, from an essay about the power of words, the author speculates about the effects, among other subsequent events, of two public speeches—by Robert Kennedy on April 4, 1968, the night Martin Luther King Jr. was killed, and by King himself in Memphis the night before that:

> After King's assassination, riots broke out in more than 100 U.S. cities—the worst destruction since the Civil War. But neither Memphis nor Indianapolis experienced that kind of damage. To this day, many believe that was due to the words spoken when so many were listening.
>
> —TIM WENDEL, "King, Kennedy, and the Power of Words"

In a cause-and-effect analysis, the writer can proceed from cause to effect, or effect to cause. This brief but efficient paragraph does both, moving first from a known cause ("King's assassination") to a known effect ("destruction" in many U.S. cities), and then from a known effect (no destruction in two cities) to a possible cause ("words spoken when so many were listening").

# INTRODUCTORY PARAGRAPHS

A well-constructed essay has a beginning, middle, and ending. Every paragraph plays an important role, but introductory paragraphs are particularly important because they represent your first chance to engage the reader.

In an introductory paragraph, you tell the reader what your essay is about—and seek to earn the reader's interest. The following famous introductory paragraph to an important document is as clear and stirring today as it was in 1776:

> When in the Course of human events, it becomes necessary for one people to dissolve the political bands which have connected them with another, and to assume among the powers of the earth, the separate and equal station to which the Laws of Nature and of Nature's God entitle them, a decent respect to the opinions of mankind requires that they should declare the causes which impel them to the separation.
>
> —Thomas Jefferson, *The Declaration of Independence*

This paragraph tells the reader exactly what's coming in the text to follow: an inventory of the reasons for the colonies' rebellion. It also seeks to justify the writer's cause and win the sympathy of the reader by invoking a higher authority: the "Laws" of God and nature trump those of Britain's King George III. Here are a few other ways to construct an introductory paragraph that may entice your readers to read on.

## Tell a story that leads into what you have to say

This introductory paragraph, from a report about research on technology and literacy, begins with two stories about how today's students read and write:

> Two stories about young people, and especially college-age students, are circulating widely today. One script sees a generation of twitterers and texters, awash in self-indulgence and narcissistic twaddle, most of it riddled with errors. The other script doesn't diminish the effects of technology, but it presents young people as running a rat race that is fueled by the Internet and its toys, anxious kids who are inundated with

mountains of indigestible information yet obsessed with making the grade, with success, with coming up with the "next big thing" but who lack the writing and speaking skills they need to do so.

—ANDREA LUNSFORD, "Our Semi-literate Youth? Not So Fast"

The author of this paragraph considers both stories she is reporting to be inaccurate; so after introducing them here, she goes on in the rest of the essay to tell alternative stories based upon her own research.

## Start with a quotation

In this example, the quotation is very short:

Our leaders have asked for "shared sacrifice." But when they did the asking, they spared me. I checked with my mega-rich friends to learn what pain they were expecting. They, too, were left untouched.

—WARREN BUFFETT, "Stop Coddling the Super-Rich"

The brief quotation in this paragraph is a reference to the following statement on the deficit by then president Barack Obama on July 16, 2011: "Simply put, it will take a balanced approach, shared sacrifice, and a willingness to make unpopular choices on all our parts." Warren Buffett could have quoted this entire statement in his introductory paragraph, of course, but Buffett's main rhetorical strategy here is to be direct and to the point.

## Ask a question—or questions

This strategy should be used sparingly, but it works especially well when you want to begin with a touch of humor—or otherwise suggest that you don't have all the answers. In this opening paragraph, a food critic explores new territory:

I've always wondered about dog food. Is a Gaines-burger really like a hamburger? Can you fry it? Does dog food "cheese" taste like real cheese"? Does Gravy Train actually make gravy in the dog's bowl, or is that brown liquid just dissolved crumbs? And exactly what *are* by-products?

—ANN HODGMAN, "No Wonder They Call Me a Bitch"

Sound appetizing? Even if your subject doesn't exactly appeal to everyone, a strong opening paragraph like this can leave your readers eager for more—or at least willing to hear you out.

# CONCLUDING PARAGRAPHS

The final paragraph of an essay should be just as satisfying as the opening paragraph. The conclusion of your essay is your last chance to drive home your point and to leave the reader with a sense of closure. Here are a few ways this is commonly done.

### Restate your main point

Remind the reader what you've said, but don't just repeat your point. Add a little something new. In this passage from the closing paragraph of an essay on becoming a scientist, the writer explicitly restates the point he has been making throughout the essay—and then concludes with a qualification:

> My confessional instead is intended to illustrate an important principle I've seen unfold in the careers of many successful scientists. It is quite simple: put passion ahead of training . . . But don't just drift through courses in science hoping that love will come to you. Maybe it will, but don't take the chance. As in other big choices in your life, there is too much at stake. Decision and hard work based on enduring passion will never fail you.
>
> —EDWARD O. WILSON, "First Passion, Then Training"

Throughout his essay, Wilson's point has to do with the power of passion; after repeating it in this closing paragraph, however, he adds the qualification that "decision and hard work" are also necessary to ensure success in any profession.

### Show the broader significance of your subject

In an essay about why *The Oprah Winfrey Show* remains the most popular English-language program in Saudi Arabia, with reruns broadcast twice daily by satellite from Dubai, Jeff Jacoby comes to the following conclusion:

> Is it any wonder that women trapped in a culture that treats them so wretchedly idolize someone like Oprah, who epitomizes so much that is absent from their lives? A nation that degrades its women degrades itself, and Oprah's message is an antidote to degradation. Why do they

love her? Because all the lies of the Wahhabists cannot stifle the truth she embodies: The blessings of liberty were made for women, too.

—Jeff Jacoby, "Watching Oprah from Behind the Veil"

Liberty for all, of course, is a much greater issue than why a particular television show is popular with a particular audience. By linking his limited topic to this broader one, the author greatly enlarges its significance.

## End with a recommendation

This strategy is especially appropriate when you're concluding an argument. Before coming to the conclusion stated in the following paragraph, the author, a sportswriter, has made the claim that student athletes should be paid for their "work":

> The republic will survive. Fans will still watch the NCAA tournament. Double-reverses will still be thrilling. Alabama will still hate Auburn. Everybody will still hate Duke. Let's do what's right and re-examine what we think is wrong.
>
> —Michael Rosenberg, "Let Stars Get Paid"

Not only is he recommending pay for college athletes, the author of this paragraph asks the reader to rethink, and totally revise, the conventional wisdom that says paying them is morally wrong. (For an essay that comes to precisely the opposite conclusion, see p. 521.)

# ⇥5⇤

## DESCRIPTION

D ESCRIPTION* is the pattern of writing that appeals most directly to the senses by showing us the physical characteristics of a subject—what it looks like, or how it sounds, smells, feels, or tastes. A good description *shows* us such characteristics; it doesn't just tell us about them. Description is especially useful for making an ABSTRACT or vague subject—such as freedom or truth or death—more CONCRETE or definite.

For example, if you were describing an old cemetery, you might say that it was a solemn and peaceful place. In order to show the reader what the cemetery actually looked or sounded like, however, you would need to focus on the physical aspects of the scene that evoked these more abstract qualities—the marble gravestones, the earth and trees, and perhaps the mourners at the site of a new grave.

Such concrete, physical details are the heart of any description. Those details can be presented either objectively or subjectively. Consider the following caption for a photograph from the website of Arlington National Cemetery:

> Six inches of snow blanket the rolling Virginia hillside as mourners gather at a fresh burial site in Arlington National Cemetery outside Washington, D.C. Rows of simple markers identify the more than 250,000 graves that make up the military portion of the cemetery. Visited annually by more than four million people, the cemetery conducts nearly 100 funerals each week.

In an OBJECTIVE description like this, the author stays out of the picture. The description shows what a detached observer would see and hear—snow, rolling hills, graves, and mourners—but it does not say what the observer thinks or feels *about* those things.

*Words printed in SMALL CAPITALS are defined in the Glossary/Index.

A **SUBJECTIVE** description, on the other hand, presents the author's thoughts and feelings along with the physical details of the scene or subject, as in this description by novelist John Updike of a cemetery in the town where he lived:

> The stones are marble, modernly glossy and simple, though I suppose that time will eventually reveal them as another fashion, dated and quaint. Now, the sod is still raw, the sutures of turf are unhealed, the earth still humped, the wreaths scarcely withered . . . . I remember my grandfather's funeral, the hurried cross of sand the minister drew on the coffin lid, the whine of the lowering straps, the lengthening, cleanly cut sides of clay, the thought of air, the lack of air forever in the close dark space lined with pink satin. . . .
>
> —JOHN UPDIKE, "Cemeteries"

This intimate description is far from detached. Not only does it give us a close-up view of the cemetery itself, it also reports the sensations that the newly dug graves evoke in the author's mind.

Whether the concrete details of a description are presented from a subjective or an objective POINT OF VIEW, every detail should contribute to some DOMINANT IMPRESSION that the writer wants the description to make upon the reader. The dominant impression we get from Updike's description, for example, is of the "foreverness" of the place. Consequently, every detail in Updike's description—from the enduring marble of the headstones to the dark, satin-lined interior of his grandfather's coffin—contributes to the sense of airless eternity that Updike recalls from his grandfather's funeral.

Joseph Krivda's description of the Vietnam War memorial on p. 79 is both subjective and objective.

Updike's references to the "raw" sod and to unhealed "sutures" in the turf show how such figures of speech as METAPHOR, SIMILE, and PERSONIFICATION can be used to make a description more vivid and concrete. This is because we often describe something by telling what it is like. A thump in your closet at night sounds like a fist hitting a table. A friend's sharp words cut like a knife. The seams of turf on new graves are like the stitches closing a wound.

As Updike's description narrows in on his grandfather's grave, we get a feeling of suffocation that directly supports the main point that the author is making about the nature of death. Death, as Updike conceives it, is no abstraction; it is the slow extinction of personal life and breath.

Updike's painful reverie is suddenly interrupted by his young son, who is learning to ride a bicycle in the peaceful cemetery. As Updike tells the story of their joyful afternoon together, the gloom of the cemetery fades into the background—as descriptive writing often does. Description frequently plays a supporting role within other PATTERNS OF WRITING; it may serve, for example, to set the scene for a NARRATIVE (as in Updike's essay) or it may provide the background for an ARGUMENT about the significance of a national cemetery.

Almost as important as the physical details in a description is the order in which those details are presented. Beginning with the glossy stones of the cemetery and the earth around them, Updike's description comes to focus on the interior of a particular grave. It moves from outside to inside and from the general to the specific. A good description can proceed from outside in, or inside out, top to bottom, front to back, or in any other direction—so long as it moves systematically

The dominant impression of a description of a swimming pool, p. 86, is one of nostalgia.

in a way that is in keeping with the dominant impression it is supposed to give, and that supports the main point the description is intended to make.

In the following description of a boy's room, the writer is setting the stage for the larger narrative—in this case, a fairy tale:

> The room was so spare one could see everything at a glance: a closet door with a lock on it, a long table with five perfect constructions—three ships, two dragons—nothing else on the table but a neat stack of stainless-steel razor-blades. What defined all the rest, of course, was that immense desk and chair. They made it seem that the room itself was from a picture book, or better yet, a stage-set, for across one end hung a dark green curtain. Beyond that, presumably, the professor's son crouched, hiding. My gaze stopped and froze on an enormous bare foot that protruded, unbeknownst to its owner, no doubt, from behind the curtain. It was the largest human foot I'd ever seen or imagined . . . .
>
> —JOHN GARDNER, *Freddy's Book*

This description of the lair of a boy giant is pure fantasy, of course. What makes it appear so realistic is the systematic way in which Gardner presents the objects in the room. First we see the closet door, a feature we might find in any boy's bedroom. Next comes the lock. Even an ordinary boy might keep the contents of his closet under lock and key. The long table with the models and razor-blades is the first hint that something unusual may be at play. And when we see the oversized desk and chair, we truly begin to suspect that this is no ordinary room and no ordinary boy. But it is not until our gaze falls upon the enormous foot protruding from beneath the curtain that we know for sure we have entered the realm of make-believe.

Fanciful as the details of Gardner's description may be, his systematic method of presenting them is instructive for composing more down-to-earth descriptions. Also, by watching how Gardner presents the details of Freddy's room from a consistent VANTAGE POINT, we can see how he builds up to a dominant impression of awe and wonder.

## A BRIEF GUIDE TO WRITING A DESCRIPTION

As you write a description, you need to identify who or what you're describing, say what your subject looks or feels like, and indicate the traits you plan to focus on. Cherokee Paul McDonald makes these basic moves of description in the beginning of his essay in this chapter:

> He was a lumpy little guy with baggy shorts, a faded T-shirt and heavy
> sweat socks falling down over old sneakers. . . . Covering his eyes and
> part of his face was a pair of those stupid-looking '50s-style wrap-
> around sunglasses.
>
> —CHEROKEE PAUL MCDONALD, "A View from the Bridge"

McDonald identifies what he's describing (a "little guy"); says what his subject
looks like ("lumpy," "with baggy shorts, a faded T-shirt and heavy sweat
socks"); and hints at characteristics (his "stupid-looking" sunglasses) that he
might focus on. Here is one more example from this chapter:

> But the center of it all was that gleaming, glorious swimming pool. Mem-
> ories of Dreamland, drenched in the smell of chlorine, Coppertone, and
> french fries, were what almost everyone who grew up in Portsmouth
> took with them as the town declined.
>
> —SAM QUINONES, "Dreamland"

The following guidelines will help you to make these basic moves as you draft
a description—and to come up with your subject; consider your purpose and audience; generate ideas; state your point; create a dominant impression of your subject; use figurative language; and arrange the details of your description effectively.

## Coming Up with a Subject

A primary resource for finding a subject is your own experience.
You will often want to describe something familiar from your
past—the lake in which you learned to swim, the neighborhood
where you grew up, a person from your hometown. Also consider more recent
experiences or less familiar subjects that you might investigate further, such
as crowd behavior at a hockey game, an unusual T-shirt, or a popular bookstore. Whatever subject you choose, be sure that you will be able to describe
it vividly for your readers by appealing to their senses.

For a taste of the unusual, Ann Hodgman describes pet food on p. 107.

## Considering Your Purpose and Audience

Your PURPOSE in describing something—whether to view your subject objectively, express your feelings about it, convince the reader to visit it (or not), or
simply to amuse your reader—will determine the details you include. Before

you start composing, decide whether your purpose will be primarily objective (as in a lab report) or subjective (as in a personal essay about your grandmother's cooking). Although both approaches provide information, an OBJECTIVE description presents its subject impartially, whereas a SUBJECTIVE description conveys the writer's personal response to the subject.

Whatever your purpose, you need to take into account how much your AUDIENCE already knows (or does not know) about your subject. For example, if you want to describe to someone who has never been on your campus the mad rush that takes place when classes change, you're going to have to provide some background: the main quadrangle with its sun worshipers, the brick-and-stone classroom buildings on either side, the library looming at one end. On the other hand, if you were to describe this same locale to fellow students, you could skip the background description and go directly to the mob scene.

## Generating Ideas: Asking What Something Looks, Sounds, Feels, Smells, and Tastes Like

Good descriptive writing is built on CONCRETE particulars rather than ABSTRACT qualities. So don't just write, "It was a dark and stormy night"; make your reader see, hear, and feel the wind and the rain, as E. B. White does at the end of "Once More to the Lake," pp. 7–13. To come up with specific details, observe your subject, ask questions, and take notes. Experience your subject as though you were a reporter on assignment or a traveler in a strange land.

One of your richest sources of ideas for a description—especially if you are describing something from the past—is memory. Ask friends or parents to help you remember details accurately and truthfully. Jog your own memory by asking, "What *did* the place (or object) look like exactly? What did it sound like? What did it smell or taste like?" Recovering the treasures of your memory is a little like fishing: think back to the spots you knew well; bait the hook by asking these key sensory questions; weigh and measure everything you pull up. Later on, you can throw back the ideas you can't use.

In "The Miss Dennis School of Writing," p. 98, Alice Steinbach draws upon her memories of a favorite teacher.

## Templates for Describing

The following templates can help you to generate ideas for a description and then to start drafting. Don't take these as formulas where you just have to fill in the blanks. There are no easy formulas for good writing. But these templates can help you plot out some of the key moves of description and thus may serve as good starting points.

> ► The main physical characteristics of X are _____, _____, and _____.
>
> ► From the perspective of _____, however, X could be described as _____.
>
> ► In some ways, namely _____, X resembles _____; but in other ways, X is more like _____.
>
> ► X is not at all like _____ because _____.
>
> ► Mainly because of _____ and _____, X gives the impression of being _____.
>
> ► From this description of X, you can see that _____.

For more techniques to help you generate ideas and start writing a descriptive essay, see Chapter 3.

## Stating Your Point

We usually describe something to someone for a reason. Why are you describing bloody footprints in the snow? You need to let the reader know, either formally or informally. One formal way is to include an explicit THESIS STATEMENT: "This description of Washington's ragged army at Yorktown shows that the American general faced many of the same challenges as Napoleon in the winter battle for Moscow, but Washington turned them to his advantage."

> E. B. White makes his point about time and mortality with a single chilling phrase (p. 13, par. 13).

Or your reasons can be stated more informally. If you are writing a descriptive travel essay, for example, you might state your point as a personal observation: "Chicago is an architectural delight in any season, but I prefer to visit from April through October because of the city's brutal winters."

## Creating a Dominant Impression

Some descriptions appeal to several senses: the sight of fireflies, the sound of crickets, the touch of a hand—all on a summer evening. Whether you appeal to a single sense or several, make sure they all contribute to the

DOMINANT IMPRESSION you want your description to make upon the reader. For example, if you want an evening scene on the porch to convey an impression of danger, you probably won't include details about fireflies and crickets. Instead, you might call the reader's attention to dark clouds in the distance, the rising wind, crashing thunder, and the sound of footsteps drawing closer. In short, you will choose details that play an effective part in creating your dominant impression: a sense of danger and foreboding.

Even though you want to create a dominant impression, don't begin your description with a general statement of what that impression is supposed to be. Instead, start with descriptive details, and let your readers form the impression for themselves. A good description doesn't *tell* readers what to think or feel; it *shows* them point by point. The dominant impression that John Gardner creates in his systematic description of Freddy's room, for instance, is a growing sense of awe and wonder. But he does so by taking us step by step into unfamiliar territory. If you were describing an actual room or other place—and you wanted to create a similar dominant impression in your reader's mind—you would likewise direct the reader's gaze to more familiar objects first (table, chairs, fireplace) and then to increasingly unfamiliar ones (a shotgun, polar bear skins on the floor, an elderly lady mending a reindeer harness).

> Judith Ortiz Cofer's description of her grandmother's house, in "More Room," p. 114, conveys enchantment.

## Using Figurative Language

Figures of speech can help to make almost any description more vivid or colorful. The three figures of speech you are most likely to use in composing a description are similes, metaphors, and personification.

SIMILES tell the reader what something looks, sounds, or feels like, using *like* or *as*: "Suspicion climbed all over her face, like a kitten, but not so playfully" (Raymond Chandler, *Farewell, My Lovely*).

METAPHORS make implicit comparisons, without *like* or *as*: "All the world's a stage" (William Shakespeare, *As You Like It*). Like similes, metaphors have two parts: the subject of the description (*world*) and the thing (*stage*) to which that subject is being implicitly compared.

PERSONIFICATION assigns human qualities to inanimate objects, as Sylvia Plath does in her poem "Mirror," in which she has the mirror speak as a person would: "I have no preconceptions. / Whatever I see I swallow immediately."

## Arranging the Details from a Consistent Vantage Point

The physical configuration of whatever you're describing will usually suggest a pattern of organization. Descriptions of places are often organized by direction—north to south, front to back, left to right, inside to outside, near to far, top to bottom. If you were describing a room, for example, you might use an outside-to-inside order, starting with the door or the door knob.

An object or person can also suggest an order of arrangement. If you were describing a large fish, for instance, you might let the anatomy of the fish guide your description, moving from its glistening scales to the mouth, eyes, belly, and tail. When constructing a description, you can go from whole to parts, or parts to whole; from most important to least important features (or vice versa); from largest to smallest, specific to general, or concrete to abstract—or vice versa.

Whatever organization you choose, be careful to maintain a consistent VANTAGE POINT. In other words, be sure to describe your subject from one position or perspective—across the room, from the bridge, face-to-face, under the bed, and so on. Do not include details that you are unable to see, hear, feel, smell, or taste from your particular vantage point. Before you fully reveal any objects or people that lie outside the reader's line of sight—such as a boy giant behind a curtain—you will need to cross the room and fling open the door or curtain that conceals them. If your vantage point (or that of your NARRATOR) changes while you are describing a subject, be sure to let your reader know that you have moved from one location to another, as in the following description of a robbery: "After I was pushed behind the counter of the Quik-Mart, I could no longer see the three men in ski masks, but I could hear them yelling at the owner to open up the register."

# EDITING FOR COMMON ERRORS IN DESCRIPTIVE WRITING

Like other kinds of writing, description uses distinctive patterns of language and punctuation—and thus invites typical kinds of errors. The following tips will help you to check for and correct these common errors in your own descriptive writing.

## Check descriptive details to make sure they are concrete

► When I visited Great Pond, the lake in E. B. White's essay, it was so ~~amazing and incredible~~ <u>clear and deep</u> that floating on it in a boat seemed like floating on air.

*Amazing* and *incredible* are ABSTRACT terms; *clear* and *deep* describe the water in more CONCRETE terms.

► The Belgrade region is famous for its ~~charming views~~ <u>panoramic views of fields, hills, and woodlands.</u>

The revised sentence says more precisely what makes the views charming.

## Check for filler words like *very, quite, really,* and *truly*

► The lake was ~~very much secluded~~ <u>fifteen miles</u> from the nearest village.

## Check that adjectives appear in the right order

Subjective adjectives (those that reflect the writer's own opinion) go before objective adjectives (those that are strictly factual): write "fabulous four-door Chevrolet" rather than "four-door fabulous Chevrolet." Beyond that, adjectives usually go in the following order: number, size, shape, age, color, nationality.

► The streets of Havana were lined with many ~~old, big~~ <u>big, old</u> American cars.

## Check for common usage errors

### UNIQUE, PERFECT

Don't use *more* or *most, less* or *least,* or *very* before words like *unique, equal, perfect,* or *infinite.* Either something is unique or it isn't.

► Their house at the lake was a ~~very~~ unique place.

### AWESOME, COOL, INCREDIBLE

Not only are these modifiers too abstract, they're overused. You probably should delete them or replace them with fresher words no matter how grand the scene you're describing.

► The Ohio River is ~~an awesome river~~ approximately 981 miles long.

# A Cheesy Label

When you describe something, you tell what its main attributes and characteristics are. A cheese, for instance, can be strong or mild in taste, hard or soft in texture, white or yellow in color—and anywhere in between. Made in Wisconsin, the Italian-style cheese described on this label is moderately strong, hard, and white. It also costs $6.39. An effective description emphasizes the most distinctive qualities of its subject, however. The folks in the marketing department at the Sartori Company ("Established 1939") recognize this. Inspired by the name of their product *MontAmoré*, which means *"Mount Love"* in French, they skip over the cheese's more common features and go to the seductive specifics. This cheese is "sweet, creamy, and fruity." It also has a spicy aftertaste ("finishes with a playful bite"). As the label warns, "prepare to fall in love."

## JOSEPH KRIVDA

# THE WALL

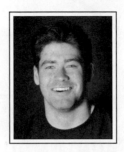

JOSEPH KRIVDA is from Kensington, Maryland, and is a student at the University of Notre Dame. He is an Army ROTC cadet, pursuing a major in biological sciences with a minor in philosophy. After graduation, he plans to attend medical school and become a physician in the United States Army Medical Corps. "The Wall," which was published in *Fresh Writing*, University of Notre Dame's journal of student writing, was inspired by Krivda's visits to the National Mall in Washington, D.C., combined with his family's military background and interest in military history. In this essay, Krivda describes the Vietnam Veterans Memorial and makes a larger point about the way memorials reflect our complex and sometimes conflicting feelings about war itself.

## The Wall

The Vietnam War Memorial on the National Mall in Washington, D.C., stands out from the structures surrounding it, but not because it actually stands out.[1] In fact, this monument is not very monumental at all. While the World War II Memorial lies in the center of the Mall with complex fountains and wreathed pillars representing the fifty states, the Vietnam War Memorial is a singular, long, black wall built into the ground, bearing the names of the war's dead. There is no victory being celebrated, no commemoration of defended freedom, but a simple display of respect to those who gave their lives for a country's broken call.

A single sentence provides CONCRETE details about the memorial's appearance

The Vietnam War was hugely controversial, with much of America opposing it. American men were fighting and dying to "stop the spread of communism," but to many Americans, we were losing thousands upon thousands of American lives to protect a country we had no business protecting (Ankony). The war was also rampant with drug abuse, a problem that greatly affected its veterans. There were no systems in place to help Vietnam veterans like there were after World War II, and many returned to a place with an antiwar culture. These vets often ended up homeless and in dire conditions (Ankony).

This paragraph describes the "controversial" nature of the Vietnam War itself

Why would we, as a nation, build a memorial for this? The answer is simple. American soldiers gave their lives for their country. No matter what the context was surrounding the war, brave men gave the ultimate sacrifice and deserve to be remembered for it. Maya Lin, as an undergraduate student, understood this perfectly when

1. Any opinions present in this essay belong to the author and do not represent the views of the United States Army [Krivda's note].

she submitted her "nihilistic slab of stone," as it was called by James Webb, a decorated Vietnam veteran and politician (Wills), for a design contest commissioned by the United States government in 1981.[2] After it was announced that her design had won the contest, it immediately received strong opposition from many, including James Webb. Despite this opposition, Lin held firm to her design.

While Lin is paying tribute to the casualties of the Vietnam War, Lin's design and the way it contrasts with other war memorials captures America's general dislike of the war. The wall was not constructed on a hill for all to see, nor is it freestanding. Lin designed it to be built into the ground, like a common retaining wall one would see

4

2. Webb was Marine Lieutenant and a platoon leader who was awarded the Navy Cross, Silver Star, two Bronze Stars, and two Purple Hearts for his heroism in Vietnam. He then graduated from Georgetown Law School and went on to become the Secretary of the Navy and a Senator of Virginia (Drew).

in a suburban backyard, making it very insignificant compared to the Washington Monument, Lincoln Memorial,
and World War II Memorial that surround it. All three of
these monuments are in the center of the Mall while the
Vietnam Memorial is off to the north side, away from a
tourist's typical walking path.

The contrast between the Vietnam and World War II    5 •••••
Memorials is telling. The World War II Memorial has an
elaborate structure that seems to glorify the war. It cele-
brates our victory over fascism, making anyone who
walks around it feel proud to be an American; the Vietnam Memorial, on the other hand, has quite a different
effect. When one walks down that black wall, reading the
names of those who sacrificed themselves for a battle that
they ultimately lost, one feels a wave of sadness sap the
excitement out of a day visiting the monuments. The
simplicity of the structure gives it its power—power that
can be seen at the memorial every day through the tears
shed by veterans taking in their fallen brothers' names.
Its lack of ornament gives it a solemn feel that facilitates
reflection on those we have lost and the sacrifice they
made. It does not glorify war, but pressures one to ponder
why we were even in Vietnam and why those men had
to die.

It's hard to drive through downtown Washington,    6
D.C., without passing an old man with a scraggly beard
and camo jacket holding a brown cardboard sign with
something like "Homeless. Vietnam Vet. Please Help. God
Bless" written on it in black Sharpie. After World War II,
new systems like the G.I. Bill, which provided veterans
with money for education, home loans, health care, and
unemployment benefits, were put in place to help

Uses COMPARISON
(Chapter 10) to
capture the
"simplicity" of the
memorial

veterans, and hiring veterans was highly encouraged. But apparently we forgot about this after the Vietnam War. Not much changed in these veteran benefit programs to account for the differences between the two wars, both in terms of what veterans experienced while in combat and society's attitudes toward the war. Maya Lin's memorial design recognizes this in its color scheme. The wall is black the whole way down, representing the war and how it was a dark time for those involved, but the names of the ones who were lost appear in white. This shows how those who served are the ones meant to be remembered. It shows veterans that they and their fallen comrades are being memorialized, not the war itself. The color white suggests that each soldier was a light in a time of darkness, and because every name is the same color, that light includes all veterans whether they are senators or men begging on a street corner.

To explain the colors of the wall, Krivda uses the SIMILE of light and darkness

While the majority of the details on the memorial  7 suggest an antiwar perspective, there is one subtle detail that cannot be ignored. The memorial is in the shape of a wide "V." This wide "V" is positioned so that one leg points at the Lincoln Memorial and the other at the Washington Monument. This addresses the war's complexity. Even though there will always inevitably be casualties of war, when it comes down to it, war is often a necessary evil to protect the values that George Washington and Abraham Lincoln fought to put in place: our freedom and equality. As the World War II Memorial shows, victories against oppression and genocide, coupled with the upholding of freedom and equality, can justify war. The Vietnam War Memorial silently shouts this at us, as if to say the original intentions of the war justified it, but as the war progressed, the accumulation of white names pulled it out of the main section of the Mall and into the ground.

The Vietnam War Memorial makes many arguments as to what constitutes a truly great memorial. Maya Lin went through with her design despite opposition because she knew that it was something special. The memorial being built into the ground and off to the side of the National Mall's main drag shows America's opposition to troops in Vietnam. The white names on a black surface testify that the soldiers were the ones to be memorialized, not the war itself or anything the war could have gained for us as a nation. Finally, its wide "V" shape pointing to the Washington Monument and the Lincoln Memorial remind us that if freedom and equality are in jeopardy, fighting can be necessary. The Vietnam War Memorial shows us that even on a national level, we can recognize our mistakes and attempt to heal our wounds.

8 • Krivda combines description and ARGUMENT (Chapter 13), to conclude that the wall is a "truly great" memorial

Works Cited

Ankony, Robert. "Perspectives." *Vietnam Magazine*, 13 June 2015, www.robertankony.com/publications /perspectives. Accessed 12 Oct. 2014.

Drew, Elizabeth. "The Jim Webb Story." Review of *A Time to Fight: Reclaiming a Fair and Just* America, by Jim Webb. *The New York Review of Books*, 26 June 2008, www .nybooks.com/articles/2008/06/26/the-jim -webb-story. Accessed 7 Dec. 2014.

United States, Department of Veterans Affairs. "VA History." *U.S. Department of Veterans Affairs*, United States Government, 17 Nov. 2014, www.va.gov/about _va/vahistory.asp. Accessed 7 Dec. 2014.

Wills, Denise Kersten. "The Vietnam Memorial's History." *The Washingtonian*, 1 Nov. 2007, www.washingtonian .com/2007/11/01/the-vietnam-memorials-history, Accessed 12 Oct. 2014.

# SAM QUINONES

# DREAMLAND

SAM QUINONES (b. 1958) is a journalist known for his reporting on Mexico and the many intersections of Mexican and American culture. A native of Claremont, California, Quinones graduated from the University of California, Berkeley, before becoming a journalist at the *Orange County Register*, a daily newspaper in California, and later, the *Los Angeles Times*. His books, beginning with *True Tales from Another Mexico* (2001), combine reportage and storytelling. In *Dreamland: The True Tale of America's Opiate Epidemic* (2015), Quinones uses Portsmouth, Ohio, to illustrate how a once-idyllic small-town America has been devastated in recent decades by both economic decline and an epidemic of addiction to opiates. In the following selection, which is the prologue to the book, Quinones uses abstract and concrete details to describe Dreamland, the "gleaming, glorious swimming pool" that for many was the place of "chlorine, Coppertone, and french fries."

I N 1929, three decades into what were the great years for the blue-collar town      1
of Portsmouth, on the Ohio River, a private swimming pool opened and
they called it Dreamland.

The pool was the size of a football field. Over the decades, generations of     2
the town grew up at the edge of its crystal-blue water.

Dreamland was the summer babysitter. Parents left their children at the      3
pool every day. Townsfolk found respite from the thick humidity at Dreamland and then went across the street to the A&W stand for hot dogs and root
beer. The pool's french fries were the best around. Kids took the bus to the
pool in the morning, and back home in the afternoon. They came from schools
all over Scioto County and met each other and learned to swim. Some of them
competed on the Dreamland Dolphins swim team, which practiced every
morning and evening. WIOI, the local radio station, knowing so many of its
listeners were sunbathing next to their transistor radios at Dreamland, would
broadcast a jingle—"Time to turn so you won't burn"—every half hour.

The vast pool had room in the middle for two concrete platforms, from      4
which kids sunned themselves, then dove back in. Poles topped with flood-
lights rose from the platforms for swimming at night. On one side of the pool
was an immense lawn where families set their towels. On the opposite side
were locker rooms and a restaurant.

Dreamland could fit hundreds of people, and yet, magically, the space      5
around it kept growing and there was always room for more. Jaime Williams,
the city treasurer, owned the pool for years. Williams was part owner of one
of the shoe factories that were at the core of Portsmouth's industrial might.
He bought more and more land, and for years Dreamland seemed to just get
better. A large picnic area was added, and playgrounds for young children.
Then fields for softball and football, and courts for basketball and shuffle-
board, and a video arcade.

For a while, to remain white only, the pool became a private club and the      6
name changed to the Terrace Club. But Portsmouth was a largely integrated
town. Its chief of police was black. Black and white kids went to the same
schools. Only the pool remained segregated. Then, in the summer of 1961, a
black boy named Eugene McKinley drowned in the Scioto River, where he was
swimming because he was kept out of the pool. The Portsmouth NAACP
pushed back, held a wade-in, and quietly they integrated the pool. With inte-

gration, the pool was rechristened Dreamland, though blacks were never made to feel particularly comfortable there.

Dreamland did wash away class distinctions, though. In a swimming 7 suit, a factory worker looked no different from the factory manager or clothing-shop owner. Wealthy families on Portsmouth's hilltop donated money to a fund that would go to pay for summer passes for families from the town's East End, down between the tracks and the Ohio River. East End river rats and upscale hilltoppers all met at Dreamland.

California had its beaches. Heartland America spent its summers at 8 swimming pools, and, down at a far end of Ohio, Dreamland took on an out-sized importance to the town of Portsmouth. A family's season pass was only twenty-five dollars, and this was a prized possession often given as a Christmas present. Kids whose families couldn't afford that could cut a neighbor's grass for the fifteen cents that a daily pool pass cost.

Page 75 explains how to describe something from a consistent vantage point like this.

Friday swim dances began at midnight. They hauled out a jukebox and 9 kids spent the night twisting by the pool. Couples announced new romances by walking hand in hand around Dreamland. Girls walked home from those dances and families left their doors unlocked. "The heat of the evening combined with the cool water was wonderful," one woman remembered. "It was my entire world. I did nothing else. As I grew up and had my own children, I took them, too."

In fact, the cycle of life in Portsmouth was repeated over and over at 10 Dreamland. A toddler spent her first years at the shallow end watched by her parents, particularly her mother, who sat on a towel on the concrete near the water with other young moms. When the child left elementary school, she migrated out to the middle section of Dreamland as her parents retreated to the grass. By high school, she was hanging out on the grass around the pool's ten-foot deep end, near the high dive and the head lifeguard's chair, and her parents were far away. When she married and had children, she returned to the shallow end of Dreamland to watch over her own children, and the whole thing began again.

"My father, a Navy Vet from WWII, insisted that his 4 children learn 11 not only how to swim but how not to be afraid of water," one man wrote. "My younger sister jumped off the 15-foot high diving board at age 3. Yes, my father, myself & brother were in the water just in case. Sister pops up out of the water and screams . . . 'Again!'"

For many years, Dreamland's manager, Chuck Lorentz, a Portsmouth 12 High School coach and strict disciplinarian, walked the grounds with a yardstick, making sure teenagers minded his "three-foot rule" and stayed that far apart. He wasn't that successful. It seems half the town got their first kiss at the pool, and plenty lost their virginity in Dreamland's endless grass.

Lorentz's son, meanwhile, learned to swim before he could walk and 13 became a Dreamland lifeguard in high school. "To be the lifeguard in that chair, you were right in the center of all the action, all the strutting, all the flirting," said John Lorentz, now a retired history professor. "You were like a king on a throne."

Through these years, Portsmouth also supported two bowling alleys, a 14 JCPenney, a Sears, and a Montgomery Ward[1] with an escalator, and locally owned Marting's Department Store, with a photo studio where graduating seniors had their portraits taken. Chillicothe Street bustled. Big U.S.-made sedans and station wagons lined the street. People cashed their checks at the Kresge's[2] on Saturdays, and the owners of Morgan Brothers Jewelry, Herrmann's Meats, Counts' Bakery, and Atlas Fashion earned a middle-class living. Kids took the bus downtown to the movie theater or for cherry Cokes at Smith's Drugstore and stayed out late trick-or-treating on Halloween. On Friday and Saturday nights, teenagers cruised Chillicothe Street, from Staker's Drugs down to Smith's, then turned around and did it again.

Throughout the year, the shoe factories would deduct Christmas Club 15 money from each worker's paycheck. Before Christmas, they issued each worker a check and he would cash it at the bank. Chillicothe Street was festive then. Bells rang as shoppers went shoulder to shoulder, watching the mechanical puppets in displays in store windows painted with candy canes, Christmas trees, and snowmen. Marting's had a Santa on its second floor.

1. A national chain of department stores in business from 1872 to 2001. An online version operates today as Wards.

2. A national chain of stores no longer in business, known for selling merchandise at low prices.

So, in 1979 and 1980, Portsmouth felt worthy to be selected an All- 16
American City. The town had more than forty-two thousand people then.
Very few were wealthy, and the U.S. Labor Department would have gauged
many Portsmouthians poor. "But we weren't aware of it, nor did we care," one
woman recalled. Its industry supported a community for all. No one had pools
in their backyards. Rather, there were parks, tennis and basketball courts, and
window-shopping and levees to slide down. Families ice-skated at Millbrook
Park in winter and picnicked at Roosevelt Lake in summer, or sat late into the
evening as their kids played Kick the Can in the street.

"My family used to picnic down by the Ohio River in a little park, where 17
my dad would push me so high on the swings I thought I'd land in Kentucky,"
another woman said.

All of this recreation let a working-class family feel well-off. But the 18
center of it all was that gleaming, glorious swimming pool. Memories of
Dreamland, drenched in the smell of chlorine, Coppertone, and french fries,
were what almost everyone who grew up in Portsmouth took with them as the
town declined.

Two Portsmouths exist today. One is a town of abandoned buildings at 19
the edge of the Ohio River. The other resides in the memories of thousands in
the town's diaspora who grew up during its better years and return to the
actual Portsmouth rarely, if at all.

When you ask them what the town was back then, it was Dreamland. 20

## FOR DISCUSSION

1. After its opening in Portsmouth, Ohio, in 1929, Dreamland, the immense swimming pool described in detail by Sam Quinones, "took on an outsized importance
   to the town" (8). Why? What was so significant about the pool to the townspeople—
   and to Quinones himself as a reporter writing about "Heartland America" (8)?

2. What were some of the sources of the "industrial might" of a town like Portsmouth in the years leading up to its designation in 1979 as an "All-American City"
   (5, 16)? How and why has the region changed since then?

3. How and how well did the town of Portsmouth deal with the racial integration of
   Dreamland in 1961 (6), according to Quinones?

4. According to Quinones, how did a members-only swimming pool "wash away class distinctions" in the town (7)? What other places can you think of that might have a similar effect?

## STRATEGIES AND STRUCTURES

1. In its heyday, says Quinones, the pool at Dreamland was "vast" (4). Point to some of the specific details in his description that convey the pool's immense size and any other physical attributes of the pool that you noticed.

2. What other ABSTRACT qualities—for example, a sense of timelessness—do Quinones and the townspeople associate with Dreamland? Cite details in the text that you find particularly effective at capturing these less CONCRETE aspects of the place.

3. Most of Quinones's description is devoted to the pool. Where does he describe other parts of the town? What DOMINANT IMPRESSION of the place does he convey here? What do all the names of stores and businesses (14) contribute to this impression? Why is it relevant, for example, that one department store had an escalator?

4. Quinones is not only describing a place and time but also the inhabitants' *recollections* of that place and time. Which particular memories and associations do you find most compelling? Why?

5. How and how well do the specific physical details and memories in Quinones's description contribute to the idea of Portsmouth as a place in a dream? Why might Quinones seek to give this impression?

## WORDS AND FIGURES OF SPEECH

1. For purposes of capturing a place and region as they were "back then," why is "Dreamland" a more descriptive name than, say, "Terrace Club" (6, 20)?

2. The manager of Dreamland often carried a yardstick to enforce his "three-foot rule" (12). Explain the PUN on *rule* here. How well did the rule work?

3. "Time to turn so you won't burn" (3)—whose slogan was this, according to Quinones? What does it tell the reader about life in the summer during Portsmouth's heyday?

4. For many of the townspeople, their memories of Dreamland are "drenched in the smell of chlorine, Coppertone, and french fries" (18). How and how well do these three terms sum up Quinones's description?

5. The word *diaspora* (19) usually refers to the movement or migration of an entire people from their ancestral homeland. By using this term in a description of present-day Portsmouth, what is Quinones suggesting about the scope and scale of the town's decline?

### FOR WRITING

1. In a single paragraph, Quinones describes an entire "cycle of life" in Portsmouth of an earlier day (10). Write a paragraph describing such a cycle of a place in your past. Organize it by time, as Quinones does—and give it a beginning, middle, and ending that circles back to the beginning.

2. Write a description of a swimming pool, amusement park, or other place of recreation that you particularly associate with growing up. Choose details that convey not only what the place meant to you but also to the larger community. Be sure to indicate how it has changed over the years.

## CHEROKEE PAUL MCDONALD

# A VIEW FROM THE BRIDGE

CHEROKEE PAUL MCDONALD (b. 1949) is a fiction writer and journalist. His memoir, *Into the Green* (2001), recounts his months of combat as an U.S. Army lieutenant in Vietnam. One of the themes of the book, says McDonald, "is hate the war, but don't hate the soldier." After Vietnam, McDonald served for ten years on the police force of Fort Lauderdale, Florida, an experience that he has drawn upon in several crime novels and that he describes graphically in *Blue Truth* (1991). McDonald is also a fisherman and the father of three children, roles that come together in the following descriptive essay about a boy who helps the author see familiar objects in a new light. The essay was first published in 1990 in *Sunshine*, a Florida sporting magazine.

•⊢────────────────────────────────⊣•

I WAS COMING UP ON THE LITTLE BRIDGE in the Rio Vista neighborhood of   1
Fort Lauderdale, deepening my stride and my breathing to negotiate the slight incline without altering my pace. And then, as I neared the crest, I saw the kid.

He was a lumpy little guy with baggy shorts, a faded T-shirt, and heavy   2
sweat socks falling down over old sneakers.

Partially covering his shaggy blond hair was one of those blue baseball   3
caps with gold braid on the bill and a sailfish patch sewn onto the peak. Covering his eyes and part of his face was a pair of those stupid-looking '50s-style
wrap-around sunglasses.

He was fumbling with a beat-up rod and reel, and he had a little bait   4
bucket by his feet. I puffed on by, glancing down into the empty bucket as I
passed.

"Hey, mister! Would you help me, please?"   5

The shrill voice penetrated my jogger's concentration, and I was deter-   6
mined to ignore it. But for some reason, I stopped.

With my hands on my hips and the sweat dripping from my nose I asked,   7
"What do you want, kid?"

"Would you please help me find my shrimp? It's my last one and I've   8
been getting bites and I know I can catch a fish if I can just find that shrimp.
He jumped outta my hand as I was getting him from the bucket."

Exasperated, I walked slowly back to the kid, and pointed.   9

"There's the damn shrimp by your left foot. You stopped me for *that*?"   10

As I said it, the kid reached down and trapped the shrimp.   11

"Thanks a lot, mister," he said.   12

I watched as the kid dropped the baited hook down into the canal. Then   13
I turned to start back down the bridge.

That's when the kid let out a "Hey! Hey!" and the prettiest tarpon I'd   14
ever seen came almost six feet out of the water, twisting and turning as he fell
through the air.

"I got one!" the kid yelled as the fish hit the water with a loud splash and   15
took off down the canal.

I watched the line being burned off the reel at an alarming rate. The kid's   16
left hand held the crank while the extended fingers felt for the drag setting.

"No, kid!" I shouted. "Leave the drag alone . . . just keep that damn rod   17
tip up!"

Then I glanced at the reel and saw there were just a few loops of line left   18
on the spool.

"Why don't you get yourself some decent equipment?" I said, but before    19
the kid could answer I saw the line go slack.

"Ohhh, I lost him," the kid said. I saw the flash of silver as the fish turned.    20

"Crank, kid, crank! You didn't lose him. He's coming back toward you.    21
Bring in the slack!"

The kid cranked like mad, and a beautiful grin spread across his face.    22

"He's heading in for the pilings," I said. "Keep him out of those pilings!"    23

The kid played it perfectly. When the fish made its play for the pilings,    24
he kept just enough pressure on to force the fish out. When the water exploded
and the silver missile hurled into the air, the kid kept the rod tip up and the
line tight.

As the fish came to the surface and began a slow circle in the middle of    25
the canal, I said, "Whooee, is that a nice fish or what?"

The kid didn't say anything, so I said, "Okay, move to the edge of the    26
bridge and I'll climb down to the seawall and pull him out."

When I reached the seawall I pulled in the leader, leaving the fish lying    27
on its side in the water.

"How's that?" I said.    28

"Hey, mister, tell me what it looks like."    29

"Look down here and check him out," I said, "He's beautiful."    30

But then I looked up into those stupid-looking sunglasses and it hit me.    31
The kid was blind.

"Could you tell me what he looks like, mister?" he said again.    32

"Well, he's just under three, uh, he's about as long as one of your arms,"    33
I said. "I'd guess he goes about 15, 20 pounds. He's mostly silver, but the silver
is somehow made up of *all* the colors, if you know what I mean." I stopped.
"Do you know what I mean by colors?"

The kid nodded.    34

"Okay. He has all these big scales, like armor all over his body. They're    35
silver too, and when he moves they sparkle. He has a strong body and a large
powerful tail. He has big round eyes, bigger than a quarter, and a lower jaw that
sticks out past the upper one and is very tough. His belly is almost white and
his back is a gunmetal gray. When he jumped he came out of the water about
six feet, and his scales caught the sun and flashed it all over the place."

By now the fish had righted itself, and I could see the bright-red gills as    36
the gill plates opened and closed. I explained this to the kid, and then said,
more to myself, "He's a beauty."

"Can you get him off the hook?" the kid asked. "I don't want to kill him."    37

I watched as the tarpon began to slowly swim away, tired but still    38
alive.

By the time I got back up to the top of the bridge the kid had his line    39
secured and his bait bucket in one hand.

He grinned and said, "Just in time. My mom drops me off here, and she'll    40
be back to pick me up any minute."

He used the back of one hand to wipe his nose.    41

"Thanks for helping me catch that tarpon," he said, "and for helping me    42
to see it."

I looked at him, shook my head, and said, "No, my friend, thank you for    43
letting *me* see that fish."

I took off, but before I got far the kid yelled again.    44

"Hey, mister!"    45

I stopped.    46

"Someday I'm gonna catch a sailfish and a blue marlin and a giant tuna    47
and all those big sportfish!"

As I looked into those sunglasses I knew he probably would. I wished I    48
could be there when it happened.


**FOR DISCUSSION**

1. Which of the five senses does Cherokee Paul McDonald appeal to in his
   **DESCRIPTION** of the tarpon (35)? In this essay as a whole?

2. How much does the jogger seem to know about fish and fishing? About boys?

3. What is the attitude of the jogger toward the "kid" before he realizes the boy is
   blind (31)? As a reader, what is your attitude toward the jogger? Why?

4. How does the jogger feel about the kid when they part? How do you feel about the
   jogger? What, if anything, changes your view of him?

5. How does meticulously describing a small piece of the world help the grumpy jogger to see the world anew?

## STRATEGIES AND STRUCTURES

1. McDonald serves as eyes for the boy (and us). Which physical details in his description of the scene at the bridge do you find to be visually most effective?

2. McDonald's description is part of a **NARRATIVE**. At first, the **NARRATOR** seems irritable and in a hurry. What makes him slow down? How does his behavior change? Why?

3. The narrator does not realize the boy is blind until paragraph 31, but we figure it out much sooner. What descriptive details lead us to realize that the boy is blind?

4. McDonald, of course, knew when he wrote this piece that the boy couldn't see. Why do you think he wrote from the **POINT OF VIEW** of the jogger, who doesn't know at first? How does he restrict the narrator's point of view in paragraph 6? Elsewhere in the essay?

5. How does the narrator's physical **VANTAGE POINT** change in paragraph 27? Why does this alter the way he sees the boy?

6. "No, my friend," says the jogger, "thank you for letting *me* see that fish" (43). So who is helping whom to see in this essay? How? Cite examples.

## WORDS AND FIGURES OF SPEECH

1. **METONYMY** is a **FIGURE OF SPEECH** in which a word or object stands in for another associated with it. How might the blind boy's cap or sunglasses be seen as examples of metonymy?

2. Point out words and phrases in this essay—for example, "sparkle"—that refer to sights or acts of seeing (35).

3. What possible meanings are suggested by the word "view" in McDonald's title?

4. Besides its literal meaning, how else might we take the word "bridge" here? Who or what is being "bridged"?

## FOR WRITING

1. Suppose you had to describe a flower, bird, snake, butterfly, or other plant or animal to a blind person. In a paragraph, describe the object—its colors, smell, texture, movement, how the light strikes it—in sufficient physical detail so that the person could form an accurate mental picture of what you are describing.

2. Write an extended description of a scene in which you see a familiar object, person, or place in a new light because of someone else who brings a fresh viewpoint to the picture. For example, you might describe the scene at the dinner table when you bring home a new girlfriend or boyfriend. Or you might describe taking a tour of your campus, hometown, neighborhood, or workplace with a friend or relative who has never seen it before.

ALICE STEINBACH

# THE MISS DENNIS SCHOOL OF WRITING

ALICE STEINBACH (1933–2012) was a freelance writer whose essays and travel sketches often deal with what she called "lessons from a woman's life." As a reporter for the *Baltimore Sun*, where she won a Pulitzer Prize for feature writing in 1985, Steinbach wrote a column about her ninth-grade creative writing teacher. It became the title piece in a collection of personal essays, *The Miss Dennis School of Writing* (1996). Here the "lesson" is both a writing lesson and a life lesson. Miss Dennis taught that good descriptive writing (her specialty) makes the reader see what the writer sees. She also taught her students to find their unique personal voices. Steinbach's distinctive voice can be heard in her vivid descriptions of her former teacher. It is a perspective, she has said, that "tends to look at people with a child's eye."

"**W**HAT KIND OF WRITING DO YOU DO?" asked the novelist sitting to my    1
left at a writer's luncheon.

"I work for a newspaper in Baltimore," he was told.    2

"Oh, did you go to journalism school?"    3

"Well, yes."    4

"Columbia?" he asked, invoking the name of the most prestigious jour-    5
nalism school in the country.

"Actually, no," I heard myself telling him. "I'm one of the lucky ones. I    6
am a graduate of the Miss Dennis School of Writing."

Unimpressed, the novelist turned away. Clearly it was a credential that    7
did not measure up to his standards. But why should it? He was not one of the
lucky ones. He had never met Miss Dennis, my ninth-grade creative writing
teacher, or had the good fortune to be her student. Which meant he had never
experienced the sight of Miss Dennis chasing Dorothy Singer around the
classroom, threatening her with a yardstick because Dorothy hadn't paid
attention and her writing showed it.

"You want to be a writer?" Miss Dennis would yell, out of breath from all    8
the running and yardstick-brandishing. "Then pay attention to what's going
on around you. Connect! You are not Switzerland—neutral, aloof, uninvolved.
Think Italy!"

Miss Dennis said things like this. If you had any sense, you wrote them    9
down.

"I can't teach you how to write, but I can tell you how to look at things,    10
how to pay attention," she would bark out at us, like a drill sergeant confronting a group of undisciplined, wet-behind-the-ears[1] Marine recruits. To drive
home her point, she had us take turns writing a description of what we saw on
the way to school in the morning. Of course, you never knew    Concrete details
which morning would be your turn so—just to be on the safe    (p. 72) help to drive
side—you got into the habit of looking things over carefully every    home the point of
                                                                     any description.
morning and making notes: "Saw a pot of red geraniums sitting in the sunlight
on a white stucco porch; an orange-striped cat curled like a comma beneath a
black van; a dark gray cloud scudding across a silver morning sky."

---

1. Young and inexperienced.

It's a lesson that I have returned to again and again throughout my writ- 11
ing career. To this day, I think of Miss Dennis whenever I write a certain kind
of sentence. Or to be more precise, whenever I write a sentence that actually
creates in words the picture I want readers to see.

Take, for instance, this sentence: Miss Dennis was a small, compact 12
woman, about albatross height—or so it seemed to her students—with short,
straight hair the color of apricots and huge eyeglasses that were always slipping down her nose.

Or this one: Miss Dennis always wore a variation of one outfit—a dark- 13
colored, flared woolen skirt, a tailored white blouse and a cardigan sweater,
usually black, thrown over her shoulders and held together by a little pearl
chain.

Can you see her? I can. And the image of her makes me smile. Still.        14

But it was not Miss Dennis's appearance or her unusual teaching 15
method—which had a lot in common with an out-of-control terrier—that
made her so special. What set her apart was her deep commitment to liberating the individual writer in each student.

"What lies at the heart of good writing," she told us over and over again, 16
"is the writer's ability to find his own unique voice. And then to use it to tell
an interesting story." Somehow she made it clear that we were interesting
people with interesting stories to tell. Most of us, of course, had never even
known we had a story to tell, much less an interesting one. But soon the stories just started bubbling up from some inner wellspring.

Finding the material, however, was one thing; finding the individual 17
voice was another.

Take me, for instance. I arrived in Miss Dennis's class trailing all sorts of 18
literary baggage. My usual routine was to write like Colette on Monday, one of
the Brontë sisters on Wednesday, and Mark Twain[2] on Friday.

Right away, Miss Dennis knocked me off my high horse.                      19

---

2. Sidonie-Gabrielle Colette (1873–1954), French novelist known for her depictions of female
sexuality; Charlotte Brontë (1816–1855), Emily Brontë (1818–1848), and Anne Brontë
(1820–1849), British writers of early Romantic novels; Mark Twain (1835–1910), American
novelist and essayist known for his works of wit and satire.

"Why are you telling other people's stories?" she challenged me, peering   20
up into my face. (At fourteen I was already four inches taller than Miss Dennis.) "You have your own stories to tell."

I was tremendously relieved to hear this and immediately proceeded to   21
write like my idol, E. B. White.[3] Miss Dennis, however, wasn't buying.

"How will you ever find out what you have to say if you keep trying to   22
say what other people have already said?" was the way she dispensed with
my E. B. White impersonation. By the third week of class, Miss Dennis knew
my secret. She knew I was afraid—afraid to pay attention to my own inner
voice for fear that when I finally heard it, it would have nothing to say.

What Miss Dennis told me—and I have carefully preserved these words   23
because they were then, and are now, so very important to me—was this:
"Don't be afraid to discover what you're saying in the act of saying it." Then, in
her inimitably breezy and endearing way, she added: "Trust me on this one."

From the beginning, she made it clear to us that it was not "right" or   24
"wrong" answers she was after. It was thinking.

"Don't be afraid to go out on a limb,"[4] she'd tell some poor kid struggling   25
to reason his way through an essay on friendship or courage. And eventually—
once we stopped being afraid that we'd be chopped off out there on that limb—
we needed no encouragement to say what we thought. In fact, after the first
month, I can't remember ever feeling afraid of failing in her class. Passing or
failing didn't seem to be the point of what she was teaching.

Miss Dennis spent as much time, maybe more, pointing out what was   26
right with your work as she did pointing out what was wrong. I can still hear
her critiquing my best friend's incredibly florid essay on nature. "You are a
very good observer of nature," she told the budding writer. "And if you just
write what you see without thinking so much about adjectives and comparisons, we will see it through your attentive eyes."

3. American essayist and children's author (1899–1985), admired for his elegant style and
attention to detail.
4. "To go out on a limb" is an expression that means to take a risk. A person climbing a tree
is safer staying close to the trunk; going out on a limb increases the risk of falling.

By Thanksgiving vacation I think we were all a little infatuated with 27 Miss Dennis. And beyond that, infatuated with the way she made us feel about ourselves—that we were interesting people worth listening to.

I, of course, fancied I had a special relationship with her. It was certainly 28 special to me. And, to tell the truth, I knew she felt the same way.

The first time we acknowledged this was one day after class when I 29 stayed behind to talk to her. I often did that and it seemed we talked about everything—from the latest films to the last issue of the *New Yorker*. The one thing we did not talk about was the sadness I felt about my father's death. He had died a few years before and, although I did not know it then, I was still grieving his absence. Without knowing the details, Miss Dennis somehow picked up on my sadness. Maybe it was there in my writing. Looking back I see now that, without my writing about it directly, my father's death hovered at the edges of all my stories.

But on this particular day I found myself talking not about the movies or 30 about writing but instead pouring out my feelings about the loss of my father. I shall never forget that late fall afternoon: the sound of the vanilla-colored blinds flap, flap, flapping in the still classroom; sun falling in shafts through the windows, each ray illuminating tiny galaxies of chalk dust in the air; the smell of wet blackboards; the teacher, small with apricot-colored hair, listening intently to a young girl blurting out her grief. These memories are stored like vintage photographs.

The words that passed between the young girl and the attentive 31 teacher are harder to recall. With this exception. "One day," Miss Dennis told me, "you will write about this. Maybe not directly. But you will write about it. And you will find that all this has made you a better writer and a stronger person."

After that day, it was as if Miss Dennis and I shared something. We 32 never talked again about my father but spent most of our time discussing our mutual interests. We both loved poetry and discovered one afternoon that each of us regarded Emily Dickinson with something approaching idolatry. Right then and there, Miss Dennis gave me a crash course in why Emily Dickinson's poems worked. I can still hear her talking about the "spare, slanted beauty" in Dickinson's unique choice of words. She also told me about the rather cloistered life led by this New England spinster, noting that nonetheless Emily Dickinson[5] knew the world as few others did. "She found her world within the word," is the way I remember Miss Dennis putting it. Of course, I could be making that part up.

That night, propped up in bed reading Emily Dickinson's poetry, I won-   33 dered if Miss Dennis, a spinster herself, identified in some way with the woman who wrote:

> Wild nights—Wild nights!
> Were I with thee
> Wild Nights should be
> Our luxury!

It seems strange, I know, but I never really knew anything about Miss Dennis'   34 life outside of the classroom. Oh, once she confided in me that the initial "M" in her name stood for Mildred. And I was surprised when I passed by the teachers' lounge one day and saw her smoking a cigarette, one placed in a long, silver cigarette holder. It seemed an exceedingly sophisticated thing to do and it struck me then that she might be more worldly than I had previously thought.

But I didn't know how she spent her time or what she wanted from life   35 or anything like that. And I never really wondered about it. Once I remember talking to some friends about her age. We guessed somewhere around fifty— which seemed really old to us. In reality, Miss Dennis was around forty.

It was Miss Dennis, by the way, who encouraged me to enter some writ-   36 ing contests. To my surprise, I took first place in a couple of them. Of course, taking first place is easy. What's hard is being rejected. But Miss Dennis helped me with that, too, citing all the examples of famous writers who'd been rejected time and time again. "Do you know what they told George Orwell[6] when they rejected *Animal Farm*?" she would ask me. Then without waiting for

5. American poet (1830–1886) who wrote almost 1,800 poems (and many letters). In later years, Dickinson seldom left her family home in Amherst, Massachusetts.

6. British novelist and essayist (1903–1950). Much of his major work, including the novel *Animal Farm* (1945), reflects his opposition to repressive governments.

a reply, she'd answer her own question: "The publisher told him, 'It is impossible to sell animal stories in the U.S.A.'"

When I left her class at the end of the year, Miss Dennis gave me a present: a book of poems by Emily Dickinson. I have it still. The spine is cracked and the front cover almost gone, but the inscription remains. On the inside flyleaf, in her perfect Palmer Method handwriting,[7] she had written: "Say what you see. Yours in Emily Dickinson, Miss Dennis."    37

She had also placed little checks next to two or three poems. I took this to mean she thought they contained a special message for me. One of those checked began this way:    38

> Hope is the thing with feathers
> That perches in the soul . . .

I can remember carefully copying out these lines onto a sheet of paper, one which I carried around in my handbag for almost a year. But time passed, the handbag fell apart and who knows what happened to the yellowing piece of paper with the words about hope.

The years went by. Other schools and other teachers came and went. But one thing remained constant: My struggle to pay attention to my own inner life; to hear a voice that I would recognize finally as my own. Not only in my writing but in my life.    39

Only recently, I learned that Miss Dennis had died at the age of fifty. When I heard this, it occurred to me that her life was close to being over when I met her. Neither of us knew this, of course. Or at least I didn't. But lately I've wondered if she knew something that day we talked about sadness and my father's death. "Write about it," she said. "It will help you."    40

And now, reading over these few observations, I think of Miss Dennis. But not with sadness. Actually, thinking of Miss Dennis makes me smile. I think of her and see, with marked clarity, a small, compact woman with apricot-colored hair. She is with a young girl and she is saying something.    41

She is saying: "Pay attention."    42

---

7. A form of standardized handwriting that was popular around 1900 but is rarely taught today.

## FOR DISCUSSION

1. When some teachers say, "Pay attention," they mean "Pay attention to what I am saying." According to her former pupil, Alice Steinbach, what did Miss Dennis mean when she told students to pay attention (8)?

2. It was neither Miss Dennis's appearance nor her teaching methods that made her so special as a teacher of writing, says Steinbach, but "her deep commitment to liberating the individual writer in each student" (15). How did Miss Dennis accomplish this feat in Steinbach's case?

3. Steinbach poses a direct question to the reader in paragraph 14: "Can you see her?" Well, can you? And if so, what exactly do you see—and hear? For example, what color was Miss Dennis's hair?

4. Steinbach thinks of her old teacher whenever she writes a sentence "that actually creates in words the picture I want readers to see" (11). This is precisely what good **DESCRIPTIVE** writing does, although it may appeal to other senses as well as sight. How did Miss Dennis teach this kind of writing?

5. Writing about old teachers who die can be an occasion for sentimentality or excessively emotional writing. Do you think Steinbach's tribute to her former teacher is overly emotional, or does she successfully avoid sentimentality? If she avoids it, in your opinion, explain how she does so. If not, explain why you think she doesn't. Find places in her essay that support your view.

## STRATEGIES AND STRUCTURES

1. Point out several descriptive passages in Steinbach's essay that follow her principle of creating in words what she wants the reader to see.

2. Why do you think Steinbach, looking back over her recollections of Miss Dennis, refers to them as "observations" (41)?

3. Description seldom stands alone. Often it shades into **NARRATION**, as here. Thus Miss Dennis, who greatly valued the writer's eye, urged the student, once she found her unique way of looking at the world, to use it "to tell an interesting story" (16). Besides Miss Dennis's, whose story is Steinbach telling? How interesting do you find *that* narrative?

4. What **DOMINANT IMPRESSION** of Miss Dennis do we get from Steinbach's description of her in paragraphs 12 through 14 and 41? Of Steinbach herself?

5. How informative do you find Steinbach's essay as a lesson on how to write, particularly on how to write good description? Where does Steinbach **ANALYZE THE PROCESS**?

## WORDS AND FIGURES OF SPEECH

1. Which is more **CONCRETE**, to say that a woman has "hair the color of apricots" or to say that she is a redhead or blonde (12)? Which is more specific?

2. The orange-striped cat in young Steinbach's description of her walk to school is "curled like a comma" beneath a van (10). Such stated **COMPARISONS**, frequently using *like* or *as*, are called **SIMILES**. Implied comparisons, without like or as, are called **METAPHORS**. What metaphoric comparison does Steinbach make in the same description? What is she comparing to what?

3. Steinbach compares Miss Dennis to an "albatross" and "an out-of-control terrier" (12, 15). Besides describing Miss Dennis, what do these fanciful comparisons tell you about her former writing pupil?

4. Steinbach arrived in Miss Dennis's class "trailing all sorts of literary baggage" (18). To what is she comparing herself here?

5. How would you describe the words that Steinbach uses in paragraph 30 to describe the afternoon? Concrete or **ABSTRACT**? Specific or general?

## FOR WRITING

1. On your next walk to or around school, pay close attention to your surroundings. Take notes, as young Steinbach does in paragraph 10. Describe what you see in a paragraph that "creates in words the picture" you want your reader to see (11). Make it as free of literary or other baggage as you can, and try to select details that contribute to a single dominant impression.

2. Write a profile—a description of a person that not only tells but shows a piece of that person's life story—of one of your favorite (or most despised) teachers or coaches. Try to give your reader a clear sense of what that person looks like; of what he or she wears, says, and does; and of the dominant impression he or she makes on others. Be sure to show how you interact with that person and what he or she has (or has not) taught you.

ANN HODGMAN

# NO WONDER THEY CALL ME A BITCH

ANN HODGMAN (b. 1956) is a freelance writer and former food critic for *Eating Well* magazine. Besides playing goalie on a women's hockey team, she is the author of more than 40 children's books, several cookbooks, and two memoirs: *The House of a Million Pets* (2007) and *How to Die of Embarrassment Every Day* (2011). For reasons soon to be apparent, the following "tasteless" essay from 1990 did not appear in Hodgman's food column, "Sweet and Sour," but in the satiric magazine *Spy*, for which Hodgman was a contributing editor. A spoof on taste testing, it takes a blue ribbon for less than appetizing descriptions that appeal to the grosser senses.

<hr />

I'VE ALWAYS WONDERED ABOUT DOG FOOD. Is a Gaines-burger really like a hamburger? Can you fry it? Does dog food "cheese" taste like real cheese? Does Gravy Train actually make gravy in the dog's bowl, or is that brown liquid just dissolved crumbs? And exactly what *are* by-products?

1

Having spent the better part of a week eating dog food, I'm sorry to say that I now know the answers to these questions. While my dachshund, Shortie, watched in agonies of yearning, I gagged my way through can after can of stinky, white-flecked mush and bag after bag of stinky, fat-drenched nuggets. And now I understand exactly why Shortie's breath is so bad.

Of course, Gaines-burgers are neither mush nor nuggets. They are, rather, a miracle of beauty and packaging—or at least that's what I thought when I was little. I used to beg my mother to get them for our dogs, but she always said they were too expensive. When I finally bought a box of cheese-flavored Gaines-burgers—after twenty years of longing—I felt deliciously wicked.

"Dogs love real beef," the back of the box proclaimed proudly. "That's why Gaines-burgers is the only beef burger for dogs with real beef and no meat by-products!" The copy was accurate: meat by-products did not appear in the list of ingredients. Poultry by-products did, though—right there next to preserved animal fat.

One Purina spokesman told me that poultry by-products consist of necks, intestines, undeveloped eggs and other "carcass remnants," but not feathers, heads, or feet. When I told him I'd been eating dog food, he said, "Oh, you're kidding! Oh, *no!*" (I came to share his alarm when, weeks later, a second Purina spokesman said that Gaines-burgers *do* contain poultry heads and feet—but not undeveloped eggs.)

Up close my Gaines-burger didn't much resemble chopped beef. Rather, it looked—and felt—like a single long, extruded piece of redness that had been chopped into segments and formed into a patty. You could make one at home if you had a Play-Doh Fun Factory.

I turned on the skillet. While I waited for it to heat up I pulled out a shred of cheese-colored material and palpated it. Again, like Play-Doh, it was quite malleable. I made a little cheese bird out of it; then I counted to three and ate the bird.

There was a horrifying rush of cheddar taste, followed immediately by the dull tang of soybean flour—the main ingredient in Gaines-burgers. Next I tried a piece of red extrusion. The main difference between the meat-flavored and cheese-flavored extrusions is one of texture. The "cheese" chews like fresh Play-Doh, whereas the "meat" chews like Play-Doh that's been sitting out on a rug for a couple of hours.

Frying only turned the Gaines-burger black. There was no melting, no    9
sizzling, no warm meat smells. A cherished childhood illusion was gone. I
flipped the patty into the sink, where it immediately began leaking rivulets of
red dye.

As alarming as the Gaines-burgers were, their soy meal began to seem    10
like an old friend when the time came to try some *canned* dog foods. I decided
to try the Cycle foods first. When I opened them, I thought about how rarely I
use can openers these days, and I was suddenly visited by a long-forgotten
sensation of can-opener distaste. *This* is the kind of unsavory place can openers spend their time when you're not watching! Every time you open a can of,
say, Italian plum tomatoes, you infect them with invisible particles of by-
product.

I had been expecting to see the usual homogeneous scrapple inside, but    11
each can of Cycle was packed with smooth, round, oily nuggets. As if someone
at Gaines had been tipped off that a human would be tasting the stuff, the four
Cycles really were different from one another. Cycle-1, for puppies, is wet and
soyish. Cycle-2, for adults, glistens nastily with fat, but it's passably edible—
a lot like some canned Swedish meatballs I once got in a care package at college. Cycle-3, the "lite" one, for fatties, had no specific flavor; it just tasted
like dog food. But at least it didn't make me fat.

Cycle-4, for senior dogs, had the smallest nuggets. Maybe old dogs can't    12
open their mouths as wide. This kind was far sweeter than the other three
Cycles—almost like baked beans. It was also the only one to contain "dried
beef digest," a mysterious substance that the Purina spokesman defined as
"enzymes" and my dictionary defined as "the products of digestion."

Next on the menu was a can of Kal Kan Pedigree with Chunky Chicken.    13
Chunky *chicken*? There were chunks in the can, certainly—big, purplish-
brown chunks. I forked one chunk out (by now I was becoming more callous)
and found that while it had no discernible chicken flavor, it wasn't bad except
for its texture—like meat loaf with ground-up chicken bones.

In the world of canned dog food, a smooth consistency is a sign of low    14
quality—lots of cereal. A lumpy, frightening, bloody, stringy horror is a sign
of high quality—lots of meat. Nowhere in the world of wet dog foods was this
demonstrated better than in the fanciest I tried—Kal Kan's Pedigree Select
Dinners. These came not in a can but in a tiny foil packet with a picture of an
imperious Yorkie. When I pulled open the container, juice spurted all over my

hand, and the first chunk I speared was trailing a long gray vein. I shrieked and went instead for a plain chunk, which I was able to swallow only after taking a break to read some suddenly fascinating office equipment catalogues. Once again, though, it tasted no more alarming than, say, canned hash.

Still, how pleasant it was to turn to *dry* dog food! Gravy Train was the       15
first I tried, and I'm happy to report that it really does make a "thick, rich, real beef gravy" when you mix it with water. Thick and rich, anyway. Except for a lingering rancid-fat flavor, the gravy wasn't beefy, but since it tasted primarily like tap water, it wasn't nauseating either.

My poor dachshund just gets plain old Purina Dog Chow, but Purina also       16
makes a dry food called Butcher's Blend that comes in Beef, Bacon & Chicken flavor. Here we see dog food's arcane semiotics at its best: a red triangle with a *T* stamped into it is supposed to suggest beef; a tan curl, chicken; and a brown *S*, a piece of bacon. Only dogs understand these messages. But Butcher's Blend does have an endearing slogan: "Great Meaty Tastes—without bothering the Butcher!" *You know, I wanted to buy some meat, but I just couldn't bring myself to bother the butcher . . .*

Purina O.N.E. ("Optimum Nutritional Effectiveness") is targeted at peo-       17
ple who are unlikely ever to worry about bothering a tradesperson. "We chose chicken as a primary ingredient in Purina O.N.E. for several reasonings," the long, long essay on the back of the bag announces. Chief among these reasonings, I'd guess, is the fact that chicken appeals to people who are—you know— *like us.* Although our dogs do nothing but spend eighteen-hour days alone in the apartment, we still want them to be *premium* dogs. We want them to cut down on red meat, too. We also want dog food that comes in a bag with an attractive design, a subtle typeface, and no kitschy pictures of slobbering golden retrievers.

Besides that, we want a list of the Nutritional Benefits of our dog food—       18
and we get it on O.N.E. One thing I especially like about this list is its constant references to a dog's "hair coat," as in "Beef tallow is good for the dog's skin and hair coat." (On the other hand, beef tallow merely provides palatability, while the dried beef digest in Cycle provides palatability *enhancement.*)

I hate to say it, but O.N.E. was pretty palatable. Maybe that's because it       19
has about 100 percent more fat than, say, Butcher's Blend. Or maybe I'd been duped by the packaging; that's been known to happen before.

As with people food, dog snacks taste much better than dog meals.  20
They're better looking too. Take Milk-Bone Flavor Snacks. The loving-hands-
at-home prose describing each flavor is colorful; the writers practically choke
on their own exuberance. Of bacon they say, "It's so good, your dog will think
it's hot off the frying pan." Of liver: "The only taste your dog wants more than
liver—is even more liver!" Of poultry: "All those farm fresh flavors deliciously
mixed in one biscuit. Your dog will bark with delight!" And of vegetable: "Gar-
dens of taste! Specially blended to give your dog that vegetable flavor he
wants—but can rarely get!"

Well, I may be a sucker, but advertising this emphatic just doesn't con-  21
vince me. I lined up all seven flavors of Milk-Bone Flavor Snacks on the floor.
Unless my dog's palate is a lot more sensitive than mine—and considering
that she steals dirty diapers out of the trash and eats them, I'm loath to think
it is—she doesn't detect any more difference in the seven flavors than I did
when I tried them.

I much preferred Bonz, the hard-baked, bone-shaped snack stuffed with  22
simulated marrow. I liked the bone part, that is; it tasted almost exactly like
the cornmeal it was made of. The mock marrow inside was a bit more problematic: in addition to looking like the sludge that collects in the treads of my
running shoes, it was bursting with tiny hairs.

I'm sure you have a few dog food questions of your own. To save us time,  23
I've answered them in advance.

Q. *Are those little cans of Mighty Dog actually branded with the sizzling word*  24
BEEF, *the way they show in the commercials?*

A. You should know by now that that kind of thing never happens.  25

Q. *Does chicken-flavored dog food taste like chicken-flavored cat food?*  26

A. To my surprise, chicken cat food was actually a little better—more  27
chickeny. It tasted like inferior canned pâté.

Q. *Was there any dog food that you just couldn't bring yourself to try?*  28

A. Alas, it was a can of Mighty Dog called Prime Entree with Bone Mar-  29
row. The meat was dark, dark brown, and it was surrounded by gelatin that
was almost black. I knew I would die if I tasted it, so I put it outside for the
raccoons.

## FOR DISCUSSION

1. Ann Hodgman's discourse on dog food may be a humorous, tongue-in-cheek play on conventional food reviews, but as **DESCRIPTIVE** writing do you agree that it is truly disgusting? Which do you find more effectively nauseating, her description of the tastes and textures of dry dog food or canned?

2. Most of Hodgman's "research" is done in her own laboratory kitchen. Where else does she go for information? Do you think her studies qualify her to speak expertly on the subject? How about vividly?

3. How do you suppose Hodgman knows what Play-Doh chews like after it's been "sitting out on a rug for a couple of hours"—that is, as opposed to fresh Play-Doh (8)?

4. What childhood fantasy does Hodgman fulfill by writing this essay? How does the reality **COMPARE** with the fantasy?

5. Do you find Hodgman's title in bad taste? Why or why not? How about her entire essay?

6. What question would you ask Hodgman about her research? For example, *Q: Why are you asking these unsavory questions?* A: Somebody has to honor those who do basic research in a new field.

## STRATEGIES AND STRUCTURES

1. "When I pulled open the container, juice spurted all over my hand, and the first chunk I speared was trailing a long gray vein" (14). Can you see, smell, and taste it? Cite other examples of Hodgman's descriptive skills and her direct appeal (if that's the right word) to the senses.

2. Notice the major shift that occurs when the description moves from canned dog food to dry. Where does the shift occur? Why does she find the change so "pleasant"? When does she shift again—to snacks?

3. Why do you suppose Hodgman never tells us why she is describing the ingredients, tastes, and textures of dog food with such scrupulous accuracy and **OBJECTIVITY**? What is her **PURPOSE** in writing this piece, and how might her scrupulous objectivity be appropriate for that purpose?

4. Why do you think Hodgman shifts to a question-and-answer format at the end of her essay?

5. Hodgman is a professional food critic. What **CONCRETE** and specific words from her professional vocabulary does she use?

6. What is the DOMINANT IMPRESSION created by Hodgman's description of Bonz in paragraph 22?

7. Hodgman not only describes herself at work in her laboratory kitchen, she ANALYZES THE PROCESS of doing basic food research there. Besides tasting, what are some of the other steps in the process?

## WORDS AND FIGURES OF SPEECH

1. Hodgman refers to "some suddenly fascinating office equipment catalogues" that divert her from tasting Kal Kan's best (14). Is this IRONY?

2. How does your dictionary DEFINE "dried beef digest" (12)? Where else does Hodgman use the technical language of the industry she is SATIRIZING?

3. Hodgman says her Gaines-burger, when fried and flipped into the sink, "began leaking rivulets of red dye" (9). Is this scientific detachment or HYPERBOLE?

4. The opposite of intentional exaggeration is UNDERSTATEMENT. In Hodgman's analysis of the simulated marrow in Bonz, would "problematic" qualify as an example (22)?

5. Hodgman says Kal Kan Pedigree with Chunky Chicken tasted "like meat loaf with ground-up chicken bones" (13). Is this a SIMILE, or do you suppose the chicken could be literally chunky because of the bones?

## FOR WRITING

1. While Hodgman gags her way through sample after sample of premium dog food, her dachshund, Shortie, looks on "in agonies of yearning" (2). Describe the "data" in Hodgman's taste experiment from Shortie's POINT OF VIEW. How might Gaines-burgers and Kal Kan Pedigree with Chunky Chicken taste to him? Is Hodgman right to say that Shortie cannot distinguish among the seven flavors of Milk-Bone Flavor Snacks? What would Shortie's palate tell us?

2. Conduct a program of research similar to Hodgman's but in the field of junk food. Write an unbiased description of your findings. Or, if you prefer, forget the taste tests, and follow Hodgman's lead in analyzing the claims of food advertisers. Choose a category of food products—gummy worms, breath mints, canned soup, frozen pizza, breakfast cereal, cookies—and study the packaging carefully. Write an essay in which you describe how the manufacturers of your samples typically describe their products.

# MORE ROOM

JUDITH ORTIZ COFER (1952–2016) wrote poetry, fiction, and nonfiction, including both memoirs and essays. Throughout her childhood, Ortiz Cofer traveled back and forth between her birthplace, Hormigueros, Puerto Rico, and Paterson, New Jersey, where her immediate family moved in the 1950s before relocating to Georgia. A graduate of Augusta College and Florida Atlantic University, Ortiz Cofer devoted much of her career to teaching English and creative writing at the University of Georgia. Much of her writing is an autobiographical exploration of what she calls "the Puerto Rican diaspora." Her last memoir, *The Cruel Country* (2015), is about her return to Puerto Rico after her mother is diagnosed with cancer. In "More Room," from Ortiz Cofer's memoir *Silent Dancing* (1990), the description of her grandmother Mamá's home in Puerto Rico becomes a loving portrait of Mamá herself, the larger-than-life "queen" of the household.

MY GRANDMOTHER'S HOUSE is like a chambered nautilus; it has many rooms, yet it is not a mansion. Its proportions are small and its design simple. It is a house that has grown organically, according to the needs of its inhabitants. To all of us in the family it is known as *la casa de Mamá*.[1] It is the place of our origin; the stage for our memories and dreams of Island life.

I remember how in my childhood it sat on stilts; this was before it had a downstairs. It rested on its perch like a great blue bird, not a flying sort of bird, more like a nesting hen, but with spread wings. Grandfather had built it soon after their marriage. He was a painter and housebuilder by trade, a poet and meditative man by nature. As each of their eight children were born, new rooms were added. After a few years, the paint did not exactly match, nor the materials, so that there was a chronology to it, like the rings of a tree, and Mamá could tell you the history of each room in her *casa*, and thus the genealogy of the family along with it.

Her room is the heart of the house. Though I have seen it recently, and both woman and room have diminished in size, changed by the new perspective of my eyes, now capable of looking over countertops and tall beds, it is not this picture I carry in my memory of Mamá's *casa*. See p. 75 for tips on moving from outside to inside in a description. Instead, I see her room as a queen's chamber where a small woman loomed large, a throne-room with a massive four-poster bed in its center which stood taller than a child's head. It was on this bed where her own children had been born that the smallest grandchildren were allowed to take naps in the afternoons; here too was where Mamá secluded herself to dispense private advice to her daughters, sitting on the edge of the bed, looking down at whoever sat on the rocker where generations of babies had been sung to sleep. To me she looked like a wise empress right out of the fairy tales I was addicted to reading.

Though the room was dominated by the mahogany four-posters, it also contained all of Mamá's symbols of power. On her dresser instead of cosmetics there were jars filled with herbs: *yerba buena, yerba mala*,[2] the making of purgatives and teas to which we were all subjected during childhood crises. She had a steaming cup for anyone who could not, or would not, get up to face

1. Mama's house.
2. Good herbs, bad herbs.

life on any given day. If the acrid aftertaste of her cures for malingering did not get you out of bed, then it was time to call *el doctor*.

And there was the monstrous chifforobe she kept locked with a little golden key she did not hide. This was a test of her dominion over us; though my cousins and I wanted a look inside that massive wardrobe more than anything, we never reached for that little key lying on top of her Bible on the dresser. This was also where she placed her earrings and rosary at night. God's word was her security system. This chifforobe was the place where I imagined she kept jewels, satin slippers, and elegant sequined, silk gowns of heartbreaking fineness. I lusted after those imaginary costumes. I had heard that Mamá had been a great beauty in her youth, and the belle of many balls. My cousins had other ideas as to what she kept in that wooden vault: its secret could be money (Mamá did not hand cash to strangers, banks were out of the question, so there were stories that her mattress was stuffed with dollar bills, and that she buried coins in jars in her garden under rosebushes, or kept them in her inviolate chifforobe); there might be that legendary gun salvaged from the Spanish-American conflict over the Island. We went wild over suspected treasures that we made up simply because children have to fill locked trunks with something wonderful.

On the wall above the bed hung a heavy silver crucifix. Christ's agonized head hung directly over Mamá's pillow. I avoided looking at this weapon suspended over where her head would lay; and on the rare occasions when I was allowed to sleep on that bed, I scooted down to the safe middle of the mattress, where her body's impression took me in like a mother's lap. Having taken care of the obligatory religious decoration with a crucifix, Mamá covered the other walls with objects sent to her over the years by her children in the States. *Los Nueva Yores*[3] were represented by, among other things, a postcard of Niagara Falls from her son Hernán, postmarked, Buffalo, N.Y. In a conspicuous gold frame hung a large color photograph of her daughter Nena, her husband and their five children at the entrance to Disneyland in California. From us she had gotten a black lace fan. Father had brought it to her from a tour of duty with the Navy in Europe (on Sundays she would remove it from its hook on the wall to fan herself at Sunday mass). Each year more items were added

3. The New Yorkers.

as the family grew and dispersed, and every object in the room had a story attached to it, a *cuento* which Mamá would bestow on anyone who received the privilege of a day alone with her. It was almost worth pretending to be sick, though the bitter herb purgatives of the body were a big price to pay for the spirit revivals of her story-telling.

Mamá slept alone on her large bed, except for the times when a sick 7 grandchild warranted the privilege, or when a heartbroken daughter came home in need of more than herbal teas. In the family there is a story about how this came to be.

When one of the daughters, my mother or one of her sisters, tells the 8 *cuento* of how Mamá came to own her nights, it is usually preceded by the qualifications that Papá's exile from his wife's room was not a result of animosity between the couple, but that the act had been Mamá's famous bloodless coup for her personal freedom. Papá was the benevolent dictator of her body and her life who had had to be banished from her bed so that Mamá could better serve her family. Before the telling, we had to agree that the old man was not to blame. We all recognized that in the family Papá was as an *alma de Dios*,[4] a saintly, soft-spoken presence whose main pleasures in life, such as writing poetry and reading the Spanish large-type editions of *Reader's Digest*, always took place outside the vortex of Mamá's crowded realm. It was not his fault, after all, that every year or so he planted a babyseed in Mamá's fertile body, keeping her from leading the active life she needed and desired. He loved her and the babies. Papá composed odes and lyrics to celebrate births and anniversaries and hired musicians to accompany him in singing them to his family and friends at extravagant pig-roasts he threw yearly. Mamá and the oldest girls worked for days preparing the food. Papá sat for hours in his painter's shed, also his study and library, composing the songs. At these celebrations he was also known to give long speeches in praise of God, his fecund wife, and his beloved island. As a middle child, my mother remembers these occasions as a time when the women sat in the kitchen and lamented their burdens, while the men feasted out in the patio, their rum-thickened voice rising in song and praise for each other, *compañeros* all.[5]

4. Literally, "soul of God"; a good person.

5. Close friends.

It was after the birth of her eighth child, after she had lost three at birth    9
or in infancy, that Mamá made her decision. They say that Mamá had had a
special way of letting her husband know that they were expecting, one that
had begun when, at the beginning of their marriage, he had built her a house
too confining for her taste. So, when she discovered her first pregnancy, she
supposedly drew plans for another room, which he dutifully executed. Every
time a child was due, she would demand, *more space, more space.* Papá acceded
to her wishes, child after child, since he had learned early that Mamá's
renowned temper was a thing that grew like a monster along with a new belly.
In this way Mamá got the house that she wanted, but with each child she lost
in heart and energy. She had knowledge of her body and perceived that if she
had any more children, her dreams and her plans would have to be permanently forgotten, because she would be a chronically ill woman, like Flora with
her twelve children: asthma, no teeth, in bed more than on her feet.

And so, after my youngest uncle was born, she asked Papá to build a large    10
room at the back of the house. He did so in joyful anticipation. Mamá had
asked him special things this time: shelves on the walls, a private entrance. He
thought that she meant this room to be a nursery where several children could
sleep. He thought it was a wonderful idea. He painted it his favorite color, sky
blue, and made large windows looking out over a green hill and the church
spires beyond. But nothing happened. Mamá's belly did not grow, yet she
seemed in a frenzy of activity over the house. Finally, an anxious Papá
approached his wife to tell her that the new room was finished and ready to be
occupied. And Mamá, they say, replied: "Good, it's for *you.*"

And so it was that Mamá discovered the only means of birth control    11
available to a Catholic woman of her time: sacrifice. She gave up the comfort
of Papá's sexual love for something she deemed greater: the right to own and
control her body, so that she might live to meet her grandchildren—me among
them—so that she could give more of herself to the ones already there, so that
she could be more than a channel for other lives, so that even now that time
has robbed her of the elasticity of her body and of her amazing reservoir of
energy, she still emanates the kind of joy that can only be achieved by living
according to the dictates of one's own heart.

## FOR DISCUSSION

1. Mamá's house in Puerto Rico was originally built on stilts to avoid high water, but the lower level got filled in anyway. Why? How is the new room different from the older additions?

2. Mamá exercises "dominion" over all her house and family (5). What is the source of her power? What role(s) does Papá play in the household?

3. When Papá is preparing birthday odes and patriotic hymns to be sung at annual feasts, what are the women in the family doing? What is Ortiz Cofer suggesting here about the culture she is describing?

4. What larger point is Ortiz Cofer making about women and families by describing the physical changes in her grandmother's home?

## STRATEGIES AND STRUCTURES

1. Ortiz Cofer describes the outside of her grandmother's house before moving to the inside. What specific details does she focus on? What do they suggest about the nature of the dwelling—and its principal inhabitants?

2. Once she moves inside the house, which room does Ortiz Cofer single out? What particular details does she focus on here, and what do they contribute to her description of Mamá?

3. Ortiz Cofer is not so much describing her grandmother's house as it is today as the house as it exists in her memory. How is this "picture" different from present-day reality (3)? How and how well does she capture the place from the viewpoint of a child?

4. In addition to describing her grandmother's house and its contents, "More Room" tells the story of a "bloodless coup" (8). What coup? How does this **NARRATIVE** relate to Ortiz Cofer's description of the place?

## WORDS AND FIGURES OF SPEECH

1. "Build three more stately mansions, O my soul. / As the swift seasons roll!" So begins the final stanza of "The Chambered Nautilus" (1858) by Oliver Wendell Holmes. How does Ortiz Cofer make use of this **ALLUSION**?

2. Her grandmother's house, says Ortiz Cofer, was "the place of our origin" (1). In what multiple senses is she using this phrase?

3. Why does Ortiz Cofer use "babyseed" (8) instead of "sperm" or some other word to describe her grandmother's plight?

4. Mamá's room, says Ortiz Cofer, is the "heart" of the house (3). What are the implications of this metaphor?

### FOR WRITING

1. Write a paragraph or two in which you compare the present-day aspects of a house, room, or other place with the aspects of that place as you picture it in memory.

2. Write a detailed description of a place—it can even be of a whole town—that uses the physical features of the place to reveal the character of its inhabitants and the tensions (and harmonies) among them.

# ⊰ 6 ⊱

# NARRATIVE

NARRATIVE* writing tells a story; it reports "what happened." All of the essays in this chapter are narratives, telling about what happened to one young pilot on September 11, 2001, for example, and to one African American man when he refused to give up his seat on a bus in North Carolina in the 1940s. There is a big difference, however, between having something "happen" and writing about it, between an event and telling about an event.

In real life, events often occur randomly or chaotically. But in a narrative, they must be told or shown in some orderly sequence (the PLOT), by a particular person (the NARRATOR), from a particular perspective (the POINT OF VIEW), within a definite time and place (the SETTING). Let's look more closely at each of these elements.

Suppose we wanted to tell a story about a young woman sitting alone eating a snack. Our opening line might go something like this:

Little Miss Muffet sat on a tuffet, eating her curds and whey.

Here, in the first line of a well-known nursery rhyme, we have someone (Miss Muffet) who is doing something (eating) at a particular time (the past) in a particular place (on a tuffet). The problem with our narrative is that it isn't very interesting. We have a character and a setting, but we don't really have a plot.

A good plot requires more than just sitting and eating. Plot can be achieved by introducing a conflict into the action, bringing the tension to a high point (the CLIMAX), then releasing the tension—in other words, by giving

*Words printed in SMALL CAPITALS are defined in the Glossary/Index.

the action of the story a beginning, middle, and end. In our story about Miss Muffet, we could achieve the necessary conflict by introducing an intruder:

Along came a spider and sat down beside her . . .

You know what's coming next, but you can still feel the tension building up before we resolve the conflict and release the rising tension in the final line of our story:

And frightened Miss Muffet away.

Well, that's better. We have a sequence of events now. Moreover, those events occur in our narrative in some sort of order—chronologically. But the events also have to be linked together in some meaningful way. In this case, the appearance of the intruder actually *causes* the departure of the heroine. There are many ways to connect the events in a narrative, but CAUSE AND EFFECT is one good approach (see Chapter 12).

Mary Mebane, p. 157, tells how segregation laws caused her to "live with terror."

We said earlier that a narrative must have a narrator. That narrator may be directly involved in the action of the narrative or may only report it. Do we have one here? Yes, we do; it is the narrator who refers to Miss Muffet as "her." But this narrator is never identified, and he or she plays no part in the action. Let's look at a narrator who does—Stephen King, in a passage from a narrative about an accident that almost killed him some years ago:

> Most of the sight lines along the mile-long stretch of Route 5 that I walk are good, but there is one place, a short steep hill, where a pedestrian heading north can see very little of what might be coming his way. I was three-quarters of the way up this hill when the van came over the crest. It wasn't on the road; it was on the shoulder. My shoulder. I had perhaps three-quarters of a second to register this.
>
> —STEPHEN KING, "On Impact"

Notice that the "I" in this piece is King himself, and he is very much involved in the action of the story he is telling. In fact, he is about to be hit by the van coming over the crest of the hill. That would introduce a conflict into his walk along Route 5, wouldn't it?

By narrating this story from a FIRST-PERSON point of view, King is putting himself in the center of the action. If he had said instead, "The van was closing in on him fast," we would have a THIRD-PERSON narrative, and the narrator would be reporting the action from the sidelines instead of bearing the brunt of it. What makes a chilling story here is that King is not only showing us what happened to him, he is showing us what he was thinking as he suddenly realized that the van was almost on top of him: "It wasn't on the road; it was on the shoulder. My shoulder." We look in as the narrator goes, in a few swift phrases, from startled disbelief to horrified certainty.

Another way in which King creates a compelling story is by using direct speech, or DIALOGUE. When King tells about his first day back at work, he lets his wife speak to us directly: "I can rig a table for you in the back hall, outside the pantry. There are plenty of outlets—you can have your Mac, the little printer, and a fan." Quoting direct speech like this helps readers to imagine the characters as real people.

But why does King end his narrative back at the writing desk? Because he knows that stories serve a larger PURPOSE than just telling what happened. The larger purpose of King's story is to make a point about writing and the writer's life. The van almost killed him, but writing, King demonstrates, helped him to recover and keeps him going.

> Yiyun Li, p. 152, uses dialogue to explain why she changed her ideas about marriage.

Well-told stories are almost always told for some reason. The searing tale you heard earlier about Miss Muffet, for example, was told to make a point about narrative structure. A brief, illustrative story like this is called an ANEC-DOTE. All stories should have a point, but anecdotes in particular are used in all kinds of writing to give examples and to illustrate the greater subject at hand—writing, for instance.

When you use a story to make a point, don't forget to remind the reader exactly what that point is. When Junot Díaz tells about thieves breaking into his family's apartment in "The Money," he is also making a point about how police respond differently to crime depending on where it takes place. Normally, Díaz writes, the police would have been called to investigate such an incident; in his old neighborhood, however, going to the police "would have been about as useless as crying." Don't keep your reader in the dark. When your purpose is to explain something, don't get so wound up in the web of telling a good story that you forget to say what the moral is.

# A BRIEF GUIDE TO WRITING A NARRATIVE

As you write a **NARRATIVE**, you need to say who or what the narrative is about, where it takes place, and what is happening. Mary Mebane makes these basic moves of narration in the following lines from her essay in this chapter:

> On this Saturday morning Esther and I set out for town for our music lesson. We were going on our weekly big adventure, all the way across town. . . . We walked the two miles from Wildwood to the bus line.
> —MARY MEBANE, "The Back of the Bus"

Mebane says *who* her story is about ("Esther and I"), *where* it takes place (on the bus line), and *what* is happening as the story opens (the two teenagers are heading for a "big adventure").

The following guidelines will help you to make these basic moves as you draft a narrative—and to come up with a subject for your story, consider your purpose and audience, state your point, and organize the specific details and events of your story into a compelling plot by using chronology, transitions, verb tenses, and dialogue.

## Coming Up with a Subject

When you enjoy a well-told story, it is often because the author presents an everyday event in an interesting or even dramatic way. To come up with a subject for a story of your own, think of events, both big and small, that you have experienced. You might write a good story about a perfectly ordinary occurrence, such as buying a car, applying for a job, arguing with a friend—or even just doing your homework.

"No, no, no," the writer Frank McCourt, author of *Angela's Ashes*, used to say to his students when they complained that nothing had happened to them when they got home the night before. "What did you do when you walked in?" McCourt would ask. "You went through a door, didn't you? Did you have anything in your hands? A book bag? You didn't carry it with you all night, did you? Did you hang it on a hook? Did you throw it across the room and your mom yelled at you for it?" Even mundane details like these can provide the material for a good story if you use them to show what people said and did—and exactly where, why, and how they said and did it.

Lynda Barry builds a narrative around the ordinary events of a school day (p. 166).

## Considering Your Purpose and Audience

As you compose a narrative, think hard about the audience you want to reach and the PURPOSE your narrative is intended to serve. Suppose you are emailing a friend about a visit to an electronics store in order to convince her to take advantage of the great deals you found there. You might tell your story this way: "When I walked into ComputerDaze, I couldn't believe my eyes. Tablet computers everywhere! And the cheap prices! I went home with a tablet under each arm." Or suppose you are writing a column in a computer magazine, and the purpose of your story is to show readers how to shop for a tablet. You might write: "The first hurdle I encountered was the numbing variety of brands and models."

Whatever your purpose, think about how much your audience is likely to know about your subject so you can judge how much background information you need to give, what terms you need to DEFINE, and so on. If you are writing an ANECDOTE, make sure it is appropriate for your audience and illustrates your larger point.

## Generating Ideas: Asking What Happened—and Who, Where, When, How, and Why

How do you come up with the raw materials for a narrative? To get started, ask yourself the questions that journalists typically ask when developing a story: who, what, where, when, how, and why? Your immediate answers will give you the beginnings of a narrative, but keep asking the questions over and over again. Try to recall lots of particular details, both visual and auditory. As the writer John Steinbeck once advised, "Try to remember [the situation] so clearly that you can see things: what colors and how warm or cold and how you got there . . . what people looked like, how they walked, what they wore, what they ate."

You will also want your readers to know *why* you're telling this particular story, so it's important to select details that support your point. For example, if you're trying to show why your sister is the funniest person in your family, your story might include specific, vivid details about the sound of her voice, her amusing facial expressions, and a practical joke she once pulled.

## Templates for Narrating

The following templates can help you to generate ideas for a narrative and then to start drafting. Don't take these as formulas where you just have to fill in the blanks. There are no easy formulas for good writing. But these templates can help you plot out some of the key moves of narration and thus may serve as good starting points:

▶ This is a story about _____.

▶ My story takes place in _____ when _____.

▶ As the narrative opens, X is in the act of _____.

▶ What happened next was _____, followed by _____ and _____.

▶ At this point, _____ happened.

▶ The climax of these events was _____.

▶ When X understood what had happened, he/she/they said, "_____."

▶ The last thing that happened to X was _____.

▶ My point in telling this story is to show that _____.

For more techniques to help you generate ideas and start writing a narrative essay, see Chapter 3.

## Stating Your Point

If you are writing a personal story about your sister, you might reveal your point implicitly through the details of the story. However, in much of the narrative writing you do as a student, you will want to state your point explicitly. If you are writing about information technology for a communications class, for example, you might include the story about going to an electronics store, and you would probably want to explain why in a THESIS STATEMENT like this: "Go into any computer store today, and you will discover that information technology is the main product of American business."

## Developing a Plot Chronologically

As a general rule, arrange events in chronological order so your readers don't have to figure out what happened when. Chronology alone, however, is insufficient for organizing a good narrative. Events need to be related in such a way that one leads directly to, or causes, another. Taken together, the events should have a beginning, middle, and end. Then your narrative will form a complete action: a PLOT.

One of the best ways to plot a narrative is to set up a situation; introduce a conflict; build up the dramatic tension until it reaches a high point, or CLIMAX; then release the tension and resolve the conflict. Even the little horror story about Miss Muffet is satisfying because it's tightly plotted with a clear sense of completion at the close.

## Using Transitions and Verb Tenses

When you write a narrative, you will often incorporate direct references to time: *first, last, immediately, not long after, next, while, then, once upon a time*. References like these can be boring in a narrative if they become too predictable, as in *first, second, third*.

Steve Hendrix, p. 138, shifts between past and present as he writes about a pilot who flew on September 11.

But used judiciously, such TRANSITIONS provide smooth links from one event to another, as do other connecting words and phrases like *thus, therefore, consequently, what happened next, before I knew it,* and so on.

In addition to clear transitions, your verb tenses can help you to connect events in time. Remember that all actions that happen more or less at the same time in your narrative should be in the same tense: "I *was* three-quarters of the way up this hill when the van *came* over the crest. It *wasn't* on the road; it *was* on the shoulder." Don't shift tenses needlessly; but when you *do* need to indicate that one action happened before another, be sure to change tenses accordingly and accurately. If you need to shift out of chronological order altogether—you might shift back in time in a FLASHBACK or shift forward in time in a FLASH-FORWARD—be sure to make the leap clear to your readers.

## Maintaining a Consistent Point of View

As you construct a narrative, you need to maintain a logical and consistent POINT OF VIEW. In a narrative written in the FIRST PERSON ("I" or "we"), like Stephen King's, the NARRATOR can be both an observer of the scene ("Most of the sight lines along the mile-long stretch of Route 5 that I walk are good") *and* a participant in the action ("I had perhaps three-quarters of a second to register this"). In a narrative written in the THIRD PERSON ("he," "she," "it," or "they"), as is the case in most articles and history books, the narrator is often merely an observer, though sometimes an all-knowing one.

Whether you write in the first or third person, don't attribute perceptions to yourself or your narrator that are physically impossible. If you are narrating a story from the front seat of your car, don't pretend to see what is going on three blocks away. If you do claim to see (or know) more than you reasonably can from where you sit, your credibility with the reader will soon be strained.

## Adding Dialogue

You can introduce the points of view of other people into a story by using DIALOGUE. In a story about her childhood, for example, Annie Dillard lets her mother speak for herself: "Lie on your back," her mother tells young Dillard. "Look at the clouds and figure out what they look like."

As a first-person narrator, Dillard might have written, "My mother told me to look at the clouds and figure out what they look like." But these words would be a step removed from the person who said them and so would lack the immediacy of direct dialogue. If you let people in your narrative speak for themselves, your characters will come to life, and your whole narrative will have a greater dramatic impact.

# EDITING FOR COMMON ERRORS IN NARRATIVE WRITING

Like other kinds of writing, narrative uses distinctive patterns of language and punctuation—and thus invites typical kinds of errors. The following tips will help you to check for and correct these errors in your narrative writing.

### Check that verb tenses accurately indicate when actions occur

Because narrative writing focuses on actions and events, it relies heavily on verbs. Make sure verb tenses accurately indicate when actions take place. Don't get confused about when to use the simple past (She *arrived* at school), the present perfect (She *has arrived* at school), and the past perfect (She *had arrived* at school).

Use the simple past to indicate actions that were completed at a specified time in the past.

▶ He ~~has~~ completed the assignment this morning.

Use the present perfect to indicate actions begun and completed at some unspecified time in the past, or actions begun in the past and continuing into the present.

▶ The recession ~~comes~~ has come to an end.
▶ The recession ~~goes~~ has gone on for more than five years now.

Use the past perfect to indicate actions completed by a specific time in the past or before another past action occurred.

▶ The alligators arrived next, but by then the palm rats <u>had</u> moved out.

## Check dialogue to be sure it's punctuated correctly

Narrative writing often includes the direct quotation of what people say. Punctuating dialogue can be challenging because you have to deal with the punctuation in the dialogue itself and also with any punctuation necessary to integrate the dialogue into the text.

Commas and periods always go inside the quotation marks.

- ▶ "Perspective is hard to define," my art history professor said.
- ▶ She noted that in a painting by Jacob Lawrence "perspective means one thing."

Semicolons and colons always go outside the quotation marks.

- ▶ But in a Cubist painting by Picasso, she said, "it means quite another"; then she went on to explain the differences.
- ▶ The painting presents the landscape "in layers": from the tops of mountains to the undersides of leaves in the same picture.

Question marks, exclamation points, and dashes go *inside* the quotation marks if they are part of the quoted text but *outside* if they are not part of the quoted text.

- ▶ The teacher asked, "Sam, how would you define perspective in art?"
- ▶ Did you say, "Divine perspective"?

## A Book Cover

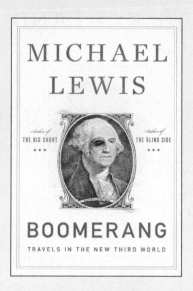

When you write a narrative, you tell what happened in a particular time and place. In the narrative illustrated on the cover of this book by best-selling author Michael Lewis, somebody has given George Washington a black eye. Lewis's title, *Boomerang*, implies that the wound is self-inflicted. Has George done something that's coming back to hit him in the face? Since the mug shot on this book cover is from a dollar bill, the offense must have been economic. A good narrative does more than simply tell what happened; it gives the story a plot with a beginning, middle, and end. Lewis traces the rise and fall of the global economy before and after 2008. How will the story end? As indicated on this book cover, Lewis concludes that the boomerang effect of excessive borrowing and lending by the United States is harming the economy and may leave the dollar with a semi-permanent black eye. A boom in the economy, on the other hand, would likely keep the dollar strong—and the boomerang from coming back to hit George.

## MELISSA UNBANKES

# THE KING AND I

MELISSA UNBANKES is a student at Yuba Community College in Marysville, California. She dreamed of becoming a rock star or a librarian, but as an adult, a complete lack of musical talent eventually led her to pursue a degree in English. She wrote this essay for her first-year writing course in which her assignment was to write a memoir about a person or event of personal significance. In this essay, Unbankes tells the story of her relationship with her grandmother—and her grandmother's relationship with an Elvis Presley figurine.

## The King and I

"I want you to have this," said my grandmother, holding out to me a rectangular purple box. "I bought it at Graceland." Her voice was quiet, almost reverent. I'd heard her talk of her trip before. My grandmother loved to travel, but Graceland always had a special significance for her. I had the sense that she considered it a pilgrimage, the trip that every true Elvis fan must take at least once. "It's numbered, see? It's a limited edition." She opened the box as she spoke, sliding out the styrofoam shell. "I bought it at the gift shop." She paused for a moment before separating the styrofoam, her movements slow and careful. There was a feeling in the room like a held breath. "You want to make sure to keep the certificate. That's how you prove it's real." I nodded eagerly. I would have promised anything, including carrying the certificate at all times, if it meant I could see what was in the box. She reached into the packaging, lifting out a figurine. "I knew you would like it, because it's porcelain, and it's Elvis."

I collected dolls, a hobby I shared with my grandmother; she had given me my first porcelain doll years before. She turned the figurine so I could see it, and my heart sank. It was Elvis, there was no doubt about that, but it wasn't the Elvis I admired. This was Elvis in a white jumpsuit. Fat Elvis. The Elvis of velvet paintings. Tacky Elvis. She handed me the figurine and I stared down at it, noting that Elvis had almost perfect circles of rouge on each cheek. Like a clown, I thought glumly. I handed it back to her as quickly as I thought was polite, muttering something about how cool it was. She admired it for a moment longer before placing it back into the box. "You can put it in your corner cabinet."

1

DIALOGUE captures the grandmother's character

First-person POINT OF VIEW reveals Unbankes's thoughts and feelings as a teenager

2

I protested immediately, telling her I could never 3
accept the responsibility for displaying such a precious
object. It should be put away, I explained, somewhere safe.
In fact, I told her, I was probably much too irresponsible
to even keep something that valuable in my possession. It
was no use. In the end I left with a cardboard box con-
taining the Elvis figurine and several other pieces of
memorabilia she thought I would like. I placed the box on
the top shelf of my closet, hoping my grandmother would
never ask where it was.

> Unbankes develops the PLOT by retelling a series of events

To say my grandmother loved Elvis would be like 4
describing the ceiling of the Sistine Chapel[1] as a nice little
mural. She was devoted, and she shared her devotion with
me on Friday afternoons. My grandmother was a school-
bus driver, and on Fridays, instead of going to day care, I
would ride her bus until the end of her route. One by one
the other passengers would leave, until it was just me and
my grandmother. Then she would turn on the radio. It
was district policy not to use the radio if students were
on the bus, so being there in the empty bus with the
music blaring gave me a kind of subversive thrill.

My grandmother always chose the oldies station, 5
"greatest hits of the '50s and '60s." I would lie across the
bench seat, feeling the bus engine rumbling underneath
me, singing along to Buddy Holly and Little Richard, the
Platters and the Drifters, and of course, Elvis. It always
came back to Elvis. My grandmother would talk between
songs, telling stories from her childhood, intertwined
with bits of trivia about the music. Some of the stories
she told me were probably not age-appropriate. My

1. Considered to be one of the greatest examples of Renaissance art,
the ceiling of the Sistine Chapel was painted by the artist Michelangelo.
The chapel is part of the Vatican in Rome, Italy.

favorite was how she would sneak out to concerts, enlisting her sisters to help push my great-grandfather's car down the road so she could race it (starting the engine in front of the house would have gotten her caught immediately, she told me). I thought that was the smartest thing I had ever heard, and filed it away for future use. As a child I was used to being talked *at* instead of *to*, but I never felt like that with her. My grandmother talked the same way to everyone; she had no filter.

Valta Jean, or "Jeannie," as she was usually called, was my best friend in those years, but by the time she gave me the Elvis figurine we had grown apart. When I was younger, I had admired how unconventional she was; now those same qualities were deeply embarrassing. I had loved listening to her talk. Now it seemed as if she talked too much, asking embarrassing questions in front of my friends. Her spontaneity grated. I never knew when she

6

FLASHBACKS bring narrative back to Unbankes's teenage years

would show up, carrying a bag of thrift store finds or items she had "rescued" from the side of the road. She went barefoot all the time, carrying a pair of shoes in her purse if she needed them. She smoked constantly and wore stretchy nylon pants and brightly patterned shirts. She was, in a word, tacky. While I loved her very much, I sometimes wished I could keep her hidden away like my Elvis albums.

Like most teenagers, my sense of self was very                    7
much a public production, something that had to be carefully maintained. My own love for Elvis was something that didn't fit, a tiny crack in the facade of cool, and my grandmother threatened to blow it wide open. I eventually got over my grandiose sense of teenage self-interest, but my relationship with my grandmother was never as close as it was in my childhood. I no longer found her embarrassing, only frustrating. Why, I wondered, couldn't she just *act* like a normal person? But that was never her way. She had no need to hide away pieces of herself.

There is a Japanese practice of repairing pottery,               8
called *kintsugi*, where broken pieces of pottery are mended with gold or a gold lacquer. It's an art form that is meant to call attention to the breaks instead of hiding them, making the repair part of the history of the object. When I first read about it, I could not understand why anyone would want to display a broken cup or bowl. How could something so obviously flawed be an object of beauty? Then a few years ago at a small gallery, I saw a collection of kintsugi pottery and I finally understood. While the original pottery was beautiful, the repaired pottery had been transformed into something unique. After seeing the kintsugi pieces, the perfect pieces of pottery seemed somehow unfinished, blank canvases. I saw many beautiful pieces of art on display that day, but the "flawed" pieces are the ones that linger in my memory.

Explicit COMPARISON (Chapter 10) of Unbankes's grandmother with the Elvis figurine

Reference to "pieces" anticipates DEFINITION of *kintsugi* in next paragraph

My grandmother died recently, and while looking
for old photos of her, I found the box she had given me so
many years ago. Tacky Elvis was in there. Officially, he's
"Mississippi Benefit Elvis in Concert, number 1551 of a
limited edition of 20,000" (I kept the certificate), but he'll
always be Tacky Elvis in my mind. My memory of his
appearance was fairly accurate, and my tastes haven't
changed so much that I can appreciate it as a work of art.
But there is something about Elvis in all his jumpsuited
glory that recalls my grandmother like none of the more
tasteful, classically beautiful porcelain dolls she gave me
over the years ever could.

There were other items in the box. There was a
matching commemorative plate; either my grandmother
never showed it to me or my mind had blocked out the
horror for all these years. Along with some books and
magazines, I found two empty candy boxes with Elvis on
the cover, a reproduction gold record, a golden watch with
Elvis on the face, and, at the very bottom of the box, a *TV
Guide* celebrating Elvis as entertainer of the century. I had
to laugh at the strange collection, so imperfectly assembled, so perfectly my grandmother.

Tacky Elvis now has a place of honor on my
bookshelf—no more hiding in the closet. I play my Elvis
albums proudly (in digital form now), singing along loudly
in the car. My oldest daughter finds it slightly embarrassing; she's getting to the age where anything I do is
increasingly uncool. "It's okay," I tell her. "Someday, these
will be the things you miss." She shakes her head,
unconvinced. "Heartbreak Hotel" comes on, and I tell her
about the first time I heard this song, about the bus,
about my grandmother and her wild stories, and of
course, I tell her about Elvis. It always comes back to
Elvis.

9

10

11 •··· Conclusion
resolves conflict
between
Unbankes and her
grandmother

# F-16 PILOT WAS READY TO GIVE HER LIFE ON SEPT. 11

STEVE HENDRIX (b. 1964) is a journalist from Americus, Georgia, who traveled around the world and published his freelance work widely before becoming a staff writer at the *Washington Post*. The sections of the paper in which his work has appeared—Travel, Style, Book World, and the Sunday magazine—give an idea of his range as a writer. As the *Post* explains, "What his stories have had in common (in addition to awful first-draft spelling) was the goal of taking readers to a place they might never visit otherwise." In "F-16 Pilot Was Ready to Give Her Life on Sept. 11," Hendrix takes his readers to the sky above Washington, D.C., on a bright September morning when an Air Force fighter pilot found herself scrambling for a suicide mission: she was given orders to use her unarmed plane to stop a hijacked airliner headed for the White House. Hendrix's narrative, written in the third person, appeared in the *Post* on the tenth anniversary of September 11.

ASHINGTON—LATE IN THE MORNING of the Tuesday that changed 1
everything, Lt. Heather "Lucky" Penney was on a runway at Andrews
Air Force Base and ready to fly. She had her hand on the throttle of an F-16[1] and
she had her orders: Bring down United Airlines Flight 93. The day's fourth
hijacked airliner seemed to be hurtling toward Washington. Penney, one of the
first two combat pilots in the air that morning, was told to stop it.

The one thing she didn't have as she roared into the crystalline sky was 2
live ammunition. Or missiles. Or anything at all to throw at a hostile aircraft.

Except her own plane. So that was the plan. 3

Because the surprise attacks were unfolding, in that innocent age, faster 4
than they could arm war planes, Penney and her commanding officer went up
to fly their jets straight into a Boeing 757.

"We wouldn't be shooting it down. We'd be ramming the aircraft," 5
Penney recalls of her charge that day. "I would essentially be a kamikaze pilot."

*Maj. Heather Penney in 2011.*

1. A single-engine fighter aircraft used by the U.S. Air Force.

For years, Penney, one of the first generation of female combat pilots in   6
the country, gave no interviews about her experiences on Sept. 11 (which
included, eventually, escorting Air Force One[2] back into Washington's suddenly highly restricted airspace).

But 10 years later, she is reflecting on one of the lesser-told tales of that   7
endlessly examined morning: how the first counterpunch the U.S. military
prepared to throw at the attackers was effectively a suicide mission.

"We had to protect the airspace any way we could," she said last week in   8
her office at Lockheed Martin,[3] where she is a director in the F-35 program.[4]

Penney, now a major but still a petite blonde with a Colgate grin, is no   9
longer a combat flier. She flew two tours in Iraq and she serves as a part-time
National Guard pilot, mostly hauling VIPs around in a military Gulfstream.[5]
She takes the stick of her own vintage 1941 Taylorcraft tail-dragger whenever
she can.

But none of her thousands of hours in the air quite compare with the   10
urgent rush of launching on what was supposed to be a one-way flight to a
midair collision.

### First of Her Kind

She was a rookie in the autumn of 2001, the first female F-16 pilot they'd ever   11
had at the 121st Fighter Squadron of the D.C. Air National Guard. She had
grown up smelling jet fuel. Her father flew jets in Vietnam and still races them.
Penney got her pilot's license when she was a literature major at Purdue. She
planned to be a teacher. But during a graduate program in American studies,
Congress opened up combat aviation to women.

"I signed up immediately," Penney says. "I wanted to be a fighter pilot   12
like my dad."

On that Tuesday, they had just finished two weeks of air combat training   13
in Nevada. They were sitting around a briefing table when someone looked in

2. The airplane that transports the U.S. president, along with staff and/or journalists.

3. A U.S.-based aerospace, defense, and security technology company. It is the largest con-
tractor for the U.S. government.

4. A Lockheed Martin project that is developing a new model of fighter plane, the F-35.

5. A type of aircraft.

*Col. John Penney and his daughter Maj. Heather Penney, in a family photo. Penney was inspired to become a fighter pilot by her father.*

to say a plane had hit the World Trade Center in New York. When it happened once, they assumed it was some yahoo in a Cessna.[6] When it happened again, they knew it was war.

See pp. 127–28 for help with making transitions in time.

But the surprise was complete. In the monumental confusion of those first hours, it was impossible to get clear orders. Nothing was ready. The jets were still equipped with dummy bullets from the training mission.

As remarkable as it seems now, there were no armed aircraft standing by and no system in place to scramble them over Washington. Before that morning, all eyes were looking outward, still scanning the old Cold War threat paths for planes and missiles coming over the polar ice cap.

6. Before it was the name of a company operating a search engine and Internet portal, a yahoo was a noisy and unsophisticated person who caused problems out of foolishness and incompetence. A Cessna is a type of aircraft made by the company of the same name.

"There was no perceived threat at the time, especially one coming from  16
the homeland like that," says Col. George Degnon, vice commander of the
113th Wing at Andrews. "It was a little bit of a helpless feeling, but we did
everything humanly possible to get the aircraft armed and in the air. It was
amazing to see people react."

Things are different today, Degnon says. At least two "hot-cocked"  17
planes are ready at all times, their pilots never more than yards from the
cockpit.

A third plane hit the Pentagon, and almost at once came word that a  18
fourth plane could be on the way, maybe more. The jets would be armed within
an hour, but somebody had to fly now, weapons or no weapons.

"Lucky, you're coming with me," barked Col. Marc Sasseville.  19

They were gearing up in the pre-flight life-support area when Sasseville,  20
struggling into his flight suit, met her eye.

"I'm going to go for the cockpit," Sasseville said.  21

She replied without hesitating.  22

"I'll take the tail."  23

It was a plan. And a pact.  24

### "Let's Go!"

Penney had never scrambled a jet before. Normally the pre-flight is a half-  25
hour or so of methodical checks. She automatically started going down the
list.

"Lucky, what are you doing? Get your butt up there and let's go!" Sas-  26
seville shouted.

She climbed in, rushed to power up the engines, screamed for her ground  27
crew to pull the chocks.[7] The crew chief still had his headphones plugged into
the fuselage as she nudged the throttle forward. He ran along pulling safety
pins from the jet as it moved forward.

She muttered a fighter pilot's prayer—"God, don't let me [expletive]  28
up"—and followed Sasseville into the sky.

---

7. Chocks are the rubber wedges used to keep the wheels of a plane (or any other vehicle)
from rolling. Pulling them allows the plane to move freely.

They screamed over the smoldering Pentagon, heading northwest at 29 more than 400 mph, flying low and scanning the clear horizon. Her commander had time to think about the best place to hit the enemy.

"We don't train to bring down airliners," said Sasseville, now stationed 30 at the Pentagon. "If you just hit the engine, it could still glide and you could guide it to a target. My thought was the cockpit or the wing."

He also thought about his ejection seat. Would there be an instant just 31 before impact?

"I was hoping to do both at the same time," he says. "It probably wasn't 32 going to work, but that's what I was hoping."

Penney worried about missing the target if she tried to bail out. 33

"If you eject and your jet soars through without impact . . ." she trails 34 off, the thought of failing more dreadful than the thought of dying.

But she didn't have to die. She didn't have to knock down an airliner full 35 of kids and salesmen and girlfriends. They did that themselves.

It would be hours before Penney and Sasseville learned that United 93 36 had already gone down in Pennsylvania, an insurrection by hostages willing to do just what the two Guard pilots had been willing to do: Anything. And everything.

"The real heroes are the passengers on Flight 93 who were willing to 37 sacrifice themselves," Penney says. "I was just an accidental witness to history."

She and Sasseville flew the rest of the day, clearing the airspace, escort- 38 ing the president, looking down onto a city that would soon be sending them to war.

Later, as the Penney family checked in on each other from around the 39 country, they marveled at the other fateful twist on the extraordinary events: the possibility that Penney's own father could well have been in the cockpit of her airliner target.

John Penney was a captain at United Airlines at the time. He had been 40 flying East Coast routes all the previous month. The daughter had no way of knowing whether the father was airborne or not.

"We talked about the possibility that I could have been on the plane," 41 Col. John Penney said. "She knew I was flying that kind of rotation. But we never fell down and emotionally broke apart or anything like that. She's a fighter pilot; I'm a fighter pilot."

Penney is a single mom of two girls now. She still loves to fly. And she    42
still thinks often of that extraordinary ride down the runway a decade ago.

"I genuinely believed that was going to be the last time I took off," she    43
says. "If we did it right, this would be it."

## FOR DISCUSSION

1. Steve Hendrix speaks of the days before September 11, 2001, as an "innocent age" (4). How accurate is this description? According to Hendrix, how have security conditions changed since then?

2. According to Hendrix's narrative, how did national security conditions on 9/11 affect the mission of Lt. Heather "Lucky" Penney?

3. The "real heroes" of the day, said Penney, were the passengers of United Airlines Flight 93, who wrestled control of the plane from the terrorists and brought it down in a field in Pennsylvania. She was only an "accidental witness to history" (37). Is Penney being too modest here? Why or why not?

4. What other outcomes might Penney's story have had on "the Tuesday that changed everything" (1)? How might those different outcomes have affected Hendrix's narrative?

5. Would it have made a difference in the telling or impact of Hendrix's narrative if his "rookie" pilot had been male instead of female (11)? Why or why not?

## STRATEGIES AND STRUCTURES

1. In the introduction to his narrative (paragraphs 1–4), Hendrix refers to events that happened on 9/11. Then, in paragraphs 5–12, he uses a **FLASH-FORWARD** to capture events that occurred "10 years later" (7). Point out other places in his narrative where Hendrix goes back and forth in time like this. Why do you think he adopted this strategy?

2. As it turns out, Penney and her commanding officer did not have to fly their planes into United Flight 93. How does Hendrix nonetheless make their tale one of heroic dedication and sacrifice? Point to specific passages in the text that support this reading.

3. Hendrix constructs the mission of Penney and her commanding officer as "effectively a suicide mission" (7). How and how well does he (and they) effectively

eliminate the possibility that his central characters might save themselves at the last minute?

4. Hendrix's narrative includes lines of dialogue spoken mostly by Penney and her commanding officer. How appropriate is the dialogue to the particular story he is telling? Why do you think so?

## WORDS AND FIGURES OF SPEECH

1. Heather Penney's nickname is "Lucky" (1). Is the name well deserved? Why or why not?

2. On 9/11, Penney's commanding officer "barked" orders at her (19), and she "roared into the crystalline sky" in her F-16 jet fighter (2). The two pilots then "screamed over the smoldering Pentagon" (29). Where else in his narrative does Hendrix use action words like these? Are they appropriate to the story he is telling, or do they border on CLICHÉ? Or both? Explain.

3. With what is Colonel Degnon comparing airplanes when he says that two are always "hot-cocked" and ready to fly (17)? How apt do you find the comparison?

4. Hendrix refers to Penney's adventures on 9/11 as "one of the lesser-told tales of that endlessly examined morning" (7). Does calling his account a "tale" enhance or diminish its credibility? Why might he make a point of noting that the tale is "lesser-told"?

5. In Hendrix's narrative, Lt. Penney is presented as a hero. Should she have been treated as the "heroine" instead? Why or why not?

## FOR WRITING

1. Are you aware of any "lesser-told tales" of September 11, 2001, that deserve to be shared? In a brief narrative, tell that story—or any other story of the day that you think is particularly worth recalling. If appropriate, give your narrative a hero—or at least a central character. Be sure to include dialogue.

2. Heather Penney refers to the passengers on United Airlines Flight 93 as "heroes" (37). Find some articles on the subject, either from the *Washington Post* (where this article appeared) or another newspaper, and write a narrative telling what happened on that flight. Consider focusing on the actions of one or two passengers, whether or not you treat what they did as heroic.

# THE MONEY

JUNOT DÍAZ (b. 1968) is a novelist, short-story writer, essayist, and recipient of both MacArthur and Guggenheim fellowships. Born in the Dominican Republic, Díaz moved with his family to New Jersey when he was six years old. Since earning degrees from Rutgers and Cornell, Díaz has authored the following works of fiction: *Drown* (1996), his debut collection of short stories; his first novel, the Pulitzer Prize–winning *The Brief Wondrous Life of Oscar Wao* (2007); and a second story collection, *This Is How You Lose Her* (2012). "The Money" first appeared in the *New Yorker* (2011); Díaz describes the narrative as "an essay on the one time my family apartment was broken into while we were away on vacation and how I solved the Mystery of the Stupid Morons." He teaches writing at the Massachusetts Institute of Technology and serves as the fiction editor for *Boston Review*, a publication that covers politics, culture, and literature.

ALL THE DOMINICANS I KNEW IN THOSE DAYS sent money home. My mother certainly did. She didn't have a regular job outside of caring for us five kids so she scrimped the loot together from whatever came her way. My father was always losing his forklift jobs so it wasn't like she had a steady flow ever. But my mother would rather have died than not send money back home to my grandparents in Santo Domingo.[1] They were alone down there and those remittances, beyond material support, were a way, I suspect, for Mami to negotiate the absence, the distance caused by our diaspora. Hard times or not she made it happen. She chipped dollars off from the cash Papi gave her for our daily expenses, forced our already broke family to live even broker. In those times when nobody gave a damn about nutrition we alone among our friends never had juice, soda, snacks in our apartment. Not ever. And you can forget about eating at McDonald's or having clothes with real labels. The family lived tight and that was how she built the nut that she sent home every six months or so to the grandparents.

We're not talking about a huge amount either. Two, maybe three hundred dollars. But in the Santo Domingo of those years, in the neighborhood in which my abuelos lived, that 300 smackers was the difference between life with meat and life without, between electricity and stone age. All of us kids knew where that money was hidden too—our apartment wasn't huge—but we all also knew that to touch it would have meant a violence approaching death. I, who could take the change out of my mother's purse without even thinking, couldn't have brought myself to even look at that forbidden stash.

So what happened? Exactly what you would think. The summer I was twelve my family went away on a "vacation"—one of my father's half-baked get-to-know-our-country-better, sleep-in-the-van extravaganzas—and when we returned to Jersey, exhausted, battered, we found our front door unlocked. Stuff was knocked over, including the empty Presidente can my mother considered a decoration. My parents' room, which was where the thieves had concentrated their search, looked like it had been tornado-tossed. The thieves had kept it simple; they'd snatched a portable radio, some of my Dungeons & Dragons[2] hardcovers and of course: the remittances my mother had kept hidden back in a drawer.

1. Capital of the Dominican Republic and its largest city.
2. A fantasy role-playing game in which players take on specific roles and personalities.

It's not like the robbery came as some huge surprise. In our neighbor-   4
hood cars and apartments were always getting jacked and the kid stupid
enough to leave a bike unattended for more than a tenth of a second was the
kid who was never going to see that bike again. There was no respect. Everybody got hit; no matter who you were, eventually it was your turn.

And that summer it was ours.                                             5

Still we took the burglary pretty hard. When you're a recent immigrant   6
and you've put up with a lot of bullshit because of it, it's easy to feel targeted.
Like it wasn't just a couple of assholes that had it in for you but the whole
neighborhood—hell, maybe the whole country.

I felt that for certain and felt shame too, wondered if it was something  7
we'd done, but I was also pissed. I was at the stage in my nerdery when I
thought Dungeons & Dragons was going to be my life so the loss of those
books was akin to having my kidney nicked while I slept.

No one took the robbery as hard as my mom, though. My father for his    8
part shrugged it off, wasn't his money or his parents after all; went right back
to running the streets but my mother stayed angry in a Hulkish way none of
us seen before. You would have thought the thieves had run off with 10 million
dollars, how she was carrying on. It was bad. She cursed the neighborhood, she
cursed the country, she cursed my father and of course she cursed us kids,
swore that the only reason that the robbery happened was because we had run
our gums[3] to our idiot friends and they had done it. Something we all denied
of course. And at least once a day, usually while we were eating, she'd say: I
guess your abuelos are going to starve now.

Just in case we kids didn't feel impotent and responsible enough.        9

Anyway, this is where the tale should end, right? Wasn't as if there was  10
going to be any CSI-style[4] investigation or anything. Should have been bye-
See p. 127 for more
on ways to end your
narrative. bye money, bye-bye Dungeon Masters Guide. Except that a couple
of days later I was moaning about the robbery to these guys I was
hanging with at that time and they were cursing sympathetically
and out of nowhere it struck me. You know when you get one of those moments
of almost mental clarity? When the nictitating membrane obscuring the world

3. An idiom meaning to tell more than one should.

4. *Crime Scene Investigation*, a drama television series that ran from 2000 to 2015.

suddenly lifts? That's what happened. For no reason whatsoever I realized that these two dopes that I called my friends had done it. They'd broken into the apartment while we were away and taken our shit. I couldn't have been any more sure if you'd shown me a video of them doing it. They were shaking their heads, mouthing all the right words but I could see the way they looked at each other, those Raskolnikov[5] glances. I *knew*.

Now it wasn't like I could publicly denounce these dolts or go to the police. That would have been about as useless as crying. Here's what I did: I asked the main dope to let me use his bathroom (we were in front of his apartment) and while I pretended to piss I unlatched the window and then we all headed down to the community pool as usual. But while they dove in I pretended to forget something back home. Ran back to the dope's apartment, slid open the bathroom window and in broad daylight wriggled my skinny ass into his apartment; his mom was of course at work.

Where the hell did I get these ideas? I have not a clue. I guess I was reading way too much Encyclopedia Brown and the Three Investigators[6] in those days. What can I tell you—that's just the kind of moron I was.

Because if mine had been the normal neighborhood this is when the cops would have been called and my ass would have been caught *burglarizing*. Oh the irony—imagine me trying to explain that one to my mother. But no matter: mine wasn't a normal neighborhood and so no one called anybody. The dolt's family had been in the U.S. all their lives and they had a ton of stuff in their apartment, a TV in every room, but I didn't have to do a great amount of searching. I popped up the dolt's mattress and underneath I found my D&D books and also most of my mother's money. He had thoughtfully kept it in the same envelope. Walked out the front door and on the run back to my apartment I kept waiting for the SWAT team to zoom up but it never happened.

And that was how I solved the Case of the Stupid Morons. My one and only case.

The next day at the pool the dolt announced that someone had broken into *his* apartment and stolen all of *his* savings. This place is full of thieves, he complained bitterly and I was like: No kidding.

11

12

13

14

15

---

5. In Fyodor Dostoyevsky's novel *Crime and Punishment*, Raskolnikov is the protagonist who commits murder.

6. Juvenile fiction that features boy detectives who solve mysteries.

Took me two days to return the money to my mother. Truth was I was   16
seriously considering keeping it. I'd never had that much money in hand and
who in those days didn't want a Colecovision?[7] But in the end the guilt got to
me and I gave it to her and told her what had happened. I guess I was expecting
my mother to run around in joy, to crown me her favorite son, to at least cook
me my favorite meal. Nada. She just looked at the money and then at me and
went back to her bedroom and put it back in its place. I'd wanted a party or at
least to see her happy but there was nothing. Just two hundred and some odd
dollars and fifteen hundred or so miles—that's all there was.

### FOR DISCUSSION

1. "When you're a recent immigrant," writes Junot Díaz, "it's easy to feel targeted"
   (6). Is Díaz right to say that feeling targeted by everybody, "maybe the whole
   country," is a normal part of the immigrant experience in America (6)? Why or
   why not?

2. Judging from Díaz's **DESCRIPTION** of the neighborhood they lived in, why were he
   and his family likely to get burglarized "eventually," no matter what they did (4)?

3. The burglary, Díaz says, came as no "huge surprise" (4). Why did the family, particularly Díaz's mother, take the burglary "pretty hard" anyway (6)?

4. After Díaz returned the stolen money to his mother, he hoped she would celebrate
   his exploits and reward him. Instead, she did nothing (16). Why do you think
   Díaz's mother reacted in this way?

### STRATEGIES AND STRUCTURES

1. Díaz presents his narrative in part as a detective story—the "Case of the Stupid
   Morons" (14). Point out other detective-story elements in his narrative. How and
   how effectively does he use them? How seriously?

2. Díaz says that all of a sudden he just "*knew*" who the thieves were (10). Is his
   explanation of how he solved the case sufficient, or should he have provided more
   narrative clues for the reader? Explain.

3. "Anyway this is where the tale should end, right?" (10). To whom is this question
   addressed? Why do you think Díaz asks it? What assumptions is he making about
   his audience?

7. A video-game unit for home entertainment. It first appeared in 1982.

4. Where else does Díaz call attention to the fact that he is writing a narrative? What is the apparent purpose of such elements in the story?

5. Díaz does not construct his narrative as just another family's tale of victimization, yet he doesn't exactly provide a happy ending either. How does his story COMPARE and CONTRAST with the kind where the hero is celebrated at the end?

### WORDS AND FIGURES OF SPEECH

1. Before her "loot" gets "jacked" by the two "dopes" in Díaz's story, his mother is stashing away money to send to her parents in the Dominican Republic (1, 4, 10). Point to other examples of Díaz's use of slang. How does this language add to (or detract from) his account?

2. "Raskolnikov glances" are *guilty* glances, like those of Rodion Raskolnikov, the uneasy perpetrator of murder in Fyodor Dostoyevsky's novel *Crime and Punishment* (1866). Where else in his narrative does Díaz make ALLUSIONS to his reading and other intellectual pursuits? What do they reveal about his youthful self (10)?

3. In his story, Díaz sprinkles in Spanish words, untranslated ("abuelos," "nada," "Papi"). Why do you think he mixes languages this way? What, if anything, would be lost if he did not?

4. Díaz refers to the theft of his mother's money as both a "robbery" and a "burglary" (4, 6). What are the differences in the legal meanings of these two terms? Should Díaz have pointed this out? Why or why not?

### FOR WRITING

1. Write a narrative about your (or a friend's or family member's) adventures in your neighborhood. Try to give a sense of how people talk as well as how they act.

2. Díaz's mother sends money to her parents in the Dominican Republic, which makes a huge difference in the quality of their life. Do a little research on the practice of sending money home, and write an essay about its significance, both social and economic. Or, alternatively, if you are aware of someone who sends money home to family or friends outside the United States, tell the story of that person and the recipients.

3. Solved any criminal or other "cases" recently? Write a narrative about the experience, and give it some of the shape and flavor of a detective story.

YIYUN LI

# ORANGE CRUSH

YIYUN LI (b. 1972) is a Chinese American writer who grew up in Beijing, China. In 1996, after attending Peking University, Li moved to the United States to study medicine at the University of Iowa, earning master's degrees in both immunology and the writing of creative nonfiction. Li's first collection of short stories, *A Thousand Years of Good Prayers* (2005), won numerous literary awards, and in 2009 she published her first novel, *The Vagrants*, followed by *Gold Boy, Emerald Girl* (2010), and, most recently, *Kinder Than Solitude* (2014). In 2010, she was awarded a prestigious MacArthur Fellowship. "Orange Crush" first appeared in the food and culture section of the *New York Times Magazine* in 2006. It tells the story of Li's encounter, as a teenager in China, with a new space-age drink from America—Tang.

---

D URING THE WINTER IN BEIJING, where I grew up, we always had orange     1
and tangerine peels drying on our heater. Oranges were not cheap. My father, who believed that thrift was one of the best virtues, saved the dried

peels in a jar; when we had a cough or cold, he would boil them until the water took on a bitter taste and a pale yellow cast, like the color of water drizzling out of a rusty faucet. It was the best cure for colds, he insisted.

I did not know then that I would do the same for my own children, pre- 2 ferring nature's provision over those orange- and pink- and purple-colored medicines. I just felt ashamed, especially when he packed it in my lunch for the annual field trip, where other children brought colorful flavored fruit drinks— made with "chemicals," my father insisted.

The year I turned sixteen, a new product caught my eye. Fruit Treasure, 3 as Tang[1] was named for the Chinese market, instantly won everyone's heart. Imagine real oranges condensed into a fine powder! Equally seductive was the TV commercial, which gave us a glimpse of a life that most families, including mine, could hardly afford. The kitchen was spacious and brightly lighted, whereas ours was a small cube—but at least we had one; half the people we knew cooked in the hallways of their apartment buildings, where every family's dinner was on display and their financial states assessed by the number of meals with meat they ate every week. The family on TV was beautiful, all three of them with healthy complexions and toothy, carefree smiles (the young parents I saw on my bus ride to school were those who had to leave at six or even earlier in the morning for the two-hour commute and who had to carry their children, half-asleep and often screaming, with them because the only child care they could afford was that provided by their employers).

The drink itself, steaming hot in an expensive-looking mug that was 4 held between the child's mittened hands, was a vivid orange. The mother talked to the audience as if she were our best friend: "During the cold winter, we need to pay more attention to the health of our family," she said. "That's why I give my husband and my child hot Fruit Treasure for extra warmth and vitamins." The drink's temperature was the only Chinese aspect of the commercial; iced drinks were considered unhealthful and believed to induce stomach disease.

As if the images were not persuasive enough, near the end of the ad an 5 authoritative voice informed us that Tang was the only fruit drink used by

1. An orange-flavored powdered drink mix first marketed in the United States in 1959.

NASA for its astronauts—the exact information my father needed to prove his theory that all orange-flavored drinks other than our orange peel water were made of suspicious chemicals.

Until this point, all commercials were short and boring, with catchy 6 phrases like "Our Product Is Loved by People Around the World" flashing on screen. The Tang ad was a revolution in itself: the lifestyle it represented—a more healthful and richer one, a Western luxury—was just starting to become legitimate in China as it was beginning to embrace the West and its capitalism.

Even though Tang was the most expensive fruit drink available, its sales 7 soared. A simple bottle cost seventeen yuan, a month's worth of lunch money. A boxed set of two became a status hostess gift. Even the sturdy glass containers that the powder came in were coveted. People used them as tea mugs, the orange label still on, a sign that you could afford the modern American drink. Even my mother had an empty Tang bottle with a snug orange nylon net over it, a present from one of her fellow schoolteachers. She carried it from the office to the classroom and back again as if our family had also consumed a full bottle.

The truth was, our family had never tasted Tang. Just think of how many 8 oranges we could buy with the money spent on a bottle, my father reasoned. His resistance sent me into a long adolescent melancholy. I was ashamed by our lack of style and our life, with its taste of orange peel water. I could not wait until I grew up and could have my own Tang-filled life.

To add to my agony, our neighbor's son brought over his first girlfriend, 9 for whom he had just bought a bottle of Tang. He was five years older and a college sophomore; we had nothing in common and had not spoken more than ten sentences. But this didn't stop me from having a painful crush on him. The beautiful girlfriend opened the Tang in our flat and insisted that we all try it. When it was my turn to scoop some into a glass of water, the fine orange powder almost choked me to tears. It was the first time I had drunk Tang, and the taste was not like real oranges but stronger, as if it were made of the essence of all the oranges I had ever eaten. This would be the love I would seek, a boy unlike my father, a boy who would not blink to buy a bottle of Tang for me. I looked at the beautiful girlfriend and wished to replace her.

My agony and jealousy did not last long, however. Two months later the 10 beautiful girlfriend left the boy for an older and richer man. Soon after, the boy's mother came to visit and was still outraged about the Tang. For tips on developing a plot, see p. 127. "What a waste of money on someone who didn't become his wife!" she said.

"That's how it goes with young people," my mother said. "Once he has a  11 wife, he'll have a better brain and won't throw his money away."

"True. He's just like his father. When he courted me, he once invited me  12 to an expensive restaurant and ordered two fish for me. After we were married, he wouldn't even allow two fish for the whole family for one meal!"

That was the end of my desire for a Tangy life. I realized that every  13 dream ended with this bland, ordinary existence, where a prince would one day become a man who boiled orange peels for his family. I had not thought about the boy much until I moved to America ten years later and discovered Tang in a grocery store. It was just how I remembered it—fine powder in a sturdy bottle—but its glamour had lost its gloss because, alas, it was neither expensive nor trendy. To think that all the dreams of my youth were once contained in this commercial drink! I picked up a bottle and then returned it to the shelf.

### FOR DISCUSSION

1. Yiyun Li was sixteen when she first heard about Tang, or "Fruit Treasure," as the American drink mix was marketed in her native China (3). How significant is the author's age to her story? Explain.

2. Why was Li's father against spending family money on the prestigious new drink? Was his position justified? Why or why not?

3. What happened to Li when she tasted Tang for the first time?

4. Why does Li change her mind about the importance of Tang in her life? What brings an end to her "agony and jealousy" (10)?

5. What life lesson does Li take from her early experience? How is her perspective on her experience influenced by her later life in America? Explain.

### STRATEGIES AND STRUCTURES

1. Why does Li begin her story with a DESCRIPTION of the orange and tangerine peels that her father saves to treat family coughs and colds—and of the water that

results when he boils them (1)? What role does this "orange peel water" play throughout her NARRATIVE?

2. What is the function of the TV commercial in Li's narrative (3–6)? Why does she describe it in such detail?

3. How does Li's crush on the neighbor's son contribute to the PLOT of her story?

4. Where and how effectively does Li use DIALOGUE? Explain.

5. In the last paragraph of her narrative, Li jumps ahead ten years in time. What is the PURPOSE of this FLASH-FORWARD? How does she anticipate this ending in the second paragraph of her story?

6. In her personal coming-of-age story, what point is Li making about the dreams of youth in general? How does she use CAUSE-AND-EFFECT analysis to help her make that point?

## WORDS AND FIGURES OF SPEECH

1. Li gives her narrative the name of an American soft drink. Why? How does she connect this and the other "vivid orange" crush in her narrative to the "painful crush" she experienced as an adolescent (4, 9)?

2. How effective is Li's choice of a powdered American drink mix as a METAPHOR for the changes in her life and in the "lifestyle" of her native country (6)? Explain.

3. Explain the PUN in Li's reference to a "Tangy life" (13).

4. The Tang ad, says Li, was "a revolution" (6). What are the implications of this term, especially in a Communist culture such as China's?

5. What cultural differences do you find reflected in the different names for Tang in America and in China? Explain.

## FOR WRITING

1. Have you or anyone you know ever purchased a product because you thought it would change your life? In a paragraph or two, tell about your encounter with this product and whether or not it met your expectations.

2. Write a narrative about an infatuation you've had with a particular person or lifestyle—or perhaps a person who represented a lifestyle. Tell what you did to act on your infatuation and how you got over it—or didn't.

3. Write a coming-of-age narrative about someone—such as a sibling, friend, or neighbor—whom you have seen change and grow over a period of time. Focus on specific actions and events that show your subject in the process of maturing.

## MARY MEBANE

# THE BACK OF THE BUS

MARY MEBANE (1933–1992) was born outside of Durham, North Carolina; her father was a farmer and her mother worked in a tobacco factory. She earned a PhD from the University of North Carolina and became a professor of English at the University of Wisconsin–Milwaukee. In 1971 on the op-ed page of the *New York Times*, Mebane told the story of a bus ride from Durham, North Carolina, to Orangeburg, South Carolina, that "realized for me the enormousness of the change" that had occurred since the passage of the Civil Rights Act of 1964. That bus ride was the germ of two autobiographical volumes, *Mary* (1981) and *Mary Wayfarer* (1983). The essay reprinted here is a complete chapter from the first book. It is a personal narrative of another, earlier bus ride that Mebane had taken during the 1940s, when the segregation laws were still in place. Mebane said she wrote this piece because she "wanted to show what it was like to live under legal segregation *before* the Civil Rights Act of 1964."

HISTORICALLY, MY LIFETIME IS IMPORTANT because I was part of the last   1
generation born into a world of total legal segregation[1] in the Southern
United States. When the Supreme Court outlawed segregation in the public
schools in 1954, I was twenty-one. When Congress passed the Civil Rights
Act of 1964, permitting blacks free access to public places, I was thirty-one.
The world I was born into had been segregated for a long time—so long, in
fact, that I never met anyone who had lived during the time when restrictive
laws were not in existence, although some people spoke of parents and others
who had lived during the "free" time. As far as anyone knew, the laws as they
then existed would stand forever. They were meant to—and did—create a
world that fixed black people at the bottom of society in all aspects of human
life. It was a world without options.

Most Americans have never had to live with terror. I had had to live with   2
it all my life—the psychological terror of segregation, in which there was a
special set of laws governing your movements. You violated them at your
peril, for you knew that if you broke one of them, knowingly or not, physical
terror was just around the corner, in the form of policemen and jails, and in
some cases and places white vigilante mobs formed for the exclusive purpose
of keeping blacks in line.

It was Saturday morning, like any Saturday morning in dozens of South-   3
ern towns.

The town had a washed look. The street sweepers had been busy since   4
six o'clock. Now, at eight, they were still slowly moving down the streets,
white trucks with clouds of water coming from underneath the swelled tubu-
lar sides. Unwary motorists sometimes got a windowful of water as a truck
passed by. As it moved on, it left in its wake a clear stream running in the gut-
ters or splashed on the wheels of parked cars.

Homeowners, bent over industriously in the morning sun, were out   5
pushing lawn mowers. The sun was bright, but it wasn't too hot. It was morning and it was May. Most of the mowers were glad that it was finally getting
warm enough to go outside.

---

1. Government policy that barred African Americans from white neighborhoods, schools, and
other facilities and required that African Americans sit in separate sections from whites in
public spaces like buses and movie theaters.

Traffic was brisk. Country people were coming into town early with their    6
produce; clerks and service workers were getting to the job before the stores
opened at ten o'clock. Though the big stores would not be open for another
hour or so, the grocery stores, banks, open-air markets, dinettes, were already
open and filling with staff and customers.

Everybody was moving toward the heart of Durham's downtown, which    7
waited to receive them rather complacently, little knowing that in a decade the
shopping centers far from the center of downtown Durham would create a
ghost town in the midst of the busiest blocks on Main Street.

Some moved by car, and some moved by bus. The more affluent used    8
cars, leaving the buses mainly to the poor, black and white, though there were
some businesspeople who avoided the trouble of trying to find a parking place
downtown by riding the bus.

I didn't mind taking the bus on Saturday. It wasn't so crowded. At night    9
or on Saturday or Sunday was the best time. If there were plenty of seats, the
blacks didn't have to worry about being asked to move so that a white person
could sit down. And the knot of hatred and fear didn't come into my stomach.

I knew the stop that was the safety point, both going and coming. Leaving    10
town, it was the Little Five Points, about five or six blocks north of the main
downtown section. That was the last stop at which four or five people might
get on. After the stop, the driver could sometimes pass two or three stops
without taking on or letting off a passenger. So the number of See pp. 125–26 for
seats on the bus usually remained constant on the trip from town more on the "who,
to Braggtown. The nearer the bus got to the end of the line, the where, and when."
more I relaxed. For if a white passenger got on near the end of the line, often to
catch the return trip back and avoid having to stand in the sun at the bus stop
until the bus turned around, he or she would usually stand if there were not
seats in the white section, and the driver would say nothing, knowing that the
end of the line was near and that the standee would get a seat in a few minutes.

On the trip to town, the Mangum Street A&P[2] was the last point at which    11
the driver picked up more passengers than he let off. These people, though
they were just a few blocks from the downtown section, preferred to ride the
bus downtown. Those getting on at the A&P were usually on their way to work

---

2. Chain of supermarkets; originally called the Great Atlantic & Pacific Tea Company.

at the Duke University Hospital—past the downtown section, through a residential neighborhood, and then past the university, before they got to Duke Hospital.

So whether the driver discharged more passengers than he took on near  12
the A&P on Mangum was of great importance. For if he took on more passengers than got off, it meant that some of the newcomers would have to stand. And if they were white, the driver was going to have to ask a black passenger to move so that a white passenger could sit down. Most of the drivers had a rule of thumb, though. By custom the seats behind the exit door had become "colored" seats, and no matter how many whites stood up, anyone sitting behind the exit door knew that he or she wouldn't have to move.

The disputed seat, though, was the one directly opposite the exit door. It  13
was "no-man's-land." White people sat there, and black people sat there. It all depended on whose section was fuller. If the back section was full, the next black passenger who got on sat in the no-man's-land seat; but if the white section filled up, a white person would take the seat. Another thing about the white people: they could sit anywhere they chose, even in the "colored" section. Only the black passengers had to obey segregation laws.

On this Saturday morning Esther[3] and I set out for town for our music  14
lesson. We were going on our weekly big adventure, all the way across town, through the white downtown, then across the railroad tracks, then through the "colored" downtown, a section of run-down dingy shops, through some fading high-class black neighborhoods, past North Carolina College, to Mrs. Shearin's house.

We walked the two miles from Wildwood to the bus line. Though it was  15
a warm day, in the early morning there was dew on the grass and the air still had the night's softness. So we walked along and talked and looked back constantly, hoping someone we knew would stop and pick us up.

I looked back furtively, for in one of the few instances that I remembered  16
my father criticizing me severely, it was for looking back. One day when I was walking from town he had passed in his old truck. I had been looking back and had seen him. "Don't look back," he had said. "People will think that you want

---

3. Mebane's sister.

them to pick you up." Though he said "people," I knew he meant men—not the men he knew, who lived in the black community, but the black men who were not part of the community, and all of the white men. To be picked up meant that something bad would happen to me. Still, two miles is a long walk and I occasionally joined Esther in looking back to see if anyone we knew was coming.

Esther and I got to the bus and sat on one of the long seats at the back that faced each other. There were three such long seats—one on each side of the bus and a third long seat at the very back that faced the front. I liked to sit on a long seat facing the side because then I didn't have to look at the expressions on the faces of the whites when they put their tokens in and looked at the blacks sitting in the back of the bus. Often I studied my music, looking down and practicing the fingering. I looked up at each stop to see who was getting on and to check on the seating pattern. The seating pattern didn't really bother me that day until the bus started to get unusually full for a Saturday morning. I wondered what was happening, where all these people were coming from. They got on and got on until the white section was almost full and the black section was full. 17

There was a black man in a blue windbreaker and a gray porkpie hat sitting in no-man's-land, and my stomach tightened. I wondered what would happen. I had never been on a bus on which a black person was asked to give a seat to a white person when there was no other seat empty. Usually, though, I had seen a black person automatically get up and move to an empty seat farther back. But this morning the only empty seat was beside a black person sitting in no-man's-land. 18

The bus stopped at Little Five Points and one black got off. A young white man was getting on. I tensed. What would happen now? Would the driver ask the black man to get up and move to the empty seat farther back? The white man had a businessman's air about him: suit, shirt, tie, polished brown shoes. He saw the empty seat in the "colored" section and after just a little hesitation went to it, put his briefcase down, and sat with his feet crossed. I relaxed a little when the bus pulled off without the driver saying anything. Evidently he hadn't seen what had happened, or since he was just a few stops from Main Street, he figured the mass exodus there would solve all the problems. Still, I was afraid of a scene. 19

The next stop was an open-air fruit stand just after Little Five Points,  20
and here another white man got on. Where would he sit? The only available
seat was beside the black man. Would he stand the few stops to Main Street or
would the driver make the black man move? The whole colored section tensed,
but nobody said anything. I looked at Esther, who looked apprehensive. I
looked at the other men and women, who studiously avoided my eyes and
everybody else's as well, as they maintained a steady gaze at a far-distant land.

Just one woman caught my eye; I had noticed her before, and I had been  21
ashamed of her. She was a stringy little black woman. She could have been
forty; she could have been fifty. She looked as if she were a hard drinker. Flat
black face with tight features. She was dressed with great insouciance in a
tight boy's sweater with horizontal lines running across her flat chest. It pulled
down over a nondescript skirt. Laced-up shoes, socks, and a head rag completed her outfit. She looked tense.

The white man who had just gotten on the bus walked to the seat in no-  22
man's-land and stood there. He wouldn't sit down, just stood there. Two adult
males, living in the most highly industrialized, most technologically advanced
nation in the world, a nation that had devastated two other industrial giants in
World War II[4] and had flirted with taking on China in Korea. Both these men,
either of whom could have fought for the United States in Germany or Korea,
faced each other in mutual rage and hostility. The white one wanted to sit
down, but he was going to exert his authority and force the black one to get up
first. I watched the driver in the rearview mirror. He was about the same age
as the antagonists. The driver wasn't looking for trouble, either.

"Say there, buddy, how about moving back," the driver said, meanwhile  23
driving his bus just as fast as he could. The whole bus froze—whites at the
front, blacks at the rear. They didn't want to believe what was happening was
really happening.

The seated black man said nothing. The standing white man said nothing.  24

"Say, buddy, did you hear me? What about moving on back." The driver  25
was scared to death. I could tell that.

---

4. The United States and its allies defeated "industrial giants" Germany and Japan, as well as
Italy, in World War II (1939–45).

"These is the niggers' seats!" the little lady in the strange outfit started        26
screaming. I jumped. I had to shift my attention from the driver to the frieze
of the black man seated and white man standing to the articulate little woman
who had joined in the fray.

"The government gave us these seats! These is the niggers' seats." I was        27
startled at her statement and her tone. "The president said that these are the
niggers' seats!" I expected her to start fighting at any moment.

Evidently the bus driver did, too, because he was driving faster and        28
faster. I believe that he forgot he was driving a bus and wanted desperately to
pull to the side of the street and get out and run.

"I'm going to take you down to the station, buddy," the driver said.        29

The white man with the briefcase and the polished brown shoes who had        30
taken a seat in the "colored" section looked as though he might die of embarrassment at any moment.

As scared and upset as I was, I didn't miss a thing.        31

By that time we had come to the stop before Main Street, and the black        32
passenger rose to get off.

"You're not getting off, buddy. I'm going to take you downtown." The        33
driver kept driving as he talked and seemed to be trying to get downtown as
fast as he could.

"These are the niggers' seats! The government plainly said these are the        34
niggers' seats!" screamed the little woman in rage.

I was embarrassed at the use of the word "nigger" but I was proud of the        35
lady. I was also proud of the man who wouldn't get up.

The bus driver was afraid, trying to hold on to his job but plainly not        36
willing to get into a row with the blacks.

The bus seemed to be going a hundred miles an hour and everybody was        37
anxious to get off, though only the lady and the driver were saying anything.

The black man stood at the exit door; the driver drove right past the A&P        38
stop. I was terrified. I was sure that the bus was going to the police station to
put the black man in jail. The little woman had her hands on her hips and she
never stopped yelling. The bus driver kept driving as fast as he could.

Then, somewhere in the back of his mind, he decided to forget the whole        39
thing. The next stop was Main Street, and when he got there, in what seemed
to be a flash of lightning, he flung both doors open wide. He and his black

antagonist looked at each other in the rearview mirror; in a second the wind-breaker and porkpie hat were gone. The little woman was standing, preaching to the whole bus about the government's gift of these seats to the blacks; the man with the brown shoes practically fell out of the door in his hurry; and Esther and I followed the hurrying footsteps.

We walked about three doors down the block, then caught a bus to the     40
black neighborhood. Here we sat on one of the two long seats facing each other, directly behind the driver. It was the custom. Since this bus had a route from a black neighborhood to the downtown section and back, passing through no white residential areas, blacks could sit where they chose. One minute we had been on a bus in which violence was threatened over a seat near the exit door; the next minute we were sitting in the very front behind the driver.

The people who devised this system thought that it was going to last     41
forever.

## FOR DISCUSSION

1. Why does the bus driver threaten to drive to the police station according to Mary Mebane? What was his official duty under segregation?

2. Why does the businessman with the briefcase and brown shoes take the separate seat in the back of the bus instead of the place on the bench across from the exit? Was he upholding or violating segregation customs by doing so?

3. What is the main confrontation of the **NARRATIVE**? What emotion(s) does it arouse in young Mebane and her sister as witnesses?

4. Who are the "people" to whom Mebane refers in paragraph 41?

5. Why does Mebane claim a national significance for the events of her private life as narrated here? Is her **CLAIM** justified? How does this claim relate to her **PURPOSE** for writing?

## STRATEGIES AND STRUCTURES

1. In which paragraph does Mebane begin telling the story of the bus ride? Why do you think she starts with the routine of the street sweepers and the homeowners doing yard work?

2. List several passages in Mebane's text that seem to be told from young Mary's **POINT OF VIEW**. Then list others that are told from the point of view of the adult

author looking back at an event in her youth. Besides time, what is the main difference in their perspectives?

3. Why does Mebane refer to the black passenger who confronts the bus driver as "the windbreaker and porkpie hat" (39)? Whose point of view is she capturing? Is she showing or telling here—and what difference does it make in her essay?

4. How does Mebane use the increasing speed of the bus to show rather than tell about the precariousness of the segregation system?

5. Mebane interrupts her narrative of the events of that Saturday morning in paragraphs 10 through 13. What is she explaining to her **AUDIENCE**, and why is it necessary that she do so? Where else does she interrupt her narrative with **EXPOSITION**?

## WORDS AND FIGURES OF SPEECH

1. Why does Mebane refer to the seat across from the exit as a "no-man's land" (13)? What does this term mean?

2. Mebane **COMPARES** the seated black man and the standing white man to a "frieze," a decorative horizontal band, often molded or carved, along the upper part of a wall (26). Why is the **METAPHOR** appropriate here?

3. Look up "insouciance" in your dictionary (21). Does the use of this word prepare you for the rebellious behavior of the "stringy" little woman (21)? How?

4. What are the two possible meanings of "scene" (19)? How might Mebane's personal narrative be said to illustrate both kinds?

5. Which of the many meanings of "articulate" in your dictionary best fits the woman who screams back at the bus driver (26)?

## FOR WRITING

1. In a brief **ANECDOTE**, recount a ride you have taken on a bus, train, plane, roller coaster, boat, or other vehicle. Focus on the vehicle itself and the people who were on it with you.

2. Write a personal narrative about an experience you had with racial tension in a public place. Be sure to describe the physical place and tell what you saw and heard and did there.

**LYNDA BARRY**

# THE SANCTUARY OF SCHOOL

LYNDA BARRY (b. 1956) is a cartoonist, novelist, and teacher of writing. She was born in Wisconsin but spent most of her adolescence in Seattle, where she supported herself at age 16 as a janitor. As a student at Evergreen State College in Olympia, Washington, Barry began drawing *Ernie Pook's Comeek*, the comic strip for which she is perhaps best known. Her first novel, *Cruddy* (2000), was about a teenager and her troubled family life "in the cruddiest part of town." In "The Sanctuary of School," which first appeared in the education section of the *New York Times* in January 1992, Barry tells how she first discovered the therapeutic value of art— and of good teachers. This narrative about her early school days also carries a pointed message for those who would cut costs in the public school system by eliminating art from the curriculum.

I WAS SEVEN YEARS OLD the first time I snuck out of the house in the dark. It was winter and my parents had been fighting all night. They were short on money and long on relatives who kept "temporarily" moving into our house because they had nowhere else to go.

My brother and I were used to giving up our bedroom. We slept on the   2
couch, something we actually liked because it put us that much closer to the
light of our lives, our television.

At night when everyone was asleep, we lay on our pillows watching it   3
with the sound off. We watched Steve Allen's[1] mouth moving. We watched
Johnny Carson's[2] mouth moving. We watched movies filled with gangsters
shooting machine guns into packed rooms, dying soldiers hurling a last gre-
nade, and beautiful women crying at windows. Then the sign-off finally came
and we tried to sleep.

The morning I snuck out, I woke up filled with a panic about needing to   4
get to school. The sun wasn't quite up yet but my anxiety was so fierce that I
just got dressed, walked quietly across the kitchen and let myself out the back
door.

It was quiet outside. Stars were still out. Nothing moved and no one was   5
in the street. It was as if someone had turned the sound off on the world.

I walked the alley, breaking thin ice over the puddles with my shoes. I   6
didn't know why I was walking to school in the dark. I didn't think about it. All
I knew was a feeling of panic, like the panic that strikes kids when they realize
they are lost.

That feeling eased the moment I turned the corner and saw the dark out-   7
line of my school at the top of the hill. My school was made up of about 15
nondescript portable classrooms set down on a fenced concrete lot in a run-
down Seattle neighborhood, but it had the most beautiful view of the Cascade
Mountains. You could see them from anywhere on the playfield and you could
see them from the windows of my classroom—Room 2.

I walked over to the monkey bars and hooked my arms around the cold   8
metal. I stood for a long time just looking across Rainier Valley. The sky was
beginning to whiten and I could hear a few birds.

In a perfect world my absence at home would not have gone unnoticed. I would   9
have had two parents in a panic to locate me, instead of two parents in a panic

---

1. American actor and musician (1921–2000) best known for his work on late night television.

2. American comedian and television personality (1924–2005) who hosted *The Tonight Show*
for thirty years.

to locate an answer to the hard question of survival during a deep financial and emotional crisis.

But in an overcrowded and unhappy home, it's incredibly easy for any child 10 to slip away. The high levels of frustration, depression, and anger in my house made my brother and me invisible. We were children with the sound turned off. And for us, as for the steadily increasing number of neglected children in this country, the only place where we could count on being noticed was at school.

"Hey there, young lady. Did you forget to go home last night?" It was 11 Mr. Gunderson, our janitor, whom we all loved. He was nice and he was funny and he was old with white hair, thick glasses and an unbelievable number of keys. I could hear them jingling as he walked across the playfield. I felt incredibly happy to see him.

He let me push his wheeled garbage can between the different portables 12 as he unlocked each room. He let me turn on the lights and raise the window shades and I saw my school slowly come to life. I saw Mrs. Holman, our school secretary, walk into the office without her orange lipstick on yet. She waved.

I saw the fifth-grade teacher, Mr. Cunningham, walking under the 13 breezeway eating a hard roll. He waved.

And I saw my teacher, Mrs. Claire LeSane, walking toward us in a red 14 coat and calling my name in a very happy and surprised way, and suddenly my throat got tight and my eyes stung and I ran toward her crying. It was something that surprised us both.

It's only thinking about it now, 28 years later, that I realize I was crying 15 from relief. I was with my teacher, and in a while I was going to sit at my desk, with my crayons and pencils and books and classmates all around me, and for the next six hours I was going to enjoy a thoroughly secure, warm and stable world. It was a world I absolutely relied on. Without it, I don't know where I would have gone that morning.

Mrs. LeSane asked me what was wrong and when I said "Nothing," she 16 seemingly left it at that. But she asked me if I would carry her purse for her, an honor above all honors, and she asked if I wanted to come into Room 2 early and paint.

She believed in the natural healing power of painting and drawing for troubled 17 children. In the back of her room there was always a drawing table and an easel

with plenty of supplies, and sometimes during the day she would come up to you for what seemed like no good reason and quietly ask if you wanted to go to the back table and "make some pictures for Mrs. LeSane." We all had a chance at it—to sit apart from the class for a while to paint, draw and silently work out impossible problems on 11 × 17 sheets of newsprint.

Drawing came to mean everything to me. At the back table in Room 2, I learned to build myself a life preserver that I could carry into my home. 18

When you tell a
story, it should have
a point (p. 127).

We all know that a good education system saves lives, but   19
the people of this country are still told that cutting the budget for
public schools is necessary, that poor salaries for teachers are all
we can manage and that art, music and all creative activities must be the first
to go when times are lean.

Before- and after-school programs are cut and we are told that public schools   20
are not made for baby-sitting children. If parents are neglectful temporarily or
permanently, for whatever reason, it's certainly sad, but their unlucky children must fend for themselves. Or slip through the cracks. Or wander in a dark
night alone.

We are told in a thousand ways that not only are public schools not   21
important, but that the children who attend them, the children who need them
most, are not important either. We leave them to learn from the blind eye of a
television, or to the mercy of "a thousand points of light"[3] that can be as far
away as stars.

I was lucky. I had Mrs. LeSane. I had Mr. Gunderson. I had an abundance   22
of art supplies. And I had a particular brand of neglect in my home that allowed
me to slip away and get to them. But what about the rest of the kids who
weren't as lucky? What happened to them?

By the time the bell rang that morning I had finished my drawing and   23
Mrs. LeSane pinned it up on the special bulletin board she reserved for drawings from the back table. It was the same picture I always drew—a sun in the
corner of a blue sky over a nice house with flowers all around it.

Mrs. LeSane asked us to please stand, face the flag, place our right hands   24
over our hearts and say the Pledge of Allegiance. Children across the country
do it faithfully. I wonder now when the country will face its children and say a
pledge right back.

---

3. In his inaugural address on January 20, 1989, President George H. W. Bush used this
phrase to refer to "all the community organizations that are spread like stars throughout the
Nation, doing good."

## FOR DISCUSSION

1. As a seven-year-old leaving home in the dark in a fit of panic and anxiety, why did young Barry instinctively head for her school?

2. Why does Barry say, "We were children with the sound turned off" (10)? Who fails to hear them?

3. Barry always drew the same picture when she sat at the art table in the back of Mrs. LeSane's classroom. What's the significance of that picture? Explain.

4. Why does Barry refer to the Pledge of Allegiance in the last paragraph of her essay?

## STRATEGIES AND STRUCTURES

1. Why does Lynda Barry begin her **NARRATIVE** with an account of watching television with her brother? Where else does she refer to watching TV? Why?

2. Most of Barry's narrative takes place at her school, which she pictures in some detail. Which of these physical details do you find most revealing, and how do they help to present the place as a "sanctuary"?

3. Point out several places in her narrative where Barry characterizes Mrs. LeSane, Mr. Gunderson, and others through their gestures and bits of **DIALOGUE**. What do these small acts and brief words reveal about the people Barry is portraying?

4. What does young Barry's sense of panic and anxiety contribute to the **PLOT** of her narrative?

5. Where and how does Barry's narrative morph into an **ARGUMENT** about public schools in America? What's the point of that argument, and where does she state it most directly?

## WORDS AND FIGURES OF SPEECH

1. Is Barry speaking literally or metaphorically (or both) when she refers to children who "wander in a dark night alone" (20)? How and how well does she pave the way for this statement at the end of her narrative?

2. What does Barry mean when she says that the "points of light" in a child's life can be "as far away as stars" (21)? How and where does the word *light* take on different implications during the course of her narrative?

3. Barry characterizes her old school as a *sanctuary* instead of, for example, a *haven* or *safehouse*. Why do you think she chooses this term? Is it apt? Why or why not?

4. Why does Barry refer to the "blind eye" of television (21)?

**FOR WRITING**

1. In a few paragraphs, tell about a time when you found school to be a sanctuary, or the opposite. Be sure to DESCRIBE the physical place and what people said and did there.

2. Write a narrative essay in which you use your experience at school to make a point about the importance of some aspect of the school curriculum that you fear may be changed or lost. If possible, expand your argument to include schools in general, not just your own.

# ⇥ 7 ⇤

# EXAMPLE

I**T'S** difficult to write about any subject, however familiar, without giving EXAMPLES.* Take hiccups, for example. The most prolonged case of hiccups in a human being is that of an Iowa man who hiccupped from 1922 to 1990. We know this is a true case because it is documented in the *Guinness World Records*, which is a compendium of examples, however unique. A typical entry consists of a category (largest pizza, oldest cat, longest bout of hiccups) and a person or thing that fits that category.

This is what examples are and do: they're individuals (a man from Iowa who hiccupped for 68 years) taken out of a larger category or group (serious cases of hiccupping) to represent the whole group. Nobody knows for sure what causes hiccups—eating too fast is only one possibility—but why we use examples in writing is pretty clear.

For most of us, it is easier to digest a piece of pie than the whole pie at once. The same goes for examples. Good examples are *representative:* they exhibit all of the main, important characteristics of the group they exemplify. That is, they give the flavor of the whole subject in a single bite. This makes it easier for the reader to grasp (if not swallow) what we have to say—assuming, of course, that our examples are interesting and compelling. Or at least vivid.

> Through one family's eviction, Matthew Desmond (p. 206) comments on poverty in America.

Good examples vivify—or give life to—a subject by making general statements ("cats can live a long time") more specific ("the oldest cat on record is Creme Puff of Austin, Texas, who lived to be 38 years old"). They also help

---

*Words printed in SMALL CAPITALS are defined in the Glossary/Index.

to make **ABSTRACT** concepts more **CONCRETE**. In the following humorous passage, Dave Barry is explaining the abstract concept of "neat stuff":

> By "neat," I mean "mechanical and unnecessarily complex." I'll give you an example. Right now I'm typing these words on an *extremely* powerful computer. It's the latest in a line of maybe ten computers I've owned, each one more powerful than the last. My computer is chock full of RAM and ROM and bytes and megahertzes and various other items that enable a computer to kick data-processing butt. It is probably capable of supervising the entire U.S. air-defense apparatus while simultaneously processing the tax return of every resident of Ohio. I use it mainly to write a newspaper column.
>
> —DAVE BARRY, "Guys vs. Men"

Abstractions are concepts, such as "neat stuff," that are more or less detached from our five senses. Concrete examples, such as Barry's computer, help to make them more immediately perceptible, especially to our eyes and ears.

As the *Guinness World Records* demonstrates, concrete examples can be interesting in their own right. In most kinds of writing, however, we do not use examples for their own sake but to make a point. Barry's point here is that "guys like neat stuff" and that this characteristic distinguishes them from "men," who are generally "way too serious" to care about mere stuff, however neat. Elsewhere in "Guys vs. Men," Barry uses a similar concrete example to distinguish guys from women: "Guys do not have a basic need to rearrange furniture. Whereas a woman who could cheerfully use the same computer for fifty-three years will rearrange her furniture on almost a weekly basis, sometimes in the dead of night."

Whether or not you agree with Barry's conclusions about masculinity and other issues of gender, his examples make an entertaining, if not absolutely decisive, argument. How many examples are sufficient to prove your point? As with other kinds of evidence, that will depend on the complexity of your subject, the nature of your audience, and your purpose in writing. Are you merely seeking to convince readers that guys like "mechanical and

*Example* 175

unnecessarily complex" devices? Or are you saying that guys are behaviorally different from women in fundamental ways? (For this, even Barry feels the need to qualify: "I realize that I'm making gender-based generalizations here, but my feeling is that if God did not want us to make gender-based generalizations, She would not have given us genders.")

Sometimes a single example can suffice—and even provide a focal point for an essay or an entire book—if it is truly representative and sufficiently appealing to your audience. Take the example of J. P. Morgan's nose, for instance. In her introduction to *Morgan, American Financier* (1999), the biographer Jean Strouse discusses the difficulties she faced in writing a life of the banker who almost single-handedly ran the American economy a hundred years ago. In addition to the sheer bulk of biographical material, there were countless stories and legends that had grown up around Morgan.

Strouse did not solve the problem of organizing all this material by focusing on Morgan's unusual nose; but she did effectively use the nose example to introduce the legendary nature of her subject to her readers:

> Even Morgan's personal appearance gave rise to legend. He had a skin disease called rhinophyma that in his fifties turned his nose into a hideous purple bulb. One day the wife of his partner Dwight Morrow reportedly invited him to tea. She wanted her daughter Anne to meet the great man, and for weeks coached the girl about what would happen. Anne would come into the room and say good afternoon; she would not stare at Mr. Morgan's nose, she would not say anything about his nose, and she would leave.

That "one day" came, as Strouse tells the story, and the Morrows' young daughter, Anne, played her part flawlessly. Mrs. Morrow, however, had more difficulty:

> Mrs. Morrow and Mr. Morgan sat on a sofa by the tea tray. Anne came in, said hello, did not look at Morgan's nose, did not say anything about his nose, and left the room. Sighing in relief, Mrs. Morrow asked, "Mr. Morgan, do you take one lump or two in your nose?"

The usefulness of this story as a way to show how examples can help to organize and focus our writing is only enhanced by the fact that this story never actually happened.

When she grew up, Anne Morrow went on to become the writer Anne Morrow Lindbergh, wife of aviator Charles Lindbergh, who made the first solo transatlantic flight. "This ridiculous story has not a grain of truth in it," Mrs. Lindbergh told Morgan's biographer many years later; but "it is so funny I am sure it will continue."

Brief NARRATIVES, or ANECDOTES, such as the story of Mrs. Morrow and J. P. Morgan's nose, often make good organizing examples because they link generalities or abstractions—gender differences, principles of biography—to specific people and concrete events. By citing just this one story among the many inspired by Morgan's appearance and personality, Strouse accomplishes several things with one stroke: she paints a clear picture of how his contemporaries regarded the man whose life story she is introducing; she shows how difficult it was to see her controversial subject through the legends that enshrouded him; and she finds a focal point for organizing the introduction to her entire book. Evidently, Strouse has a good nose for examples.

# A BRIEF GUIDE TO WRITING
# AN ESSAY BASED ON EXAMPLES

As you write an essay based on examples, you need to identify your subject, say what its main characteristics are, and give specific instances that exhibit those characteristics. The editors of the *Onion* make these basic moves in the following tongue-in-cheek passage from an essay in this chapter:

> In total, 347 individual acts of sin were committed at the bake sale, with nearly every attendee committing at least one of the seven deadly sins as outlined by Gregory the Great in the Fifth Century.
>
> —THE ONION, "All Seven Deadly Sins Committed at Church Bake Sale"

*Example* 177

The editors of the *Onion* identify their subject ("the seven deadly sins"), define it or state its main characteristics ("as outlined by Gregory the Great"), and give specific instances that exhibit these characteristics ("347 individual acts of sin").

The following guidelines will help you to make these basic moves as you draft an exemplification essay. They will also help you to ensure that your examples fit your purpose and audience, are sufficient to make your point, are truly representative of your subject, and are effectively organized with appropriate transitions.

## Coming Up with a Subject

To come up with a subject for your essay, take any subject you're interested in—the presidency of Abraham Lincoln, for example—and consider whether it can be narrowed down to focus on a specific aspect of the subject (such as Lincoln's humor in office) for which you can find a reasonable number of examples. Then choose examples that show the characteristics of that narrower topic. In this case, a good example of the presidential humor might be the time a well-dressed lady visited the White House and inadvertently sat on Lincoln's hat. "Madame," the president is supposed to have responded, "I could have told you it wouldn't fit."

If you have personal knowledge of your topic, you may already have many exemplary facts or stories about it. Or you may need to do some research. As you look for examples, choose ones that represent the qualities and characteristics you're trying to illustrate—and that are most likely to appeal to your AUDIENCE.

> The author of "My Technologically Challenged Life," p. 184, had all the examples she needed at home and at work.

## Considering Your Purpose and Audience

Before you begin writing, think about your PURPOSE. Is it to entertain? inform? persuade? For instance, the purpose of "All Seven Deadly Sins Committed at Church Bake Sale" on page 190 is to entertain, so the writer offers humorous examples of incidents at the bake sale. But if you were writing about the bake sale in order to persuade others to participate next time, you might offer examples of the money earned at various booths, how much fun participants had, and the good causes the money will be used for. In every case, your purpose determines the kinds of examples you use.

Before you select examples, you need to take into account how much your AUDIENCE already knows about your topic and how sympathetic they are likely to be to your position. If you are writing to demonstrate that the health of Americans has declined over the past decade, and your audience consists of doctors and nutritionists, a few key examples would probably suffice. For a general audience, however, such as your classmates, you would need to give more background information and cite more (and more basic) examples. And if your readers are unlikely to view your topic as you do, you will have to work even harder to come up with convincing examples.

## Generating Ideas: Finding Good Examples

Try to find examples that display as many of the typical characteristics of your topic as possible. Suppose you were writing an essay on the seven deadly sins, and you decided to focus on wrath. Getting angry is a basic characteristic of wrath, but anger and wrath are not the same thing. Wrath is habitual anger that is often directed toward someone or something in particular; therefore, a good example of wrath would need to display this quality. As a superhero, The Hulk not only gets angry, he gets angry often; and he goes after whomever or whatever is making him angry. Thus, The Hulk would probably be a good example of wrath.

## Templates for Exemplifying

The following templates can help you to generate ideas for an exemplification essay and then to start drafting. Don't take these as formulas where you just have to fill in the blanks. There are no easy formulas for good writing. But these templates can help you plot out some of the key moves of exemplification and thus may serve as good starting points.

*Example* 179

► About X, it can generally be said that _____; a good example would be _____.

► The main characteristics of X are _____ and _____, as exemplified by _____, _____, and _____.

► For the best example(s) of X, we can turn to _____.

► Additional examples of X include _____, _____, and _____.

► From these examples of X, we can conclude that _____.

For more techniques to help you generate ideas and start writing with examples, see Chapter 3.

## Stating Your Point

In an exemplification essay, you usually state your point directly in a **THESIS STATEMENT** in your introduction. For example:

> College teams depend more on teamwork than on star athletes for success.
>
> The health of most Americans has declined in the last ten years.
>
> The Italian army's desert campaign of World War II was the result of a number of tactical errors.

Each of these thesis statements calls for specific examples to support it. How many examples do you need—and what kinds?

## Using Sufficient Examples

As you select examples to support a thesis, you can use either multiple brief examples or one or two extended examples. The approach you take will depend, in part, on the kind of generalization you're making. Multiple examples work

For an essay made
up almost entirely of
examples, see p. 200. well when you are dealing with different aspects of a large topic (battle strategy in a world war) or with trends involving large numbers of people (college athletes, Americans' declining health). Extended examples work better when you are writing about a particular case, such as a single scene in a novel.

Keep in mind that sufficiency isn't strictly a matter of numbers. Often a few good examples will suffice, which is what sufficiency implies: enough to do the job, and no more. In other words, whether or not your examples are sufficient to support your thesis is not determined by the number of examples but by how persuasive those examples seem to your readers. Choose examples that you think they will find vivid and convincing.

## Using Representative Examples

Be sure that your examples fairly and accurately support the point you're making. In an essay on how college athletic teams depend on teamwork, for instance, you would want to choose examples from several teams and sports. Similarly, if you are trying to convince readers that a general made many tactical errors in a strategic battle, you would need to show a number of errors from different points in the battle. And if you're exemplifying an **ABSTRACT** concept, such as wrath, be sure to choose **CONCRETE** examples that possess all of its distinguishing characteristics.

It is also good to avoid using highly unusual examples. In an essay about the benefits of swimming every day, for instance, Michael Phelps might not be the best example since he is not a typical swimmer. Better to cite several swimmers who have a more typical routine to demonstrate the benefits of swimming.

## Organizing Examples and Using Transitions

Once you have stated your thesis and chosen your examples, you need to put them in some kind of order. You might present them in order of increasing importance or interest, perhaps saving the best for last. Or if you have a large

*Example* 181

number of examples, you might organize them into categories. Or you might arrange them chronologically, if you are citing errors made during a political campaign, for example.

Regardless of the organization you choose, you need to relate your examples to each other and to the point you're making by using clear TRANSI-TIONS and other connecting words and phrases. You can always use the phrases *for example* and *for instance*. But consider using other transitions as well, such as *more specifically, exactly, precisely, thus, namely, indeed, that is, in other words, in fact, in particular*: "Better health care, in fact, has led to a dramatic improvement in the general treatment of diabetes." Or try using a RHETORICAL QUESTION, which you then answer with an example: "So what factor has contributed the most to the declining health of Americans?"

# EDITING FOR COMMON ERRORS
# IN EXEMPLIFICATION

Exemplification invites certain typical errors, especially with lists or series of examples. The following tips will help you to check and correct your writing for these common problems.

### When you list a series of examples, make sure they are parallel in structure

- ▶ Animals avoid predators in many ways. They travel in groups, move fast, blend~~ing~~ in with their surroundings, and look~~ing~~ threatening.

### Edit out *etc., and so forth,* or *and so on* when they don't add useful information to your sentence

- ▶ Animals typically avoid predators by traveling in groups, moving fast, <u>and</u> blending in with their surroundings~~, etc~~.

## Check your use of *i.e.* and *e.g.*

These abbreviations of Latin phrases are often used interchangeably to introduce examples, but they do not mean the same thing: *i.e.* means "that is" and *e.g.* means "for example." Since most of your readers do not likely speak Latin, it is a good idea to use the English equivalents.

▶ The tree sloth is an animal that uses protective coloring to hide—~~i.e.~~ that is, it lets green algae grow on its fur in order to blend in with the tree leaves.

▶ Some animals use protective coloring to hide—~~e.g.~~ for example, the tree sloth.

# A Lighted Billboard

By illuminating only one of the spotlights on this billboard, a utility company sets a good example for consumers—and gives a "for instance" of the general point it is making here. You can use examples to shed light on almost any subject by making abstract concepts (energy conservation) more concrete (turning off extra lights) and by focusing the reader's attention on a particular illuminating instance or illustration of your subject.

MONICA WUNDERLICH

# MY TECHNOLOGICALLY CHALLENGED LIFE

MONICA WUNDERLICH'S "My Technologically Challenged Life" appeared in *Delta Winds* (2004), an anthology of student writing published each year by the English department of San Joaquin Delta College in Stockton, California. Wunderlich first wrote the essay as an assignment for an English course. It gives many humorous examples of the difficulties she has encountered with ordinary technology (or the lack of it) in her everyday life. At the nursing facility where the author worked while attending college, however, the lack of up-to-date equipment was no laughing matter—as Wunderlich's more disturbing examples make clear.

## My Technologically Challenged Life

It probably seems easy for someone to use a computer to solve a task or call a friend on a cellular phone for the solution. I, however, do not have access to such luxuries. My home, workplace, and automobile are almost barren of anything electronic. It's not as if I don't want technology in my life, but I feel as if technology has taken on the role of a rabbit, and I am the fox with three legs that just can't seem to get it. And after many useless attempts at trying to figure it out, I have almost given up.

In my house, technology does not exist, at least not for my parents. In fact it was 1995 when my father finally had to part with his beloved rotary phone,[1] not because it was worn out, but because it would not work with the new automated menus that companies were using. Reaching an actual person was difficult the old way because of the physical impossibility of being able to *push* 1, 2, or 3 when a phone possesses no buttons. It was quite embarrassing, especially since I was fifteen and all of my friends had "normal" phones. My dad's biggest argument was that "it's a privacy issue. No one can tap into our phone calls and listen to our conversations." Well, the last time I had checked, none of us were trafficking dope.

I also had the privilege of not using a computer. It was hard going through high school without one, for I had many teachers who demanded many essays from me. Yet I had no way to type them. My sister was in the same boat, so we tried tag-teaming[2] my parents into getting us a

1

Three-category organization promises multiple examples and suggests the order in which they'll appear

2

Example: rotary phone

3

Example: no computer

1. *Rotary phone*: A dial-faced style of telephone widely used throughout the twentieth century.

2. *Tag-teaming*: A wrestling term referring to two people working as a team in alternate turns.

computer. But to no avail. We kept getting things like "they're too expensive," or "we have no room for one," or "we'll get one later." Later! My parents should have just said NEVER! So my sister and I resorted to spending hours at our friends' houses, because their parents were nice to them and bought computers. The only problem was that our friends had lives and weren't always around at our disposal. So Plan B for essay completion was using a cheesy electronic word processor that my dad had borrowed from my *grandparents* to supposedly "help us out." This beast of a machine wasn't much help, though, because it was a pain in the neck to use. It had a teeny tiny little screen that wouldn't show the entire typed line, so by the time the line was printed, I'd find about ten uncorrected mistakes, and I'd have to start over. However, nothing is permanent and walls do come down, and so be it—the Wunderlichs buy their first computer! Two years after I graduate high school. As of yet, we still do not have the Internet.

My job is another place where technology is lacking. I work in a home for the elderly, and I take care of about eight to ten patients a night. I have to take some of these patients' vital signs, and I speak on behalf of anyone who has ever worked in the medical profession when I say that the most efficient way to take vital signs is electronically. However, my employers do not grant us the equipment for electronic vitals. We are still using glass thermometers, which are not only a waste of time (3 seconds vs. 3 minutes for an oral temperature), but they are extremely dangerous. Residents are known to bite down on the thermometers, exposing themselves to harmful mercury. I can't even begin to count how many thermometers I have

Example: glass thermometers

dropped and broken since I've worked there. One time I dropped a thermometer and didn't realize I had broken it. So I picked it up to shake it down, but instead I flung mercury everywhere. An electronic thermometer just makes more sense when trying to make the residents' environment as safe as possible.

We also have to use manual blood pressure cuffs. They're just the normal cuffs that are wrapped around the arm, pumped up, and read using the bouncing needle. The problem is that none of our blood pressure cuffs are calibrated correctly, and the needles are way out of kilter. This makes it impossible to get an accurate reading. An ingenious solution would be digital cuffs, but that is highly unlikely. Actually, the home did try to supply some digital cuffs, but they were stolen. One man's sticky fingers equals inconvenience for the rest of us, and the home no longer supplied us with such time-saving technology. Using manual equipment is hard not only for us but also for the nurses. The care home does not allow feeding machines in the facility, yet people who need to be fed by a stomach tube are still admitted. This means that the nurses have to allot a special time from their med pass to hook up a syringe to the patient's stomach tube and pour their "steak dinner in a can" down the tube little by little. This tedious process takes about twenty minutes, and nurses don't really have twenty minutes to throw around, so it really crowds their schedules. If we had feeding machines, the nurses would only have to change a bag when a machine beeps. Problem solved if things went my way.

Another part of my life that is technologically crippled is my car. As much as I like my car, I still think it could use a few more bells and whistles. I drive a 2002

5 •···· Example: manual blood pressure cuffs

•···· Example: no feeding machines

6

RHETORICAL QUESTION indicates more examples to come

⋯⋯• Volkswagen Jetta, which would probably make the reader think, "Oh, a new car. There must be plenty of technology in that new car?" My answer to that is "No, there isn't." The only technology is the 5 billion standard airbags for when I do something really stupid. Other than that I have to shift it manually. If I want to roll down my window, I have to turn a crank. My car did not come with a CD player, so I shelled out $500 for one. I've had this stereo since last May, and I still can't figure out how to set the

Examples are presented in a cluster: manual transmission and windows, after-market stereo, faulty engine light, no GPS

⋯⋯• clock or preset stations. Volkswagen technology could not stop my car from exercising its "check engine light" once every three weeks. Even though the design techs included a cute warning light, my blood still boiled every time the light would come on proudly, and I made yet another pilgrimage to the dealership . . . on my day off. It would be nice if my car came equipped with one of those Global Positioning System things as well. I am really good at getting lost, and if I had one of these systems a year ago, I would not have found myself driving over both the Bay Bridge and the Golden Gate Bridge when I was supposed to be on the Richmond Bridge. (Ironically enough, I did this during the weekend that terrorists were supposed to be blowing up the Bay and Golden Gate Bridges.) And if I had had any passengers while tempting fate that day, I could have kept them distracted from the fact that we were lost (and possibly going to die) by letting them watch a movie on one of those in-car DVD players. But of course I don't have an in-car DVD player, so my hypothetical passengers would probably have been frantic.

No matter how much technology is out there, I seem to be getting through the day without most of it. It would seem hard to imagine someone else living without

7

such modern conveniences, and, yes, at times I feel very primitive. However, I am slowly catching on to what's new out there even though incorporating every modern convenience into my day is out of the question. I am learning even though it is at a snail's pace. Hopefully I'll have it all figured out by the time cars fly, or else I will be walking.

Final example: flying cars

# ALL SEVEN DEADLY SINS COMMITTED AT CHURCH BAKE SALE

THE *ONION* is a SATIRICAL newspaper that originated in Madison, home of the University of Wisconsin. In a typical issue, the paper pokes fun at everything from politics ("Obama Practices Looking-Off-Into-Future Pose") and American lifestyles ("TV Helps Build Valuable Looking Skills") to medicine ("Colonoscopy Offers Non-Fantastic Voyage through Human Body") and religion (which is what this selection is about—sort of). According to the Roman Catholic Church, there are basically two types of sins: "venial" ones that are easily forgiven, and "deadly" ones that, well, are not. In the sixth century, Pope Gregory the Great identified what he took to be the seven worst of the worst: pride, envy, wrath, sloth, avarice (or greed), gluttony, and lust. In this tongue-in-cheek news release from a church bake sale in Gadsden, Alabama, the *Onion* reporter finds concrete, specific examples of each of them.

G ADSDEN, AL—The seven deadly sins—avarice, sloth, envy, lust, gluttony, 1
pride, and wrath—were all committed Sunday during the Page 179 explains how to state the point of your example. twice-annual bake sale at St. Mary's of the Immaculate Conception Church.

In total, 347 individual acts of sin were committed at the bake sale, with 2
nearly every attendee committing at least one of the seven deadly sins as outlined by Gregory the Great in the Fifth Century.

"My cookies, cakes, and brownies are always the highlight of our church 3
bake sales, and everyone says so," said parishioner Connie Barrett, 49, openly
committing the sin of pride. "Sometimes, even I'm amazed by how well my
goodies turn out."

Fellow parishioner Betty Wicks agreed. 4

"Every time I go past Connie's table, I just have to buy something," said 5
the 245-pound Wicks, who commits the sin of gluttony at every St. Mary's
bake sale, as well as most Friday nights at Old Country Buffet. "I simply can't
help myself—it's all so delicious."

The popularity of Barrett's mouth-watering wares elicited the sin of 6
envy in many of her fellow vendors.

"Connie has this fantastic book of recipes her grandmother gave her, and 7
she won't share them with anyone," church organist Georgia Brandt said.
"This year, I made white-chocolate blondies and thought they'd be a big hit.
But most people just went straight to Connie's table, got what they wanted,
and left. All the while, Connie just stood there with this look of smug satisfaction on her face. It took every ounce of strength in my body to keep from going
over there and really telling her off."

While the sins of wrath and avarice were each committed dozens of 8
times at the event, Barrett and longtime bake-sale rival Penny Cox brought
them together in full force.

"Penny said she wanted to make a bet over whose table would make the 9
most money," said Barrett, exhibiting avarice. "Whoever lost would have to
sit in the dunk tank at the St. Mary's Summer Fun Festival. I figured it's for
such a good cause, a little wager couldn't hurt. Besides, I always bring the
church more money anyway, so I couldn't possibly lose."

Moments after agreeing to the wager, Cox became wrathful when Barrett, 10
the bake sale's co-chair, grabbed the best table location under the pretense of

having to keep the coffee machine full. Cox attempted to exact revenge by reporting an alleged Barrett misdeed to the church's priest.

"I mentioned to Father Mark [O'Connor] that I've seen candles at Con- 11
nie's house that I wouldn't be surprised one bit if she stole from the church's storage closet," said Cox, who also committed the sin of sloth by forcing her daughter to set up and man her booth while she gossiped with friends. "Perhaps if he investigates this, by this time next year, Connie won't be co-chair of the bake sale and in her place we'll have someone who's willing to rotate the choice table spots."

The sin of lust also reared its ugly head at the bake sale, largely due to the 12
presence of Melissa Wyckoff, a shapely 20-year-old redhead whose family recently joined the church. While male attendees ogled Wyckoff, the primary object of lust for females was the personable, boyish Father Mark.

Though attendees' feelings of lust for Wyckoff and O'Connor were never 13
acted on, they did not go unnoticed.

"There's something not right about that Melissa Wyckoff," said envious   14
and wrathful bake-sale participant Jilly Brandon, after her husband Craig
offered Wyckoff one of her Rice Krispie treats to "welcome [her] to the parish." "She might have just moved here from California, but that red dress of
hers should get her kicked out of the church."

According to St. Mary's treasurer Beth Ellen Coyle, informal church-   15
sponsored events are a notorious breeding ground for the seven deadly sins.

"Bake sales, haunted houses, pancake breakfasts . . . such church events   16
are rife with potential for sin," Coyle said. "This year, we had to eliminate the
'Guess Your Weight' booth from the annual church carnival because the envy
and pride had gotten so out of hand. Church events are about glorifying God,
not violating His word. If you want to do that, you're no better than that cheap
strumpet Melissa Wyckoff."

### FOR DISCUSSION

1. The *Onion* reporter gives bake-sale-specific **EXAMPLES** for each of the Deadly
   Sins. How well do you think these examples represent the sins they're meant to
   illustrate?

2. Statistics is the science of analyzing numerical examples. In all, says *Onion*
   reporter, parishioners at the St. Mary's bake sale committed "347 individual acts
   of sin" (2). Anything suspicious about these stats? How do you suppose they were
   determined?

3. All of the seven deadly sins are identified in the first paragraph of the *Onion*'s
   spoof. In what order are they explained after that? Which one does the watchful
   reporter come back to at the end?

4. Which specific deadly sin is the only one unacted upon at the bake sale? Who
   inspired it?

### STRATEGIES AND STRUCTURES

1. Pope Gregory might object that the *Onion*'s examples are a bit trivial. But how
   **CONCRETE** and specific are they?

2. **SATIRE** is writing that makes fun of vice or folly for the **PURPOSE** of exposing and
   correcting it. To the extent that the *Onion* is satirizing the behavior of people at
   "church-sponsored events," what less-than-truly-deadly "sins" is the paper actually making fun of (15)?

3. A *spoof* is a gentle parody or mildly satirical imitation. What kind of writing or reporting is the *Onion* spoofing here? Who is the AUDIENCE for this spoof?

4. As a Catholic priest, "boyish Father Mark" would probably say that all the other deadly sins are examples of pride (12). How might pride be thought of as the over-archingly general "deadly sin"?

5. As a "news" story, this one has elements of NARRATIVE. What are some of them, specifically?

## WORDS AND FIGURES OF SPEECH

1. What, exactly, is a "strumpet" (16)?

2. *Deadly* (or *mortal*) sins are to be distinguished from *venial* sins. According to your dictionary, what kind of sins would be venial sins? Give several examples.

3. Give a SYNONYM for each of the following words: "avarice," "sloth," "gluttony," and "wrath" (1).

4. Another word for *pride* is *hubris*. What language does it derive from? What's the distinction between the two?

5. *Hypocrisy* is not one of the seven deadly sins, but how would you DEFINE it? Which of the St. Mary's parishioners might be said to commit *this* sin?

## FOR WRITING

1. Imagine a strip mall called the Seven Deadly Sins Shopping Center, where each item on Pope Gregory's list is represented by a store selling ordinary products and services. Draw up a list of store names that would exemplify each of the seven deadlies—for example, Big Joe's Eats for gluttony. You might also compose some signs or other advertising to place in the windows of each shop.

2. Using examples, write an essay entitled "All Seven Deadly Sins Committed at _____." Fill in the blank with any venue you choose—"School Cafeteria," for example, or "College Library." Give at least one example for each offense.

3. According to somebody's critical theory, the characters on *Gilligan's Island* each represent one of the seven deadly sins. If you've seen enough reruns of the show to have an opinion, write an essay either questioning or supporting this reading.

JANET WU

# HOMEWARD BOUND

JANET WU is an award–winning reporter in Boston and New York. Wu was 12 years old when she first met her Chinese grandmother. Her father had escaped China during the Communist revolution at the end of World War II, and for the next 25 years, because of strained relations between China and the United States, Chinese Americans were not allowed to return to their homeland. "Homeward Bound," first published in the *New York Times Magazine* (1999), is about Wu's visits with a relative she did not know she had. In this essay, Wu looks at the vast differences between two cultures through a single, extended example—the ancient practice, now outlawed, of breaking and binding the feet of upper-class Chinese girls. These "lotus feet" were once a symbol of status and beauty.

M Y GRANDMOTHER HAS BOUND FEET. Cruelly tethered since her birth, 1
they are like bonsai trees, miniature versions of what should have been. She is a relic even in China, where foot binding was first banned more than 80 years ago when the country could no longer afford a population that

had to be carried. Her slow, delicate hobble betrays her age and the status she held and lost.

My own size 5 feet are huge in comparison. The marks and callouses they bear come from running and jumping, neither of which my grandmother has ever done. The difference between our feet reminds me of the incredible history we hold between us like living bookends. We stand like sentries on either side of a vast gulf.

For most of my childhood, I didn't even know she existed. My father was a young man when he left his family's village in northern China, disappearing into the chaos of the Japanese invasion and the Communist revolution[1] that followed. He fled to Taiwan and eventually made his way to America, alone. To me, his second child, it seemed he had no family or history other than his American-born wife and four children. I didn't know that he had been writing years of unanswered letters to China.

I was still a young girl when he finally got a response, and with it the news that his father and six of his seven siblings had died in those years of war and revolution. But the letter also contained an unexpected blessing: somehow his mother had survived. So 30 years after he left home, and in the wake of President Nixon's visit,[2] my father gathered us up and we rushed to China to find her.

I saw my grandmother for the very first time when I was 12. She was almost 80, surprisingly alien and shockingly small. I searched her wrinkled face for something familiar, some physical proof that we belonged to each other. She stared at me the same way. Did she feel cheated, I wondered, by the distance, by the time we had not spent together? I did. With too many lost years to reclaim, we had everything and nothing to say. She politely listened as I struggled with scraps of formal Chinese and smiled as I fell back on

1. The Japanese invasion of China began in the late 1930s and lasted until Japan surrendered to the Allied forces at the close of World War II. In the years following this surrender, the Chinese Nationalist and Communist parties battled for control, with the communists seizing power in 1949.

2. In 1972, Richard Nixon became the first U.S. president to meet with Communist leaders on Chinese soil, opening relations between countries that had been enemies since the revolution.

"Wo bu dong" ("I don't understand you"). And yet we communicated something strange and beautiful. I found it easy to love this person I had barely met.

The second time I saw her I was 23, arriving in China on an indulgent 6 post-graduate-school adventure, with a Caucasian boyfriend in tow. My grandmother sat on my hotel bed, shrunken and wise, looking as if she belonged in a museum case. She stroked my asymmetrically cropped hair. I touched her feet, and her face contorted with the memory of her childhood pain. "You are lucky," she said. We both understood that she was thinking of far more than the bindings that long ago made her cry. I wanted to share even the smallest part of her life's journey, but I could not conceive of surviving a dynasty and a revolution, just as she could not imagine my life in a country she had never seen. In our mutual isolation of language and experience, we could only gaze in wonder, mystified that we had come to be sitting together.

Janet Wu uses narrative to organize her examples. See p. 176 for more on this technique.

I last saw her almost five years ago. At 95, she was even smaller, and her 7 frailty frightened me. I was painfully aware that I probably would never see her again, that I would soon lose this person I never really had. So I mentally logged every second we spent together and jockeyed with my siblings for the chance to hold her hand or touch her shoulder. Our departure date loomed like some kind of sentence. And when it came, she broke down, her face bowed into her gnarled hands. I went home, and with resignation awaited the inevitable news that she was gone.

But two months after that trip, it was my father who died. For me, his 8 loss was doubly cruel: his death deprived me of both my foundation and the bridge to my faraway grandmother. For her, it was the second time she had lost him. For the 30 years they were separated, she had feared her son was dead. This time, there was no ambiguity, no hope. When she heard the news, my uncle later wrote us, she wept quietly.

When I hear friends complain about having to visit their nearby rela- 9 tives, I think of how far away my grandmother is and how untouched our relationship remains by the modern age. My brief handwritten notes are agonizingly slow to reach her. When they do arrive, she cannot read them. I cannot call her. I cannot see, hear or touch her.

But last month my mother called to tell me to brush up on my Chinese. 10 Refusing to let go of our tenuous connection to my father's family, she has decided to take us all back to China in October for my grandmother's 100th birthday. And so every night, I sit at my desk and study, thinking of her tiny doll-like feet, of the miles and differences that separate us, of the moments we'll share when we meet one last time. And I beg her to hold on until I get there.

## FOR DISCUSSION

1. Janet Wu's feet are calloused from exercise. What does this difference between her feet and her grandmother's show about the differences in their lives?

2. Why does Wu touch her grandmother's feet in paragraph 6? What is her grandmother's response? What happens to the "vast gulf" between them (2)?

3. What is the CONCRETE EXAMPLE Wu's essay is organized around? How does this example illustrate the differences between her and her grandmother, and their connection as family? Refer to particular passages.

## STRATEGIES AND STRUCTURES

1. Where does Wu mention her grandmother's feet for the last time in her essay? How does this mention serve as an example of bridging two disparate thoughts?

2. Wu is separated from her grandmother by culture, physical distance, and time. Point out several of the many references to time and the passage of time in her essay. How do these references help Wu to organize her essay?

3. Wu's NARRATIVE takes an unexpected turn in paragraph 8. What is it? How does the physical frailty of her grandmother contribute to the IRONY of this turn of events?

4. A big part of the cultural difference that separates Wu and her grandmother is language. List some of the examples Wu gives of this separation. Why do you think Wu says, in the last paragraph of her essay, that "every night, I sit at my desk and study" (10)?

5. Wu uses the example of her grandmother's bound feet as the basis of an extended COMPARISON AND CONTRAST. Besides feet, what is she comparing to what? What specific similarities and differences does she touch on? What other examples does she use?

## WORDS AND FIGURES OF SPEECH

1. Explain the PUN(s), or play(s) on words, in Wu's title.

2. Wu compares her grandmother's feet to "bonsai trees" (1). What is a bonsai, and what do the grandmother's feet have in common with one?

3. Wu says her wrinkled, shrunken grandmother looks like she belongs in "a museum case" (6). Why? To what is she comparing her grandmother?

4. If Wu and her grandmother are "living bookends," what do they hold between them (2)? What connection(s) between books and "history" does Wu's use of this METAPHOR imply (2)?

5. When is Wu using her grandmother's bound feet as a metaphor, and when are the feet simply serving her as a literal example? Cite specific passages.

## FOR WRITING

1. In a paragraph or two, give several examples of distinctive traits, gestures, or physical features shared by members of your family.

2. Write a personal narrative about a meeting between you and a relative or family friend that exemplifies both the differences separating you and the ties binding you together. Use lots of examples to illustrate those similarities and differences.

**RICHARD LEDERER**

# ENGLISH IS A CRAZY LANGUAGE

RICHARD LEDERER (b. 1938) taught for many years at St. Paul's, a boarding school in New Hampshire. He retired in 1989 to carry on his "mission as a user-friendly English teacher" by writing and speaking extensively and humorously about the peculiarities of the English language. He coined the term *verbivore* to describe those who, like himself, "devour words." Lederer is the author of *Get Thee to a Punnery* (1988) and *Anguished English* (1989), among other books. This essay, made up of one example after another, is the opening chapter of his best-selling *Crazy English* (1989).

•⟩————————————————————————————⟨•

ENGLISH IS THE MOST WIDELY SPOKEN LANGUAGE in the history of our 1 planet, used in some way by at least one out of every seven human beings around the globe. Half of the world's books are written in English, and the majority of international telephone calls are made in English. English is the language of over 60 percent of the world's radio programs, many of them beamed, ironically, by the Russians, who know that to win friends and influence nations, they're best off using English. More than 70 percent of international mail is written and addressed in English, and 80 percent of all computer text is stored in English. English has acquired the largest vocabulary of all the world's languages, perhaps as many as two million words, and has generated one of the noblest bodies of literature in the annals of the human race.

Nonetheless, it is now time to face the fact that English is a crazy 2 language.

In the crazy English language, the blackbird hen is brown, blackboards 3 can be blue or green, and blackberries are green and then red before they are ripe. Even if blackberries were really black and blueberries really blue, what are strawberries, cranberries, elderberries, huckleberries, raspberries, boysenberries, mulberries, and gooseberries supposed to look like?

For tips on when and how to use multiple examples like these, see pp. 179–80.

To add to the insanity, there is no butter in buttermilk, no egg in egg- 4 plant, no grape in grapefruit, neither worms nor wood in wormwood, neither pine nor apple in pineapple, neither peas nor nuts in peanuts, and no ham in a hamburger. (In fact, if somebody invented a sandwich consisting of a ham patty in a bun, we would have a hard time finding a name for it.) To make matters worse, English muffins weren't invented in England, french fries in France, or danish pastries in Denmark. And we discover even more culinary madness in the revelations that sweetmeat is candy, while sweetbread, which isn't sweet, is made from meat.

In this unreliable English tongue, greyhounds aren't always grey (or 5 gray); panda bears and koala bears aren't bears (they're marsupials); a woodchuck is a groundhog, which is not a hog; a horned toad is a lizard; glowworms are fireflies, but fireflies are not flies (they're beetles); ladybugs and lightning bugs are also beetles (and to propagate, a significant proportion of ladybugs must be male); a guinea pig is neither a pig nor from Guinea (it's a South American rodent); and a titmouse is neither mammal nor mammaried.

Language is like the air we breathe. It's invisible, inescapable, indispens- 6 able, and we take it for granted. But when we take the time, step back, and listen to the sounds that escape from the holes in people's faces and explore the paradoxes and vagaries of English, we find that hot dogs can be cold, darkrooms can be lit, homework can be done in school, nightmares can take place in broad daylight, while morning sickness and daydreaming can take place at night, tomboys are girls, midwives can be men, hours—especially happy hours and rush hours—can last longer than sixty minutes, quicksand works *very* slowly, boxing rings are square, silverware can be made of plastic and table-cloths of paper, most telephones are dialed by being punched (or pushed?), and most bathrooms don't have any baths in them. In fact, a dog can go to the bathroom under a tree—no bath, no room; it's still going to the bathroom. And doesn't it seem at least a little bizarre that we go to the bathroom in order to go to the bathroom?

Why is it that a woman can man a station but a man can't woman one, that a man can father a movement but a woman can't mother one, and that a king rules a kingdom but a queen doesn't rule a queendom? How did all those Renaissance men reproduce when there don't seem to have been any Renaissance women? 7

A writer is someone who writes, and a stinger is something that stings. But fingers don't fing, grocers don't groce, hammers don't ham, and humdingers don't humding. If the plural of *tooth* is *teeth*, shouldn't the plural of *booth* be *beeth*? One goose, two geese—so one moose, two meese? One index, two indices—one Kleenex, two Kleenices? If people ring a bell today and rang a bell yesterday, why don't we say that they flang a ball? If they wrote a letter, perhaps they also bote their tongue. If the teacher taught, why isn't it also true that the preacher praught? Why is it that the sun shone yesterday while I shined my shoes, that I treaded water and then trod on soil, and that I flew out to see a World Series game in which my favorite player flied out? 8

If we conceive a conception and receive at a reception, why don't we grieve a greption and believe a beleption? If a horsehair mat is made from the hair of horses and a camel's hair brush from the hair of camels, from what is a mohair coat made? If a vegetarian eats vegetables, what does a humanitarian eat? If a firefighter fights fire, what does a freedom fighter fight? If a weightlifter lifts weights, what does a shoplifter lift? If *pro* and *con* are opposites, is congress the opposite of progress? 9

Sometimes you have to believe that all English speakers should be committed to an asylum for the verbally insane. In what other language do people drive in a parkway and park in a driveway? In what other language do people recite at a play and play at a recital? In what other language do privates eat in the general mess and generals eat in the private mess? In what other language do men get hernias and women get hysterectomies? In what other 10 language do people ship by truck and send cargo by ship? In what other language can your nose run and your feet smell?

How can a slim chance and a fat chance be the same, "what's going on?" 11 and "what's coming off?" be the same, and a bad licking and a good licking be the same, while a wise man and a wise guy are opposites? How can sharp speech and blunt speech be the same and *quite a lot* and *quite a few* the same, while *overlook* and *oversee* are opposites? How can the weather be hot as hell one day and cold as hell the next?

If *button* and *unbutton* and *tie* and *untie* are opposites, why are *loosen* and 12 *unloosen* and *ravel* and *unravel* the same? If *bad* is the opposite of *good, hard* the opposite of *soft,* and *up* the opposite of *down,* why are *badly* and *goodly, hardly* and *softly,* and *upright* and *downright* not opposing pairs? If harmless actions are the opposite of harmful actions, why are shameless and shameful behavior the same and pricey objects less expensive than priceless ones? If appropriate and inappropriate remarks and passable and impassable mountain trails are opposites, why are flammable and inflammable materials, heritable and inheritable property, and passive and impassive people the same and valuable objects less treasured than invaluable ones? If *uplift* is the same as *lift up,* why are *upset* and *set up* opposite in meaning? Why are *pertinent* and *impertinent, canny* and *uncanny,* and *famous* and *infamous* neither opposites nor the same? How can *raise* and *raze* and *reckless* and *wreckless* be opposites when each pair contains the same sound?

Why is it that when the sun or the moon or the stars are out, they are 13 visible, but when the lights are out, they are invisible, and that when I wind up my watch, I start it, but when I wind up this essay, I shall end it?

English is a crazy language. 14

## FOR DISCUSSION

1. Most of the time, Richard Lederer is illustrating his main point that "English is a crazy language" (2). But what does he say about its widespread influence? What **EXAMPLES** does he give?

2. Do you think English is as crazy as Lederer says it is? Why or why not? Give several examples to support your opinion.

3. How seriously do you think Lederer actually intends for us to take the general proposition of his essay? Why do you think he gives so many crazy examples?

4. In paragraph 6, Lederer refers to two related aspects of the English language that all of his examples might be said to illustrate. What are these aspects? Where else in his essay does Lederer actually name the aspects of English he is exemplifying?

## STRATEGIES AND STRUCTURES

1. What is the PURPOSE of the opening paragraph of Lederer's essay? How does the opening paragraph color the rest of what he says about the craziness of the English language?

2. Lederer's essay is made up almost entirely of clusters of examples. What do the examples in paragraph 3 have in common? Are the examples in paragraph 4 more like those in paragraph 3 or paragraph 5? Explain.

3. In paragraph 8, Lederer pretends to be upset with irregular verbs and irregular plurals of nouns. Which are examples of which? Make a list of his examples for both categories.

4. Which examples have to do primarily with gender? What connects all the examples in paragraph 12?

5. Lederer gives his essay the form of a logical ARGUMENT. The proposition he intends to prove is stated in paragraph 2. Where does he state it again as a conclusion? Is the argument in between primarily INDUCTIVE (reasoning from specific examples to a general conclusion) or DEDUCTIVE (reasoning from general principles to a more specific conclusion)? Explain.

## WORDS AND FIGURES OF SPEECH

1. In American English, a *rant* is a form of vehement speech; in British English, a rant can also mean an outburst of wild merriment. Which meaning or meanings apply to Lederer's essay?

2. A *misnomer* is a term that implies a meaning or interpretation that is actually untrue or inaccurate—"koala bears," for example, are marsupials (5). Choose one of the following misnomers that Lederer mentions and explain why you think the object it refers to has this inaccurate name—and why the name persists: "eggplant," "peanut," "french fries," "horned toad," "firefly," and "guinea pig" (4, 5).

3. How does your dictionary DEFINE the word "vagaries" (6)? How is it related to the word "vagabonds"?

4. Lederer "winds up" his essay in paragraph 13. Could he be said, just as accurately, to "wind it down"?

## FOR WRITING

1. Write an essay illustrating the craziness of some language other than English—one you speak and/or have studied. For example, one way to say you're welcome in French is "Je vous en prie," which means, literally, "I beg of you."

2. For all its "craziness," Lederer asserts that "English is the most widely spoken language in the history of our planet" (1). Write an essay that supports or contests this proposition. Be sure to include sufficient examples of who uses the language, where, and for what purposes.

**MATTHEW DESMOND**

# COLD CITY

MATTHEW DESMOND teaches sociology and ethnography at Harvard University. He is the author of four books and numerous articles about race, social class, educational inequality, and poverty in America. In *Evicted: Poverty and Profit in the American City* (2016), Desmond examines why an increasing number of people—more than one in eight renters during the worst years of the economic recession that began in 2007—are being forced from their homes in Milwaukee, Wisconsin, and similar cities. Displaying their typical "vulnerability and desperation, as well as their ingenuity and guts," the people in "Cold City," the prologue to *Evicted*, are representative examples of those hit hardest by the housing crisis.

---

JORI AND HIS COUSIN WERE CUTTING UP, tossing snowballs at passing cars. From Jori's street corner on Milwaukee's near South Side, cars driving on Sixth Street passed squat duplexes with porch steps ending at a sidewalk edged in dandelions. Those heading north approached the Basilica of St. Josaphat, whose crowning dome looked to Jori like a giant overturned plunger. It was January of 2008, and the city was experiencing the snowiest winter on record.

Every so often, a car turned off Sixth Street to navigate Arthur Avenue, hemmed in by the snow, and that's when the boys would take aim. Jori packed a tight one and let it fly. The car jerked to a stop, and a man jumped out. The boys ran inside and locked the door to the apartment where Jori lived with his mother, Arleen, and younger brother, Jafaris. The lock was cheap, and the man broke down the door with a few hard-heeled kicks. He left before anything else happened. When the landlord found out about the door, she decided to evict Arleen and her boys. They had been there eight months.

The day Arleen and her boys had to be out was cold. But if she waited any 2 longer, the landlord would summon the sheriff, who would arrive with a gun, a team of boot-footed movers, and a folded judge's order saying that her house was no longer hers. She would be given two options: truck or curb. "Truck" would mean that her things would be loaded into an eighteen-footer and later checked into bonded storage. She could get everything back after paying $350. Arleen didn't have $350, so she would have opted for "curb," which would mean watching the movers pile everything onto the sidewalk. Her mattresses. A floor-model television. Her copy of *Don't Be Afraid to Discipline*. Her nice glass dining table and the lace tablecloth that fit just-so. Silk plants. Bibles. The meat cuts in the freezer. The shower curtain. Jafaris's asthma machine.

Arleen took her sons—Jori was thirteen, Jafaris was five—to a homeless 3 shelter, which everyone called the Lodge so you could tell your kids, "We're staying at the Lodge tonight," like it was a motel. The two-story stucco building could have passed for one, except for all the Salvation Army signs. Arleen stayed in the 120-bed shelter until April, when she found a house on Nineteenth and Hampton, in the predominantly black inner city, on Milwaukee's North Side, not far from her childhood home. It had thick trim around the windows and doors and was once Kendal green, but the paint had faded and chipped so much over the years that the bare wood siding was now exposed, making the house look camouflaged. At one point someone had started repainting the house plain white but had given up mid-brushstroke, leaving more than half unfinished. There was often no water in the house, and Jori had to bucket out what was in the toilet. But Arleen loved that it was spacious and set apart from other houses. "It was quiet," she remembered. "And five-twenty-five for a whole house, two bedrooms upstairs and two bedrooms downstairs. It was my favorite place."

After a few weeks, the city found Arleen's favorite place "unfit for human     4
habitation," removed her, nailed green boards over the windows and doors,
and issued a fine to her landlord. Arleen moved Jori and Jafaris into a drab
apartment complex deeper in the inner city, on Atkinson Avenue, which she
soon learned was a haven for drug dealers. She feared for her boys, especially
Jori—slack-shouldered, with pecan-brown skin and a beautiful smile—who
would talk to anyone.

Arleen endured four summer months on Atkinson before moving into a     5
bottom duplex unit on Thirteenth Street and Keefe, a mile away. She and the
boys walked their things over. Arleen held her breath and tried the lights,
smiling with relief when they came on. She could live off someone else's electricity bill for a while. There was a fist-sized hole in a living-room window, the
front door had to be locked with an ugly wooden plank dropped into metal
brackets, and the carpet was filthy and ground in. But the kitchen was spacious
and the living room well lit. Arleen stuffed a piece of clothing into the window
hole and hung ivory curtains.

The rent was $550 a month, utilities not included, the going rate in 2008     6
for a two-bedroom unit in one of the worst neighborhoods in America's
fourth-poorest city. Arleen couldn't find a cheaper place, at least not one fit
for human habitation, and most landlords wouldn't rent her a smaller one on
account of her boys. The rent would take 88 percent of Arleen's $628-a-
month welfare check. Maybe she could make it work. Maybe they could at
least stay through winter, until crocuses and tulips stabbed through the
thawed ground of spring, Arleen's favorite season.

There was a knock at the door. It was the landlord, Sherrena Tarver.     7
Sherrena, a black woman with bobbed hair and fresh nails, was loaded down
with groceries. She had spent $40 of her own money and picked up the rest at
a food pantry. She knew Arleen needed it.

Arleen thanked Sherrena and closed the door. Things were off to a good     8
start.

✳ ✳ ✳

Even in the most desolate areas of American cities, evictions used to be rare.     9
They used to draw crowds. Eviction riots erupted during the Depression,[1]

1. Reference to the Great Depression, the greatest economic depression in the United States
(and many other parts of the world) in the 20th century, that began with a stock market crash
in 1929 and lasted about a decade.

even though the number of poor families who faced eviction each year was a fraction of what it is today. A *New York Times* account of community resistance to the eviction of three Bronx families in February 1932 observed, "Probably because of the cold, the crowd numbered only 1,000." Sometimes neighbors confronted the marshals directly, sitting on the evicted family's furniture to prevent its removal or moving the family back in despite the judge's orders. The marshals themselves were ambivalent about carrying out evictions. It wasn't why they carried a badge and a gun.

These days, there are sheriff squads whose full-time job is to carry out   10 eviction and foreclosure orders. There are moving companies specializing in evictions, their crews working all day, every weekday. There are hundreds of data-mining companies that sell landlords tenant screening reports listing past evictions and court filings. These days, housing courts swell, forcing commissioners to settle cases in hallways or makeshift offices crammed with old desks and broken file cabinets—and most tenants don't even show up. Low-income families have grown used to the rumble of moving trucks, the early-morning knocks at the door, the belongings lining the curb.

Families have watched their incomes stagnate, or even fall, while their   11 housing costs have soared. Today, the majority of poor renting families in America spend over half of their income on housing, and at least one in four dedicates over 70 percent to paying the rent and keeping the lights on. Millions of Americans are evicted every year because they can't make rent. In Milwaukee, a city of fewer than 105,000 renter households, landlords evict roughly 16,000 adults and children each year. That's sixteen families evicted through the court system daily. But there are other ways, cheaper and quicker ways, for landlords to remove a family than through court order. Some landlords pay tenants a couple hundred dollars to leave by the end of the week. Some take off the front door. Nearly half of all forced moves experienced by renting families in Milwaukee are "informal evictions" that take place in the shadow of the law. If you count all forms of involuntary building condemnations—you discover that between 2009 and 2011 more than 1 in 8 Milwaukee renters experienced a forced move.

There is nothing special about Milwaukee when it comes to eviction.   12 The numbers are similar in Kansas City, Cleveland, Chicago, and other cities. In 2013, 1 in 8 poor renting families nationwide were unable to pay all of their rent, and a similar number thought it was likely they would be evicted soon....

See p. 180 for the importance of using representative examples.

The evictions take place throughout the city, embroiling not only land-  13
lords and tenants but also kin and friends, lovers and ex-lovers, judges and
lawyers, dope suppliers and church elders. Eviction's fallout is severe. Losing
a home sends families to shelters, abandoned houses, and the street. It invites
depression and illness, compels families to move into degrading housing in
dangerous neighborhoods, uproots communities, and harms children. Eviction
reveals people's vulnerability and desperation, as well as their ingenuity and
guts.

Fewer and fewer families can afford a roof over their head. This is among  14
the most urgent and pressing issues facing America today, and acknowledging
the breadth and depth of the problem changes the way we look at poverty. For
decades, we've focused mainly on jobs, public assistance, parenting, and mass
incarceration. No one can deny the importance of these issues, but something
fundamental is missing. We have failed to fully appreciate how deeply housing
is implicated in the creation of poverty. Not everyone living in a distressed
neighborhood is associated with gang members, parole officers, employers,
social workers, or pastors. But nearly all of them have a landlord.

### FOR DISCUSSION

1. In "Cold City," Arleen and her two sons are presented as a typical example of
   "poor renting families in America" who often get evicted from their homes (11).
   How common, according to Matthew Desmond, are cases like theirs? Why do they
   occur?

2. Decades ago, according to Desmond, evictions "used to draw crowds" of supporters for the evictees (9). How and why have things changed since then?

3. Arleen and her family get evicted, on one occasion, as the indirect result of the
   boys' throwing snowballs at cars. Does the punishment fit the crime here? Why or
   why not?

4. When Arleen moves the family to Atkinson Avenue, she "feared for her boys,
   especially Jori" (4). Why is she afraid? How justified are her fears?

5. "Cold City" is the prologue to an entire book on the subject of eviction. Judging
   from this introduction, what do you think the methods and point of view of the
   book are likely to be? Does this sampling make you want to read the book? Why or
   why not?

## STRATEGIES AND STRUCTURES

1. Desmond divides his essay into two parts: the specific case of Arleen, Jori, and Jafaris (1–8)—followed by his own general observations on the issue of eviction in America (9–14). Is this a good strategy? Why do you think he adopts this order instead of, say, presenting his observations first and then the example?

2. A good example exhibits the typical characteristics of the group it exemplifies. What are some of the main characteristics Desmond ascribes to Arleen and her family?

3. Desmond uses an example (Arleen and family) within an example (Milwaukee). What group does the city of Milwaukee exemplify? Is it a good example? Why or why not?

4. Why do you think Desmond ends his narrative of Arleen's troubles with the appearance of a new landlord bearing gifts for her and her family (7–8)?

5. Desmond uses a mix of strategies in addition to exemplification. Where and how does he analyze CAUSE AND EFFECT? The PROCESS of eviction itself?

## WORDS AND FIGURES OF SPEECH

1. Since Milwaukee, in Desmond's essay, is experiencing its "snowiest winter on record," "Cold City" is a reference to the weather (1). What else does this PUN refer to?

2. Desmond never gives Arleen's last name. Should he have? Why or why not?

3. Evictees, according to Desmond, can either *truck* or *curb* (2). How appropriate are these terms for the options they designate? How does the list of examples at the end of paragraph 2 help to make Desmond's explanation more concrete?

4. Among Arleen's possessions is a book entitled *Don't Be Afraid to Discipline* (2). Why do you think Desmond makes an ALLUSION to Arleen's reading? What does this example tell us about her as a mother?

5. At one point, Arleen takes her boys to a homeless shelter. Why is it called "the Lodge" (3)?

6. Point out places in his essay where Desmond addresses the reader directly as "you." Why do you think he uses the second person here instead of sticking to the more conventional third-person *he, she,* or *they*?

**FOR WRITING**

1.  Are you aware of someone who has been evicted? Write a case study of that person or persons that gives numerous examples of their experience.

2.  Desmond's broader subject here is not just eviction but poverty in America. Write a case history of someone you know whose experience exemplifies this larger subject.

3.  Have you ever had difficulty finding appropriate housing? What were some of the causes of those difficulties? Write an essay about this experience—and its causes and conditions—including examples of what you went through.

## ANN HOOD

# LONG BEAUTIFUL HAIR

ANN HOOD (b. 1956) is a novelist, essayist, and teacher of writing at the New School in New York City and at New York University. A native of Warwick, Rhode Island, Hood graduated from the University of Rhode Island with a BA in English and went on to study American literature in graduate school at NYU. On April 18, 2002, Hood's five-year-old daughter Grace contracted a virulent form of strep and died suddenly. Books such as *The Knitting Circle* (2007), *Comfort: A Journey Through Grief* (2008), and *The Red Thread* (2010) explore this loss. At first glance, "Long Beautiful Hair" appears to provide examples of different haircuts that would be relatable to anyone who has had a bad hair day. The depth and direction of Hood's analysis changes, however, when she recalls a "hair pact" with her daughter. "Long Beautiful Hair" first appeared in the Spring 2010 issue of *Amoskeag*, the literary journal of Southern New Hampshire University.

I BLAME KATHY CONNOR for over 30 years of hair disasters. When I met her, back in 1975, I was a hair virgin. I had very long, dirty blond locks that had remained exactly that long for my entire 19 years. Kathy took one look, lifted a hank of hair in her hands, and examined it. "Your hair," she said, "is a mess. Dry. Damaged. Split." Kathy was one of those people who seem infinitely wiser and older than everyone else. She did not wear jeans or Izod shirts. She liked Frank Sinatra music. She knew how to prepare flank steak and cherries jubilee. So when she delivered my hair diagnosis, I listened.

"You need to cut it," she said. I began to sweat. My hair, thick and high-lighted with gold streaks that I carefully painted on every six weeks, was my best feature.

"Like a trim?" I managed to ask. Once a year, I went to the hair salon at the Jordan Marsh department store and let a hairdresser cut an inch or two. This, I believed, kept my tresses looking good. Apparently, I was wrong.

Kathy leaned in for a closer examination. Her face filled with disgust. "At least six inches," she announced.

If only I had been the kind of 19-year-old who did not listen to someone simply because she knew the words to "My Kind of Town,"[1] this story would have ended right there in the living room of the Alpha Xi Delta sorority. Instead, I followed Kathy to the telephone and let her make an appointment for me with a man named Tony at a salon in nearby Providence. A week later, I walked onto South Main Street a different person. My long, beautiful hair had been cut into a Dorothy Hamill wedge.[2] Even worse, as the blond locks fell to the floor, I was left with what lay beneath them: mousy brown roots.

"You look so much better," Kathy said, swinging her own still-long hair. She had gotten a one-inch trim. I had been scalped.

"Uh-huh," I said, peering at my reflection in various store windows as we walked by them. I was skinny back then, and with my hair so short and wearing my standard uniform of khaki pants and a polo shirt, I no longer looked like a pretty girl. To be honest, I didn't look much like a girl at all.

1. A song about the city of Chicago made popular by Frank Sinatra.

2. Dorothy Hamill is a U. S. figure skater who won a gold medal in the 1976 Olympics. Her short, wedge-like hairstyle became popular in the 1970s.

That haircut stayed with me throughout college. Whenever I tried to 8
grow it out, I got weird wings on the sides of my face that made me look like
the Flying Nun. I tried to adapt to the change: I replaced my Long & Silky
shampoo with Short & Sassy. I painted on highlights more frequently, trying
to make the best of a bad situation. I pretended I was glad that I attracted
attention because of my wit and smarts, rather than a gorgeous head of hair.
Truth be told, I missed the weight of all that hair on my shoulders. I missed
the way boys grabbed onto it when we kissed. I even missed my split ends,
which I held up in the sunlight on lazy afternoons, a book open on my lap, and
pulled apart.

After college, when I interviewed with airlines for a job as a flight atten- 9
dant, the woman at United told me the highlights had to go. "Too brassy," she
said, with the same tone of distaste as Kathy Connor.

To remedy my so-called brassy hair, Tony (don't ask me why I went back 10
to him) stripped it completely and recolored it a dishwater-dull ash blond. It
was my first real chemical process. And it was just the beginning. War had
been declared; my hair was now the enemy.

Shortly after visiting Tony, I decided to grow it long again, thereby kick- 11
ing off a protracted, torturous growing-out process. Over the next few years,
I tried bangs, braids, and bobs. (Why? Because one hairdresser
said I had to "go short to go long.") I had perms, highlights, low-
lights, root color, and foils. Once I even got the top spiked, which
left me with a mullet that could be fixed only by chopping my hair
short again. All this was in an effort to have my hair resemble what it had
looked like before I met Kathy Connor. But no matter what I did, my 19-year-
old self's hair remained elusive.

For advice on when and how to use extended examples, see p. 179.

Or it did until one day when, at the age of 30, I wandered into a fancy 12
New York City salon, saw a beautiful, long-haired stylist named Joy, and told
her: "I want your hair." Joy did not believe that you had to go short in order to
go long. She worked her magic, and within a few months I had long, gentle layers of blond hair—exactly the way I had wanted it.

I had missed this Me in my decade of short and medium-length hair. Call 13
me shallow and narcissistic, but I liked the way men admired it. I liked walking
down a city street in my jeans, cowboy boots, and black leather jacket. And,
yes, abundant blond hair.

That should have been the end of my hair saga. Goal achieved; move on  14
to the next thing. But life is not so simple. And so, at age 35, I found myself
once again sitting in a hair salon, wearing a kimono and a towel pinned around
my shoulders. I was pregnant, and suddenly my hair was dull and uncoopera-
tive again. The products that once gave it volume made it so full that I looked
like a country-western singer. And my doctor said no hair color until the baby
was born.

"To the collarbone," I told the stylist. She lifted her scissors and cut.  15

By the time I had my second baby, a few years later, my hair was as short as  16
a British schoolboy's. And, surprisingly, I was OK with that. It was much easier to
care for and kind of sexy, I decided. Plus, it was blonder than ever before.

That second baby was a girl, whom my husband and I named Grace. And  17
she was blessed with the real thing: pale blond hair that never betrays you by
turning brown. To keep her tangles under control, we cut her hair chin-length
in a chic cut that had longer points in front.

When Grace turned five, she announced that she wanted long hair. It  18
would be beautiful, I thought. Fine and golden. "You grow yours, too," Grace
said. "We'll be even more the same." Grace looked exactly like me. "Deal," I
told her. She didn't have to know how I kept my own hair blond. We sealed our
plan with a sticky kiss.

Grace and I did not get very far in our journey. Before her hair reached  19
her shoulders, she got a virulent form of strep and died within 36 hours. The
day of her funeral, my hairdresser, Jenny, came to our house to fix my hair.

"Cut it," I told her.  20

"Really?" Jenny asked. Her eyes were red and puffy from crying.  21

I couldn't bear to tell her the deal Grace and I had made. I couldn't bear  22
to keep my end of it, alone now. "Really," I said.

Jenny cut it, and for the next two years, as grief kept me in its terrible  23
grasp, I kept it short and dark, as if even my hair had to wear my sorrow.

Time passed. Somehow, it does that. And one spring day in 2007, five years  24
after Grace's death, I walked into a new salon and told the owner, Kim, that I
wanted to grow out my hair. And I wanted it to be blond. Although that might
sound as if I had not traveled very far at all, in fact, that day turned out to be
one of the first tentative steps I took back into the world.

Patiently, over the next year, Kim trimmed and shaped so that the 25
growing-out process did not make me look too bad. "You'll be able to wear a
ponytail this summer," she said. She was right. That summer I walked along
the ocean with my wet hair pulled back. By winter it fell below my collarbone.
And now it hangs gently down my back.

Thirty-one years ago, I was a 19-year-old without the self-confidence to 26
ignore bad advice. The fact that, at 50, I have the same hair that I so foolishly
relinquished decades earlier does not mean that I am holding on to my youth
or am unable to grow older gracefully. No. It means that I am a woman who
has teased and sprayed and snipped her way through the decades, to finally
land at the place where she feels most herself: as an unapologetic, long-haired
blond; as a mother who lost her daughter, slowly, slowly reclaiming the torn
pieces of herself.

### FOR DISCUSSION

1. When she was nineteen, says Ann Hood, a "friend" instructed her to cut off her
   long hair (1—4). Hood did as she was told. Why? What should she have done?

2. Hood spent the next decade fretting over the loss of her hair—and trying fruit-
   lessly to get it back. "Call me shallow and narcissistic," she writes (13). Is this a fair
   assessment? Why or why not?

3. As her "hair saga" unfolds, Hood provides several examples of times she had her
   hair shorn or otherwise altered (11, 14—16). Explain what each example adds to her
   story.

4. That she still wants, more than 30 years later, to have "the same hair" she had at
   nineteen, says Hood, "does not mean that I am holding on to my youth or am
   unable to grow older gracefully" (26). What *does* it exemplify about her? Explain.

### STRATEGIES AND STRUCTURES

1. Hood gives no hint at the beginning of her essay that she will be writing, in part,
   about her reaction to her daughter's death. Should she have? Why or why not?

2. Hood presents major hair events of her life in chronological order. How and how
   effectively does this way of organizing her examples help to draw the reader into
   her analysis?

3. Point out specific passages in her essay where Hood focuses on the CAUSES AND EFFECTS of her hair troubles. Which passages do you find particularly revealing? Why?

4. In the last paragraph of her essay, Hood allows her hair to grow back. Why? What is she exemplifying here about the nature of grief and loss? How and how well does Hood's final example of her obsession with long hair help to tie up the loose ends, so to speak, in the NARRATIVE part of her essay?

## WORDS AND FIGURES OF SPEECH

1. Hood's hair references can be seen as instances of METONOMY: her hair is to be associated with, or "stands in for," something of which it is a part. What might that might be? Explain.

2. A *saga* is an epic tale, usually about the adventures of Vikings or other Norsemen (14). Is it inappropriate for Hood to use this term for a mere hair story? Why or why not?

3. What are the implications, in context, of each of the following terms: *virgin* (1), *betrays* (17), *journey* (19)?

4. The "torn pieces" in the last sentence of Hood's essay refer explicitly to her grief over the loss of her daughter. What else might they recall? Explain.

## FOR WRITING

1. In a paragraph or two, write about an occasion when you allowed someone to convince you to do something that went against your better judgment. Be sure to explain what caused you to give in despite your misgivings.

2. Write an essay that gives numerous examples of the difficulties or triumphs you experienced as the result of trying to maintain a particular image of yourself or of someone else. Cite specific physical details and attributes as appropriate.

# ⇥8⇤

# CLASSIFICATION

WHEN we CLASSIFY* things, we say what categories they belong to. Dogs, for instance, can be classified as Great Danes, Labrador retrievers, Chihuahuas, and so on. A category is a group with similar characteristics. Thus, to be classified as a Labrador, a dog must be sturdily built, have soft jaws, and have a yellow, black, or chocolate coat—these are the characteristics, among others, that distinguish its group or breed.

Dogs, like anything else, can be classified in more than one way. We can also classify dogs as working dogs, show dogs, and mutts that make good family pets. Or simply as small, medium, and large dogs—or as males and females. The categories into which we divide any subject will depend upon the basis on which we classify it. In the case of dogs, our principle of classification is often by breed, but it can also be by role, size, sex, or some other principle.

No matter your subject or your principle of classification, the categories in your system must be inclusive and not overlap. You wouldn't classify dogs as hunting dogs, show dogs, or retrievers, because some dogs, such as most family pets, would be left out—while others, such as Irish setters, would belong to more than one category, since setters are both hunting dogs and retrievers.

As Robert Sussman notes on p. 264, humans, too, can be classified.

The categories in any classification system will vary with who is doing the classifying and for what PURPOSE. A teacher divides a group of thirty students according to grades: A, B, C, D, and F. A basketball coach might divide the same group of students into forwards, guards, and centers. The director of a student drama group would have another set of criteria. Yet all three systems

*Words printed in SMALL CAPITALS are defined in the Glossary/Index.

are valid for the purposes they are intended to serve. And classification must serve some larger purpose, or it becomes an empty game.

Systems of classification can help us organize our thoughts about the world around us. They can also help us organize our thoughts in writing, whether in a single paragraph or a whole essay. For example, you might organize a paragraph by introducing your subject, dividing it into types, and then giving the distinguishing features of each type. Here is a paragraph that follows such a pattern. The subject is lightning:

> There are several types of lightning named according to where the discharge takes place. Among them are intracloud lightning, by far the most common type, in which the flash occurs within the thundercloud; air-discharge lightning, in which the flash occurs between the cloud and the surrounding air; and cloud-to-ground lightning, in which the discharge takes place between the cloud and the ground.
> —Richard Orville, "Bolts from the Blue"

This short paragraph could be the opening of an essay that goes on to discuss each of the three types of lightning in order, devoting a paragraph or more to each type. If the author's purpose were simply to help us understand the different types, he would probably spend more time on the first kind of lightning—perhaps coming back to it in detail later in his essay—because "intracloud lightning" is the most common variety.

In this case, however, Richard Orville, a meteorologist at Texas A&M University, chose to develop his essay by writing several additional paragraphs on the third type of lightning, "in which the discharge takes place between the cloud and the ground." Why emphasize this category?

Meteorologists classify storms—especially hurricanes, tornadoes, and thunderstorms—not only to understand them but also to predict where they are most likely to occur. As Orville says, his main point in classifying lightning is to "tell what parts on the ground will be most threatened by the lightning activity." Based on this information, the meteorologist can then warn people to take shelter. He can also alert the power companies, so they can deploy power crews more effectively, or reroute electricity away from a power plant even before it is hit.

Given this purpose—to predict weather activity so he can issue accurate warnings and advisories—Orville first classifies his subject into types based on the location of the electrical discharge, or "flash." He then devotes most of his essay to the third type of lightning (cloud-to-ground) because it is the most dangerous kind—to property, to natural resources such as forests, and to people.

Meteorologists divide the subject of lightning into groups or kinds—intracloud, air-discharge, cloud-to-ground. This is the equivalent of classifying dogs by dividing them into distinct breeds. Meteorologists also sort individual bolts of lightning according to the group or kind they belong to: "The bolt of lightning that just destroyed the oak tree in your yard was the cloud-to-ground kind." This is the equivalent of saying that a particular dog is a Lab or a husky or a Portuguese water dog. In this chapter, we will use the term *classification* whether we are dividing a subject into groups or sorting individuals according to the group they belong to—because in either case we are organizing a subject into categories.

# A BRIEF GUIDE TO WRITING
# A CLASSIFICATION ESSAY

As you write a classification essay, you need to identify your subject and explain the basis on which you're classifying it. David Brooks makes these basic moves of classification in this first paragraph from one of his opinion pieces:

> The world can be divided in many ways—rich and poor, democratic and authoritarian—but one of the most striking is the divide between the societies with an individualist mentality and the ones with a collectivist mentality.
>
> —DAVID BROOKS, "Harmony and the Dream"

Brooks identifies his subject (societies of the world) and explains the basis on which he is classifying it (their basic philosophies, or "mentalities").

The following guidelines will help you to make these basic moves as you draft a classification essay. They'll also help you to come up with your subject and to select categories that fit your purpose and audience, are effectively organized, support your main point, and are sufficiently inclusive yet don't overlap.

## Coming Up with a Subject

Almost any subject—lightning, convertibles, TV dramas—can be classified in some way. As you consider subjects to classify, think about what you might learn from doing so—your PURPOSE for classifying. For example, you might want to classify something in order to evaluate it (Which dog breeds are appropriate for families with young children?); to determine causes (Was the crash due to mechanical failure, weather, or pilot error?); or to make sense of events (What kinds of economic recessions has the United States historically experienced?). Choose a subject that interests you, but also ask yourself, "Why is this subject worth classifying?"

## Considering Your Purpose and Audience

The specific traits you focus on and the categories you divide your subject into will be determined largely by your purpose and audience. Suppose the roof of your town's city hall blows off in a hurricane, and your PURPOSE is to write an article for your neighborhood newsletter explaining what kind of roof will stay on best in the next hurricane. In this case, you'd look closely at such traits as weight and wind resistance and pay less attention to such traits as color or energy efficiency.

Once you've determined the kind of roof that has the highest wind rating, you probably will not have a hard time convincing your AUDIENCE (some of whom also lost their roofs) that this is the kind to buy. However, since your audience of homeowners may not be experts in roofing materials, you'll want to DEFINE any technical terms and use language they're familiar with. Keep in mind that readers will not always agree with the way you classify a subject. So you may need to explain why they should accept the criteria you've used.

# Generating Ideas:
# Considering What Categories There Are

Once you have a subject in mind and a reason for classifying it, consider what categories there are and choose the ones that best suit your purpose and audience. For example, if your purpose is to evaluate different kinds of movies for a film course, you might classify them by genre—drama, comedy, romance, horror, thriller, or musical. But if you are reviewing movies for the campus newspaper, you would probably base your classification on quality, perhaps dividing them into these five categories: "must see," "excellent," "good," "mediocre," and "to be avoided at all costs."

When you devise categories for a classification essay, make sure they adhere to a consistent principle (or basis) of classification. For example, if the basis of your movie classification is "movies appropriate for young children," you might use categories such as "good for all ages," "preschool," "six and up," and "not suitable for children." But you should avoid mixing such categories with those based on genre or quality. In other words, you wouldn't use "drama," "excellent," and "not suitable for children" as the categories.

# Templates for Classifying

The following templates can help you to generate ideas for a classification essay and then to start drafting. Don't take these as formulas where you just have to fill in the blanks. There are no easy formulas for good writing. But these templates can help you plot out some of the key moves of classification and thus may serve as good starting points.

> ► X can be classified on the basis of _____.

> ► Classified on the basis of _____, some of the most common types of X are _____, _____, and _____.

> ► X can be divided into two basic types, _____ and _____.

> ► Experts in the field typically divide X into _____, _____, and _____.

> ▶ This particular X clearly belongs in the \_\_\_\_\_ category, since it is \_\_\_\_\_,
>   \_\_\_\_\_, and \_\_\_\_\_.
>
> ▶ \_\_\_\_\_ and \_\_\_\_\_ are examples of this type of X.
>
> ▶ By classifying X in this way, we can see that \_\_\_\_\_.

For more techniques to help you generate ideas and start writing a classification essay, see Chapter 3.

## Organizing a Classification Essay

In the opening paragraphs of your essay, tell the reader what you're classifying and why, and explain your classification system. If you were writing an essay classifying types of environmentally friendly cars, for example, you might use an introduction like this:

> If you are considering buying an environmentally friendly car, you need to know which types of fueling are available in order to find a car that meets your goals for a green lifestyle. Green cars can best be divided into the following categories: petrol cars, diesel cars, electric cars, hybrid cars, and biofuel cars. If you understand these five basic types and the differences among them, you can make an informed decision for the good of both the environment and your wallet.

Typically, the body of a classification essay is devoted to a point-by-point discussion of each of the categories that make up your classification system. Thus if you are classifying green cars, you would spend a paragraph, or at least several sentences, explaining the most important characteristics of each type.

Once you've laid out the categories in some detail, remind the reader of the point you are making. The point of classifying cars by fuel type, for example, is to help readers choose the green car that best meets their goals for an environmentally friendly lifestyle.

## Stating Your Point

When you compose a classification essay, you should have in mind what you learned about your subject by classifying it in a particular way. Tell the reader in a THESIS STATEMENT what your main point is and why you're dividing up your subject as you do. Usually, you'll want to state your main point in the introduction as you explain your classification system. In the opening paragraph of the essay on green cars, for instance, the main point is stated in the last sentence: "If you can understand these five basic types . . . you can make an informed decision."

## Choosing Significant Characteristics

Whatever classification system you use, base your categories on the most significant characteristics of your subject—ones that explain something important about it. For example, you probably would not discuss color when classifying environmentally friendly cars because this attribute does not tell the reader anything about a car's impact on the environment. After all, every kind of car comes in more or less the same colors. Instead, you would probably use such attributes as fuel type, miles-per-gallon, and types of emissions—traits that differentiate, say, a hybrid car from other kinds of green cars.

## Choosing Categories That Are Inclusive and Don't Overlap

When you divide your subject into categories, those categories must be inclusive enough to cover most cases, and they must not overlap. For example, classifying ice cream into chocolate and vanilla alone isn't very useful because this system leaves out many other important kinds, such as strawberry, pistachio, and rum raisin. The categories in a good classification system include all kinds: for instance, no-fat, low-fat, and full-fat ice cream. And they should not overlap. Thus, chocolate, vanilla, homemade, and Ben and Jerry's do not make a good classification system because the same scoop of ice cream could fit into more than one category.

# EDITING FOR COMMON ERRORS IN A CLASSIFICATION ESSAY

Classification invites problems with listing groups or traits. Here are some common errors to check for and correct when you write a classification essay.

## When you list categories or traits in a classification system, make sure they are parallel in form

- ▶ How much income tax you pay each year depends largely on whether your income is taxed as wages or ~~you have a lot of~~ capital gains.

- ▶ Capital gains are classified according to whether the earnings are long-term (more than a year) or ~~are produced over the~~ short-term (a year or less).

## Check that traits used to describe or define categories are in the following order: size, age, color, region

- ▶ His preferred type of headgear was ~~Panama, old, big, white~~ <u>big, old, white Panama</u> hats.

## Potato Proverb

When you classify things, you tell what categories they fall into. According to this inscription on a blackboard outside the Perfect Potato restaurant in Brooklyn, New York, all things "in this world" can be classified as those that are potatoes and those that are not potatoes. A binary (two-part) system like this can be useful when you want to classify individuals and groups according to whether they exhibit a particular trait—being a potato, for example, or being tall (basketball players), having a high concentration of fluoride (toothpaste), or allowing pets (hotel rooms).

Depending upon your purpose and audience, however, your classification system may need to include a number of different categories, each defined by a variety of traits. Suppose you're writing about the best potato varieties to use for making not only french fries but also potato salad and other dishes. For this purpose, you might classify potatoes according to the following system from the *Huffington Post* in the article "A Guide to Every Type of Potato You Need to Know": starchy (Idaho Russet, for example), waxy (Red Bliss), and all-purpose (Yukon Gold).

## ERIC A. WATTS

# THE COLOR OF SUCCESS

ERIC A. WATTS wrote the following essay about racial stereotyping when he was a sophomore at Brown University. In it, Watts argues that African Americans who criticize one another for "acting white" and who say that success based on academic achievement is "not black" are misclassifying themselves as "victims." After tracing the historical roots of this "outdated" system, Watts assesses its damaging effects and examines more recent ways of classifying and achieving success that are based more on economics than race. "The Color of Success" originally appeared in the Brown *Alumni Monthly*.

## The Color of Success

When I was a black student at a primarily white high school, I occasionally confronted the stereotypes and prejudice that some whites aimed at those of my race. These incidents came as no particular surprise—after all, prejudice, though less prevalent than in the past, is ages old.

1

> Introduces the general topic of the essay: false categories

What did surprise me during those years was the profound disapproval that some of my black peers expressed toward my studious behavior. "Hitting the books," expressing oneself articulately, and, at times, displaying more than a modest amount of intelligence—these traits were derided as "acting white."

2

> Identifies the particular false category that he will emphasize

Once, while I was traveling with other black students, a young woman asked me what I thought of one of our teachers. My answer, phrased in what one might call "standard" English, caused considerable discomfort among my audience. Finally, the young woman exploded: "Eric," she said, "stop talking like a white boy! You're with us now!"

3

> Gives the first in a series of traits that define "acting white"

Another time, again in a group of black students, a friend asked how I intended to spend the weekend. When I answered that I would study, my friend's reaction was swift: "Eric, you need to stop all this studying; you need to stop acting so white." The others laughed in agreement.

4

Signithea Fordham's 1986 ethnographic study of a mostly black high school in Washington, D.C., *Black Students' School Success,* concluded that many behaviors associated with high achievement—speaking standard English, studying long hours, striving to get good grades—were regarded as "acting white." Fordham further

5

concluded that "many black students limit their academic success so their peers won't think they are 'acting white.'"

Rejects "acting-white" as a valid category

Frankly, I never took the "acting white" accusation seriously. It seemed to me that certain things I valued—hard work, initiative, articulateness, education—were not solely white people's prerogative.

Trouble begins, however, when students lower their standards in response to peer pressure. Such a retreat from achievement has potentially horrendous effects on the black community.

Watts's purpose in examining a false classification system is to examine its harmful effects

Even more disturbing is the rationale behind the "acting white" accusation. It seems that, on a subconscious level, some black students wonder whether success—in particular, academic success—is a purely white domain.

In his essay "On Being Black and Middle Class," in *The Content of Our Character* (1990), Shelby Steele, a black scholar at San Jose State University, argues that certain "middle-class" values—the work ethic, education, initiative—by encouraging "individualism," encourage identification with American society, rather than with race. The ultimate result is integration.

Analyzes CAUSES that led to self-stereotyping

But, Steele argues, the racial identification that emerged during the 1960s, and that still persists, urges middle-class blacks to view themselves as an embattled minority: to take an adversarial stance toward the mainstream. It emphasizes ethnic consciousness over individualism.

Steele says that this form of black identification emerged in the civil rights effort to obtain full racial equality, an effort that demanded that blacks present themselves (by and large) as a racial monolith: a single mass with the common experience of oppression. So blackness became virtually synonymous with victimization and the characteristics associated with it: lack of education and poverty.

I agree with Steele that a monolithic form of racial identification persists. The ideas of the black as a victim and the black as inferior have been too much entrenched in cultural imagery and too much enforced by custom and law not to have damaged the collective black psyche.

This damage is so severe that some black adolescents still believe that success is a white prerogative—the white "turf." These young people view the turf as inaccessible, both because (among other reasons) they doubt their own abilities and because they generally envision whites as, if not outspoken racists, people who are mildly interested in "keeping blacks down."

The result of identifying oneself as a victim can be, "Why even try? It's a white man's world."

Several years ago I was talking to an old friend, a black male. He justified dropping out of school and failing to look for a job on the basis of one factor: the cold, heartless, white power structure. When I suggested that such a power structure might indeed exist, but that opportunity for blacks was at an unprecedented level, he laughed. Doomed, he felt, to a life of defeat, my friend soon eased his melancholy with crack.

The most frustrating aspect of the "acting white" accusation is that its main premise—that academic and subsequent success are "white"—is demonstrably false. And so is the broader premise: that blacks are the victims of whites.

12

13

14 •··· States the main damaging effect of believing in the stereotypes

15

•···· Gives an example from personal experience

16

Attacks the premises of the "victims" argument

That academic success is "not black" is easily seen     17
as false if one takes a brisk walk through the Brown
University campus and looks at the faces one passes.
Indeed, the most comprehensive text concerning blacks
in decades, *A Common Destiny* (1989), states, "Despite
large gaps . . . whether the baseline is the 1940s, 1950s, or
1960s, the achievement outcomes . . . of black schooling
have greatly improved." That subsequent success in the
world belongs to blacks as well as whites is exemplified
today by such blacks as Jesse Jackson, Douglas Wilder,
Norman Rice, Anne Wortham, Sara Lawrence Lightfoot,
David Dinkins, August Wilson, Andrew Young . . .

The idea of a victimized black race is slowly becom-     18
ing outdated. Today's black adolescents were born after
the *Brown v. Board of Education* decision of 1954; after the
passage of the Civil Rights Act; after the Economic
Opportunity Act of 1964. With these rulings and laws,
whites' attitudes toward blacks have also greatly
improved. Although I cannot say that my life has been
free of racism on the part of whites, good racial relations
in my experience have far outweighed the bad. I refuse to
apologize for or retreat from this truth.

Argues that racial conditions in America have changed

The result of changes in policies and attitudes has     19
been to provide more opportunities for black Americans
than at any other point in their history. As early as 1978,
William Julius Wilson, in *The Declining Significance of
Race,* concluded that "the recent mobility patterns of
blacks lend strong support to the view that economic
class is clearly more important than race in predetermin-
ing . . . occupational mobility."

Anticipates objections to his position

There are, of course, many factors, often     20
socioeconomic, that still impede the progress of blacks.

High schools in black neighborhoods receive less local, state, and federal support than those in white areas; there is evidence that the high school diplomas of blacks are little valued by employers.

We should rally against all such remaining racism, confronting particularly the economic obstacles to black success. But we must also realize that racism is not nearly as profound as it once was, and that opportunities for blacks (where opportunity equals jobs and acceptance for the educated and qualified) have increased. Furthermore, we should know that even a lack of resources is no excuse for passivity.

Concludes by saying what should be done

21

As the syndicated columnist William Raspberry (who is black) says, it is time for certain black adolescents to "shift their focus": to move from an identity rooted in victimization to an identity rooted in individualism and hard work.

22

Simply put, the black community must eradicate the "you're-acting-white" syndrome. Until it does, black Americans will never realize their potential.

23

# MOTHER TONGUE

AMY TAN (b. 1952), a native of Oakland, California, is the author of seven novels, most recently *The Valley of Amazement* (2013). In her best-selling first novel, *The Joy Luck Club* (1989), Tan used all of the different forms of the English language she had spoken since childhood with her mother, whose native language was Chinese. In "Mother Tongue," which first appeared in the *Threepenny Review* (1990), Tan not only uses her family's different "Englishes," she classifies them into their various kinds and explains how each type lends itself to a different form of communication.

I AM NOT A SCHOLAR of English or literature. I cannot give you much more than personal opinions on the English language and its variations in this country or others. 1

I am a writer. And by that definition, I am someone who has always loved language. I am fascinated by language in daily life. I spend a great deal of my time thinking about the power of language—the way it can evoke an emotion, a visual image, a complex idea, or a simple truth. Language is the tool of my trade. And I use them all—all the Englishes I grew up with. 2

Recently, I was made keenly aware of the different Englishes I do use. I 3 was giving a talk to a large group of people, the same talk I had already given to half a dozen other groups. The nature of the talk was about my writing, my life, and my book, *The Joy Luck Club*. The talk was going along well enough, until I remembered one major difference that made the whole talk sound wrong. My mother was in the room. And it was perhaps the first time she had heard me give a lengthy speech, using the kind of English I have never used with her. I was saying things like, "The intersection of memory upon imagination" and "There is an aspect of my fiction that relates to thus-and-thus"—a speech filled with carefully wrought grammatical phrases, burdened, it suddenly seemed to me, with nominalized forms, past perfect tenses, conditional phrases, all the forms of standard English that I had learned in school and through books, the forms of English I did not use at home with my mother.

Just last week, I was walking down the street with my mother, and I 4 again found myself conscious of the English I was using, the English I do use with her. We were talking about the price of new and used furniture and I heard myself saying this: "Not waste money that way." My husband was with us as well, and he didn't notice any switch in my English. And then I realized why. It's because over the twenty years we've been together I've often used the same kind of English with him, and sometimes he even uses it with me. It has become our language of intimacy, a different sort of English that relates to family talk, the language I grew up with.

So you'll have some idea of what this family talk I heard sounds like, I'll 5 quote what my mother said during a recent conversation which I videotaped and then transcribed. During this conversation, my mother was talking about a political gangster in Shanghai who had the same last name as her family's, Du, and how the gangster in his early years wanted to be adopted by her family, which was rich by comparison. Later, the gangster became more powerful, far richer than my mother's family, and one day showed up at my mother's wedding to pay his respects. Here's what she said in part:

"Du Yusong having business like fruit stand. Like off the street kind. He 6 is Du like Du Zong—but not Tsung-ming Island people. The local people call putong, the river east side, he belong to that side local people. That man want to ask Du Zong father take him in like become own family. Du Zong father wasn't look down on him, but didn't take seriously, until that man big like become a mafia. Now important person, very hard to inviting him. Chinese way, came only to show respect, don't stay for dinner. Respect for making big celebration, he shows up. Mean gives lots of respect. Chinese custom. Chinese social life that way. If too important won't have to stay too long. He come to my wedding. I didn't see, I heard it. I gone to boy's side, they have YMCA dinner. Chinese age I was nineteen."

You should know that my mother's expressive command of English ⁷ belies how much she actually understands. She reads the *Forbes*[1] report, listens to *Wall Street Week*, converses daily with her stockbroker, reads all of Shirley MacLaine's[2] books with ease—all kinds of things I can't begin to understand. Yet some of my friends tell me they understand 50 percent of what my mother says. Some say they understand 80 to 90 percent. Some say they understand none of it, as if she were speaking pure Chinese. But to me, my mother's English is perfectly clear, perfectly natural. It's my mother tongue. Her language, as I hear it, is vivid, direct, full of observation and imagery. That was the language that helped shape the way I saw things, expressed things, made sense of the world.

Lately, I've been giving more thought to the kind of English my mother speaks. ⁸ Like others, I have described it to people as "broken" or "fractured" English. But I wince when I say that. It has always bothered me that I can think of no way to describe it other than "broken," as if it were damaged and needed to be fixed, as if it lacked a certain wholeness and soundness. I've heard other terms used, "limited English," for example. But they seem just as bad, as if everything is limited, including people's perceptions of the limited English speaker.

I know this for a fact, because when I was growing up, my mother's ⁹ "limited" English limited *my* perception of her. I was ashamed of her English. I believed that her English reflected the quality of what she had to say. That is, because she expressed them imperfectly her thoughts were imperfect. And I had plenty of empirical evidence to support me: the fact that people in department stores, at banks, and at restaurants did not take her seriously, did not

1. Business magazine.
2. American film actress (b. 1934) who has written a number of memoirs.

give her good service, pretended not to understand her, or even acted as if they did not hear her.

My mother has long realized the limitations of her English as well. When 10 I was fifteen, she used to have me call people on the phone to pretend I was she. In this guise, I was forced to ask for information or even to complain and yell at people who had been rude to her. One time it was a call to her stockbroker in New York. She had cashed out her small portfolio and it just so happened we were going to go to New York the next week, our very first trip outside California. I had to get on the phone and say in an adolescent voice that was not very convincing, "This is Mrs. Tan."

And my mother was standing in the back whispering loudly, "Why he 11 don't send me check, already two weeks late. So mad he lie to me, losing me money."

And then I said in perfect English, "Yes, I'm getting rather concerned. 12 You had agreed to send the check two weeks ago, but it hasn't arrived."

Then she began to talk more loudly. "What he want, I come to New York 13 tell him front of his boss, you cheating me?" And I was trying to calm her down, make her be quiet, while telling the stockbroker, "I can't tolerate any more excuses. If I don't receive the check immediately, I am going to have to speak to your manager when I'm in New York next week." And sure enough, the following week there we were in front of this astonished stockbroker, and I was sitting there red-faced and quiet, and my mother, the real Mrs. Tan, was shouting at his boss in her impeccable broken English.

We used a similar routine just five days ago, for a situation that was far 14 less humorous. My mother had gone to the hospital for an appointment, to find out about a benign brain tumor a CAT scan had revealed a month ago. She said she had spoken very good English, her best English, no mistakes. Still, she said, the hospital did not apologize when they said they had lost the CAT scan and she had come for nothing. She said they did not seem to have any sympathy when she told them she was anxious to know the exact diagnosis, since her husband and son had both died of brain tumors. She said they would not give her any more information until the next time and she would have to make another appointment for that. So she said she would not leave until the doctor called her daughter. She wouldn't budge. And when the doctor finally called her daughter, me, who spoke in perfect English—lo and behold—we had assurances the CAT scan would be found, promises that a conference call on Monday would be held, and apologies for any suffering my mother had gone through for a most regrettable mistake.

I think my mother's English almost had an effect on limiting my possi- 15 bilities in life as well. Sociologists and linguists probably will tell you that a person's developing language skills are more influenced by peers. But I do think that the language spoken in the family, especially in immigrant families which are more insular, plays a large role in shaping the language of the child. And I believe that it affected my results on achievement tests, IQ tests, and the SAT. While my English skills were never judged as poor, compared to math, English could not be considered my strong suit. In grade school I did moderately well, getting perhaps B's, sometimes B-pluses, in English and scoring perhaps in the sixtieth or seventieth percentile on achievement tests. But those scores were not good enough to override the opinion that my true abilities lay in math and science, because in those areas I achieved A's and scored in the ninetieth percentile or higher.

This was understandable. Math is precise; there is only one correct 16 answer. Whereas, for me at least, the answers on English tests were always a judgment call, a matter of opinion and personal experience. Those tests were constructed around items like fill-in-the-blank sentence completion, such as,

See p. 225 on choosing categories that don't overlap.

"Even though Tom was _____, Mary thought he was _____." And the correct answer always seemed to be the most bland combinations of thoughts, for example, "Even though Tom was shy, Mary thought he was charming," with the grammatical structure "even though" limiting the correct answer to some sort of semantic opposites, so you wouldn't get answers like, "Even though Tom was foolish, Mary thought he was ridiculous." Well, according to my mother, there were very few limitations as to what Tom could have been and what Mary might have thought of him. So I never did well on tests like that.

The same was true with word analogies, pairs of words in which you 17 were supposed to find some sort of logical, semantic relationship—for example, "*Sunset* is to *nightfall* as _____ is to _____." And here you would be presented with a list of four possible pairs, one of which showed the same kind of relationship: *red* is to *stoplight*, *bus* is to *arrival*, *chills* is to *fever*, *yawn* is to *boring.* Well, I could never think that way. I knew what the tests were asking, but I could not block out of my mind the images already created by the first pair, "*sunset* is to *nightfall*"—and I would see a burst of colors against a darkening sky, the moon rising, the lowering of a curtain of stars. And all the other pairs of words—red, bus, stoplight, boring—just threw up a mass of confusing images, making it impossible for me to sort out something as logical as saying: "A sunset precedes nightfall" is the same as "a chill precedes a fever." The only way I would have gotten that answer right would have been to imagine an associative situation, for example, my being disobedient and staying out past sunset, catching a chill at night, which turns into feverish pneumonia as punishment, which indeed did happen to me.

I have been thinking about all this lately, about my mother's English, about   18
achievement tests. Because lately I've been asked, as a writer, why there are not more Asian Americans represented in American literature. Why are there few Asian Americans enrolled in creative writing programs? Why do so many Chinese students go into engineering? Well, these are broad sociological questions I can't begin to answer. But I have noticed in surveys—in fact, just last week—that Asian students, as a whole, always do significantly better on math achievement tests than in English. And this makes me think that there are other Asian-American students whose English spoken in the home might also be described as "broken" or "limited." And perhaps they also have teachers who are steering them away from writing and into math and science, which is what happened to me.

Fortunately, I happen to be rebellious in nature and enjoy the challenge   19
of disproving assumptions made about me. I became an English major my first year in college, after being enrolled as pre-med. I started writing nonfiction as a freelancer the week after I was told by my former boss that writing was my worst skill and I should hone my talents toward account management.

But it wasn't until 1985 that I finally began to write fiction. And at first I   20
wrote using what I thought to be wittily crafted sentences, sentences that would finally prove I had mastery over the English language. Here's an example from the first draft of a story that later made its way into *The Joy Luck Club*, but without this line: "That was my mental quandary in its nascent state." A terrible line, which I can barely pronounce.

Fortunately, for reasons I won't get into today, I later decided I should   21
envision a reader for the stories I would write. And the reader I decided upon
was my mother, because these were stories about mothers. So with this reader
in mind—and in fact she did read my early drafts—I began to write stories
using all the Englishes I grew up with: the English I spoke to my mother, which
for lack of a better term might be described as "simple"; the English she used
with me, which for lack of a better term might be described as "broken"; my
translation of her Chinese, which could certainly be described as "watered
down"; and what I imagined to be her translation of her Chinese if she could
speak in perfect English, her internal language, and for that I sought to pre-
serve the essence, but neither an English nor a Chinese structure. I wanted to
capture what language ability tests can never reveal: her intent, her passion,
her imagery, the rhythms of her speech and the nature of her thoughts.

Apart from what any critic had to say about my writing, I knew I had   22
succeeded where it counted when my mother finished reading my book and
gave me her verdict: "So easy to read."

### FOR DISCUSSION

1. Into what two basic categories does Amy Tan **CLASSIFY** all the Englishes that she
   uses in writing and speaking?

2. How many Englishes did Tan learn at home from conversing with her mother, a
   native speaker of Chinese? How does she distinguish among them?

3. According to Tan, what are the significant characteristics of "standard" English
   (3)? How and where did she learn standard English?

4. Tan tells us that she envisions her mother as the **AUDIENCE** for her stories, using
   "all the Englishes I grew up with" in writing them (21). For what audience did Tan
   write this essay? How would you classify the English she uses in it?

### STRATEGIES AND STRUCTURES

1. Why do you think Tan begins her essay with the disclaimer that she is "not a
   scholar" of the English language (1)? How does she otherwise establish her authority on the subject? How well does she do it?

2. Tan first gives **EXAMPLES** of "family talk" and only later classifies them (4, 21).
   Why do you think she follows this order? Why not give the categories first, then
   the specific examples?

3. What specific kind of English, by Tan's classification, is represented by paragraph 6 of her essay?

4. Besides classifying Englishes, Tan also includes NARRATIVES about using them. What do the narratives contribute to her essay? How would the essay be different without the stories?

5. In which paragraphs is Tan advancing an ARGUMENT about achievement tests? What is her point here, and how does she use her different Englishes to support that point?

## WORDS AND FIGURES OF SPEECH

1. Explain the PUN in Tan's title. What does it tell us about the essay?

2. By what standards, according to Tan, is "standard" English to be established and measured (3)?

3. What are some of the implications of using such terms as *broken* or *fractured* to refer to nonstandard forms of speech or writing (8)?

4. Do you find "simple" to be better or worse than "broken"? How about "watered down" (21)? Explain.

5. Tan does not give a term for the kind of English she uses to represent her mother's "internal language" (21). What name would you give it? Why?

## FOR WRITING

1. Many families have private jokes, code words, gestures, even family whistles. In a paragraph or two, give examples of your family's private speech or language. How does each function within the family? In relation to the family and the outside world?

2. How many different Englishes (and other languages) do you use at home, at school, among friends, and elsewhere? Write an essay classifying them, giving the characteristics of each, and explaining how and when each is used.

JACK HITT

# THE DOLLAR-STORE ECONOMY

JACK HITT (b. 1957) grew up in Charleston, South Carolina, and graduated from the University of the South in Sewanee, Tennessee, in 1979. His articles and essays appear frequently in such magazines as *Rolling Stone*, *Wired*, and *Outside*. As a contributing editor to the *New York Times*, *Harper's*, and *This American Life*, Hitt has covered everything from undergraduate drinking and presidential politics to Internet spam and featherless chickens. He is the author, most recently, of *Bunch of Amateurs: A Search for the American Character* (2012). In "The Dollar-Store Economy" (*New York Times*, 2011), Hitt classifies retail outlets in "the basement of American capitalism." Like an archeologist digging through "the detritus of a hyperproductive global manufacturing system," he divides this "stratum" into various levels—and uncovers a new breed of shopper inspired by the recession.

•┝─────────────────────────────────────────────────────────┤•

HEATHER MANN WRITES a blog called Dollar Store Crafts, which evolved 1
from her occasional trips to the extreme-discount dollar stores near her
home in Salem, Oregon. Her readers admire her gift for buying really cheap

stuff and then making cool and beautiful things from the pile. Her knockoff "alien abduction lamp" is jury-rigged from a small light fixture, two plastic bowls (flying saucer), a clear acrylic tumbler (tractor beam) and a small plastic toy cow (abductee)—all purchased for about five bucks.

As we entered her favorite store, a Dollar Tree in Salem, Mann warned me that I'd have to hustle to keep up with her. "Look at these," she said. "Cute." Before I could even examine her find—a rack of smushy yellow chickens on sticks (plastic toy? garden ornament? edible peeps?)—she had ricocheted down another aisle, where I found her studying a prominent display garishly pushing a superabsorbent shammy. Mann noted that this was not the famously kitschy ShamWow! but a very cheap imitation called, merely, Wow. The display boasted, "As Seen on TV."

"As in, you've seen the *real* ad on TV," she said.

All around, the stacks of products and aisles of merchandise screamed a technicolor siren song. I found four AA batteries for my tape recorder for a dollar ($5.49 when I spotted them the next day at RadioShack), and dish towels that might have sold for $5 elsewhere were just a buck. Mann now brandished something called a "wineglass holder" the way Jacques Cousteau might have held up a starfish. It was a small aluminum device meant to clip onto your plastic picnic plate "for hands-free dining and socializing." At a price of four for a dollar, it's a good deal if your world is overrun with miserly wine connoisseurs.

When I looked up, Mann was already around the corner, having fun with a bottle of discount detergent boasting a "bingo bango mango" scent. Just up the way was a bin of brown bags marked either "A Surprise for a Boy" or "A Surprise for a Girl." Mann's five-year-old niece accompanied us on our tour and was crazed with excitement over these, and the truth is, we were all in the same exact mood. All around us, See p. 222 on how your purpose affects your classification. strange things hung here and there, urging us on an unending treasure hunt. Perhaps, like me, you have driven by and occasionally stopped in a dollar store and assumed that there were two kinds of customers, those there for the kitschy pleasure of it all—the Heather Manns of the world—and those for whom the dollar store affords a low-rent version of the American Consumer Experience, a place where the poor can splurge. That's true. But current developments in this, the low end of retail, suggest that a larger shift in the American consumer market is under way.

*A young woman scans an aisle in a Dollar Tree store.*

We are awakening to a dollar-store economy. For years the dollar store has not   6
only made a market out of the detritus of a hyperproductive global manufacturing system, but it has also made it appealing—by making it amazingly
cheap. Before the market meltdown of 2008 and the stagnant, jobless recovery
that followed, the conventional wisdom about dollar stores—whether one of
the three big corporate chains (Dollar General, Family Dollar and Dollar Tree)
or any of the smaller chains (like "99 Cents Only Stores") or the world of
independents—was that they appeal to only poor people. And while it's true
that low-wage earners still make up the core of dollar-store customers
(42 percent earn $30,000 or less), what has turned this sector into a nearly
recession-proof corner of the economy is a new customer base. "What's driving the growth," says James Russo, a vice president with the Nielsen Company, a consumer survey firm, "is affluent households."

The affluent are not just quirky D.I.Y.[1] types. These new customers are   7
people who, though they have money, feel as if they don't, or soon won't. This

1. Abbreviation for "do it yourself."

anxiety—sure to be restoked by the recent stock-market gyrations and generally abysmal predictions for the economy—creates a kind of fear-induced pleasure in selective bargain-hunting. Rick Dreiling, the chief executive of Dollar General, the largest chain, with more than 9,500 stores, calls this idea the New Consumerism. "Savings is fashionable again," Dreiling told me. "A gallon of Clorox bleach, say, is $1.44 at a drugstore or $1.24 at a grocery store, and you pay a buck for it at the Dollar General. When the neighbors come over, they can't tell where you bought it, and you save anywhere from 20 to 40 cents, right?"

Financial anxiety—or the New Consumerism, if you like—has been a boon to dollar stores. Same-store sales, a key measure of a retailer's health, spiked at the three large, publicly traded chains in this year's first quarter—all were up by at least 5 percent—while Walmart had its eighth straight quarterly decline. Dreiling says that much of Dollar General's growth is generated by what he calls "fill-in trips"—increasingly made by wealthier people. Why linger in the canyons of Wal-Mart or Target when you can pop into a dollar store? Dreiling says that 22 percent of his customers make more than $70,000 a year and added, "That 22 percent is our fastest-growing segment." 8

This growth has led to a building campaign. At a time when few businesses seem to be investing in new equipment or ventures or jobs, Dreiling's company announced a few months ago that it would be creating 6,000 new jobs by building 625 new stores this year. Kiley Rawlins, vice president for investor relations at Family Dollar, said her company would add 300 new stores this year, giving it more than 7,000 in 44 states. 9

And yet, how do dollar stores expand and make impressive returns, all the while dealing in an inventory that still largely retails for a few dollars? How does a store sell four AA batteries for $1? In part this market takes advantage of the economy degrading all around it. When I asked Dreiling about the difference in the cost of RadioShack batteries, he said that "RadioShack is probably in a better spot in the same shopping center," while Dollar General might be in a "C+, B site." RadioShack pays the high rent, while the dollar stores inhabit a "no-frills box." 10

The dollar-store combination has more to it than low store rents and really cheap products. The labor force needed to run a dollar store is a tiny, low-wage staff. Do the math of Dreiling's announcement: 6,000 jobs divided by 625 stores equals about 10 jobs per store. 11

Perhaps this is all merely our grandparents' Woolworth's[2] five-and- 12
dime updated by inflation to a dollar and adapted, like any good weed, to distressed areas of the landscape. But a new and eroding reality in American life
underwrites this growing market. Yet even deep discounters have limits. In
early June, Dollar General predicted that its sales growth would slow slightly
for the rest of the year. Dreiling told analysts in a conference call that his company would be very careful about raising prices, even though its costs for fuel
and such were rising. "This sounds almost silly," he said, "but a $1 item going
to $1.15 in our channel is a major change for our customer." Such delicate price
sensitivity suggests what is changing. Howard Levine, the chief executive of
Family Dollar, said to me, although "not necessarily a good thing for our country, more and more people are living paycheck to paycheck."

Profit margins have always been thin in the dollar stores. But now that they 13
are competing for the shrinking disposable income of the middle class, there is
a new kind of consultant out there—the dollar-store fixer. Bob Hamilton
advises the troubled independent-dollar-store manager on the tactics needed
to survive and thrive in the dollar-store economy. One afternoon he drove me
to Beaverton, Oregon, to give me a tour of a Dollar Tree store whose layout
and strategy he thinks is exemplary in its competitive cunning.

In Hamilton's view, the secret of a good dollar store is an obsessive man- 14
ager who can monitor 8,000 to 10,000 items, constantly varying product display tactics, and sense the changing interests of a local customer base. This
frenzied drama requires a sharp eye for tiny details. "The market is moving all
the time," Hamilton said as we entered the store. Right away, he threw up his
arms, thrilled. This was just before Easter, and he pointed out the big holiday
display practically in the doorway, an in-our-face explosion of color and
delight that herded us away from the exit. "The natural inclination is to move
to the right," Hamilton said, nodding at the cash registers on the left. The hunt
was on.

Hamilton pointed out that the aisles are about two inches wider than 15
two shopping carts, which themselves are comically tiny, giving the buyer a

2. The original five-and-dime discount chain that sold general merchandise in stores across
the United States for most of the 20th century.

*An aisle in a dollar store in North Arlington, New Jersey*

sense that even a small pile of goods is lavish. Despite the dollar store's reputation for shoddy products, the *mise-en-scène* nevertheless suggests a kind of luxury, if only of quantity. "The first thing you feel is this thing is packed with merchandise," Hamilton said, pointing out the high shelves along the walls. Helium balloons strained upward, everywhere. Any empty wall space was filled with paper signage proclaiming savings or "$1" and framing the store's goods.

But wait! There, in the middle of the aisle, was a tower of candy boxes, 16 razored open and overflowing with cheap sweets. "They do this a lot with facial tissue or back-to-school items," Hamilton said. But it was blocking the aisle—a deadly error in his view. Worse are the managers who deliberately create cul-de-sacs by closing off the back of an aisle with goods. "You have to turn around and come back!" Hamilton said, shaking his head in disbelief. "You just watch the customers, and they will skip the aisle, every one of them."

The idea, Hamilton explained, is to create a kind of primal experience     17
and a certain meditative flow. "My theory was to get them in a pattern, and
they will just go up and down and go, 'Oh, I forgot I need that,' and pick it up."

At one point in the tour, Hamilton spotted patches of bare shelf space     18
and was practically ashamed. His model store was committing egregious mistakes. "This is probably the worst aisle we've been down," he whispered. He
dashed to a single barren metal hook and pointed in horror. "They have an
empty peg! People are thinking, I'm getting the last one!" The stuffed bins, the
boxes on wood pallets sitting on the floor, the merchandise piled to the
ceiling—all this breeds an excited sense that everything just got here and
you're getting to it first.

"You always keep things full," he said. And always keep the higher part     19
of the shelves engorged with product. "People buy at eye level," he added.
Hamilton advised that products should be hung in vertical strips so that in a
walk up the aisle, the eye can distinguish one item from the next. We arrived
to a back wall covered entirely in plastic, pillar after pillar of household cleaning supplies, a kaleidoscopic blaze of primary colors. Bob Hamilton was one
happy man.

"Shopping is our hunting and gathering," says Sharon Zukin, a professor     20
of sociology at Brooklyn College who specializes in consumer culture and suggests that the dollar-store experience is a mere updating of our evolutionary
instincts. "This bare-bones aesthetic puts across the idea that there is nothing
between you the consumer and the goods that you desire. You are a bargain
hunter, and it's not like a bazaar or open-market situation in other regions of
the world. It doesn't require personal haggling between the shopkeeper and
the shoppers. Right? The price is set, and it's there for the taking. In many
cases the cartons there have not been unpacked! You are getting the product
direct from the anonymous large-scale producer. You have bagged the deer:
you have your carton of 36 rolls of toilet paper."

As strange as sociological metaphors sound in this context, this is very     21
close to how the corporate chain executives describe the next stage of dollar-
store evolution, as they try to please their new, more affluent customer. Both
Dollar General and Family Dollar are moving toward uniformity in their design
and layout, throwing off the serendipity that came of buying random lots and
salvage goods and was so admired by, say, crafts bloggers. The new design has

opened up the front of the stores "for those whose trip is all about, 'I'm getting what I need and getting out,'" said Rawlins of Family Dollar. As a result, the design of the store is no longer catch-as-catch-can but built around groupings of products that all make sense for the mission-oriented hunter. Store designers call these groupings "adjacencies" and draw them up in fine detail in an architectural schematic called a planogram. Toys, wrapping paper and gift cards, for instance, are laid out in a logical sequence that has been revealed by elaborate customer research and designed with precision.

"A hundred percent of our stores are planogrammed," Dreiling of Dollar    22
General says. "We used to have what was called 'flex space,' and 25 percent of the store was where the store manager could put in whatever they wanted." No more. "Everything is planogrammed now."

"Today we have very little in terms of closeouts," said Family Dollar's    23
Rawlins. "Forty-five percent of our merchandise are national brands that we carry every day." Even though the goods are still deeply discounted, the stores will begin to have a similar look and layout—like the higher-end stores already do. Same inventory, same layout, same experience—from coast to coast.

As all these stores expand into really cheap food, they are creating their own    24
store brands. Just as A&P long ago, or Target more recently, pronounced its market significance by creating store brands like Ann Page or Archer Farms foods, Family Dollar now sells Family Gourmet packaged meals, and Dollar General promotes its line of discounted packaged foods with the bucolic handle Clover Valley.

\* \* \*

What does all this mean for the independent dollar stores? Is there a place for    25
them in the evolving dollar-store economy? There is, but only if they are willing to hustle for pennies.

I called JC Sales, one of the big warehouse suppliers of independent dol-    26
lar stores located south of Los Angeles, and talked to Wally Lee, director of marketing and technology. He agreed there was little room for error now. If I wanted to open a dollar store, I asked him, where would he suggest I locate it? "Right next to a Wal-Mart or a Target," he said. And how large should my new store be? "If you want to be profitable, start with an 8,000-square-foot store," he said. "That is the most optimally profitable among all our customers." Stores can be as small as 1,000 square feet and go up to 20,000, but Lee

implied that there is practically an algorithm of size, labor and expenses—8,000 to 10,000 square feet is profitability's sweet spot. But it's not all science, Lee said. The very absence of a planogram is the other advantage independents can have.

"You need to have a good store manager who loves to talk to people," Lee said. "If it is a Spanish market, then it has to be a Spanish manager to speak to them to see what their needs are. If you don't do that, you'll never beat anybody else." 27

In other words, even as the corporate chains standardize their inventory and planogram their stores down to the last Wow shammy, the independents flourish by retaining a Bob Hamilton-like sensibility—the sense that the market is in motion—with managers buzzing about the store, constantly tweaking the inventory, moving stuff around, ordering things that people request, changing the lineup again, trying out a different placement, listening, yakking, and hand-trucking more product onto the floor. 28

In the basement of American capitalism, you can see the invisible hand at work, except it's not invisible. It's actually your hand. 29

The streamlining of the big dollar stores opens up, for other outlets, their original source of cheap merchandise: distressed goods, closeouts, overstock, salvage merchandize, department-store returns, liquidated goods, discontinued lines, clearance items, ex-catalog stock, freight-damaged goods, irregulars, salvage cosmetics, test-market items and bankruptcy inventories. 30

This secondary market supplies another stratum of retail chains below the dollar-store channel, one of the best known being Big Lots. Hamilton explained that if these guys don't sell the merchandise, it bumps on down the line to another level known as liquidators. 31

Hamilton drove me out to Steve's Liquidators outside Portland, Oregon. It was marked by only a sign on the road. The store itself was an unadorned massive warehouse, with not even a sign over the door, a Euclidean concrete cube painted a bright lime green with lemon yellow trim. 32

As we entered, a scruffy man exited, pushing a busted cart—each palsied wheel pulling in a different direction—into a busy parking lot brimming with older-model automobiles. Inside, the store could not have been more spare, a decrepit imitation of a standard suburban grocery store. Exposed warehouse ceilings above, and below, an unfinished shop floor occupied by metal indus- 33 trial shelving with aisles wide and deep enough to forklift in the goods. Here is where food products minutes away from expiration hover, on the cusp of becoming compost.

A pallet of giant restaurant-grade cans formed a giant ingot of eggplant   34
in tomato sauce. Hamilton examined the cans, each dented and dinged, labels torn—all still sitting on a wooden pallet, partly in its shrink-wrap. "Must have fallen off a truck," he mused. There were sparse fruits and vegetables and rows of salvaged canned goods. Scattered throughout and along the sides were whatever else had been left behind at the dollar stores and then the closeout stores and maybe even the thrift shops—dozens of princess night lights, a single mattress leaning against a wall, a pallet of car oil, an array of carpets, a thousand boxes of the same generic cornflakes, a leaf blower. Back in the car, I asked Hamilton where the merchandise would go if it didn't sell here.

"The Dumpster," he said.   35

## FOR DISCUSSION

1. Why, according to Jack Hitt, are Americans, even affluent ones, shopping more and more frequently in dollar stores? Is his assessment accurate? Explain.

2. Do you agree that "shopping is our hunting and gathering" (20)? Why or why not?

3. Hitt says that the economy represented by dollar stores, particularly the larger chains, is "evolving" (25). In what ways? For what **PURPOSE** do species usually evolve?

4. Dollar stores have low profit margins, so how do the successful ones make money (13)? What are some of the earmarks of a successful dollar store, according to Hitt?

## STRATEGIES AND STRUCTURES

1. What is Hitt's main purpose in exploring the lower ranks of retail outlets in America? Where does he first state the general point he is making by **CLASSIFYING** different types of discount stores?

2. Hitt divides dollar stores into two basic categories. What are they, and what are some of the main traits that distinguish the two types?

3. If independent dollar stores constitute "the basement of American capitalism," what is the sub-sub-sub-basement (29)? Where does a chain like Big Lots fit in

this secondary classification system? How about Steve's Liquidators outside Portland, Oregon (32)? Explain.

4. By what specific traits does Hitt distinguish among various types in the "stratum of retail chains below the dollar-store channel" (31)? Point out several EXAMPLES, including ones that occupy an entire paragraph.

5. As Hitt delves into the nether regions of the dollar-store economy, he talks about encounters with various guides, such as the crafts blogger Heather Mann (1–5). How and how well do these ANECDOTES help the reader sort out and understand the different categories Hitt is identifying?

### WORDS AND FIGURES OF SPEECH

1. Comment on the IRONY of Hitt's reference to a Dollar Tree store that is "exemplary in its competitive cunning" (13).

2. The French term *mise-en-scène* (literally "put in the scene") refers to the staging of a play (15). Why does Hitt appropriate this term from the theater to DESCRIBE a dollar store in Beaverton, Oregon?

3. "You have bagged the deer," says the sociology professor whom Hitt cites as an expert on consumer culture (20). What deer? Explain her METAPHOR.

4. Google "invisible hand" and Adam Smith, the Scottish philosopher who coined it (29). What did Smith mean by the term, and how has it come to be used by modern economists?

5. At the bottom of the dollar-store food chain, Hitt finds dated goods "on the cusp of becoming compost" (33). In what sense is he using the word *cusp* in an essay about trends in retailing?

### FOR WRITING

1. Visit a Sears, Walmart, or other department store and make a list of the main categories of goods and services it provides as suggested by the store's signage, including "planograms."

2. Choose a "stratum" (high-end, low-end, middle, other) of retail outlets, including car dealerships, and write an essay classifying the different kinds of businesses you find in that stratum. Mention particular people you encounter, and try to relate your classification to the economy in general.

# STOP CODDLING THE SUPER-RICH

Warren Buffett (b. 1930) is the CEO of Berkshire Hathaway, a holding company headquartered in Omaha, Nebraska. One of the richest men in the world and widely regarded as the most successful investor of his generation, the "Sage of Omaha" has pledged to donate approximately 99 percent of his wealth to charitable causes. He once said, "I want to give my kids just enough so that they would feel that they could do anything, but not so much that they would feel like doing nothing." Except for owning a private jet named *The Indefensible*, Buffett lives modestly in a house he purchased in 1957 for $31,500. In "Stop Coddling the Super-Rich" (*New York Times*, 2011), Buffett uses a classification system based on income (and equity) to argue for an increase in taxes for the wealthiest Americans, classifying them in general as "those making more than $1 million." A version of this "Buffett rule" was considered by the U.S. Senate as part of the Paying a Fair Share Act of 2012, but it failed to attract enough votes to move forward.

Our leaders have asked for "shared sacrifice." But when they did the asking, they spared me. I checked with my mega-rich friends to learn what pain they were expecting. They, too, were left untouched.

While the poor and middle class fight for us in Afghanistan, and while most Americans struggle to make ends meet, we mega-rich continue to get our extraordinary tax breaks. Some of us are investment managers who earn billions from our daily labors but are allowed to classify our income as "carried interest," thereby getting a bargain 15 percent tax rate. Others own stock index futures for 10 minutes and have 60 percent of their gain taxed at 15 percent, as if they'd been long-term investors.

These and other blessings are showered upon us by legislators in Washington who feel compelled to protect us, much as if we were spotted owls or some other endangered species. It's nice to have friends in high places.

To belong to a particular species, one must exhibit *all* its significant traits, p. 225. Billionaires are rare but not endangered.

Last year my federal tax bill—the income tax I paid, as well as payroll taxes paid by me and on my behalf—was $6,938,744. That sounds like a lot of money. But what I paid was only 17.4 percent of my taxable income—and that's actually a lower percentage than was paid by any of the other 20 people in our office. Their tax burdens ranged from 33 percent to 41 percent and averaged 36 percent.

If you make money with money, as some of my super-rich friends do, your percentage may be a bit lower than mine. But if you earn money from a job, your percentage will surely exceed mine—most likely by a lot.

To understand why, you need to examine the sources of government revenue. Last year about 80 percent of these revenues came from personal income taxes and payroll taxes. The mega-rich pay income taxes at a rate of 15 percent on most of their earnings but pay practically nothing in payroll taxes. It's a different story for the middle class: typically, they fall into the 15 percent and 25 percent income-tax brackets, and then are hit with heavy payroll taxes to boot.

Back in the 1980s and 1990s, tax rates for the rich were far higher, and my percentage rate was in the middle of the pack. According to a theory I sometimes hear, I should have thrown a fit and refused to invest because of the elevated tax rates on capital gains and dividends.

I didn't refuse, nor did others. I have worked with investors for 60 years  8
and I have yet to see anyone—not even when capital gains rates were 39.9 percent in 1976–77—shy away from a sensible investment because of the tax
rate on the potential gain. People invest to make money, and potential taxes
have never scared them off. And to those who argue that higher rates hurt job
creation, I would note that a net of nearly 40 million jobs were added between
1980 and 2000. You know what's happened since then: lower tax rates and far
lower job creation.

Since 1992, the I.R.S. has compiled data from the returns of the 400  9
Americans reporting the largest income. In 1992, the top 400 had aggregate
taxable income of $16.9 billion and paid federal taxes of 29.2 percent on that
sum. In 2008, the aggregate income of the highest 400 had soared to
$90.9 billion—a staggering $227.4 million on average—but the rate paid had
fallen to 21.5 percent.

The taxes I refer to here include only federal income tax, but you can be  10
sure that any payroll tax for the 400 was inconsequential compared to income.
In fact, 88 of the 400 in 2008 reported no wages at all, though every one of
them reported capital gains. Some of my brethren may shun work but they all
like to invest. (I can relate to that.)

I know well many of the mega-rich and, by and large, they are very decent  11
people. They love America and appreciate the opportunity this country has
given them. Many have joined the Giving Pledge, promising to give most of
their wealth to philanthropy. Most wouldn't mind being told to pay more in
taxes as well, particularly when so many of their fellow citizens are truly
suffering.

Twelve members of Congress will soon take on the crucial job of rear-  12
ranging our country's finances.[1] They've been instructed to devise a plan that
reduces the 10-year deficit by at least $1.5 trillion. It's vital, however, that
they achieve far more than that. Americans are rapidly losing faith in the ability of Congress to deal with our country's fiscal problems. Only action that is

1. Reference to the Congress's Joint Select Committee on Deficit Reduction (popularly known
as the "Supercommittee"), which was unable to come to an agreement on how best to handle
the U.S. budget deficit and disbanded in November 2011.

immediate, real, and very substantial will prevent that doubt from morphing into hopelessness. That feeling can create its own reality.

Job one for the 12 is to pare down some future promises that even a rich America can't fulfill. Big money must be saved here. The 12 should then turn to the issue of revenues. I would leave rates for 99.7 percent of taxpayers unchanged and continue the current 2-percentage-point reduction in the employee contribution to the payroll tax. This cut helps the poor and the middle class, who need every break they can get.                                                     13

But for those making more than $1 million—there were 236,883 such households in 2009—I would raise rates immediately on taxable income in excess of $1 million, including, of course, dividends and capital gains. And for those who make $10 million or more—there were 8,274 in 2009—I would suggest an additional increase in rate.                                                     14

My friends and I have been coddled long enough by a billionaire-friendly Congress. It's time for our government to get serious about shared sacrifice.                                                     15

### FOR DISCUSSION

1. Why does Warren Buffett think legislators in Washington should stop "coddling" the country's richest taxpayers? Do you agree? Why or why not?

2. According to Buffett, how has the federal tax system changed since the 1980s? Should he have said more about the causes of those changes, or is he wise to leave them largely unspecified? Explain.

3. What economic "theory" is Buffett referring to in paragraph 7? Why does he think this view of investment is incorrect? What EVIDENCE does he give?

4. According to Buffett, what specific actions should Congress take in order to do "the crucial job of rearranging our country's finances" (12)? Why does Buffett think these steps are especially needed now?

### STRATEGIES AND STRUCTURES

1. An income tax system is, by definition, a CLASSIFICATION system. As laid out by Buffett, what are some of the principle categories of the present system of classifying taxpayers and their incomes in the United States?

2. How and how well does Buffett use these various categories to support his ARGUMENT that the system needs to be changed? Point out specific EXAMPLES in the text that you find particularly effective.

3. When and where does Buffett use mainly ANECDOTAL evidence to make his case? When does he turn to statistics? Should he have included more (or fewer) numbers? Explain.

4. Many wealthy people, says Buffett, "classify our income as 'carried interest'" (2). How and how well does this example support Buffett's claim that such a classification system is faulty?

5. "I know well many of the 'mega-rich' and, by and large, they are very decent people" (11). How and how well does Buffett establish his credibility as someone qualified to speak authoritatively about each of these categories? Explain.

## WORDS AND FIGURES OF SPEECH

1. If the "mega-rich," according to Buffett's classification system, are "those who make $10 million or more" (14), how does the system DEFINE the merely "super-rich"?

2. *Coddled* is a word usually reserved for children. What does it mean, and why does Buffett use the term to refer to a particular economic class (or classes)?

3. In Buffett's accounting of the traits and conditions that define the super-rich, what are the implications of the word *blessings* (3)? Of "showered" (3)?

4. Why does Buffett put "shared sacrifice" in quotation marks at the beginning of his essay but not at the end (1, 15)?

## FOR WRITING

1. Check out the Internal Revenue Service's website at www.irs.gov. Make a list of the main categories of information and services on the site.

2. Many banks and lending institutions in the United States identify a category of customers whom they call the "mass affluent." Write a classification essay about this socioeconomic group that explains its common traits and divides this general category into subgroups. Be sure to explain why bankers and stockbrokers might be particularly interested in this segment of the American population.

JULIO M. OTTINO AND GARY SAUL MORSON

# BUILDING A BRIDGE BETWEEN ENGINEERING AND THE HUMANITIES

JULIO M. OTTINO (b. 1951) and GARY SAUL MORSON (b. 1948) jointly authored the essay "Building a Bridge between Engineering and the Humanities," which was first published in the *Chronicle of Higher Education* (2016). Ottino grew up in La Plata, Argentina, and pursued a career as an artist before moving to the United States to earn a PhD in chemical engineering; today, he is dean of the Robert R. McCormick School of Engineering and Applied Sciences at Northwestern University. Morson, originally from New York City, once planned to be a physicist; he now teaches Slavic Literature and the History of Ideas, also at Northwestern. Both scholars are members of the American Academy of Arts and Sciences. In their essay, they argue for interdisciplinary studies centered on what is shared by scientists and artists alike—the creative process.

THE ENGINEERING FIELD IS BOOMING these days. Society regards it as an essential part of innovation, and colleges promote a degree in it as an entry into a fruitful, sustaining career. The humanities, by contrast, are in peril, with fewer students each year.

We want to bridge this divide and help create a system where the two areas are not separate but are essential to each other. One of us began his studies in art and is now dean of an engineering school, and the other is an expert in Russian literature who originally planned to study physics.

We know that engineering and the humanities differ not just in subject matter but in the very kinds of thinking they encourage. So the question is not just what information from each domain might be useful to the other, but also what each could learn by imagining the world in a whole new way.

See p. 225 for more on thesis statements in classification essays.

In the United States, we are uniquely positioned to bring these two cultures together because, unlike in Europe and South America, students here are expected to learn much more than their specialty. This makes interdisciplinary interactions involving the left brain—analytical, convergent, and quantitative skills associated with science and engineering—and right brain—artistic and humanistic abilities—easier to achieve. Doing so will result in much more talented and versatile engineers and humanists, but it will require vast changes at every level.

By its very nature, engineering is creative and directed to human uses. All too often, however, engineering education postpones or overlooks both. Instead, it is presented as a process of absorption, followed only much later by the production of something new.

Students master routine solving of well-understood problems. Textbooks present current knowledge as timeless truths, as if they had been handed down by divine revelation. Students are told to be creative only at the very end of their studies, in a senior thesis or a design project. Imagine if poets were trained to identify meters but to suspend actually using them to create a poem for several years.

Fortunately, teaching in engineering has evolved significantly over the past decade or so, though not in all places and not all at the same rate. Instead of simply passing on knowledge, the best programs now try to foster experiential learning. Teams rule, and in place of homogenous courses with all engineers in the same discipline, new courses pull together teams from multiple disciplines, including many outside of engineering.

In the arts and humanities, creative and metaphorical thinking come into 8 play early on. Basic literature courses do not teach mastery of a body of material—not just because there is no such body but because it isn't clear what "mastery of material" would mean. Literature does not aspire to transfer information per se; one must get personally involved.

Like literature, engineering sometimes works not by satisfying recog- 9 nized needs but by creating the needs it satisfies. From the first day of class, the good literature professor does not try to transfer knowledge about poems but models the process of imaginative interpretation of a poem. Good literature lectures are a form of improvisational performance exhibiting what it is like to experience a story, a novel, or a great painting, and arrive at an interpretation. That is the real lesson, not the interpretation itself.

What if more engineers contemplated their work similarly? By the same 10 token, if humanists understood how scientists and engineers think, and if they were not mystified by mathematics, experimentation, and the testing characteristic of those disciplines, they would appreciate their own distinctive ways of thinking and grasp opportunities to contribute something distinctive.

The Russian Formalist critic Victor Shklovsky argued that art demands 11 we reverse the usual process of learning. When we acquire a skill, we normally practice it until it is automatic. Learning is, in this sense, a process of familiarization. But sometimes it is important to experience something that has long grown familiar as if for the first time.

Or, as Shklovsky explains, we need to defamiliarize the familiar: "The 12 purpose of art is to impart the sensation of things as they are perceived and not as they are already known. The technique of art is to make objects 'unfamiliar.'"

Acquiring the habit of overcoming habitual perception is one process 13 that brings engineering and the arts together. It is how great writers impart human experience in new ways, and it is how engineers innovate. Technology does not proceed along a preordained single path, as one might suppose from a textbook or problem-solving approach. Like literature, engineering sometimes works not by satisfying recognized needs but by creating the needs it satisfies. And that is also like literature: Tolstoy[1] did not satisfy someone's need for a novel called *Anna Karenina*.

1. Leo Tolstoy (1828–1910), Russian novelist, author of *War and Peace* and *Anna Karenina* most notably.

But Tolstoy did provide his readers with a glimpse into Anna's inner life.  14
Similarly, engineering thrives by going beyond the technical into the realm of
its human users. More and more, engineering education is recognizing the
importance of understanding devices, systems, and processes in terms of the
people who use them.

At the heart of human-centered design is empathy, and empathy is what  15
literature, above all, is good at teaching. When you read a great novel, you
identify with a character, experience what she is experiencing, follow her
thoughts and feelings moment by moment from within. You do this with
people of a different culture, age, gender, social class, nationality, profession,
and religion. You do it with several characters in the course of one long novel,
and not just once, but countless times, until it becomes a habit. Empathy
creates better people and better technical innovations for people to use.

So how do we ensure that more skillful innovators emerge from academe?  16

Boosting enrollments in STEM[2] is not enough. An educational system  17
that merges humanities and sciences, creating whole-brain engineers and sci-
entifically inspired humanists, fosters more than just innovation. It yields
more-flexible individuals who adapt to unanticipated changes as the world
evolves unpredictably.

But it is easy to see why existing systems encourage the opposite. One  18
reason is funding. Most doctoral students in engineering are paid to go to
school, with funding provided by government grants. The demand for results,
the expanding list of compliance mechanisms, and the gravitational pull
toward meeting narrow program goals create a closed system that allows little
time or attention for ancillary pursuits. This process discourages whole-
brainers from even applying.

Alternative graduate programs should cultivate the whole-brain experi-  19
ence that is more often seen at the undergraduate level. One avenue is to
provide courses that bring different modes of thinking, rather than moving
students in parallel, noninteractive tracks. At our institution we have encouraged that kind of thinking in courses that link engineers with artists, both
within our university and with the School of the Art Institute of Chicago.

It should not be rare to have graduate students in science and engineer-  20
ing in literature, philosophy, and history of science courses. It should be the

2. Abbreviation for the disciplines of science, technology, engineering, and mathematics.

norm. It is in the augmentation of possibilities—the things we never knew existed—where remarkable opportunities exist at the intersection of engineering and humanities. The possibilities are vast.

## FOR DISCUSSION

1. According to Julio Ottino and Gary Saul Morson, why is the field of engineering enjoying a boom these days, while the humanities, in their view, are out of favor with students and the public? How accurate is this view in your experience? Explain.

2. Ottino and Morson are not suggesting that, as fields of study, engineering and the humanities should be put in the same class or category. What are they suggesting?

3. Why is the United States "uniquely positioned," in the view of Ottino and Morson, to bridge the gap between the different "cultures" of the two "areas" they are exploring (2, 4)? Are they right? Why or why not?

4. According to Ottino and Morson, why is the "mastery of a body of material" *not* the purpose of taking a literature course (8)? What *is* the purpose in their view? In yours?

5. Ottino and Morson suggest that we can learn about life and others from the study of great literature, such as the novel *Anna Karenina* by the Russian writer Leo Tolstoy. Does it matter that Anna and other characters in literature are not real people? Why or why not?

## STRATEGIES AND STRUCTURES

1. Ottino and Morson refer to their own educational backgrounds in paragraph 2. What is their **PURPOSE** in doing this—and why so near the beginning of their essay?

2. Engineers, according to Ottino and Morson, are traditionally **CLASSIFIED** as "left-brain" thinkers, while poets and other creative types are "right brain" (4). What are some of the more important distinguishing features of the two classes? Point to places in the text where Ottino and Morson cite specific characteristics of each group.

3. Ottino and Morson are advocating a third kind of thinking—"whole brain" (17). What are the main characteristics of this type? Where and how do Ottino and Morson identify this group?

4. In addition to classifying thinkers according to their brain types, Ottino and Morson **COMPARE AND CONTRAST** the two types. How effective is this strategy for supporting their argument in favor of a third class of thinker? Explain.

5. Ottino and Morson's essay appeared in the *Chronicle of Higher Education*, a publication that describes itself as a "source of news, information, and jobs for college and university faculty members and administrators." How appropriate, for such an **AUDIENCE**, is their argument about the need for a kind of thinking that uses both sides of the brain? Why do you think so?

## WORDS AND FIGURES OF SPEECH

1. Although they are writing, in part, about engineers and engineering, Ottino and Morson are not calling for bridges of iron and steel. Explain the **METAPHOR** of their title, "Building a Bridge."

2. STEM is an acronym for Science, Technology, Engineering, and Mathematics (17). What are acronyms and how are they formed? Do you think such linguistic innovations are usually more the province of engineers or of humanists? Explain.

3. Look up *discipline* in the *Online Etymology Dictionary*. What is the root meaning of the word, and how did it come to mean an academic field of study? Why might Ottino and Morson avoid using it?

4. Ottino and Morson quote the Russian formalist critic Victor Shklovsky on "the purpose of art" (12). What's the purpose of this **ALLUSION**? How and how well does it apply to their subject?

5. The word *engineer* is related, etymologically, to the word *ingenious*, meaning "clever, resourceful." Look up the root meanings of the two terms, and explain how they might be used to support the argument that humanities majors should know more about what goes on in STEM courses.

## FOR WRITING

1. In a paragraph, **DEFINE** *empathy* (15) and explain why having this particular characteristic might be good for both humanists and scientists.

2. Write an essay about a course you took (or are taking) in which the instructor modeled (or failed to model) the qualities and characteristics of a person skilled in that field of study. Be sure to specify what some of those most important qualities were and how that person conveyed them to you and your classmates.

# THE MYTH OF RACE

ROBERT WALD SUSSMAN (1941–2016) was a primatologist and anthropologist who devoted decades to studying macaques—a primate group that includes more than 23 species of monkeys—and lemurs. A native of Brooklyn, New York, Sussman completed his PhD at Duke University in 1972 and then joined the anthropology department at Washington University in St. Louis. Among his principal interests was, as he put it, "the evolution of human and nonhuman primate behavior and the ways in which the study of primates can help us understand the biological basis of human behavior." Sussman is best remembered for his book *The Myth of Race: The Troubling Persistence of an Unscientific Idea* (2014), in which he asserts that the commonly understood notion of race is a social construct. In the following excerpt, he explains that classification of human beings by race is a cultural myth, not a biological fact.

•⟩────────────────────────────────────────────────⟨•

R ACISM IS A PART OF OUR EVERYDAY LIVES. Where you live, where you go to     1
school, your job, your profession, who you interact with, how people interact with you, your treatment in the healthcare and justice systems are all

affected by your race. For the past 500 years people have been taught how to interpret and understand racism. We have been told that there are very specific things that relate to race, such as intelligence, sexual behavior, birth rates, infant care, work ethics and abilities, personal restraint, life span, law-abidingness, aggression, altruism, economic and business practices, family cohesion, and even brain size. We have learned that races are structured in a hierarchical order and that some races are better than others. Even if you are not a racist, your life is affected by this ordered structure. We are born into a racist society.

What many people do not realize is that this racial structure is not based   2 on reality. Anthropologists have shown for many years now that there is no biological reality to human race. There are no major complex behaviors that directly correlate with what might be considered human "racial" characteristics. There is no inherent relationship between intelligence, law-abidingness, or economic practices and race, just as there is no relationship between nose size, height, blood group, or skin color and any set of complex human behaviors. However, over the past 500 years, we have been taught by an informal, mutually reinforcing consortium of intellectuals, politicians, statesmen, business and economic leaders, and their books that human racial biology is real and that certain races are biologically better than others. These teachings have led to major injustices to Jews and non-Christians during the Spanish Inquisition[1]; to blacks, Native Americans, and others during colonial times; to African Americans during slavery and reconstruction; to Jews and other Europeans during the reign of the Nazis in Germany; and to groups from Latin America and the Middle East, among others, during modern political times.

I am not going to dwell upon all of the scientific information that has   3 been gathered by anthropologists, biologists, geneticists, and other scientists concerning the fact that there are no such things as human biological races. This has been done by many people over the past fifty or so years. What I am going to do is describe the history of our myth of race and racism....

---

1. A campaign in 15th-century Spain to enforce and maintain Catholic orthodoxy. Its history is controversial, but it is associated with the persecution, expulsion, and murder of thousands of people, principally Jews and Muslims, but many others, as well.

Before beginning this story, however, it is important to understand how   4
scientists define the concept of race. How is race defined in *biological* terms?
What do we mean by the term *race* when describing population variation in
large mammals such as humans? Do the criteria used in describing these variations hold when we examine human population variation? In biological terms,

In addition to classi-
fying, Sussman is
defining key terms
such as "race" and
"species."

the concept of race is integrally bound to the process of evolution
and the origin of species. It is part of the process of the formation
of new species and is related to subspecific differentiation. However, because conditions can change and subspecies can and do
merge (Alan Templeton, 2013), this process does not necessarily lead to the
development of new species. In biology, a species is defined as a population of
individuals who are able to mate and have viable offspring; that is, offspring
who are also successful in reproducing. The formation of new species usually
occurs slowly over a long period of time. For example, many species have a
widespread geographic distribution with ranges that include ecologically
diverse regions. If these regions are large in relationship to the average distance of migration of individuals within the species, there will be more mating, and thus more exchange of genes, within than between regions. Over very
long periods of time (tens of thousands of years), differences would be expected
to evolve between distant populations of the same species. Some of these
variations would be related to adaptations to ecological differences within the
geographic range of the populations, while others might be purely random.
Over time, if little or no mating (or genetic exchange) occurs between these
distant populations, genetic (and related morphological)[2] differences will
increase. Ultimately, over tens of thousands of years of separation, if little or
no mating takes place between separate populations, genetic distinctions can
become so great that individuals of the different populations could no longer
mate and produce viable offspring. The two populations would now be considered two separate species. This is the process of speciation. However, again,
none of these criteria require that speciation will ultimately occur.

Since speciation develops very slowly, it is useful to recognize interme-   5
diate stages in this process. Populations of a species undergoing differentiation would show genetic and morphological variation due to a buildup of

2. When Sussman uses the word *genetic*, he is referring to the actual genes or DNA that
determine the characteristics of a living thing. The term *morphological* refers to the study of
the form and structure of a living thing, which is determined by its genetic makeup.

genetic differences but would still be able to breed and have offspring that could successfully reproduce. They would be in various stages of the process of speciation but not yet different species. In biological terminology, it is these populations that are considered "races" or "subspecies" (Williams 1973; Amato and Gatesy 1994; Templeton 1998, 2013). Basically, subspecies within a species are geographically, morphologically, and genetically distinct populations but still maintain the possibility of successful interbreeding (Smith, Chiszar, and Montanucci 1997). Thus, using this biological definition of race, we assume that races or subspecies are populations of a species that have genetic and morphological differences due to barriers to mating. Furthermore, little or no mating (or genetic exchange) between them has persisted for extremely long periods of time, thus giving the individuals within the population a common and separate evolutionary history.

Given advances in molecular genetics, we now have the ability to examine populations of species and subspecies and reconstruct their evolutionary histories in an objective and explicit fashion. In this way, we can determine the validity of the traditional definition of human races "by examining the patterns and amount of genetic diversity found within and among human populations" (Templeton 1998, 633) and by comparing this diversity with other large-bodied mammals that have wide geographic distributions. In other words, we can determine how much populations of a species differ from one another and how these divergences came about.    6

A commonly used method to quantify the amount of within- to among-group genetic diversity is through examining molecular data, using statistics measuring genetic differences within and between populations of a species. Using this method, biologists have set a minimal threshold for the amount of genetic differentiation that is required to recognize subspecies (Smith, Chiszar, and Montanucci 1997). Compared to other large mammals with wide geographic distributions, human populations do not reach this threshold. In fact, even though humans have the widest distribution, the measure of human genetic diversity (based on sixteen populations from Europe, Africa, Asia, the Americas, and the Australia-Pacific region) falls well below the threshold used to recognize races for other species and is among the lowest value known for large mammalian species. This is true even if we compare humans to chimpanzees (Templeton 2013).    7

Using a number of molecular markers, Templeton (1998, 2013), further, has shown that the degree of isolation among human populations that would    8 have been necessary for the formation of biological subspecies or races never occurred during the 200,000 years of modern human evolution. Combined genetic data reveal that from around one million years ago to the last tens of thousands of years, human evolution has been dominated by two evolutionary forces: (1) constant population movement and range expansion; and (2) restrictions on mating between individuals only because of distance. Thus, there is no evidence of fixed, long-term geographic isolation between populations. Other than some rare, temporary isolation events, such as the isolation of the aborigines of Australia, for example, the major human populations have been interconnected by mating opportunities (and thus genetic mixture) during the last 200,000 years (as long as modern humans, *Homo sapiens*, have been around). As summarized by Templeton (1998, 647), who is among the world's most recognized and respected geneticists,

> because of the extensive evidence for genetic interchange through population movements and recurrent gene flow going back at least hundreds of thousands of years ago, there is only one evolutionary lineage of humanity and there are no subspecies or races. . . . Human evolution and population structure has been and is characterized by many locally differentiated populations coexisting at any given time, but with sufficient contact to make all of humanity a single lineage sharing a common, long-term evolutionary fate.

Thus, given current scientific data, biological races do not exist among modern humans today, and they have never existed in the past. Given such clear scientific evidence as this and the research data of so many other biologists, anthropologists, and geneticists that demonstrate the nonexistence of biological races among humans, how can the "myth" of human races still persist? If races do not exist as a biological reality, why do so many people still believe that they do? In fact, even though biological races do not exist, the concept of race obviously is still a reality, as is racism. These are prevalent and persistent elements of our everyday lives and generally accepted aspects of our culture. Thus, the concept of human races is real. It is not a biological reality, however, but a cultural one. Race is not a part of our biology, but it is definitely a part of our culture. Race and racism are deeply ingrained in our history.

## References

Amato G., and J. Gatesy. 1994. PCR Assays of Variable Nucleotide Sites for Identification of Conservation Units. In B. Schierwater, B. Streit, G. P. Wagner, and R. DeSalle, eds., *Molecular Ecology and Evolution: Approaches and Applications*, 215–226. Basel: Birkhäser Verlag.

Smith, H. M., D. Chiszar, and R. R. Montanucci. 1997. Subspecies and Classification. *Herpetological Review* 28:13–16.

Templeton. A. R. 1998. Human Races: A Genetic and Evolutionary Perspective. *American Anthropologist* 100:632–650.

———. 2013. Biological Races in Humans. *Studies in History and Philosophy of Science Part C: Studies in History and Philosophy of Biological and Biomedical Sciences* 44:262–271.

Williams, B. J. 1973. *Evolution and Human Origins: An Introduction to Physical Anthropology*. New York: Harper & Row.

### FOR DISCUSSION

1. "The formation of new species," says Robert Wald Sussman, "usually occurs slowly over a long period of time" (4). How long? Why is the process of evolving a new species so slow?

2. According to Sussman, two conditions must be met if a new species is to develop. First, members of a population must be physically separated from one another. What is the second condition?

3. Over the last 200,000 years of their existence, modern humans have been separated by "population movement and range expansion," and they have been isolated by "restrictions on mating between individuals only because of distance" (8). Why then, according to Sussman and the other experts he cites, have humans nevertheless remained a single species, without developing subspecies or "races"?

4. If "the concept of race" is a "reality" to many people, as Sussman says, does it matter that there is no biological basis for this concept (9)? Why or why not?

5. "Taxonomy" (or the science of CLASSIFICATION) divides all living things into six general categories. What are they, and how are modern human beings (*Homo sapiens*) classified within this general system?

## STRATEGIES AND STRUCTURES

1. Sussman's basic point is that race is a cultural myth rather than a scientific fact. To develop this **THESIS**, he launches immediately into a scientific **DEFINITION** of "the concept of race" (4). Is this a good way to begin? Why or why not?

2. The concept of race is closely related to that of "species." How and where does Sussman define this basic term in the scientific classification of all living things?

3. As the basis for a biological classification system, how significant and distinctive is being "able to mate and have viable offspring" (4)? Explain.

4. In scientific classification systems, races are not species but "subspecies" (5). What's the difference, according to Sussman? Where and how does he develop this distinction?

5. In addition to redefining race in terms of species and subspecies, Sussman also analyzes "the process of speciation" (4). How and how well does his use of **PROCESS ANALYSIS** support his thesis about the misclassification of human beings?

## WORDS AND FIGURES OF SPEECH

1. "Racism," says Sussman, "is a part of our everyday lives" (1). Ultimately, Sussman is writing about *racism* in addition to *race*. What's the difference between these two closely related terms?

2. *On the Origin of Species* (1859) is the title of the monumental book by Charles Darwin that laid the foundation for the field of modern evolutionary biology. Where and why does Sussman **ALLUDE** to this groundbreaking work?

3. The modern word *taxonomy* derives from a Greek term meaning, in part, "arrangement." How and how well does this ancient meaning help to explain the modern one?

4. What is a *myth*, and why might Sussman use the term when writing that there is "no biological reality to human race" (2)?

5. How and how well might the term *myth* apply to the subject of racism in general? Explain.

## FOR WRITING

1. Citing Sussman and other sources, write an essay on how the scientific classification of human beings and their relatives should bear upon our views of race.

2. Not long ago, ancestors of modern humans would have been referred to as *hominids*. Today, scientists are more likely to call them *hominins* instead. Look up the meanings and history of these two terms, and write an essay explaining the issues they illustrate in the modern, scientific classification of human beings.

# ⁂9⁂

# PROCESS ANALYSIS

THE essays in this chapter are examples of **PROCESS ANALYSIS**\* or "how to" writing. Basically, there are two kinds of process analysis: *directive* and *explanatory*. A directive process analysis explains how to make or do something— for instance, how to throw a boomerang. ("Bring the boomerang back behind you and snap it forward as if you were throwing a baseball."—howstuffworks. com) An explanatory process analysis explains how something works; it tells you what makes the boomerang come back.

Both kinds of analysis break a process into the sequence of actions that lead to its end result. In her sassy memoir *Bossypants*, for example, the comedian Tina Fey explains how to do improvisational comedy by breaking the process into four basic rules. "The first rule of improvisation," Fey writes, "is AGREE. Always agree and SAY YES." Then "add something of your own" (rule 2), continue to make positive statements (rule 3), and treat all "mistakes" as "opportunities" (rule 4).

The end result of improvisational comedy is the audience's laughter. Here's an example of how Fey follows her own "rules" to achieve this end:

> If I start a scene as what I think is very clearly a cop riding a bicycle, but you think I am a hamster in a hamster wheel, guess what? Now I'm a hamster in a hamster wheel. I'm not going to stop everything to explain that it was really supposed to be a bike. Who knows? Maybe I'll end up being a police hamster who's been put on "hamster wheel" duty because I'm "too much of a loose cannon" in the field. In improv there are no

---

\*Words printed in SMALL CAPITALS are defined in the Glossary/Index.

mistakes, only beautiful happy accidents. And many of the world's greatest discoveries have been by accident. I mean, look at the Reese's Peanut
Butter Cup, or Botox.

—Tina Fey, *Bossypants*

In a directive process analysis, you typically use the second-person pronoun
(*you*) because you're giving instructions directly to the reader. Sometimes the
*you* is understood, as in a recipe: *[you] combine the milk with the
eggs, then add a pinch of salt and the juice of one lemon.* In an explanatory process analysis, you typically use the third-person pronouns
(*he, she, it*) because you're giving information *about* something:

Allegra Goodman,
p. 300, uses second-
person point of view
to tell you how to be
a good writer.

> The uneven force caused by the difference in speed between the two
> wings applies a constant force at the top of the spinning boomer-
> ang. . . . Like a leaning bicycle wheel, the boomerang is constantly turn-
> ing to the left or right, so that it travels in a circle and comes back to its
> starting point.
>
> —HOWSTUFFWORKS.COM

Sometimes a process is best explained by *showing* how it works, so you may
want to add diagrams or drawings to the written text. An analysis of how to
throw a boomerang, for example, might benefit from a clearly labeled diagram.

*Bring behind head, then snap forward*

Most processes that you analyze will be linear rather than cyclical. Even if the process is repeatable, your analysis will proceed chronologically step by step, stage by stage to an end result that is different from the starting point. Consider this explanatory analysis of how fresh oranges are turned into orange juice concentrate:

> As the fruit starts to move along a concentrate plant's assembly line, it is first culled. . . . Moving up a conveyer belt, oranges are scrubbed with detergent before they roll on into juicing machines. There are several kinds of juicing machines, and they are something to see. One is called the Brown Seven Hundred. Seven hundred oranges a minute go into it and are split and reamed on the same kind of rosettes that are in the centers of ordinary kitchen reamers. The rinds that come pelting out the bottom are integral halves, just like the rinds of oranges squeezed in a kitchen. Another machine is the Food Machinery Corporation's FMC In-line Extractor. It has a shining row of aluminum teeth. When an orange tumbles in, the upper jaw comes crunching down on it while at the same time the orange is penetrated from below by a perforated steel tube. As the jaws crush the outside, the juice goes through the perforations in the tube and down into the plumbing of the concentrate plant. All in a second, the juice has been removed and the rind has been crushed and shredded beyond recognition.
>
> From either machine, the juice flows on into a thing called the finisher, where seeds, rag, and pulp are removed. The finisher has a big stainless-steel screw that steadily drives the juice through a fine-mesh screen. From the finisher, it flows on into holding tanks.
>
> —JOHN McPHEE, *Oranges*

John McPhee divides the process of making orange juice concentrate from fresh fruit into five stages: (1) culling, (2) scrubbing, (3) extracting, (4) straining, (5) storing. When you plan an essay that analyzes a process, make a list of all the stages or phases in the process you are analyzing. Make sure that they are separate and distinct and that you haven't left any out. When you are satisfied that your list is complete, you are ready to decide upon the order in which you will present the steps.

The usual order of process analysis is chronological, beginning with the earliest stage of the process (the culling of the split and rotten oranges from the rest) and ending with the last, or with the finished product (concentrated orange juice in holding tanks). Notice that after they leave the conveyer belt, McPhee's oranges come to a fork in the road. They can go in different directions, depending upon what kind of juicing machine is being used. McPhee briefly follows the oranges into one kind of juicer and then comes back to the other. He has stopped time and forward motion for a moment. Now he picks them up again and proceeds down the line: "from either machine, the juice flows on into a thing called the finisher" where it is strained. From the straining stage, the orange concentrate goes into the fifth (and final) holding stage, where it is stored in large tanks.

An early stage in becoming a man, says Jon Katz, p. 294, is learning to show no fear.

Another lesson to take away from McPhee: if the order of the process you are analyzing is controlled by a piece of machinery or other mechanism, let it work for you. McPhee, in fact, lets several machines—conveyor belt, extractor, and finisher—help him organize his analysis.

Some stages in a process analysis may be more complicated than others. Suppose you are explaining to someone how to replace a light switch. You might break the process down into six stages: (1) select and purchase the new switch; (2) turn off the power at the breaker box; (3) remove the switch plate; (4) disconnect the old switch and install the new one; (5) replace the switch plate; (6) turn the power back on. Obviously, one of these stages—"disconnect the old switch and install the new one"—is more complicated than the others. When this happens, you can break down the more complicated stage into smaller steps, as McPhee does with his analysis of the production of orange juice concentrate.

The most complicated stage in McPhee's process analysis is the third one, extracting. He breaks it into the following steps: (1) an orange enters the extractor; (2) it is crushed by the extractor's steel jaws; (3) at the same time, the orange is "penetrated from below by a perforated steel tube"; (4) the extracted juice flows on to the next stage of the process. All of this happens "in a second," says McPhee; but for purposes of analysis and explanation, the steps must be presented in sequence, using such TRANSITIONS

as "when," "while at the same time," "all in a second," "from . . . to," "next,"
and "then."

McPhee's process analysis is explanatory; it tells how orange juice concentrate is made. When you are telling someone how to do something (a directive process analysis), the method of breaking the process into
steps and stages is the same. Here's how our analysis of how to
change a light switch might break down the most complicated
step in the process, the one where the old switch is removed and
replaced. The transitions and other words that signal the order
and timing of the steps *within* this stage are printed in italics:

Edward O. Wilson
uses this kind of
process analysis to
explain how to
become a scientist,
p. 288.

> To remove the old switch, *first* unscrew the two terminal screws on the
> sides. *If* the wires are attached to the back of the switch, *instead* clip off
> the old wires as close to the switch as possible. As necessary, strip the
> insulation from the ends of the wires *until* approximately half an inch is
> exposed. *Next*, unscrew the green grounding screw, *and* disconnect the
> bare wire attached to it. You are *now* ready to remove the old switch and
> replace it with the new one. *Either* insert the ends of the insulated wires
> into the holes on the back of the new switch, *or* bend the ends of the
> wires around the terminal screws *and* tighten the screws. *Reattach* the
> bare wire to the green terminal. *Finally*, secure the new switch by tight-
> ening the two long screws at top and bottom into the ears on the old
> switch box.

Explaining this stage in our analysis is further complicated because we have to
stop the flow of information (with "if . . . instead"; "either . . . or . . . and") to
go down a fork in the road—the wires can be attached either to the screws on
the sides of the switch or to holes in the rear—before getting back on track.
And we now have to signal a move on to the next stage: "Once the new switch
is installed, replacing the switch plate is a snap."

Actually, this simple next-to-last stage (before turning the power back
on) requires a *twist* of the little screw in the center of the switch plate, which
can serve to remind us that the forward movement of a process analysis, step
by step, from beginning to end, is much like the twisting and turning of the

PLOT in a NARRATIVE—a process is a sequence of events or actions. You are the NARRATOR, and you are telling the exciting story of how something is made or done or how it works. Also as with a narrative, you will want your process analysis to make a point so the reader knows why you're analyzing the process and what to expect. When Tina Fey analyzes how to do improv, for example, she is also careful to explain that "the rules of improvisation appealed to me not only as a way of creating comedy, but as a worldview."

You may simply conclude your story with the product or end result of the process you've been analyzing. But you may want to round out your account by summarizing the stages you have just gone through or by encouraging the reader to follow your directions—"Changing a light switch yourself is easy, and it can save money"—or by explaining why the process is important. The production of orange juice concentrate, for example, transformed Florida's citrus industry. In what is called "the old fresh-fruit days," 40 percent of the oranges grown in Florida were left to rot in the fields because they couldn't travel well. "Now," as McPhee notes, "with the exception of split and rotten fruit, all of Florida's orange crop is used." This is not exactly the end product of the process McPhee is analyzing, but it is an important consequence and one that makes technical advances in the citrus industry seem more worth reading about.

One other detail, though a minor one, in McPhee's analysis that you may find interesting: when all that fresh fruit was left to rot on the ground because it couldn't be shipped and local people couldn't use it all, the cows stepped in to help. Thus McPhee notes that in the days before orange juice concentrate, "Florida milk tasted like orangeade." Details like this may not make the process you are analyzing clearer or more accurate, but they may well make the reader more interested in the process itself.

# A BRIEF GUIDE TO WRITING
# A PROCESS ANALYSIS

As you write a PROCESS ANALYSIS, you need to say what process you're analyzing and to identify some of its most important steps. These moves are fundamental to any process analysis. Allegra Goodman makes these basic moves in her essay in this chapter:

> Forthwith, some advice for those of you who have always wanted to write.... To begin, don't write about yourself.... [I]f you want to be a writer, start by writing about other people.... Find a peaceful place to work.... Read widely.... value your own time.
>
> —ALLEGRA GOODMAN, "So, You Want to Be a Writer? Here's How."

Goodman identifies the process she's analyzing (how "to be a writer") and indicates the most important steps that make up the process (write "about other people," "find a peaceful place to work," "read widely," "value your own time").

The following guidelines will help you to make these basic moves as you draft a process analysis. They will also help you to choose a process to analyze, divide it into steps, and put those steps in order, using appropriate transitions and pronouns.

## Coming Up with a Subject

Your first challenge is to find a process worth analyzing. You might start by considering processes you are already familiar with, such as running a marathon, training a puppy, or playing a video game. Or you might think about processes you are interested in and want to learn more about. Do you wonder how bees make honey, how to tune a guitar, how to change the oil in a car engine, or how the oil and gas in your car are produced and refined? Whatever process you choose, you will need to understand it fully yourself before you can explain it clearly to your readers.

## Considering Your Purpose and Audience

When your PURPOSE is to tell readers how to do something, a basic set of instructions will usually do the job, as when you give someone the recipe for your Aunt Mary's famous pound cake. When, however, you want your AUDIENCE to understand, not duplicate, a complicated process—such as the chemistry that makes a cake rise—your analysis should be explanatory. So instead of giving instructions ("add the sugar to the butter"), you would go over the inner workings of the process in some detail, telling readers, for example, what happens when they add baking powder to the cake mixture.

The nature of your audience will also influence the information you include. How much do your intended readers already know about the process? Why might they want to know more, or less? If you are giving a set of instructions, will they require any special tools or equipment? What problems are they likely to encounter? Will they need to know where to find more information on your topic? Asking questions like these will help you select the appropriate steps and details.

## Generating Ideas: Asking How Something Works

When you analyze a process, the essential question to ask yourself is *how*. How does a cake rise? How do I back out of the garage? To get started, ask yourself a

Or pick a lock (p. 304)? Or benefit from suffering (p. 312)?

"how" question about your subject, research the answer (if necessary), and write down all the steps involved. For instance, "How do I back out of the garage?" might result in a list like this: put the car in reverse, step on the gas, turn the key in the ignition, look in the rearview mirror. Although this list includes all the essential steps for backing a car out of a garage, you wouldn't want your reader to follow them in this order. Once you have a complete list of steps, think about the best order in which to present them to your reader. Usually it will be chronological: turn the key in the ignition, put the car in reverse, look in the rearview mirror, and step lightly on the gas pedal.

Also think about whether you should demonstrate the process—or a complex part of it—visually. If you decide to include one or more diagrams or drawings, make sure there are words to accompany each visual. Either DESCRIBE what the visual shows, or label the parts of a diagram (the parts of an engine, for instance).

## Templates for Analyzing a Process

The following templates can help you to generate ideas for an essay that analyzes a process and then to start drafting. Don't take these as formulas where you just have to fill in the blanks. There are no easy formulas for good writing. But these templates can help you plot out some of the key moves of process analysis and thus may serve as good starting points.

> ▶ In order to understand how process X works, we can divide it into the following steps: \_\_\_\_\_, \_\_\_\_\_, and \_\_\_\_\_.
>
> ▶ The various steps that make up X can be grouped into the following stages: \_\_\_\_\_, \_\_\_\_\_, and \_\_\_\_\_.
>
> ▶ The end result of X is \_\_\_\_\_.
>
> ▶ In order to repeat X, you must first \_\_\_\_\_; then \_\_\_\_\_ and \_\_\_\_\_; and finally \_\_\_\_\_.
>
> ▶ The tools and materials you will need to replicate X include \_\_\_\_\_, \_\_\_\_\_, and \_\_\_\_\_.
>
> ▶ The most important reasons for understanding/repeating X are \_\_\_\_\_, \_\_\_\_\_, and \_\_\_\_\_.

For more techniques to help you generate ideas and start writing a process analysis, see Chapter 3.

## Putting the Steps in Order

When you write about a process, you must present its main steps in order. If the process is a linear one, such as backing out of a garage or driving to a particular address in Dallas, you simply start at the earliest point in time and move forward chronologically, step by step, to the end result. If the process is cyclical, such as what's happening in your car engine as you drive, you will have to pick a logical point in the process and then proceed through the rest of the cycle. If, however, the process you are analyzing does not follow a chronology, try arranging the steps from most important to least important, or the other way around.

## Stating Your Point

A good process analysis should have a point to make, and that point should be clearly expressed in a THESIS STATEMENT. Make sure your thesis statement identifies the process, indicates its end result, and tells the reader why you're analyzing it. For example:

> You cannot understand how the Florida citrus industry works without understanding how fresh orange juice gets processed into "concentrate."
>
> —JOHN MCPHEE, *Oranges*

McPhee's thesis statement clearly tells the reader what process he's analyzing (making "concentrate" from fresh oranges), its end result (orange juice concentrate), and why he is analyzing it (to understand the Florida citrus industry).

## Using Appropriate Transitions

As you move from one step to another, include clear TRANSITIONS, such as *next, from there, after five minutes,* and *then.* Because the actions and events that make up a process are repeatable, you will frequently use expressions such as *usually, normally, in most cases,* and *whenever.* Also, use transitions like *sometimes, rarely,* and *in one instance* to note any deviations from the normal order.

## Using Appropriate Pronouns

In addition to appropriate transition words, be careful to use pronouns that fit the kind of analysis you are writing. In an explanatory process analysis, you will focus on the things (oranges) and activities (culling and scrubbing) that make up the process. Thus, you will usually write about the process in the third person (*he, she, it,* and *they*), as John McPhee does: "Moving up a conveyor belt, oranges are scrubbed with detergent before *they* roll on into the juicing machines." In a directive process analysis, by contrast, you are telling the reader directly how to do something as when Tina Fey tells readers how to do improv comedy. So you should typically use the second person (*you*):

"When you're improvising . . . *you* are required to agree with whatever your partner has created."

## Concluding a Process Analysis

A process analysis is not complete until it explains how the process ends— and the significance of that result. For example, in concluding a process analysis about training a puppy, you might say not only what the result will be but why it is important or desirable: "A well-trained dog will behave when guests visit, won't destroy your carpeting and furniture, and will make less work for you in the long run." In the case of processing oranges into concentrate, John McPhee concludes his essay by telling readers not only that the process yielded a new, concentrated form of orange juice, but that it totally changed the Florida citrus industry and saved much of the crop from going to waste—or winding up as orange-flavored milk.

# EDITING FOR COMMON ERRORS
# IN A PROCESS ANALYSIS

Like other kinds of writing, process analysis uses distinctive patterns of language and punctuation—and thus invites typical kinds of errors. The following tips will help you to check for (and correct) these common errors when you analyze a process in your own writing.

### Check to ensure you've used the right pronouns

When you're explaining how something works or is done, make sure you use mostly third-person pronouns (*he, she, it, they*). When you're explaining how to do something, make sure you emphasize the second-person pronoun (*you*).

Here, readers are being told how oranges are processed by others.

▶ When fresh oranges are turned into concentrate, ~~you first scrub them~~ they are first scrubbed with detergent.

Here, readers are being told how to make orange concentrate for themselves.

▶ To turn fresh oranges into concentrate, ~~they are first scrubbed~~ <u>you must first</u>
<u>scrub them</u> with detergent.

## Check your verbs to make sure you haven't shifted needlessly between the indicative and the imperative moods

▶ According to my mother's recipe, ~~add~~ the nuts <u>are added</u>, and then the cinna-
mon is sprinkled on top.

▶ According to my mother's recipe, add the nuts, and then <u>sprinkle</u> the cinna-
mon ~~is sprinkled~~ on top.

# How to Use a Deck-Fastening Tool

When you analyze a process, you explain how to do something, such as fasten planks to make a deck or walkway. This set of instructions for the Camo® Marksman Pro® deck-fastening tool divides the fastening process into the following steps, indicated in both English and Spanish: *set* (*prepare*) the tool in place across the board that you want to fasten; *load* (*cargue*) the tool by inserting a stainless steel screw in each end; and *drive* (*atornille*) the screws into the plank with an electric drill. In addition to giving instructions like this, a process analysis can also explain how something works or is made, as shown in the last panel in black and white. The purpose of using this highly specialized tool is to hold screws at just the right angle for driving them into the wooden planks. This way the planks will be securely fastened and the screws will be more or less invisible from the top, finished side of the new deck.

**PEGAH MORADI**

# SPLITTING HAIRS

Pegah Moradi is from Haymarket, Virginia, and is a student at Cornell University pursuing an interdisciplinary major in computer science and government. She is an opinion columnist for *The Cornell Daily Sun* and an editor for *The Cornell Lunatic*, the university's humor magazine. After graduation, Moradi hopes to attend graduate school to study technology, law, and politics. "Splitting Hairs," which was published in *The Cornell Daily Sun* (2016), uses process analysis to explore themes related to appearance and identity, as demonstrated by Moradi's own relationship with her mother and their shared curly hair.

## Splitting Hairs

I started straightening my own hair when I was in the seventh grade. Before then, I would ask my mother to do it for me. We started when I was just six, sitting cross-legged on our out-of-place Tabriz rugs in our quaint little Boise home. My mother would plug in a thick, two-inch ironing wand. While we waited for it to warm, she would pull my hair out from its elastic prison and begin to torture away its tangles. She would brush. I would scream.

I hated my hair. That's an uncomfortable thing for me to think, let alone write. I think it's accurate though; I hated it. Once I was old enough to take care of it myself, I tied it up in as tight of a ponytail as possible until my curls were flattened by sheer tension. When it got long enough, I would force the ponytail into a Professor McGonagall–style bun,[1] hiding as much of it as possible. I used to brush through it right after I showered, when it was sopping wet, watching as it would straighten out with every brush, then squirm its way back into coils, sort of like how a worm contorts its smooth body into kinks and knots.

Straightening my hair became a skill. My mother and I moved on from the wand to a flat iron. We learned words like *anti-frizz* and *heat-protectant*. We were told about the pricier names like *Chi* and *Biolage*.[2] We traded secrets and shampoos. I'm told I have the same hair as my

1

2

3

> Introduces straightening, the first phase of the hair-care process

> This SIMILE provides a clear picture of what her hair looked like

1. In the *Harry Potter* series, Professor Minerva McGonagall is head-mistress of Hogwarts School; she wears her hair in a bun beneath her witch's hat.

2. Hair-care products sold, respectively, under the brand names Ultra and Matrix.

father, but at this point he hardly has any hair at all. I feel as though I have the same hair as my mother, if you think about hair in a more abstract sense, as in, we don't have the same curl type, but we have the same hair history. My mother told me how she resented her hair growing up, how her mother sat her down and brushed her hair just like my mother brushed mine. How she would cry, but how mothers in 1970s Iran were far less tolerant of whining kids.

> An important part of the process, especially for a writer, is learning the language of hair care

Combatting our curls was our shared language. My           4
mother is graceful, while I have walked into a pole more than once in the past month. She is conventionally feminine, while I spent most of my childhood eating dirt and wearing cargo capris. Nevertheless, I would watch as my mother spent an hour with her arms up in the air, parting her hair and brushing down her tightly wound spirals.

> Moradi figures out how to straighten her hair by watching her mother do it

Near the end of my sophomore year of high school,        5
I walked into my mom's hair salon of choice like a man with a plan, clutching a photo of Carey Mulligan[3] that I printed off of the Internet and a book I had to read for world history class. I was going to get a keratin treatment and make my hair permanently straight, then cut it like Mulligan in the hit 2011 crime drama *Drive*. A few important notes: this plan seemed absolutely horrible to everyone who knew me, I have never seen the movie *Drive*, and my stylist found out I was friends with one of her clients and kept noting how handsome he was the entire time she was doing my hair. Despite these minor setbacks, I left the salon that night running my fingers

3. As Irene in *Drive* (2011), the British actress Carey Mulligan wears her hair in a blond bob.

through my new off-brand—Carey Mulligan hair and feeling a resounding sense of victory. After I had had straight
hair for several months, my mother decided to get the
treatment too.

Over a year ago I stopped straightening my hair, 6
partly because I was bored of it, partly because I felt fake.
I didn't want to hate my hair anymore. Why did I even
hate it so much? I cut off the permanently straight parts
and I read an entire book on curly hair. I took up a new
skill. I figured out how curls should be cut. I googled
videos on how to style spirals straight out of the shower.
I read about what foods to eat for shinier hair. It's a different kind of language, I think. It's easier to speak.

The new word I learned was *free*. As in, *sulfate-free* 7
and *paraben-free*. My mother asks if I want to go back to
the keratin treatment anytime soon. I say no. Her permanent straightener is wearing off. You can start to see her
curls again.

> Entering a new
> phase of the
> process—
> self-acceptance

# FIRST PASSION, THEN TRAINING

Edward Osborne Wilson (b. 1929) is a renowned biologist and ecologist, and an advocate for biodiversity. Twice awarded the Pulitzer Prize for general nonfiction—for *On Human Nature* (1979) and *The Ants* (1991)—Wilson is a professor emeritus at Harvard University, where he also received his PhD. Now retired from classroom teaching, he has published, on average, one book a year. *Letters to a Young Scientist* (2013), a book of 20 letters in which Wilson shares stories and insights about his profession, begins with the following essay. In "First Passion, Then Training," Wilson recalls his boyhood love of spiders and snakes as the first step in a process that would lead him to his life's calling: to become a scientist.

•>————————————————————————————<•

I BELIEVE IT WELL HELP for me to start with this letter by telling you who I really am. This requires your going back with me to the summer of 1943, in the midst of the Second World War. I had just turned fourteen, and my hometown, the little city of Mobile, Alabama, had been largely taken over by the buildup of a wartime 1

**Zoology**

*Merit badge symbol for "Zoology" from the* Boy Scout Handbook, *fourth edition (1940).*

shipbuilding industry and military air base. Although I rode my bicycle around the streets of Mobile a couple of times as a potential emergency messenger, I remained oblivious to the great events occurring in the city and world. Instead, I spent a lot of my spare time—not required to be at school—earning merit badges in my quest to reach the Eagle rank in the Boy Scouts of America. Mostly, however, I explored nearby swamps and forests, collecting ants and butterflies. At home I attended to my menagerie of snakes and black widow spiders.

Global war meant that very few 2 young men were available to serve as counselors at nearby Boy Scout Camp Pushmataha. The recruiters, having heard of my extracurricular activities, had asked me, I assume in desperation, to serve as the nature counselor. I was, of course, delighted with the prospect of a free summer camp experience doing approximately what I most wanted to do anyway. But I arrived at Pushmataha woefully underaged and underprepared in much of anything but ants and butterflies. I was nervous. Would the other scouts, some older than I, laugh at what I had to offer? Then I had an inspiration: *snakes.* Most people are simultaneously frightened, riveted, and instinctively interested in snakes. It's in the genes. I didn't realize it at the time, but the south-central Gulf coast is home to the largest variety of snakes in North America, upward of forty species. So upon arrival I got some of the other campers to help me build some cages from wooden crates and window screen. Then I directed all residents of the camp to join me in a summer-long hunt for snakes whenever their regular schedules allowed.

Thereafter, on an average of several times a day, the cry rang out from 3 somewhere in the woods: Snake! Snake! All within hearing distance would rush to the spot, calling to others, while I, snake-wrangler-in-chief, was fetched.

If nonvenomous, I would simply grab it. If venomous, I would first press 4
it down just behind the head with a stick, roll the stick forward until its head
was immobile, then grasp it by the neck and lift it up. I'd then identify it for
the gathering circle of scouts and deliver what little I knew about the species
(usually very little, but they knew less). Then we would walk to headquarters
and deposit it in a cage for a residence of a week or so. I'd deliver short talks
at our zoo, throw in something new I learned about local insects and other
animals. (I scored zero on plants.) The summer rolled by pleasantly for me and
my small army.

The only thing that could interrupt this happy career was, of course, a 5
snake. I have since learned that all snake specialists, scientists and amateurs
alike, apparently get bitten at least once by a venomous snake. I was not to be
an exception. Halfway through the summer I was cleaning out a cage that contained several pygmy rattlesnakes, a venomous but not deadly species. One
coiled closer to my hand than I'd realized, suddenly uncoiled, and struck me on
the left index finger. After first aid in a doctor's office near the camp, which
was too late to do any good, I was sent home to rest my swollen left hand and
arm. Upon returning to Pushmataha a week later, I was instructed by the adult
director of the camp, as I already had been by my parents, that I was to catch
no more venomous snakes.

At the end of the season, as we all prepared to leave, the director held a 6
popularity poll. The campers, most of whom were assistant snake hunters,
placed me second, just behind the chief counselor. I had found my life's work.
Although the goal was not yet clearly defined then in my adolescent mind, I
was going to be a scientist—and a professor.

Through high school I paid very little attention to my classes. Thanks to 7
the relatively relaxed school systems of south Alabama in wartime, with over-
worked and distracted teachers, I got away with it. One memorable day at
Mobile's Murphy High School, I captured with a sweep of my hand and killed
twenty houseflies, then lined them up on my desk for the next hour's class to
find. The following day the teacher, a young lady with considerable aplomb,
congratulated me but kept a closer eye on me thereafter. That is all I remember, I am embarrassed to say, about my first year in high school.

I arrived at the University of Alabama shortly after my seventeenth 8
birthday, the first member of my family on either side to attend college. I had

by this time shifted from snakes and flies to ants. Now determined to be an entomologist and work in the outdoors as much as possible, I kept up enough effort to make A's. I found that not very difficult (it is, I'm told, *very* different today), but soaked up all the elementary and intermediate chemistry and biology available.

Harvard University was similarly tolerant when I arrived as a Ph.D. student in 1951. I was considered a prodigy in field biology and entomology, and was allowed to make up the many gaps in general biology left from my happy days in Alabama. The momentum I built up in my southern childhood and at Harvard carried through to an appointment at Harvard as assistant professor. There followed more than six decades of fruitful work at this great university.

I've told you my Pushmataha-to-Harvard story not to recommend my kind of eccentricity (although in the right circumstances it could be of advantage); and I disavow my casual approach to early formal education. I grew up in a different age. You, in contrast, are well into a different era, where opportunity is broader but more demanding.

My confessional instead is intended to illustrate an important principle I've seen unfold in the careers of many successful scientists. It is quite simple: put passion ahead of training. Feel out in any way you can what you most want to do in science, or technology, or some other science-related profession. Obey that passion as long as it lasts. Feed it with the knowledge the mind needs to grow. Sample other subjects, acquire a general education in science, and be smart enough to switch to a greater love if one appears. But don't just drift through courses in science hoping that love will come to you. Maybe it will, but don't take the chance. As in other big choices in your life, there is too much at stake. Decision and hard work based on enduring passion will never fail you.

For more details on directive process analysis, see p. 272.

## FOR DISCUSSION

1. As a renowned biologist and science writer, Edward O. Wilson is not recommending "passion" as a substitute for "training" in the process of pursuing a career in science. What is he recommending with regard to passion? Explain.

2. Wilson grew up in Mobile, Alabama, on the south-central Gulf Coast. What about this location contributed to his youthful imagination and his interest in snakes?

3. For students today, says Wilson, opportunity is "broader but more demanding" than in the "different age" in which he grew up (10). What differences is he referring to? Is his assessment correct? Why or why not?

4. What advice does Wilson offer the aspiring student of science at the end of his essay? Is it good advice? Why or why not?

## STRATEGIES AND STRUCTURES

1. In the process of pursuing a successful career in science, the first step, according to Wilson, is "passion." What are the next steps in the process?

2. Much of Wilson's analysis for how to become a scientist comes at the end of his essay. Why here instead of the beginning? How and how well does Wilson build up to his **PROCESS ANALYSIS** rather than down from it?

3. Wilson's essay takes the form of a letter. Letters are usually addressed to someone whom the writer knows personally. Point out passages in Wilson's letter that establish a familiar relationship between writer and reader. Why do you think Wilson adopts this strategy?

4. The series of steps that make up a process analysis usually lead to an end result, product, or goal. In Wilson's analysis, the end result of the process is to make a scientist out of the youthful enthusiast. How and where does Wilson first catch sight of this goal? Why, at first, is it not more "clearly defined" for him (6)?

5. Most of Wilson's essay consists of an account of how he became interested in science, particularly biology, and where that interest led. Given his intended **AUDIENCE** (the young scientist, or would-be scientist), why might he take this **NARRATIVE** approach to his subject? How and how well does this strategy work for him?

## WORDS AND FIGURES OF SPEECH

1. What are the implications of Wilson's use of the word *confessional* (11) to describe the point of view and tone of his essay?

2. Referring to the "eccentricity" (10) of his career is an **UNDERSTATEMENT** on Wilson's part given his professional success. Where else in his essay—and to what effect—does he use this figure of speech?

3. According to the dictionary definition, what is a *prodigy* (9)? As described in this essay by his older self, how and how well does young Wilson fit the standard definition?

## FOR WRITING

1. Write a process analysis that explains how you acquired a passion for something. Be sure to explain what is involved in committing yourself to that activity or pursuit.

2. Write a letter, whether to someone you know personally or do not know well, that tells "who I really am" by recounting an experience that embarrassed you or required you to be further "instructed" (5).

JON KATZ

# HOW BOYS BECOME MEN

JON KATZ (b. 1947) is a mystery writer and media critic. A former executive producer for *CBS Morning News,* he has also written a number of books about dogs, including *Katz on Dogs* (2005) and *Soul of a Dog* (2009), as well as columns for *Rolling Stone, HotWired,* and slashdot.org, a website dedicated to "News for Nerds." For Katz, the Internet is different from other, more traditional media, such as books and newspapers, because it is interactive. Interactivity, however, is not a trait that most men come by naturally in their personal lives, says Katz. Why? Because "sensitivity" has been beaten out of them as boys. Katz analyzes this male maturation process in "How Boys Become Men," first published in 1993 in *Glamour,* a magazine for young women.

T WO NINE-YEAR-OLD BOYS, neighbors and friends, were walking home from 1 school. The one in the bright blue windbreaker was laughing and swinging a heavy-looking book bag toward the head of his friend, who kept ducking and stepping back. "What's the matter?" asked the kid with the bag, whooshing it over his head. "You chicken?"[1]

His friend stopped, stood still and braced himself. The bag slammed into the side of his face, the thump audible all the way across the street where I stood watching. The impact knocked him to the ground, where he lay mildly stunned for a second. Then he struggled up, rubbing the side of his head. "See?" he said proudly. "I'm no chicken." 2

No. A chicken would probably have had the sense to get out of the way. This boy was already well on the road to becoming a *man*, having learned one of the central ethics of his gender: Experience pain rather than show fear. 3

Women tend to see men as a giant problem in need of solution. They tell us that we're remote and uncommunicative, that we need to demonstrate less machismo and more commitment, more humanity. But if you don't understand something about boys, you can't understand why men are the way we are, why we find it so difficult to make friends or to acknowledge our fears and problems. 4

See p. 279 for tips on putting the steps of a process in order.

Boys live in a world with its own Code of Conduct, a set of ruthless, unspoken, and unyielding rules: 5

Don't be a goody-goody.

Never rat.[2] If your parents ask about bruises, shrug.

Never admit fear. Ride the roller coaster, join the fistfight, do what you have to do. Asking for help is for sissies.

Empathy is for nerds. You can help your best buddy, under certain circumstances. Everyone else is on his own.

Never discuss anything of substance with anybody. Grunt, shrug, dump on teachers, laugh at wimps, talk about comic books. Anything else is risky.

---

1. An idiom in American English that means "coward" or "afraid."

2. An idiom in American English for a person who informs authorities (parent, teacher, police, etc.) about the activities of another person.

Boys are rewarded for throwing hard. Most other activities—reading, befriend-ing girls, or just thinking—are considered weird. And if there's one thing boys don't want to be, it's weird.

More than anything else, boys are supposed to learn how to handle 6 themselves. I remember the bitter fifth-grade conflict I touched off by elbow-ing aside a bigger boy named Barry and seizing the cafeteria's last carton of chocolate milk. Teased for getting aced out by a wimp, he had to reclaim his place in the pack. Our fistfight, at recess, ended with my knees buckling and my lip bleeding while my friends, sympathetic but out of range, watched resignedly.

When I got home, my mother took one look at my swollen face and 7 screamed. I wouldn't tell her anything, but when my father got home I cracked and confessed, pleading with them to do nothing. Instead, they called Barry's parents, who restricted his television for a week.

The following morning, Barry and six of his pals stepped out from behind 8 a stand of trees. "It's the rat," said Barry.

I bled a little more. *Rat* was scrawled in crayon across my desk. 9

They were waiting for me after school for a number of afternoons to fol- 10 low. I tried varying my routes and avoiding bushes and hedges. It usually didn't work.

I was as ashamed for telling as I was frightened. "You did ask for it," said 11 my best friend. Frontier Justice has nothing on Boy Justice.

In panic, I appealed to a cousin who was several years older. He followed 12 me home from school, and when Barry's gang surrounded me, he came barrel-ing toward us. "Stay away from my cousin," he shouted, "or I'll kill you."

After they were gone, however, my cousin could barely stop laughing. 13 "You were afraid of *them*?" he howled. "They barely came up to my waist."

Men remember receiving little mercy as boys; maybe that's why it's 14 sometimes difficult for them to show any.

"I know lots of men who had happy childhoods, but none who have 15 happy memories of the way other boys treated them," says a friend. "It's a macho marathon from third grade up, when you start butting each other in the stomach."

"The thing is," adds another friend, "you learn early on to hide what you 16 feel. It's never safe to say, 'I'm scared.' My girlfriend asks me why I don't talk more about what I'm feeling. I've gotten better at it, but it will *never* come naturally."

You don't need to be a shrink to see how the lessons boys learn affect   17
their behavior as men. Men are being asked, more and more, to show sensitivity, but they dread the very word. They struggle to build their increasingly
uncertain work lives but will deny they're in trouble. They want love, affec-
tion, and support but don't know how to ask for them. They hide their weaknesses and fears from all, even those they care for. They've learned to be wary
of intervening when they see others in trouble. They often still balk at being
stigmatized as weird.

Some men get shocked into sensitivity—when they lose their jobs, their   18
wives, or their lovers. Others learn it through a strong marriage, or through
their own children.

It may be a long while, however, before male culture evolves to the point   19
that boys can learn more from one another than how to hit curve balls. Last
month, walking my dog past the playground near my house, I saw three boys
encircling a fourth, laughing and pushing him. He was skinny and rumpled,
and he looked frightened. One boy knelt behind him while another pushed him
from the front, a trick familiar to any former boy. He fell backward.

When the others ran off, he brushed the dirt off his elbows and walked   20
toward the swings. His eyes were moist and he was struggling for control.

"Hi," I said through the chain-link fence. "How ya doing?"   21

"Fine," he said quickly, kicking his legs out and beginning his swing.   22

## FOR DISCUSSION

1. In order to explain how boys become men, Jon Katz must first explain how boys become boys. By what specific "rules" does this process occur, according to him (5)?

2. Is Katz right, do you think, in his **PROCESS ANALYSIS** of how boys are brought up? Why or why not?

3. The end result of how they learn to behave as boys, says Katz, is that men find it difficult "to make friends or to acknowledge our fears and problems" (4). They lack "sensitivity" (18). Do you agree? In your experience, is Katz's analysis accurate or inaccurate? Explain.

4. According to Katz, women are puzzled by "male culture" (19). How, in his view, do women regard men? Do you agree or disagree with this analysis? Why?

5. What evidence, if any, can you find in Katz's essay to indicate that the author has learned as an adult male to behave in ways he was not taught as a boy? By what processes, according to Katz, do men sometimes learn such new kinds of behavior?

## STRATEGIES AND STRUCTURE

1. Katz tells the story in paragraphs 1 and 2 of a boy who prefers to get knocked down rather than be called a "chicken." Why do you think he begins with this incident? What stage or aspect of the boy-training process is he illustrating?

2. The longest of the **ANECDOTES** that Katz tells to show how boys learn to behave is the one about himself. Where does it begin and end? By what process or processes is he being taught here?

3. What is the role of the older cousin in the **NARRATIVE** Katz tells about himself as a boy? How does the cousin's response in paragraph 13 illustrate the process Katz is analyzing?

4. Where else in his essay does Katz tell a brief story to illustrate what he is saying about how boys are trained? How do these stories support his main point? What would the essay be like without any of the stories?

5. "If you don't understand something about boys, you can't understand why men are the way we are . . ." (4). To whom is Katz speaking here? What **PURPOSES** might he have for explaining the male maturation process to this particular **AUDIENCE**?

6. Besides analyzing the processes by which boys learn to behave according to a rigid "Code of Conduct," Katz's essay also analyzes the lasting effects caused by this early training (5). What are some of these effects?

## WORDS AND FIGURES OF SPEECH

1. How does your dictionary define "machismo" (4)? What language(s) does it derive from?

2. To feel *sympathy* for someone means to have feelings and emotions similar to theirs. What does "empathy" mean (5)?

3. How does Katz's use of the various meanings of the words "chicken" and "rat" help him to make his point about how boys become men (1–3, 5, 8–9)?

4. Verbal **IRONY** is the use of one word or phrase to imply another with a quite different meaning. What's ironic about the boy's reply to Katz's question in paragraph 22?

## FOR WRITING

1. Write a brief Code of Conduct like the one in paragraph 5 that lays out the unspoken rules of the "culture," male or female, in which you grew up.

2. Write an essay that analyzes the process of how boys become men, as *you* see it. Or, alternatively, write an analysis of the process(es) by which *girls* are typically socialized to become women in America or somewhere else. Draw on your own personal experience, or what you know from others, or both. Feel free to use **ANECDOTES** and other elements of narrative as appropriate to illustrate your analysis.

ALLEGRA GOODMAN

# SO, YOU WANT TO BE
# A WRITER? HERE'S HOW.

ALLEGRA GOODMAN (b. 1967) is a novelist and short-story writer who wrote and illustrated her first novel at the age of seven. After growing up in Honolulu, she studied at Harvard, then earned a PhD in English from Stanford University. Her most recent novels include *The Chalk Artist* (2017), *The Cookbook Collector* (2010), and *The Other Side of the Island* (2008). "If there's one thing I've learned over the years," says Goodman, who is fascinated by the writing process, "it's the value of revision. I write draft after draft, rereading, rethinking, rephrasing every step of the way." In the following essay, published in the *Boston Globe* in 2008, Goodman gives advice on the process of becoming a writer.

WHEN PEOPLE HEAR THAT I'M A NOVELIST, I get one comment more than any other. "I'm a physician (or a third-grade teacher, or a venture capitalist) but what I really want to do is write." A mother of three muses: "I've always loved writing since I was a little girl." A physicist declares, "I've got a great idea for a mystery-thriller-philosophical-love story—if I only had the time." I nod, resisting the temptation to reply: "And I have a great idea for a unified field theory—if I just had a moment to work it out on paper."

Book sales are down, but creative writing enrollments are booming. The   2
longing to write knows no bounds. A lactation consultant[1] told me, "I have a story inside of me. I mean, I know everybody has a story, but I really have a story."

Forthwith, some advice for those of you who have always wanted to   3
write, those with best-selling ideas, and those who really have a story.

To begin, don't write about yourself. I'm not saying you're uninterest-   4
ing. I realize that your life has been so crazy no one could make this stuff up. But if you want to be a writer, start by writing about other people. Observe their faces, and the way they wave their hands around. Listen to the way they talk. Replay conversations in your mind—not just the words, but the silences as well. Imagine the lives of others. If you want to be a writer, you need to get over yourself. This is not just an artistic choice; it's a moral choice. A writer attempts to understand others from the inside.

Find a peaceful place to work. Peace does not necessarily entail an artists'   5
colony or an island off the coast of Maine. You might find peace in your base-ment, or at a cafe in Davis Square,[2] or amid old ladies rustling magazines at the public library. Peace is not the same as quiet. Peace means you avoid checking your e-mail every ten seconds. Peace means you are willing to work offline, screen calls, and forget your to-do list for an hour. If this is difficult, turn off your Web browser, or try writing without a computer altogether. Treat your-self to pen and paper and make a mess, crossing out sentences, crumpling pages, inserting paragraphs in margins. Remember spiral-bound notebooks, and thank-you notes with stamps? Handwriting is arcane in all the best ways. Writing in ink doesn't feel like work; it feels like secret diaries and treasure maps and art.

> Let readers know when they will need special equipment, as in the fifth template on p. 279.

Read widely, and dissect books in your mind. What, exactly, makes   6
David Sedaris[3] funny? How does George Orwell[4] fill us with dread? If you want

---

1. Someone who advises mothers about nursing their infants.

2. Central intersection in Somerville, Massachusetts, a city north of Boston.

3. Best-selling American author (b. 1956), known for his witty autobiographical writing.

4. British novelist and essayist (1903–1950), whose novel *1984* is a foreboding story of a repressive totalitarian government.

to be a novelist, read novels new and old, satirical, experimental, Victorian, American. Read nonfiction as well. Consider how biographers select details to illuminate a life in time. If you want to write nonfiction, study histories and essays, but also read novels and think about narrative, and the novelist's artful release of information. Don't forget poetry. Why? Because it's good to go where words are worshipped, and essential to remember that you are not a poet. Lyric poets linger on a mood or fragmentary phrase; prose writers must move along to tell their story, and catch their train.

And this is true for everyone, but especially for women: If you don't value   7 your own time, other people won't either. Trust me, you can't write a novel in stolen minutes outside your daughter's tap class. Virginia Woolf[5] declared that a woman needs a room of her own. Well, the room won't help, if you don't shut the door. Post a note. "Book in progress, please do not disturb unless you're bleeding." Or these lines from Samuel Taylor Coleridge,[6] which I have adapted for writing mothers: " . . . Beware! Beware! / Her flashing eyes, her floating hair! Weave a circle round her thrice, / And close your eyes with holy dread, / For she on honey-dew hath fed, / and drunk the milk of Paradise."

### FOR DISCUSSION

1. Why, according to Allegra Goodman, should aspiring writers write about other people instead of themselves? Do you think this is sensible advice? Why or why not?

2. What **PROCESS** is Goodman **ANALYZING** exactly—how to write or how to become a writer? Is her analysis explanatory or directive? Explain.

3. Why does Goodman recommend writing by hand in ink?

4. Why does Goodman think all writers should study poetry? Is she right? Why or why not?

5. What special advice does Goodman have for women writers? Why, in her view, do they need such advice even more than men do?

5. British novelist and essayist (1882–1941). In her book *A Room of One's Own* (1929), Woolf noted that "a woman must have money and a room of her own if she is to write fiction."

6. British Romantic poet and critic (1772–1834). Goodman adapts lines from his poem "Kubla Khan" (1816), which Coleridge claimed he was unable to complete after being interrupted by a knock at the door during its composition.

## STRATEGIES AND STRUCTURES

1. What is the end result of the process that Goodman is analyzing? Where and how does she first introduce it?

2. In the beginning of her essay, Goodman tells about all the people she has met who want to be writers. Is this an effective way to begin? Why or why not?

3. Goodman tells us early on who she has in mind as her main AUDIENCE for the advice she gives. Who is it? In what ways is her essay directed toward this audience? Explain.

4. Goodman divides the process that she is analyzing into four basic stages. What are they? Does she use chronology to organize them? If not, how are they organized?

5. Into what steps is the reading stage of the process further broken down? What about the other stages? Why does Goodman break them down in this way?

6. Why does Goodman end her analysis with the words of another writer? Is this an effective strategy? Why or why not?

7. In paragraph 6, Goodman COMPARES the writer of prose to the writer of poetry. Which kind of writer—or aspiring writer—is her advice aimed at? How does she DEFINE the kind of writer she has in mind?

## WORDS AND FIGURES OF SPEECH

1. Why is writing about other people rather than oneself a "moral" choice, according to Goodman (4)? What's moral about it?

2. The writer, says Goodman, needs "a peaceful place to work" (5). How does she define "peaceful"?

3. Why does Goodman use the word "arcane" instead of *old-fashioned* or *outmoded* to DESCRIBE handwriting (5)?

4. What does Goodman mean by "artful" when she uses it to describe how the novelist releases information in a NARRATIVE (6)?

5. Explain the ALLUSION to Virginia Woolf in the last paragraph of Goodman's essay. What PURPOSE does it serve in her analysis?

## FOR WRITING

1. In a paragraph or two, analyze the process you follow for managing your time when you write.

2. Write an essay analyzing the process you have gone through so far in learning how to be a writer. Be sure to say how much further you have to go in order to reach your goal and what advice you have for other writers.

PHILIP WEISS

# HOW TO GET OUT OF A LOCKED TRUNK

PHILIP WEISS (b. 1955) is an investigative journalist and former columnist for the *New York Observer*. He has also been a contributor to the *Jewish World Review, Esquire*, and the *New York Observer*, where he began the blog *Mondoweiss*, a now independent website that covers developments in Israel, Palestine, and relevant American foreign policy. Weiss is the author of the political novel *Cock-A-Doodle-Doo* (1995) and the investigative work *American Taboo: A Murder in the Peace Corps* (2004). About to be married when he wrote "How to Get Out of a Locked Trunk" for *Harper's* (1992), Weiss obsessively analyzes his way out of the trunks of locked cars, a strange fixation that suggests his bachelor self may be carrying some extra baggage. The essay also analyzes how Weiss got out of his condition.

O N A HOT SUNDAY LAST SUMMER my friend Tony and I drove my rental car, a '91 Buick, from St. Paul to the small town of Waconia, Minnesota, forty miles southwest. We each had a project. Waconia is Tony's boyhood home, and his sister had recently given him a panoramic postcard of Lake Waconia as seen from a high point in the town early in the century. He wanted to duplicate the photograph's vantage point, then hang the two pictures together in his house in Frogtown. I was hoping to see Tony's father, Emmett, a retired mechanic, in order to settle a question that had been nagging me: Is it possible to get out of a locked car trunk?

We tried to call ahead to Emmett twice, but he wasn't home. Tony   2
thought he was probably golfing but that there was a good chance he'd be back by the time we got there. So we set out.

I parked the Buick, which was a silver sedan with a red interior, by the   3
graveyard near where Tony thought the picture had been taken. He took his picture and I wandered among the headstones, reading the epitaphs. One of them was chillingly anti-individualist. It said, "Not to do my will, but thine."

Trunk lockings had been on my mind for a few weeks. It seemed to me   4
that the fear of being locked in a car trunk had a particular hold on the American imagination. Trunk lockings occur in many movies and books—from *Goodfellas* to *Thelma and Louise* to *Humboldt's Gift*.[1] And while the highbrow national newspapers generally shy away from trunk lockings, the attention they receive in local papers suggests a widespread anxiety surrounding the subject. In an afternoon at the New York Public Library I found numerous stories about trunk lockings. A Los Angeles man is discovered, bloodshot, banging the trunk of his white Eldorado following a night and a day trapped inside; he says his captors went on joyrides and picked up women. A forty-eight-year-old Houston doctor is forced into her trunk at a bank ATM and then the car is abandoned, parked near the Astrodome.[2] A New Orleans woman tells police she gave birth in a trunk while being abducted to Texas. Tests undermine her story, the police drop the investigation. But so what if it's a fantasy? That only shows the idea's hold on us.

Every culture comes up with tests of a person's ability to get out of a   5
sticky situation. The English plant mazes. Tropical resorts market those straw

---

1. *Humboldt's Gift* (1975), a novel by Saul Bellow about a spiritually empty writer whose life is reawakened by a mob member; *Goodfellas* (1990), a gangster movie; *Thelma and Louise* (1991), a road movie about two women trying to escape oppressive marriages.

2. A large sports arena in Houston, Texas.

finger-grabbers that tighten their grip the harder you pull on them, and Viennese intellectuals gave us the concept of childhood sexuality—figure it out, or remain neurotic for life.

At least you could puzzle your way out of those predicaments. When they slam the trunk, though, you're helpless unless someone finds you. You would think that such a common worry should have a ready fix, and that the secret of getting out of a locked trunk is something we should all know about.  6

I phoned experts but they were very discouraging.  7

"You cannot get out. If you got a pair of pliers and bat's eyes, yes. But you have to have a lot of knowledge of the lock," said James Foote at Automotive Locksmiths in New York City.  8

Jim Frens, whom I reached at the technical section of *Car and Driver*[3] in Detroit, told me the magazine had not dealt with this question. But he echoed the opinion of experts elsewhere when he said that the best hope for escape would be to try and kick out the panel between the trunk and the backseat. That angle didn't seem worth pursuing. What if your enemies were in the car, crumpling beer cans and laughing at your fate? It didn't make sense to join them.  9

The people who deal with rules on auto design were uncomfortable with my scenarios. Debra Barclay of the Center for Auto Safety, an organization founded by Ralph Nader,[4] had certainly heard of cases, but she was not aware of any regulations on the matter. "Now, if there was a defect involved—" she said, her voice trailing off, implying that trunk locking was all phobia. This must be one of the few issues on which she and the auto industry agree. Ann Carlson of the Motor Vehicle Manufacturers Association became alarmed at the thought that I was going to play up a non-problem: "In reality this very rarely happens. As you say, in the movies it's a wonderful plot device," she said. "But in reality apparently this is not that frequent an occurrence. So they have not designed that feature into vehicles in a specific way."  10

When we got to Emmett's one-story house it was full of people. Tony's sister, Carol, was on the floor with her two small children. Her husband, Charlie, had  11

3. A monthly magazine for car enthusiasts.

4. American attorney and political activist (b. 1934) who was an early advocate of automobile safety.

one eye on the golf tournament on TV, and Emmett was at the kitchen counter, trimming fat from meat for lunch. I have known Emmett for fifteen years. He looked better than ever. In his retirement he had sharply changed his diet and lost a lot of weight. He had on shorts. His legs were tanned and muscular. As always, his manner was humorous, if opaque.

Tony told his family my news: I was getting married in three weeks. 12 Charlie wanted to know where my fiancée was. Back East, getting everything ready. A big-time hatter was fitting her for a new hat.

Emmett sat on the couch, watching me. "Do you want my advice?" 13

"Sure." 14

He just grinned. A gold tooth glinted. Carol and Charlie pressed him to 15 yield his wisdom.

Finally he said, "Once you get to be thirty, you make your own mistakes." 16

He got out several cans of beer, and then I brought up what was on 17 my mind.

Emmett nodded and took off his glasses, then cleaned them and put them 18 back on.

We went out to his car, a Mercury Grand Marquis, and Emmett opened 19 the trunk. His golf clubs were sitting on top of the spare tire in a green golf bag. Next to them was a toolbox and what he called his "burglar tools," a set of elbowed rods with red plastic handles he used to open door locks when people locked their keys inside.

Tony and Charlie stood watching. Charlie is a banker in Minneapolis. He 20 enjoys gizmos and is extremely practical. I would describe him as unflappable. That's a word I always wanted to apply to myself, but my fiancée had recently informed me that I am high-strung. Though that surprised me, I didn't quarrel with her.

For a while we studied the latch assembly. The lock closed in much the 21 same way that a lobster might clamp on to a pencil. The claw portion, the jaws of the lock, was mounted inside the trunk lid. When you shut the lid, the jaws locked on to the bend of a U-shaped piece of metal mounted on the body of the car. Emmett said my best bet would be to unscrew the bolts. That way the U-shaped piece would come loose and the lock's jaws would swing up with it still in their grasp.

"But you'd need a wrench," he said.                                                    22

It was already getting too technical. Emmett had an air of endless      23
patience, but I felt defeated. I could only imagine bloodied fingers, cracked
teeth. I had hoped for a simple trick.

Charlie stepped forward. He reached out and squeezed the lock's jaws.   24
They clicked shut in the air, bound together by heavy springs. Charlie now
prodded the upper part of the left-hand jaw, the thicker part. With a rough
flick of his thumb, he was able to force the jaws to snap open. Great.

Unfortunately, the jaws were mounted behind a steel plate the size of   25
your palm in such a way that while they were accessible to us, standing outside the car, had we been inside the trunk the plate would be in our way, blocking the jaws.

This time Emmett saw the way out. He fingered a hole in the plate. It was   26
no bigger than the tip of your little finger. But the hole was close enough to the
latch itself that it might be possible to angle something through the hole from
inside the trunk and nudge the jaws apart. We tried with one of my keys. The
lock jumped open.

It was time for a full-dress test. Emmett swung the clubs out of the    27
trunk, and I set my can of Schmidt's on the rear bumper and climbed in. Everyone gathered around, and Emmett lowered the trunk on me, then pressed it
shut with his meaty hands. Total darkness. I couldn't hear the people outside.
I thought I was going to panic. But the big trunk felt comfortable. I was pressed
against a sort of black carpet that softened the angles against my back.

I could almost stretch out in the trunk, and it seemed to me I could make   28
them sweat if I took my time. Even Emmett, that sphinx, would give way to
curiosity. Once I was out he'd ask how it had been and I'd just grin. There were
some things you could only learn by doing.

It took a while to find the hole. I slipped the key in and angled it to one   29
side. The trunk gasped open.

Emmett motioned the others away, then levered me out with his big     30
right forearm. Though I'd only been inside for a minute, I was disoriented—as
much as anything because someone had moved my beer while I was gone, setting it down on the cement floor of the garage. It was just a little thing, but I
could not be entirely sure I had gotten my own beer back.

Charlie was now raring to try other cars. We examined the latch on his    31
Toyota, which was entirely shielded to the trunk occupant (i.e., no hole in the
plate), and on the neighbor's Honda (ditto). But a 1991 Dodge Dynasty was
doable. The trunk was tight, but its lock had a feature one of the mechanics I'd
phoned described as a "tailpiece": a finger-like extension of the lock mechanism itself that stuck out a half inch into the trunk cavity; simply by twisting
the tailpiece I could free the lock. I was even faster on a 1984 Subaru that had
a little lever device on the latch.

We went out to my rental on Oak Street. The Skylark was in direct sun    32
and the trunk was hot to the touch, but when we got it open we could see that
its latch plate had a perfect hole, a square in which the edge of the lock's jaw
appeared like a face in a window.

The trunk was shallow and hot. Emmett had to push my knees down    33
before he could close the lid. This one was a little suffocating. I imagined being
trapped for hours, and even before he had got it closed I regretted the decision
with a slightly nauseous feeling. I thought of Edgar Allan Poe's live burials,[5]
and then about something my fiancée had said more than a year and a half
before. I had been on her case to get married. She was divorced, and at every
opportunity I would reissue my proposal—even during a commercial. She'd
interrupted one of these chirps to tell me, in a cold, throaty voice, that she had
no intention of ever going through another divorce: "This time, it's death
out." I'd carried those words around like a lump of wet clay.

As it happened, the Skylark trunk was the easiest of all. The hole was    34
right where it was supposed to be. The trunk popped open, and I felt great
satisfaction that we'd been able to figure out a rule that seemed to      "As it happened" is
apply about 60 percent of the time. If we publicized our success,         one example of
                                                                          Weiss's use of
it might get the attention it deserved. All trunks would be fitted        transitions, p. 280.
with such a hole. Kids would learn about it in school. The grip of the fear
would relax. Before long a successful trunk-locking scene would date a movie
like a fedora[6] dates one today.

5. American author (1809–1849) known for his eerie short stories and poems; his story "The
Premature Burial" recounts the terror of a man buried alive.

6. Brimmed men's hat popular from the 1920s through the 1950s, often worn by gangsters
and detectives in movies from that era.

When I got back East I was caught up in wedding preparations. I live in   35
New York, and the wedding was to take place in Philadelphia. We set up camp
there with five days to go. A friend had lent my fiancée her BMW, and we
drove it south with all our things. I unloaded the car in my parents' driveway.
The last thing I pulled out of the trunk was my fiancée's hat in its heavy cardboard shipping box. She'd warned me I was not allowed to look. The lid was
free but I didn't open it. I was willing to be surprised.

When the trunk was empty it occurred to me I might hop in and give it a   36
try. First I looked over the mechanism. The jaws of the BMW's lock were
shielded, but there seemed to be some kind of cable coming off it that you
might be able to manipulate so as to cause the lock to open. The same cable
that allowed the driver to open the trunk remotely . . .

I fingered it for a moment or two but decided I didn't need to test out the   37
theory.

## FOR DISCUSSION

1. So, according to Philip Weiss, how *do* you get out of a locked trunk? How, according to his fiancée, do you get out of a marriage? What is the implication of Weiss's
   addressing these two problems in the same essay?
2. Of the cars he tests, which one alarms Weiss most yet turns out to be the easiest
   to get out of? Why is he so alarmed, do you think? Why is he so anxious to find a
   "simple trick" that will fit all instances (23)?
3. Why does Weiss say, "There were some things you could only learn by doing"
   (28)? What might some of them be?
4. Why do you think Weiss refrains from taking a peek at his fiancée's new hat, since
   the lid is "free" and the box would be so easy to open (35)? Incidentally, how does
   Weiss know that the lid is free?

## STRATEGIES AND STRUCTURES

1. What is Weiss's **PURPOSE** in **ANALYZING THE PROCESS** of getting out of a locked
   trunk? What **AUDIENCE** does Weiss think will be interested in his analysis? Why?
2. Weiss's essay is divided into three parts—paragraphs 1 through 10, 11 through 34,
   and 35 through 37. In which section does Weiss most fully analyze the process of
   getting out of a locked car trunk? Is his analysis explanatory or directive? Explain.

3. Why do you think the last section of Weiss's essay is the shortest? How—and how effectively—does it bring the essay to a satisfying conclusion?

4. What is Weiss's purpose in citing several "experts" in paragraphs 7 through 10? What is Emmett's role in the big experiment?

5. "It's a wonderful plot device," Weiss quotes one expert as saying about being locked in a car trunk (10). Is she right? Where in his essay is Weiss telling a story, and where is he analyzing a process? Give specific EXAMPLES from the text.

6. Like NARRATIVES, which often report events chronologically, process analyses are often organized in the chronological order of the steps or stages of the process that is being analyzed. Where does Weiss use chronology either to tell a story or to analyze a process? Give specific examples from the text.

### WORDS AND FIGURES OF SPEECH

1. The lock on the trunk of Emmett's Mercury Grand Marquis, says Weiss, "closed in much the same way that a lobster might clamp on to a pencil" (21). How effective do you find this SIMILE for explaining how this particular trunk locks? Where else does Weiss use FIGURES OF SPEECH as a tool of process analysis?

2. A phobia is an irrational fear (10). Point out specific EXAMPLES in his essay where Weiss (or his persona) might be said to exhibit phobic behavior. What's he afraid of?

3. To whom is Weiss referring when he mentions "Viennese intellectuals" (5)? Why is he ALLUDING to them? Why does he allude to Poe in paragraph 33?

4. "Not to do my will, but thine" (3). What are the implications of this inscription, which Weiss reads on a tombstone at the beginning of his essay?

5. "Case," "reissue," "chirp," and "death out" (33): why does Weiss use these words in the ANECOTE about his proposals? What about "willing" (35)?

### FOR WRITING

1. Has anyone you know ever exhibited phobic behavior? Explain how the phobia manifested itself and what specific steps the victim took to deal with it.

2. "Every culture," writes Weiss, "comes up with tests of a person's ability to get out of a sticky situation" (5). Have you ever been in such a situation? How did you get out of it? Write an essay analyzing the process.

# WHAT SUFFERING DOES

DAVID BROOKS (b. 1961) is a political and cultural commentator best known for his op-ed columns in the *New York Times* and his appearances on *PBS NewsHour*. Brooks earned his BA at the University of Chicago, where he studied history and contributed satirical pieces to student publications. After graduating, he worked as a reporter in Chicago and, later, as a journalist and editor at the *Wall Street Journal*. He is the author of several books, including *The Social Animal* (2011) and, most recently, *The Road to Character* (2015). In "What Suffering Does," first published in the *New York Times* (2014), Brooks examines the process by which individuals fashion their own characters through the moral choices they make in response to the events of their lives.

O VER THE PAST FEW WEEKS, I've found myself in a bunch of conversations  1
in which the unspoken assumption was that the main goal of life is to maximize happiness. That's normal. When people plan for the future, they often talk about all the good times and good experiences they hope to have.

We live in a culture awash in talk about happiness. In one three-month period last year, more than 1,000 books were released on Amazon on that subject.

But notice this phenomenon. When people remember the past, they       2
don't only talk about happiness. It is often the ordeals that seem most significant. People shoot for happiness but feel formed through suffering.

Now, of course, it should be said that there is nothing intrinsically enno-       3
bling about suffering. Just as failure is sometimes just failure (and not your path to becoming the next Steve Jobs[1]) suffering is sometimes just destructive, to be exited as quickly as possible.

But some people are clearly ennobled by it. Think of the way Franklin       4
Roosevelt came back deeper and more empathetic after being struck with polio. Often, physical or social suffering can give people an outsider's perspective, an attuned awareness of what other outsiders are enduring.

But the big thing that suffering does is it takes you outside of precisely       5
that logic that the happiness mentality encourages. Happiness wants you to think about maximizing your benefits. Difficulty and suffering sends you on a different course.

First, suffering drags you deeper into yourself. The theologian Paul Til-       6
lich wrote that people who endure suffering are taken beneath the routines of life and find they are not who they believed themselves to be. The For advice on how to put things in order, see p. 279.
agony involved in, say, composing a great piece of music or the
grief of having lost a loved one smashes through what they
thought was the bottom floor of their personality, revealing an area below, and then it smashes through that floor revealing another area.

Then, suffering gives people a more accurate sense of their own limita-       7
tions, what they can control and cannot control. When people are thrust down into these deeper zones, they are forced to confront the fact they can't determine what goes on there. Try as they might, they just can't tell themselves to stop feeling pain, or to stop missing the one who has died or gone. And even when tranquillity begins to come back, or in those moments when grief eases, it is

---

1. Entrepreneur and inventor (1955−2011) who cofounded Apple, Inc., and was its chief executive. The fact that he did not graduate from college is often mentioned both by his detractors and his fans.

not clear where the relief comes from. The healing process, too, feels as though it's part of some natural or divine process beyond individual control.

People in this circumstance often have the sense that they are swept up    8
in some larger providence. Abraham Lincoln suffered through the pain of conducting a civil war, and he came out of that with the Second Inaugural. He emerged with this sense that there were deep currents of agony and redemption sweeping not just through him but through the nation as a whole, and that he was just an instrument for transcendent tasks.

It's at this point that people in the midst of difficulty begin to feel a call.    9
They are not masters of the situation, but neither are they helpless. They can't determine the course of their pain, but they can participate in responding to it. They often feel an overwhelming moral responsibility to respond well to it. People who seek this proper rejoinder to ordeal sense that they are at a deeper level than the level of happiness and individual utility. They don't say, "Well, I'm feeling a lot of pain over the loss of my child. I should try to balance my hedonic account by going to a lot of parties and whooping it up."

The right response to this sort of pain is not pleasure. It's holiness. I    10
don't even mean that in a purely religious sense. It means seeing life as a moral drama, placing the hard experiences in a moral context and trying to redeem something bad by turning it into something sacred. Parents who've lost a child start foundations. Lincoln sacrificed himself for the Union. Prisoners in the concentration camp with psychologist Viktor Frankl[2] rededicated themselves to living up to the hopes and expectations of their loved ones, even though those loved ones might themselves already be dead.

Recovering from suffering is not like recovering from a disease. Many    11
people don't come out healed; they come out different. They crash through the logic of individual utility and behave paradoxically. Instead of recoiling from the sorts of loving commitments that almost always involve suffering, they throw themselves more deeply into them. Even while experiencing the worst and most lacerating consequences, some people double down on vulnerability.

---

2. Austrian neurologist and psychiatrist (1905–1997). In his book *Man's Search for Meaning* (1946), Frankl narrates his experiences as a concentration camp inmate and how those experiences shaped his theories on human psychology.

They hurl themselves deeper and gratefully into their art, loved ones and commitments.

The suffering involved in their tasks becomes a fearful gift and very dif- 12 ferent than that equal and other gift, happiness, conventionally defined.

### FOR DISCUSSION

1. According to David Brooks, what does suffering do to—and for—us? What is the end result of the process as he analyzes it? Is this a desirable result? Why?

2. "We live in a culture awash in talk about happiness," says Brooks (1). What "culture," exactly, do you think he is referring to?

3. Is Brooks right that the "fearful gift" of suffering is a neglected subject in our conversations and reading (12)? If so, what do you think accounts for this neglect and what might be some of the consequences of it?

4. With suffering, says Brooks, the process of recovery "is not like recovering from a disease" (11). Why not? What differences does he see in the two forms of healing? How useful is this distinction? Explain.

5. Essays on suffering often refer to the biblical figure of Job. Do some research on the *Book of Job*, and explain why its hero is often presented as a model of patience under suffering. Should Brooks have mentioned the story? Why or why not?

### STRATEGIES AND STRUCTURES

1. The first step in the process of suffering (and recovery from it), says Brooks, is that "suffering drags you deeper into yourself" (6). What are the other main steps in the process, and where in his essay, exactly, does Brooks identify them?

2. According to Brooks, the "right response" to suffering is not, as it might be in the case of achieving happiness, to replicate the process (10). What is it? Does Brooks's explanation serve as a fitting conclusion to his essay? Why or why not?

3. Brooks gives several EXAMPLES of historical figures who were, in his view, transformed by suffering. Which ones do you find particularly effective (or ineffective)? Why?

4. Brooks COMPARES AND CONTRASTS suffering with happiness but does not give equal weight to each subject. Why not?

## WORDS AND FIGURES OF SPEECH

1. To say that we are "awash" in talk about a particular subject is an intentional overstatement, or **HYPERBOLE** (1). Why might Brooks use this **FIGURE OF SPEECH** at the beginning of his essay?

2. Although Brooks is writing about serious concepts, he often uses simple, informal language—such as "bunch" (1), "big thing" (5), "bottom floor" (6), "whooping it up" (9). How do such terms affect the **TONE** of his essay? Is this level of **DICTION** inappropriate in a discourse on such a serious topic? Explain.

3. If not in its "purely religious sense," how then, exactly, is Brooks **DEFINING** the key word *holiness* in his essay (10)? Is the word appropriate, or should he have chosen a different term? Why or why not?

4. In the last phrase of his essay, Brooks again opposes the benefits of suffering to the benefits of happiness "conventionally defined" (12). Why do you think he ends with this qualifier?

## FOR WRITING

1. Write an essay about a painful or otherwise difficult experience you (or someone you know) successfully recovered from. Explain the process and its various steps, including the end result. Explain how you were changed (or not) by the experience.

2. Write an essay about a historical figure (or figures) as a model of the transformative power of suffering. Give not only the end result of that person's suffering, but the process by which he or she arrived at that result.

# ⇒ 10 ⇐

# COMPARISON AND CONTRAST

I F you are thinking of buying a new car, you will probably want to do some
COMPARISON* shopping. You might compare the Mazda Miata to the Mit-
subishi Eclipse, for example: both are sporty convertibles with similar features in about the same price range. If you're in the market for a convertible,
you would be wasting your time getting a quote on a van or pickup. That
would be comparing apples to oranges, and true comparisons can be made
only among like kinds. Your final decision, however, will be based more on
differences (in acceleration, fuel economy, trunk space) than on the similarities. Your comparison, that is, will also entail CONTRAST. Strictly speaking, a
*comparison* looks at both the similarities and the differences between two subjects, whereas a *contrast* looks mainly at the differences.

Drawing comparisons in writing is a lot like comparison shopping. It
points out similarities in different subjects and differences in similar ones.
Consider the following comparison between two items we might normally
think of as identical:

> The common yo-yo is crudely made, with a thick shank between two
> widely spaced wooden disks. The string is knotted or stapled to the
> shank. With such an instrument nothing can be done except the simple
> up-down movement. My yo-yo, on the other hand, was a perfectly bal-
> anced construction of hard wood, slightly weighted, flat, with only a six-
> teenth of an inch between the halves. The string was not attached to the
> shank, but looped over it in such a way as to allow the wooden part to
> spin freely on its own axis. The gyroscopic effect thus created kept the
> yo-yo stable in all attitudes.
>
> —FRANK CONROY, *Stop-Time*

*Words printed in SMALL CAPITALS are defined in the Glossary/Index.

Why is Frank Conroy comparing yo-yos here? He is not going to buy one, nor is he telling the reader what kind to buy. Conroy is making a larger point: all yo-yos are not created equal. They may look alike and they may all go up and down on a string, but he points out meaningful differences between them. There are good yo-yos, Conroy is saying, and bad yo-yos.

Once Conroy has brought together like kinds (apples to apples, yo-yos to yo-yos) and established in his own mind a basis for comparing them (the "common" kind versus "my" kind), he can proceed in one of two ways. He can dispense his information in "chunks" or in "slices" (as when selling bologna). These basic methods of organizing a comparison or contrast are sometimes called the subject-by-subject and the point-by-point methods. The subject-by-subject method treats several aspects of one subject, then discusses the same aspects of the other. So the author provides chunks of information all about one subject before moving on to the other subject. Point-by-point organization shifts back and forth between each subject, treating each point of similarity and difference before going on to the next one.

Dan Treadway uses the subject-by-subject method in "Football vs. Asian Studies," p. 328.

In his comparison, Conroy uses the subject-by-subject method. He first gives several traits of the inferior, "common" yo-yo ("crudely made," string fixed to the shank, only goes up and down); then he gives contrasting traits of his superior yo-yo ("perfectly balanced," string loops over the shank, "spins freely on its own axis"). Now let's look at an example of a comparison that uses the point-by-point method to compare two great basketball players, Wilt ("the Stilt") Chamberlain and Bill Russell:

> Russell has been above all a team player—a man of discipline, self-denial and killer instinct; in short, a *winner*, in the best American Calvinist tradition. Whereas Russell has been able somehow to squeeze out his last ounce of ability, Chamberlain's performances have been marked by a seeming nonchalance—as if, recognizing his Gigantistic fate, he were more concerned with personal style than with winning. "I never want to set records. The only thing I strive for is perfection," Chamberlain has said.
>
> —Jamey Larner, "David vs. Goliath"

Paragraph by paragraph, Jamey Larner goes on like this, alternating "slices" of information about each player: Chamberlain's free throws were always uncertain; Russell's were always accurate in the clutch. Chamberlain was efficient; Russell was more so. Chamberlain was fast; Russell was faster. Chamberlain was Goliath at 7-feet-3-inches tall; Russell was David at 6-feet-9. The fans expected Chamberlain to lose; they expected Russell to win.

Point by point, Larner goes back and forth between his two subjects, making one meaningful (to basketball fans) distinction after another. But why, finally, is he bringing these two players together? What's his reason for comparing them at all? Larner has a point to make, just as Conroy does when he compares two yo-yos and just as you should when you draw comparisons in your writing. The author compares these two in order to ARGUE that although the giant Chamberlain was "typecast" by the fans to lose to Russell the giant-killer, it was Wilt "the Stilt," defying all expectations, who arguably became the greatest basketball player ever. (This decision was made without consulting Michael Jordan or LeBron James.)

Whether you use chunks or slices, you can take a number of other hints from Conroy and Larner. First, choose subjects that belong to the same general class or category: two toys, two athletes, two religions, two mammals. You might point out many differences between a mattress and motorcycle, but any distinctions you make between them are not likely to be meaningful because there is little logical basis for comparing them.

Gary Soto compares his family's perceptions of ethnic groups, p. 350, when he tries to figure out whom to marry.

Even more important, you need to have a good reason for bringing your subjects together in the first place—and a main point to make about them. Then, whether you proceed subject by subject or point by point, stick to two and only two subjects at a time.

And, finally, don't feel that you must always give equal weight to similarities and differences. You might want to pay more attention to the similarities if you wish to convince your parents that a two-seater convertible actually has a lot in common with the big, safe SUV they want you to consider—they both have wheels, brakes, and an engine, for example. But you might want to emphasize the differences between your two subjects if the similarities are readily apparent, as between two yo-yos and two basketball stars.

# A BRIEF GUIDE TO WRITING
# A COMPARISON-AND-CONTRAST ESSAY

As you begin to write a comparison, you need to identify your subjects, state the basis on which you're comparing them, and indicate whether you plan to emphasize their similarities or their differences. Jennine Capó Crucet makes these basic moves of comparison in the second paragraph of her essay in this chapter:

> I was a first-generation college student as well as the first in our family to be born in America—my parents were born in Cuba—and we didn't yet know that families were supposed to leave pretty much right after they unloaded your stuff from the car.
>
> —JENNINE CAPÓ CRUCET, "Taking My Parents to College"

Crucet identifies her subjects (she and her parents), states the basis on which she is comparing them (generational characteristics), and indicates that she is planning to emphasize their differences (she was born in America and went to college; her parents were born in Cuba and didn't).

Here is one more example from this chapter:

> They were two strong men, these oddly different generals, and they represented the strengths of two conflicting currents that, through them, had come into final collision.
>
> —BRUCE CATTON, "Grant and Lee: A Study in Contrasts"

The following guidelines will help you to make these basic moves as you draft a comparison. They will also help you to come up with two subjects to compare, present their similarities and differences in an organized way, and state your point in comparing them.

## Coming Up with Your Subjects

The first thing you need to do when composing a comparison essay is to choose two subjects that are different in significant ways but that also have enough in common to provide a solid basis of comparison. A cruise ship and a jet, for instance, are very different machines; but both are modes of transportation, and that shared characteristic can become the basis for comparing them.

When you look for two subjects that have shared characteristics, don't stretch your comparison too far. The Duchess in Lewis Carroll's *Alice in Wonderland* compares mustard to flamingos because they "both bite." In the real world, however, there's no point in bringing two subjects together when the differences between them are far more significant than the similarities. Better to compare mustard and ketchup or flamingos and roseate spoonbills (another type of pink bird).

## Considering Your Purpose and Audience

Suppose that you are comparing smartphones because the screen cracked on your old one and you need to replace it. In this case, your PURPOSE is to evaluate them and decide which smartphone fits your needs best. However, if you were writing the comparison for *Consumer Reports*, you would be comparing and contrasting smartphones in order to inform readers about their various functions and capabilities.

With comparisons, one size does not fit all. Whether you're writing a comparison to inform, to evaluate, or for some other purpose, always keep the specific needs of your AUDIENCE in mind. How much do your readers already know about your topic? Why should they want or need to know more? What distinctions can you make that they haven't already thought of?

Deborah Tannen's audience is teachers in her essay "Gender in the Classroom," p. 356.

## Generating Ideas: Asking How Two Things Are Alike or Different

Once you have a clear basis for comparing two subjects—flamingos and roseate spoonbills are both large pink birds; mustard and ketchup are both condiments; cruise ships and jets are both modes of transportation—look for specific points of comparison between them. Ask yourself: How, specifically, are my two subjects alike? How are they different?

As you answer these questions, make a point-by-point list of the similarities and differences between your subjects. When you draw up your list, make sure you look at the same elements in both subjects. For example, if you are comparing two smartphone models, you might list such elements as the price, size, and accessories available for each one. Preparing such a list will help you to determine whether your two subjects are actually worth comparing—and will also help you to get the similarities and differences straight in your own mind before attempting to explain them to your audience.

## Templates for Comparing

The following templates can help you to generate ideas for a comparison and then to start drafting. Don't take these as formulas where you just have to fill in the blanks. There are no easy formulas for good writing. But these templates can help you plot out some of the key moves of comparison and contrast and thus may serve as good starting points.

> ► X and Y can be compared on the grounds that both are _____.

> ► Like X, Y is also _____, _____, and _____.

> ► Although X and Y are both _____, the differences between them far outweigh the similarities. For example, X is _____, _____, and _____, while Y is _____, _____, and _____.

> ► Unlike X, Y is _____.

> ► Despite their differences, X and Y are basically alike in that _____.

> ► At first glance, X and Y seem _____; however, a closer look reveals _____.

> ► In comparing X and Y, we can see that _____.

For more techniques to help you generate ideas and start writing a comparison essay, see Chapter 3.

## Organizing a Comparison

As we discussed earlier, there are fundamentally two ways to organize a comparison: point by point or subject by subject. With a point-by-point organization (like Larner's comparison of Wilt Chamberlain and Bill Russell), you discuss each point of comparison (or contrast) between your two subjects before going on to the next point. With the subject-by-subject method, you discuss each subject individually, making a number of points about one subject and then covering more or less the same points about the other subject. This is the organization Conroy follows in his comparison of yo-yos.

Which method of organization should you use? You will probably find that the point-by-point method works best for beginning and ending an essay, while the subject-by-subject method serves you well for longer stretches in the main body.

One reason for using the subject-by-subject method to organize most of your essay is that the point-by-point method, when relentlessly applied, can make the reader a little seasick as you jump back and forth from your first subject to your second. With the subject-by-subject method, you do not have to give equal weight to both subjects. The subject-by-subject method is, thus, indispensable for treating a subject in depth, whereas the point-by-point method is an efficient way to establish a basis of comparison at the beginning, to remind readers along the way why two subjects are being compared, and to sum up your essay at the end.

Jeff Jacoby begins with the point-by-point method on p. 332.

## Stating Your Point

Your main point in drawing a comparison will determine whether you emphasize similarities or differences. For instance, if your thesis is that there are certain fundamental qualities that all successful coaches share—and you're comparing the best coaches from your own high school days to make this point—you will focus on the similarities among them. However, if you're comparing blind dates to make the point that it's difficult to be prepared for a blind date because no two are alike, you would focus on the differences among the blind dates you've had.

Whatever the main point of your comparison might be, state it clearly right away in an explicit THESIS STATEMENT: "Blind dates are inherently unpredictable; since no two are alike, the best way to go into one is with no expectations at all." Be sure to indicate to readers which you are going to emphasize—the similarities or differences between your subjects. Then, in the body of your essay, use specific points of comparison to show those similarities or differences and to prove your main point.

## Providing Sufficient Points of Comparison

No matter how you organize a comparison essay, you will have to provide a sufficient number of points of comparison between your subjects to demonstrate that they are truly comparable and to justify your reasons for comparing them. How many points of comparison are enough to do the job?

Sufficiency isn't strictly a matter of numbers. It depends, in part, on just how inclined your audience is to accept (or reject) the main point your comparison is intended to make. If you are comparing subjects that your readers are not familiar with, you may have to give more examples of similarities or differences than you would if your readers already knew a lot about your subjects. For instance, if you're comparing the racing styles of cyclists Bradley Wiggins and Mark Cavendish, readers who think the Tour de France is a vacation package are going to require more (and more basic) points of comparison than avid cycling fans will.

To determine how many points of comparison you need to make, consider your intended readers, and choose the points of comparison you think they will find most useful, interesting, or otherwise convincing. Then give a sufficient number to get your larger point across, but not so many that you run the comparison into the ground.

# EDITING FOR COMMON ERRORS
# IN COMPARISONS

Like other kinds of writing, comparison uses distinctive patterns of language and punctuation—and thus invites typical kinds of errors. The following tips will help you to check for (and correct) these common errors when you make comparisons in your own writing.

## Make sure all comparisons are complete

Comparisons examine at least two things at once. Check to make sure you've identified both of them; otherwise, readers may not fully understand what is being compared.

► When you enter a chapel, there is more solitude and calm <u>than in the world outside</u>.

► Most public chapels are not as quiet <u>as those attached to monasteries</u>.

## Check that all comparisons are grammatically consistent

When you compare items, they should be grammatically parallel—that is, similar in grammatical form. The original version of this sentence unintentionally compares churches to a country.

► In Italy the churches seemed even older than <u>those in</u> France.

## Check for common errors in usage

*GOOD, WELL, BETTER*

*Good* is an adjective; *well* is the adverb form. *Better* can be either an adjective or an adverb.

► Celeste plays the clarinet ~~good~~ *well*, but Angela plays even *better*.

## BETWEEN, AMONG

Use *between* when you're comparing two items; use *among* when you're comparing three or more.

▸ *Between* France and Germany, Germany has the larger economy.

▸ *Among* all the countries in the euro zone, Germany has the largest economy.

# Buses, Bikes, and Cars

When you compare and contrast, you show the similarities and differences among related subjects. Buses, cars, and bikes are related subjects—all are common means of transportation—and in this visual comparison from the website of the Cycling Promotion Fund, an organization that promotes cycling across communities in Australia, they're shown as transporting the same number of passengers. The big difference here, of course, is in the number of vehicles that appear with the large group of people in each photo: at least 100 cars, just as many bicycles, but only one long bus. We draw comparisons in order to make a larger point, and in this case, the one here aligns with the fund's mission: to make cities biker friendly, to fight climate change, and to reduce congestion. If more people used public transit and rode bikes, we could save fuel and perhaps leave a smaller carbon footprint.

## DAN TREADWAY

# FOOTBALL VS. ASIAN STUDIES

DAN TREADWAY wrote "Football vs. Asian Studies" as a senior majoring in communication studies at the University of Texas, Austin. Far from comparing apples to oranges, his essay uses strategies of comparison to uncover unexpected similarities between sports and academics at a large state university. "Sadly," argues Treadway, an associate editor of the *Daily Texan*, those similarities are generally ignored. "Football vs. Asian Studies" was a finalist in a student writing contest sponsored in 2010 by the *Nation* magazine.

## Football vs. Asian Studies

The University of Texas football team is among the [1] best in the nation. It has been a beloved part of the university since 1894, and has grown each year since its inception. The program is seemingly larger than life, making more money last year than any other athletic program in history. Its place at this university is defined and unquestioned. If one attends the University of Texas, it's impossible to not know about the importance of the football team.

*The University of Texas Asian Studies program is one* [2] *of the best in the nation. It's been a part of the university since 1994, and is already among the most distinguished academic departments of its kind. Its place at this university is defined to those who know about the major, but it's quite possible to study on campus for four years and never become aware of the fact that the Asian Studies program even exists.*

> Italics indicate change from subject A (football) to subject B (Asian Studies)

The football team is comprised of eighty-five [3] student-athletes who receive full scholarships to attend the university.

*While there is limited funding for those who study* [4] *abroad, the Department of Asian Studies does not have the funds to offer scholarships specifically aimed at students within the major to help them pay for classes at UT.*

> Covers the same points in the same order, here and throughout, for each subject

To bolster the team's defense, the University [5] recently recruited Will Muschamp, the former defensive coordinator at Auburn University, to stabilize the shaky unit. Muschamp was offered a salary of $425,000 annually to bring his unique services to the program. Entering only his third year at the University, Muschamp has already become a team favorite among players and fans alike.

*To bolster an incomplete Asian Studies program, stu-*    6
*dents along with faculty lobbied tirelessly for the university to*
*adopt a class that would teach the Vietnamese language. After*
*two years of diligent campaigning, the university decided to*
*add the language to the curriculum in the Department of*
*Asian Studies in 2006. Dr. Hoang Ngo was selected to teach*
*both the regular and advanced Vietnamese courses at the Uni-*
*versity. He was offered a salary of a little more than $45,000*
*for his unique services. Ngo quickly became a favorite among*
*his students for his knowledge and patience.*

Football is the most popular spectator sport in the    7
state of Texas without rival. The sport's importance to
our heritage is well known and documented.

*Vietnamese is the third-most-spoken language in the*    8
*state of Texas behind English and Spanish. This is a fact that*
*is not well known or documented.*

Under head coach Mack Brown, the Longhorns    9
football program has soared to new heights. In the past
decade, the Longhorns have won more games than in any
other ten-year stretch in the program's history. Brown's
smart coaching and savvy recruiting have built a seemingly unstoppable athletic machine in the city of Austin.
His success has distinguished this era of Texas football
as the golden age, unmatched by teams from past
generations.

*Under Dr. Hoang Ngo, the Vietnamese language course*    10
*had grown quite popular in a short period of time. According*
*to Nickie Tran, a former student in Ngo's class, "[Teaching the*
*Vietnamese language] is important because if you talk to a lot*
*of second-generation Asian-Americans, you hear it's hard for*
*them to retain their native language." Teaching Vietnamese*

> Frequent repetition of phrases establishes a firm basis of comparison

at the University of Texas has enabled this generation of
Vietnamese-Americans to develop a special connection to generations past.

Mack Brown recently received a $2.1 million pay          11
raise on his $3 million base salary to reward all of his suc-
cess. The University of Texas's football program is
thriving—last year it generated $120 million in revenue.

*Dr. Ngo has now moved back to Vietnam to seek new*          12
*employment. The Vietnamese language program at UT has*
*been discontinued. A casualty of budget cuts, the administra-*          Frames Asian
*tion felt that the program was expendable because of its small*          Studies as a
*size—its absence will save the university approximately*          bargain by
*$50,000 a year.*          comparison

A 2009 study revealed that less than 50 percent of          13
football players at the University of Texas ultimately
graduated and received a degree.

*With the elimination of the Vietnamese language pro-*          14
*gram, dozens of students will be forced to take courses in a dif-*
*ferent foreign language so that they may fulfill their academic*
*requirement and graduate with a degree.*

Come September, when students come back to          15
campus, the most popular sport in Texas will be put on
display before an ecstatic crowd of more than 100,000
screaming people in Darrell K. Royal-Texas Memorial
Stadium, which recently received $179 million in
renovations.

*Come September, when students come back to campus,*          16          Conclusion
*the third most spoken language in Texas will no longer be*          emphasizes points
*taught due to budgetary constraints and sadly, hardly anybody*          of contrast
*will ask questions or even notice.*          between the two
          subjects

JEFF JACOBY

# WATCHING OPRAH
# FROM BEHIND THE VEIL

JEFF JACOBY (b. 1959) is a columnist for the *Boston Globe*. Before turning to journalism, Jacoby practiced law, worked on a political campaign, assisted the president of Boston University, and hosted a television show, *Talk of New England*. In 2004 he received the Thomas Paine Award from the libertarian Institute for Justice, presented to journalists dedicated "to the preservation and championing of individual liberty." First published in the *Globe* (2008), "Watching Oprah from Behind the Veil" compares the life and circumstances of an American icon with those of the Arab women who have made her show the most popular English-language program in Saudi Arabia.

---

S HE HAS BEEN CALLED the most influential woman of our time. They are 1 among the most disempowered women on earth.

   She is a self-made billionaire, with worldwide interests that range from 2 television to publishing to education. They are forbidden to get a job without the permission of a male "guardian," and the overwhelming majority of them are unemployed.

She has a face that is recognized the world over. They cannot leave home  3
without covering their face and obscuring their figure in a cloak.

She is famous for her message of confidence, self-improvement, and spiritual  4
uplift. They are denied the right to make the simplest decisions, treated by law like
children who cannot be trusted with authority over their own well-being.

She, of course, is Oprah Winfrey. They are the multitude of Saudi Ara-  5
bian women whose devotion to her has made *The Oprah Winfrey Show*—
broadcast twice daily on a Dubai-based satellite channel—the highest-rated
English-language program in the kingdom.

A recent *New York Times* story—"Veiled Saudi Women Are Discovering  6
an Unlikely Role Model in Oprah Winfrey"—explored the appeal of America's
iconic talk-show host for the marginalized women of the Arabian peninsula.

"In a country where the sexes are rigorously separated, where topics like  7
sex and race are rarely discussed openly, and where a strict code of public
morality is enforced by religious police," the *Times* noted, "Ms. Winfrey provides many young Saudi women with new ways of thinking about the way
local taboos affect their lives. . . . Some women here say Ms. Winfrey's assurances to her viewers—that no matter how restricted or even abusive their
circumstances may be, they can take control in small ways and create lives of
value—help them find meaning in their cramped, veiled existence."

And so they avidly analyze Oprah's clothes and hairstyles, and circulate  8
"dog-eared copies" of her magazine, *O*, and write letters telling her of their
dreams and disappointments. Many undoubtedly dream of doing
what she did—freeing themselves from the shackling circumstances into which they were born and rising as high as their talents can take them.

> Jacoby is now using
> the subject-by-
> subject method,
> p. 318.

But the television star never faced the obstacles that confront her Saudi fans.  9

That is not to minimize the daunting odds Oprah overcame. She was  10
born to an unwed teenage housemaid in pre-civil rights Mississippi, and spent
her first years in such poverty that at times she wore dresses made from potato
sacks. She was sexually molested as a child, and ran away from home as a
young teen. It was a squalid beginning, one that would have defeated many
people not blessed with Oprah's intelligence and drive and native gifts.

But whatever else may be said of Oprah's life, it was never crippled by  11
Wahhabism, the fundamentalist strain of Islam that dominates Saudi Arabia
and immiserates Saudi women in ruthless gender apartheid. Strict sex

segregation is the law of the land. Women are forbidden to drive, to vote, to freely marry or divorce, to appear in public without a husband or other male guardian, or to attend university without their father's permission. They can be jailed—or worse—for riding in a car with a man to whom they are unrelated. Their testimony in court carries less weight than a man's. They cannot even file a criminal complaint without a male guardian's permission—not even in cases of domestic abuse, when it is their "guardian" who has attacked them.

Could Oprah herself have surmounted such pervasive repression?          12

Some Saudi women manage to find jobs, but Wahhabist opposition   13
is fierce. In 2006, Youssef Ibrahim reported in the *New York Sun* on Nabil Ramadan, the owner of a fast-food restaurant in Ranoosh who hired two women to take telephone orders. Within twenty-four hours, the religious police had him arrested and shut down the restaurant for "promoting lewdness." Ramadan was sentenced by a religious court to ninety lashes on his back and buttocks.

Is it any wonder that women trapped in a culture that treats them so   14
wretchedly idolize someone like Oprah, who epitomizes so much that is absent from their lives? A nation that degrades its women degrades itself, and Oprah's message is an antidote to degradation. Why do they love her? Because all the lies of the Wahhabists cannot stifle the truth she embodies: The blessings of liberty were made for women, too.

### FOR DISCUSSION

1. According to Jeff Jacoby, why do Oprah Winfrey and her show appeal to so many women in Saudi Arabia?

2. What particular lesson about living in "restricted or even abusive" circumstances does Oprah have to teach these women (7)?

3. What obstacles do Saudi women face that Oprah did not, even though she grew up poor in "pre-civil rights Mississippi" (10)?

4. What is the root cause, according to Jacoby, of the "ruthless gender apartheid" that many Saudi women must contend with (11)?

### STRATEGIES AND STRUCTURES

1. Do you think Jacoby's intended **AUDIENCE** for this **COMPARISON** essay is mostly female, mostly male, or both? Why do you think so?

2. On what basis is Jacoby comparing some of "the most disempowered women on earth" to the "influential" Oprah Winfrey (1)? What common ground do they share?

3. Why does Jacoby wait until the fifth paragraph to name his subjects? What is the effect of referring to them at first as "she" and "they"? What does this contribute to his comparison?

4. Does Jacoby rely more on the point-by-point or subject-by-subject method for organizing his comparison? Is this method of organization effective for this essay? Explain.

5. What is the main point of Jacoby's comparison? Where does he state it most directly?

6. What are some of Jacoby's most effective points of comparison? Does he give a sufficient number of them to support his point? Explain.

7. Jacoby includes a brief **NARRATIVE** about Oprah's life in paragraph 10. What purpose does this story serve in his comparison? Where else does Jacoby incorporate narrative in his essay?

## WORDS AND FIGURES OF SPEECH

1. Though many Arab women wear veils, Jacoby is not simply referring to their attire in his title. Explain the **METAPHOR** of the phrase "from behind the veil."

2. Why does Jacoby put the word *guardian* in quotation marks (2)?

3. "Immiserates," meaning makes miserable, might not be a word you hear every day (11). Why not? Should Jacoby have used a more common word? Explain.

4. "Apartheid" is a term that refers to a systematic policy of discrimination based on race (11). How valid do you find Jacoby's use of this term in the context of gender? Explain.

## FOR WRITING

1. Compile a list of the points of comparison you would make if you were comparing Oprah Winfrey to those who watched her show and read her magazine in the United States.

2. Write an essay comparing the characteristics and values of an influential (or notorious) public figure with those of a particular group of his or her most avid admirers (or detractors).

# TAKING MY PARENTS TO COLLEGE

JENNINE CAPÓ CRUCET (b. 1981) is a novelist and short-story writer. Crucet grew up in Hialeah, a neighborhood in Miami, Florida. In describing her writing, she says that it "has been shaped by South Florida, its people and its landscape, and by the stories of Cuba repeated to me almost daily by my parents and *abuelos.*" Her debut story collection, *How to Leave Hialeah* (2009), won the Iowa Short Fiction Prize and John Gardner Book Award, among others. Her first novel, *Make Your Home among Strangers* (2015), tells the story of a young woman born to Cuban immigrants who, after leaving her home in Miami to attend college, faces challenges personally and academically. In addition to her writing, Crucet is an assistant professor of English and Ethnic Studies at the University of Nebraska in Lincoln. In her essay "Taking My Parents to College," published in the *New York Times* (2015), Crucet describes her first days at Cornell University, when she felt clueless and alone compared to her peers.

I T WAS A SIMPLE QUESTION, but we couldn't find the answer in any of the paperwork the college had sent. How long was my family supposed to stay for orientation? This was 1999, so Google wasn't really a verb yet, and we were a low-income family (according to my new school) without regular Internet access.

I was a first-generation college student as well as the first in our family to be born in America—my parents were born in Cuba—and we didn't yet know that families were supposed to leave pretty much right after they unloaded your stuff from the car.

We all made the trip from Miami, my hometown, to what would be my new home at Cornell University. Shortly after arriving on campus, the five of us—my parents, my younger sister, my abuela and me—found ourselves listening to a dean end his welcome speech with the words: "Now, parents, please: Go!"

Almost everyone in the audience laughed, but not me, and not my parents. They turned to me and said, "What does he mean, *Go?*" I was just as confused as they were: We thought we *all* needed to be there for freshman orientation—the whole family, for the entirety of it. My dad had booked their hotel through the day after my classes officially began. They'd used all their vacation days from work and had been saving for months to get me to school and go through our orientation.

> The opening sentence of this paragraph identifies the subjects of comparison.

Every afternoon during that week, we had to go back to the only department store we could find, the now-defunct Ames, for some stupid thing we hadn't known was a necessity, something not in our budget: shower shoes, extra-long twin sheets, mesh laundry bags. Before the other families left, we carefully watched them—they knew what they were doing—and we made new shopping lists with our limited vocabulary: *Those things that lift up the bed*, we wrote. *That plastic thing to carry stuff to the bathroom.*

My family followed me around as I visited department offices during course registration. *Only four classes?* they asked, assuming I was mistakenly taking my first semester too easy. They walked with me to buildings I was supposed to be finding on my own. They waited outside those buildings so that we could all leave from there and go to lunch together.

The five of us wandered each day through the dining hall's doors. "You guys are still here!" the over-friendly person swiping ID cards said after day three. "They sure are!" I chirped back, learning via the cues of my hallmates that I was supposed to want my family gone. But it was an act: We sat together at meals—amid all the other students, already making friends—my mom placing a napkin and fork at each place, setting the table as we did at home.

I don't even remember the moment they drove away. I'm told it's one of 8 those instances you never forget, that second when you realize you're finally on your own. But for me, it's not there—perhaps because, when you're the first in your family to go to college, you never truly feel like they've let you go.

They did eventually leave—of course they did—and a week into classes, 9 I received the topics for what would be my first college paper, in an English course on the modern novel. I might as well have been my non-English-speaking grandmother trying to read and understand them: The language felt that foreign. I called my mom at work and in tears told her that I had to come home, that I'd made a terrible mistake.

She sighed into the phone and said: "Just read me the first question. 10 We'll go through it a little at a time and figure it out."

I read her the topic slowly, pausing after each sentence, waiting for her 11 to say something. The first topic was two paragraphs long. I remember it had the word *intersectionalities* in it. And the word *gendered*. And maybe the phrase *theoretical framework*. I waited for her response and for the ways it would encourage me, for her to tell me I could do this, that I would eventually be the first in my family to graduate from college.

"You're right," she said after a moment. "You're screwed." 12

Other parents—parents who have gone to college themselves—might 13 have known at that point to encourage their kid to go to office hours, or to the writing center, or to ask for help. But my mom thought I was as alone as I feared.

"I have no idea what any of that means," she said. "I don't even know 14 how it's a *question*."

While my college had done an excellent job recruiting me, I had no road 15 map for what I was supposed to do once I made it to campus. I'd already embarrassed myself by doing things like asking my R.A. what time the dorm closed for the night. As far as I knew, there'd been no mandatory meeting geared toward first-generation students like me: Aside from a check-in with my financial aid officer when she explained what work-study was (I didn't know and worried it meant I had to join the army or something) and where she had me sign for my loans, I was mostly keeping to myself to hide the fact that I was a very special kind of lost. I folded the sheet with the paper topics in half and put it in my desk drawer.

"I don't know what you're gonna do," my mom almost laughed. "Maybe—    16
have you looked in the dictionary?"

I started crying harder, my hand over the receiver.                    17

"You still there?" she eventually asked, clearly hiding her own tears. I    18
murmured *Mmmhmm.*

"Look, just stick it out up there until Christmas," she said. "We have no    19
more vacation days this year. We can't take off any more time to go get you."

"O.K.," I swallowed. I started breathing in through my nose and out    20
through my mouth, calming myself. "I can do that," I said.

My mom laughed for real this time and said, "Mamita, you don't really    21
have a choice."

She didn't say this in a mean way. She was just telling me the truth.    22
"This whole thing was your idea, remember?" she said. Then she told me she had to go, that she needed to get back to work.

So I got back to work, too, and *Get back to work* became a sort of mantra    23
for me. I tackled the paper with the same focus that had landed me, to everyone's surprise—even my own—at Cornell in the first place. I did O.K. on it, earning a "B−/C" (I never found out how a grade could have a slash in it, but now that I'm an English professor I understand what he was trying to say). The professor had covered the typed pages with comments and questions, and it was in his endnote that he listed the various campus resources available to me.

My mom didn't ask outright what grade I earned—she eventually    24
stopped asking about assignments altogether—and I learned from my peers that grades were something that I didn't have to share with my parents the way I had in high school.

My grades were the first of many elements of my new life for which they    25
had no context and which they wouldn't understand. With each semester, what I was doing became, for them, as indecipherable as that paper topic; they didn't even know what questions to ask. And that, for me, is the quintessential quality of the first-generation college student's experience. It's not even knowing what you don't know.

## FOR DISCUSSION

1. When Jennine Capó Crucet went off to college, she didn't know that her family was not supposed to come and stay through the entire orientation period. Was she the only one to blame? Why or why not?

2. Crucet started college in 1999. By contrast, she implies, first-generation students today would likely have a better idea of what to expect than she did. Do you agree? Explain.

3. Crucet tells us that she succeeded at her studies in time. How did she do with regard to the strange language that was such a source of anxiety to her in the beginning? How do we know?

4. In Crucet's comparison, what are some of the main differences between her parents and those of many of her fellow classmates? What strengths (if any) does Crucet ascribe to her family (particularly her mother)?

## STRATEGIES AND STRUCTURES

1. Crucet begins her essay by **COMPARING AND CONTRASTING** her family, including herself, with those families that "knew what they were doing" (5). By the end of her essay, who is she mostly contrasting with whom? Where and why does her focus shift during the course of her essay?

2. Where does Crucet explicitly compare her subsequent life in college to the set of topics she was given for her first college paper? What is her point in making the comparison? Is it effective for this purpose? Why or why not?

3. When Crucet's English professor returns her first paper, he has covered it "with comments and questions" and given her a grade of B−/C (23). What else does her professor provide in his endnote? Why and how is this relevant to the story she is telling?

4. Crucet's essay includes many elements of **NARRATIVE**. Do these elements support (or fail to support) the comparisons she is making? Be sure to comment on her use of **DIALOGUE**, particularly in the phone conversation with her mother.

5. Crucet ends her essay with a **DEFINITION**: "And that, for me, is the quintessential quality of the first-generation college student's experience. It's not even knowing what you don't know" (25). She notes that her definition is particular to her experience with the addition of "for me." Does this make her definition more or less persuasive? Explain.

**WORDS AND FIGURES OF SPEECH**

1. *Abuela* (3) is the word for grandmother in Spanish. Should Crucet have given an English translation when she first uses the term in her essay? Why or why not?

2. *Indecipherable* (25) is usually applied to forms of writing, often in code, that the reader cannot understand. To whom or what is Crucet applying it? Is this an apt use of the term? Why or why not?

3. Throughout her college years, says Crucet, "*Get back to work*" became her "mantra" (23). Look up the term in a dictionary. How and how well does it apply to Crucet's trials and tribulations—to those of college in general?

4. In ancient Greek philosophy, the word *quintessence* is referred to a "fifth essence" in addition to earth, air, fire, and water, which were thought to be the four essential elements of the physical universe. Look up the term and explain what Crucet means by a "quintessential quality" (25).

**FOR WRITING**

1. Education, Crucet implies, is all about asking questions. In a paragraph or two, respond to this idea; be sure, however, to say what else, if anything, "getting an education" entails in your view.

2. Starting college is a new experience for anyone, whether or not they are the first member of their family to attend. Write an essay about your experience (or that of someone you know) going to college. Compare the experience in detail to that of your (or their) classmates.

**BRUCE CATTON**

# GRANT AND LEE:
# A STUDY IN CONTRASTS

BRUCE CATTON (1899–1979) was a distinguished historian of the Civil War
and winner of both the Pulitzer Prize and the National Book Award for *A
Stillness at Appomattox* (1953). Among Catton's many other Civil War
books are *This Hallowed Ground* (1956), *The Army of the Potomac* (1962),
*Terrible Swift Sword* (1963), and *Grant Takes Command* (1969). It was not,
said Catton, "the strategy or political meanings" of the Civil War that most
fascinated him, but the "almost incomprehensible emotional experience
which this war brought to our country." First published in the essay collection *The American Story* (1955), "Grant and Lee: A Study in Contrasts"
looks at two great Americans—one "the modern man emerging," the other
seemingly from "the age of chivalry."

WHEN ULYSSES S. GRANT AND ROBERT E. LEE MET in the parlor of a modest   1
house at Appomattox Court House, Virginia, on April 9, 1865, to work out the terms for the surrender of Lee's Army of Northern Virginia, a great chapter in American life came to a close, and a great new chapter began.

These men were bringing the Civil War[1] to its virtual finish. To be sure,   2
other armies had yet to surrender, and for a few days the fugitive Confederate government would struggle desperately and vainly, trying to find some way to go on living now that its chief support was gone. But in effect it was all over when Grant and Lee signed the papers. And the little room where they wrote out the terms was the scene of one of the poignant, dramatic contrasts in American history.

They were two strong men, these oddly different generals, and they rep-   3
resented the strengths of two conflicting currents that, through them, had come into final collision.

Back of Robert E. Lee was the notion that the old aristocratic concept   4
might somehow survive and be dominant in American life.

Lee was tidewater Virginia,[2] and in his background were family, culture,   5
and tradition . . . the age of chivalry transplanted to a New World which was making its own legends and its own myths. He embodied a way of life that had come down through the age of knighthood and the English country squire. America was a land that was beginning all over again, dedicated to nothing much more complicated than the rather hazy belief that all men had equal rights and should have an equal chance in the world. In such a land Lee stood for the feeling that it was somehow of advantage to human society to have a pronounced inequality in the social structure. There should be a leisure class, backed by ownership of land; in turn, society itself should be keyed to the land as the chief source of wealth and influence. It would bring forth (according to this ideal) a class of men with a strong sense of obligation to the community; men

1. Fought between "the Union" (Northern states that stayed loyal to the federal government under President Abraham Lincoln) and "the Confederacy" (eleven slave-holding Southern states and their sympathizers that formed a separate government under Jefferson Davis; 1861–1865).

2. Coastal region of eastern Virginia. Jamestown, the first British colony in North America, was settled in this region in 1607.

who lived not to gain advantage for themselves, but to meet the solemn obligations which had been laid on them by the very fact that they were privileged. From them the country would get its leadership; to them it could look for the higher values—of thought, of conduct, of personal deportment—to give it strength and virtue.

Lee embodied the noblest elements of this aristocratic ideal. Through him, 6 the landed nobility justified itself. For four years, the Southern states had fought a desperate war to uphold the ideals for which Lee stood. In the end, it almost seemed as if the Confederacy fought for Lee; as if he himself was the Confederacy . . . the best thing that the way of life for which the Confederacy stood could ever have to offer. He had passed into legend before Appomattox. Thousands of tired, underfed, poorly clothed Confederate soldiers, long since past the simple enthusiasm of the early days of the struggle, somehow considered Lee the symbol of everything for which they had been willing to die. But they could not quite put this feeling into words. If the Lost Cause, sanctified by so much heroism and so many deaths, had a living justification, its justification was General Lee.

Grant, the son of a tanner on the Western frontier, was everything Lee 7 was not. He had come up the hard way and embodied nothing in particular except the eternal toughness and sinewy fiber of the men who grew up beyond the mountains. He was one of a body of men who owed reverence and obeisance to no one, who were self-reliant to a fault, who cared hardly anything for the past but who had a sharp eye for the future.

These frontier men were the precise opposites of the tidewater aristocrats. 8 Back of them, in the great surge that had taken people over the Alleghenies[3] and into the opening Western country, there was a deep, implicit dissatisfaction with a past that had settled into grooves. They stood for democracy, not from any reasoned conclusion about the proper ordering of human society, but simply because they had grown up in the middle of democracy and knew how it worked. Their society might have privileges, but they would be privileges each man had won for himself. Forms and patterns meant nothing. No man was born to anything, except perhaps to a chance to show how far he could rise. Life was competition.

Yet along with this feeling had come a deep sense of belonging to a 9 national community. The Westerner who developed a farm, opened a shop, or set up in business as a trader, could hope to prosper only as his own community

---

3. Mountain range that runs from north-central Pennsylvania to southwestern Virginia.

prospered—and his community ran from the Atlantic to the Pacific and from Canada down to Mexico. If the land was settled, with towns and highways and accessible markets, he could better himself. He saw his fate in terms of the nation's own destiny. As its horizons expanded, so did his. He had, in other words, an acute dollars-and-cents stake in the continued growth and development of his country.

And that, perhaps, is where the contrast between Grant and Lee becomes most striking. The Virginia aristocrat, inevitably, saw himself in relation to his own region. He lived in a static society which could endure almost anything except change. Instinctively, his first loyalty would go to the locality in which that society existed. He would fight to the limit of endurance to defend it, because in defending it he was defending everything that gave his own life its deepest meaning.

The Westerner, on the other hand, would fight with an equal tenacity for the broader concept of society. He fought so because everything he lived by was tied to growth, expansion, and a constantly widening horizon. What he lived by would survive or fall with the nation itself. He could not possibly stand by unmoved in the face of an attempt to destroy the Union. He would combat it with everything he had, because he could only see it as an effort to cut the ground out from under his feet.

So Grant and Lee were in complete contrast, representing two diametrically opposed elements in American life. Grant was the modern man emerging; beyond him, ready to come on the stage, was the great age of steel and machinery, of crowded cities and a restless burgeoning vitality. Lee might have ridden down from the old age of chivalry, lance in hand, silken banner fluttering over his head. Each man was the perfect champion of his cause, drawing both his strengths and his weaknesses from the people he led.

Yet it was not all contrast, after all. Different as they were—in background, in personality, in underlying aspiration—these two great soldiers had much in common. Under everything else, they were marvelous fighters. Furthermore, their fighting qualities were really very much alike.

A balanced comparison includes both similarities and differences.

Each man had, to begin with, the great virtue of utter tenacity and fidelity. Grant fought his way down the Mississippi Valley in spite of acute personal discouragement and profound military handicaps. Lee hung on in the trenches at Petersburg after hope itself had died. In each man there was an

*Union general Ulysses S. Grant, 1864. Photograph by Mathew Brady.*

*Confederate general Robert E. Lee, 1860.*

indomitable quality . . . the born fighter's refusal to give up as long as he can still remain on his feet and lift his two fists.

Daring and resourcefulness they had, too; the ability to think faster and move faster than the enemy. These were the qualities which gave Lee the dazzling campaigns of Second Manassas and Chancellorsville and won Vicksburg for Grant. 15

Lastly, and perhaps greatest of all, there was the ability, at the end, to turn quickly from war to peace once the fighting was over. Out of the way these two men behaved at Appomattox came the possibility of a peace of reconciliation. It was a possibility not wholly realized, in the years to come, but which did, in the end, help the two sections to become one nation again . . . after a war whose bitterness might have seemed to make such a reunion wholly impossible. No part of either man's life became him more than the part he played in this brief meeting in the McLean house at Appomattox. Their behavior there put all succeeding generations of Americans in their debt. Two great Americans, Grant and Lee—very different, yet under everything very much alike. Their encounter at Appomattox was one of the great moments of American history. 16

### FOR DISCUSSION

1. Bruce Catton writes that generals Lee and Grant represented two conflicting currents of American culture. What were these currents? What **CONTRASTING** qualities and ideals does Catton associate with each man?

2. What qualities, according to Catton, did Grant and Lee have in common? What did these shared qualities enable each man to accomplish?

3. With Lee's surrender, says Catton, "a great new chapter" of American history began (1). What characteristics of the new era does Catton anticipate in his **DESCRIPTION** of Grant?

4. Catton does not describe, in any detail, how Grant and Lee behaved as they worked out the terms of peace at Appomattox. What does he imply about the conduct of the two men in general?

### STRATEGIES AND STRUCTURES

1. Beginning with paragraph 3, Catton provides specific details to illustrate the contrast between the two generals. How does Catton organize his contrast—point by

point or subject by subject? In what paragraphs does he turn to the similarities between the two men, and how are they organized?

2. Which sentence in the final paragraph brings together both the differences and the similarities outlined in the preceding paragraphs? How does this paragraph recall the opening paragraphs of the essay? Why might Catton end with an echo of his beginning?

3. Catton does not really give specific reasons for the Confederacy's defeat. What general explanation does he hint at, however, when he associates Lee with a "static society" and Grant with a society of "restless burgeoning vitality" (10, 12)? What is Catton's purpose in drawing this extensive comparison?

4. In comparing and contrasting the two generals in this essay, Catton also describes two regional types. What are some of the specific personal characteristics Catton ascribes to Grant and Lee that, at the same time, make them representative figures?

## WORDS AND FIGURES OF SPEECH

1. Catton describes the parlor where Grant and Lee met as the "scene" of a "dramatic" contrast, and he says that a new era was ready to come on stage (2). What view of history is suggested by these METAPHORS?

2. What does Catton mean by "the Lost Cause" in paragraph 6?

3. What is the precise meaning of "obeisance" (7)? Why might Catton choose this term instead of the more common *obedience* when describing General Grant?

4. Look up any of the following words that you would like to know more about: "fugitive" (2), "poignant" (2), "chivalry" (5), "sinewy" (7), "implicit" (8), "tenacity" (11), "diametrically" (12), "acute" (14), "profound" (14), "indomitable" (14). What words would you substitute to help make the TONE of the essay less formal?

## FOR WRITING

1. Photographs of Grant and Lee are included with this essay. Consider what each photograph contributes to your understanding of the men and their roles in history. Write several paragraphs comparing and contrasting the two photographs and what they reveal about each man.

2. Write an essay comparing and contrasting a pair of important historical or public figures with whom you are familiar—Thomas Jefferson and Alexander Hamilton or Hillary Clinton and Michelle Obama, for example.

# GARY SOTO

# LIKE MEXICANS

GARY SOTO (b. 1952), who grew up in Fresno, California, taught creative writing at the University of California at Riverside. He is the author of eleven books of poetry, numerous stories for children and young adults, and several novels, including *Nickel and Dime* (2000), *Poetry Lover* (2001), and *Amnesia in a Republican Country* (2003). Soto's memoir, *Living up the Street* (1985), won an American Book Award. In "Like Mexicans," from *Small Faces* (1986), another collection of reminiscences about growing up in the barrio, Soto compares his future wife's Japanese American family with his own Mexican American one.

•⊢————————————————————————————⊣•

M Y GRANDMOTHER GAVE ME BAD ADVICE AND GOOD ADVICE when I was in 1 my early teens. For the bad advice, she said that I should become a barber because they made good money and listened to the radio all day. "Honey, they don't work como burros," she would say every time I visited her. She made the sound of donkeys braying. "Like that, honey!" For the good advice, she said that I should marry a Mexican girl. "No Okies, hijo"—she would say—"Look, my son. He marry one and they fight every day about I don't know what and I don't know what." For her, everyone who wasn't Mexican, black, or Asian were Okies. The French were Okies, the Italians in suits were Okies. When I asked about Jews, whom I had read about, she asked for a picture. I rode home on my bicycle and returned with a calendar depicting the important races of the world. "Pues si, son Okies tambien!"[1] she said, nodding her head. She waved the calendar away and we went to the living room where she lectured me on the virtues of the Mexican girl: first, she could cook and, second, she acted like a woman, not a man, in her husband's home. She said she would tell me about a third when I got a little older.

I asked my mother about it—becoming a barber and marrying Mexican.   2
She was in the kitchen. Steam curled from a pot of boiling beans, the radio was on, looking as squat as a loaf of bread. "Well, if you want to be a barber—they say they make good money." She slapped a round steak with a knife, her glasses slipping down with each strike. She stopped and looked up. "If you find a good Mexican girl, marry her of course." She returned to slapping the meat and I went to the backyard where my brother and David King were sitting on the lawn feeling the inside of their cheeks.

"This is what girls feel like," my brother said, rubbing the inside of his   3
cheek. David put three fingers inside his mouth and scratched. I ignored them and climbed the back fence to see my best friend, Scott, a second-generation Okie. I called him and his mother pointed to the side of the house where his bedroom was, a small aluminum trailer, the kind you gawk at when they're flipped over on the freeway, wheels spinning in the air. I went around to find Scott pitching horseshoes.

I picked up a set of rusty ones and joined him. While we played, we   4
talked about school and friends and record albums. The horseshoes scuffed up dirt, sometimes ringing the iron that threw out a meager shadow like a sundial. After three argued-over games, we pulled two oranges apiece from his tree and started down the alley still talking school and friends and record albums. We pulled more oranges from the alley and talked about who we would marry. "No offense, Scott," I said with an orange slice in my mouth,

1. Well yes, they're Okies, too.

"but I would never marry an Okie." We walked in step, almost touching, with a sled of shadows dragging behind us. "No offense, Gary," Scott said, "but I would *never* marry a Mexican." I looked at him: a fang of orange slice showed from his munching mouth. I didn't think anything of it. He had his girl and I had mine. But our seventh-grade vision was the same: to marry, get jobs, buy cars and maybe a house if we had money left over.

We talked about our future lives until, to our surprise, we were on the 5 downtown mall, two miles from home. We bought a bag of popcorn at Penney's and sat on a bench near the fountain watching Mexican and Okie girls pass. "That one's mine," I pointed with my chin when a girl with eyebrows arched into black rainbows ambled by. "She's cute," Scott said about a girl with yellow hair and a mouthful of gum. We dreamed aloud, our chins busy pointing out girls. We agreed that we couldn't wait to become men and lift them onto our laps.

But the woman I married was not Mexican but Japanese. It was a surprise 6 to me. For years, I went about wide-eyed in my search for the brown girl in a white dress at a dance. I searched the playground at the baseball diamond. When the girls raced for grounders, their hair bounced like something that couldn't be caught. When they sat together in the lunchroom, heads pressed together, I knew they were talking about us Mexican guys. I saw them and dreamed them. I threw my face into my pillow, making up sentences that were good as in the movies.

But when I was twenty, I fell in love with this other girl who worried my 7 mother, who had my grandmother asking once again to see the calendar of the Important Races of the World. I told her I had thrown it away years before. I took a much-glanced-at snapshot from my wallet. We looked at it together, in silence. Then Grandma reclined in her chair, lit a cigarette, and said, "Es pretty." She blew and asked with all her worry pushed up to her forehead: "Chinese?"

I was in love and there was no looking back. She was the one. I told my 8 mother who was slapping hamburger into patties. "Well, sure if you want to marry her," she said. But the more I talked, the more concerned she became. Later I began to worry. Was it all a mistake? "Marry a Mexican girl," I heard my mother say in my mind. I heard it at breakfast. I heard it over math problems, between Western Civilization and cultural geography. But then one afternoon while I was hitchhiking home from school, it struck me like a baseball in the back: my mother wanted me to marry someone of my own social class—a poor girl. I considered my fiancée, Carolyn, and she didn't look poor, though I knew she came from a family of farm workers and pull-yourself-up-by-your-bootstraps ranchers. I asked my brother, who was marrying Mexican poor that fall, if I should marry a poor girl. He screamed "Yeah" above his terrible guitar playing in his bedroom. I considered my sister who had married Mexican. Cousins were dating Mexican. Uncles were remarrying poor women. I asked Scott, who was still my best friend, and he said, "She's too good for you, so you better not."

I worried about it until Carolyn took me home to meet her parents. We  9 drove in her Plymouth until the houses gave way to farms and ranches and finally her house fifty feet from the highway. When we pulled into the drive, I panicked and begged Carolyn to make a U-turn and go back so we could talk about it over a soda. She pinched my cheek, calling me a "silly boy." I felt better, though, when I got out of the car and saw the house: the chipped paint, a cracked window, boards for a walk to the back door. There were rusting cars near the barn. A tractor with a net of spiderwebs under a mulberry. A field. A bale of barbed wire like children's scribbling leaning against an empty chicken coop. Carolyn took my hand and pulled me to my future mother-in-law who was coming out to greet us.

We had lunch: sandwiches, potato chips, and iced tea. Carolyn and her  10 mother talked mostly about neighbors and the congregation at the Japanese Methodist Church in West Fresno. Her father, who was in khaki work clothes, excused himself with a wave that was almost a salute and went outside. I heard a truck start, a dog bark, and then the truck rattle away.

Carolyn's mother offered another sandwich, but I declined with a shake  11 of my head and a smile. I looked around when I could, when I was not saying over and over that I was a college student, hinting that I could take care of her daughter. I shifted my chair. I saw newspapers piled in corners, dusty cereal boxes and vinegar bottles in corners. The wallpaper was bubbled from rain that had come in from a bad roof. Dust. Dust lay on lamp shades and window sills. These people are just like Mexicans, I thought. Poor people.

> Soto is clearly stating his basis of comparison, pp. 320–21.

Carolyn's mother asked me through Carolyn if I would like a *sushi*. A  12 plate of black and white things were held in front of me. I took one, wide-eyed, and turned it over like a foreign coin. I was biting into one when I saw a kitten crawl up the window screen over the sink. I chewed and the kitten opened its mouth of terror as she crawled higher, wanting in to paw the leftovers from our plates. I looked at Carolyn who said that the cat was just showing off. I looked up in time to see it fall. It crawled up, then fell again.

We talked for an hour and had apple pie and coffee, slowly. Finally, we 13 got up with Carolyn taking my hand. Slightly embarrassed, I tried to pull away but her grip held me. I let her have her way as she led me down the hallway with her mother right behind me. When I opened the door, I was startled by a kitten clinging to the screen door, its mouth screaming "cat food, dog biscuits, *sushi.* . . . " I opened the door and the kitten, still holding on, whined in the language of hungry animals. When I got into Carolyn's car, I looked back: the cat was still clinging. I asked Carolyn if it were possibly hungry, but she said the cat was being silly. She started the car, waved to her mother, and bounced us over the rain-pocked drive, patting my thigh for being her lover baby. Carolyn waved again. I looked back, waving, then gawking at a window screen where there were now three kittens clawing and screaming to get in. Like Mexicans, I thought. I remembered the Molinas and how the cats clung to their screens—cats they shot down with squirt guns. On the highway, I felt happy, pleased by it all. I patted Carolyn's thigh. Her people were like Mexicans, only different.

### FOR DISCUSSION

1. After **COMPARING** his future wife's family to his own, Gary Soto concludes that they are much alike, "only different" (13). How and how well does this conclusion summarize the main point of Soto's comparison? Explain.

2. How does Soto's grandmother **DEFINE** an "Okie" (1)? Why doesn't she want him to marry one?

3. Why does Soto say that his grandmother gave him bad and good advice (1)? Which is which, and why?

4. "It was a surprise to me," says Soto about marrying a girl of Japanese descent (6). Why didn't he marry a Mexican girl, as his grandmother advised?

5. What does Soto imply about ethnic and racial stereotypes when he refers to the calendar showing the "Important Races of the World" (1, 7)? Why does his grandmother ask for the calendar again?

## STRATEGIES AND STRUCTURES

1. Before comparing them with Japanese Americans, Soto explains what Mexican Americans are "like." What are some of the specifics by which he characterizes himself and his family? What is his **PURPOSE** for citing these particular traits?

2. We meet Carolyn's family in paragraph 10. How has Soto already prepared us to expect more similarities than differences between the two families? Cite details by which Soto explains what Carolyn's people are "like."

3. Why does Soto refer so often to the kittens of Carolyn's family's house? What role do they play in his comparison?

4. Besides giving advice, Soto's grandmother, like all the other adult women in the essay, is engaged in what activity? Why do you think Soto focuses on this?

5. Soto's comparison of two American families has many elements of **NARRATIVE**. Who is the **NARRATOR**: a young man growing up in a Mexican American neighborhood, an older man looking back at him, or both? Explain.

## WORDS AND FIGURES OF SPEECH

1. What is the effect of Soto's **DESCRIPTION** of the orange slice in Scott's mouth as a "fang" (4)? Why do you think he says, "I didn't think anything of it" (4)?

2. What does Soto mean by the term "social class" in paragraph 8?

3. Why do you think Soto compares *sushi* to a foreign coin (12)? Give examples of other **SIMILES** like this one in his essay.

4. What is the derivation of Soto's grandmother's favorite ethnic slur, "Okies"?

## FOR WRITING

1. Write a paragraph comparing and contrasting your family with that of a close friend, spouse, or partner. Choose one specific point of comparison—how or what they eat, how they interact within their family, how they celebrate special occasions, and so forth.

2. Whether or not you grew up in a racially or ethnically diverse neighborhood, you may recall friends and acquaintances who differed from each other in social, economic, physical, religious, or other ways. Write an essay comparing and contrasting several of these friends.

## DEBORAH TANNEN

# GENDER IN THE CLASSROOM

DEBORAH TANNEN (b. 1945) is a professor of linguistics at Georgetown University. She specializes, as she says, in "the language of everyday conversation." "Gender in the Classroom," which originally appeared in the *Chronicle of Higher Education*, grew out of her research for *You Just Don't Understand* (1990), a book about the various conversational styles of men and women. In the United States, says Tannen, the sexes bond differently. Women do it by talking with each other about their troubles; men do it by exchanging "playful insults." In this essay, Tannen compares and contrasts the various behaviors that result from gender-related styles of talking and then explains how she adjusts her teaching methods to accommodate these behaviors.

---

W HEN I RESEARCHED AND WROTE MY LATEST BOOK, *You Just Don't Understand: Women and Men in Conversation,* the furthest thing from my mind was reevaluating my teaching strategies. But that has been one of the direct benefits of having written the book.

The primary focus of my linguistic research always has been the lan- 2 guage of everyday conversation. One facet of this is conversational style: how different regional, ethnic, and class backgrounds, as well as age and gender, result in different ways of using language to communicate. *You Just Don't Understand* is about the conversational styles of women and men. As I gained more insight into typically male and female ways of using language, I began to suspect some of the causes of the troubling facts that women who go to single-sex schools do better in later life, and that when young women sit next to young men in classrooms, the males talk more. This is not to say that all men talk in class, nor that no women do. It is simply that a greater percentage of discussion time is taken by men's voices.

The research of sociologists and anthropologists such as Janet Lever, 3 Marjorie Harness Goodwin, and Donna Eder has shown that girls and boys learn to use language differently in their sex-separate peer groups. Typically, a girl has a best friend with whom she sits and talks, frequently telling secrets. It's the telling of secrets, the fact and the way that they talk to each other, that makes them best friends. For boys, activities are central: Their best friends are the ones they do things with. Boys also tend to play in larger groups that are hierarchical. High-status boys give orders and push low-status boys around. So boys are expected to use language to seize center stage: by exhibiting their skill, displaying their knowledge, and challenging and resisting challenges.

These patterns have stunning implications for classroom interaction. 4 Most faculty members assume that participating in class discussion is a necessary part of successful performance. Yet speaking in a classroom is more congenial to boys' language experience than to girls', since it entails putting oneself forward in front of a large group of people, many of whom are strangers and at least one of whom is sure to judge speakers' knowledge and intelligence by their verbal display.

Another aspect of many classrooms that makes them more hospitable to 5 most men than to most women is the use of debate-like formats as a learning tool. Our educational system, as Walter Ong[1] argues persuasively in his book *Fighting for Life* (Cornell University Press, 1981), is fundamentally male in that

1. Cultural historian, philosopher, and Jesuit priest (1912–2003).

the pursuit of knowledge is believed to be achieved by ritual opposition: public display followed by argument and challenge. Father Ong demonstrates that ritual opposition—what he calls "adversativeness" or "agonism"—is fundamental to the way most males approach almost any activity. (Consider, for example, the little boy who shows he likes a little girl by pulling her braids and shoving her.) But ritual opposition is antithetical to the way most females learn and like to interact. It is not that females don't fight, but that they don't fight for fun. They don't *ritualize* opposition.

Anthropologists working in widely disparate parts of the world have 6 found contrasting verbal rituals for women and men. Women in completely unrelated cultures (for example, Greece and Bali) engage in ritual laments: spontaneously produced rhyming couplets that express their pain, for example, over the loss of loved ones. Men do not take part in laments. They have their own, very different verbal ritual: a contest, a war of words in which they vie with each other to devise clever insults.

When discussing these phenomena with a colleague, I commented that I 7 see these two styles in American conversation: Many women bond by talking about troubles, and many men bond by exchanging playful insults and put-downs, and other sorts of verbal sparring. He exclaimed: "I never thought of this, but that's the way I teach: I have students read an article, and then I invite them to tear it apart. After we've torn it to shreds, we talk about how to build a better model."

This contrasts sharply with the way I teach: I open the discussion of 8 readings by asking, "What did you find useful in this? What can we use in our own theory building and our own methods?" I note what I see as weaknesses in the author's approach, but I also point out that the writer's discipline and purposes might be different from ours. Finally, I offer personal anecdotes illustrating the phenomena under discussion and praise students' anecdotes as well as their critical acumen.

These different teaching styles must make our classrooms wildly differ- 9 ent places and hospitable to different students. Male students are more likely to be comfortable attacking the readings and might find the inclusion of personal anecdotes irrelevant and "soft." Women are more likely to resist discussion they perceive as hostile, and, indeed, it is women in my classes who are most likely to offer personal anecdotes.

A colleague who read my book commented that he had always taken for 10 granted that the best way to deal with students' comments is to challenge them: this, he felt, was self-evident, sharpens their minds and helps them develop debating skills. But he had noticed that women were relatively silent in his classes, so he decided to try beginning discussion with relatively open-ended questions and letting comments go unchallenged. He found, to his amazement and satisfaction, that more women began to speak up.

Though some of the women in his class clearly liked this better, perhaps 11 some of the men liked it less. One young man in my class wrote in a question-naire about a history professor who gave students questions to think about and called on people to answer them: "He would then play devil's advo-cate . . . i.e., he debated us. . . . That class *really* sharpened me intellectually. . . . We as students do need to know how to defend ourselves." This young man valued the experience of being attacked and challenged publicly. Many, if not most, women would shrink from such a "challenge," experiencing it as a public humiliation.

A professor at Hamilton College told me of a young man who was upset 12 because he felt his class presentation had been a failure. The professor was puzzled because he had observed that class members had listened attentively and agreed with the student's observations. It turned out that it was this very agreement that the student interpreted as failure: Since no one had engaged his ideas by arguing with him, he felt they had found them unworthy of attention.

So one reason men speak in class more than women is that many of them 13 find the "public" classroom setting more conducive to speaking, whereas most women are more comfortable speaking in private to a small group of people they know well. A second reason is that men are more likely to be comfortable with the debate-like form that discussion may take. Yet another reason is the different attitudes toward speaking in class that typify women and men.

Students who speak frequently in class, many of whom are men, assume 14 that it is their job to think of contributions and try to get the floor to express them. But many women monitor their participation not only to get the floor but to avoid getting it. Women students in my class tell me that if they have spoken up once or twice, they hold back for the rest of the class because they don't want to dominate. If they have spoken a lot one week, they will remain silent the next. These different ethics of participation are, of course, unstated, so those who speak freely assume that those who remain silent have nothing to say, and those who are reining themselves in assume that the big talkers are selfish and hoggish.

When I looked around my classes, I could see these differing ethics and 15 habits at work. For example, my graduate class in analyzing conversation had twenty students, eleven women and nine men. Of the men, four were foreign students: two Japanese, one Chinese, and one Syrian. With the exception of the three Asian men, all the men spoke in class at least occasionally. The biggest talker in the class was a woman, but there were also five women who never spoke at all, only one of whom was Japanese. I decided to try something different.

I broke the class into small groups to discuss the issues raised in the 16 readings and to analyze their own conversational transcripts. I devised three ways of dividing the students into groups: one by the degree program they were in, one by gender, and one by conversational style, as closely as I could guess it. This meant that when the class was grouped according to conversational style, I put Asian students together, fast talkers together, and quiet students together. The class split into groups six times during the semester, so they met in each grouping twice. I told students to regard the groups as examples of interactional data and to note the different ways in which they participated in the different groups. Toward the end of the term, I gave them a questionnaire asking about their class and group participation.

I could see plainly from my observation of the groups at work that 17 women who never opened their mouths in class were talking away in the small groups. In fact, the Japanese woman commented that she found it particularly hard to contribute to the all-woman group she was in because "I was overwhelmed by how talkative the female students were in the female-only group." This is particularly revealing because it highlights that the same person who can be "oppressed" into silence in one context can become the talkative "oppressor" in another. No one's conversational style is absolute; everyone's style changes in response to the context and others' styles.

Some of the students (seven) said they preferred the same-gender 18 groups; others preferred the same-style groups. In answer to the question "Would you have liked to speak in class more than you did?" six of the seven who said yes were women; the one man was Japanese. Most startlingly, this response did not come only from quiet women; it came from women who had indicated they had spoken in class never, rarely, sometimes, and often. Of the eleven students who said the amount they had spoken was fine, seven were men. Of the four women who checked "fine," two added qualifications indicating it wasn't completely fine: One wrote in "maybe more," and one wrote, "I have an urge to participate often but feel I should have something more interesting/relevant/wonderful/intelligent to say!"

I counted my experiment a success. Everyone in the class found the small groups interesting, and no one indicated he or she would have preferred that the class not break into groups. Perhaps most instructive, however, was the fact that the experience of breaking into groups, and of talking about participation in class, raised everyone's awareness about classroom participation. After we had talked about it, some of the quietest women in the class made a few voluntary contributions, though sometimes I had to insure their participation by interrupting the students who were exuberantly speaking out.    19

Americans are often proud that they discount the significance of cultural differences: "We're all individuals," many people boast. Ignoring such issues as gender and ethnicity becomes a source of pride: "I treat everyone the same." But treating people the same is not equal treatment if they are not the same.    20

The classroom is a different environment for those who feel comfortable putting themselves forward in a group than it is for those who find the prospect of doing so chastening, or even terrifying. When a professor asks, "Are there any questions?," students who can formulate statements the fastest have the greatest opportunity to respond. Those who need significant time to do so have not really been given a chance at all, since by the time they are ready to speak, someone else has taken the floor.    21

In a class where some students speak out without raising hands, those who feel they must raise their hands and wait to be recognized do not have equal opportunity to speak. Telling them to feel free to jump in will not make them feel free; one's sense of timing, of one's rights and obligations in a classroom, are automatic, learned over years of interaction. They may be changed over time, with motivation and effort, but they cannot be changed on the spot. And everyone assumes his or her own way is best. When I asked my students how the class could be changed to make it easier for them to speak more, the    22 most talkative woman said she would prefer it if no one had to raise hands, and a foreign student said he wished people would raise their hands and wait to be recognized.

My experience in this class has convinced me that small-group interac-   23
tion should be part of any class that is not a small seminar. I also am convinced that having the students become observers of their own interaction is a crucial part of their education. Talking about ways of talking in class makes students aware that their ways of talking affect other students, that the motivations they impute to others may not truly reflect others' motives, and that the behaviors they assume to be self-evidently right are not universal norms.

The goal of complete equal opportunity in class may not be attainable,   24
but realizing that one monolithic classroom-participation structure is not

A comparison       equal opportunity is itself a powerful motivation to find more
should also make a  diverse methods to serve diverse students—and every classroom
point, pp. 323–24.
                   is diverse.

## FOR DISCUSSION

1. According to Deborah Tannen, speaking up in class is typically more "congenial" to whom, women or men (4)? What accounts for this difference, according to her **COMPARISON** of the "language experience" (4)?

2. Men, says Tannen, "ritualize opposition"; women don't (5). Why not? What is the difference, according to the authorities she cites, between how men fight and how women fight? Do you agree?

3. One of Tannen's colleagues teaches by asking students to read an article and then "tear it apart" (7). How does Tannen say this compares with the way she teaches?

4. Tannen **CONTRASTS** the "ethics of [class] participation" by men with those of women (14). What differences does she find? What are the consequences of their being "unstated" (14)?

5. In paragraph 18, Tannen presents the results of her questionnaire about class and group participation. What are some of those results? What do you think of her findings?

6. Tannen says that her research in the conversation of men and women caused her to change her classroom teaching strategies. What are some of the changes she made? How compelling do you find her reasons for making them?

## STRATEGIES AND STRUCTURES

1. Tannen's title announces that she is comparing men and women on the basis of their classroom behavior. Where does she first indicate the aspects of behavior she will focus on? What are some of them?

2. This essay appeared in the *Chronicle of Higher Education*, a periodical read mostly by educators. How does Tannen tailor her essay to suit this AUDIENCE? How might this essay be different if she had written it for first-year college students?

3. In paragraph 13, Tannen sums up two of the points of comparison that she has previously made. What are they, and why do you think she summarizes them here? What new point of comparison does she then introduce, and how does she develop it in the next paragraph(s)?

4. "No one's conversational style is absolute," says Tannen; "everyone's style changes in response to the context and others' styles" (17). How does the EXAMPLE of the Japanese woman in her class illustrate the principle that people have different styles of conversation in different situations?

5. Tannen is advancing an ARGUMENT about equal opportunity in the classroom (24). What is her main argument? How and how well does she support her position?

6. "I broke the class into small groups," says Tannen (16). Where else in her essay do you find Tannen telling an ANECDOTE? How do the NARRATIVE elements in her essay support the comparison she is making in it?

## WORDS AND FIGURES OF SPEECH

1. Roughly speaking, one's "sex" is biological while one's "gender" is not, or not entirely. Why do you think Tannen uses the second term rather than the first?

2. "Behavior" usually functions as a collective noun, as in the sentence "Their behavior last night was atrocious." Why do you suppose social scientists like Tannen often use the plural form, "behaviors," in their writing (23)?

3. Tannen's writing style is peppered with compound nouns and nouns used as adjectives—for example, "single-sex schools" and "sex-separate peer groups" (2, 3). Point out other expressions like these.

4. What is the meaning of the word "hierarchical" (3), and why does Tannen use it to refer to boys?

5. What is the difference between "ritual opposition" as Tannen uses the term and just plain opposition (5)? What other behaviors does Tannen cite that might be considered rituals?

**FOR WRITING**

1. How do Tannen's observations on gender in the classroom compare with your own? Write a paragraph comparing and contrasting some aspect of the classroom behaviors of the two genders.

2. Tannen comments on the differences in the ways girls and boys use language to make friends. How do Tannen's observations square with your experience of making friends while growing up? Write an essay in which you compare and contrast how you made friends with the way, as you recall, the "opposite" gender did so. Give specific examples and include anecdotes when possible.

# ⇒11⇐

# DEFINITION

WHEN you **DEFINE**\* something, you tell what it is—and what it is not—as in the following famous definitions:

Happiness is a warm puppy.
—CHARLES M. SCHULZ

Man is a biped without feathers.
—PLATO

Hope is the thing with feathers.
—EMILY DICKINSON

Golf is a good walk spoiled.
—MARK TWAIN

All of these model definitions, you'll notice, work in the same way. They place the thing to be defined (happiness, man, hope, golf) into a general class (puppy, biped, thing, walk) and then add characteristics (warm, without feathers, with feathers, spoiled) that distinguish it from others in the same class.

This is the kind of defining—by general class and characteristics—that dictionaries do. *The American Heritage Dictionary*, for example, defines the word *scepter* as "a staff held by a sovereign . . . as an emblem of authority." Here the general class is "staff," and the characteristics that differentiate it

---

\*Words printed in **SMALL CAPITALS** are defined in the Glossary/Index.

from other staffs—such as those carried by shepherds—are "held by a sovereign" and "as an emblem of authority."

The problem with a basic dictionary definition like this is that it often doesn't tell us everything we need to know. You might begin an essay with one, but you are not going to get very far with a topic unless you *extend* your definition. One way to give an extended definition is to name other similar items in the same category as the item you are defining.

Take the term *folklore*, for example. A standard definition of *folklore* is "the study of traditional materials." This basic definition is not likely to enlighten anyone who is not already familiar with what those "materials" are, however. So one folklorist defines his field by listing a host of similar items that all belong to it:

> Folklore includes myths, legends, folktales, jokes, proverbs, riddles, chants, charms, blessings, curses, oaths, insults, retorts, taunts, teases, toasts, tongue-twisters, and greeting and leave-taking formulas (e.g., see you later, alligator). It also includes folk costumes, folk dance, folk drama (and mime), folk art, folk belief (or superstition), folk medicine, folk instrumental music (e.g., fiddle tunes), folksongs (e.g., lullabies, ballads), folk speech (e.g., to paint the town red), and names (e.g., nicknames and place names).
>
> —Alan Dundes, *The Study of Folklore*

Dundes's extended definition does not stop here; it goes on to include "latrinalia (writings on the walls of public bathrooms)," "envelope sealers (e.g., SWAK—Sealed With A Kiss)," "comments made after body emissions (e.g., after burps or sneezes)," and many others items that populate the field he is defining.

Another way to extend a basic definition is to specify additional characteristics of the item or idea you are defining. *Hydroponic tomatoes*, for example, are tomatoes grown mostly in water. Food expert Raymond Sokolov further defines this kind of tomato as one that is "mass-produced, artificially ripened, mechanically picked, and long-hauled." "It has no taste," he says, "and it won't go splat" (all additional negative characteristics). *Organic tomatoes*, by contrast, says

Dave Barry extends the definition of the term *guys* in "Guys vs. Men," p. 380.

Sokolov, are to be defined as tomatoes that are "squishable, blotchy, tart, and sometimes green-dappled."

To extend your definition further, you might give SYNONYMS for the word or concept you're defining, or trace its ETYMOLOGY, or word history. *Tomatoes*, for example, are commonly defined as "vegetables," but an extended definition might point out that they are actually synonymous with "berries" or "fleshy fruits" and that they derive their name from the Nahuatl word *tomatl*. How do we know this last obscure fact? Because most standard dictionaries include etymologies along with basic definitions. Etymologies trace the origins of a word and sometimes can help organize an entire essay.

For example, here is the beginning of an essay by biologist Stephen Jay Gould on the concept of evolution:

> The exegesis [interpretation] of evolution as a concept has occupied the lifetimes of a thousand scientists. In this essay, I present something almost laughably narrow in comparison—an exegesis of the word itself. I shall trace how organic change came to be called *evolution*. The tale is complex and fascinating as a pure antiquarian exercise in etymological detection. But more is at stake, for a past usage of this word has contributed to the most common, current misunderstanding among laymen of what scientists mean by evolution.
>
> —STEPHEN JAY GOULD, *Ever Since Darwin*

The misunderstanding to which this paragraph refers is the idea that *evolution* means "progress." Among scientists, the term signifies simply "organic change," adaptation—without any implication of improvement.

Gould could make this point by tracing the history of evolution "as a concept"; but that might take another scientific lifetime, and he is only writing an essay. So he chooses the much narrower topic of tracing the origins of "the word itself." Following the etymology of a key term like this is an efficient way to reach a larger conclusion—in this case, the modern scientific understanding of evolution. And it can provide a road map for organizing the rest of an essay as a tale of "detection" that uncovers and explains how various related terms have been used in the past.

There is no set formula for writing good definitions, but there are some questions to keep in mind when you are working on one: What is the essential nature or main use of the thing you are defining? What are its distinguishing characteristics? How is it different from other things like it? And, perhaps most important, why do your readers need to know about it, and what point do you want to make?

# A BRIEF GUIDE TO WRITING A DEFINITION ESSAY

As you write a definition, you need to identify your subject, assign it to a general class, and specify particular characteristics that distinguish it from others in that same class.

> We're often told that happiness is an illusion, and some of us believe it, despite the experience of our own lives. Happiness is obviously not an illusion, because we've all felt it, not once but many times.
>
> —MICHAEL CRICHTON, "Happiness"

Crichton identifies the term he is defining (happiness), assigns it to a general class (realities), and specifies a particular characteristic ("we've all felt it") that distinguishes his subject from others like it (illusions that seem real but aren't).

Basic definitions like this can be useful in almost any kind of essay. To define a concept in depth, however, you will need to explain why you're defining it—Crichton's purpose in defining happiness is to explain how to achieve it—and to extend your definition by adding other distinguishing characteristics, by giving synonyms, and by tracing the etymology of key terms. The following guidelines will help you to make these and other key moves of definition as you draft an essay.

## Coming Up with a Subject

When you compose a definition essay, a good strategy is to look for a concept or term that you think has been defined incorrectly or inadequately—as Gould and Crichton do with *evolution* and *happiness*—or that is complex enough in meaning to leave room for discussion and debate. For example: What constitutes *racism* or *sexual harassment*? What characterizes *friendship*? What is *intelligent design*? Whatever term you choose, you will need to discover its essential characteristics (such as the trust and loyalty involved in friendship) and make a specific point about it.

## Considering Your Purpose and Audience

When you define something, you may be conveying useful information, demonstrating that you understand the term's meaning, arguing for a particular definition, or just entertaining the reader. Keep your PURPOSE in mind as you construct your definition, and adapt the TONE of your essay accordingly—objective when you want to inform, persuasive when you are arguing, humorous when you want the reader to smile.

Also consider why your AUDIENCE might want (or be reluctant) to know more about your term and what it means. How might the reader already define the term? What information can you supply to make it easier for the reader to understand your definition, or be more receptive to it? For example, a definition of *acid* in a lab manual for chemistry students would be considerably different from a definition of *acid* for a general audience. Whatever term you are defining, be sure to focus on those aspects of it that your audience is most likely to find interesting and useful.

## Generating Ideas: Asking What Something Is—and Is Not

In order to define a term or concept, you need to know what its distinguishing characteristics are—what makes it different from other things in the same general class. For instance, suppose you wanted to define what a bodybuilder is. It might occur to you to say that bodybuilders are athletes who need to maintain a certain weight and to build up muscle strength. But these characteristics also apply to runners and swimmers. Among these three types of athletes, however, only bodybuilders train primarily for muscle definition and bulk. In other words, training for muscle definition and bulk is a characteristic that distinguishes bodybuilders from other athletes. Runners and swimmers need strong muscles, too, but what distinguishes them is their speed on the track or in the pool, characteristics that do *not* apply to bodybuilders. As you list the essential characteristics for your term, remember that definitions set up boundaries. They say, in effect: "This is the territory occupied by my concept, and everything outside these boundaries is something else."

In "Blue-Collar Brilliance," p. 405, Mike Rose questions traditional definitions of intelligence.

Once you have identified the distinguishing characteristics for your term or concept, you can construct a basic definition of it—and then extend it from there. So a good basic definition of a bodybuilder might be "an athlete who trains primarily for muscle definition and bulk."

## Templates for Defining

The following templates can help you to generate ideas for a definition and then to start drafting. Don't take these as formulas where you just have to fill in the blanks. There are no easy formulas for good writing. But these templates can help you plot out some of the key moves of definition and thus may serve as good starting points.

> ► In general, X can be defined as a kind of _____.
>
> ► What specifically distinguishes X from others in this category is _____.
>
> ► Other important distinguishing characteristics of X are _____, _____, and _____.
>
> ► X is often used to mean _____, but a better synonym would be _____ or _____.
>
> ► One way to define X is as the opposite of _____, the distinguishing characteristics of which are _____, _____, and _____.
>
> ► If we define X as _____, we can then define Y as _____.
>
> ► By defining X in this way, we can see that _____.

For more techniques to help you generate ideas and start writing effective definitions, see Chapter 3.

## Stating Your Point

In any definition essay, you need to explain the point your definition is intended to make. A **THESIS STATEMENT**—usually in the introduction of your essay and perhaps reiterated with variations at the end—is a good way to do this. The following example is from an essay defining a farmer, written by Craig Schafer, a student at Ohio State who grew up on a farm in the Midwest: "By definition, a farmer is someone who tills the soil for a living, but I define a true farmer according to his or her attitudes toward the land." This is a good thesis statement because it defines the subject in an interesting way that may draw the reader in to the rest of the essay.

## Adding Other Distinguishing Characteristics

Of all the ways you can extend a basic definition, perhaps the most effective is simply to specify additional characteristics that set your subject apart. To support his definition of a farmer as a person with certain attitudes toward the land, Schafer goes on to specify what those attitudes are, devoting a paragraph to each: A farmer is a born optimist, planting his crops "with no assurances that nature will cooperate." A farmer is devoted to the soil, sifting it through his fingers and "sniffing the fresh clean aroma of a newly plowed field." A farmer is self-denying, with a barn that is often "more modern than his house." And so on. As you compose a definition essay, make sure you provide enough characteristics to identify your subject thoroughly and completely.

## Using Synonyms and Etymologies

Another way to extend a definition is by offering **SYNONYMS**. For example, if you were defining *zine* for readers who are unfamiliar with the term, you might say that it is short for *magazine*. You could then explain which characteristics of magazines apply to zines and which ones don't. Both zines and magazines, you might point out, include printed articles and artwork; but zines, unlike magazines, are typically self-published, are photocopied and bound by hand, have very small circulations and are rarely sold at newsstands, and include both original work and work appropriated from other sources.

Often you can extend the definition of a term by tracing its history, or **ETYMOLOGY**. This is what one engineer did when he asked: "Who are we who have been calling ourselves engineers since the early nineteenth century?" Here's part of his answer:

> The word *engineering* probably derives from the Latin word *ingeniatorum*. In 1325 a contriver of siege towers was called by the Norman word *engy-nours*. By 1420 the English were calling a trickster a *yngynore*. By 1592 we find the word *enginer* being given to a designer of phrases—a wordsmith.
>
> —JOHN H. LIENHARD, "The Polytechnic Legacy"

Knowing the history of a word and its variations can help you with a current definition. You can find the etymology of a word in most dictionaries.

## CORRECTING COMMON ERRORS IN DEFINITIONS

Like other kinds of writing, definitions use distinctive patterns of language and punctuation—and thus invite typical kinds of errors. The following tips will help you to check for (and correct) these common errors in your own definitions.

### Make sure that words referred to as words are in italics

- ▶ An expert in evolution, Gould defines the term *evolution* by explaining how it has been misused.

- ▶ Often used as a synonym for *progress*, says Gould, *evolution* simply means change.

### Be sure each basic definition includes the general class to which the term belongs

- ▶ Engineering <u>is a professional field that</u> applies science for practical purposes.

- ▶ A thoroughbred is <u>a breed of horse</u> capable of racing at high speeds for long distances.

Without *professional field* and *breed of horse*, the preceding sentences are statements about their subjects rather than definitions of them.

## Check for common usage errors

*IS WHERE, IS WHEN*

*Where* and *when* should not be used to introduce definitions.

- ▶ Engineering is ~~where you put~~ the practice of putting science to use.
- ▶ A recession is ~~when~~ the economic condition in which both prices and sales go down.

*COMPRISE, COMPOSE*

*Comprise* means "to consist of." *Compose* means "to make up." The whole *comprises* the parts; the parts *compose* the whole.

- ▶ The federal government ~~composes~~ comprises three branches.
- ▶ Three branches ~~comprise~~ compose the federal government.

# Social Media Explained with Donuts

SOCIAL MEDIA EXPLAINED

TWITTER — I'M EATING A #DONUT

FACEBOOK — I LIKE DONUTS

FOURSQURE — THIS IS WHERE I EAT DONUTS

INSTAGRAM — HERE'S A VINTAGE PHOTO OF MY DONUT

YOU TUBE — HERE I AM EATING A DONUT

LINKED N — MY SKILLS INCLUDE DONUT EATING

PINTEREST — HERE'S A DONUT RECIPE

LAST FM — NOW LISTENING TO "DONUTS"

G+ — I'M A GOOGLE EMPLOYEE WHO EATS DONUTS.

When you define something, you explain what general category it belongs to; then you give specific characteristics (and examples) of your subject that distinguish it from others in that same category. *Twitter* and *YouTube*, for example—like the other technologies defined by donuts here—both belong to the general category *social media*. As with selecting a donut, however, it is the differences that really define them. With *Twitter*, you're limited to 140-character messages. With *YouTube*, you can post actual videos of yourself engaged in some activity. ("Here I am eating a donut.") Videos on *YouTube*, however, are always posted after the fact. If you want to tell people what's happening in real time, *Twitter*, though plainer, may be the better selection. ("I'm eating a #donut.") Ultimately, the best medium to choose is the one that best suits the purpose or need your message is intended to serve. Ditto for definitions—and for donuts.

## MATT TREACY

# SHE

MATT TREACY is an art producer living and working in Richmond, Virginia. A partner and engineer at two Richmond-based production studios, he also manages the non-profit entertainment company Free Jambalaya, Inc. and builds websites for a number of local and national clients. He wrote this essay in his Rhetoric 101 class at Hampden-Sydney College, a liberal arts college for men in Virginia. His teacher asked students to write about a person, to "create for your reader a sense not only of what or who the person is or was but also why the person should be of interest to your reader." Treacy writes of his mother, focusing on how she "always shingled lessons" into his mind, "leaving each one slightly raised for prying up later on."

### She

Mom says, "If you go a day without using your hands, you die." It's a principle that influences the way I do things. Nothing is ever futile. The most horrible chores ever devised by the devil in the days of man do not even leave me with a gutted feeling anymore, though God knows they used to. Repainting a chicken shed or lying prostrate to the sun on a steel roof is never as bad as it sounds; you've used your hands, and at least *that's* worthwhile. My mother has always shingled lessons into my mind, leaving each one slightly raised for prying up later on. There was never a day when we didn't do some meaningless household task just to pass the time. She always used her hands. On top of an adamant refusal to learn the first thing about technology, manual labor just fits her. She used her hands when She shot the groundhog who had one of her zucchinis in its mouth. She used her hands when crunching rabbits under the blunt end of a hatchet for some of the best stew in the Western hemisphere. She used her hands to hang the stockings, even when my sister and I knew better than to believe in a fat guy in a red suit. In the past I have questioned her claim of devotion to me, but there were always ethics to be spaded out of the dirt she was normally covered in, sandy values scraping the back of my neck during a rough hug before bed. Loving me is something She has always done, but with a sharp manner that hides the tenderness I sometimes cry for.

My Mother is not a woman so much as she is a field of energy. Mom is a force, a kind of aura that only takes human form to be that much more intimidating. An order to cut the grass is not a request but an international

**Defines the using-your-hands "principle" by giving EXAMPLES**

**Defines "my mom" (*She*) by saying what she is and what she is not**

1

2

doctrine, and She sits at the helm of an aircraft carrier just waiting for a rebellious child to give her reason for an atomic strike. Making us cut the grass is her method of control. There lies, somewhere beneath the tile of our kitchen, a proverbial bag of chores just waiting to be opened, like Pandora's Box. I am in constant fear that, one day, a refusal to mow will burst that bag wide open and spill hell into my life, so I do whatever I'm told. These responsibilities have become more of a tradition than a job, so I can't mind them; God forbid I break that custom. The sun bakes me like a scone on early August days, but smiles down on the Mother weeding eggplant, and the neighbors selling lemonade under an oak. She works like a madwoman in the garden, and still keeps an eye on whichever unlucky child has a job outside. When all is said and done, the yard has grown to the heavens, leaving me to give it the haircut of a lifetime under the omniscient eye from amongst the bean rows. It is a task that takes a light-year, but after three hours in the field I'll gladly accept the neighbor's lemonade, no matter what's floating in it. The common image is me standing at attention and She a drill sergeant inspecting my work, looking for any surviving dandelion to give me away. I imagine She would love to find a single uncut weed to justify beating the shag out of me with the garden hose. But then, smiling a smile that would have wilted the grass anyway, She goes to get a beer and watch me finish off the front yard.

There are some unexplainable phenomena between the two of us. These things I've grown accustomed to but have never understood. It's all to do with her. No one else

Ultimately, Treacy is not only defining a relationship but saying "how weird" it is

can really grasp just how weird our relationship is, because no one else has ever gone through another like it. The first clue that our mother-son bond was stronger than most was the day I came home to a chaotic scene and She immediately informed me, "Way to go baby, you let the emu out." That night I did homework in electrified silence, forcing down home-grown garden squash and awaiting her return. Finally the door screamed and I prepared for a verbal thrashing only to be greeted with a hug. Everything was forgotten. The homework lay strewn on the table and the snow fell as She unfolded a story that would eventually go down in family lore. It was not a story like the boring epics that college professors pride themselves on, but a *story*. It was like something told by five different people at Thanksgiving with sporadic inter-jections thrown in through mouthfuls of mashed potatoes

Uses story of escaped emu to explain what a NARRATIVE is and how to tell one

and venison. There was a plot line, rising action, a climax, blood, and plenty of cursing. By the time she finished and I had chewed my lip raw, the escaped emu had been recap-tured somehow by a turkey call and something resem-bling a German infantry tactic. I sat there in awe, swallowing repeatedly to wet my vocal cords back into coherence. "That's the most incredible thing I've ever heard," I managed to gasp, unable to get the image of my mom pulling a tackle on a bird from the Cretaceous period out of my mind. The amount of respect She lost for me that night was more than made up by my amazement and overwhelming love for this woman who brought down ostriches. Even being sentenced to double grass-cutting duty and cooking for a week didn't really sting that much. After all, I'd be using my hands.

So many times She would ruin my chances for fun.   4
So many times I was caught when it seemed I could not
be, and so many times I would be forced to dry dishes
instead of climbing hay bales in the fields. Of course there
will always be hay, and there will always be home. She
will always be there weeping me away to college and willing me back with that same aura of power that surrounds
her. Each time I will argue, but apparently dishes will
never just dry themselves. And each time that I think I'm
too tired to get up and turn off the dorm room TV, I will
think of my mother and stumble over in the pitch black to
use my hands at least one more time that day.

Concludes by
returning to the
basic principle of
using your hands
as defined at the
essay's beginning

# GUYS VS. MEN

DAVE BARRY (b. 1947) is a widely published humorist. After graduating from Haverford College, he found work as a journalist, eventually becoming a columnist for the *Miami Herald,* where he won a Pulitzer Prize for commentary in 1988. He is the author of many humor books, including *Dave Barry's Complete Guide to Guys* (1995), the introduction of which is included here. Despite its title, "Guys vs. Men" is not a comparative study of these two basic types of males. Men and manhood have been written about far too much already, says Barry. But guys and guyhood are neglected topics, and even though he "can't define exactly what it means to be a guy," Barry's essay lays out "certain guy characteristics" that distinguish his quarry from other warm-blooded animals in the field.

---

T HIS IS A BOOK ABOUT GUYS. It's *not* a book about men. There are already  1
way too many books about men, and most of them are *way* too serious.

    *Men* itself is a serious word, not to mention *manhood* and *manly.* Such  2
words make being male sound like a very important activity, as opposed to what it primarily consists of, namely, possessing a set of minor and frequently unreliable organs.

But men tend to attach great significance to Manhood. This results in 3
certain characteristically masculine, by which I mean stupid, behavioral patterns that can produce unfortunate results such as violent crime, war, spitting,
and ice hockey. These things have given males a bad name.[1] And the "Men's
Movement," which is supposed to bring out the more positive aspects of
Manliness, seems to be densely populated with loons and goobers.[2]

So I'm saying that there's another way to look at males: not as aggressive 4
macho dominators; not as sensitive, liberated, hugging drummers; but as *guys*.

And what, exactly, do I mean by "guys"? I don't know. I haven't thought 5
that much about it. One of the major characteristics of guyhood is that we
guys don't spend a lot of time pondering our deep innermost
feelings. There is a serious question in my mind about whether
guys actually *have* deep innermost feelings, unless you count, for
example, loyalty to the Detroit Tigers,[3] or fear of bridal showers.

> Giving synonyms is
> always a good way
> to define a key term,
> p. 371.

But although I can't define exactly what it means to be a guy, I can 6
describe certain guy characteristics, such as:

## Guys Like Neat Stuff

By "neat," I mean "mechanical and unnecessarily complex." I'll give you an 7
example. Right now I'm typing these words on an *extremely* powerful computer. It's the latest in a line of maybe ten computers I've owned, each one
more powerful than the last. My computer is chock full of RAM and ROM and
bytes and megahertzes and various other items that enable a computer to kick
data-processing butt. It is probably capable of supervising the entire U.S.
air-defense apparatus while simultaneously processing the tax return of every
resident of Ohio. I use it mainly to write a newspaper column. This is an activity wherein I sit and stare at the screen for maybe ten minutes, then, using
only my forefingers, slowly type something like:

*Henry Kissinger[4] looks like a big wart.*

1. Specifically, "asshole" [Barry's note].
2. An expression that is used to refer to people with silly ideas and little common sense.
3. Major league baseball team that last won the World Series in 1984.
4. Henry Kissinger (b. 1923), U.S. secretary of state 1973–1977.

I stare at this for another ten minutes, have an inspiration, then amplify the original thought as follows:

> *Henry Kissinger looks like a big fat wart.*

Then I stare at that for another ten minutes pondering whether I should try to work in the concept of "hairy."

This is absurdly simple work for my computer. It sits there, humming 8 impatiently, bored to death, passing the time between keystrokes via brain-teaser activities such as developing a Unified Field Theory of the universe and translating the complete works of Shakespeare into rap.[5]

In other words, this computer is absurdly overqualified to work for me, 9 and yet soon, I guarantee, I will buy an *even more powerful* one. I won't be able to stop myself, I'm a guy.

Probably the ultimate example of the fundamental guy drive to have neat 10 stuff is the Space Shuttle. Granted, the guys in charge of this program *claim* it has a Higher Scientific Purpose, namely to see how humans function in space. But of course we have known for years how humans function in space: They float around and say things like: "Looks real good, Houston!"

No, the real reason for the existence of the Space Shuttle is that it is one 11 humongous and spectacularly gizmo-intensive item of hardware. Guys can tinker with it practically forever, and occasionally even get it to work, and use it to place *other* complex mechanical items into orbit, where they almost immediately break, which provides a great excuse to send the Space Shuttle up *again*. It's Guy Heaven.

Other results of the guy need to have stuff are Star Wars,[6] the recrea- 12 tional boating industry, monorails, nuclear weapons, and wristwatches that indicate the phase of the moon. I am not saying that women haven't been involved in the development or use of this stuff. I'm saying that, without guys, this stuff probably would not exist; just as, without women, virtually every piece of furniture in the world would still be in its original position. Guys do

---

5. To be or not? I got to *know*. Might kill myself by the end of the *show* [Barry's note].

6. Popular term for the Strategic Defense Initiative, a 1980s-era program to develop a space-based antimissile system for the United States.

not have a basic need to rearrange furniture. Whereas a woman who could cheerfully use the same computer for fifty-three years will rearrange her furniture on almost a weekly basis, sometimes in the dead of night. She'll be sound asleep in bed, and suddenly, at 2 a.m., she'll be awakened by the urgent thought: *The blue-green sofa needs to go perpendicular to the wall instead of parallel, and it needs to go there* RIGHT NOW. So she'll get up and move it, which of course necessitates moving other furniture, and soon she has rearranged her entire living room, shifting great big heavy pieces that ordinarily would require several burly men to lift, because there are few forces in Nature more powerful than a woman who needs to rearrange furniture. Every so often a guy will wake up to discover that, because of his wife's overnight efforts, he now lives in an entirely different house.

(I realize that I'm making gender-based generalizations here, but my 13 feeling is that if God did not want us to make gender-based generalizations, She would not have given us genders.)

## Guys Like a Really Pointless Challenge

Not long ago I was sitting in my office at the *Miami Herald*'s Sunday magazine, 14 *Tropic*, reading my fan mail[7] when I heard several of my guy coworkers in the hallway talking about how fast they could run the forty-yard dash. These are guys in their thirties and forties who work in journalism, where the most demanding physical requirement is the ability to digest vending-machine food. In other words, these guys have absolutely no need to run the forty-yard dash.

But one of them, Mike Wilson, was writing a story about a star 15 high-school football player who could run it in 4.38 seconds. Now if Mike had written a story about, say, a star high-school poet, none of my guy coworkers would have suddenly decided to find out how well they could write sonnets. But when Mike turned in his story, they became *deeply* concerned about how fast they could run the forty-yard dash. They were so concerned that the magazine editor, Tom Shroder, decided that they should get a stopwatch and go out to a nearby park and find out. Which they did, a bunch of guys taking off their shoes and running around barefoot in a public park on company time.

---

7. Typical fan letter: "Who cuts your hair? Beavers?" [Barry's note].

This is what I heard them talking about, out in the hall. I heard Tom, who   16
was thirty-eight years old, saying that his time in the forty had been 5.75 seconds. And I thought to myself: This is ridiculous. These are middle-aged guys,
supposedly adults, and they're out there *bragging* about their performance in
this stupid juvenile footrace. Finally I couldn't stand it anymore.

"Hey!" I shouted. "*I* could beat 5.75 seconds."   17

So we went out to the park and measured off forty yards, and the guys   18
told me that I had three chances to make my best time. On the first try my
time was 5.78 seconds, just three-hundredths of a second slower than Tom's,
even though, at forty-five, I was seven years older than he. So I just *knew* I'd
beat him on the second attempt if I ran really, really hard, which I did for a
solid ten yards, at which point my left hamstring muscle, which had not yet
shifted into Sprint Mode from Mail-Reading Mode, went, and I quote, "pop."

I had to be helped off the field. I was in considerable pain, and I was obvi-   19
ously not going to be able to walk right for weeks. The other guys were very
sympathetic, especially Tom, who took the time to call me at home, where I
was sitting with an ice pack on my leg and twenty-three Advil in my blood-
stream, so he could express his concern.

"Just remember," he said, *"you didn't beat my time."*   20

There are countless other examples of guys rising to meet pointless   21
challenges. Virtually all sports fall into this category, as well as a large part
of U.S. foreign policy ("I'll bet you can't capture Manuel Noriega!"[8] "Oh
YEAH??")

## Guys Do Not Have a Rigid and Well-Defined Moral Code

This is not the same as saying that guys are bad. Guys *are* capable of doing bad   22
things, but this generally happens when they try to be Men and start becoming
manly and aggressive and stupid. When they're being just plain guys, they aren't
so much actively *evil* as they are *lost*. Because guys have never really grasped the
Basic Human Moral Code, which I believe was invented by women millions of
years ago when all the guys were out engaging in some other activity, such as

---

8. Manuel Noriega (b. 1934), Panamanian dictator removed from power by armed U.S.
intervention in 1989.

seeing who could burp the loudest. When they came back, there were certain rules that they were expected to follow unless they wanted to get into Big Trouble, and they have been trying to follow these rules ever since, with extremely irregular results. Because guys have never *internalized* these rules. Guys are similar to my small auxiliary backup dog, Zippy, a guy dog[9] who has been told numerous times that he is *not* supposed to (1) get into the kitchen garbage or (2) poop on the floor. He knows that these are the rules, but he has never really understood *why*, and sometimes he gets to thinking: Sure, I am *ordinarily* not supposed to get into the garbage, but obviously this rule is not meant to apply when there are certain extenuating[10] circumstances, such as (1) somebody just threw away some perfectly good seven-week-old Kung Pao Chicken, and (2) I am home alone.

And so when the humans come home, the kitchen floor has been transformed into Garbage-Fest USA, and Zippy, who usually comes rushing up, is off in a corner disguised in a wig and sunglasses, hoping to get into the Federal Bad Dog Relocation Program before the humans discover the scene of the crime.    23

When I yell at him, he frequently becomes so upset that he poops on the floor.    24

Morally, most guys are just like Zippy, only taller and usually less hairy. Guys are *aware* of the rules of moral behavior, but they have trouble keeping these rules in the forefronts of their minds at certain times, especially the present. This is especially true in the area of faithfulness to one's mate. I realize, of course, that there are countless examples of guys being faithful to their mates until they die, usually as a result of being eaten by their mates immediately following copulation. Guys outside of the spider community, however, do not have a terrific record of faithfulness.    25

I'm not saying guys are scum. I'm saying that many guys who consider themselves to be committed to their marriages will stray if they are confronted with overwhelming temptation, defined as "virtually any temptation."    26

---

9. I also have a female dog, Earnest, who *never* breaks the rules [Barry's note].

10. I am taking some liberties here with Zippy's vocabulary. More likely, in his mind, he uses the term *mitigating* [Barry's note].

Okay, so maybe I *am* saying guys are scum. But they're not *mean-spirited*   27
scum. And few of them—even when they are out of town on business trips, far
from their wives, and have a clear-cut opportunity—will poop on the floor.

## FOR DISCUSSION

1. Dave Barry starts to **DEFINE** what he means by "guys" and then says, "I don't
   know. I haven't thought that much about it" (5). He's being funny, right? Does his
   extended definition of *guys* lead you to believe that he has thought intelligently
   about what guys are? How so?

2. Males, says Barry, can be divided into two basic classes. What are the distinguishing characteristics of each?

3. To write his humor column, Barry doesn't ever need to buy a new, more powerful
   computer. But he says in paragraph 9 that he will do it anyway. What principle of
   guy behavior is he illustrating here?

4. In paragraph 12, Barry develops his definition of guys as neat-stuff-buying animals by **CONTRASTING** them with women. How does he define women in this
   paragraph? Do you think his definition is accurate? If not, how would you revise
   what he says?

5. Do you agree or disagree with Barry that "virtually all" sports fall into the "pointless challenge" category (21)? What about U.S. foreign policy?

6. Guys, says Barry, "are similar" to his dog Zippy (22). This is a definition by **ANALOGY**.
   What specific characteristics, according to Barry, do guys and Zippy have in common?
   Do you think the **COMPARISON** is just? In what one way does even Barry admit that
   unleashed guys are generally superior to dogs?

## STRATEGIES AND STRUCTURES

1. Beginning in paragraph 6, Barry defines guys by citing three of their distinguishing
   "guy characteristics." What are they? How does Barry use these characteristics to
   organize his entire essay?

2. In Barry's definition, guys belong to the class of males who like challenges. But this
   is still a very broad class, so Barry narrows it down further by adding the qualifier
   "pointless." Following this logic, why can't the high-school poet in paragraph 15 be
   defined as a guy? Point out other examples of this logic of elimination in Barry's
   essay, such as his definition of guys as "scum" in paragraph 26.

3. Why do you think Barry is so careful to specify the gender of God in paragraph 13? What AUDIENCE does he have in mind here?

4. From reading Barry's title, you might expect "Guys vs. Men" to be primarily a comparison and contrast essay. Where and *why* does Barry switch from drawing a comparison between the two kinds of males to defining one kind to the exclusion of the other?

5. Barry's humor often comes from his use of specific examples, as in "violent crime, war, spitting, and ice hockey" (3). Point out where his EXAMPLES help define specific terms. What would this essay be like *without* all the examples? What is Barry's PURPOSE in being (or pretending to be) so rigorous?

## WORDS AND FIGURES OF SPEECH

1. How does Barry define "male" (2)? How about "manly" (2)? So, according to Barry's definitions, is "manly male" an OXYMORON?

2. How would you define "loons" (3)? How do they differ from "goobers" (3)?

3. Why does Barry capitalize "Big Trouble" in paragraph 22?

4. Translate the following Barry phrase into standard English: "one humongous and spectacularly gizmo-intensive item of hardware" (11).

## FOR WRITING

1. Barry is considered to be a humorist. How would you define one? Make a list of the distinguishing characteristics that make a good humorist in your view, and give examples of humorists who you think represent these characteristics. (You might want to use Barry as an example, or not.)

2. How would you define "guys"? What characteristics does Barry leave out? Can a female be a "guy" (as in "When we go shopping, my grandmother is just one of the guys")? Write an essay setting forth your definition of "guys." Or choose another gender term (such as *men, women, girls,* or *girlfriends*), and write an essay that gives "another way to look" at gender through your definition of this term.

# SE HABLA ESPAÑOL

TANYA MARIA BARRIENTOS (b. 1960) is a novelist, a former columnist for the *Philadelphia Inquirer*, and presently a communications director at the Robert Wood Johnson Foundation. With a journalism degree from the University of Missouri, she is the author of the novels *Frontera Street* (2002) and *Family Resemblance* (2003). "Se Habla Español" was first published in the bilingual magazine *Latina* (2004). Her title refers to the sign, often seen in store windows, announcing that "Spanish is spoken" here. In this essay, Barrientos raises a basic question of self-definition and ethnic identity: Can a woman born in Guatemala who grew up in the United States speaking English instead of Spanish be legitimately considered Latina?

---

T HE MAN ON THE OTHER END OF THE PHONE LINE is telling me the classes I've called about are first-rate: native speakers in charge, no more than six students per group. I tell him that will be fine and yes, I've studied a bit of Spanish in the past. He asks for my name and I supply it, rolling the double "r" in "Barrientos" like a pro. That's when I hear the silent snag, the momentary hesitation I've come to expect at this part of the exchange. Should I go into it again? Should I explain, the way I have to half a dozen others, that I am Guatemalan by birth but *pura gringa*[1] by circumstance?

This will be the sixth time I've signed up to learn the language my parents speak to each other. It will be the sixth time I've bought workbooks and notebooks and textbooks listing 501 conjugated verbs in alphabetical order, in hopes that the subjunctive tense will finally take root in my mind. In class I will sit across a table from the "native speaker," who will wonder what to make of me. "Look," I'll want to say (but never do). "Forget the dark skin. Ignore the obsidian eyes. Pretend I'm a pink-cheeked, blue-eyed blonde whose name tag says 'Shannon.'" Because that is what a person who doesn't innately know the difference between *corre, corra,* and *corrí*[2] is supposed to look like, isn't it?

I came to the United States in 1963 at age three with my family and immediately stopped speaking Spanish. College-educated and seamlessly bilingual when they settled in west Texas, my parents (a psychology professor and an artist) wholeheartedly embraced the notion of the American melting pot. They declared that their two children would speak nothing but *inglés.* They'd read in English, write in English, and fit into Anglo society beautifully.

It sounds politically incorrect now. But America was not a hyphenated nation back them. People who called themselves Mexican Americans or Afro Americans were considered dangerous radicals, while law-abiding citizens were expected to drop their cultural baggage at the border and erase any lingering ethnic traits.

To be honest, for most of my childhood I liked being the brown girl who defied expectations. When I was seven, my mother returned my older brother and me to elementary school one week after the school year had already begun. We'd been on vacation in Washington, D.C., visiting the Smithsonian, the Capitol, and the home of Edgar Allan Poe. In the Volkswagen on the way home,

1. Completely non-Latina. *Pura* is Spanish for "pure"; *gringa,* the feminine form of *gringo,* is used to refer to someone of non-Latino background.

2. Verb forms of "run."

I'd memorized "The Raven," and I would recite it with melodramatic flair to any poor soul duped into sitting through my performance. At the school's office, the registrar frowned when we arrived.

"You people. Your children are always behind, and you have the nerve to bring them in late?"   6

"My children," my mother answered in a clear, curt tone, "will be at the top of their classes in two weeks."   7

The registrar filed our cards, shaking her head.   8

I did not live in a neighborhood with other Latinos, and the public school I attended attracted very few. I saw the world through the clear, cruel vision of a child. To me, speaking Spanish translated into being poor. It meant waiting tables and cleaning hotel rooms. It meant being left off the cheerleading squad and receiving a condescending smile from the guidance counselor when you said you planned on becoming a lawyer or a doctor. My best friends' names were Heidi and Leslie and Kim. They told me I didn't seem "Mexican" to them, and I took it as a compliment. I enjoyed looking into the faces of Latino store clerks and waitresses and, yes, even our maid and saying *"Yo no hablo español."*[3] It made me feel superior. It made me feel American. It made me feel white. I thought if I stayed away from Spanish, stereotypes would stay away from me.   9

Then came the backlash. During the two decades when I'd worked hard to isolate myself from the stereotype I'd constructed in my own head, society shifted. The nation changed its views on ethnic identity. College professors started teaching history through African American and Native American eyes. Children were told to forget about the melting pot and picture America as a multicolored quilt instead. Hyphens suddenly had muscle, and I was left wondering where I fit in.   10

Stereotypes cite defining traits that are false or oversimplified. Frank Conroy is careful not to do this with yo-yos (pp. 317–18).

The Spanish language was supposedly the glue that held the new Latino community together. But in my case it was what kept me apart. I felt awkward among groups whose conversations flowed in and out of Spanish. I'd be asked a question in Spanish and I'd have to answer in English, knowing this raised a mountain of questions. I wanted to call myself Latina, to finally take pride, but it felt like a lie. So I set out to learn the language that people assumed I already knew.   11

3. I don't speak Spanish.

After my first set of lessons, I could function in the present tense. *"Hola,* [12]
*Paco. ¿Qué tal? ¿Qué color es tu cuaderno? El mío es azul."*[4] My vocabulary built
quickly, but when I spoke, my tongue felt thick inside my mouth—and if I
needed to deal with anything in the future or the past, I was sunk. I enrolled in
a three-month submersion program in Mexico and emerged able to speak like
a sixth-grader with a solid C average. I could read Gabriel García Márquez[5]
with a Spanish-English dictionary at my elbow, and I could follow 90 percent
of the melodrama on any given telenovela.[6] But true speakers discover my
limitations the moment I stumble over a difficult construction, and that is
when I get the look. The one that raises the wall between us. The one that
makes me think I'll never really belong. Spanish has become a litmus test
showing how far from your roots you've strayed.

My bilingual friends say I make too much of it. They tell me that my [13]
Guatemalan heritage and unmistakable Mayan features are enough to legiti-
mize my membership in the Latin American club. After all, not all Poles
speak Polish. Not all Italians speak Italian. And as this nation grows more
and more Hispanic, not all Latinos will share one language. But I don't believe
them.

There must be other Latinas like me. But I haven't met any. Or, I should [14]
say, I haven't met any who have fessed up. Maybe they are secretly struggling
to fit in, the same way I am. Maybe they are hiring tutors and listening to tapes
behind locked doors, just like me. I wish we all had the courage to come out of
our hiding places and claim our rightful spot in the broad Latino spectrum.
Without being called hopeless gringas. Without having to offer apologies or
show remorse.

If it will help, I will go first. [15]

*Aquí estoy.*[7] Spanish-challenged and *pura* Latina. [16]

---

4. Hello, Paco. How are you? What color is your notebook? Mine is blue.

5. Columbian novelist and short-story writer (1928–2014).

6. Spanish-language TV soap opera.

7. Here I am.

## FOR DISCUSSION

1. Tanya Maria Barrientos is not a native speaker of Spanish, though both of her parents were. Why didn't they encourage her to learn the language as a child? Should they have? Why or why not?

2. According to Barrientos, how were "hyphenated" Americans DEFINED when she and her family first came to the United States from Guatemala in 1963 (4)? How did young Barrientos define Latinos who spoke Spanish?

3. In the decades following her arrival in the United States, says Barrientos, societal views toward ethnic identity "shifted" (10). What are some of the more significant aspects of that shift, according to Barrientos?

4. In your opinion, is Barrientos a legitimate member of "the Latin American club" (13)? That is, can she and others with similar backgrounds rightfully define themselves as Latinas or Latinos? Why or why not?

## STRATEGIES AND STRUCTURES

1. What is Barrientos's PURPOSE in "Se Habla Español": to explain why she does not speak Spanish with the fluency of a native speaker? to persuade readers that she is a true Latina? to define the ambiguous condition of being both "Spanish-challenged and *pura* Latina" (16)? Explain.

2. Is Barrientos's essay aimed mainly at a multilingual AUDIENCE or a largely English-speaking one? Why do you think so?

3. How does Barrientos use the Spanish language itself to help define who and what she is? Give several examples that you find particularly effective.

4. Where and how does Barrientos construct a stereotypical definition of "Latin American"? Where and how does she reveal the shortcomings of this definition?

5. Barrientos's essay includes many NARRATIVE elements. What are some of them, and how do they help her to define herself and her condition?

## WORDS AND FIGURES OF SPEECH

1. Once defined as a "melting-pot," the United States, says Barrientos, is now a "multicolored quilt" (10). What are some of the implications of this shift in METAPHORS for national diversity?

2. When Barrientos refers to the Spanish language as "glue," is she avoiding CLICHÉS or getting stuck in one (11)? Explain.

3. In printing, a *stereotype* was a cast metal plate used to reproduce blocks of type or crude images. How does this early meaning of the term carry over into the modern definition as Barrientos uses it (10)?

4. Barrientos sometimes groups herself with other "Latinos," sometimes with other "Latinas" (9, 14). Why the difference?

### FOR WRITING

1. Write a paragraph or two about an incident in which someone defined you on the basis of your choice of words, your accent, or some other aspect of your speech or appearance.

2. Write an essay about your experience learning, or attempting to learn, a language other than your native tongue—and how that experience affected your own self-definition or cultural identity.

GEETA KOTHARI

# IF YOU ARE WHAT YOU EAT, THEN WHAT AM I?

GEETA KOTHARI (b. 1962) is the nonfiction editor of the *Kenyon Review* and director of the Writing Center at the University of Pittsburgh. She is the editor of *Did My Mama Like to Dance? and Other Stories about Mothers and Daughters* (1994). Her stories and essays have appeared in various newspapers and journals, including the *Toronto South Asian Review* and the *Kenyon Review,* from which these complete sections of a longer article are taken. Kothari's essay (1999) presents a problem in personal definition. The Indian food she eats, says Kothari, is not really Indian like her mother's; nor is the American food she eats really American like her husband's. So, Kothari wonders, if we are defined by what we eat—and the culture it represents—how are she and her culture to be defined?

To belong is to understand the tacit codes of the people you live with.
—MICHAEL IGNATIEFF, *Blood and Belonging*

T HE FIRST TIME MY MOTHER AND I OPEN A CAN OF TUNA, I am nine years old.  1
We stand in the doorway of the kitchen, in semidarkness, the can tilted toward daylight. I want to eat what the kids at school eat: bologna, hot dogs, salami—foods my parents find repugnant because they contain pork and meat byproducts, crushed bone and hair glued together by chemicals and fat. Although she has never been able to tolerate the smell of fish, my mother buys the tuna, hoping to satisfy my longing for American food.

Indians, of course, do not eat such things.  2

The tuna smells fishy, which surprises me because I can't remember  3
anyone's tuna sandwich actually smelling like fish. And the tuna in those sandwiches doesn't look like this, pink and shiny, like an internal organ. In fact, this looks similar to the bad foods my mother doesn't want me to eat. She is silent, holding her face away from the can while peering into it like a half-blind bird.

For tips on writing pithy definitions like this, see pp. 369–70.

"What's wrong with it?" I ask.  4

She has no idea. My mother does not know that the tuna everyone else's  5
mothers made for them was tuna *salad*.

"Do you think it's botulism?"  6

I have never seen botulism, but I have read about it, just as I have read  7
about but never eaten steak and kidney pie.

There is so much my parents don't know. They are not like other par-  8
ents, and they disappoint me and my sister. They are supposed to help us negotiate the world outside, teach us the signs, the clues to proper behavior: what to eat and how to eat it.

We have expectations, and my parents fail to meet them, especially my  9
mother, who works full-time. I don't understand what it means, to have a mother who works outside and inside the home; I notice only the ways in which she disappoints me. She doesn't show up for school plays. She doesn't make chocolate-frosted cupcakes for my class. At night, if I want her attention, I have to sit in the kitchen and talk to her while she cooks the evening meal, attentive to every third or fourth word I say.

We throw the tuna away. This time my mother is disappointed. I go to    10
school with tuna eaters. I see their sandwiches, yet cannot explain the dis-
crepancy between them and the stinking, oily fish in my mother's hand. We do
not understand so many things, my mother and I.

When we visit our relatives in India, food prepared outside the house is care-    11
fully monitored. In the hot, sticky monsoon months in New Delhi and Bom-
bay, we cannot eat ice cream, salad, cold food, or any fruit that can't be peeled.
Definitely no meat. People die from amoebic dysentery, unexplained fevers,
strange boils on their bodies. We drink boiled water only, no ice. No sweets
except for jalebi, thin fried twists of dough in dripping hot sugar syrup. If
we're caught outside with nothing to drink, Fanta, Limca, Thums Up (after
Coca-Cola is thrown out by Mrs. Gandhi[1]) will do. Hot tea sweetened with
sugar, served with thick creamy buffalo milk, is preferable. It should be boiled,
to kill the germs on the cup.

My mother talks about "back home" as a safe place, a silk cocoon frozen    12
in time where we are sheltered by family and friends. Back home, my sister
and I do not argue about food with my parents. Home is where they know all
the rules. We trust them to guide us safely through the maze of city streets for
which they have no map, and we trust them to feed and take care of us, the way
parents should.

Finally, though, one of us will get sick, hungry for the food we see our    13
cousins and friends eating, too thirsty to ask for a straw, too polite to insist on
properly boiled water.

At my uncle's diner in New Delhi, someone hands me a plate of aloo    14
tikki, fried potato patties filled with mashed channa dal and served with a
sweet and a sour chutney. The channa, mixed with hot chilies and spices,
burns my tongue and throat. I reach for my Fanta, discard the paper straw, and
gulp the sweet orange soda down, huge drafts that sting rather than soothe.

When I throw up later that day (or is it the next morning, when a stom-    15
achache wakes me from deep sleep?), I cry over the frustration of being singled

1. Coca-Cola was banned in India for 20 years beginning in the mid-1970s, when Indira
Gandhi was prime minister, because the company would not reveal its formula to the government. Fanta, Limca, and Thums Up are other soft drinks popular in India.

out, not from the pain my mother assumes I'm feeling as she holds my hair back from my face. The taste of orange lingers in my mouth, and I remember my lips touching the cold glass of the Fanta bottle.

At that moment, more than anything, I want to be like my cousins.     16

In New York, at the first Indian restaurant in our neighborhood, my father     17
orders with confidence, and my sister and I play with the silverware until the steaming plates of lamb biryani arrive.

What is Indian food? my friends ask, their noses crinkling up.     18

Later, this restaurant is run out of business by the new Indo-Pak-     19
Bangladeshi combinations up and down the street, which serve similar food. They use plastic cutlery and Styrofoam cups. They do not distinguish between North and South Indian cooking, or between Indian, Pakistani, and Bangladeshi cooking, and their customers do not care. The food is fast, cheap, and tasty. Dosa, a rice flour crepe stuffed with masala potato, appears on the same trays as chicken makhani.

Now my friends want to know, Do you eat curry at home?     20

One time my mother makes lamb vindaloo for guests. Like dosa, this is a     21
South Indian dish, one that my Punjabi[2] mother has to learn from a cookbook. For us, she cooks everyday food—yellow dal, rice, chapati, bhaji. Lentils, rice, bread, and vegetables. She has never referred to anything on our table as "curry" or "curried," but I know she has made chicken curry for guests. Vindaloo, she explains, is a curry too. I understand then that curry is a dish created for guests, outsiders, a food for people who eat in restaurants.

I look around my boyfriend's freezer one day and find meat: pork chops,     22
ground beef, chicken pieces, Italian sausage. Ham in the refrigerator, next to the homemade bolognese sauce. Tupperware filled with chili made from ground beef and pork.

He smells different from me. Foreign. Strange.     23

I marry him anyway.     24

2. Native of the state of Punjab, in northern India.

He has inherited blue eyes that turn gray in bad weather, light brown 25
hair, a sharp pointy nose, and excellent teeth. He learns to make chili with
ground turkey and tofu, tomato sauce with red wine and portobello mush-
rooms, roast chicken with rosemary and slivers of garlic under the skin.

He eats steak when we are in separate cities, roast beef at his mother's 26
house, hamburgers at work. Sometimes I smell them on his skin. I hope he
doesn't notice me turning my face, a cheek instead of my lips, my nose wrinkled at the unfamiliar, musky smell.


I have inherited brown eyes, black hair, a long nose with a crooked bridge, and 27
soft teeth with thin enamel. I am in my twenties, moving to a city far from my
parents, before it occurs to me that jeera, the spice my sister avoids, must
have an English name. I have to learn that haldi = turmeric, methi = fenugreek.
What to make with fenugreek, I do not know. My grandmother used to make
methi roti for our breakfast, cornbread with fresh fenugreek leaves served
with a lump of homemade butter. No one makes it now that she's gone, though
once in a while my mother will get a craving for it and produce a facsimile
("The cornmeal here is wrong") that only highlights what she's really missing:
the smells and tastes of her mother's house.

I will never make my grandmother's methi roti or even my mother's 28
unsatisfactory imitation of it. I attempt chapati; it takes six hours, three phone
calls home, and leaves me with an aching back. I have to write translations down:
jeera = cumin. My memory is unreliable. But I have always known garam = hot.

If I really want to make myself sick, I worry that my husband will one day 29
leave me for a meat-eater, for someone familiar who doesn't sniff him suspi-
ciously for signs of alimentary infidelity.

Indians eat lentils. I understand this as absolute, a decree from an 30
unidentifiable authority that watches and judges me.

So what does it mean that I cannot replicate my mother's dal? She and 31
my father show me repeatedly, in their kitchen, in my kitchen. They coach me
over the phone, buy me the best cookbooks, and finally write down their
secrets. Things I'm supposed to know but don't. Recipes that should be, by
now, engraved on my heart.

Living far from the comfort of people who require no explanation for 32
what I do and who I am, I crave the foods we have shared. My mother convinces
me that moong is the easiest dal to prepare, and yet it fails me every time:
bland, watery, a sickly greenish yellow mush. These imperfect imitations
remind me only of what I'm missing.

But I have never been fond of moong dal. At my mother's table it is the 33
last thing I reach for. Now I worry that this antipathy toward dal signals something deeper, that somehow I am not my parents' daughter, not Indian, and
because I cannot bear the touch and smell of raw meat, though I can eat it
cooked (charred, dry, and overdone), I am not American either.

I worry about a lifetime purgatory in Indian restaurants where I will 34
complain that all the food looks and tastes the same because they've used the
same masala.

## FOR DISCUSSION

1. How does Geeta Kothari DEFINE "meat byproducts" (1)? Why is she so concerned
   with different kinds of food? Who or what is she trying to define?

2. How do Kothari and her mother define "back home" in paragraph 12?

3. Why is Kothari angry with herself in paragraphs 15 and 16? What "rule" has she
   momentarily forgotten?

4. Kothari's friends ask for a definition of Indian food in paragraph 18. How does she
   answer them (and us)?

5. What's wrong, from Kothari's POINT OF VIEW, with the "Indo-Pak-Bangladeshi"
   restaurants that spring up in her neighborhood (19)?

6. Marriage is an important event in anyone's biography, but why is it especially
   central in Kothari's case?

## STRATEGIES AND STRUCTURES

1. How does Kothari go about answering the definition question that she raises in
   her title? Give specific examples of her strategy. What point is she making in
   answering this question?

2. Why does Kothari recall the tuna incident in paragraphs 1 through 10? What does
   this ANECDOTE illustrate about her relationship with her mother? About her
   "Americanness"?

3. Why does Kothari introduce the matter of heredity in paragraphs 25 and 27? How do these paragraphs anticipate the reference to "something deeper" in paragraph 33?

4. According to Kothari, is culture something we inherit or something we learn? How do paragraphs 31 and 32 contribute to her definition of culture?

5. Kothari's essay is largely made up of specific EXAMPLES, particularly culinary ones. How do they relate to the matters of personal and cultural identity she is defining? Should she have made these connections more explicit? Why?

## WORDS AND FIGURES OF SPEECH

1. What is usually meant by the saying "You are what you eat"? How is Kothari interpreting this adage?

2. What does Kothari mean by "alimentary infidelity" (29)? What ANALOGY is she drawing here?

3. What is "purgatory" (34)? Why does Kothari end her essay with a reference to it?

4. *Synecdoche* is the FIGURE OF SPEECH that substitutes a part for the whole. What part does Kothari substitute for what whole when she uses the phrase "meat-eater" (29)? Can we say her entire essay works by means of synecdoche? Explain.

5. Kothari provides both the Indian word and its English equivalent for several terms in her essay—"garam" for "hot" in paragraph 28, for example. Why? What do these translations contribute to her definition of cultural identity? Point out several other examples in the text.

## FOR WRITING

1. Write an extended definition of your favorite type of food. Be sure to relate how your food and food customs help to define who you are.

2. Food and food customs are often regional, as Kothari points out. Write an essay in which you define one of the following: New England, Southern, or Midwestern cooking; California cuisine; Tex-Mex, French, or Chinese food; fast food; or some other distinctive cuisine.

3. Write an essay about food and eating in your neighborhood. Use the food customs of specific individuals and groups to help define them—personally, ethnically, socially, or in some other way.

# THE EXTRAORDINARY
# CHARACTERISTICS OF DYSLEXIA

JACK HORNER (b. 1946) grew up in Shelby, Montana, and studied geology and zoology at the University of Montana. He is a professor at Montana State University and curator of paleontology at the Museum of the Rockies, which has the largest collection of dinosaur remains in the United States. A technical advisor for the *Jurassic Park* movies, Horner was the first person to discover dinosaur eggs in the Western Hemisphere. In "The Extraordinary Characteristics of Dyslexia" (published in 2008 by the International Dyslexia Association in *Perspectives on Language and Literacy*), Horner bypasses the usual symptoms of dyslexia and defines it as a way of understanding the world that, in some respects, may be superior to more "normal" ways.

•>——————————————————————————————————————<•

E ACH OF US can narrate an early experience of failure in schools. Because of 1 it, most of us have known some form of peer persecution. But what most non-dyslexics don't know about us, besides the fact that we simply process information differently, is that our early failures often give us an important edge as we grow older. It is not uncommon that we "dyslexics" go on to succeed at the highest of levels.

I don't care much for the word *dyslexia*. I generally think of "us" as spatial thinkers and non-dyslexics as linear thinkers, or people who could be most often described as being *dys-spatios*. For spatial thinkers, reading is clearly necessary but overrated. Most of us would rather write about our own adventures than read about someone else's. Most spatial thinkers are extremely visual, highly imaginative, and work in three dimensions, none of which have anything to do with time. Linear thinkers (*dys-spatics*) generally operate in a two-dimensional world where time is of the utmost importance. We spatial thinkers fail tests given by linear thinkers because we don't think in terms of time or in terms of written text. Instead, our perception is multidimensional, and we do best when we can touch, observe, and analyze. If we were to give spatial tests to linear thinkers, they would have just as much trouble with our tests as we do with theirs. It is unfortunate that we are the minority and have to deal with the linear-thinkers' exams in order to enter the marketplace to find jobs. Even though we often fail or do miserably on these linear-thinker tests, we often end up in life achieving exceptional accomplishments. From the perspective of the linear thinkers, we spatial thinkers seem to "think outside the box," and this accounts for our accomplishments. However, we think outside the box precisely because we have never been in one. Our minds are not clogged up by preconceived ideas acquired through excessive reading. We are, therefore, free to have original thoughts enhanced by personal observations.

Page 369 explains how to define a term by saying what it is not.

In 1993, I was inducted into the American Academy of Achievement, an organization started in 1964, that annually brings together the highest achievers in America with the brightest American high-school students. The achievers included United States presidents, Nobel Laureates, movie stars, sports figures, and other famous people. The high school students were winners of the best scholarships like the Rhodes, the Westinghouse, the Truman, and so on. In other words, it was supposed to be a meeting of the best of the best according to the linear thinkers who "judge" such things. The idea was that the achievers would somehow, over the course of a three-day meeting, influence the students, and push them on to extraordinary achievement. Interestingly, however, most of us "achievers" admitted that we would never have qualified to be in such a student group. The largest percentage of the achievers were actually people who had difficulties in school and didn't get scholarships, or awards, or other accolades. Most of the achievers were spatial thinkers, while most of the students were linear thinkers. From 1964 until 2000, less than half a dozen students broke the barrier to be inducted at the American Academy of Achievement's annual get-together. How could it be that so many promising students, judged by the linear thinkers themselves, failed to reach the highest levels of achievement?

I think the answer is simple. Linear thinkers are burdened by high expec-    4
tations from everyone, including themselves. They go out and get good jobs, but they seldom follow their dreams because dream-following is risk-taking, and risk-taking carries the possible burden of failure.

We spatial thinkers have known failure our entire lives and have grown    5
up without expectations, not from our teachers, often not from our parents, and sometimes, not even from ourselves. We don't meet the expectations of linear thinkers and are free to take risks. We are the people who most often follow our dreams, who think differently, spatially, inquisitively.

Personally, I think dyslexia and the consequences of dyslexia—learning    6
to deal with failure—explains my own success. From my failures, I've learned where I need help, such as reading and math. But I've also learned from my accomplishments what I'm better at than the linear thinkers. When I'm teaching linear thinkers here at Montana State University, I know to be patient, as they have just as hard a time with spatial problems as I have with linear ones. We both have learning talents and learning challenges, but I would never think of trading my spatial way of thinking for their linear way of thinking. I think dyslexia is an extraordinary characteristic, and it is certainly not something that needs to be fixed, or cured, or suppressed! Maybe it's time for a revolution! Take us out of classes for special ed, and put us in classes for spatial ed, taught of course, by spatial thinkers!

## FOR DISCUSSION

1. Jack Horner says that "non-dyslexics" are "linear thinkers" (2). What does he mean by this **DEFINITION**? Do you think it's accurate? Why or why not?

2. On the other hand, says Horner, people who are called *dyslexic* are actually "spatial thinkers" (2). Again, what does he mean, and how accurate is this definition?

3. Why does Horner think that his spatial perspective has helped him to succeed in his life and career?

4. Why does he think linear thinkers, including "many promising students," even when judged by other linear thinkers, "failed to reach the highest levels of achievement" (3)?

## STRATEGIES AND STRUCTURES

1. What is Horner's **PURPOSE** in defining dyslexia in positive terms as having "extraordinary characteristics"?

2. In addition to spatial thinkers, what other **AUDIENCE** might Horner and the International Dyslexia Association be interested in reaching? Explain.

3. Nowhere in his essay does Horner cite a standard textbook definition of *dyslexia*. In addition to the extraordinary characteristics, should he have included the ordinary ones in his definition as well? Why or why not?

4. Beside being "spatial thinkers," people with dyslexia have other distinguishing characteristics, according to Horner. What are some of them? Which ones seem particularly effective for extending his basic definition?

5. Horner uses his own life and career as an **EXAMPLE**. How and how well does that example help to explain what it means, in his view, to be dyslexic?

## WORDS AND FIGURES OF SPEECH

1. New words are often coined by **ANALOGY** with words that already exist (for example, *workaholic* and *alcoholic*). How does Horner derive the word "dys-spatics" (2)?

2. Thinking "outside the box" is a **CLICHÉ** (2). Should Horner have avoided the phrase? Why or why not?

3. What are the implications of *burdened* (4)? Is Horner being **IRONIC** here?

4. Explain the **PUN** in "spatial ed" (6).

## FOR WRITING

1. Write a paragraph or two explaining how "an early experience of failure in schools" or "peer persecution" has "given you an important edge" now (1).

2. Write a definition essay explaining what dyslexia is, what its causes are thought to be, and how it's usually treated. Be sure to cite your sources—and, if appropriate, an interesting case or two, whether "extraordinary" or typical.

# BLUE-COLLAR BRILLIANCE

MIKE ROSE (b. 1944) is a professor of education at the UCLA Graduate School of Education and Information Studies. When he was seven, Rose moved with his parents from Altoona, Pennsylvania, to Los Angeles, where his mother worked as a waitress, and he "watched the cooks and waitresses and listened to what they said." After graduating from Loyola University, Rose earned advanced degrees from the University of Southern California and UCLA. His books on language, literacy, and cognition include *The Mind at Work: Valuing the Intelligence of the American Worker* (2004) and *Back to School: Second Chances at Higher Ed* (2012). Based on years of teaching and close observations of the workplace, Rose is convinced that people can be smart in many different ways. In "Blue-Collar Brilliance," from the *American Scholar* (2009), he offers a definition of intelligence that does not separate the mind from the body—a shortcoming, in his view, of more conventional definitions.

M Y MOTHER, ROSE MERAGLIO ROSE (ROSIE), shaped her adult identity as a 1 waitress in coffee shops and family restaurants. When I was growing up in Los Angeles during the 1950s, my father and I would occasionally hang out at the restaurant until her shift ended, and then we'd ride the bus home with her. Sometimes she worked the register and the counter, and we sat there; when she waited booths and tables, we found a booth in the back where the waitresses took their breaks.

There wasn't much for a child to do at the restaurants, and so as the 2 hours stretched out, I watched the cooks and waitresses and listened to what they said. At mealtimes, the pace of the kitchen staff and the din from customers picked up. Weaving in and out around the room, waitresses warned *behind you* in impassive but urgent voices. Standing at the service window facing the kitchen, they called out abbreviated orders. *Fry four on two,* my mother would say as she clipped a check onto the metal wheel. Her tables were *deuces, four-tops,* or *six-tops* according to their size; seating areas also were nicknamed. The *racetrack,* for instance, was the fast-turnover front section. Lingo conferred authority and signaled know-how.

Rosie took customers' orders, pencil poised over pad, while fielding 3 questions about the food. She walked full tilt through the room with plates stretching up her left arm and two cups of coffee somehow cradled in her right hand. She stood at a table or booth and removed a plate for this person, another for that person, then another, remembering who had the hamburger, who had the fried shrimp, almost always getting it right. She would haggle with the cook about a returned order and rush by us, saying, *He gave me lip, but I got him.* She'd take a minute to flop down in the booth next to my father. *I'm all in,* she'd say, and whisper something about a customer. Gripping the outer edge of the table with one hand, she'd watch the room and note, in the flow of our conversation, who needed a refill, whose order was taking longer to prepare than it should, who was finishing up.

I couldn't have put it in words when I was growing up, but what I observed 4 in my mother's restaurant defined the world of adults, a place where competence was synonymous with physical work. I've since studied the working hab-

Page 371 offers advice on using synonyms to start a definition.

its of blue-collar workers and have come to understand how much my mother's kind of work demands of both body and brain. A waitress acquires knowledge and intuition about the ways and the rhythms of the restaurant business. Waiting on seven to nine tables, each with two to six customers, Rosie devised memory strategies so that she could remember who ordered what. And because she knew the average time it took to prepare different dishes, she could monitor an order that was taking too long at the service station.

Like anyone who is effective at physical work, my mother learned *to work*  5 *smart*, as she put it, *to make every move count*. She'd sequence and group tasks: What could she do first, then second, then third as she circled through her station? What tasks could be clustered? She did everything on the fly, and when problems arose—technical or human—she solved them within the flow of work, while taking into account the emotional state of her co-workers. Was the manager in a good mood? Did the cook wake up on the wrong side of the bed? If so, how could she make an extra request or effectively return an order?

And then, of course, there were the customers who entered the restau-  6 rant with all sorts of needs, from physiological ones, including the emotions that accompany hunger, to a sometimes complicated desire for human contact. Her tip depended on how well she responded to these needs, and so she became adept at reading social cues and managing feelings, both the customers' and her own. No wonder, then, that Rosie was intrigued by psychology. The restaurant became the place where she studied human behavior, puzzling over the problems of her regular customers and refining her ability to deal with people in a difficult world. She took pride in *being among the public*, she'd say. *There isn't a day that goes by in the restaurant that you don't learn something.*

My mother quit school in the seventh grade to help raise her brothers and  7 sisters. Some of those siblings made it through high school, and some dropped out to find work in railroad yards, factories, or restaurants. My father finished a grade or two in primary school in Italy and never darkened the schoolhouse door again. I didn't do well in school, either. By high school I had accumulated a spotty academic record and many hours of hazy disaffection. I spent a few years on the vocational track, but in my senior year I was inspired by my English teacher and managed to squeak into a small college on probation.

My freshman year was academically bumpy, but gradually I began to see  8 formal education as a means of fulfillment and as a road toward making a living. I studied the humanities and later the social and psychological sciences

*Rosie solved technical and human problems on the fly.*

and taught for ten years in a range of situations—elementary school, adult education courses, tutoring centers, a program for Vietnam veterans who wanted to go to college. Those students had socioeconomic and educational backgrounds similar to mine. Then I went back to graduate school to study education and cognitive psychology and eventually became a faculty member in a school of education.

Intelligence is closely associated with formal education—the type of    9 schooling a person has, how much and how long—and most people seem to move comfortably from that notion to a belief that work requiring less schooling requires less intelligence. These assumptions run through our cultural history, from the post—Revolutionary War period, when mechanics were characterized by political rivals as illiterate and therefore incapable of participating in government, until today. More than once I've heard a manager label his workers as "a bunch of dummies." Generalizations about intelligence, work, and social class deeply affect our assumptions about ourselves and each other, guiding the ways we use our minds to learn, build knowledge, solve problems, and make our way through the world.

Although writers and scholars have often looked at the working class, they have generally focused on the values such workers exhibit rather than on the thought their work requires—a subtle but pervasive omission. Our cultural iconography promotes the muscled arm, sleeve rolled tight against biceps, but no brightness behind the eye, no image that links hand and brain.

One of my mother's brothers, Joe Meraglio, left school in the ninth grade to work for the Pennsylvania Railroad. From there he joined the Navy, returned to the railroad, which was already in decline, and eventually joined his older brother at General Motors where, over a 33-year career, he moved from working

*This famous poster by J. Howard Miller, later called "Rosie the Riveter," was created to boost morale among factory workers during World War II. "Our cultural iconography," writes Mike Rose, "promotes the muscled arm, sleeve rolled tight against biceps, but no brightness behind the eye, no image that links hand and brain." With the feminist movement of the 1960s and later, however, "Rosie" came to represent what Rose himself calls "blue-collar brilliance"—a blending of muscle and intelligence.*

on the assembly line to supervising the paint-and-body department. When I was a young man, Joe took me on a tour of the factory. The floor was loud—in some places deafening—and when I turned a corner or opened a door, the smell of chemicals knocked my head back. The work was repetitive and taxing, and the pace was inhumane.

Still, for Joe the shop floor provided what school did not; it was *like* 12 *schooling,* he said, a place where *you're constantly learning.* Joe learned the most efficient way to use his body by acquiring a set of routines that were quick and preserved energy. Otherwise he would never have survived on the line.

As a foreman, Joe constantly faced new problems and became a consum- 13 mate multi-tasker, evaluating a flurry of demands quickly, parceling out physical and mental resources, keeping a number of ongoing events in his mind, returning to whatever task had been interrupted, and maintaining a cool head under the pressure of grueling production schedules. In the midst of all this, Joe learned more and more about the auto industry, the technological and social dynamics of the shop floor, the machinery and production processes, and the basics of paint chemistry and of plating and baking. With further promotions, he not only solved problems but also began to find problems to solve: Joe initiated the redesign of the nozzle on a paint sprayer, thereby eliminating costly and unhealthy overspray. And he found a way to reduce energy costs on the baking ovens without affecting the quality of the paint. He lacked formal knowledge of how the machines under his supervision worked, but he had direct experience with them, hands-on knowledge, and was savvy about their quirks and operational capabilities. He could experiment with them.

In addition, Joe learned about budgets and management. Coming off the 14 line as he did, he had a perspective of workers' needs and management's demands, and this led him to think of ways to improve efficiency on the line while relieving some of the stress on the assemblers. He had each worker in a unit learn his or her co-workers' jobs so they could rotate across stations to relieve some of the monotony. He believed that rotation would allow assemblers to get longer and more frequent breaks. It was an easy sell to the people on the line. The union, however, had to approve any modification in job duties, and the managers were wary of the change. Joe had to argue his case on a number of fronts, providing him a kind of rhetorical education.

Eight years ago I began a study of the thought processes involved in work    15
like that of my mother and uncle. I catalogued the cognitive demands of a
range of blue-collar and service jobs, from waitressing and hair styling to
plumbing and welding. To gain a sense of how knowledge and skill develop, I
observed experts as well as novices. From the details of this close examination, I tried to fashion what I called "cognitive biographies" of blue-collar
workers. Biographical accounts of the lives of scientists, lawyers, entrepreneurs, and other professionals are rich with detail about the intellectual
dimension of their work. But the life stories of working-class people are few
and are typically accounts of hardship and courage or the achievements
wrought by hard work.

Our culture—in Cartesian fashion[1]—separates the body from the mind,    16
so that, for example, we assume that the use of a tool does not involve abstraction. We reinforce this notion by defining intelligence solely on grades in
school and numbers on IQ tests. And we employ social biases pertaining to a
person's place on the occupational ladder. The distinctions among blue, pink,
and white collars carry with them attributions of character, motivation, and
intelligence. Although we rightly acknowledge and amply compensate the play
of mind in white-collar and professional work, we diminish or erase it in con-
siderations about other endeavors—physical and service work particularly.
We also often ignore the experience of everyday work in administrative delib-
erations and policymaking.

But here's what we find when we get in close. The plumber seeking lever-    17
age in order to work in tight quarters and the hair stylist adroitly handling
scissors and comb manage their bodies strategically. Though work-related
actions become routine with experience, they were learned at some point
through observation, trial and error, and, often, physical or verbal assistance
from a co-worker or trainer. I've frequently observed novices talking to themselves as they take on a task, or shaking their head or hand as if to erase an
attempt before trying again. In fact, our traditional notions of routine
performance could keep us from appreciating the many instances within
routine where quick decisions and adjustments are made. I'm struck by the

1. After French philospher René Descartes (1596–1650), who proposed the dualism of mind
and body.

*With an eighth-grade education, Joe (hands together) advanced to supervisor of a G.M. paint-and-body department.*

thinking-in-motion that some work requires, by all the mental activity that can be involved in simply getting from one place to another: the waitress rushing back through her station to the kitchen or the foreman walking the line.

The use of tools requires the studied refinement of stance, grip, balance, and fine-motor skills. But manipulating tools is intimately tied to knowledge of what a particular instrument can do in a particular situation and do better than other similar tools. A worker must also know the characteristics of the material one is engaging—how it reacts to various cutting or compressing devices, to degrees of heat, or to lines of force. Some of these things demand judgment, the weighing of options, the consideration of multiple variables, and, occasionally, the creative use of a tool in an unexpected way. 18

In manipulating material, the worker becomes attuned to aspects of the environment, a training or disciplining of perception that both enhances knowledge and informs perception. Carpenters have an eye for length, line, and angle; mechanics troubleshoot by listening; hair stylists are attuned to shape, texture, and motion. Sensory data merge with concept, as when an auto mechanic relies on sound, vibration, and even smell to understand what cannot be observed. 19

Planning and problem solving have been studied since the earliest days of  20
modern cognitive psychology and are considered core elements in Western
definitions of intelligence. To work is to solve problems. The big difference
between the psychologist's laboratory and the workplace is that in the former
the problems are isolated and in the latter they are embedded in the real-time
flow of work with all its messiness and social complexity.

Much of physical work is social and interactive. Movers determining  21
how to get an electric range down a flight of stairs require coordination, negotiation, planning, and the establishing of incremental goals. Words, gestures,
and sometimes a quick pencil sketch are involved, if only to get the rhythm
right. How important it is, then, to consider the social and communicative
dimension of physical work, for it provides the medium for so much of work's
intelligence.

Given the ridicule heaped on blue-collar speech, it might seem odd to  22
value its cognitive content. Yet, the flow of talk at work provides the channel
for organizing and distributing tasks, for troubleshooting and problem solving, for learning new information and revising old. A significant amount of
teaching, often informal and indirect, takes place at work. Joe Meraglio saw
that much of his job as a supervisor involved instruction. In some service
occupations, language and communication are central: observing and interpreting behavior and expression, inferring mood and motive, taking on the
perspective of others, responding appropriately to social cues, and knowing
when you're understood. A good hair stylist, for instance, has the ability to
convert vague requests (*I want something light and summery*) into an appropriate cut through questions, pictures, and hand gestures.

Verbal and mathematical skills drive measures of intelligence in the West-  23
ern Hemisphere, and many of the kinds of work I studied are thought to require
relatively little proficiency in either. Compared to certain kinds of white-collar
occupations, that's true. But written symbols flow through physical work.

Numbers are rife in most workplaces: on tools and gauges, as measure-  24
ments, as indicators of pressure or concentration or temperature, as guides to
sequence, on ingredient labels, on lists and spreadsheets, as markers of quantity and price. Certain jobs require workers to make, check, and verify calcu-
lations, and to collect and interpret data. Basic math can be involved, and some
workers develop a good sense of numbers and patterns. Consider, as well,

what might be called material mathematics: mathematical functions embodied in materials and actions, as when a carpenter builds a cabinet or a flight of stairs. A simple mathematical act can extend quickly beyond itself. Measuring, for example, can involve more than recording the dimensions of an object. As I watched a cabinetmaker measure a long strip of wood, he read a number off the tape out loud, looked back over his shoulder to the kitchen wall, turned back to his task, took another measurement, and paused for a moment in thought. He was solving a problem involving the molding, and the measurement was important to his deliberation about structure and appearance.

In the blue-collar workplace, directions, plans, and reference books rely on illustrations, some representational and others, like blueprints, that require training to interpret. Esoteric symbols—visual jargon—depict switches and receptacles, pipe fittings, or types of welds. Workers themselves often make sketches on the job. I frequently observed them grab a pencil to sketch something on a scrap of paper or on a piece of the material they were installing.     25

Though many kinds of physical work don't require a high literacy level, more reading occurs in the blue-collar workplace than is generally thought, from manuals and catalogues to work orders and invoices, to lists, labels, and forms. With routine tasks, for example, reading is integral to understanding production quotas, learning how to use an instrument, or applying a product. Written notes can initiate action, as in restaurant orders or reports of machine malfunction, or they can serve as memory aids.     26

True, many uses of writing are abbreviated, routine, and repetitive, and they infrequently require interpretation or analysis. But analytic moments can be part of routine activities, and seemingly basic reading and writing can be cognitively rich. Because workplace language is used in the flow of other activities, we can overlook the remarkable coordination of words, numbers, and drawings required to initiate and direct action.     27

If we believe everyday work to be mindless, then that will affect the work we create in the future. When we devalue the full range of everyday cognition, we offer limited educational opportunities and fail to make fresh and meaningful instructional connections among disparate kinds of skill and knowledge. If we think that whole categories of people—identified by class or occupation—are not that bright, then we reinforce social separations and cripple our ability to talk across cultural divides.     28

Affirmation of diverse intelligence is not a retreat to a softhearted defini- 29
tion of the mind. To acknowledge a broader range of intellectual capacity is to
take seriously the concept of cognitive variability, to appreciate in all the Rosies
and Joes the thought that drives their accomplishments and defines who they
are. This is a model of the mind that is worthy of a democratic society.

### FOR DISCUSSION

1. Is Mike Rose correct when he says that DEFINITIONS of human intelligence should
   not be based solely "on grades in school and numbers on IQ tests" (16)? Why or
   why not?

2. According to Rose, how *should* intelligence be defined, especially among workers
   whose tasks are not "closely associated with formal education" (9)? What would
   he add to more traditional definitions?

3. Why is Rose concerned with definitions of intelligence that consider "everyday
   work to be mindless" (28)? What EFFECTS are such misguided (in his view) con-
   ceptions likely to have on society "in the future" (28)?

4. What does Rose mean by the "concept of cognitive variability" (29), and where—
   aside from watching his mother wait tables in a restaurant—did he likely learn
   about it?

### STRATEGIES AND STRUCTURES

1. Why does Rose begin his essay with an account of his mother's experience as a
   waitress (1–6)? Where else does he use elements of NARRATIVE to support his
   definition of intelligence? How effective are they? Explain.

2. What are some of the main traits of "blue-collar brilliance" as Rose defines it?
   Point to specific passages in the text where he identifies those traits.

3. "There wasn't much for a child to do at the restaurants," says Rose, "and so as the
   hours stretched out, I watched the cooks and waitresses and listened to what they
   said" (2). How does his childhood role as an observer at his mother's restaurant
   anticipate the adult role that Rose adopts as a scholar who tells "the life stories of
   working-class people" (15)?

4. "I couldn't have put it into words," Rose says of this early experience of the workplace (4). How *did* he learn to put his observations into words, and what kind of
   language does he typically use to do it? Point to specific examples in the text.

5. Rose's definition of blue-collar intelligence is based on "a model of the mind" that, he claims at the end of his essay, is "worthy of a democratic society" (29). How and how well does Rose anticipate this ARGUMENT? Should he have stated this major point more directly earlier? Why or why not?

6. Rose's essay first appeared in the *American Scholar*, a journal aimed at readers who are interested in intellectual subjects beyond their narrow fields of expertise. How appropriate are the language and writing style of his essay to this intended AUDIENCE? Explain.

## WORDS AND FIGURES OF SPEECH

1. How and how well does Rose capture the "lingo" of the workplace (2)? Point to specific words and phrases in the text.

2. SYNONYMS are different words that have essentially the same meaning. What is Rose defining when he refers to "a place where competence was synonymous with physical work" (4)?

3. Look up the word *iconography* in your dictionary (10). Who or what did it pertain to before the rock stars and television celebrities of today?

4. Rose says that he has long observed blue-collar workers for the purpose of writing their "cognitive biographies" (15). Judging from the context in which he uses it, what does Rose mean by this term? Which parts of his essay (if any) would you point to as examples of this type of writing? Why?

## FOR WRITING

1. Spend an hour or so watching and listening to the workers in a diner, factory, store, hair salon, or other workplace environment. Take notes on what they say and do, and write a paragraph or two capturing the scene as Rose does in the opening paragraphs of his essay.

2. Write an essay explaining how a group of workers you have observed, blue-collar or otherwise, defines some important aspect of their work. For example, you might explain how they define competency in their field—or failure, loyalty, or some other broad concept. Cite particular cases and conversations in some detail.

# ⊹12⊹

## CAUSE AND EFFECT

I F you were at home on vacation and read in the morning paper that the physics building at your school had burned, your first questions would probably be about the *effects* of the fire: "How much damage was done? Was anyone hurt?" Once you knew what the effects were—the building burned to the ground, but the blaze broke out in the middle of the night when nobody was in it—your next questions would likely be about the *causes*: "What caused the fire? Lightning? A short circuit in the electrical system? An arsonist's match?"

If the newspaper went on to say that the fire was set by your old roommate, Larry, you would probably have some more questions, such as "Why did Larry do it? What will happen to Larry as a result of his action?" When you write a **CAUSE-AND-EFFECT*** essay, you answer fundamental questions like these about the *what* and *why* of an event or phenomenon. The questions may be simple, but answering them fully and adequately may require you to consider a variety of possible causes and effects—and to distinguish one type of cause from another.

In our example, Larry struck a match, which caused the building to catch fire. That effect in turn caused another effect—the building burned down. Larry's striking the match is the *immediate* cause of the fire—the one closest to the event in time. A *remote* cause, on the other hand, might be Larry's failure on a physics test two weeks earlier. But which cause is the *main* cause, the most important one, and which causes are less important—merely *contributing*? Was Larry depressed and angry before he took the physics test? What were his feelings toward his father, the physics professor? Often you will need to run through a whole chain of related causes and effects like these before deciding to emphasize one or two.

*Words printed in SMALL CAPITALS are defined in the Glossary/Index.

How do you make sure that the causes you choose to emphasize actually account for the particular event or phenomenon you're analyzing? Two basic conditions have to be met to prove causation. A main cause has to be both *necessary* and *sufficient* to produce the effect in question. That is, it must be shown that (1) the alleged cause *always* accompanies the effect, and (2) that the alleged cause (and only the alleged cause) has the power to produce the effect. Let's look at these conditions in the following passage from a 2009 article on statistics in the *New York Times*. The author is recalling a time before the Salk vaccine defeated polio:

> For example, in the late 1940s, before there was a polio vaccine, public health experts in America noted that polio cases increased in step with the consumption of ice cream and soft drinks. . . . Eliminating such treats was even recommended as part of an anti-polio diet. It turned out that polio outbreaks were most common in the hot months of summer, when people naturally ate more ice cream. . . .
>
> —STEVE LOHR, "For Today's Graduates,
> Just One Word: Statistics"

The health experts who thought that ice cream and soft drinks *caused* polio failed to distinguish between causation and mere correlation. Although out-breaks of polio always seemed to be accompanied by an increase in the consumption of cool summer treats, ice cream and soft drinks did not actually have the power to cause the disease. And though the *heat* was the clear cause of the increased consumption of ice cream and soft drinks, Jonas Salk and his colleagues suspected that nor-mal summer weather was not sufficiently harmful to induce paralysis. Eventu-ally they isolated the *main* cause—the poliomyelitis virus. This tiny killer met both tests for true causality: it appeared in every case, and it was the only factor capable of producing the dire effect ascribed to it. It was both necessary and sufficient.

Tim Wendel makes this distinction in "King, Kennedy, and the Power of Words," p. 433.

As Dr. Salk knew from the beginning, mere sequences in time—cases of polio increase as, or immediately after, the consumption of ice cream and soft drinks increases—is not sufficient to prove causation. This mistake in causal analysis is commonly referred to as the *post hoc, ergo propter hoc*

FALLACY, Latin for "after this, therefore because of this." Salk understood the two conditions that must be met before causation may be accurately inferred.

These two conditions can be expressed as a simple formula:

B cannot have happened without A;
Whenever A happens, B must happen.

When we are dealing with psychological and social rather than purely physical factors, the main cause may defy simple analysis. Or it may turn out that there are a number of causes working together. Suppose we looked for an answer to the following question: Why does Maria smoke? This looks like a simple question, but it is a difficult one to answer because there are so many complicated reasons a young woman like Maria might smoke. The best way for a writer to approach this kind of causal analysis might be to list as many of the contributing causes as he or she can turn up:

| | |
|---:|:---|
| MARIA: | I smoke because I need to do something with my hands. |
| MARIA'S BOYFRIEND: | Maria smokes because she thinks it looks cool. |
| MEDICAL DOCTOR: | Because Maria has developed a physical addiction to tobacco. |
| PSYCHOLOGIST: | Because of peer pressure. |
| SOCIOLOGIST: | Because Maria is Hispanic; in recent years tobacco companies have spent billions in advertising to attract more Hispanic smokers. |

When you list particular causes like this, be as specific as you can. When you list effects, be even more specific. Instead of saying "Smoking is bad for your health," be particular. In an essay on the harm of tobacco, for example, Erik Eckholm provides a grim effect. "The most potentially tragic victims," he writes, "are the infants of mothers who smoke. They are more likely than the babies of nonsmoking mothers to be born underweight and thus to encounter death or disease at birth or during the initial months of life."

In singling out the effects of smoking upon unwitting infants, Eckholm uses an EXAMPLE that might be just powerful enough to convince some smokers to quit. Though your examples may not be as dramatic as Eckholm's, they must be specific to be powerful. And they must be selected with your AUDIENCE in mind. In the previous example, Eckholm addresses young women who smoke. If he were writing for a middle-aged audience, however, he might point out that the incidence of cancer and heart disease is 70 percent higher among one-pack-a-day men and women than among nonsmokers.

Your audience needs to be taken into account when you analyze causes and effects because, among other reasons, you are usually making an ARGUMENT about the causes or effects of a phenomenon or event. Thus, you must carry the reader step by step through some kind of proof. Your explanation may be instructive, amusing, or startling; but if your analysis is to make the point you want it to make, it must also be persuasive.

# A BRIEF GUIDE TO WRITING A CAUSE-AND-EFFECT ESSAY

When you analyze causes or effects, you explain why something happened or what its results are. So as you write a cause-and-effect essay, you need to identify your subject and indicate which you plan to emphasize—causes or effects. Myriam Márquez makes these basic moves in the opening paragraphs of her essay in this chapter:

> When I'm shopping with my mother or standing in line with my stepdad to order fast food or anywhere else we might be together, we're going to speak Spanish. . . . Let me explain why we haven't adopted English as our official family language.
>
> —MYRIAM MÁRQUEZ, "Why and When
> We Speak Spanish in Public"

Márquez identifies the subject of her analysis (speaking Spanish in public) and indicates that she plans to emphasize the causes of this phenomenon ("why").

Whether you emphasize causes or effects, remember that the effect of one event may become the cause of a subsequent event, forming a CAUSAL CHAIN that you will need to follow link by link in order to fully analyze why something happened. For example: Two cars collide, killing the driver of the second car. The first driver's excessive speed is the cause; the death of the second driver is the effect. That effect, in turn, causes another one—the children of the second driver grow up without that parent.

Elisa Gonzales traces a chain of causes and effects in "Family History," p. 428.

The following guidelines will help you make the basic moves of cause and effect as you draft an essay. They will also help you come up with your subject, explain why you're analyzing causes and effects, distinguish between different kinds of causes, and present your analysis in an organized way.

## Coming Up with a Subject

To find a subject for an essay that analyzes cause and effect, start with your own curiosity—about the physical world or about history, sociology, or any other field that interests you. Look for specific phenomena or events—climate change, President Truman's decision to drop the atomic bomb on Japan in 1945, the rising cost of health care in the United States—that you find intriguing. In order to narrow your subject down into a topic that is specific enough to investigate within the time allotted by your instructor, begin by asking yourself what its main causes (or effects) are likely to be. You may need to do some research on your subject; you'll find guidelines for doing research in the Appendix of this book.

## Considering Your Purpose and Audience

As you examine particular causes and effects, think about why you're analyzing them. Is your PURPOSE to inform your readers? Amuse them? ARGUE that one set of causes (or effects) is more likely than another? One writer, for example, may try to persuade readers that autism is caused by inherent biological factors, while another writer might argue for environmental causes.

You'll also need to consider the AUDIENCE you want to reach. Are your readers already familiar with the topic, or will you need to provide background information and DEFINE unfamiliar terms? Are they likely to be receptive to the point you're making, or opposed to it? An article on the causes of autism may have a very different slant depending on whether the intended readers are parents of autistic children, medical doctors, psychologists, or the general public.

Myriam Márquez, p. 445, assumes a reader who knows little about her subject.

## Generating Ideas: Asking Why, What, and What If

When you want to figure out what caused something, the essential question to ask is *why*. Why does a curveball drop as it crosses home plate? Why was Napoleon defeated in his invasion of Russia in 1812? If, on the other hand, you want to figure out what the effects of something are, or will be, then the basic question to ask is *what*, or *what if*. What will happen if the curveball fails to drop? What effect did the weather have on Napoleon's campaign?

As you ask *why* or *what* about your subject, keep in mind that a single effect may have multiple causes, or vice versa. Be sure to write down as many causes or effects as you can think of. If you were to ask why the U.S. financial system almost collapsed in the fall of 2008, for example, you would need to consider a number of possible causes, including recklessness on Wall Street, vastly inflated real estate values, subprime mortgages offered to unqualified borrowers, and a widespread credit crunch. Similarly, if you were analyzing the effects of the financial crisis, you would need to consider several of them, such as widespread unemployment, falling stock prices, and the loss of consumer confidence.

## Templates for Analyzing Causes and Effects

The following templates can help you to generate ideas for a cause-and-effect essay and then to start drafting. Don't take these as formulas where you just have to fill in the blanks. There are no easy formulas for good writing. But these templates can help you plot out some of the key moves of cause and effect and thus may serve as good starting points.

▶ The main cause/effect of X is _____.

▶ X would also seem to have a number of contributing causes, including _____, _____, and _____.

▶ One effect of X is _____, which in turn causes _____.

▶ Some additional effects of X are _____, _____, and _____.

▶ Although the causes of X are not known, we can speculate that a key factor is _____.

▶ X cannot be attributed to mere chance or coincidence because _____.

▶ Once we know what causes X, we are in a position to say that _____.

For more techniques to help you generate ideas and start writing a cause-and-effect analysis, see Chapter 3.

## Stating Your Point

As you draft an essay that analyzes cause and effect, tell readers at the outset whether you are going to focus on causes or effects—or both. Also make clear what your main point, or **THESIS**, is. For example, if you are analyzing the causes of the financial meltdown in the United States in 2008, you might signal your main point in a **THESIS STATEMENT** like this one:

> The main cause of the financial meltdown in the United States in 2008 was the freezing of credit, which made it impossible for anyone to borrow money.

Once you have stated your thesis, you are ready to present evidence that supports it.

## Distinguishing One Type of Cause from Another

To help your reader understand how a number of causes work together to produce a particular effect, you can distinguish among causes based on their relative importance in producing the effect and on their occurrence in time.

**MAIN AND CONTRIBUTING CAUSES.** The *main cause* is the one that has the greatest power to produce the effect. It must be both necessary to cause the effect and sufficient to do so. On August 1, 2007, a bridge collapsed on Interstate 35W in Minneapolis, Minnesota. Most investigators now agree that the main cause of the collapse was a flaw in the bridge's design. A *contributing cause* is a secondary cause—it helps to produce the effect but is not sufficient to do it alone. In the Minnesota bridge collapse, a contributing cause was the weight of construction supplies and equipment on the bridge at the time. Although it would have been wise to locate at least some of the construction equipment off the bridge, the added weight alone did not cause the collapse. As one investigator pointed out, "If the bridge had not been improperly designed, everybody says it would have held up that weight easily."

**IMMEDIATE AND REMOTE CAUSES.** The *immediate cause* is the one closest in time and most directly responsible for producing the effect, whereas *remote causes* are less apparent and more removed in time. The immediate cause of the financial meltdown of 2008 was the drying up of credit, but several remote causes were in play as well, such as subprime lending, the burst in the housing bubble, and recklessness on Wall Street.

Keep in mind, however, that these two ways of distinguishing causes aren't mutually exclusive. For example, the weight of the construction equipment on the bridge was both a contributing cause and an immediate one—though not the main cause, it immediately triggered the collapse of the bridge.

As you link together causes and effects, be careful not to confuse causation with coincidence. Just because one event (increased sales of soft drinks) comes before another (higher incidence of polio) does not mean the first event actually caused the second.

## Organizing a Cause-and-Effect Essay

One way to present the effects of a given cause is by arranging them in chronological order. If you were tracing the effects of the credit crisis of 2008, for example, you would start with the crisis itself (the freezing of credit) and then proceed chronologically, detailing its effects in the order in which they occurred: first several investment banks collapsed, then the stock market plummeted, then the federal government stepped in with a massive bailout, and so on.

Reverse chronological order, in which you begin with a known effect and work backward through the possible causes, can also be effective. In the case of the Minnesota bridge collapse, you would start with the collapse itself (the known effect) and work backward in time through all of the possible causes: heavy construction equipment overloaded the bridge; the bridge structure was already weakened by corrosion; corrosion had not been discovered because of lack of inspections and maintenance; the capacity of the bridge was reduced at the outset by an error in design.

Sonia Sotomayor travels back in time to examine the causes of adversity in her life, p. 454.

Often you will want to organize your analysis around various types of causes or effects. You might, for instance, explore the immediate cause before moving on to the remote causes, or vice versa. Or you might explore the contributing causes before the main cause, or vice versa. Whatever method you choose, be sure to organize your analysis in a way that makes the relationship between causes and effects as clear to your reader as possible.

# EDITING FOR COMMON ERRORS IN A CAUSE-AND-EFFECT ANALYSIS

Like other kinds of writing, a cause-and-effect analysis uses distinctive patterns of language and punctuation—and thus invites typical kinds of errors. The following tips will help you to check for (and correct) these common errors when you analyze causes and effects in your own writing.

## Check your verbs to make sure they clearly express causation

Some verbs express causation clearly and directly, whereas other verbs merely imply that one thing causes another.

| VERBS THAT EXPRESS CAUSATION | VERBS THAT IMPLY CAUSATION |
|---|---|
| account for | follow |
| bring about | happen |
| cause | imply |
| effect | involve |
| make | implicate |
| result | influence |

Using verbs that clearly express causation makes your analysis more precise.

▶ The collapse of the bridge on Interstate 35W ~~involved~~ <u>was caused by</u> faulty design.

## Check for common usage errors

### AFFECT, EFFECT

In cause-and-effect analysis, *affect* is a verb meaning "influence." *Effect* is usually a noun meaning "result," but it can also be a verb meaning "bring about."

▶ Failing the course did not *affect* his graduation.

▶ Failing the course did not have the *effect* he feared most.

▶ Failing the course, however, did *effect* a change in his class standing.

### REASON IS BECAUSE, REASON WHY

Both of these expressions are redundant. In the first case, use *that* instead of *because*. In the second, use *reason* alone.

▶ The reason the bridge collapsed was ~~because~~ <u>that</u> it was poorly designed.

▶ Faulty design is the reason ~~why~~ the bridge collapsed.

## Polar Bear Blues

In this poster, sponsored by WWF, a world wildlife foundation, a polar bear sleeps on a seedy backstreet. The sign in the background suggests that one cause of his predicament is global warming. How has global warming left the bear in such a bad state? The fine print at the bottom of the poster explains: "Animals around the world are losing their habitats due to climate change. By choosing a hybrid or fuel-efficient car, you can help prevent this. Take action right now." When you analyze causes and effects, follow the lead of the WWF: identify the particular effect you plan to look into (homeless polar bear) and the causes of this effect (loss of habitat due to climate change). You may also want to explain how readers can prevent undesirable causes and their effects "right now"—so that polar bears and other animals can get back to their own neighborhoods.

ELISA GONZALES

# FAMILY HISTORY

ELISA GONZALES wrote "Family History" for an undergraduate writing class at Yale University. In it, she explores the causes and effects of bipolar disorder in two members of the same family. Gonzales does not try to determine if such psychological conditions are inherited, but she does find sufficient evidence in her family's history to suggest that the effects of one person's disorder may become causes of the same disorder in another family member. "Family History," along with other work by Gonzales, won the 2011 Norman Mailer College Writing prize, sponsored jointly by the National Council of Teachers of English and the Mailer Center.

Family History

By the time I am diagnosed with bipolar disorder type II, I have known Dr. Bradley for years. I know that he is divorced with two children, that he dated a beautiful Russian nurse who quit last year under obscure circumstances, that he colors his hair to stop the gray from infringing on his catalogue-model looks. He delivered my littlest sister, now seven, and he cried when my youngest brother died after several days in an incubator, his lungs hesitantly fluttering like moth wings before they finally deflated. Dr. Bradley has spent years counseling my mother after suicide attempts. In many ways, he knows us better than my closest friends who, blithe and unsuspecting, have always accepted my selective disclosures about my family. So when he pauses, clears his throat, and asks if I have a family history of bipolar disorder, I stare at him without speaking. It seems impossible that he doesn't know about my father.

For several minutes, I have trouble comprehending what he's saying, though he's kind and clear. Based on what I've told him—that I've had to leave parties because the urge to scream was so uncontrollable I felt I might disintegrate, that I've stayed up for days without speaking or going to class, that I've frightened my boy-friend with my bursts of rage—bipolar disorder seems probable. It often manifests in people around my age, especially in creative high-achieving people. There is no blood test; he will give me medication, a combination of new antipsychotic drugs and traditional lithium pills, and see if I improve. Confirming my family history is the last piece of the diagnosis. Heredity strikes most

1 ••••• First line introduces a serious effect of yet unknown cause(s)

••••• Probes for possible causes of the disorder

2

••••• Gives specific effects that might confirm the diagnosis

people as soon as they look in the mirror, in how much the jawline protrudes or how adamantly the earlobes crease, so I should not be so surprised at being confronted with my own history. Studying a chart of the cardiovascular system, I briefly wonder if I have always known that I carried with me more than my father's curly hair and dry sense of humor. But this is impossible, and far too mystical for the sterility of the exam table. It is true, though, that I have always feared my father, not just the physical reality of him—those thick hands that have left bruises around my throat and shoved my mother's teeth through her cheeks—but the lingering effects of his presence.

When I was six, I went to the kitchen expecting breakfast and found my father frying Sesame Street videotapes in the cast-iron skillet. The charred plastic littered the kitchen for days and smoke stained the walls for the whole summer, until my father was released from his month-long stay in the hospital and repainted the entire house as penance. He also mended the holes he'd made in the walls and bought a new couch to replace the one he'd gutted with a butcher knife one night while we were sleeping. To celebrate, we ate store-bought pecan pie in a kitchen that smelled of fresh white paint. He talked about repairing the furnace and my sister showed him the stuffed dog named Rosie she'd gotten for her birthday. Although this cycle—destruction, then rehabilitation—has happened many times, I have always recalled the precision of his hands as he stood so calmly by the stove stirring twisted plastic with a metal spatula.

A month before my diagnosis, my sister and I fought about who would use the car, a typical sibling

Introduces a significant probable cause of the disorder

Implies that immediate effects of one disorder may be remote causes of the other

fight, except in its escalation. I started screaming and threw a book at her head, threatening to call the police on her and report the car stolen if she took it. When she moved toward the door, I got a knife from the kitchen and told her I would slash the tires before I would let her leave. She stopped arguing with me to say, disbelievingly, "You're just like Daddy." I wanted to tell her that I couldn't be like him because he is crazy and I am not. Instead, I began to weep soundlessly, collapsing to the ground, my mouth gaping and silent. Now, in the exam room, I feel that type of ache again, beyond expression because no noise can cure it. It is here that I realize my entire life has converged in a dark pattern newly revealed.

> Suggests a cause-and-effect relationship between the two disorders

When my father was nineteen—the same age I am now—he cut up houseplants in precise segments and neatly ate a plateful with a fork before his brother found him and rushed him to the hospital. Later that month, after the doctors bandied around the word "schizophrenia" for a while, he received his own proper diagnosis. In 1979, lithium pharmacology had been approved for the treatment of manic depression, as bipolar disorder was called then, so his illness was manageable if he took his pills. But he never liked lithium, or the other medications his doctors prescribed. I wonder if I too will feel blunted and blurred without other forces sharpening themselves on my mind. Dr. Bradley asks if I have any questions before he writes me a prescription, and I say no. I am familiar with the required monthly checkups and learned the difference between the words "manic" and "maniac" when I was seven. Years before I grew up a little and participated in the national spelling bee, I was awed by the crucial distinction created through the addition of an *A*.

5

> Gives early symptoms of the father's disorder

> Anticipates possible future effects

> Suggests that the old name for the disorder confused cause and effect

The strangest part of hearing the diagnosis is that I    6
suddenly want something I haven't wanted in years: to
talk to my father. I know that he ran away after the doctors told him the news and his brothers found him four
days later on a beach in California, but I know nothing
else. I would like to call my father and say, "I know I've
always hated you, but as it turns out, I'm just like you."
Perhaps he would tell me how he felt when he found out,
if he slept on the beach and wandered through a shabby
town looking for the anonymity that would let him lose
his label, or if he blurted his diagnosis to people to try it
out. Mostly, I would like to know if he would have come
back, had they not found him, or if instead he would have
woken up and walked into the ocean one day, the only
person to separate the sky from all that water. The lure
of water in the lungs, of the non-breathing world, is one
that I too will face in the months after the diagnosis.

But my father and I haven't exchanged more than a    7
few words since I was fourteen, when he tried to strangle
me, saying that he had brought me into this world and he
could take me out of it. After that, he left us, hauled out
by police officers and kept away by court orders; I no
longer know his number. I will not call him, nor mention
when I see him for a few minutes at Christmas that I am
also bipolar. Yet months after, when I am assigned *Paradise Lost* for a class, I will start to cry upon reading a
piece of the poet's invocation:

> *though fallen on evil days,*
> *on evil days though fallen, and evil tongues;*
> *in darkness, and with dangers compass'd round,*
> *and solitude; yet not alone.*

Confronts one of the worst remote effects she may face

Ends with a positive effect of the discovery that her condition is shared

TIM WENDEL

# KING, KENNEDY, AND THE POWER OF WORDS

TIM WENDEL (b. 1956) is a novelist, sportswriter, and teacher of writing. He was born in Philadelphia and grew up in Lockport, New York. After graduating from Syracuse University as a journalism major, Wendel earned an MFA from Johns Hopkins University, where he now teaches writing. His articles and essays have appeared in *Esquire, Go, Gargoyle*, the *New York Times*, the *Washington Post*, and *USA Today*. Author of *Summer of '68: The Season That Changed Baseball, and America, Forever* (2012), among other books, Wendel believes that American discourse, especially political discourse, has changed significantly in the decades since the assassinations of John F. Kennedy, Martin Luther King Jr., and Robert F. Kennedy. In "King, Kennedy, and the Power of Words" (from the website of the *American Scholar*, April 2012), Wendel analyzes some of the specific causes and effects of those changes, particularly what he sees as the tendency of politicians today to slip into "passive-voice mode."

T HE NIGHT OF APRIL 4, 1968, presidential candidate Robert Kennedy received the news that Martin Luther King Jr. had been assassinated. Kennedy was about to speak in Indianapolis and some in his campaign wondered if they should go ahead with the rally. 1

Moments before Kennedy climbed onto a flatbed truck to address the crowd, which had gathered in a light rain, press secretary Frank Mankiewicz gave the candidate a sheet of paper with ideas of what he might say. Kennedy slid it into his pocket without looking at it. Another aide approached with more notes and the candidate waved him away. 2

"Do they know about Martin Luther King?" Kennedy asked those gathered on the platform. No, came the reply. 3

After asking the crowd to lower its campaign signs, Kennedy told his audience that King had been shot and killed earlier in Memphis. Gasps went up from the crowd and for a moment everything seemed ready to come apart. Indianapolis might have joined other cities across America that burned on that awful night. 4

But then Kennedy, beginning in a trembling, halting voice, slowly brought the people back around and somehow held them together. Listening to the speech decades later is to be reminded of the real power of words. How they can heal, how they can still bring us together, but only if they are spoken with conviction and from the heart. 5

Compare what we often hear from politicians today to what Kennedy said on that tragic night in Indianapolis. He told the crowd how he "had a member of my family killed"—a reference to his brother John, who had been assassinated less than five years before. 6

Later on, Kennedy recited a poem by Aeschylus, which he had memorized long before that trying night in Indianapolis: 7

> Even in our sleep, pain which cannot forget
> Falls drop by drop upon the heart,
> Until, in our own despair, against our will,
> Comes wisdom through the awful grace of God.

Kennedy's heartfelt speech came only hours after King's last address. The night before, the civil rights leader had reluctantly taken to the dais at the 8

*Martin Luther King Jr.*

Mason Temple in Memphis. The weather that evening had been miserable—thunderstorms and tornado warnings. As a result, King arrived late and was just going to say a few words and then tell everyone to please go home.

Visibly tired and with no notes in hand, King stumbled at first. The shutters hitting against the temple walls sounded like gun shots to him. So much so that King's friend, the Reverend Billy Kyles, found a custodian to stop the noise. Only then, at the crowd's urging, did the words begin to come together for King. 9

"We've got some difficult days ahead," he said that night. "But it really doesn't matter with me now. Because I've been to the mountaintop." 10

King closed by telling the crowd, "We as a people will get to the Promised Land. So I'm happy tonight. I'm not worried about anything. I'm not fearing any man. . . ." 11

Novelist Charles Baxter contends that the greatest influence on American writing and discourse in recent memory can be traced back to the phrase 12

"Mistakes were made." Of course, that's from Watergate and the shadowy intrigue inside the Nixon White House.[1] In his essay "Burning Down the House,"

Remote causes are discussed on p. 424.

Baxter compares that "quasi-confessional passive-voice-mode sentence" to what Robert E. Lee said after the battle of Gettysburg and the disastrous decision of Pickett's Charge.[2]

"All of this has been my fault," the Confederate general said. "I asked more of the men than should have been asked of them." 13

In Lee's words, and those of King and Kennedy, we hear a refreshing candor and directness that we miss today. In 1968, people responded to what King and Kennedy told them. During that tumultuous 24-hour period in 1968, people cried aloud and chanted in Memphis. Words struck a chord in Indianapolis, too, and decades later former mayor (and now U.S. Senator) Richard Lugar[3] told writer Thurston Clarke that Kennedy's speech was "a turning point" for his city. 14

After King's assassination, riots broke out in more than 100 U.S. cities— the worst destruction since the Civil War. But neither Memphis nor Indianapolis experienced that kind of damage. To this day, many believe that was due to the words spoken when so many were listening. 15

### FOR DISCUSSION

1. Beginning with the title of his essay, Tim Wendel CLAIMS that words have "power." To do what, according to his analysis?

2. When and how, in Wendel's view, can words have the EFFECT he ascribes to them? Under what circumstances, and spoken by whom? Explain.

1. Shortly after President Richard Nixon (1913–1994), a Republican, began his second term in office, it was discovered that operatives of his campaign had broken into offices of the Democratic Party in the Watergate office complex in June 1972. The resulting scandal, popularly known as Watergate, prompted Nixon to resign from office in 1974.

2. On July 3, 1863, Confederate commander Robert E. Lee ordered General George Pickett to lead an infantry assault against Union positions at Gettysburg, Pennsylvania. The attack failed, and the battle of Gettysburg was lost. Many historians consider this to be the turning point of the Civil War.

3. Lugar's term as a senator ended in 2013.

3. Why, according to Wendel, did the cities of Memphis and Indianapolis escape destruction, by and large, during the riots that followed the assassination of Martin Luther King Jr. in April 1968? Is his analysis of CAUSE AND EFFECT correct? Why or why not?

4. Wendel's essay is ultimately about RHETORIC, which can be defined as the use of words to move an audience to action or belief. According to Wendel, "American writing and discourse" have changed since April 1968 (12). How does he explain the causes of this effect?

## STRATEGIES AND STRUCTURES

1. Wendel's essay was written for Martin Luther King Day. How and how well do his words speak to that occasion? Explain.

2. Wendel criticizes the rhetoric of "politicians today"; but aside from alluding to "the Nixon White House," he does not name names (6, 12). Should he have? Why or why not?

3. "To this day, many believe that [the absence of rioting] was due to the words spoken when so many were listening" (15). As proof of this conclusion about cause and effect, Wendel cites three main EXAMPLES of speech and speeches by King, Kennedy, and Robert E. Lee. Is this evidence sufficient to make his point? Why or why not?

4. Wendel does not mention that on June 5, 1968, just two months after the death of Martin Luther King Jr., the other man who had spoken so eloquently that night— Robert Kennedy—was himself shot while campaigning for the presidency, and he died the next day. Is this a glaring omission, or does it contribute in some way to the rhetorical effect of Wendel's essay? Explain.

## WORDS AND FIGURES OF SPEECH

1. The word *awful* comes up twice in Wendel's essay (4, 7). In what different senses does he use it?

2. Martin Luther King Jr. said he had been to the "mountaintop" (10). What mountaintop was he referring to? Explain the ALLUSION.

3. Look up *discourse* in your dictionary (12). In what sense is Wendel using the term here?

4. Why does Wendel refer to the phrase "mistakes were made" as a "quasi-confessional passive-voice-mode sentence" (12)? What is passive about this verbal phrase, and how does it fit in with Wendel's overall argument about the use of words by public figures?

### FOR WRITING

1. Martin Luther King Jr.'s famous "I Have a Dream" speech is reprinted in Chapter 14. Comb through King's speech and make a list of the words and phrases that confirm (or call into question) the power of words when "spoken with conviction and from the heart" (5).

2. Choose one (or more) of the classic speeches or essays in Chapter 14, and write an analysis of how the author achieves (or fails to achieve) an intended effect on the audience. For example, the writer might seek to establish his or her credibility by convincing readers that they are listening to a person of good moral character—or of great feeling or intellect. Cite specific passages from the text to support your analysis.

MARISSA NUÑEZ

# CLIMBING THE GOLDEN ARCHES

MARISSA NUÑEZ (b. 1974) was nineteen when she wrote this essay about working for McDonald's. Nuñez started at the bottom (the "fried products" station) and worked her way up to management training. "Climbing the Golden Arches" not only tells the story of this ascent, it also analyzes the effects, personal and professional, of learning to do a job, dealing with the public, and being part of a team. An essay about making choices and becoming oneself, "Climbing the Golden Arches" originally appeared in *New Youth Connections* (1997), a magazine that publishes work by student authors.

TWO YEARS AGO, while my cousin Susie and I were doing our Christmas 1
shopping on Fourteenth Street, we decided to have lunch at McDonald's.
"Yo, check it out," Susie said. "They're hiring. Let's give it a try." I 2
looked at her and said, "Are you serious?" She gave me this look that made it
clear that she was.
After we ate our food, I went over to the counter and asked the manager 3
for two applications. I took them back to our table and we filled them out.
When we finished, we handed them in to the manager and he told us he'd be
calling.
When Susie and I got home from school one day about a month later, my 4
mother told us that McDonald's had called. They wanted to interview us both.
We walked straight over there. They asked us why we wanted to work at

McDonald's and how we felt about specific tasks, like cleaning the bathrooms. Then they told us to wait for a while. Finally the manager came out and said we had the job.

When we got outside, I looked over at Susie and laughed because I hadn't  5 thought it would work. But I was happy to have a job. I would be able to buy my own stuff and I wouldn't have to ask my mother for money anymore.

A week and a half later we went to pick up our uniforms (a blue and white  6 striped shirt with blue pants or a blue skirt) and to find out what days we'd be working. We were also told the rules and regulations of the work place. "No stealing" was at the top of the list. A couple of the others were: "Leave all your problems at home" and "Respect everyone you work with."

Before you can officially start working, you have to get trained on every  7 station. I started on "fried products," which are the chicken nuggets, chicken sandwiches, and Filet-o-Fish. Then I learned to work the grill, which is where we cook the burgers. Next was the assembly table where we put all the condi-ments (pickles, onions, lettuce, etc.) on the sandwiches. After all that, you have to learn the french fry station. Then finally you can learn to work the register. It was a month before I could be left alone at any station.

The most difficult thing was learning how to work the grill area. We use a  8 grill called a clamshell, which has a cover. It cooks the whole burger in forty-four seconds without having to flip it over. At first I didn't like doing this. Either I wouldn't lay the meat down right on the grill and it wouldn't cook all the way through or I would get burned. It took a few weeks of practicing before I got the hang of it. Now, after a lot more practice, I can do it with no problem.

My first real day at work was a lot of fun. The store had been closed for  9 remodeling and it was the grand opening. A lot of people were outside waiting for the store to open. I walked around just to get the feel of things before we let the customers come in. I was working a register all by myself. My cousin was at the station next to me and we raced to see who could get the most cus-tomers and who could fill the orders in fifty-nine seconds. I really enjoyed myself.

Page 418 analyzes how and why one event causes or results from another.

Susie worked for only three months after our grand opening,  10 but I stayed on. I liked having a job because I was learning how to be a responsible person. I was meeting all kinds of people and learning a lot about them. I started making friends with my co-workers and getting to know many of the customers on a first-name basis. And I was in charge of my own money for the first time. I didn't have to go asking Mom for money when I wanted something anymore. I could just go and buy it.

Working at McDonald's does have its down side. The worst thing about the job is that the customers can be real jerks sometimes. They just don't seem to understand the pressure we're under. At times they will try to jerk you or make you look stupid. Or they will blame you for a mistake they made. If you don't watch and listen carefully, some of them will try to short-change you for some money.

The most obnoxious customer I ever had came in one day when it was really busy. She started saying that one of my co-workers had overcharged her. I knew that wasn't the case, so I asked her what the problem was. She told me to mind my own business, so I told her that she was my business. She started calling me a "Spanish b-tch" and kept on calling me names until I walked away to get the manager. If I had said anything back to her, I would have gotten in trouble.

Another time, a woman wanted to pay for a $2.99 Value Meal with a $100 bill. No problem, we changed it. She walked away from the counter with her food and then came back a few minutes later saying we had given her a counterfeit $20 bill in her change. We knew it was a lie. She wouldn't back down and even started yelling at the manager. He decided that we should call the cops and get them to settle it. That got her so mad that she threw her tray over the counter at us. Then she left. Of course, not all our customers are like this. Some are very nice and even take the time to tell the manager good things about me.

Sometimes we make up special events to make the job more fun for everyone. For example, we'll have what we call a "battle of the sexes." On those days, the women will work the grill area and the french fry station and all the other kitchen jobs and the men will work the registers. For some reason, the guys usually like to hide in the grill area. The only time they'll come up front and pretend they are working there is to see some female customer they are interested in. Still, they always act like working the grill is so much harder than working the register. I say the grill is no problem compared to working face-to-face with customers all day. After a battle of the sexes, the guys start to give the girls more respect because they see how much pressure we're under.

Every six months, our job performance is reviewed. If you get a good review, you get a raise and sometimes a promotion. After my first six months on the job I got a raise and was made a crew trainer. I became the one who would show new employees how to work the register, fry station, and, yes, even the grill area. 15

When I made a year and a half, I was asked if I would like to become a manager-trainee. To move to that level, your performance has to be one hundred percent on all stations of the store. That means doing every job by the book with no shortcuts. The managers have to trust you, and you have to set a good example for your co-workers. I was so happy. Of course I said yes. 16

Now that I've been there two years, the managers trust me to run a shift by myself. I am working to get certified as a manager myself. To do that I have to attend a class and take an exam, and my manager and supervisor have to observe the way I work with everyone else and grade my performance. I have been in the program for nine months now and expect to get certified this month. I'm thinking about staying on full-time after I graduate from high school. 17

Working at McDonald's has taught me a lot. The most important thing I've learned is that you have to start at the bottom and work your way up. I've learned to take this seriously—if you're going to run a business, you need to know how to do all the other jobs. I also have more patience than ever and have learned how to control my emotions. I've learned to get along with all different kinds of people. I'd like to have my own business someday, and working at McDonald's is what showed me I could do that. 18

## FOR DISCUSSION

1. Marissa Nuñez had been working for McDonald's for two years when she wrote this essay. What **EFFECTS** did the experience have on her? What were some of the main **CAUSES** of those effects?

2. What particular work experiences did Nuñez find most instructive? How did they help bring about the personal changes she mentions?

3. What does Nuñez hope to become by working at McDonald's? How does she expect to accomplish that goal?

4. What do you think of Nuñez's response to the customer who calls her a name?

5. This essay was originally published in a magazine for teenagers. How does it appeal to the attitudes and values of that AUDIENCE?

## STRATEGIES AND STRUCTURES

1. In paragraph 10, Nuñez sums up what she is learning in her new job. Where does she sum up what she *has* learned? If Nuñez had left out these two paragraphs, how would the focus and direction of her essay be changed?

2. How does the following sentence, which comes approximately halfway through her essay, help Nuñez to present different aspects of her work experience: "Working at McDonald's does have its down side" (11)? What sort of causes is she analyzing now? What effect do they have on her?

3. "Climbing the Golden Arches" also tells a story. What is the role of the "most obnoxious customer" and of the woman who throws her tray (12, 13)? What roles do these people play in her analysis of causes and effects?

4. Nuñez's essay covers a two-year work period that might be broken down into application, apprenticeship, "officially working," management training, future plans. Where does each stage begin and end? How effective do you find this strategy for organizing this analysis?

5. The phases of Nuñez's NARRATIVE resemble the steps or stages of much PROCESS ANALYSIS, or how-to writing (Chapter 9). Why is this? Besides examining the effects on her life of working at McDonald's, what process or processes does she analyze by telling her story?

## WORDS AND FIGURES OF SPEECH

1. Why does Nuñez put "battle of the sexes" in quotation marks (14)?

2. What does the word "station" mean in connection with restaurant work (7)?

3. Explain the METAPHOR in Nuñez's title. What figurative meaning does the word *arches* take on in an account of someone's career goals? How about *golden* arches?

4. How does Nuñez DEFINE the word *fun* in this essay (9, 14)? What specific EXAMPLES does she give? What does her distinctive use of the word indicate about her attitude toward work?

## FOR WRITING

1. Write a letter of application for your ideal job. Explain your qualifications, your career goals, and how you expect to achieve them.

2. Write a personal narrative of your work experience or some other experience that taught you a lot. Break it into phases, if appropriate, and explain how specific aspects and events of the experience caused you to become who you are. In other words, tell what happened to you, but also analyze the specific EFFECTS the experience had on you and your life.

**MYRIAM MÁRQUEZ**

# WHY AND WHEN WE SPEAK
# SPANISH IN PUBLIC

MYRIAM MÁRQUEZ is the executive editor of *El Nuevo Herald*, a sister publication of the *Miami Herald* and currently the largest-circulation Spanish-language daily newspaper in the United States. Born in Cuba, Márquez fled to the United States with her parents in 1959. After graduating from the University of Maryland, where she studied journalism and political science, Márquez worked for eighteen years at the *Orlando Sentinel* before joining the staff of the *Herald* in 2005. In "Why and When We Speak Spanish in Public" (*Orlando Sentinel*, 1999), Márquez examines the causes and effects of her family's decision not to adopt English as "our official family language."

•┝━━━━━━━━━━━━━━━━━━━━━━━━━━━━━━━━━━━━━━━┥•

W HEN I'M SHOPPING WITH MY MOTHER or standing in line with my step-   1
dad to order fast food or anywhere else we might be together, we're
going to speak to one another in Spanish.

That may appear rude to those who don't understand Spanish and over-  2
hear us in public places.

Those around us may get the impression that we're talking about them.  3
They may wonder why we would insist on speaking in a foreign tongue, especially if they knew that my family has lived in the United States
for forty years and that my parents do understand English and
speak it, albeit with difficulty and a heavy accent.

A true cause must
be sufficient *and*
necessary (p. 418) to
produce an alleged
effect.

Let me explain why we haven't adopted English as our offi-  4
cial family language. For me and most of the bilingual people I
know, it's a matter of respect for our parents and comfort in our cultural roots.

It's not meant to be rude to others. It's not meant to alienate anyone or  5
to balkanize America.

It's certainly not meant to be un-American—what constitutes an  6
"American" being defined by English speakers from North America.

Being an American has very little to do with what language we use during  7
our free time in a free country. From its inception, this country was careful not
to promote a government-mandated official language.

We understand that English is the common language of this country and  8
the one most often heard in international-business circles from Peru to Nor-
way. We know that, to get ahead here, one must learn English.

But that ought not mean that somehow we must stop speaking in our  9
native tongue whenever we're in a public area, as if we were ashamed of who
we are, where we're from. As if talking in Spanish—or any other language, for
that matter—is some sort of litmus test used to gauge American patriotism.

Throughout this nation's history, most immigrants—whether from  10
Poland or Finland or Italy or wherever else—kept their language through the
first generation and, often, the second. I suspect that they spoke among themselves in their native tongue—in public. Pennsylvania even provided voting
ballots written in German during much of the 1800s for those who weren't
fluent in English.

In this century, Latin American immigrants and others have fought for  11
this country in U.S.-led wars. They have participated fully in this nation's
democracy by voting, holding political office, and paying taxes. And they have
watched their children and grandchildren become so "American" that they
resist speaking in Spanish.

You know what's rude?     12

When there are two or more people who are bilingual and another person     13
who speaks only English and the bilingual folks all of a sudden start speaking
Spanish, which effectively leaves out the English-only speaker. I don't tolerate
that.

One thing's for sure. If I'm ever in a public place with my mom or dad     14
and bump into an acquaintance who doesn't speak Spanish, I will switch to
English and introduce that person to my parents. They will respond in English
and do so with respect.

### FOR DISCUSSION

1. Even though they have lived in the United States for many years, Myriam Márquez
   and her parents have not adopted English as their "official family language" (4).
   Should they have? Why or why not?

2. Márquez defends her family's right to speak Spanish among themselves, but she
   nevertheless insists that "one must learn English" (8). Why? What are the consequences of doing so—and of not doing so—in her view?

3. "I don't tolerate that," Márquez says of people who continue to speak Spanish in
   the presence of others who speak only English (13). Why does she think this is
   "rude" (12)? Do you agree? Why or why not?

### STRATEGIES AND STRUCTURES

1. Márquez gives specific **EFFECTS** ("we're going to speak to one another in Spanish")
   before she gives particular **CAUSES** ("respect for our parents and comfort in our
   cultural roots") (1, 4). Is this a logical order of presentation? Why or why not?

2. Why does Márquez cite immigrants from Poland, Finland, Italy, and "wherever
   else" (10)? Is this additional evidence sufficient to justify her **CLAIM** that it's okay
   for her family to speak their native language in public? Why or why not?

3. Márquez makes a point of saying that immigrants from Latin America have "fought
   for this country" and "participated fully in this nation's democracy by voting,
   holding political office, and paying taxes" (11). What potential objection to her
   claim is she anticipating here?

4. How and how effectively does Márquez use elements of **NARRATIVE** to develop her
   analysis of causes and effects? Point to specific passages in the text that support
   your answer.

## WORDS AND FIGURES OF SPEECH

1. To "balkanize" means to divide a region into small, less powerful states (5). Where does the meaning of this word come from, and how appropriate is Márquez's use of the term here?

2. A "litmus test" is a test in which the outcome is based on only one factor (9). Why might Márquez be reluctant to apply such an either/or test to a person's "patriotism" (6)?

3. Why does Márquez make a point of describing certain behavior as "rude" (2, 12)? How does her choice of this word affect her credibility as someone who can judge when social behavior is proper or not?

### FOR WRITING

1. In a paragraph or two, explain why it would or would not be rude to continue speaking rapidly in English (or some other language) in the presence of others who have difficulty understanding the language being spoken.

2. Write an essay analyzing how and why you and your family (or friends) might speak or behave in a fashion that could seem exclusive to others but that is not intended to be disrespectful. Give specific circumstances under which you think such conduct would and would not be appropriate.

# GET A KNIFE, GET A DOG, BUT GET RID OF GUNS

MARY TYLER "MOLLY" IVINS (1944–2007) was a journalist and author. Born in California and raised in Houston, Texas, Ivins received a BA from Smith College and an MA in journalism from Columbia University. She became nationally famous as a syndicated political columnist at the *Fort Worth Star-Telegram*—a local daily newspaper serving Forth Worth, Texas, and its surrounding areas—where "Get a Knife, Get a Dog, but Get Rid of Guns" first appeared. It was later included in *Nothin' but Good Times Ahead* (1993), Ivins's collection of essays examining American politics. An unapologetic liberal, Ivins used humor to address serious issues and delighted especially in exposing politics at its worst. The essay begins, characteristically, with jokes before she gets to her point: a misinterpretation of the U.S. Constitution's Second Amendment can cause needless carnage and a loss of the very "security" that guns are said to provide.

G UNS. EVERYWHERE GUNS. 1
    Let me start this discussion by pointing out that I am not antigun. 2
I'm proknife. Consider the merits of the knife.

In the first place, you have to catch up with someone in order to stab 3
him. A general substitution of knives for guns would promote physical fitness.
We'd turn into a whole nation of great runners. Plus, knives don't ricochet.
And people are seldom killed while cleaning their knives.

As a civil libertarian, I, of course, support the Second Amendment. And 4
I believe it means exactly what it says:

*A well-regulated militia being necessary to the security of a free state, the* 5
*right of the people to keep and bear arms shall not be infringed.* Fourteen-year-old
boys are not part of a well-regulated militia. Members of wacky religious cults
are not part of a well-regulated militia. Permitting unregulated citizens to
have guns is destroying the security of this free state.

I am intrigued by the arguments of those who claim to follow the judi- 6
cial doctrine of original intent. How do they know it was the dearest wish
of Thomas Jefferson's heart that teenage drug dealers should cruise the
cities of this nation perforating their fellow citizens with assault rifles?
Channeling?

There is more hooey spread about the Second Amendment. It says quite 7
clearly that guns are for those who form part of a well-regulated militia, that
is, the armed forces, including the National Guard. The reasons for keeping
them away from everyone else get clearer by the day.

The comparison most often used is that of the automobile, another lethal 8
object that is regularly used to wreak great carnage. Obviously, this society is
full of people who haven't enough common sense to use an automobile properly. But we haven't outlawed cars yet.

We do, however, license them and their owners, restrict their use to 9
presumably sane and sober adults, and keep track of who sells them to whom.
At a minimum, we should do the same with guns.

In truth, there is no rational argument for guns in this society. This is no 10
longer a frontier nation in which people hunt their own food. It is a crowded,
overwhelmingly urban country in which letting people have access to guns is
a continuing disaster. Those who want guns—whether for target shooting,
hunting, or potting rattlesnakes (get a hoe)—should be subject to the same

restrictions placed on gun owners in England, a nation in which liberty has survived nicely without an armed populace.

The argument that "guns don't kill people" is patent nonsense. Anyone who has ever worked in a cop shop knows how many family arguments end in murder because there was a gun in the house. Did the gun kill someone? No. But if there had been no gun, no one would have died. At least not without a good foot race first. Guns do kill. Unlike cars, that is all they do.

Michael Crichton makes an interesting argument about technology in his thriller *Jurassic Park*. He points out that power without discipline is making this society into a wreckage. By the time someone who studies the martial arts becomes a master—literally able to kill with bare hands—that person has also undergone years of training and discipline. But any fool can pick up a gun and kill with it.

"A well-regulated militia" surely implies both long training and long discipline. That is the least, the very least, that should be required of those who are permitted to have guns, because a gun is literally the power to kill. For years I used to enjoy taunting my gun-nut friends about their psychosexual hang-ups—always in a spirit of good cheer, you understand. But letting the noisy minority in the NRA[1] force us to allow this carnage to continue is just plain insane.

I do think gun nuts have a power hang-up. I don't know what is missing in their psyches that they need to feel they have the power to kill. But no sane society would allow this to continue.

Ban the damn things. Ban them all.

You want protection? Get a dog.

## FOR DISCUSSION

1. "Guns. Everywhere guns" (1). Is Molly Ivins right? Just how common are guns in American society? How do you know?

2. The Second Amendment, which Ivins quotes in full, has been variously interpreted since it was first written over two hundred years ago. Why? What aspects of the wording, structure, or other features of the text leave (or do not leave) its meaning open to debate?

1. National Rifle Association.

3. Ivins mentions "the judicial doctrine of original intent" as one way of interpreting the Second Amendment and other parts of the Constitution (6). What is this doctrine and how does it affect the reading and understanding of a written text?

4. Suppose Thomas Jefferson could come back to life for a moment and say, "No. You're wrong. I personally did intend that teenage drug dealers should be free to cruise the streets with guns" (6). How would you address this point of view if you were arguing in favor of gun regulation, as Ivins is?

### STRATEGIES AND STRUCTURES

1. Ivins begins her essay by proclaiming that she is not "antigun" but, rather, a "civil libertarian." What does this label imply? Why is it important to her ARGUMENT?

2. In Ivins's analysis, the effect of having guns everywhere is the destruction of "the security of this free state" (5). What, in her view, is the main CAUSE (or causes)? Point to specific passages in the text.

3. What is the point of Ivins's COMPARISON of guns with cars? Where does she state it most directly? How convincing do you find this comparison as part of her larger argument about gun control? Explain.

4. How convincing do you find Ivins's argument? Could she have provided more EVIDENCE to further support her CLAIM? Explain.

### WORDS AND FIGURES OF SPEECH

1. Ivins uses humor throughout much of her essay. Are her comic TONE and DICTION appropriate for such a serious subject? Explain.

2. What are the implications of the term *channeling* as Ivins uses it to suggest how one might know what Thomas Jefferson meant by certain words (6)?

3. "There is more hooey spread about the Second Amendment" (7). Does her use of this term—a way of referring to something as nonsense—weaken Ivins's argument or strengthen it? Explain.

4. Explain the significance of Ivins's use of the imperative voice ("get," and "get rid") in her title and elsewhere in her essay, particularly the ending.

**FOR WRITING**

1. In a paragraph, explain the meaning of the Second Amendment as you understand it. Be sure to say why you read the text this way.

2. In a paragraph or two, explain what effect your reading of the Second Amendment would (or should) have upon gun control legislation in America—and why.

# MY BELOVED WORLD

SONIA SOTOMAYOR (b. 1954) is an associate justice of the Supreme Court of the United States, a position she has held since 2009, following her nomination by then-president Barack Obama. Sotomayor was born in the Bronx to parents who moved from Puerto Rico to New York. Her only goal when growing up, she has said, was to graduate from college. Indeed, she achieved that goal: after graduating as the valedictorian of her high school, Sotomayor attended Princeton University and Yale Law School. Her ensuing legal career has been a steady ascent: assistant district attorney, U.S. District Court judge, U.S. Court of Appeals judge, and now a justice of the Supreme Court, where she is the third woman to be appointed. This reading is the prologue to her memoir *My Beloved World* (2013)—here, Sotomayor writes about the adversity she faced in her childhood and how hardship shaped her life for the better. As she says, "difficulty can tap unsuspected strengths."

I WAS NOT YET EIGHT YEARS OLD when I was diagnosed with diabetes. To my    1
family, the disease was a deadly curse. To me, it was more a threat to the
already fragile world of my childhood, a state of constant tension punctuated
by explosive discord, all of it caused by my father's alcoholism and my mother's response to it, whether family fight or emotional flight. But the disease
also inspired in me a kind of precocious self-reliance that is not uncommon in
children who feel the adults around them to be unreliable.

There are uses to adversity, and they don't reveal themselves until    2
tested. Whether it's serious illness, financial hardship, or the simple constraint of parents who speak limited English, difficulty can tap unsuspected
strengths. It doesn't always, of course: I've seen life beat people down until
they can't get up. But I have never had to face anything that could overwhelm
the native optimism and stubborn perseverance I was blessed with.

At the same time, I would never claim to be self-made—quite the con-    3
trary: at every stage of my life, I have always felt that the support I've drawn
from those closest to me has made the decisive difference between success
and failure. And this was true from the beginning. Whatever their limitations
and frailties, those who raised me loved me and did the best they knew how.
Of that I am sure.

The world that I was born into was a tiny microcosm of Hispanic    4
New York City. A tight few blocks in the South Bronx bounded the lives of
my extended family: my grandmother, matriarch of the tribe, and her second
husband, Gallego, her daughters and sons. My playmates were my cousins.
We spoke Spanish at home, and many in my family spoke virtually no
English. My parents had both come to New York from Puerto Rico in 1944,
my mother in the Women's Army Corps, my father with his family in search
of work as part of a huge migration from the island, driven by economic
hardship.

My brother, now Juan Luis Sotomayor Jr., M.D., but to me forever Junior,    5
was born three years after I was. I found him a nuisance as only a little brother
can be, following me everywhere, mimicking my every gesture, eavesdropping
on every conversation. In retrospect, he was actually a quiet child who made
few demands on anyone's attention. My mother always said that compared
with me, caring for Junior was like taking a vacation. Once, when he was still
tiny and I wasn't much bigger, my exasperation with him inspired me to lead

him into the hallway outside the apartment and shut the door. I don't know how much later it was that my mother found him, sitting right where I'd left him, sucking his thumb. But I do know I got walloped that day.

But that was just domestic politics. On the playground, or once he started 6 school at Blessed Sacrament with me, I watched out for him, and any bully thinking of messing with him would have to mix it up with me first. If I got beat up on Junior's account, I would settle things with him later, but no one was going to lay a hand on him except me.

Around the time that Junior was born, we moved to a newly constructed 7 public housing project in Soundview, just a ten-minute drive from our old neighborhood. The Bronxdale Houses sprawled over three large city blocks: twenty-eight buildings, each seven stories tall with eight apartments to a floor. My mother saw the projects as a safer, cleaner, brighter alternative to the decaying tenement where we had lived. My grandmother Abuelita, however, saw this move as a venture into far and alien territory, *el jurutungo viejo* for all practical purposes. My mother should never have made us move, she said, because in the old neighborhood there was life on the streets and family nearby; in the projects we were isolated.

I knew well enough that we were isolated, but that condition had more to 8 do with my father's drinking and the shame attached to it. It constrained our lives as far back as my memory reaches. We almost never had visitors. My cousins never spent the night at our home as I did at theirs. Even Ana, my mother's best friend, never came over, though she lived in the projects too, in the building kitty-corner from ours, and took care of my brother, Junior, and me after school. We always went to her place, never the other way around.

The only exception to this rule was Alfred. Alfred was my first cousin— 9 the son of my mother's sister, Titi Aurora. And just as Titi Aurora was much older than Mami, and more of a mother to her than a sister, Alfred, being sixteen years older than I, acted more as an uncle to me than a cousin. Sometimes my father would ask Alfred to bring him a bottle from the liquor store. We counted on Alfred a lot, in part because my father avoided driving. This annoyed me, as it clearly contributed to our isolation—and what's the point of having a car if you never drive it? I didn't understand until I was older that his drinking was probably the reason.

My father would cook dinner when he got home from work; he was an 10 excellent cook and could re-create from memory any new dish he encountered as well as the Puerto Rican standards he no doubt picked up in Abuelita's kitchen. I loved every dish he made without exception, even his liver and onions, which Junior hated and shoveled over to me when Papi's back was turned. But as soon as dinner was over, the dishes still piled in the sink, he would shut himself in the bedroom. We wouldn't see him again until he came out to tell us to get ready for bed. It was just Junior and I every night, doing homework and not much else. Junior wasn't much of a conversationalist yet. Eventually, we got a television, which helped to fill the silence.

My mother's way of coping was to avoid being at home with my father. 11 She worked the night shift as a practical nurse at Prospect Hospital and often on weekends too. When she wasn't working, she would drop us off at Abuelita's or sometimes at her sister Aurora's apartment and then disappear for hours with another of my aunts. Even though my mother and I shared the same bed every night (Junior slept in the other room with Papi), she might as well have been a log, lying there with her back to me. My father's neglect made me sad, but I intuitively understood that he could not help himself; my mother's neglect made me angry at her. She was beautiful, always elegantly dressed, seemingly strong and decisive. She was the one who moved us to the projects. Unlike my aunts, she chose to work. She was the one who insisted we go to Catholic school. Unfairly perhaps, because I knew nothing then of my mother's own story, I expected more from her.

However much was said at home, and loudly, much also went unsaid, and 12 in that atmosphere I was a watchful child constantly scanning the adults for cues and listening in on their conversations. My sense of security depended on what information I could glean, any clue dropped inadvertently when they didn't realize a child was paying attention. My aunts and my mother would gather in Abuelita's kitchen, drinking coffee and gossiping. "*¡No me molestes!*[1] Go play in the other room now," an aunt would say, shooing me away, but I overheard much regardless: how my father had broken the lock on Titi Gloria's liquor cabinet, ruining her favorite piece of furniture; how whenever Junior and I slept over with our cousins, my father would phone every fifteen minutes all

1. Don't bother me!

night long, asking, "Did you feed them? Did you give them a bath?" I knew well enough that my aunts and my grandmother were all prone to exaggeration. It wasn't really every fifteen minutes, but Papi did call a lot, as I gathered from my aunts' exasperated and mechanically reassuring side of the conversations.

See p. 424 for more on main and contributing causes.

The gossip would then take a familiar turn, my grandmother saying something like "Maybe if Celina ever came home, he wouldn't be drinking every night. If those kids had a mother who ever cooked a meal, Juli wouldn't be worrying about them all night." As much as I adored Abuelita—and no one resented my mother's absence more than I did—I couldn't bear this constant blaming. Abuelita was unconditionally loyal to blood kin. Her sons' wives were not outside the ambit of her protection, but they didn't enjoy the same immunity from prosecution. And often my mother's efforts to please Abuelita—whether a generously chosen gift or her ready services as a nurse—went dimly acknowledged. Even being Abuelita's favorite, I felt exposed and unmoored when she criticized my mother, whom I struggled to understand and forgive myself. In fact, she and I wouldn't achieve a final reconciliation before working on it for many years.

My surveillance activities became family legend the Christmas that Little Miss Echo arrived. I had seen the doll with its concealed tape recorder advertised on television and begged for it. It was the hottest gift of the season, and Titi Aurora had searched far and wide for a store that still had one in stock. I sent my cousin Miriam into the kitchen with the doll to bug the adults' conversation, knowing that I would have been immediately suspect. But before anything could be recorded, Miriam cracked and gave me up at the first question, and I got walloped anyway.

One overheard conversation had a lasting effect, though I now remember it only dimly. My father was sick: he had passed out, and Mami took him to the hospital. Tío Vitín and Tío Benny came to get Junior and me, and they were talking in the elevator about how our home was a pigsty, with dishes in the sink and no toilet paper. They spoke as if we weren't there. When I realized what they were saying, my stomach lurched with shame. After that I washed the dishes every night, even the pots and pans, as soon as we finished dinner. I also dusted the living room once a week. Even though no one ever came over, the house was always clean. And when I went shopping with Papi on Fridays, I made sure we bought toilet paper. And milk. More than enough milk.

The biggest fight my parents ever had was because of the milk. At din- 16
nertime, Papi was pouring a glass for me, and his hands were shaking so badly
the milk spilled all over the table. I cleaned up the mess, and he tried again
with the same result. "Papi, please don't!" I kept repeating. It was all I could do
to keep myself from crying; I was utterly powerless to stop him. "Papi, I don't
want any milk!" But he didn't stop until the carton was empty. When my
mother got home from work later and there was no milk for her coffee, all hell
broke loose. Papi was the one who had spilled the milk, but I was the one who
felt guilty.

## FOR DISCUSSION

1. As a child, Sonia Sotomayor and her family lived, she says, in "a state of constant
tension punctuated by explosive discord" (1). As Sotomayor analyzes them here,
what were some of the main CAUSES of that tension and discord?

2. Her father's "neglect" of her as a child, writes Sotomayor, made her "sad," but her
mother's "neglect" made her "angry" (11). Why did such similar causes have such
different emotional EFFECTS upon young Sotomayor?

3. As she was growing up, Sotomayor struggled with material poverty, illness, and,
after the early death of her father, a mother who remained emotionally distant
from her. What, according to Sotomayor, allowed her to overcome this adversity?

4. In her preface to *My Beloved World*, Sotomayor says that her main purpose in writing the book was "to make my hopeful example accessible." Is the example she
offers in this reading actually "hopeful," despite all the hardships? Is it "accessible?" Explain.

5. Sotomayor says she was "a watchful child" (12). What caused her to be this way in
particular? Point to specific passages in the text to support your answer.

## STRATEGIES AND STRUCTURES

1. How do the first three paragraphs of Sotomayor's text serve as an introduction to
the rest? In particular, how do they indicate that she is doing more here than just
telling a story? Point to specific passages in the text that signal her wider intentions to the reader.

2. Sotomayor is writing about the "uses to adversity," as well as the causes of it in her early life (2). The causes she analyzes are rich in detail. Where and how does she examine the useful effects of those causes?

3. In her next-to-last paragraph, Sotomayor recalls overhearing a conversation that had a "lasting effect" upon her (15). To what extent might her account of this conversation be said to represent the entire chapter? How and how well does her analysis of causes and effects in this passage serve her stated purpose of presenting a "hopeful example" to the reader?

4. "People who live in difficult circumstances need to know that happy endings are possible." Why, then, do you think she ends the chapter with a scene of tension, where "all hell broke loose" (15)?

## WORDS AND FIGURES OF SPEECH

1. Given the many difficulties she had to overcome, the title of Sotomayor's book *My Beloved World* sounds like an example of IRONY. Is it? Explain.

2. Sotomayor writes "the world that I was born into was a tiny microcosm of Hispanic New York City" (4). The term *microcosm* means "little world." How might this entire early chapter be seen as a microcosm of her entire life story?

3. Unlike her mother, says Sotomayor, her father enjoyed "immunity from prosecution" by her sometimes critical grandmother (13). Where else in her text does Sotomayor's language and perspective reflect her background as a lawyer and judge? Point to specific words and phrases.

## FOR WRITING

1. In two or three paragraphs, recall a difficult relationship that affected you in your early years. What do you think caused the relationship to be difficult, and how did you achieve (or fail to achieve) a "final reconciliation" with that person (13)?

2. Write an essay about hardships in your childhood or early youth. Explain the lasting effects such adversity had upon you and what you learned.

# ⇒13⇐

# ARGUMENT

A RGUMENT* is the strategic use of language to convince an AUDIENCE to agree with you on an issue or to act in a way that you think is right—or at least to hear you out, even if they disagree with you. You can convince people in three ways: (1) by appealing to their sense of reason, (2) by appealing to their emotions, and (3) by appealing to their sense of ethics (their standards of what constitutes proper behavior). The essays in this chapter illustrate all three appeals.

When you appeal to a reader's sense of reason, you don't simply declare, "Be reasonable; agree with what I say." You must supply solid EVIDENCE for your claim in the form of facts, examples, statistics, expert testimony, and personal experience. And you must use logical reasoning in presenting that evidence. There are basically two kinds of logical reasoning: INDUCTION and DEDUCTION. When we use induction, we reason from particulars to generalities: "You and your neighbors own guns; it's possible that many other families in the neighborhood own guns." When we deduce something, we reason from general premises to particular conclusions: "All guns are dangerous; your family is in danger because you have one in your house."

> John McWhorter, p. 490, uses induction when he concludes that words take on meanings beyond their literal definitions.

Of course, a proposition can be logically valid without necessarily being true. If "all guns are dangerous," then logically a particular gun must be dangerous as well. Given this general premise (or assumption) about guns, the conclusion about any particular gun's being dangerous is a valid conclusion. The same is true of the following argument: "*No* guns are dangerous; this particular gun is *not* dangerous." This is a valid argument, too; but here, again, not everyone will accept the first (or major) premise about guns in general. Most

*Words printed in SMALL CAPITALS are defined in the Glossary/Index.

real-life debates, in fact, take place because rational people disagree about the truth of one or more of the premises on which their conclusions are based.

Whether an argument uses induction or deduction, it must make an arguable statement or CLAIM. Take, for example, the idea that the world's leaders "should start an international campaign to promote imports from sweatshops." Nicholas D. Kristof argued in favor of this controversial proposition in an article published in the *New York Times* entitled "Let Them Sweat." Kristof's essay is an instructive example of how all the techniques of argumentation can work together.

Kristof knows that arguing in favor of sweatshops is likely to be an unpopular position. Like any writer with a point to make, especially a controversial one, he needs to win the reader's trust. One way to do this is to anticipate objections that the reader might raise. So before anyone can accuse him of being totally out of his head for promoting sweatshops, Kristof writes: "The Gentle Reader will think I've been smoking Pakistani opium. But sweatshops are the only hope of kids like Ahmed Zia, 14, here in Attock, a gritty center for carpet weaving."

Right away, Kristof is hoping to convince his audience that they are hearing the words of an ethical person who deserves their attention. Next, he tugs at the readers' heartstrings:

> Ahmed earns $2 a day hunched over the loom, laboring over a rug that will adorn some American's living room. It is a pittance, but the American campaign against sweatshops could make his life much more wretched by inadvertently encouraging mechanization that could cost him his job.
>
> "Carpet-making is much better than farm work," Ahmed said. "This makes much more money and is more comfortable."

Underlying Kristof's emotional appeal in citing Ahmed's case is the logical claim that Ahmed's story is representative of the plight of most factory workers in poor countries. "Indeed," writes Kristof, "talk to Third World factory workers and the whole idea of 'sweatshops' seems a misnomer. It is farmers and brick-makers who really sweat under the broiling sun, while sweatshop workers merely glow."

The same claim—that other cases are like this one—also lies behind Kristof's second example: "But before you spurn a shirt made by someone like Kamis Saboor, eight, an Afghan refugee whose father is dead and who is the sole breadwinner in the family, answer this question: How does shunning sweatshop products help Kamis? All the alternatives for him are worse." Kristof is appealing to the reader's emotions and sense of ethics, and he is using logical reasoning. If we grant Kristof's premise that in really poor countries "all the alternatives" to sweatshop labor are worse, we must logically concede his main point that, for these workers, "a sweatshop job is the first step on life's escalator" and, therefore, that sweatshops are to be supported.

Kristof has not finished marshaling his reasons and evidence yet. To strengthen his argument, he introduces another, broader example, one that Americans are more likely to be familiar with:

> Nike has 35 contract factories in Taiwan, 49 in South Korea, only three in Pakistan, and none at all in Afghanistan—if it did, critics would immediately fulminate about low wages, glue vapors, the mistreatment of women.
>
> But the losers are the Afghans, and especially Afghan women. The country is full of starving widows who can find no jobs. If Nike hired them at 10 cents an hour to fill all-female sweatshops, they and their country would be hugely better off.
>
> Nike used to have two contract factories in impoverished Cambodia, among the neediest countries in the world. Then there was an outcry after BBC reported that three girls in one factory were under 15 years old. So Nike fled controversy by ceasing production in Cambodia.
>
> The result was that some of the 2,000 Cambodians (90 percent of them young women) who worked in three factories faced layoffs. Some who lost their jobs probably were ensnared in Cambodia's huge sex slave industry—which leaves many girls dead of AIDS by the end of their teenage years.

We can object to Kristof's premises. Can the widows of Afghanistan find no decent jobs whatsoever? Will they actually starve if they don't? Will some of the young women of Cambodia die of AIDS because Nike has pulled out of their impoverished country? (Notice that Kristof qualifies this assertion with "probably.") We can even dispute Kristof's reasoning based on statistics. In statistics, when it is not possible to poll every individual in a group of people being analyzed, sound practice requires at least a representative sampling. Has Kristof given us a truly representative sampling of *all* the workers in Third World sweatshops?

We can pick away at Kristof's logic—as have many of his critics since this article was first published. But with the exception of a court of law, a good argument does not have to prove its point beyond a shadow of a doubt. It only has to convince the reader. Whether or not you're convinced by Kristof's argument, you can learn from the tactics he uses to support his position.

# A BRIEF GUIDE TO WRITING AN ARGUMENT

When you construct an ARGUMENT, you take a position on an issue and then support that position, as Nicholas D. Kristof does in his argument in favor of sweatshops. So the first moves you need to make as you write an argument are to identify the subject or issue you are addressing and to state the claim you are making about it. Here's how Mark D. White and Robert Arp make these fundamental moves near the beginning of their argument in this chapter:

> Pop culture, such as the Batman comics and movies, provides an opportunity to think philosophically about issues and topics that parallel the real world. For instance, thinking about why Batman has never killed the Joker may help us reflect on the nation's issues with terror and torture, specifically their ethics.
> —MARK D. WHITE AND ROBERT ARP, "Should Batman Kill the Joker?"

White and Arp identify the subject of their argument (pop culture) and state their claim about it ("provides an opportunity to think philosophically about issues and topics"). Next they narrow the broad field of pop culture to a specific topic ("why Batman has never killed the Joker") and a more limited claim ("may help us reflect on the nation's issues with terror and torture").

The following guidelines will help you make these basic moves as you draft an argument. They will also help you support your claim with reasoning and evidence, avoid logical fallacies, appeal to your readers' emotions and sense of ethics, and anticipate other arguments.

## Coming Up with a Claim

Unlike a statement of fact (broccoli is a vegetable) or personal taste (I hate broccoli), a CLAIM is a statement that is debatable, that rational people can disagree with. We can all agree, for example, that pop culture has something to teach us. We might reasonably disagree, however, on what those lessons are. To come up with a claim, think of issues that are debatable: Batman is (is not) a model of ethical behavior. More debatable claims appear on pp. 495 and 515. Broccoli provides (does not provide) more health benefits than any other vegetable. Genetic factors are (are not) the main determiners of personality. The risks of climate change have (have not) been exaggerated by the scientific community. Before you decide on a particular claim, make sure it is one you actually care about enough to argue it persuasively. If you don't care much about your topic, your readers probably won't either.

## Considering Your Purpose and Audience

The **PURPOSE** of an argument is to convince other people to listen thoughtfully to what you have to say—even if they don't completely accept your views. Whatever your claim, your argument is more likely to appeal to your audience if it is tailored to their particular needs and interests. Suppose, for example, that you have a friend who habitually sends text messages while driving even though she knows it's dangerous. You think your friend should put down her phone while driving—or pull over when she needs to text. Your friend might be more likely to agree with you if, in addition to citing statistics on increased traffic deaths due to driving while texting, you also pointed out that she was setting a bad example for her younger sister.

So think about what your audience's views on the particular issue are likely to be. Of all the evidence you might present in support of your case, what kind would your intended readers most likely find reasonable and, thus, convincing?

## Generating Ideas: Finding Effective Evidence

Suppose you want to argue that the SAT is unfair because it is biased in favor of the wealthy. To support a claim like this effectively, you can use *facts, statistics, examples, expert testimony,* and *personal experience.*

**FACTS.** To argue that the SAT favors the wealthy, you might cite facts about the cost of tutors for the test: "In New York City, a company called Advantage charges $500 for 50 minutes of coaching with their most experienced tutors."

**STATISTICS.** You could cite statistics about income and text scores: "On the 2008 SAT, students with family incomes of more than $200,000 had an average math score of 570, while those with family incomes up to $20,000 had an average score of 456."

**EXAMPLES.** You could discuss a question from an actual SAT exam that might show SAT bias. The following question asks the test taker to select a pair of words whose relationship matches the relationship expressed by RUNNER : MARATHON. The choices are (A) envoy : embassy; (B) martyr : massacre; (C) oarsman : regatta; (D) referee : tournament; (E) horse : stable. The correct answer is C: an oarsman competes in a regatta, an organized boat race, in much the same way as a runner competes in a marathon. But because regattas are largely a pursuit of the wealthy, you could argue that the question favors the wealthy test taker.

**EXPERT TESTIMONY.** You might quote a statement like this one by Richard Atkinson, former president of the University of California: "Anyone involved in education should be concerned about how overemphasis on the SAT is distorting educational priorities and practices [and] how the test is perceived by many as unfair. . . ."

A works-cited list like the one on p. 512 identifies your sources.

**PERSONAL EXPERIENCE.** The following anecdote reveals, in a personal way, how the SAT favors certain socioeconomic groups: "No one in my family ever participated in a regatta—as a high school student, I didn't even know the meaning of the word. So when I took the SAT and encountered analogy questions that referred to regattas and other unfamiliar things, I barely broke 600 on the verbal aptitude section."

No matter what type of evidence you present, it must be pertinent to your argument and sufficient to convince your audience that your claim is worth taking seriously. It should also be presented to the reader in a well-organized fashion that makes sense logically.

## Templates for Arguing

The following templates can help you to generate ideas for an argument and then to start drafting. Don't take these as formulas where you just have to fill in the blanks. There are no easy formulas for good writing, though these templates can help you plot out some of the key moves of argumentation and thus may serve as good starting points.

> ► In this argument about X, the main point I want to make is _____.
>
> ► Others may say _____, but I would argue that _____.
>
> ► My contention about X is supported by the fact that _____.
>
> ► Additional facts that support this view of X are _____, _____, and _____.
>
> ► My own experience with X shows that _____ because _____.
>
> ► My view of X is supported by _____, who says that X is _____.
>
> ► What you should do about X is _____.

For more techniques to help you generate ideas and start writing an argument, see Chapter 3.

## Organizing an Argument

Any well-constructed argument is organized around a claim and support for that claim. Here is a straightforward plan that can be effective for most argument essays. You may, of course, need to supplement or modify this plan to fit a particular topic.

1. In your *introduction,* identify your topic and state your claim clearly. Indicate why you're making this claim and why the reader should be interested in it. Make sure your topic is narrow enough to be covered in the time and space allotted.

2. In the main *body* of your argument, introduce an important example or a solid piece of evidence that is likely to catch your reader's attention; then use a clear, logical organization to present the rest of your support. For example, move from your weakest point to your strongest. Or vice versa.

3. Deal with *counterarguments* at appropriate points throughout your essay.

4. In the *conclusion,* restate your claim—and why you're making it—and sum up how the evidence supports that claim.

## Narrowing and Stating Your Claim

State your claim clearly at the beginning of your argument—and take care not to claim more than you can possibly prove in one essay. "Sweatshops are acceptable," for example, is too broad to work as an arguable claim. Acceptable for whom, we might ask? Under what circumstances?

To narrow this claim, we could restate it as follows: "In very poor countries, sweatshops are acceptable." This claim could be still more restricted, however: "In very poor countries, sweatshops are acceptable *when the alternatives are even worse.*" Because it is narrower, this is a more supportable claim than the one we started with.

## Using Logical Reasoning: Induction and Deduction

In many writing situations, logical reasoning is indispensable for persuading others that your ideas and opinions are valid. As we noted in the introduction, there are two main kinds of logical reasoning: induction and deduction. Induction is reasoning from particular evidence to a general conclusion. It is based on probability and draws a conclusion from a limited number of specific cases. You reason inductively when you observe the cost of a gallon of gas at half a dozen service stations and conclude that the price of gas is uniformly high. In contrast to induction, deduction moves from general principles to a particular conclusion. You reason deductively when your car stops running and— knowing that cars need fuel, that you started with half a tank and have been driving all day—you conclude that you are out of gas.

Deductive arguments can be stated as SYLLOGISMS, which have a major premise, a minor premise, and a conclusion. For example:

> *Major premise:* All scientific theories should be taught in science classes.
> *Minor premise:* Intelligent design is a scientific theory.
> *Conclusion:* Intelligent design should be taught in science classes.

This is a valid syllogism, meaning that the conclusion follows logically from the premises. (Remember however, that *validity* in a deductive argument is not the same as *truth*.)

The great advantage of deduction over induction is that it deals with logical certainty rather than mere probability. As long as a deductive argument is properly constructed, the conclusion must be valid. The conclusion can still be untrue, however, if one or more of the premises is false. The following syllogism, for example, is properly constructed (the conclusion follows logically from the premises), but not everyone would agree that the major premise is true:

> **Major premise:** Only people who have tattoos are cool.
> **Minor premise:** Robin got a tattoo on her shoulder last weekend.
> **Conclusion:** Robin is cool.

Advertisers use this kind of faulty reasoning all the time to try to convince you that you must buy their products if you want to be a cool person. Many people, however, would consider the major premise false; there are lots of cool people who don't have tattoos at all, so the reasoning is faulty.

You can also run into trouble when you know that some of your readers may disagree with your premises but you still want to convince them to accept (or at least think seriously about) your conclusion. For example, if you are arguing that a particular firearm is not dangerous because "no guns are dangerous," many readers are likely to take exception with your reasoning. What to do?

One tactic would be to tone down your major premise. Your ultimate purpose in constructing any argument, after all, is to convince readers to accept your *conclusion*. So instead of the (obviously loaded) premise that "no guns are dangerous," you might instead restate your premise as follows: "Not all guns are dangerous." That a particular gun is safe does not necessarily follow from this premise, but more readers may be inclined to accept it—and thus more likely to take your conclusion seriously—especially if the rest of your evidence is strong.

Sherry Turkle's (p. 502) major premise is that people are always with their phones.

## Avoiding Logical Fallacies

LOGICAL FALLACIES are errors in logical reasoning. Here are some of the most common logical fallacies to watch out for:

**POST HOC, ERGO PROPTER HOC.** Latin for "after this, therefore because of this." Assuming that just because one event (such as rain) comes after another event (a rain dance), it therefore occurs *because* of the first event: "From 1995 to 2005, as the Internet grew, the number of new babies named Jennifer grew by 30 percent." The increase in "Jennifers" may have followed the spread of the Internet, but the greater Internet use didn't necessarily *cause* the increase.

**NON SEQUITUR.** A statement that has no logical connection to the preceding statement: "The early Egyptians were masters of architecture. Thus they created a vast network of trade throughout the ancient world." Since mastering architecture has little to do with expanding trade, this second statement is a *non sequitur.*

**BEGGING THE QUESTION.** Taking for granted what is supposed to be proved: "Americans should be required to carry ID cards because Americans need to be prepared to prove their identity." Instead of addressing the claim that Americans should be required to prove their identity by having an ID card that verifies it, the "because" statement takes that claim for granted.

**APPEAL TO DOUBTFUL AUTHORITY.** Citing as expert testimony the opinions of people who are not experts on the issue: "According to David Letterman, the candidate who takes Ohio will win the election." Letterman isn't an expert on politics.

**AD HOMINEM.** Latin for "to the man," a type of fallacy where someone attacks the person making an argument instead of addressing the actual issue: "She's too young to be head of the teachers' union, so why listen to her views on wages?" Saying she's too young focuses on her as a person rather than on her views on the issue.

**EITHER/OR REASONING.** Treating a complicated issue as if it had only two sides: "Either you believe that God created the universe, or you believe that the universe evolved randomly." This statement doesn't allow for possibilities outside of these two options.

**HASTY GENERALIZATION.** Drawing conclusions based on too little evidence: "In the four stories by Edgar Allan Poe that we read, the narrator is mentally ill. Poe himself must have been insane." There is not nearly enough evidence here to determine Poe's mental health.

**FALSE ANALOGY.** Making a faulty comparison: "Children are like dogs. A happy dog is a disciplined dog, and a happy child is one who knows the rules and is taught to obey them." Dogs and children aren't alike enough to assume that what is good for one is necessarily good for the other.

**RED HERRING.** Misleading readers by distracting them from the main argument: "Sure, my paper is full of spelling errors. But English is not a very phonetic language. Now if we were writing in Spanish . . ."

**OVERSIMPLIFICATION.** Assigning insufficient causes to explain an effect or justify a conclusion: "In a school budget crunch, art and music classes should be eliminated first because these subjects are not very practical." This argument is oversimplified because it doesn't admit that there are other reasons, besides practicality, for keeping a subject in the school curriculum.

## Appealing to Your Readers' Emotions

Sound logical reasoning is hard to refute, but appealing to your readers' emotions can also be an effective way to convince them to accept—or at least listen to—your argument. In a follow-up to his argument in favor of sweatshops, Nicholas D. Kristof writes:

> The miasma of toxic stink leaves you gasping, breezes batter you with filth, and even the rats look forlorn. Then the smoke parts and you come across a child ambling barefoot, searching for old plastic cups that recyclers will buy for five cents a pound.
> —NICHOLAS D. KRISTOF, "Where Sweatshops Are a Dream"

Kristof is describing a gigantic garbage dump in Phnom Penh, Cambodia, where whole families try to make a living under inhumane conditions. Compared to this "Dante-like vision of hell," Kristof argues, "sweltering at a sewing machine" seems like an unattainable dream. By making us feel the desperation of the people he describes, Kristof is clearly tugging at the readers' heartstrings—before going on to supply more facts and examples to support his claim.

# Establishing Your Own Credibility

When you construct an argument, you can use logic to show that what you have to say is valid and true. And you can appeal to your readers' emotions with genuine fervor. That might not be enough, however, if your readers don't fully trust you. Here are a few tips to help you establish trust with your readers:

- *Present issues objectively.* Acknowledge opposing points of view, and treat them fairly and accurately. If you have experience or expertise in your subject, let your readers know. For example, Kristof tells his readers, "My views on sweatshops are shaped by years living in East Asia, watching as living standards soared—including those in my wife's ancestral village in southern China—because of sweatshop jobs."

- *Pay close attention to the* TONE *of your argument.* Whether you come across as calm and reasonable or full of righteous anger, your tone will say much about your own values and motives for writing—and about you as a person.

- *Convince your readers* that you have considered their values and that you understand their concerns.

# Anticipating Other Arguments

As you construct an argument, it's important to consider viewpoints other than your own, including objections that others might raise. Anticipating other arguments, in fact, is yet another way to establish your credibility. Readers are more likely to see you as trustworthy if, instead of ignoring an opposing argument, you state it fairly and accurately and then refute it. Kristof knows that many readers will disagree with his position on sweatshops, so he acknowledges the opposition up front before going on to give his evidence for his position:

"I realize," Diane Guerrero admits, hoping to win over skeptics, "the issues are complicated" (p. 488).

> When I defend sweatshops, people always ask me: But would you want to work in a sweatshop? No, of course not. But I would want even less to pull a rickshaw. . . . I often hear the argument: Labor standards can improve wages and working conditions, without greatly affecting the eventual retail cost of goods. That's true. But . . .
>
> —NICHOLAS, D. KRISTOF, "Where Sweatshops Are a Dream"

You still may not agree with Kristof's position that sweatshops are a good idea. But you're more likely to listen to what he, or any other writer, has to say if you think that person has thought carefully about all aspects of the issue, including points of view opposed to his or her own.

# EDITING FOR COMMON ERRORS
# IN ARGUMENTS

As with other modes of writing, certain errors in punctuation and usage are common in arguments. The following guidelines will help you spot such problems and edit them appropriately.

### Check to see that you've correctly punctuated connecting words

*If, therefore, thus, consequently, however, nevertheless,* and *because* are common connecting words. When the connecting word comes at the beginning of a sentence and links the statement you're making to earlier statements, it should be followed by a comma:

- ▶ Therefore, stronger immigration laws will not be necessary.
- ▶ Consequently, the minimum drinking age should be lowered to age 18.

When the connecting word comes at the beginning of a sentence and is part of an introductory clause—a group of words that includes a subject and a verb—the entire clause should be followed by a comma:

- ▶ Because guest workers will be legally registered, stronger immigration laws will be unnecessary.
- ▶ If people are old enough to vote and go to war, they're old enough to drink responsibly.
- ▶ If recent statistics from the Department of Transportation are accurate, far fewer people die when the legal drinking age is 21 instead of 18.

When the connecting word indicates a relationship—such as cause and effect, logical sequence, or comparison—between two independent clauses, it is usually preceded by a semicolon and followed by a comma:

- ▶ Many of the best surgeons have the highest rates of malpractice; thus, the three-strikes-and-you're-out rule for taking away a doctor's license may do more harm than good.

When the connecting word comes in the middle of an independent clause, it should usually be set off by commas:

> ► A surgeon who removes the wrong leg, however, deserves a somewhat harsher penalty than one who forgets to remove a sponge.

## Check for common errors in usage

*HOWEVER, NEVERTHELESS*

Use *however* when you acknowledge a different argument but want to minimize its consequence:

> ► The surgeon may have been negligent; ~~nevertheless,~~ however, he should not lose his license because the patient lied about the dosage he was taking.

Use *nevertheless* when you acknowledge a different argument but wish to argue for a harsher consequence anyway:

> ► The surgeon may not have been negligent; ~~however,~~ nevertheless, he should lose his license because the patient died.

*IMPLY, INFER*

Use *imply* when you mean "to state indirectly":

> ► The coach's speech ~~inferred~~ implied that he expected the team to lose the game.

Use *infer* when you mean "to draw a conclusion":

> ► From the coach's speech, I ~~implied~~ inferred that the team would lose the game.

# Mysterious Warning Signs

Like many road signs—"YIELD," "STOP!" and "EXIT LANE ONLY"—a good argument catches our attention and is clear. Let this sign, which appeared in Coral Springs, Florida, be a warning of the confusion that can result when you alert a driver to a problem or issue without being clear as to what you mean. Looking at the sign, "WARNING, LOW FLYING OWLS," just what are we being warned to avoid here? On one hand, you could read the sign as saying that low flying owls are particularly vulnerable to oncoming traffic; reduce speed to protect them. If that's the argument, the message on the sign might be clearer as follows: "SLOW DOWN, LOW FLYING OWLS." On the other hand, maybe the sign is telling us the opposite—close the car windows and speed up because there are low flying owls that could come in through your car window. On a road sign, of course, there is not much room or time to go into details, so clarity is important. And in your writing, the sooner you make clear what your position is, the better the ride for the reader.

## LIZ ADDISON

# TWO YEARS ARE BETTER THAN FOUR

LIZ ADDISON argues that community colleges are "one of America's great institutions" in her essay "Two Years Are Better than Four." A graduate of Southern Maine Community College, Addison submitted her essay to a national college writing contest sponsored by the *New York Times* magazine. The topic was to respond to "What's the Matter with College," an opinion piece by the historian Rick Perlstein, published online by the *Times* in 2007. A graduate of an elite four-year university, Perlstein argued that colleges "seem to have lost their centrality" in American culture. Approximately 600 students from institutions across the country took up the challenge, and Addison's rebuttal was chosen as one of four runners-up.

## Two Years Are Better than Four

Oh, the hand wringing. "College as America used to
understand it is coming to an end," bemoans Rick
Perlstein and his beatnik friend of fallen face. Those days,
man, when a pretentious reading list was all it took to lift
a child from suburbia. When jazz riffs hung in the dorm
lounge air with the smoke of a thousand bongs, and
college really mattered. Really mattered?

Rick Perlstein thinks so. It mattered so much to
him that he never got over his four years at the University of Privilege. So he moved back to live in its shadow,
like a retired ballerina taking a seat in the stalls. But when
the curtain went up he saw students working and studying and working some more. Adults before their time.
Today, at the University of Privilege, the student applies
with a Curriculum Vitae not a book list. Shudder.

Thus, Mr. Perlstein concludes, the college
experience—a rite of passage as it was meant it to be—
must have come to an end. But he is wrong. For
Mr. Perlstein, so rooted in his own nostalgia, is looking
for himself—and he would never think to look for himself
in the one place left where the college experience of self-
discovery does still matter to those who get there. My
guess, reading between the lines, is that Mr. Perlstein has
never set foot in an American community college.

The philosophy of the community college, and I
have been to two of them, is one that unconditionally
allows its students to begin. Just begin. Implicit in this
belief is the understanding that anything and everything
is possible. Just follow any one of the 1,655 road signs, and
pop your head inside—yes, they let anyone in—and there
you will find discoveries of a first independent film, a first

1

2

3

4

Title states her claim

Sums up the position she plans to contest

The main support for her claim is personal experience

independent thought, a first independent study. This college experience remains as it should. This college brochure is not marketing for the parents—because the parents, nor grandparents, probably never went to college themselves.

Upon entry to my first community college I had but 5 one O'level to my name. These now disbanded qualifications once marked the transition from lower to upper high school in the Great British education system. It was customary for the average student to proceed forward with a clutch of O'levels, say eight or nine. On a score of one, I left school hurriedly at sixteen. Thomas Jefferson once wrote, "Everybody should have an education proportional to their life." In my case, my life became proportional to my education. But, in doing so, it had the good fortune to land me in an American community college and now, from that priceless springboard, I too seek admission to the University of Privilege. Enter on empty and leave with a head full of dreams? How can Mr. Perlstein say college does not matter anymore?

> Her claim is based on an ideal of "public service"

The community college system is America's hidden 6 public service gem. If I were a candidate for office I would campaign from every campus. Not to score political points, but simply to make sure that anyone who is looking to go to college in this country knows where to find one. Just recently, I read an article in the *New York Times* describing a "college application essay" workshop for low-income students. I was strangely disturbed that those interviewed made no mention of community college. Mr. Perlstein might have been equally disturbed, for the thrust of the workshop was no different to that of an essay coach to the affluent. "Make Life Stories Shine," beams the headline. Or, in other words, prove yourself worldly, insightful, cultured, mature, before you get to college.

Yet, down at X.Y.C.C. it is still possible to enter the college experience as a rookie. That is the understanding— that you will grow up a little bit with your first English class, a bit more with your first psychology class, a whole lot more with your first biology, physics, chemistry. That you may shoot through the roof with calculus, philosophy, or genetics. "College is the key," a young African American student writes for the umpteenth torturous revision of his college essay, "as well as hope." Oh, I wanted desperately to say, please tell him about community college. Please tell him that hope can begin with just one placement test.

7

When Mr. Perlstein and friends say college no longer holds importance, they mourn for both the individual and society. Yet, arguably, the community college experience is more critical to the nation than that of former beatnik types who, lest we forget, did not change the world. The community colleges of America cover this country college by college and community by community. They offer a network of affordable future, of accessible hope, and an option to dream. In the cold light of day, is it perhaps not more important to foster students with dreams rather than a building take-over?

8

I believe so. I believe the community college system to be one of America's uniquely great institutions. I believe it should be celebrated as such. "For those who find it necessary to go to a two-year college," begins one

9

Conclusion restates her claim as a matter of "belief"

University of Privilege admissions paragraph. None too subtle in its implication, but very true. For some students, from many backgrounds, would never breathe the college experience if it were not for the community college. Yes, it is here that Mr. Perlstein will find his college years of self-discovery, and it is here he will find that college does still matter.

**MARK D. WHITE AND ROBERT ARP**

# SHOULD BATMAN KILL THE JOKER?

MARK D. WHITE (b. 1971) is chair of the department of philosophy at the College of Staten Island of the City University of New York. Among his books is *A Philosopher Reads Marvel Comics' Civil War* (2016). ROBERT ARP (b. 1970) is a philosopher specializing in bioethics, information science, evolutionary psychology, and the philosophy of popular culture. Among his books is *1001 Ideas That Changed the Way We Think* (2013). Together, White and Arp edited *Batman and Philosophy: The Dark Knight of the Soul* (2008), a collection of essays. In "Should Batman Kill the Joker?," first published in the *Boston Globe* (2008), they argue for the value of pop culture in exploring ethical approaches to real-world issues.

B ATMAN SHOULD KILL THE JOKER. How many of us would agree with that? 1
Quite a few, we'd wager. Even Heath Ledger's Joker in *The Dark Knight* marvels at Batman's refusal to kill him. After all, the Joker is a murderous

psychopath, and Batman could save countless innocent lives by ending his miserable existence once and for all.

Of course, there are plenty of masked loonies ready to take the Joker's    2
place, but none of them has ever shown the same twisted devotion to chaos and tragedy as the Clown Prince of Crime.

But if we say that Batman should kill the Joker, doesn't that imply that    3
we should torture terror suspects if there's a chance of getting information that could save innocent lives? Of course, terror is all too present in the real world, and Batman only exists in the comics and movies. So maybe we're just too detached from the Dark Knight and the problems of Gotham City, so we can say "go ahead, kill him." But, if anything, that detachment implies that there's more at stake in the real world—so why aren't we tougher on actual terrorists than we are on the make-believe Joker?

Pop culture, such as the Batman comics and movies, provides an oppor-    4
tunity to think philosophically about issues and topics that parallel the real world. For instance, thinking about why Batman has never killed the Joker may help us reflect on the nation's issues with terror and torture, specifically their ethics.

Three major schools of ethics provide some perspective on Batman's    5
quandary.

Utilitarianism, based on the work of Jeremy Bentham and John Stuart    6
Mill,[1] would probably endorse killing the Joker, based on comparing the many lives saved against the one life lost.

Deontology, stemming largely from the writings of Immanuel Kant,[2]    7
would focus on the act of murder itself, rather than the consequences. Kant's

For advice on appealing to the reader's sense of ethics, see p. 461. position would be more ambiguous than the utilitarian's: While it may be preferable for the Joker to be dead, it may not be morally right for any person (such as Batman) to kill him. If the Joker is to

be punished, it should be through official procedures, not vigilante justice. More generally, while the Joker is evil, he is still a human being, and is thus deserving of at least a minimal level of respect and humanity.

---

1. Mill (1806–1873) and Bentham (1748–1832) were British philosophers and social reformers.

2. German philosopher (1724–1804) whose works include treatises on reason and ethics.

Finally, virtue ethics, dating back to the ancient Greeks (such as  8
Aristotle[3]), would highlight the character of the person who kills the Joker.
Does Batman want to be the kind of person that takes his enemies' lives? If he
killed the Joker, would he be able to stop there, or would every two-bit thug
get the same treatment?

Taking these three ethical perspectives together, we see that while there  9
are good reasons to kill the Joker, in terms of innocent lives saved, there are
also good reasons not to kill him, based on what killing him would mean about
Batman and his motives, mission, and character.

The same arguments apply to the debate over torture: While there are  10
good reasons to do it, based on the positive consequences that may come from
it, there are also good reasons not to, especially those based on our national
character. Many Americans who oppose torture explain their position by saying, "It's not who we are" or "We don't want to turn into them." Batman often
says the same thing when asked why he hasn't killed the Joker: "I don't want
to become that which I hate."

Applying philosophy to Batman, *South Park*, or other pop culture phe-  11
nomena may seem silly or frivolous, but philosophers have used fanciful
examples and thought experiments for centuries. The point is making philosophy accessible, and helping us think through difficult topics by casting
them in a different light.

Regardless of your position, torture is an uncomfortable and emotional  12
topic. If translating the core issue to another venue, such as Batman and the
Joker, helps us focus on the key aspects of the problem, that can only help
refine our thinking. And Batman would definitely approve of that.

3. Classical Greek philosopher (384–322 BCE) whose work was foundational to Western
philosophy and culture.

## FOR DISCUSSION

1. Mark D. White and Robert Arp do not give a final answer to the question posed in their title. Should they have? Why or why not?

2. Of the three schools of philosophy cited by White and Arp, which one(s) best support Batman's CLAIM that if he kills the Joker he will become "that which I hate" (10)? Explain your answer.

3. Are White and Arp being "silly or frivolous" when they take Batman's adventures as a serious guide to moral and ethical behavior (11)? Why or why not?

4. So *is* Batman morally and ethically right to let the Joker live? Or should he kill the Joker at the first opportunity? Why do you think so?

## STRATEGIES AND STRUCTURES

1. What AUDIENCE in particular do White and Arp have in mind when they use pop culture to examine complex ethical and philosophical questions?

2. What is White and Arp's main claim in comparing the actions and decisions of a comic book character to those that real-life leaders must make in government and society? Where in the text is that claim directly stated?

3. Throughout their ARGUMENT, White and Arp rely heavily on logical reasoning, both INDUCTIVE and DEDUCTIVE. Where in their argument do they reason inductively? Where is their reasoning more deductive? Point to specific instances of each type of reasoning.

4. "Should Batman Kill the Joker?" is primarily a moral and ethical argument. How and how well do White and Arp present themselves as knowledgeable and ethical people who deserve to be heard? Point to specific passages in the text where they establish (or fail to establish) their credibility.

5. Is it logical to say that a person who condones torture is in danger of becoming that which he or she hates? Or does such reasoning introduce a red herring, or some other LOGICAL FALLACY? Explain.

6. Arguments by ANALOGY draw comparisons, as White and Arp do in comparing Batman's dilemma to the debate over torture and terrorism. The PURPOSE of such arguments, as they say, is to help us "think through difficult topics by casting them in a different light" (11). How effective is this strategy in helping White and Arp to clarify the difficult issue of torture?

7. How do the DEFINITIONS that White and Arp provide in paragraphs 6–8 support their argument about the value of pop culture for understanding ethical and philosophical issues?

## WORDS AND FIGURES OF SPEECH

1. A "psychopath" is someone who is antisocial and self-centered to the point of having no regard for the rules of society or the needs of other people (1). In what ways does the Joker, as White and Arp DESCRIBE him, exhibit this behavior?

2. "Utilitarianism" stresses the welfare of the majority over the special interests of the few (6). How and how well does White and Arp's summary of this philosophy fit this definition?

3. "Deontology" takes its name from the Greek word for *obligation* or *duty* (7). How does this root meaning apply to the school of ethics by that name as White and Arp define it?

4. Look up the root meanings of *ethics* and *ethnic* in your dictionary. What do the two terms have in common? What does their ETYMOLOGY tell you about the nature of *ethical* arguments, as opposed to *emotional* and *logical* arguments?

## FOR WRITING

1. Choose a pop culture icon you find interesting. Write an argument for why that figure's deeds and moral standards (or lack thereof) can teach us moral, ethical, or practical lessons.

2. Write an argument condemning (or justifying) the use of torture when dealing with terrorists. Consider applying one or more of the schools of philosophy outlined by White and Arp—or any other that you choose—to make your argument.

**DIANE GUERRERO**

# MY PARENTS WERE DEPORTED

Diane Guerrero (b. 1986) is an actress best known for her roles in the television series *Orange Is the New Black* and *Jane the Virgin*. Born in New Jersey and raised in Boston, her parents and older brother are from Colombia and came to the United States before she was born. They immigrated without documentation, and though they made every effort to legalize their status, they were then deported back to Colombia. In her memoir *In the Country We Love: My Family Divided* (2016), Guerrero writes about her and her family's experience of being undocumented immigrants in the United States. In "My Parents Were Deported," which appeared in the *Los Angeles Times* (2014), Guerrero uses her family's story to argue for more justice and compassion in the immigration system.

•❯──────────────────────────────────────────────❬•

IN *ORANGE IS THE NEW BLACK*, I play Maritza Ramos, a tough Latina from the 'hood. In *Jane the Virgin*, I play Lina, Jane's best friend and a funny know-it-all who is quick to offer advice.   1

I love both parts, but they're fiction. My real story is this: I am the citi-  2
zen daughter of immigrant parents who were deported when I was 14. My
older brother was also deported.

My parents came here from Colombia during a time of great instability  3
there. Escaping a dire economic situation at home, they moved to New Jersey,
where they had friends and family, seeking a better life, and then moved to
Boston after I was born.

Throughout my childhood I watched my parents try to become legal but to  4
no avail. They lost their money to people they believed to be attorneys, but who
ultimately never helped. That meant my childhood was haunted by the fear that
they would be deported. If I didn't see anyone when I walked in the door after
school, I panicked.

And then one day, my fears were realized. I came home from school to an  5
empty house. Lights were on and dinner had been started, but my family
wasn't there. Neighbors broke the news that my parents had been taken away
by immigration officers, and just like that, my stable family life was over.

Not a single person at any level of government took any note of me. No  6
one checked to see if I had a place to live or food to eat, and at 14, I found
myself basically on my own.

While awaiting deportation proceedings, my parents remained in deten-  7
tion near Boston, so I could visit them. They would have liked to fight deportation, but without a lawyer and an immigration system that rarely gives judges
the discretion to allow families to stay together, they never had a
chance. Finally, they agreed for me to continue my education at
Boston Arts Academy, a performing arts high school, and the parents of friends graciously took me in.

See p. 471 for ways
to appeal to your
readers' emotions.

I was lucky to have good friends, but I had a rocky existence. I was always  8
insecure about being a nuisance and losing my invitation to stay. I worked a
variety of jobs in retail and at coffee shops all through high school. And, though
I was surrounded by people who cared about me, part of me ached with every
accomplishment because my parents weren't there to share my joy.

My family and I worked hard to keep our relationships strong, but too-  9
short phone calls and the annual summer visits I made to Colombia didn't
suffice. They missed many important events in my life, including my singing
recitals—they watched my senior recital on a tape I sent them instead of from

the audience. And they missed my prom, my college application process, and my graduations from high school and college.

My story is all too common. Every day, children who are U.S. citizens are   10
separated from their families as a result of immigration policies that need fixing.

I consider myself lucky because things turned out better for me than for   11
most, including some of my own family members. When my brother was deported, his daughter was just a toddler. She still had her mother, but in a single-parent household, she faced a lot of challenges. My niece made the wrong friends and bad choices. Today, she is serving time in jail, living the reality that I act out on screen. I don't believe her life would have turned out this way if her father and my parents had been here to guide and support her.

I realize the issues are complicated. But it's not just in the interest of   12
immigrants to fix the system: It's in the interest of all Americans. Children who grow up separated from their families often end up in foster care, or worse, in the juvenile justice system despite having parents who love them and would like to be able to care for them.

I don't believe it reflects our values as a country to separate children and   13
parents in this way. Nor does it reflect our values to hold people in detention without access to good legal representation or a fair shot in a court of law. President Obama has promised to act on providing deportation relief for families across the country, and I would urge him to do so quickly. Keeping families together is a core American value.

Congress needs to provide a permanent, fair legislative solution, but in   14
the meantime families are being destroyed every day, and the president should do everything in his power to provide the broadest relief possible now. Not one more family should be separated by deportation.

## FOR DISCUSSION

1. As an American citizen and the daughter of immigrant parents who were deported when she was 14, Diane Guerrero does not believe that "it reflects our values as a country to separate children and parents in this way" (13). To what extent do you agree or disagree with this CLAIM? Why?

2. Which do you think is more instrumental in establishing her credibility and winning sympathy for her position—that Guerrero is a well-known actress, or that she is a first-generation American? Why do you think so?

3. When her parents were deported, Guerrero could have elected to return to Colombia with her parents. Should she have? Why or why not?

## STRATEGIES AND STRUCTURES

1. Why do you think Guerrero begins her ARGUMENT by distinguishing between "fiction" and reality (1, 2)? Is this an effective strategy? Why or why not?

2. For the most part, Guerrero's argument takes the form of a NARRATIVE about being separated from her parents as a teenager. At what point in her essay does Guerrero switch from "my real story" to making a larger claim? What is her claim exactly, and where does she state it most clearly and directly?

3. A fair and equitable immigration system benefits not only immigrants like her parents, Guerrero argues, but the country as a whole. What reasons does she give? How and how well do they support this aspect of her claim?

4. What point is Guerrero making when she cites the EXAMPLE of her niece who is in jail? How and how well does it represent the group of people it purports to exemplify? Explain.

## WORDS AND FIGURES OF SPEECH

1. Her jailed niece, Guerrero says, is "living the reality that I act out on screen" (11). How do these words near the end of Guerrero's essay recall those of her opening paragraphs?

2. According to Guerrero, the immigration system in America needs "fixing" (10). What are the implications of this METAPHOR, and why do you think Guerrero uses it instead of simply saying that she thinks immigration policies should be changed?

3. In the final paragraph of her argument, Guerrero calls for a *solution* rather than a *fix* (14). What's the difference, if any? Is this a better choice of words? Why or why not?

## FOR WRITING

1. Tell the story of someone you know, or have heard about, who has been deported. Based on that narrative and any other EVIDENCE you choose, make the case that American immigration policies need to be reformed—or, alternatively, that the existing immigration system actually works, more or less.

2. In a carefully composed argument, support or refute this claim: "Except in cases of serious crime, separating families through deportation (or incarceration) is wrong and does more harm than good to American society." Try to include facts and figures as well as ANECDOTAL evidence in your proof.

JOHN McWHORTER

# WHY "REDSKINS" IS A BAD WORD

JOHN McWHORTER (b. 1965) is an associate professor of English and comparative literature at Columbia University, specializing in creole languages as well as the philosophy and sociology of language. A Philadelphia native, McWhorter holds degrees from Simon's Rock College, Rutgers University, New York University, and Stanford University. In addition to his teaching and appearances as a commentator on radio and television programs, he is a prolific writer, with many essays and books on linguistics and race relations, among them *Losing the Race: Self-Sabotage in Black America* (2000). In 2015, McWhorter wrote the essay "Why 'Redskins' Is a Bad Word" for *Time* magazine. Discussing the controversy surrounding this common name for athletic teams, McWhorter argues that the connotations of the word make it inherently insulting to Native Americans. "As always," he writes, "life is more than the literal."

CALIFORNIA'S BAN OF THE USE OF THE NAME "REDSKINS" by schools is likely 1
the beginning of a trend. Native Americans have been decrying the term "Redskin" as a slur for a good while now, and Washington Redskins owner Dan Snyder's refusal to change the name of the team is looking increasingly callous and antique. Many will celebrate that "Redskin" is likely starting to go the way of "Oriental" and—well, you know.

Yet some may quietly be harboring another question: What's so terri- 2
ble about referring to the fact that many Native Americans have a reddish skin tone compared to other people? It's not as if having "red" skin is a negative or even humorous trait. It isn't illogical to wonder, deep down, whether Native Americans are fashioning a controversy.

> McWhorter considers viewpoints other than his own.

They aren't, though, because words can come to have meanings quite 3
different from their literal ones, and when it comes to matters of insult and dignity, meaning counts.

For example, the term "Oriental" for Asians became impolite 25 years 4
ago. Yet it's true that Asian heritage, for Chinese, Japanese and Korean people, is in "the Orient," traditionally a Western word for Asia. One now and then hears someone, usually of a certain age, grousing that "Well, now they want to be called Asians" with an air of dismissal, as if people go around willfully creating confusion and feigning hurt.

But actually, "Oriental" came to be associated with stereotypes of the 5
people in question, such that it was felt that a new term was necessary. Long ago, the same thing happened to "Chinaman." What's wrong with calling a man from China a "Chinaman"? Nothing, in the literal sense—but as always, life is more than the literal. "Chinaman" signifies the subservient, exotified "Ah, sohhh!" figure from Charlie Chan[1] movies; out it went and few miss it. "Oriental" was next.

These things can be subtle. I once had to inform a foreign student that in 6
class discussion it was unseemly to refer to another person directly as "a Jew," rather than as "a Jewish person." To be American is to internalize that "a Jew"

---

1. A fictional detective of mystery novels in the 1920s and, later, of more than fifty films. Chan was presented as a positive, sympathetic character, but also displayed stereotypical qualities and was the object of light mockery.

*A detail view of a Washington Redskins helmet. California Governor Jerry Brown signed a bill into law banning public schools from using the term "Redskins" as a team name or mascot.*

has an air of accusation and diminishment (ironically the student was from Israel!). That makes no literal sense, but it is a reality, as it is that to many, "blacks" sounds abrupt and hostile compared to "black people."

We are faced with something analogous to what Steven Pinker has artfully called the "euphemism treadmill." When something has negative associations, the word referring to it gradually takes on implied meanings connected with that contempt. This happens under the radar, but after about a generation, the reality becomes impossible to ignore. 7

What was once called "home relief" became more politely called "welfare" after a while, for example. But it's easy to forget what a positive and even warm word "welfare" is, given the associations it had amassed by the 1970s. Today one increasingly speaks of "cash assistance," and that term will surely have the same bad odor about it among many sooner rather than later. Yet all of these terms mean the same thing literally. The literal is but one part of language as we actually live it. 8

"Crippled," for example, is in itself a neutral, descriptive term—taken    9
literally, it even harbors an element of sympathy. However, the realities of
discrimination meant that "crippled" had a less neutral connotation after a
while, upon which "handicapped" was a fine substitute. But after a while, we
needed "disabled," and of course now there is "differently abled," and indeed
there will likely be something else before long.

This, then, is why "Redskins" qualifies as a slur despite not being a literal    10
insult. Words have not only core meanings, but resonances of the kind that
may not make it into the dictionary but are deeply felt by all of us. Sometimes
we need to get back down to cases[2] with a new word.

It may not be mean to tell someone their skin happens to be reddish. But    11
it's mean to call someone a Redskin. There's a difference.

### FOR DISCUSSION

1. It is a "slur," John McWhorter argues, to call someone a name like *Redskin* just
   because "their skin happens to be reddish" (1, 10). Why does McWhorter think so? Is
   he right, being politically correct, or some combination of both? Explain your view.

2. Many linguists would agree that no words are inherently "bad," since words take
   their meanings from the people who use them. To what extent would you say
   McWhorter's ARGUMENT is (or is not) based on this premise? Explain.

3. So, should the Washington Redskins change their name? Why or why not?

### STRATEGIES AND STRUCTURES

1. How, and how effectively, does McWhorter anticipate and counter the argument that
   it's not "so terrible" to call people a name based on the color of their skin (2)? Explain.

2. To support his argument that a particular word is disrespectful and offensive—
   and, therefore, not to be used—McWhorter cites EXAMPLES of several other
   words that have taken on negative CONNOTATIONS over time. Which examples
   do you find particularly effective? Why?

4. McWhorter concludes by saying, "It may not be mean to tell someone their skin
   happens to be reddish. But it's mean to call someone a Redskin. There's a difference" (11). Is this an effective summary of his argument? Is it a good way to end the
   essay? Why or why not?

2. "Back down to cases": expression meaning to discuss closely.

## WORDS AND FIGURES OF SPEECH

1. McWhorter calls the owner of the Washington Redskins "callous and antique" for his refusal to change the name of the team (1). Do these words constitute a slur by McWhorter's **DEFINITION**? Why or why not?

2. In what sense is McWhorter using the term *mean* (11)? What else can *mean* mean (in the adjective form)? Which, if any, of these other definitions relate to McWhorter's argument?

3. McWhorter refers to a "euphemism treadmill" (7). Explain the implications of this **METAPHOR**.

4. Is McWhorter choosing his words carefully when he says that changes in meaning occur "under the radar"; or should he have edited out this **CLICHÉ** (7)? How about "bad odor" (8)? Explain.

5. Look up the term "reverse epithet." How might it be applied to *Redskins* and similar, once-pejorative words and names?

## FOR WRITING

1. At Florida State University, football fans, many of whom are Native Americans, root avidly for the "Seminoles" (or "Noles"), the historical designation (in English) of an actual tribe of Native Americans. In a paragraph or two, outline the main points you would make to support the argument that there is or is not "a difference" between this case and that of the Redskins fans.

2. In 2016, the *Washington Post* conducted a telephone poll with 504 self-identifying Native Americans; nine out of ten said they were not offended by the name *Redskins*. Look up the details of the survey, and, based on those findings, write an argument for (or against) the use of *Redskins* as a name for the football team.

# MIND AND MEDIA:
# HOW IS TECHNOLOGY INFLUENCING
# OUR MINDS—AND OUR HEARTS?

S MARTPHONES are smart, right? At a touch or swipe, they connect us to a universe of ideas and information that once would have taken ages to locate in the great libraries of the world—if they could be found at all. But access to information and intelligence, one might argue, are not necessarily the same. "Is Google Making Us Stupid?" is how the technology writer Nicholas Carr famously framed the question back in 2008 in a much-discussed cover article for *The Atlantic* magazine. Technology, he concluded, may be expanding our knowledge base, but it is also making us intellectually shallower.

What about our emotions? If access and intelligence do not always equate, neither do access and communication. Some might say that because of technology we are able to stay in touch with our friends and family who live far away, and to make new connections with people we would otherwise never meet. At the same time, you've also probably heard that we are becoming more glued to our devices, perhaps at the expense of genuine conversation. Are we ignoring the emotional needs of the people physically around us—not to mention our own deeper feelings—when we text each other from afar instead of engaging face-to-face? Or do smartphones and other technologies keep us meaningfully connected with one another at all times as never before? Maybe both realities are true.

In the following essays, **Jane McGonigal**, **Sherry Turkle**, and **Andrea Lunsford** address these and other fundamental questions about the effects of digital media and technology upon the human mind and heart, including our capacities for engaging with other people through thoughtful conversation as well as intelligent reading and writing.

JANE McGONIGAL

# BE A GAMER, SAVE THE WORLD

JANE McGONIGAL (b. 1977) is a game designer and author. She received her doctorate in performance studies from the University of California, Berkeley. Known for designing alternate reality games such as *I Love Bees* (2004), *Last Call Poker* (2005), and *World Without Oil* (2007), she was named chief creative officer at SuperBetter Labs in 2012. McGonigal is the author of *Reality Is Broken: Why Games Make Us Better and How They Can Change the World* (2011). She is also the director of game research and development at the Institute for the Future, a nonprofit organization that, according to its website, provides "practical tools, research, and programs" to help a variety of organizations reach their future goals. In "Be a Gamer, Save the World," first published in the "Life and Culture" section of the *Wall Street Journal* (2011), McGonigal argues that gaming, particularly multiplayer online gaming, can help to make the world a better place.

W E OFTEN THINK OF IMMERSIVE COMPUTER AND VIDEOGAMES—like *Farm-Ville, Guitar Hero* and *World of Warcraft*—as "escapist," a kind of passive retreat from reality. Many critics consider such games a mind-numbing waste of time, if not a corrupting influence. But the truth about games is very nearly the opposite. In today's society, they consistently fulfill genuine human needs that the real world fails to satisfy. More than that, they may prove to be a key resource for solving some of our most pressing real-world problems.

Hundreds of millions of people around the globe are already devoting larger and larger chunks of time to this alternate reality. Collectively, we spend three billion hours a week gaming. In the United States, where there are 183 million active gamers, videogames took in about $15.5 billion last year. And though a typical gamer plays for just an hour or two a day, there are now more than five million "extreme" gamers in the United States who play an average of 45 hours a week. To put this in perspective, the number of hours that gamers world-wide have spent playing *World of Warcraft* alone adds up to 5.93 million years.

These gamers aren't rejecting reality entirely, of course. They have careers, goals, schoolwork, families and real lives that they care about. But as they devote more of their free time to game worlds, they often feel that the real world is missing something.

Gamers want to know: Where in the real world is the gamer's sense of being fully alive, focused and engaged in every moment? The real world just doesn't offer up the same sort of carefully designed pleasures, thrilling challenges and powerful social bonding that the gamer finds in virtual environments. Reality doesn't motivate us as effectively. Reality isn't engineered to maximize our potential or to make us happy.

Those who continue to dismiss games as merely escapist entertainment will find themselves at a major disadvantage in the years ahead, as more gamers start to harness this power for real good. My research over the past decade at the University of California, Berkeley, and the Institute for the Future has shown that games consistently provide us with the four ingredients that make for a happy and meaningful life: satisfying work, real hope for success, strong social connections and the chance to become a part of something bigger than ourselves.

We get these benefits from our real lives sometimes, but we get them    6
almost every time we play a good game. These benefits are what positive psychologists call intrinsic rewards—we don't play games to make money,
improve our social status, or achieve any external signposts of success. And
these intrinsic rewards, studies at the University of Pennsylvania, Harvard
and U.C. Berkeley have shown, provide the foundation for optimal human
experience.

    In a good game, we feel blissfully productive. We have clear    7
goals and a sense of heroic purpose. More important, we're constantly able to see and feel the impact of our efforts on the virtual
world around us. As a result, we have a stronger sense of our own
agency—and we are more likely to set ambitious real-life goals. One recent
study found, for example, that players of *Guitar Hero* are more likely to pick up
a real guitar and learn how to play it.

"More important"
and "as a result" are
types of connecting
words (p. 473).

*Could games like* Guitar Hero *help cure cancer and end poverty?*

*Videogames make players feel like their best selves. Why not give them real problems to solve?*

When we play, we also have a sense of urgent optimism. We believe   8
wholeheartedly that we are up to any challenge, and we become remarkably
resilient in the face of failure. Research shows that gamers spend on average
80% of their time failing in game worlds, but instead of giving up, they stick
with the difficult challenge and use the feedback of the game to get better.
With some effort, we can learn to apply this resilience to the real-world challenges we face.

Games make it easy to build stronger social bonds with our friends and   9
family. Studies show that we like and trust someone better after we play a
game with them—even if they beat us. And we're more likely to help someone
in real life after we've helped them in an online game. It's no wonder that 40%
of all user time on Facebook is spent playing social games. They're a fast and
reliable way to strengthen our connection with people we care about.

Today's videogames are increasingly created on an epic scale, with com-   10
pelling stories, sweeping mythologies and massive multiplayer environments

**Game Time**

Average daily time spent among 8- to 18-year-olds

■ Playing videogames

▪ Reading books, magazines, and newspapers for pleasure

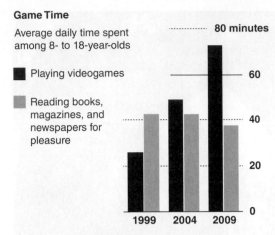

Source: Kaiser Family Foundation

that produce feelings of awe and wonder. Researchers on positive emotion have found that whenever we feel awe or wonder, we become more likely to serve a larger cause and to collaborate selflessly with others.

11 With so much blissful productivity and urgent optimism, stronger social bonds and extreme cooperation, it's not surprising that so many players feel that they become the best version of themselves in games. That's one of the reasons I believe we can take the benefits of games a step further. We can harness the power of game design to tackle real-world problems. We can empower gamers to use their virtual-world strengths to accomplish real feats. Indeed, when game communities have been matched with challenging real-world problems, they have already proven themselves capable of producing tangible, potentially worldchanging results.

12 In 2010, more than 57,000 gamers were listed as co-authors for a research paper in the prestigious scientific journal *Nature*. The gamers—with no previous background biochemistry—had worked in a 3D game environment called Foldit, folding virtual proteins in new ways that could help cure cancer or prevent Alzheimer's. The game was developed by scientists at the University of Washington who believed that gamers could outperform supercomputers at this creative task—and the players proved them right, beating the supercomputers at more than half of the game's challenges.

13 More recently, more than 19,000 players of EVOKE, an online game that I created for the World Bank Institute, undertook real-world missions to improve food security, increase access to clean energy and end poverty in more than 130 countries. The game focused on building up players' abilities to design and launch their own social enterprises.

14 After 10 weeks, they had founded more than 50 new companies—real businesses working today from South Africa and India to Buffalo, N.Y. My

favorite is Libraries Across Africa, a new franchise system that empowers local entrepreneurs to set up free community libraries. It also creates complementary business opportunities for selling patrons refreshments, WiFi access and cellphone time. The first is currently being tested in Gabon.

These examples are just the beginning of what is possible if we take 15 advantage of the power of games to make us better and change the world. Those who understand this power will be the people who invent our future. We can create rewarding, transformative games for ourselves and our families; for our schools, businesses and neighborhoods; for an entire industry or an entirely new movement.

We can play any games we want. We can create any future we can imag- 16 ine. Let the games begin.

### UNDERSTANDING THE ESSAY

1. You could argue that the claim "gamers can save the world" is a bit of an **OVERSTATEMENT**. Why do you think Jane McGonigal uses this title in an essay on the benefits of playing computer and video games?

2. At the end of paragraph 1, McGonigal's **CLAIM** has been narrowed down to a more manageable (and defensible) topic. What is it?

3. "Many critics consider such games a mind-numbing waste of time" (1). Referring to an opposing position like this in order to refute it is called "introducing a naysayer."[1] Where else in her **ARGUMENT** does McGonigal introduce naysayers? How effective is her use of this technique? Why do you say so?

4. According to McGonigal, the number of hours that gamers worldwide have spent playing a single popular game "adds up to 5.93 million years" (2). Point to other places in her essay where McGonigal uses statistics like this to support her argument. How convincing do you find this **EVIDENCE**? Why?

5. "Games," says McGonigal, "provide us with the four ingredients that make for a happy and meaningful life" (5). What are those ingredients? How might someone like David Brooks ("What Suffering Does," p. 312) respond to this claim?

6. McGonigal closes her argument with a number of **EXAMPLES**. Which examples do you find most effective? Do they support the claim that gamers have already begun to "harness" the power of gaming "for real good" (5)? Explain.

1. Graff, Gerald, and Cathy Birkenstein. *"They Say / I Say": The Moves That Matter in Academic Writing.* 3rd ed., W. W. Norton, 2017.

SHERRY TURKLE

# ROMANCE: WHERE ARE YOU? WHO ARE YOU? WAIT, WHAT JUST HAPPENED?

SHERRY TURKLE (b. 1948) is a professor of social studies at the Massachusetts Institute of Technology and the author of nine books. Turkle was born in New York and holds degrees from Radcliffe College and Harvard University, where she earned her doctorate in sociology and personal psychology. Much of her scholarly career has been devoted to studying the relationship between people and the technology they use, especially computers. Her book *The Second Self* (1984), for example, argues that computers fundamentally alter the ways we think and act. The thesis of *Alone Together* (2011) is evident in that book's subtitle: *Why We Expect More from Technology and Less from Each Other*. In the following selection from her most recent book, *Reclaiming Conversation: The Power of Talk in a Digital Age* (2015), Turkle argues that new technologies have changed the rules of our oldest preoccupation—love.

*I only ask, "How's the conversation?"*

—OPERA SINGER LUCIANO PAVAROTTI, WHEN ASKED
ABOUT RAISING ONLY DAUGHTERS

*True love is a lack of desire to check one's
smartphone in another's presence.*

—ALAIN DE BOTTON

FOR ADULTS AS FOR TEENAGERS, it comes down to this: You always expect    1
other people to have their phones with them. You expect that no matter
what else they are doing, they will see a message you sent. So, if they care
about you, you should be getting a text back. If they care. But in romantic
texting, responding to a communication with silence happens all the time. It's
the NOTHING gambit. It appeared early. As soon as texting had established
itself in flirting, there was talk about how to handle the strategy of silence.
Even in high school.

## The NOTHING Gambit

In 2008, eighteen-year-old Hannah tells me that in online flirting, "the hard-    2
est thing" is that the person you text has the option of simply not responding—
that is, of responding with NOTHING, a conversational choice not really
available in face-to-face talk. Her assessment of its effects: "It is a way of
driving someone crazy. . . . You don't exist."

Hannah explains that after a no-response, she feels a strong temptation    3
to make things worse for herself by following the online activities of the boy
who ignored her—on Facebook she can see if he's been out to dinner or a
party. In the past, you could console yourself that a person ignoring you was
perhaps busy with a family emergency. You could tell yourself all manner of
improbable stories. Now, as one of Hannah's friends puts it, "You have to cope
with the reality: they are busy with everything but you." Hannah says that this
makes rejection on social media "five times as great as regular rejection."

The NOTHING gambit is not a resolved conversation or a conversation    4
that has trailed off. It is not, Hannah insists, like "someone telling you a few
times that they are busy and then you get the picture." It is more like a

conversation with someone who simply looks away as if they don't understand that human beings need to be responded to when they speak. Online, we
give ourselves permission to behave this way.

And when it happens to you, the only way to react with dignity is to   5
pretend it didn't happen. Hannah describes the rules: If people don't respond
to you online, your job is to pretend to not notice. "I'm *not* going to be that
person who goes off on people saying, 'Why don't you get back to me, blah,
blah, blah.' . . . Not cool. I'm *not* going to be, like, 'Hello, are you still there? If
you don't want to talk, just tell me.'"

Hannah and I are talking in a circle of seven high school seniors, boys and   6
girls. When she says, "Why don't you get back to me, blah, blah, blah," everyone breaks out laughing. Hannah is doing a perfect imitation of a pathetic
loser. The behavior she describes is what no one would ever do. When someone hits you with a no-response, you meet silence with silence. Hannah is
explicit: "If people want to disappear, I'll be, like, 'Okay, I'm fine with it.'" In
fact, in Hannah's circle, the socially correct response to the NOTHING gambit
is to get aggressively busy on social media—busy enough that your activity
will be noticed by the person who has gone silent on you.

**Turkle establishes
credibility (p. 472)
by mentioning how
many people she
interviewed.**

In the early days of texting, 2008-2010, I spoke with more   7
than three hundred teens and young adults about their online
lives. I saw a generation settle into a new way of dealing with
silence from other people: namely, deny that it hurts and put
aside your understanding that if you do it to others, it will hurt them as well.
We tolerate that we are not being shown empathy. And then we tolerate that
we don't show it to others.

This style of relating is part of a larger pattern. You learn to give your   8
parents a pass when they turn to their phones instead of responding to you.
You learn to give your friends a pass when they drop in and out of conversations to talk with friends on their phones. And in flirtation, you learn to treat
NOTHING as something to put out of your mind.

You could say that in romance, being ignored is a staple and that this is   9
old wine in new bottles. But in the past, the silent treatment was a moment.
It could be the beginning of a chase or what led a suitor to abandon hope. But
it was a moment. Now, as we've seen before, a moment has turned into a
method.

## Friction-Free

Even the apps we use to find love are in formats that make it easy to ignore 10
being ignored. On Tinder, a mobile dating app, rejection is no longer rejection,
it is "swiping left," and when it happens to you, you don't even know it happened. Tinder asks, "Who is available, right now, near you, to go out for a
coffee or a drink, to maybe be your lover?" People who want to be considered
sign up, and their photograph and a brief bio appear on the system.

Once you have the app open, if you like the looks of someone, you swipe 11
right on your phone. If you're not interested, you swipe left. If I swipe right on
you and you swipe right on me, then we are notified that we have been
"matched" and can begin to communicate. But if I choose you with a right
swipe and you don't do the same for me, you simply don't appear in my visual
field again.

This is what people mean by "friction-free," the buzzword for what a life 12
of apps can bring us. Without an app, it would not be possible to reject hundreds,
even thousands of potential mates with no awkwardness. It has never been easier to think of potential romantic partners as commodities in abundance.

In this social environment, studies show a decline in the ability to form 13
secure attachments—the kind where you trust and share your life. Ironically,
our new efficient quests for romance are tied up in behavior that discourages
empathy and intimacy. The preliminaries of traditional courtship, the dinner dates that emphasized patience and deference, did not necessarily lead
to intimacy but provided practice in what intimacy requires. The new
preliminaries—the presentation of candidates as if in a game—don't offer that
opportunity.

Love talk during the chase involves new skills. You'll want a fluidity with 14
apps that will become part of your romantic game—apps for meeting, apps for
texting and messaging, apps for video chat. All of these bring the promise of
businesslike crispness to falling in love. They bring efficiency into the realm of
our intimacies. In a world where people live far away from parents and neighborhood ties, apps bring hope that they will smooth out the hard job of finding
a partner without the community connections enjoyed by previous generations. And so, the first story that young people tell about technology and
romance is that their phones have made things more efficient. But the first
story is not the whole story.

In fact, technology brings significant complications to the conversations    15
of modern romance. We feel we have permission to simply drop out. It encourages us to feel that we have infinite choice in romantic partners, a prospect
that turns out to be as stressful as it is helpful in finding a mate. It offers a
dialogue that is often not a dialogue at all because it is not unusual for people
to come to online conversations with a team of writers. You want a team
because you feel you are working in an unforgiving medium. Timing matters
and punctuation counts!

Finally, although technology offers so much to the chase—new ways to    16
meet, new ways to express interest and passion—it also makes a false promise. It is easy to think that if you feel close to someone because of their words
on a screen, you understand the person behind them. In fact, you may be overwhelmed with data but have little of the wisdom that comes with face-to-face
encounters.

Our new ways of communicating have an effect on every stage of    17
romance, from searching for love to presenting ourselves when we are hopeful
of finding it to the new complexities we encounter as we try to make it work.
In this environment, we move from "Where are you?" (the technology-
enhanced encounter) to "Who are you?" and then to "Wait, what just happened? Did I make you disappear?"

### UNDERSTANDING THE ESSAY

1. In the conventions of online flirtation and romance, explains Sherry Turkle, to
   reply to a text message with nothing at all is fundamentally different from the old-
   fashioned, face-to-face "silent treatment." What is the difference, according to
   Turkle? How and how well does her **ARGUMENT** support this key **CLAIM**?

2. Turkle's essay raises the question of "how to handle the strategy of silence" in
   online communication (1). What are some of the counterstrategies she mentions?
   How well do they work?

3. In a texting environment, according to Turkle, we've learned to "tolerate that we
   are not being shown empathy" (7). This adaptation, she says, is "part of a larger
   pattern" (8). In Turkle's analysis, what are some of the broader **CAUSES AND
   EFFECTS** of online communication?

4. To support her claims, Turkle draws on interviews not only with Hannah and her friends but with "more than three hundred teens and young adults" (7). Is this sufficient proof in your view? Why or why not?

5. The term *gambit* is from chess. A player intentionally sacrifices a piece in hopes of gaining a larger advantage in the coming play. How and how well does this METAPHOR help Turkle to DESCRIBE the online practice she is analyzing? Explain.

**ANDREA LUNSFORD**

# OUR SEMI-LITERATE YOUTH?
# NOT SO FAST

ANDREA LUNSFORD (b. 1942) is Professor Emerita of English at Stanford University and is on the faculty at the Bread Loaf School of English. After graduating from the University of Florida, Lunsford taught English at Colonial High School in Orlando before earning a PhD in rhetoric from the Ohio State University. "Our Semi-Literate Youth? Not So Fast" reports on research by Lunsford and others about trends in undergraduate writing (and thinking) as a result of increased use of digital technologies. Based on their findings, Lunsford argues, writing and literacy should be redefined for the digital age—and teachers of writing, she implies, should reconsider how they teach.

T WO STORIES ABOUT YOUNG PEOPLE, and especially college-age students, 1
are circulating widely today. One script sees a generation of twitterers and texters, awash in self-indulgence and narcissistic twaddle, most of it riddled with errors. The other script doesn't diminish the effects of technology,

but it presents young people as running a rat race that is fueled by the internet and its toys, anxious kids who are inundated with mountains of indigestible information yet obsessed with making the grade, with success, with coming up with the "next big thing," but who lack the writing and speaking skills they need to do so.

No doubt there's a grain of truth in both these depictions. But the doom-   2
sayers who tell these stories are turning a blind eye on compelling alternative narratives. As one who has spent the last 30-plus years studying the writing of college students, I see a different picture. For those who think Google is making us stupid and Facebook is frying our brains, let me sketch that picture in briefly.

Anticipating the views of opponents, p. 472, strengthens your own claims.

In 2001, I and my colleagues began a longitudinal study of writing at   3
Stanford, following a randomly selected group of 189 students from their first day on campus through one year beyond graduation; in fact, I am still in touch with a number of the students today. These students—about 12 percent of that year's class—submitted the writing they did for their classes and as much of their out-of-class writing as they wanted to an electronic database, along with their comments on those pieces of writing. Over the years, we collected nearly 15,000 pieces of student writing: lab reports, research essays, Power-Point presentations, problem sets, honors theses, email and textings (in 11 languages), blogs and journals, poems, documentaries, even a full-length play entitled *Hip-Hopera*. While we are still coding these pieces of writing, several results emerged right away. First, these students were writing A LOT, both in class and out, though they were more interested in and committed to writing out of class, what we came to call "life writing," than they were in their school assignments. Second, they were increasingly aware of those to whom they were writing and adjusted their writing styles to suit the occasion and the audience. Third, they wanted their writing to count for something; as they said to us over and over, good writing to them was performative, the kind of writing that "made something happen in the world." Finally, they increasingly saw writing as collaborative, social, and participatory rather than solitary.

So yes, these students did plenty of emailing and texting; they were   4
online a good part of every day; they joined social networking sites enthusiastically. But rather than leading to a new illiteracy, these activities seemed to help them develop a range or *repertoire* of writing styles, tones, and formats

along with a range of abilities. Here's a student sending a text message to friends reporting on what she's doing on an internship in Bangladesh (she refers in the first few words to the fact that power has been going on and off ever since she arrived): "Next up: words stolen from before the power went out\*\*\*\*~~~~Whadda-ya-know, I am back in Dhaka from the villages of Mymensingh. I'm familiar enough with the villages now that it's harder to find things that really surprise me, though I keep looking ☺." In an informal message, this students feels free to use fragments ("Next up"), slang ("whadda-ya-know"), asterisks and tildes for emphasis, and a smiley.

Now look at a brief report she sends to the faculty adviser for her internship in Bangladesh: "In June of 2003, I traveled to Dhaka, Bangladesh for 9 weeks to intern for Grameen Bank. Grameen Bank is a micro-credit institution which seeks to alleviate poverty by providing access to financial capital. Grameen Bank provides small loans to poor rural women, who then use the capital to start small businesses and sustain income generating activities." Here the student is all business, using formal academic style to begin her first report. No slang, no use of special-effects markings: just the facts, ma'am.[1] In the thousands of pieces of student writing we have examined, we see students moving with relative ease across levels of style (from the most informal to the most formal): these young people are for the most part aware of the context and audience for their writing—and they make the adjustments necessary to address them effectively.

Ah, you say, but these are students at Stanford—the crème de la crème. And I'll agree that these students were all very keen, very bright. But they were not all strong writers or communicators (though our study shows that they all improved significantly over the five years of the study) and they did not all come from privilege—in fact, a good number far from it. Still, they were part of what students on this campus call the "Stanford bubble." So let's look beyond that bubble to another study I conducted with researcher Karen Lunsford. About 18 months ago, we gathered a sample of first-year student writing from across all regions of the United States, from two-year and four-year schools, big schools and small schools, private and public. Replicating a

1. Phrase made famous by the lead detective on *Dragnet*, a 1950s TV show in which Joe Friday, a stern, no-nonsense cop, said the phrase often during witness interviews.

study I'd conducted twenty-five years ago, we read a random sample of these student essays with a fine-tooth eye, noting every formal error in every piece of writing. And what did we find? First, that the length of student writing has increased nearly three-fold in these 25 years, corroborating the fact that students today are writing more than ever before. Second, we found that while error patterns have changed in the last twenty-five years, the ratio of errors to number of words has remained stable not just for twenty-five years but for the last 100 years. In short, we found that students today certainly make errors— as all writers do—but that they are making no more errors than previous studies have documented. Different errors, yes—but more errors, no.

We found, for example, that spelling—the most prevalent error by over 7 300 percent some 25 years ago—now presents much less of a problem to writers. We can chalk up that change, of course, to spell-checkers, which do a good job overall—but still can't correct words that sound alike (to, too, two). But with technology, you win some and you lose some: the most frequent error in our recent study is "wrong word," and ironically a good number of these wrong words come from advice given by the sometimes-not-so-trusty spell-checkers. The student who seems from the context of the sentence to be trying to write "frantic," for example, apparently accepts the spell-checker's suggestion of "fanatic" instead. And finally, this recent study didn't turn up any significant interference from internet lingo—no IMHOs, no LOLs, no 2nites, no smileys. Apparently, by the time many, many students get to college, they have a pretty good sense of what's appropriate: at the very least, they know the difference between a Facebook friend and a college professor.

In short, the research my colleagues and I have been doing supports what 8 other researchers are reporting about digital technologies and learning. First, a lot of that learning (perhaps most of it) is taking place outside of class, in the literate activities (musical compositions, videos, photo collages, digital stories, comics, documentaries) young people are pursuing on their own. This is what Mimi Ito[2] calls "kid-driven learning." Second, the participatory nature of digital media allows for more—not less—development of literacies, as Henry Jenkins[3] argues compellingly.

2. Cultural anthropologist (b. 1968) who studies learning and new media.

3. Professor (b. 1958) and author of many books and articles about the role of media.

If we look beyond the hand-wringing about young people and literacy 9 today, beyond the view that paints them as either brain-damaged by technology or as cogs in the latest race to the top, we will see that the changes brought about by the digital revolution are just that: changes. These changes alter the very grounds of literacy as the definition, nature, and scope of writing are all shifting away from the consumption of discourse to its production across a wide range of genres and media, away from individual "authors" to participatory and collaborative partners-in-production; away from a single static standard of correctness to a situated understanding of audience and context and purpose for writing. Luckily, young people are changing as well, moving swiftly to join in this expanded culture of writing. They face huge challenges, of course—challenges of access and of learning ever new ways with words (and images). What students need in facing these challenges is not derision or dismissal but solid and informed instruction. And that's where the real problem may lie—not with student semi-literacy but with that of their teachers.

## WORKS CITED

Fishman, Jenn, et al. "Performing Writing, Performing Literacy." *College Composition and Communication*, vol. 57, no. 3, 2005, pp. 224–252.

Ito, Mizuko, et al. *Living and Learning with New Media: Summary of Findings from the Digital Youth Project*. MIT Press, 2009.

Ito, Mizuko, et al. *Hanging Out, Messing Around, and Geeking Out: Kids Living and Learning with New Media*. MIT Press, 2009.

Jenkins, Henry. *Confronting the Challenges of Participatory Culture: Media Education for the 21st Century*. MIT Press, 2009.

---. *Convergence Culture: When Old and New Media Collide*. NYU Press, 2008.

Lunsford, Andrea A., and Karen J. Lunsford. "'Mistakes are a Fact of Life': A National Comparative Study." *College Composition and Communication*, vol. 59, no. 4, 2008, pp. 781–807.

Rogers, Paul M. *The Development of Writers and Writing Abilities: A Longitudinal Study across and beyond the College-Span*. 2008. University of California, Santa Barbara, PhD dissertation.

## UNDERSTANDING THE ESSAY

1. When Andrea Lunsford and her colleagues did a longitudinal study of undergraduate student writing at Sanford, she says, "several results emerged right away" (3). What were some of those preliminary results?

2. The students in Lunsford's study "did plenty of" emailing, texting, and other forms of online social networking and writing (4). These "activities," however, did not lead to "a new illiteracy," Lunsford argues (4). In her view, what did they lead to? Does Lunsford offer convincing EVIDENCE to support this part of her CLAIM? Point to specific EXAMPLES in her text.

3. How might the following words and phrases in Lunsford's text be said to confirm (or disprove) what she says about "a range . . . of styles, tones, and formats" as a mark of good writing: *longitudinal* (3), *crème de la crème* (6), *just the facts, ma'am* (5), *fine-tooth eye* (6), *you win some and you lose some* (7)?

4. "Ah, you say, but these are students at Stanford" (6). Is Lunsford wise to bring up this counterargument at this point in her ARGUMENT? Why or why not?

5. A significant portion of Lunsford's argument has to do with "errors" in student writing (6). What claim is she making here? How and how well does she support that claim? Point to specific details in her argument.

6. "In short," says Lunsford near the end of her argument, "the research my colleagues and I have been doing supports what other researchers are reporting about digital technologies and learning" (8). So what larger conclusion(s) about technology and literacy do Lunsford and colleagues come to? How and how effectively is this claim supported by her earlier, narrower conclusions about student writing at particular universities?

# MIND AND MEDIA:
# HOW IS TECHNOLOGY INFLUENCING
# OUR MINDS—AND OUR HEARTS?

## ANALYZING THE ARGUMENTS

1. Among the three writers in this debate, which ones make the strongest **ARGU-MENT** about the way digital technologies are changing the way we feel, think, and act? What makes those arguments particularly convincing?

2. Among the three arguments in this debate, which one makes the strongest argument that technology may be diminishing our capacities in some way? What makes this argument effective in your view?

3. Whether or not you agree with their conclusions, which of the writers in this cluster do you find most credible? Why? What strategies do they use to establish their credibility? For example, how well do they anticipate opposing arguments? Refer to particular passages in the text.

## FOR WRITING

1. Choose a **CLAIM** from one of these three arguments that you think could use more support. Write a paragraph providing additional **EVIDENCE** to support (or refute) that claim.

2. Write an argument supporting, opposing, or both, the claim that face-to-face communication is more effective and satisfying than texting or other forms of digital communication. Feel free to cite your own experience or that of your family or friends to support your argument.

3. Write a "modest proposal" (see Jonathan Swift's "A Modest Proposal," p. 542) suggesting that society should cease to use [insert digital technology of your choice] for an entire year. Be sure to cite the specific advantages of adopting your proposal.

# MONEYBALL:
# ARE COLLEGE SPORTS
# WORTH THE PRICE?

I N 2011, the University of Miami Hurricanes ran into heavy weather: roughly half the football team was accused of accepting "gifts" for their services on the field. A year earlier, several star football players at Ohio State traded sports memorabilia for cash and tattoos. As a result, the school vacated the 2010 season and gave up scholarships under NCAA sanctions and the head coach resigned. Money and college sports: the scandals go back at least to 1947, when players on the City College of New York's basketball team began accepting bribes in exchange for point shaving. In the end, thirty-two players from seven schools were arrested. Perhaps such scandals could be avoided if college athletes were openly paid for their work like everyone else, including those rank-and-file professional athletes who make good salaries but attract fewer fans than the best college players. Should college athletes be paid what they're worth? How much is that? Or are the excesses of sportsbiz out of place in college? Should big-time college athletics be benched permanently?

In the following essays, **Michael Rosenberg**, **Joe Posnanski**, and **Laura Pappano** address—and argue how to resolve—these and other issues related to the long but turbulent marriage of money and college sports.

# LET STARS GET PAID

MICHAEL ROSENBERG (b. 1954) is a sports writer and Michigan fan who worked for the *Detroit Free Press* for twelve years before joining the staff of *Sports Illustrated* in 2012. He is the author of *War as They Knew It: Woody Hayes, Bo Schembechler, and America in a Time of Unrest* (2008). In the following sports column, which first appeared in *Sports Illustrated* (2011), Rosenberg argues that "corruption" in college sports can be reduced by changing the rules instead of simply punishing players who game the system for pay and other perks.

---

E VERY SATURDAY IN THE FALL, we pack college stadiums, raise the American flag, stand quietly as a marching band plays "The Star-Spangled Banner," and cheer for a sport that prohibits capitalism.

College athletes cannot be paid. Every American knows this. The concept is as entrenched in our bloodstreams as cholesterol. We have accepted it for so long, and gone along with the NCAA's[1] definition of right and wrong for

---

1. The National Collegiate Athletic Association, the governing body of intercollegiate sports in the United States.

so many years, that we don't even remember the reasons anymore.

They can't be paid because they can't be paid, because they just can't, because it's not allowed, because if it were allowed, then they could be paid. And they can't. Because it's not allowed. Got it?

So when Cam Newton allegedly earns $180,000 playing college football to help repair his father's church, he is a villain. When Terrelle Pryor and A. J. Green sell memorabilia, they get suspended, even though their schools openly sell memorabilia.

*Former Auburn University quarterback Cam Newton, who now plays in the NFL.*

When Robert Traylor, the poor son of a crack-addicted mother and absentee father, takes money from a booster, he gets exiled. When Reggie Bush accepts thousands of dollars from somebody who sees his pro potential, he has to return his Heisman Trophy.[2]

Stanford quarterback Andrew Luck, who probably would have been the No. 1 pick in last April's NFL Draft,[3] turned down millions to return for his senior season. Given his worth, shouldn't he be able to make money while in college?

Look, cheating is wrong. The point here is not to excuse the cheaters. I hate cheating. The point is to redefine cheating.

The 2010−2011 NCAA manual says the "Principle of Amateurism" is important because college athletics are an "avocation" and . . . hang on, here comes the punchline: "student-athletes should be protected from exploitation by professional and commercial enterprise."

Really? When an athlete sells his jersey so he can pay rent, and the NCAA suspends him, is the NCAA really protecting him? Who is the NCAA kidding?

---

2. The most prestigious award in college football, awarded annually to one player.

3. An annual event in which the teams of the National Football League (NFL) select former college football players for the upcoming season.

If major college sports did not exist, nobody would try to create them—  10
not as we know them today. The entire enterprise is preposterous. If there
were no college sports, 100 school presidents would never issue the following
press release:

> We have decided to create sports teams to represent our universities.
> We will have to admit a lot of students with inferior academic records
> solely because they can play football or basketball, but hey, we're cool
> with that. Anyway, what matters here is that we can make billions of
> dollars doing this, and we're not going to let the players have anything
> beyond room, board, meals, and a few other sundries. Not only that, but
> we will not allow ANYBODY to give them money. We have decided
> money is bad for them. It . . . uh . . . corrupts! Yes. It corrupts. Now:
> Who wants to buy a personal-seat license?

We have a system where coaches are worth $5 million a year but star  11
players are worth $40,000—a structure completely incongruous with the rest
of the sports landscape.

It's time to start over. College sports have so many redeeming qualities—  12
the sense of community, the thrill of competition, and goshdarnit, I'll even
throw "life lessons for young people" in there. Why are we so obsessed with
restraining the income of players? Who is winning here? What are we
protecting?

That NCAA manual devotes 16 pages to amateurism. We can cut it down to  13
one, with one principle: Athletes may not be paid directly with university funds.

That's it. One rule. There is your "amateurism." This way, universities  14
can spend their booster donations, TV money, and sponsorship dollars subsi-
dizing facilities, staff, operating costs, and athletic scholarships. College
athletics will continue to thrive across dozens of sports.

But those who can cash in on their fame and success will be able to do it.  15
If a wealthy South Carolina alum wants to give $50,000 a year to every Game-
cock, he can do it.

Is this fair? No, not really. If we wanted to be completely fair, then foot-  16
ball and basketball players would not be forced to subsidize non-revenue

athletes. But this is a start. It's a way to keep what we love about More types of logical fallacies appear on pp. 469–471. college athletics without unduly penalizing athletes.

Some day, we will look back on this era of college sports the 17 way we look back on Prohibition.[4] We'll see that there were some good intentions behind it, along with some misguided fears. The problem with amateurism in college sports is the same problem the nation had with Prohibition: It is impossible to enforce.

The simple fact is that college athletes want to get paid (who wouldn't?) 18 and there are literally thousands of people out there who would like to pay them. Why are we stopping this? What is the big deal? What do you think would happen if your starting quarterback was allowed to take $100,000 from somebody who enjoyed watching him play? Would the Earth crash into the sun?

I once had a remarkably circular conversation with former NCAA presi- 19 dent Myles Brand about the NCAA's amateurism rules. One of his chief arguments was this: "The fact is we don't pay students in other areas when they are engaged in activities as part of their education."

That may be (mostly) true. But colleges don't prevent their students 20 from making additional money either. If a student at the University of Southern California School of Cinematic Arts is offered $2 million to direct a major-studio movie, that student would still be allowed to take his film classes. USC wouldn't say, "Hey, that's no good. Give us your money so we can pay a professor seven figures."

This is not about whether college athletes are "exploited." That argu- 21 ment is a canard. Yes, they get a free education, and get to eat free meals, and get tutors and great weightlifting facilities. So does Kobe Bryant. (Well, he did, until last month.)

With every booster scandal, we confirm what we already suspect: Many 22 people are eager to pay these young men for their work, and the NCAA cabal won't allow it.

Should college athletes be paid? That's not really the question. No, the 23 question is this: Should college athletes be allowed to be paid? Should they be allowed to take money for doing something perfectly legal?

4. Constitutional ban on the sale and consumption of alcohol in 1919; repealed in 1933.

Of course they should. In America in 2011, why are we even debating  24
this?

Colleges have assigned themselves the role of Robin Hood: they take the  25
earnings of football and basketball players and give most of it to swimmers,
soccer players, and other not-so-popular athletes.

That's not terrible. But it is still wrong. And yet . . . well, progress comes  26
in small steps, and for now, I'm willing to let schools keep on doing that.
Really. Just loosen the rules so the most popular athletes can cash in on their
fame and success. Let them sign endorsement deals, take money from boosters, and get free tattoos and meals.

Then the NCAA can stop slapping every hand that is out and focus its  27
energy and money on academic fraud and education standards for athletes.

The republic will survive. Fans will still watch the NCAA tournament.  28
Double-reverses will still be thrilling. Alabama will still hate Auburn. Everybody will still hate Duke. Let's do what's right and reexamine what we think is
wrong.

## UNDERSTANDING THE ESSAY

1. Michael Rosenberg says he is not arguing that college athletes *should* be paid.
   What **CLAIM** *is* he making? Where does he state that claim most clearly and
   directly? What are some of the main reasons he gives to support it?

2. What action does Rosenberg want his readers to take? Where does he spell out
   that part of his **ARGUMENT**?

3. Rosenberg gives an example of circular reasoning in paragraph 3. What's faulty, in
   general, about such logic? About the reasoning, as Rosenberg sees it, of the NCAA
   president's defense of "amateurism rules" (19)? Explain.

4. "Look, cheating is wrong. The point here is not to excuse cheaters. I hate cheating"
   (7). These words are not aimed at the reader's faculties of reason but at his or her
   emotions and moral sense. Is this an effective strategy? Why or why not?

5. Rosenberg does not condone cheating in college sports, he says. Rather he wants
   "to redefine cheating" (7). How? Point to specific passages in the text.

**JOE POSNANSKI**

# COLLEGE ATHLETES
# SHOULD NOT BE PAID

JOE POSNANSKI (b. 1967) is a sports journalist and former columnist for *Sports Illustrated* who now has his own *Joe Blog*. In addition to *The Soul of Baseball* (2007), which won a Casey award for the best baseball book of the year, he is the author of *Paterno* (2012), a biography of the controversial Penn State football coach, Joe Paterno. A native of Cleveland, Posnanski is the type of sports enthusiast who, according to a colleague, "revels in sports for their own sake, but also eagerly plumbs them for metaphors for life." In "College Athletes Should Not Be Paid," which first appeared in *Sports Illustrated* (2011), Posnanski plumbs the "vital" relationship between colleges and their students and alumni—a connection, he argues, that "is at its strongest with sports."

M Y GREAT GOOD FRIEND MICHAEL ROSENBERG has a wonderful knack of 1 writing things that strike powerful disagreement inside me. It is one of his many gifts. This is not to say that I always, or even often, disagree with Michael. I don't. I think Michael's one of the best sportswriters in the country and we see things the same way the vast majority of the time. Maybe that's why when I *do* disagree with him—like I did with a Tiger Woods column he wrote a couple of years ago or the let's pay the stars of college sports piece he wrote this week—it's a pretty strong emotion, the sort of emotion that pushes me to mumble to myself and to start a new file on my computer.

There is something I have wanted to say for a while about big-time col- 2 lege athletics, but it is one of those weird thoughts that is both blindingly obvious and strangely difficult to put into words. That's why I had never written it before. It was reading Michael's piece, and this sentence in particular—"If we wanted to be completely fair, then football and basketball players would not be forced to subsidize non-revenue athletes"—that opened the door. It has been a long time since I read a sentence I more strongly disagreed with.

And that led to the words that form the heart of this piece . . . words that, 3 I have to say, surprised me: "College athletics are *not* about the players."

You are more than welcome to stop reading now.                               4

What is the question here? Let's talk about this for a second here before mov- 5 ing to the big point. Most people frame the question like so: See p. 468 for ways to state a claim so it is easier to defend. Should the best college athletes in the most successful sports be paid for all the hard work they put in and for all the revenue they help generate at colleges across America?

When the question is framed like that, it's hard to see how there are two 6 sides to the argument: *of course* they should get paid. This is America.

But, really, that's not the question, is it? I hate to bring up this old bit, 7 but to get where we are going I must: Big-time athletes do get paid. They get free college tuition. We all used to believe that was worth something (parents of college aged kids know that it's worth something). They get room and board. At the kinds of schools we are talking about, they get incredible facilities to train, the best coaching available (how much does it cost just to send your child to one of these coach's *camps*?), public relations machines to help them build their brand, national exposure, free travel, the best doctors, direct access to the professional ranks, youthful fame that can open doors for the rest of their lives, priceless experiences, and so on. How much do you think parents would pay to send their son to play four years of basketball at Duke for Mike Krzyzewski? Is there a price tag you could put on that?

*Mike Krzyzewski of Duke University instructs his players.*

I'm not saying this to make any point except that the question has to be    8
asked the right way. The question is: Should big-time college athletes (in the
revenue-producing sports, of course) get paid *more* than they do now?

I have long thought: Yes. They should. I've never believed in amateurism    9
for amateurism's sake. I've never bought into the notion that by keeping
money away from players you are doing them favors. The arcane rules of the
NCAA[1] drive me mad, just like they drive Andy Staples[2] and everyone else
mad. The occasional story that comes out about schools getting in trouble for
paying the plane fare to send a player home to his grandmother's funeral, or
anything like that, makes me so angry I wish the whole system was burned to

1. The National Collegiate Athletic Association, the governing body of college sports.

2. College football writer for the magazine *Sports Illustrated*.

the ground. I have long wished they could at least give players a stipend or something.

But here is my problem: Every time I read another story about *why* star    10
players should get paid more—and remember, we are almost always talking only about the stars, almost always talking about a few dozen players scattered across America—I come away feeling more and more like they should not. The biggest argument for paying the athletes comes down to this: College players (those stars especially) are the reason why these schools are generating so much money and so they deserve a much bigger piece of the pie. These sports are *about* them.

And you know what? I totally, completely, utterly, and thoroughly dis-    11
agree with that.

Ask yourself this: What would happen if tomorrow every single player    12
on the Auburn football team quit and reformed as a professional team called the Birmingham Bandits. Who would go to their games? Anyone? How much would those talented young men get paid?

Ask yourself this: What would happen if all the ACC basketball schools    13
dropped their players and replaced them with Division II[3] talent? Would North Carolina—Duke suddenly play in empty arenas?

Ask yourself this: Say the first, second, and third All-America Teams in    14
college football tomorrow went into the NFL.[4] They just left. How many fewer fans would the college games draw? How many fewer people would watch Texas and Tennessee and Iowa?

Ask yourself this: Why do we care about college football? We know that    15
the skill level in college football is vastly inferior to the skill level of NFL teams. Heck, many Heisman Trophy[5] winners are not even NFL prospects. Yet, by the millions, we watch. We cheer. We buy. We rejoice. We gripe. We wear. We eat. We live it. Many of us even argue that we *prefer* the quality and style of college to pro, we *like* watching those games more. But is it the quality

---

3. The Atlantic Coast Conference consists of 15 major college athletic programs; Division II teams in the NCAA compete at an intermediate (and less expensive) level.

4. National Football League.

5. Awarded annually to the single most outstanding player in college football.

and style we prefer or is it passion, youth, exuberance, and that we feel closer to the game?

No, college athletics is not *about* the players. College athletics is FOR the 16 players, but that's a different thing, and that's a distinction we don't often make. College football only works on this grand scale, I believe, because it's about the colleges. The alumni connect to it. The people in the town connect to it. The people in the state connect to it. People are proud of their connection to the University of South Carolina and Clemson, they are inspired by Alabama and Auburn, Penn State and Notre Dame and Stanford, they identify themselves through Missouri and Wisconsin and Florida and Texas A&M. The players matter because they chose those schools, they play for those schools, they win for those schools, and they lose for those schools, too. Everyone, of course, wants them to be the best players available, and some are willing to cheat the current system to get those players. But soon the players move on, and the love affair continues, just as strong, just as vital. The *connection* is what drives college football.

Otherwise, without that connection, it's just football that isn't nearly as 17 well played as the NFL.

Big-time college football . . . big-time college basketball . . . these are 18 about the schools that play them. They are about the institutions, the campuses, the landmarks, being young—the front of the jersey and not the back, as coaches love to say. This connection—fan to college—is at its strongest with sports. People might get irritated when the alumni fundraisers find them at their new address (how do they always find me?). They might not want to send in money to build a better library. But they'll buy sweatshirts, and they'll buy tickets, and they'll travel to bowl games, and they'll pay for pay-per-view, and they'll take a chartered bus to a subregional in Tulsa. This direct line to sports is how they support—and how they love—their school.

So it seems obvious to me that the money from football—revenue- 19 driving basketball too—should go to offer more and better opportunities at those colleges. That should be its singular purpose. The money from football— as much of it as possible—should pay for talented young tennis players to go to that school. It should pay to give opportunities to gifted swimmers, dedicated runners, hard-working volleyball players, and so on. The point is not how many people watch those athletes play, or how many people care about the sports they play. The point is about opportunity and education and developing people and creating a richer environment at the school. My friend Mechelle Voepel was just telling me about Caton Hill—have you heard of her? She played basketball at Oklahoma. She's now a flight surgeon in the Army, and she says basketball helped her get there. How many stories are there like that from softball and track and lacrosse and all the rest? If football is pulling in all this cash and is not offering those kinds of chances, if it is not making the colleges better places, then who needs it?

Michael in his piece does not say that the schools should pay the 20 players—at least for now. No, he makes the argument that basically they should allow boosters to pay the players, and allow the players to take whatever money and benefits and endorsements they can get. I can only imagine a college sport where high school kids hire agents and send them from school to school to cut the best deal they can make with various car dealers, CEOs, and tattoo-parlor owners. I can only imagine how many people will take the money they normally give to the school and instead spend it to get a running back they can call their very own. Maybe they can have the players wear a little patch on their shoulders with the name of the booster who gave the player the money to come to the school. That touchdown was scored by Tommy Tutone and brought to you by Bob's Trucking.

But, even that doesn't bother me much. I'm all for the NCAA loosening 21 up on the rules. No, it's the larger point. Schools are drowning *now*. I have good friends, both of them have good jobs, both of them have saved responsibly, and they have no idea how they can afford to send all three of their kids to college. No idea. And their kids are smart, they're getting some scholarship money, but the price is still overwhelming. Look around: Schools are slashing sports. They are raising tuition prices. They are cutting scholarships. Meanwhile college football and basketball—especially football—has become an arms race, with insane salaries being paid to coaches, and cathedrals built for weight training, and video equipment that the Pentagon would envy.

I'm not sure how you stop that. Maybe you can't stop it. Maybe you 22 don't even want to stop it . . . that's a whole other topic. But paying the stars seems to be sending college football careening away from anything close to the point. College football is not popular because of the stars. College football is popular because of that first word. Take away the college part, add in money, and you are left with professional minor league football and a developmental basketball league. See how many people go watch that.

## UNDERSTANDING THE ESSAY

1. Joe Posnanski begins his essay by saying what a good friend Michael Rosenberg (author of the previous essay) is to him and what a great sportswriter he is. Is this a good strategy of **ARGUMENT**, given that Posnanski is about to attack his colleague's position? Explain.

2. Reframing the question at issue is a common tactic in debate. Posnanski does this when he asks, "What is the question here?" (5). What *was* the original question? How does Posnanski reframe it, and how does this change help (if it does help) to advance his argument?

3. "Ask yourself this"—with this phrase, Posnanski introduces several what-ifs (12–15). How accurate are his conclusions in each hypothetical case? How and how well do these what-ifs prove the point he is making about the importance of college sponsorship?

4. Posnanski describes NCAA rules as *arcane* (9). Why might he choose this term rather than, say, *complicated* or *confusing*?

5. "I totally, completely, utterly, and thoroughly disagree with that" (11). What point is Posnanski disagreeing with so unequivocally here? What effect might he hope to have upon the audience by being so emphatic—and personal? Does the strategy work? Why or why not?

6. "No, college athletics is not *about* the players. College athletics is FOR the players, but that's a different thing, and that's a distinction that we don't often make" (16). What distinction is Posnanski making here? How well does he demonstrate that this distinction (and thus the conclusion of his entire argument) is valid? Explain.

LAURA PAPPANO

# HOW BIG-TIME SPORTS ATE COLLEGE LIFE

LAURA PAPPANO (b. 1962) is a journalist who writes about education, social issues, and gender (especially in sports). A graduate of Yale, she is the author of *Inside School Turnarounds* (2010) and co-author of *Playing with the Boys* (2008). The following selection (from the *New York Times*, 2012) examines how revenue-producing sports, especially football and basketball, have spilled over into all aspects of campus life, including academics. What can be done to turn back the tide? The best hope, Pappano argues on the basis of her extensive research and numerous interviews, lies in what many faculty members and academic administrators call "balance."

I T WAS A GREAT DAY TO BE A BUCKEYE. Josh Samuels, a junior from Cincinnati, dates his decision to attend Ohio State to November 10, 2007, and the chill he felt when the band took the field during a football game against Illinois. "I looked over at my brother and I said, 'I'm going here. There is nowhere else I'd rather be.'" (Even though Illinois won, 28–21.)

Tim Collins, a junior who is president of Block O, the 2,500-member 2 student fan organization, understands the rush. "It's not something I usually admit to, that I applied to Ohio State 60 percent for the sports. But the more I do tell that to people, they'll say it's a big reason why they came, too."

Ohio State boasts 17 members of the American Academy of Arts and 3 Sciences, three Nobel laureates, eight Pulitzer Prize winners, 35 Guggenheim Fellows, and a MacArthur winner. But sports rule.

"It's not, 'Oh, yeah, Ohio State, that wonderful physics department.' It's 4 football," said Gordon Aubrecht, an Ohio State physics professor.

Last month, Ohio State hired Urban Meyer to coach football for $4 mil- 5 lion a year plus bonuses (playing in the B.C.S. National Championship game nets him an extra $250,000; a graduation rate over 80 percent would be worth $150,000).[1] He has personal use of a private jet.

Dr. Aubrecht says he doesn't have enough money in his own budget to 6 cover attendance at conferences. "From a business perspective," he can see why Coach Meyer was hired, but he calls the package just more evidence that the "tail is wagging the dog."

Dr. Aubrecht is not just another cranky tenured professor. Hand-wring- 7 ing seems to be universal these days over big-time sports, specifically football and men's basketball. Sounding much like his colleague, James J. Duderstadt, former president of the University of Michigan and author of "Intercollegiate Athletics and the American University," said this: "Nine of 10 people don't understand what you are saying when you talk about research universities. But you say 'Michigan' and they understand those striped helmets running under the banner."

For good or ill, big-time sports has become the public face of the univer- 8 sity, the brand that admissions offices sell, a public-relations machine thanks to ESPN exposure. At the same time, it has not been a good year for college athletics. Child-abuse charges against a former Penn State assistant football coach brought down the program's legendary head coach and the university's president. Not long after, allegations of abuse came to light against an assistant basketball coach at Syracuse University. Combine that with the scandals

---

1. The Bowl Championship Series (BCS) selects the ten teams that compete in the NCAA championship in Division I, the highest level of play.

over boosters showering players with cash and perks at Ohio State and, allegedly, the University of Miami, and a glaring power gap becomes apparent
between the programs and the institutions that house them.

"There is certainly a national conversation going on now that I can't ever   9
recall taking place," said William E. Kirwan, chancellor of the University of
Maryland system and codirector of the Knight Commission on Intercollegiate
Athletics. "We've reached a point where big-time intercollegiate athletics is
undermining the integrity of our institutions, diverting presidents and institutions from their main purpose."

The damage to reputation was clear in a November survey         10
by Widmeyer Communications in which 83 percent of 1,000         For tips on using statistics to support an argument, see p. 466.
respondents blamed the "culture of big money" in college sports
for Penn State officials' failure to report suspected child abuse to
local law enforcement; 40 percent said they would discourage their child from
choosing a Division I institution "that places a strong emphasis on sports," and
72 percent said Division I sports has "too much influence over college life."

Has big-time sports hijacked the American campus? The word today is   11
"balance," and the worry is how to achieve it.

The explosion in televised games has spread sports fever well beyond   12
traditional hotbeds like Alabama and Ole Miss. Classes are canceled to accommodate broadcast schedules, and new research suggests that fandom can affect
academic performance. Campus life itself revolves around not just going to
games but lining up and camping out to get into them.

"It's become so important on the college campus that it's one of the   13
only ways the student body knows how to come together," said Allen Sack,
president-elect of the Drake Group, a faculty network that lobbies for academic integrity in college sports. "In China and other parts of the world, there
are no gigantic stadiums in the middle of campus. There is a laser focus on
education as being the major thing. In the United States, we play football."

Dr. Sack, interim dean of the University of New Haven's college of busi-   14
ness, was sipping orange juice at a coffee shop a few blocks from the Yale Bowl.
It was a fitting place to meet, given that when the Ivy League was formed in
1954, presidents of the eight member colleges saw where football was headed
and sought to stop it. The pact they made, according to a contemporaneous
account in the *Harvard Crimson*, aimed to ensure that players would "enjoy the

game as participants in a form of recreational competition rather than as professional performers in public spectacles."

There is nothing recreational about Division I football today, points out 15 Dr. Sack, who played for Notre Dame in the 1960s. Since then, athletic departments have kicked the roof off their budgets, looking more like independent franchises than university departments.

It is that point—"this commercial thing" in the middle of academia, as 16 Charles T. Clotfelter, a public policy professor at Duke, put it—that some believe has thrown the system out of kilter. In his recent book *Big-Time Sports in American Universities*, Dr. Clotfelter notes that between 1985 and 2010, average salaries at public universities rose 32 percent for full professors, 90 percent for presidents and 650 percent for football coaches.

The same trend is apparent in a 2010 Knight Commission report that 17 found the 10 highest-spending athletic departments spent a median of $98 million in 2009, compared with $69 million just four years earlier. Spending on high-profile sports grew at double to triple the pace of that on academics. For example, Big Ten colleges, including Penn State, spent a median of $111,620 per athlete on athletics and $18,406 per student on academics.

Division I football and basketball, of course, bring in millions of dollars a 18 year in ticket sales, booster donations, and cable deals. Penn State football is a money-maker: 2010 Department of Education figures show the team spending $19.5 million and bringing in almost $73 million, which helps support 29 varsity sports. Still, only about half of big-time programs end up in the black; many others have to draw from student fees or the general fund to cover expenses. And the gap between top programs and wannabes is only growing with colleges locked into an arms race to attract the best coaches and build the most luxurious venues in hopes of luring top athletes, and donations from happy alumni.

College sports doesn't just demand more and more money; it is demand- 19 ing more attention from fans.

Glen R. Waddell, associate professor of economics at the University of 20 Oregon, wanted to know how much. In a study published last month as part of the National Bureau of Education Research working paper series, Oregon researchers compared student grades with the performance of the Fighting Ducks, winner of this year's Rose Bowl and a crowd pleaser in their Nike uniforms in crazy color combinations and mirrored helmets.

"Here is evidence that suggests that when your football team does well,    21
grades suffer," said Dr. Waddell, who compared transcripts of over 29,700
students from 1999 to 2007 against Oregon's win-loss record. For every three
games won, grade-point average for men dropped 0.02, widening the G.P.A.
gender gap by 9 percent. Women's grades didn't suffer. In a separate survey of
183 students, the success of the Ducks also seemed to cause slacking off: students reported studying less (24 percent of men, 9 percent of women), con-
suming more alcohol (28 percent, 20 percent), and partying more (47 percent,
28 percent).

While acknowledging a need for more research, Dr. Waddell believes the    22
results should give campus leaders pause: fandom can carry an academic price.
"No longer can it be the case where we skip right over that inconvenience," he
said.

Dr. Clotfelter, too, wanted to examine study habits. He tracked articles    23
downloaded from campus libraries during March Madness, the National Collegiate Athletic Association basketball tournament. Library patrons at universities with teams in the tournament viewed 6 percent fewer articles a day as
long as their team was in contention. When a team won an upset or close
game, article access fell 19 percent the day after the victory. Neither dip was
made up later with increased downloads.

"Big-time sports," Dr. Clotfelter said, "have a real effect on the way peo-    24
ple in universities behave."

✳ ✳ ✳

Television has fed the popularity. The more professional big-time college    25
sports has become, the more nonathletes have been drawn in, said Murray
Sperber, author of *Beer and Circus: How Big-Time College Sports Has Crippled
Undergraduate Education*. "Media coverage gets into kids' heads," he said, "and
by the time they are ready to choose a college, it becomes a much bigger factor
than it was historically."

In the last ten years, the number of college football and basketball games    26
on ESPN channels rose to 1,320 from 491. This doesn't include games shown
by competitors: the Big 10 Network, Fox, CBS/Turner, Versus, and NBC. All
that programming means big games scheduled during the week and television
crews, gridlock, and tailgating on campus during the school day.

"How can you have a Wednesday night football game without shutting 27 down the university for a day or two?" asked Dr. Sack of the Drake Group with a twinge of sarcasm. He's not exactly wrong, though. Last semester, the University of Central Florida canceled afternoon classes before the televised game against the University of Tulsa. Mississippi State canceled a day of classes before a Thursday night broadcast of a football game against Louisiana State, creating an online skirmish between Bulldog fans and a blogger who suggested parents should get their tuition back.

Even Boston College bowed, canceling afternoon classes because the 28 football game against Florida State was on ESPN at 8 p.m. Janine Hanrahan, a Boston College senior, was so outraged at missing her political science class, "Immigration, Processes, and Policies," that she wrote an opinion piece headlined "B.C.'s Backwards Priorities" in the campus newspaper. "It was an indication that football was superseding academics," she explained. ("We are the national role model," a university spokesman, Jack Dunn, responded. "We are the school everyone calls to say, 'Where do you find the balance?'")

Universities make scheduling sacrifices not just for the lucrative con- 29 tracts but also because few visuals build the brand better than an appearance on ESPN's road show "College GameDay." (In November, it had John L. Hennessey, president of Stanford, out on the Oval at daybreak working the crowd.) The school spirit conveyed by cheering thousands—there were 18,000 on Francis Quadrangle at the University of Missouri, Columbia, on October 23, 2010, for "GameDay"—is a selling point to students choosing colleges. When Missouri first started recruiting in Chicago a decade ago, few prospective students had ever heard the university's nickname, "Mizzou," according to the admissions director, Barbara Rupp. "Now they know us by 'Mizzou,'" thanks in part to "GameDay." "I can't deny that," she said.

Universities play the sports card, encouraging students to think of 30 themselves as fans. A Vanderbilt admissions blog last fall featured "My Vandy Fanatic Weekend" describing the thrill of attending a basketball game and football game back to back. "One of the things we hear in the admissions office is that students these days who are serious about academics are still interested in sports," said John Gaines, director of undergraduate admissions. Mr. Gaines slipped in that its academic competitor Washington University in St. Louis is only Division III. "We always make sure we throw in a few crowd shots of people wearing black and gold" during presentations. Imagine, he is saying, "calling yourself a Commodore."

Or calling yourself a Cornhusker. A few years ago, the "Big Red Wel- 31 come" for new University of Nebraska students began including a special treat: the chance to replicate the football team's famed "tunnel walk," jogging along the snaking red carpet below Memorial Stadium, then crashing through the double doors onto the field (though without the 86,000 fans).

When Kirk Kluver, assistant dean for admissions at Nebraska's College of 32 Law, set up his information table at recruiting fairs last year, a student in Minnesota let him know he would "check out Nebraska now that you are part of the Big 10." He got the same reaction in Arizona. Mr. Kluver said applications last fall were up 20 percent, while law school applications nationally fell 10 percent.

Penn State's new president, Rodney Erickson, announced last month that he 33 wanted to lower the football program's profile. How is unclear. A Penn State spokeswoman declined to make anyone available to discuss the future besides releasing a statement from Dr. Erickson about seeking "balance."

What would balance really look like? 34

Duke officials pride themselves in offering both an excellent education 35 and a stellar sports program.

Six years ago this spring, Duke experienced its own national scandal 36 when three lacrosse players were accused of rape by a stripper hired for a party at the "lacrosse house"—a bungalow since torn down. The charges were found to be false, but the episode prompted university leaders to think hard about the relationship between academics and athletics.

Kevin M. White, the athletic director, now reports directly to the president 37 of Duke. It was part of structural changes to more healthily integrate athletics into university life, said James E. Coleman Jr., a law professor who is chairman of the faculty athletics council and was chairman of the committee that investigated the athletes' behavior. (Vanderbilt made an even stronger move in 2008, disbanding the athletics department and folding it into the student life division.) Sitting in his office on Duke's Durham, North Carolina, campus, Dr. Coleman set his lunch tray on a mountain of papers and explained the challenges. He calls sports "a public square for universities" but also acknowledges how rising commercialism comes with strings that "have become spider webs."

A 2008 report by the athletics department, "Unrivaled Ambition: A      38
Strategic Plan for Duke Athletics," praises the K-Ville bonding experience and
the "identity and cohesion," of the rivalry with U.N.C. as it describes in stressful language the facilities arms race, skyrocketing coach salaries, and the
downside of television deals.

"We no longer determine at what time we will play our games, because      39
they are scheduled by TV executives," it laments, going on to complain about
away games at 9 p.m. "Students are required to board a flight at 2 a.m., arriving back at their dorms at 4 or 5 a.m., and then are expected to go to class,
study, and otherwise act as if it were a normal school day." And: "our amateur
student-athletes take the field with a corporate logo displayed on their uniform
beside 'Duke.' "

"The key thing is to control the things you can control and make sure the      40
athletic program doesn't trump the rest of the university, as it has in some
places," Dr. Coleman said. "These presidents have to do more than pay lip
service to this notion of balance between athletics and academics." He suggests that elevating academic standards for athletes is one way to assert
university—not athletic department—control over programs.

He has also tried to foster rapport between faculty members and the      41
athletic department. "The difficulty is having faculty understand athletics," he
said. "Both sides need to cross lines. Otherwise, it becomes these two silos
with no connection." Last month, Dr. Coleman hosted a lunch that brought
together Mr. White, athletics staff members and professors on his committee.
He's also revamping a program to match faculty members with coaches, and
sends them sports-related articles to bone up on issues.

Pointed questions about oversight of its athletic program were raised at      42
Penn State's faculty senate meeting last month, and faculty involvement is the
subject of a national meeting of the Coalition on Intercollegiate Athletics at
the University of Tulsa this weekend. John S. Nichols, the group cochairman
and professor emeritus at Penn State, says professors typically ignore the
many issues that swirl around sports and influence the classroom. His list
includes decisions about recruiting and admissions, and even conference
realignments. Starting in 2013, the Big East will stretch over seven states,
meaning not just football and basketball players but all student athletes—and
some fans—will be making longer trips to away games. Dr. Nichols says it is

time to "put some checks in place" on uncontrolled growth of athletics "or consider a different model."

    To be sure, efforts to rehabilitate major college sports are not new. Amid   43 much debate, an NCAA plan to raise scholarship awards by $2,000 was being reviewed this month. Some have seen it as the athletes' due, for the money they bring in, and others as pay for play; some colleges have complained they can't afford it.

    Many are skeptical that reining in college sports is even possible; the   44 dollars are simply too attractive, the pressures from outside too great. Mr. White said that it was naïve "to think we will ever put the toothpaste back in the tube." He added, "There is an oversized, insatiable interest in sports, and college sports is part of that."

    But some decisions are in university hands.   45

    Despite Duke's ascent to basketball royalty, Cameron Indoor Stadium—   46 built in 1940, renovated in the 1980s, and at 9,300 seats one of the smallest venues for a big-time program—still gives thousands of the best seats to students. At many large programs, courtside seats and luxury boxes go to boosters. But "outsiders with money," Dr. Coleman said, can make demands and change the way the team fits in with a university. "We could easily double the size of our basketball stadium and sell it out," he said. "That will never happen. If it does, you will know Duke has gone over to the dark side."

### UNDERSTANDING THE ESSAY

1. Early in her **ARGUMENT**, Laura Pappano raises a key question in the ongoing national debate about college athletics: "Has big-time sports hijacked the American campus?" (11)? To what extent is this a **RHETORICAL QUESTION**? Explain.

2. What are the implications of the word hijacked (11)? Why do you think Pappano chose this term instead of framing her question in more neutral language? Point out other places in her essay where Pappano's word choice suggests what her own views might be.

3. A key word throughout Pappano's essay is balance (11, 28, 34). What do college and sports officials mean by the term? Why, according to Pappano, are they so concerned with balance?

4. "Balance" is an important concept in newspaper reporting as well as sports—and in argumentation. How balanced (showing both sides of the question) is Pappano's presentation of the issues she is writing about? How does she achieve (or fail to achieve) balance? Point to specific passages in her essay.

5. Although she cites specific examples of particular schools and individual students, Pappano also uses other kinds of EVIDENCE, such as statistics and expert testimony, to frame and support the argument that the balance between college sports and academics needs to be redressed. Which pieces of evidence do you find most convincing? Do the pieces add up to sufficient proof? Why or why not?

6. What is Pappano's apparent PURPOSE in returning, at the end of her argument, to the EXAMPLE of big-time basketball at Duke? How and how well has she developed the Duke example to prepare readers for this conclusion?

7. In 2015, Pappano wrote "Valuing the Ideological Roots of Women's Athletics" for *Women Change Worlds*, a blog for the Wellesley Center for Women, an institute at Wellesley College dedicated to social change for women. Find the article online and COMPARE it to Pappano's essay for the *New York Times*. How are Pappano's arguments the same and how are they different? Explain.

# MONEYBALL: ARE COLLEGE
# SPORTS WORTH THE PRICE?

## ANALYZING THE ARGUMENTS

1. Among the three writers in this debate, which one(s) make the strongest **ARGUMENT** for the value (whether monetary or moral or both) of college sports? What makes the argument(s) particularly convincing? Cite particular passages and pieces of evidence.

2. Joe Posnanski's "College Athletes Should Not Be Paid" is a direct response to Michael Rosenberg's "Let Stars Get Paid." Point out specific places where he confronts his opponent's views, and identify some of the strategies he draws on, such as using logic, appealing to the reader's emotions or sense of ethics, and citing facts and figures. Explain why you find those strategies to be especially effective here—or ineffective.

3. Whether or not you agree with their conclusions, which of these three writers do you find most credible? How do they establish their credibility? For example, which ones seem most **OBJECTIVE**, or best informed, or most committed to their subjects? Refer to particular passages in the texts.

## FOR WRITING

1. Choose a **CLAIM** from one of these three arguments that you think could use more support. Write a paragraph providing additional evidence to support (or refute) that claim.

2. Write an argument that either supports or opposes one of the following claims: (1) profits from big-time college sports help to pay for minor sports and academic programs; (2) the most vital connection between most alumni and their schools is the sports connection; (3) sports have eaten a big hole in college life. Be sure to back up your claim with copious evidence.

# ⨯14⨯

## CLASSIC ESSAYS AND SPEECHES

T HE essays and speeches in this chapter are "classics"—timeless examples of good writing across the centuries. What makes them timeless? Jonathan Swift's "A Modest Proposal," for instance, is nearly 300 years old, and the speaker is a "projector," a word we don't even use anymore in the sense that Swift used it, for a person who is full of foolish projects. However, the moral and economic issues that Swift addresses are as timely today as they were in the eighteenth century. His greedy countrymen, Swift charges—not to mention English landlords and "a very knowing American of my acquaintance"—will do anything for money (9).

## What Makes a Classic Essay or Speech?

This sense of relevance—the feeling that what the writer has to say applies directly to us and our time—is one measure of a "classic." We feel it with all the essays and speeches in this chapter, including the Declaration of Independence; Abraham Lincoln's Second Inaugural Address; Sojourner Truth's "Ain't I a Woman?"; Zora Neale Hurston's "How It Feels to Be Colored Me"; and Martin Luther King Jr.'s "I Have a Dream."

In addition to their timeless themes, the works in this chapter are classics because the writer of each one has a unique command of language and of the fundamental forms and patterns of written or spoken discourse. By taking apart these great essays and speeches, you will find that they are constructed using the same basic strategies and techniques of writing you have been studying throughout this book. All the basic patterns of writing are here—NARRATION,* DESCRIPTION, EXPOSITION, and ARGUMENT—but interwoven seamlessly to make a *text*, a written fabric of words with each strand worked carefully into the grand design.

*Words printed in SMALL CAPITALS are defined in the Glossary/Index.

Let's look more closely at Zora Neale Hurston's "How It Feels to Be Colored Me" to see how a great writer combines several of the basic patterns of writing into a well-constructed essay.

## Mixing the Patterns

Hurston's essay is built on a series of DESCRIPTIONS—of the passing parade of strangers as seen from the front porch of her childhood home in Florida; of the jazz scene at the New World Cabaret in Harlem; of a sophisticated lady sauntering down a Paris boulevard; and, finally, of the mundane contents of the "brown bag of miscellany" that, Hurston claims, made up her essential life and being (17). In addition to describing particular places, people, and objects, these passages describe Hurston's feelings about them. Taken together, Hurston is capturing the feelings she has around her own identity and her awareness of how others perceive her—as suggested by the title "How It Feels to Be Colored Me."

Written when she was in her late thirties, the essay is not only a description of what Hurston saw and felt at various times in her life, but a NARRATIVE that focuses on her growing awareness of race, including her memory from age 13 of "the very day I became colored" (2). At the beginning of her story, she is "unconscious Zora" (9) to whose mind "white people differed from colored" only in that they passed through her little town but didn't live there (4). By the end of her narrative, time has passed and she reflects on what it means to be "colored," both in her "heart as well as in the mirror" (5).

Writing in 1928, before the Civil Rights movement of the 1960s, Hurston cannot escape the racial and social distinctions of her day. Her narrative, in fact, is also an example of CLASSIFICATION. You could say that on

For a scientist's views on "the myth of race," see Robert Wald Sussman's essay on p. 264.

one level, Hurston is describing a world that is divided across racial lines. At Barnard she is a "dark rock" amidst "the thousand white persons" (10) and when attending a jazz concert her "pulse is throbbing like a war drum" while a white man sits "motionless in his seat, smoking calmly" (11). As she says, "he has only heard what I felt" (13). On another level, Hurston's classification system also divides the world into winners and losers: "I have seen that the world is to the strong regardless of a little pigmentation more or less" (6).

Hurston's **PURPOSE** in "How It Feels to Be Colored Me," is not, however, to only describe and classify, but to make the **ARGUMENT** that such skin-deep ways of dividing up humanity are worth challenging. Her **EVIDENCE** for this claim is both "cosmic"—if she is "a fragment of the Great Soul," then so is everyone else, regardless of color—and grounded in history (14, 15). When confronted with the reality of slavery, for example, Hurston takes the position that white people are in a "much more difficult" situation, historically, than she is as a person of color (8). The world is her oyster to be acquired and pried open.

It is the **COMPARISON** with which Hurston concludes her essay, however, that provides perhaps the most compelling evidence for her claim that distinctions based on race and gender don't control her—and by extension, anyone else. We are each and all, she argues, a mixed bag of essentially similar odds and ends. Empty the bags into a common heap, and each one can be refilled more or less at random "without altering the content of any greatly" (17).

To reduce Hurston's essay to a simple **SUMMARY**, however, is to miss the point of this chapter. The meanings of a densely textured essay like Hurston's are not to be extracted from the text like pulling threads from a tapestry. We can break a complex essay into its constituent parts and patterns, but the full significance and overall structure of the essay derive from the writer's seamless combination of the various elements and modes of writing into a unified whole.

# A MODEST PROPOSAL

JONATHAN SWIFT (1667–1745) was born in Ireland and educated at Trinity College, Dublin, where he was censured for breaking the rules of discipline, graduating only by "special grace." He was ordained as a clergyman in the Anglican Church in 1694 and became dean of St. Patrick's Cathedral, Dublin, in 1713. Swift's satires in prose and verse, including *Gulliver's Travels* (1726), addressed three main issues: political relations between England and Ireland; Irish social questions; and matters of church doctrine. Swift's best-known essay was published in 1729 under the full title "A Modest Proposal for Preventing the Children of Poor People in Ireland, from being a Burden to Their Parents or Country, and for Making Them Beneficial to the Publick." Using irony as his weapon, Swift explains his deep contempt for materialism and for logic without compassion.

I T IS A MELANCHOLY OBJECT to those who walk through this great town[1] or travel in the country, when they see the streets, the roads, and cabin doors, crowded with beggars of the female sex, followed by three, four, or six children, all in rags and importuning every passenger for an alms. These mothers, instead of being able to work for their honest livelihood, are forced to employ all their time in strolling to beg sustenance for their helpless infants, who, as they grow up, either turn thieves for want of work, or leave their dear native country to fight for the Pretender in Spain, or sell themselves to the Barbadoes.[2]

I think it is agreed by all parties that this prodigious number of children in the arms, or on the backs, or at the heels of their mothers, and frequently of their fathers, is in the present deplorable state of the kingdom a very great additional grievance; and therefore whoever could find out a fair, cheap, and easy method of making these children sound, useful members of the common-wealth would deserve so well of the public as to have his statue set up for a preserver of the nation.

But my intention is very far from being confined to provide only for the children of professed beggars; it is of a much greater extent, and shall take in the whole number of infants at a certain age who are born of parents in effect as little able to support them as those who demand our charity in the streets.

As to my own part, having turned my thoughts for many years upon this important subject and maturely weighed the several schemes of other projec-tors,[3] I have always found them grossly mistaken in their computation. It is true, a child just dropped from its dam may be supported by her milk for a solar year, with little other nourishment; at most not above the value of two shillings,[4] which the mother may certainly get, or the value in scraps, by her lawful occupation of begging; and it is exactly at one year old that I propose to provide for them in such a manner as instead of being a charge upon their

1. Dublin, capital city of Ireland.

2. That is, sell themselves into indentured servitude to masters in Barbados, an island colony in the West Indies. The pretender to the throne of England was James Francis Edward Stuart (1688–1766), son of the deposed James II.

3. Men whose heads were full of foolish schemes or projects.

4. The British pound sterling was made up of 20 shillings; 5 shillings made a crown.

parents or the parish, or wanting food and raiment for the rest of their lives, they shall on the contrary contribute to the feeding, and partly to the clothing, of many thousands.

There is likewise another great advantage in my scheme, that it will pre- 5 vent those voluntary abortions, and that horrid practice of women murdering their bastard children, alas, too frequent among us, sacrificing the poor inno- cent babes, I doubt, more to avoid the expense than the shame, which would move tears and pity in the most savage and inhuman breast.

The number of souls in this kingdom being usually reckoned one million 6 and a half, of these I calculate there may be about two hundred thousand cou- ple whose wives are breeders; from which number I subtract thirty thousand couples who are able to maintain their own children, although I apprehend there cannot be so many under the present distress of the kingdom; but this being granted, there will remain an hundred and seventy thousand breeders. I again subtract fifty thousand for those women who miscarry, or whose chil- dren die by accident or disease within the year. There only remain an hundred and twenty thousand children of poor parents annually born. The question therefore is, how this number shall be reared and provided for, which, as I have already said, under the present situation of affairs, is utterly impossible by all the methods hitherto proposed. For we can neither employ them in handicraft or agriculture; we neither build houses (I mean in the country) nor cultivate land. They can very seldom pick up a livelihood by stealing till they arrive at six years old, except where they are of towardly parts,[5] although I confess they learn the rudiments much earlier, during which time they can however be looked upon only as probationers, as I have been informed by a principal gen- tleman in the county of Cavan,[6] who protested to me that he never knew above one or two instances under the age of six, even in a part of the kingdom so renowned for the quickest proficiency in that art.

I am assured by our merchants that a boy or a girl before twelve years old 7 is no salable commodity; and even when they come to this age they will not yield above three pounds, or three pounds and half a crown at most on the

---

5. Having natural ability.

6. A county in northeast Ireland.

Exchange; which cannot turn to account either to the parents or the kingdom, the charge of nutriment and rags having been at least four times that value.

I shall now therefore humbly propose my own thoughts, which I hope 8 will not be liable to the least objection.

I have been assured by a very knowing American of my acquaintance in 9 London, that a young healthy child well nursed is at a year old a most delicious, nourishing, and wholesome food, whether stewed, roasted, baked, or boiled; and I make no doubt that it will equally serve in a fricassee or a ragout.

I do therefore humbly offer it to public consideration that of the hundred 10 and twenty thousand children, already computed, twenty thousand may be reserved for breed, whereof only one fourth part to be males, which is more than we allow to sheep, black cattle, or swine; and my reason is that these children are seldom the fruits of marriage, a circumstance not much regarded by our savages, therefore one male will be sufficient to serve four females. That the remaining hundred thousand may at a year old be offered in sale to the persons of quality and fortune through the kingdom, always advising the mother to let them suck plentifully in the last month, so as to render them plump and fat for a good table. A child will make two dishes at an entertainment for friends; and when the family dines alone, the fore or hind quarter will make a reasonable dish, and seasoned with a little pepper or salt will be very good boiled on the fourth day, especially in winter.

I have reckoned upon a medium that a child just born will weigh twelve 11 pounds, and in a solar year if tolerably nursed increaseth to twenty-eight pounds.

I grant this food will be somewhat dear, and therefore very proper for 12 landlords, who, as they have already devoured most of the parents, seem to have the best title to the children.

Infant's flesh will be in season throughout the year, but more plentiful in 13 March, and a little before and after. For we are told by a grave author, an eminent French physician,[7] that fish being a prolific diet, there are more children born in Roman Catholic countries about nine months after Lent than at any other season; therefore, reckoning a year after Lent, the markets will be more glutted than usual, because the number of popish infants is at least three to

---

7. François Rabelais (1494?–1553), French satirist.

one in this kingdom; and therefore it will have one other collateral advantage, by lessening the number of Papists[8] among us.

I have already computed the charge of nursing a beggar's child (in which　14 list I reckon all cottagers, laborers, and four fifths of the farmers) to be about two shillings per annum, rags included; and I believe no gentleman would repine to give ten shillings for the carcass of a good fat child, which, as I have said, will make four dishes of excellent nutritive meat, when he hath only some particular friend or his own family to dine with him. Thus the squire will learn to be a good landlord, and grow popular among the tenants; the mother will have eight shillings net profit, and be fit for work till she produces another child.

Those who are more thrifty (as I must confess the times require) may　15 flay the carcass; the skin of which artificially[9] dressed will make admirable gloves for ladies, and summer boots for fine gentlemen.

As to our city of Dublin, shambles[10] may be appointed for this purpose in　16 the most convenient parts of it, and butchers we may be assured will not be wanting; although I rather recommend buying the children alive, and dressing them hot from the knife as we do roasting pigs.

A very worthy person, a true lover of his country, and whose virtues I　17 highly esteem, was lately pleased in discoursing on this matter to offer a refinement upon my scheme. He said that many gentlemen of this kingdom, having of late destroyed their deer, he conceived that the want of venison might be well supplied by the bodies of young lads and maidens, not exceeding fourteen years of age nor under twelve, so great a number of both sexes in every country being now ready to starve for want of work and service; and these to be disposed of by their parents, if alive, or otherwise by their nearest relations. But with due deference to so excellent a friend and so deserving a patriot, I cannot be altogether in his sentiments; for as to the males, my American acquaintance assured me from frequent experience that their flesh was

8. Roman Catholics, called Papists because of their allegiance to the pope. Though Catholics made up the majority of the Irish population in this period, English Protestants controlled the government, and Catholics were subject to discrimination and oppressive policies.

9. Skillfully, artfully.

10. Slaughterhouses.

generally tough and lean, like that of our schoolboys, by continual exercise, and their taste disagreeable; and to fatten them would not answer the charge. Then as to the females, it would, I think with humble submission, be a loss to the public, because they soon would become breeders themselves: and besides, it is not improbable that some scrupulous people might be apt to censure such a practice (although indeed very unjustly) as a little bordering upon cruelty; which, I confess, hath always been with me the strongest objection against any project, how well 'soever intended.

But in order to justify my friend, he confessed that this expedient was put into his head by the famous Psalmanazar, a native of the island Formosa,[11] who came from thence to London above twenty years ago, and in conversation told my friend that in his country when any young person happened to be put to death, the executioner sold the carcass to persons of quality as a prime dainty; and that in his time the body of a plump girl of fifteen, who was crucified for an attempt to poison the emperor, was sold to his Imperial Majesty's prime minister of state, and other great mandarins of the court, in joints from the gibbet,[12] at four hundred crowns. Neither indeed can I deny that if the same use were made of several plump young girls in this town, who without one single groat[13] to their fortunes cannot stir abroad without a chair, and appear at the playhouse and assemblies in foreign fineries which they never will pay for, the kingdom would not be the worse.     18

A single extended example may be sufficient to make your point.

Some persons of a desponding spirit are in great concern about that vast number of poor people who are aged, diseased, or maimed, and I have been desired to employ my thoughts what course may be taken to ease the nation of so grievous an encumbrance. But I am not in the least pain upon that matter, because it is very well known that they are every day dying and rotting by cold and famine, and filth and vermin, as fast as can be reasonably expected. And as to the younger laborers, they are now in almost as hopeful a condition. They cannot get work, and consequently pine away for want of nourishment to a     19

11. Former name of Taiwan. George Psalmanazar (1679?–1763), a Frenchman, fooled British society for several years by masquerading as a pagan Formosan.

12. A structure for hanging a felon.

13. A British coin of the time, worth the equivalent of four cents.

degree that if at any time they are accidentally hired to common labor, they have not strength to perform it; and thus the country and themselves are happily delivered from the evils to come.

I have too long digressed, and therefore shall return to my subject. I think    20
the advantages by the proposal which I have made are obvious and many, as well as of the highest importance.

For first, as I have already observed, it would greatly lessen the number    21
of Papists, with whom we are yearly overrun, being the principal breeders of the nation as well as our most dangerous enemies; and who stay at home on purpose to deliver the kingdom to the Pretender, hoping to take their advantage by the absence of so many good Protestants, who have chosen rather to leave their country than stay at home and pay tithes against their conscience to an Episcopal curate.[14]

Secondly, the poorer tenants will have something valuable of their own,    22
which by law may be made liable to distress, and help to pay their landlord's rent, their corn and cattle being already seized and money a thing unknown.

Thirdly, whereas the maintenance of an hundred thousand children,    23
from two years old and upward, cannot be computed at less than ten shillings a piece per annum, the nation's stock will be thereby increased fifty thousand pounds per annum, besides the profit of a new dish introduced to the tables of all gentlemen of fortune in the kingdom who have any refinement in taste. And the money will circulate among ourselves, the goods being entirely of our own growth and manufacture.

Fourthly, the constant breeders, besides the gain of eight shillings ster-    24
ling per annum by the sale of their children, will be rid of the charge of maintaining them after the first year.

Fifthly, this food would likewise bring great custom to taverns, where    25
the vintners will certainly be so prudent as to procure the best receipts for dressing it to perfection, and consequently have their houses frequented by all the fine gentlemen, who justly value themselves upon their knowledge in good

---

14. Tithes are taxes or levys, traditionally 10 percent of one's income, paid to the church or other authority. Swift blamed much of Ireland's poverty on large landowners who avoided church tithes by living and spending their money abroad.

eating; and a skillful cook, who understands how to oblige his guests, will contrive to make it as expensive as they please.

Sixthly, this would be a great inducement to marriage, which all wise 26 nations have either encouraged by rewards or enforced by laws and penalties. It would increase the care and tenderness of mothers toward their children, when they were sure of a settlement for life to the poor babes, provided in some sort by the public, to their annual profit instead of expense. We should see an honest emulation among the married women, which of them could bring the fattest child to the market. Men would become as fond of their wifes during the time of their pregnancy as they are now of their mares in foal, their cows in calf, or sows when they are ready to farrow; nor offer to beat or kick them (as is too frequent a practice) for fear of a miscarriage.

Many other advantages might be enumerated. For instance, the addition 27 of some thousand carcasses in our exportation of barreled beef, the propagation of swine's flesh, and improvement in the art of making good bacon, so much wanted among us by the great destruction of pigs, too frequent at our tables, which are no way comparable in taste or magnificence to a well-grown, fat, yearling child, which roasted whole will make a considerable figure at a lord mayor's feast or any other public entertainment. But this and many others I omit, being studious of brevity.

Supposing that one thousand families in this city would be constant customers for infants' flesh, besides others who might have it at merry meetings, 28 particularly weddings and christenings, I compute that Dublin would take off annually about twenty thousand carcasses, and the rest of the kingdom (where probably they will be sold somewhat cheaper) the remaining eighty thousand.

I can think of no one objection that will possibly be raised against this 29 proposal, unless it should be urged that the number of people will be thereby much lessened in the kingdom. This I freely own, and it was indeed one principal design in offering it to the world. I desire the reader will observe, that I calculate my remedy for this one individual kingdom of Ireland and for no other that ever was, is, or I think ever can be upon earth. Therefore let no man talk to me of other expedients:[15] of taxing our absentees at five shillings a pound: of using neither clothes nor household furniture except what is of our

15. The following are all measures that Swift himself proposed in various pamphlets.

own growth and manufacture: of utterly rejecting the materials and instruments that promote foreign luxury: of curing the expensiveness of pride, vanity, idleness, and gaming in our women: of introducing a vein of parsimony, prudence, and temperance: of learning to love our country, in the want of which we differ even from Laplanders and the inhabitants of Topinamboo:[16] of quitting our animosities and factions, nor acting any longer like the Jews, who were murdering one another at the very moment their city[17] was taken: of being a little cautious not to sell our country and conscience for nothing: of teaching landlords to have at least one degree of mercy toward their tenants: lastly, of putting a spirit of honesty, industry, and skill into our shopkeepers; who, if a resolution could now be taken to buy only our native goods, would immediately unite to cheat and exact upon us in the price, the measure, and the goodness, nor could ever yet be brought to make one fair proposal of just dealing, though often and earnestly invited to it.

Therefore I repeat, let no man talk to me of these and the like expedients, till he hath at least some glimpse of hope that there will ever be some hearty and sincere attempt to put them in practice. 30

But as to myself, having been wearied out for many years with offering vain, idle, visionary thoughts, and at length utterly despairing of success, I fortunately fell upon this proposal, which, as it is wholly new, so it hath something solid and real, of no expense and little trouble, full in our own power, and whereby we can incur no danger in disobliging England. For this kind of commodity will not bear exportation, the flesh being of too tender a consistence to admit a long continuance in salt, although perhaps I could name a country[18] which would be glad to eat up our whole nation without it. 31

After all, I am not so violently bent upon my own opinion as to reject any offer proposed by wise men, which shall be found equally innocent, cheap, easy, and effectual. But before something of that kind shall be advanced in contradiction to my scheme, and offering a better, I desire the author or authors will be pleased maturely to consider two points. First, as things now 32

16. The British of Swift's time would have considered the inhabitants of Lapland (region in northern Europe) and Topinamboo (area in the jungles of Brazil) highly uncivilized.

17. Jerusalem, sacked by the Romans in 70 CE.

18. England.

stand, how they will be able to find food and raiment for an hundred thousand useless mouths and backs. And secondly, there being a round million of creatures in human figure throughout this kingdom, whose sole subsistence put into a common stock would leave them in debt two millions of pounds sterling, adding those who are beggars by profession to the bulk of farmers, cottagers, and laborers, with their wives and children who are beggars in effect; I desire those politicians who dislike my overture, and may perhaps be so bold to attempt an answer, that they will first ask the parents of these mortals whether they would not at this day think it a great happiness to have been sold for food at a year old in the manner I prescribe, and thereby have avoided such a perpetual scene of misfortunes as they have since gone through by the oppression of landlords, the impossibility of paying rent without money or trade, the want of common sustenance, with neither house nor clothes to cover them from the inclemencies of the weather, and the most inevitable prospect of entailing the like or greater miseries upon their breed forever.

I profess, in the sincerity of my heart, that I have not the least personal 33 interest in endeavoring to promote this necessary work, having no other motive than the public good of my country, by advancing our trade, providing for infants, relieving the poor, and giving some pleasure to the rich. I have no children by which I can propose to get a single penny; the youngest being nine years old, and my wife past childbearing.

## UNDERSTANDING THE ESSAY

1. Jonathan Swift's essay is celebrated for its **IRONY**, which is sometimes misdefined as saying the opposite of what is meant. But Swift is not really arguing that the people of Ireland should not eat children. What is he **ARGUING**? (Clue: see paragraph 29.) How would you define irony based on this example?

2. **SATIRE** is writing that uses humor and sarcasm to expose—and sometimes correct—wrongdoing. Who are the wrongdoers addressed in Swift's great satire?

3. Swift's projector offers what he considers a serious solution to a serious problem. How would you describe the projector's personality and **TONE** of voice? How does using the persona of the projector contribute to Swift's irony throughout the essay? Give specific examples from the text.

4. In "A Modest Proposal," the projector uses both **PROCESS ANALYSIS** (how to solve Ireland's economic woes) and **CAUSE AND EFFECT** (the causes of Ireland's poverty

and moral condition; the effects of the proposed "improvements"). How do these two modes of exposition support the projector's logical argument?

5. Swift's persona is the soul of reason, yet what he proposes is so horrible and bizarre that any reader would reject it. Why do you think Swift resorts to the METAPHOR of cannibalism? How does it help him to critique arguments that depend on pure reason, even when the situations they address are truly desperate?

**THOMAS JEFFERSON**

# THE DECLARATION
# OF INDEPENDENCE

THOMAS JEFFERSON (1743–1826) was the third president of the United States and one of the country's Founding Fathers. A lawyer by training, he was also a philosopher and scholar. Charged with drafting the Declaration of Independence (1776), he was assisted by Benjamin Franklin, John Adams, and the Continental Congress. A model of the rational thinking of the Enlightenment, the Declaration is as much a timeless essay on tyranny and human rights as a legal document announcing the colonies' break with England. The version reprinted here is published on the website of the United States National Archives, www.archives.gov.

W HEN IN THE COURSE OF HUMAN EVENTS, it becomes necessary for one    1
people to dissolve the political bands which have connected them with another, and to assume among the powers of the earth, the separate and equal station to which the Laws of Nature and of Nature's God entitle them, a decent respect to the opinions of mankind requires that they should declare the causes which impel them to the separation.

We hold these truths to be self-evident, that all men are created equal,  2
that they are endowed by their Creator with certain unalienable Rights, that
among these are Life, Liberty and the pursuit of Happiness. That to secure
these rights, Governments are instituted among Men, deriving their just pow-

See p. 468 for argu-
ing from general
premises to a spe-
cific conclusion.
ers from the consent of the governed. That whenever any Form of
Government becomes destructive of these ends, it is the Right of
the People to alter or to abolish it, and to institute new Government, laying its foundation on such principles and organizing its powers in
such form, as to them shall seem most likely to effect their Safety and Happiness. Prudence, indeed, will dictate that Governments long established should
not be changed for light and transient causes; and accordingly all experience
hath shewn, that mankind are more disposed to suffer, while evils are suffer-
able, than to right themselves by abolishing the forms to which they are accustomed. But when a long train of abuses and usurpations pursuing invariably
the same Object evinces a design to reduce them under absolute Despotism, it
is their right, it is their duty, to throw off such Government, and to provide
new Guards for their future security. Such has been the patient sufferance of
these Colonies; and such is now the necessity which constrains them to alter
their former Systems of Government. The history of the present King of Great
Britain[1] is a history of repeated injuries and usurpations, all having in direct
object the establishment of absolute Tyranny over these States. To prove this,
let Facts be submitted to a candid world.

He has refused his Assent to Laws, the most wholesome and necessary  3
for the public good.

He has forbidden his Governors to pass Laws of immediate and pressing  4
importance, unless suspended in their operation till his Assent should be
obtained; and when so suspended, he has utterly neglected to attend to them.

He has refused to pass other Laws for the accommodation of large districts  5
of people, unless those people would relinquish the right of Representation in
the Legislature, a right inestimable to them and formidable to tyrants only.

He has called together legislative bodies at places unusual, uncomfort-  6
able, and distant from the depository of their public Records, for the sole purpose of fatiguing them into compliance with his measures.

---

1. George III (ruled 1760–1820).

He has dissolved Representative Houses repeatedly, for opposing with 7 manly firmness his invasions on the rights of the people.

He has refused for a long time, after such dissolutions, to cause others to 8 be elected; whereby the Legislative powers, incapable of Annihilation, have returned to the People at large for their exercise; the State remaining in the mean time exposed to all the dangers of invasion from without, and convulsions within.

He has endeavoured to prevent the population of these States; for that 9 purpose obstructing the Laws of Naturalization of Foreigners; refusing to pass others to encourage their migration hither, and raising the conditions of new Appropriations of Lands.

He has obstructed the Administration of Justice, by refusing his Assent 10 to Laws for establishing Judiciary powers.

He has made Judges dependent on his Will alone, for the tenure of their 11 offices, and the amount and payment of their salaries.

He has erected a multitude of New Offices, and sent hither swarms of 12 Officers to harass our people, and eat out their substance.

He has kept among us, in time of peace, Standing Armies without the 13 Consent of our legislatures.

He has affected to render the Military independent of and superior to the 14 Civil power.

He has combined with others to subject us to a jurisdiction foreign to 15 our constitution, and unacknowledged by our laws; giving his Assent to their acts of pretended Legislation:

For Quartering large bodies of armed troops among us: 16

For protecting them, by a mock Trial, from punishment for any Murders 17 which they should commit on the Inhabitants of these States:

For cutting off our Trade with all parts of the world: 18

For imposing Taxes on us without our Consent: 19

For depriving us in many cases, of the benefits of Trial by Jury: 20

For transporting us beyond the Seas to be tried for pretended offenses: 21

For abolishing the free System of English Laws in a neighbouring 22 Province, establishing therein an Arbitrary government, and enlarging its Boundaries so as to render it at once an example and fit instrument for introducing the same absolute rule into these Colonies:

For taking away our Charters, abolishing our most valuable Laws, and 23 altering fundamentally the Forms of our Governments:

For suspending our own Legislatures, and declaring themselves invested 24 with power to legislate for us in all cases whatsoever.

He has abdicated Government here, by declaring us out of his Protection 25 and waging War against us.

He has plundered our seas, ravaged our Coasts, burnt our towns and 26 destroyed the lives of our people.

He is at this time transporting large Armies of foreign Mercenaries to 27 compleat the works of death, desolation and tyranny, already begun with circumstances of Cruelty & perfidy scarcely paralleled in the most barbarous ages, and totally unworthy the Head of a civilized nation.

He has constrained our fellow Citizens taken Captive on the high Seas to 28 bear Arms against their Country, to become the executioners of their friends and Brethren, or to fall themselves by their Hands.

He has excited domestic insurrections amongst us, and has endeavoured 29 to bring on the inhabitants of our frontiers, the merciless Indian Savages, whose known rule of warfare, is an undistinguished destruction of all ages, sexes and conditions.

In every stage of these Oppressions We have Petitioned for Redress in 30 the most humble terms: Our repeated Petitions have been answered only by repeated injury. A Prince whose character is thus marked by every act which may define a Tyrant, is unfit to be the ruler of a free people.

Nor have We been wanting in attentions to our British brethren. We 31 have warned them from time to time of attempts by their legislature to extend an unwarrantable jurisdiction over us. We have reminded them of the circumstances of our emigration and settlement here. We have appealed to their native justice and magnanimity, and we have conjured them by the ties of our common kindred to disavow these usurpations, which would inevitably interrupt our connections and correspondence. They too have been deaf to the voice of justice and of consanguinity. We must, therefore acquiesce in the necessity, which denounces our Separation, and hold them, as we hold the rest of mankind, Enemies in War, in Peace Friends.

We, therefore, the Representatives of the United States of America, in 32 General Congress, Assembled, appealing to the Supreme Judge of the world for the rectitude of our intentions, do, in the Name, and by Authority of the good People of these Colonies, solemnly publish and declare, That these United Colonies are, and of Right ought to be Free and Independent States; that they are Absolved from all Allegiance to the British Crown, and that all political connection between them and the State of Great Britain, is and ought to be totally dissolved; and that as Free and Independent States, they have full Power to levy War, conclude Peace, contract Alliances, establish Commerce, and to do all other Acts and Things which Independent States may of right do. And for the support of this Declaration, with a firm reliance on the protection of divine Providence, we mutually pledge to each other our Lives, our Fortunes and our sacred Honor.

### UNDERSTANDING THE ESSAY

1. Thomas Jefferson's main **PURPOSE** in the Declaration of Independence is to declare the sovereignty of the United States. How and where does he use **CAUSE AND EFFECT** to help achieve this purpose?

2. How does Jefferson **DEFINE** what it means to be a tyrant? In what way does this definition help him achieve his main purpose?

3. The Declaration of Independence presents a logical **ARGUMENT**. How and where does Jefferson use **INDUCTION** (reasoning from specific instances to a general conclusion) to make the point that King George is indeed a tyrant?

4. Once Jefferson reaches this conclusion about King George, he uses it as the minor premise of a **DEDUCTIVE** argument (from general principles to specific conclusions). The conclusion of that argument is that "these United Colonies are, and of Right ought to be Free and Independent States" (32). What is the major premise of this deductive argument? Explain.

5. Jefferson refers to the British people as "our British brethren" (31). Why? What **AUDIENCE** does he have in mind here, and why would he need to convince them that his cause is just?

6. According to Jefferson and the other signers of the Declaration, what is the purpose of government, and where does a government get its authority? What form of government do they envision for the states, and how well does the Declaration make the case for this form of government? Explain.

# AIN'T I A WOMAN?

SOJOURNER TRUTH (c. 1797–1883) is the name assumed by Isabella Baumfree, who was born into slavery in Hurley, New York, and legally freed in 1827. Truth became a celebrated speaker for the causes of both abolition and women's rights. "Ain't I a Woman?" is the title usually given to a brief extemporaneous speech that Truth delivered at the Women's Rights Convention in Akron, Ohio, in 1851. Since what was passed down is a reported version of what Truth said, the speech is a composite of her words and the recollections of two individuals who witnessed it. The version reprinted here derives from the second published version, that of abolitionist writer and speaker Frances Dana Gage, in the *National Anti-Slavery Standard* on May 2, 1863. Gage added the title phrase "Ain't I a Woman?" and many specific details to Truth's plea for equal rights for women and blacks.

WELL, CHILDREN, WHERE THERE IS SO MUCH RACKET there must be some-  1
thing out of kilter. I think that 'twixt the negroes of the South and the
women at the North, all talking about rights, the white men will be in a fix
pretty soon. But what's all this here talking about?

That man over there says that women need to be helped into carriages,  2
and lifted over ditches, and to have the best place everywhere. Nobody ever
helps me into carriages, or over mud-puddles, or gives me any best place! And
ain't I a woman? Look at me! Look at my arm! I have ploughed and
planted, and gathered into barns, and no man could head me!          *Using personal
And ain't I a woman? I could work as much and eat as much as a       experience to make
                                                                     a point is discussed
man—when I could get it—and bear the lash as well! And ain't I a woman? I    on p. 466.*
have borne thirteen children, and seen most all sold off to slavery, and when I
cried out with my mother's grief, none but Jesus heard me! And ain't I a woman?

Then they talk about this thing in the head; what's this they call it?  3
[member of audience whispers, "intellect"] That's it, honey. What's that got
to do with women's rights or negroes' rights? If my cup won't hold but a pint,
and yours holds a quart, wouldn't you be mean not to let me have my little half
measure full?

Then that little man in black there, he says women can't have as much  4
rights as men, 'cause Christ wasn't a woman! Where did your Christ come
from? Where did your Christ come from? From God and a woman! Man had
nothing to do with Him.

If the first woman God ever made was strong enough to turn the world  5
upside down all alone, these women together ought to be able to turn it back,
and get it right side up again! And now they is asking to do it, the men better
let them.

Obliged to you for hearing me, and now old Sojourner ain't got nothing  6
more to say.

## UNDERSTANDING THE ESSAY

1. What "racket" is Truth referring to in the opening paragraph of her speech? What
   is "out of kilter" in her view and that of the other women who attended the convention? What solution to this imbalance do they propose?

2. What **EVIDENCE** does Truth offer to support her **CLAIM** that women are equal to
   men? How sufficient is that evidence to prove her point? Explain.

3. If women want to set the world right again, Truth argues, "the men better let them" (5). Does this part of her ARGUMENT appeal mostly to the listener's intellect ("this thing in the head"), emotions, or sense of ethics (3)? Explain.

4. Why does Truth address her AUDIENCE as "children" (1)? Is this an effective strategy? Why or why not?

5. What is Truth's point in drawing an ANALOGY between "these women" and Eve (5)?

6. The title "Ain't I a Woman?" is also a RHETORICAL QUESTION. What is the effect of repeating it four times in this short speech?

## ABRAHAM LINCOLN

# SECOND INAUGURAL ADDRESS

ABRAHAM LINCOLN (1809–1865) was the sixteenth president of the United States. Largely self-taught, Lincoln studied law and spent eight years in the Illinois state legislature before being elected president in 1860. By the time Lincoln took office, seven states had seceded from the Union, and his first inaugural address was a conciliatory speech calling for national unity. Four years later, slavery had been abolished and the Civil War (1861–1865) was drawing to a close. Lincoln's Second Inaugural Address was delivered on March 4, 1865, two months before the war ended; several weeks after delivering these words, he was assassinated.

A T THIS SECOND APPEARING to take the oath of the presidential office, there is less occasion for an extended address than there was at the first. Then a statement, somewhat in detail, of a course to be pursued, seemed fitting and proper. Now, at the expiration of four years, during which public declarations have been constantly called forth on every point and phase of the great contest which still absorbs the attention, and engrosses the energies of the nation, little that is new could be presented. The progress of our arms, upon which all

1

else chiefly depends, is as well known to the public as to myself; and it is, I trust, reasonably satisfactory and encouraging to all. With high hope for the future, no prediction in regard to it is ventured.

On the occasion corresponding to this four years ago, all thoughts were　2 anxiously directed to an impending civil war. All dreaded it—all sought to avert it. While the inaugural address was being delivered from this place, devoted altogether to *saving* the Union without war, insurgent agents were in the city seeking to *destroy* it without war—seeking to dissolve the Union, and divide effects, by negotiation.[1] Both parties deprecated war; but one of them would *make* war rather than let the nation survive; and the other would *accept* war rather than let it perish. And the war came.

One-eighth of the whole population were colored slaves, not distributed　3 generally over the Union, but localized in the Southern part of it. These slaves constituted a peculiar and powerful interest. All knew that this interest was, somehow, the cause of the war. To strengthen, perpetuate, and extend this interest was the object for which the insurgents would rend the Union, even by war; while the government claimed no right to do more than to restrict the ter-

Page 423 suggests when to weave a cause-and-effect analysis into an argument.

ritorial enlargement of it. Neither party expected for the war, the magnitude, or the duration, which it has already attained. Neither anticipated that the *cause* of the conflict might cease with, or even before, the conflict itself should cease. Each looked for an easier triumph, and a result less fundamental and astounding. Both read the same Bible, and pray to the same God; and each invokes His aid against the other. It may seem strange that any men should dare to ask a just God's assistance in wringing their bread from the sweat of other men's faces; but let us judge not that we be not judged.[2] The prayers of both could not be answered; that of neither has been answered fully. The Almighty has His own purposes. "Woe unto the world because of offenses! for it must needs be that offenses come; but woe

---

1. Prior to the start of the Civil War, representatives from the slave-holding states attempted to convince the federal government to allow them to secede and form their own union.

2. "Let us judge not" alludes to Jesus's Sermon on the Mount ("Judge not, that ye be not judged") in Matthew 7:1; "wringing their bread from the sweat of other men's faces" alludes to God's curse on Adam ("In the sweat of thy face shalt thou eat bread") in Genesis 3:19.

to that man by whom the offense cometh!"[3] If we shall suppose that American slavery is one of those offenses which, in the providence of God, must needs come, but which, having continued through His appointed time, He now wills to remove, and that He gives to both North and South, this terrible war, as the woe due to those by whom the offense came, shall we discern therein any departure from those divine attributes which the believers in a Living God always ascribe to Him? Fondly do we hope—fervently do we pray—that this mighty scourge of war may speedily pass away. Yet, if God wills that it continue, until all the wealth piled by the bondman's two hundred and fifty years of unrequited toil shall be sunk, and until every drop of blood drawn with the lash, shall be paid by another drawn with the sword, as was said three thousand years ago, so still it must be said, "the judgments of the Lord are true and righteous altogether."[4]

With malice toward none; with charity for all; with firmness in the right, as God gives us to see the right, let us strive on to finish the work we are in; to bind up the nation's wounds; to care for him who shall have borne the battle, and for his widow, and his orphan—to do all which may achieve and cherish a just, and a lasting peace, among ourselves, and with all nations.     4

### UNDERSTANDING THE ESSAY

1. Compared to the inaugural speeches of most presidents, Abraham Lincoln's Second Inaugural Address is remarkably short. Why? What is the main **PURPOSE** of his speech, and what knowledge (and sentiment) does he assume on the part of his **AUDIENCE** in order to accomplish that purpose in so few words?

2. Lincoln calls for action "[w]ith malice toward none; with charity for all," including the people of the vanquished Southern states (4). Unlike his first inaugural address, this second one is delivered from a position of strength. How and where, then, does the author counterbalance conciliatory language like this with "firmness" (4)?

3. As he contemplates the opposing sides in the war, Lincoln reasons that "[n]either anticipated that the *cause* of the conflict might cease with, or even before, the conflict itself should cease" (3). If the still-continuing conflict is the effect, what is the great *cause* to which Lincoln refers? For what purpose does Lincoln use **CAUSE AND EFFECT** in this speech? What point is he making here?

3. From Matthew 18:7, Jesus's speech to his disciples.
4. From Psalms 19:9.

4. Toward the middle of paragraph 3 ("If we shall suppose . . ."), Lincoln uses logical reasoning to make the **ARGUMENT** that the Civil War and all its woes are, in some measure, the will of God. How valid is his reasoning here? Explain.

5. **COMPARE AND CONTRAST** Lincoln's Second Inaugural Address with Martin Luther King Jr.'s "I Have a Dream" (p. 571) as appeals to their audiences' sense of right and wrong in time of crisis. Compare the strategies each writer uses to lay out the challenges he sees ahead and to motivate his audience to meet them. Which man comes across as the more credible speaker? Explain why by pointing to specific passages in the texts.

# HOW IT FEELS
# TO BE COLORED ME

Zora Neale Hurston (1891–1960), an anthropologist, folklorist, and writer, was a central figure of the Harlem Renaissance of the 1920s and 1930s. Hurston was born in Notasulga, Alabama, and grew up in Eatonville, Florida, the daughter of a preacher and a seamstress. She received a BA from Barnard College, where she studied anthropology and developed an interest in the folk traditions that would infuse her short stories and novels, such as *Their Eyes Were Watching God* (1937). Just as Hurston was finishing her studies at Barnard, "How It Feels to Be Colored Me" was published in *World Tomorrow* (1928), a magazine founded by the Fellowship of Reconciliation, a religious group devoted to nonviolence. It was later included in *I Love Myself When I Am Laughing ... and Then Again When I Am Looking Mean and Impressive*, a volume of Hurston's writing edited by the writer Alice Walker.

I AM COLORED but I offer nothing in the way of extenuating circumstances 1 except the fact that I am the only Negro in the United States whose grandfather on the mother's side was not an Indian chief.

I remember the very day that I became colored. Up to my thirteenth year 2 I lived in the little Negro town of Eatonville, Florida. It is exclusively a colored town. The only white people I knew passed through the town going to or coming from Orlando. The native whites rode dusty horses, the Northern tourists chugged down the sandy village road in automobiles. The town knew the Southerners and never stopped cane chewing[1] when they passed. But the Northerners were something else again. They were peered at cautiously from behind curtains by the timid. The more venturesome would come out on the porch to watch them go past and got just as much pleasure out of the tourists as the tourists got out of the village.

The front porch might seem a daring place for the rest of the town, but 3 it was a gallery seat for me. My favorite place was atop the gate-post. Proscenium box for a born first-nighter. Not only did I enjoy the show, but I didn't mind the actors knowing that I liked it. I usually spoke to them in passing. I'd wave at them and when they returned my salute, I would say something like this: "Howdy-do-well-I-thank-you-where-you-goin'?" Usually automobile or the horse paused at this, and after a queer exchange of compliments, I would probably "go a piece of the way" with them, as we say in farthest Florida. If one of my family happened to come to the front in time to see me, of course negotiations would be rudely broken off. But even so, it is clear that I was the first "welcome-to-our-state" Floridian, and I hope the Miami Chamber of Commerce will please take notice.

During this period, white people differed from colored to me only in that 4 they rode through town and never lived there. They liked to hear me "speak pieces" and sing and wanted to see me dance the parse-me-la, and gave me generously of their small silver for doing these things, which seemed strange to me for I wanted to do them so much that I needed bribing to stop. Only they didn't know it. The colored people gave no dimes. They deplored any joyful tendencies in me, but I was their Zora nevertheless. I belonged to them, to the nearby hotels, to the county—everybody's Zora.

1. Chewing sugarcane.

But changes came in the family when I was thirteen, and I was sent to  5
school in Jacksonville. I left Eatonville, the town of the oleanders,² as Zora.
When I disembarked from the river-boat at Jacksonville, she was no more. It
seemed that I had suffered a sea change. I was not Zora of Orange County any
more, I was now a little colored girl. I found it out in certain ways. In my heart
as well as in the mirror, I became a fast brown—warranted not to rub nor run.

But I am not tragically colored. There is no great sorrow dammed up in my  6
soul, nor lurking behind my eyes. I do not mind at all. I do not belong to the
sobbing school of Negrohood who hold that nature somehow has given them a
lowdown dirty deal and whose feelings are all hurt about it. Even in the helter-
skelter skirmish that is my life, I have seen that the world is to the strong
regardless of a little pigmentation more or less. No, I do not weep at the
world—I am too busy sharpening my oyster knife.³

Someone is always at my elbow reminding me that I am the granddaugh-  7
ter of slaves. It fails to register depression with me. Slavery is sixty years in
the past. The operation was successful and the patient is doing well, thank
you. The terrible struggle⁴ that made me an American out of a potential slave
said "On the line!" The Reconstruction said "Get set!"; and the generation
before said "Go!" I am off to a flying start and I must not halt in the stretch to
look behind and weep. Slavery is the price I paid for civilization, and the choice
was not with me. It is a bully adventure and worth all that I have paid through
my ancestors for it. No one on earth ever had a greater chance for glory. The
world to be won and nothing to be lost. It is thrilling to think—to know that
for any act of mine, I shall get twice as much praise or twice as much blame. It
is quite exciting to hold the center of the national stage, with the spectators
not knowing whether to laugh or to weep.

The position of my white neighbor is much more difficult. No brown  8
specter pulls up a chair beside me when I sit down to eat. No dark ghost thrusts

2. Fragrant tropical flowers, common in the South.

3. Reference to the idiom "the world is my oyster," meaning that someone feels in control of
the world and able to receive anything it offers.

4. The Civil War. The Reconstruction was the period immediately following the war; one of
its effects was that northern educators came South to teach newly freed slaves.

its leg against mine in bed. The game of keeping what one has is never so exciting as the game of getting.

I do not always feel colored. Even now I often achieve the unconscious   9
Zora of Eatonville before the Hegira.[5] I feel most colored when I am thrown against a sharp white background.

For instance at Barnard. "Beside the waters of the Hudson"[6] I feel my   10
race. Among the thousand white persons, I am a dark rock surged upon, and overswept, but through it all, I remain myself. When covered by the waters, I am; and the ebb but reveals me again.

Sometimes it is the other way around. A white person is set down in our   11
midst, but the contrast is just as sharp for me. For instance, when I sit in the drafty basement that is The New World Cabaret with a white person, my color comes. We enter chatting about any little nothing that we have in common and are seated by the jazz waiters. In the abrupt way that jazz orchestras have, this one plunges into a number. It loses no time in circumlocutions, but gets

Figures of speech,   right down to business. It constricts the thorax and splits the heart
p. 74, can help to   with its tempo and narcotic harmonies. This orchestra grows ram-
make your writing   bunctious, rears on its hind legs and attacks the tonal veil with
vivid.

primitive fury, rending it, clawing it until it breaks through to the jungle beyond. I follow those heathen—follow them exultingly. I dance wildly inside myself; I yell within, I whoop; I shake my assegai[7] above my head, I hurl it true to the mark *yeeeeooww!* I am in the jungle and living in the jungle way. My face is painted red and yellow and my body is painted blue. My pulse is throbbing like a war drum. I want to slaughter something—give pain, give death to what, I do not know. But the piece ends. The men of the orchestra wipe their lips and rest their fingers. I creep back slowly to the veneer we call civilization with the last tone and find the white friend sitting motionless in his seat, smoking calmly.

5. Journey undertaken away from a dangerous situation into a more highly desirable one (literally, the flight of Muhammad from Mecca in 622 CE).

6. Barnard, an American women's college in New York City, located near the Hudson River; cf. the psalmist's "by the waters of Babylon."

7. South African hunting spear.

"Good music they have here," he remarks, drumming the table with his fingertips. 12

Music. The great blobs of purple and red emotion have not touched him. He has only heard what I felt. He is far away and I see him but dimly across the ocean and the continent that have fallen between us. He is so pale with his whiteness then and I am *so* colored. 13

At certain times I have no race, I am *me*. When I set my hat at a certain angle and saunter down Seventh Avenue, Harlem City, feeling as snooty as the lions in front of the Forty-Second Street Library, for instance. So far as my feelings are concerned, Peggy Hopkins Joyce on the Boule Mich[8] with her gorgeous raiment, stately carriage, knees knocking together in a most aristocratic manner, has nothing on me. The cosmic Zora emerges. I belong to no race nor time. I am the eternal feminine with its string of beads. 14

I have no separate feeling about being an American citizen and colored. I am merely a fragment of the Great Soul that surges within the boundaries. My country, right or wrong. 15

Sometimes, I feel discriminated against, but it does not make me angry. It merely astonishes me. How *can* any deny themselves the pleasure of my company? It's beyond me. 16

But in the main, I feel like a brown bag of miscellany propped against a wall. Against a wall in company with other bags, white, red and yellow. Pour out the contents, and there is discovered a jumble of small things priceless and worthless. A first-water diamond, an empty spool, bits of broken glass, lengths of string, a key to a door long since crumbled away, a rusty knife-blade, old shoes saved for a road that never was and never will be, a nail bent under the weight of things too heavy for any nail, a dried flower or two still a little fragrant. In your hand is the brown bag. On the ground before you is the jumble it held—so much like the jumble in the bags, could they be emptied, that all might be dumped in a single heap and the bags refilled without altering the content of any greatly. A bit of colored glass more or less would not matter. Perhaps that is how the Great Stuffer of Bags filled them in the first place—who knows? 17

8. Peggy Hopkins Joyce (1893–1957), American beauty and fashion-setter of the twenties; "Boule Mich," Boulevard Saint-Michel, a fashionable Parisian street.

## UNDERSTANDING THE ESSAY

1. Zora Neale Hurston's essay originally appeared in a magazine intended for a liberal Christian readership. How and where does she seem to be appealing directly to such an **AUDIENCE**? Point to specific passages in the text.

2. Hurston's essay tells the story of how she "became colored" (2). What happened to bring about this transformation? When and why did she feel her race most deeply?

3. Hurston refers to the front porch of her childhood home in Eatonville as a "gallery" and to the passers-by as "actors" (3). Where else in her essay does she use terms from the theater to describe her experience of race in America? What are some of the implications of such **METAPHORS**?

4. Hurston ends her essay by **COMPARING** the contents of a mixed bag of odds and ends. What is the point of this comparison, and what does it convey about Hurston's sense of personal identity?

# MARTIN LUTHER KING JR.

# I HAVE A DREAM

MARTIN LUTHER KING JR. (1929–1968) was a Baptist minister and civil rights activist known for his doctrine of nonviolent protest. A graduate of Morehouse College and Crozer Theological Seminary, he was awarded a PhD in theology from Boston University in 1955. That same year, King was selected by the local chapter of the National Association for the Advancement of Colored People (NAACP) to lead a boycott of the segregated bus system in Montgomery, Alabama. The boycott resulted in a Supreme Court ruling banning racial segregation on the city's buses. After this landmark case, King used his newly attained national stature to speak and demonstrate tirelessly in the cause of civil rights. His efforts culminated in the peaceful march on Washington, D.C., in 1963 of more than a quarter-million protesters, to whom he delivered his "I Have a Dream" address from the steps of the Lincoln Memorial. The next year King received the Nobel Peace Prize. He was assassinated on April 4, 1968, in Memphis, Tennessee.

FIVE SCORE YEARS AGO, a great American, in whose symbolic shadow we stand, signed the Emancipation Proclamation.[1] This momentous decree came as a great beacon light of hope to millions of Negro slaves who had been seared in the flames of withering injustice. It came as a joyous daybreak to end the long night of captivity.

But one hundred years later, we must face the tragic fact that the Negro is still not free. One hundred years later, the life of the Negro is still sadly crippled by the manacles of segregation and the chains of discrimination. One hundred years later, the Negro lives on a lonely island of poverty in the midst of a vast ocean of material prosperity. One hundred years later, the Negro is still languishing in the corners of American society and finds himself an exile in his own land. So we have come here today to dramatize an appalling condition.

In a sense we have come to our nation's capital to cash a check. When the architects of our republic wrote the magnificent words of the Constitution and the Declaration of Independence, they were signing a promissory note to which every American was to fall heir. This note was a promise that all men would be guaranteed the inalienable rights of life, liberty, and the pursuit of happiness.

It is obvious today that America has defaulted on this promissory note insofar as her citizens of color are concerned. Instead of honoring this sacred obligation, America has given the Negro people a bad check which has come back marked "insufficient funds." But we refuse to believe that the bank of justice is bankrupt. We refuse to believe that there are insufficient funds in the great vaults of opportunity of this nation. So we have come to cash this check—a check that will give us upon demand the riches of freedom and the security of justice. We have also come to this hallowed spot to remind America of the fierce urgency of *now*. This is no time to engage in the luxury of cooling off or to take the tranquilizing drug of gradualism. *Now* is the time to rise from the dark and desolate valley of segregation to the sunlit path of racial justice. *Now* is the time to open the doors of opportunity to all of God's children. *Now* is the time to lift our nation from the quicksands of racial injustice to the solid rock of brotherhood.

---

1. In 1863, President Abraham Lincoln signed a decree declaring that "all persons held as slaves within any States . . . shall be then, thenceforward, and forever free."

It would be fatal for the nation to overlook the urgency of the moment  5
and to underestimate the determination of the Negro. This sweltering summer
of the Negro's legitimate discontent will not pass until there is an invigorating
autumn of freedom and equality. Nineteen sixty-three is not an end, but a
beginning. Those who hope that the Negro needed to blow off steam and will
now be content will have a rude awakening if the nation returns to business as
usual. There will be neither rest nor tranquility in America until the Negro is
granted his citizenship rights. The whirlwinds of revolt will continue to shake
the foundations of our nation until the bright day of justice emerges.

But there is something that I must say to my people who stand on the  6
warm threshold which leads into the palace of justice. In the process of gaining
our rightful place we must not be guilty of wrongful deeds. Let us
not seek to satisfy our thirst for freedom by drinking from the
cup of bitterness and hatred.

See p. 472 for antici-
pating objections to
an argument.

We must forever conduct our struggle on the high plane of dignity and  7
discipline. We must not allow our creative protest to degenerate into physical
violence. Again and again we must rise to the majestic heights of meeting
physical force with soul force. The marvelous new militancy which has
engulfed the Negro community must not lead us to distrust of all white people,
for many of our white brothers, as evidenced by their presence here today,
have come to realize that their destiny is tied up with our destiny and their
freedom is inextricably bound to our freedom. We cannot walk alone.

And as we walk, we must make the pledge that we shall march ahead. We  8
cannot turn back. There are those who are asking the devotees of civil rights,
"When will you be satisfied?" We can never be satisfied as long as our bodies,
heavy with the fatigue of travel, cannot gain lodging in the motels of the
highways and the hotels of the cities. We cannot be satisfied as long as the
Negro's basic mobility is from a smaller ghetto to a larger one. We can never
be satisfied as long as a Negro in Mississippi cannot vote and a Negro in
New York believes he has nothing for which to vote. No, no, we are not satisfied, and we will not be satisfied until justice rolls down like waters and righ-
teousness like a mighty stream.

I am not unmindful that some of you have come here out of great trials  9
and tribulations. Some of you have come fresh from narrow cells. Some of you
have come from areas where your quest for freedom left you battered by the

storms of persecution and staggered by the winds of police brutality. You have been the veterans of creative suffering. Continue to work with the faith that unearned suffering is redemptive.

Go back to Mississippi, go back to Alabama, go back to Georgia, go back    10
to Louisiana, go back to the slums and ghettos of our northern cities, knowing that somehow this situation can and will be changed. Let us not wallow in the valley of despair.

I say to you today, my friends, that in spite of the difficulties and frus-    11
trations of the moment, I still have a dream. It is a dream deeply rooted in the American dream.

I have a dream that one day this nation will rise up and live out the true    12
meaning of its creed: "We hold these truths to be self-evident: that all men are created equal."

I have a dream that one day on the red hills of Georgia the sons of former    13
slaves and the sons of former slaveowners will be able to sit down together at a table of brotherhood.

I have a dream that one day even the state of Mississippi, a desert state,    14
sweltering with the heat of injustice and oppression, will be transformed into an oasis of freedom and justice.

I have a dream that my four children will one day live in a nation where    15
they will not be judged by the color of their skin but by the content of their character.

I have a dream today.    16

I have a dream that one day the state of Alabama, whose governor's lips    17
are presently dripping with the words of interposition and nullification,[2] will be transformed into a situation where little black boys and black girls will be able to join hands with little white boys and white girls and walk together as sisters and brothers.

I have a dream today.    18

I have a dream that one day every valley shall be exalted, every hill and    19
mountain shall be made low, the rough places will be made plain, and the

2. George Wallace (1919–1998), governor of Alabama, was a fierce opponent of the civil rights movement. In 1963 he defied U.S. law and mounted a campaign against the integration of Alabama public schools.

crooked places will be made straight, and the glory of the Lord shall be revealed, and all flesh shall see it together.[3]

This is our hope. This is the faith with which I return to the South. With this faith we will be able to hew out of the mountain of despair a stone of hope. With this faith we will be able to transform the jangling discords of our nation into a beautiful symphony of brotherhood. With this faith we will be able to work together, to pray together, to struggle together, to go to jail together, to stand up for freedom together, knowing that we will be free one day. [20]

This will be the day when all of God's children will be able to sing with a new meaning, "My country, 'tis of thee, sweet land of liberty, of thee I sing. Land where my fathers died, land of the pilgrim's pride, from every mountain-side, let freedom ring." [21]

And if America is to be a great nation this must become true. So let freedom ring from the prodigious hilltops of New Hampshire. Let freedom ring from the mighty mountains of New York. Let freedom ring from the heightening Alleghenies of Pennsylvania! [22]

Let freedom ring from the snowcapped Rockies of Colorado! [23]

Let freedom ring from the curvaceous peaks of California! [24]

But not only that; let freedom ring from Stone Mountain of Georgia![4] [25]

Let freedom ring from Lookout Mountain of Tennessee![5] [26]

Let freedom ring from every hill and every molehill of Mississippi. From every mountainside, let freedom ring. [27]

When we let freedom ring, when we let it ring from every village and every hamlet, from every state and every city, we will be able to speed up that day when all of God's children, black men and white men, Jews and Gentiles, Protestants and Catholics, will be able to join hands and sing in the words of the old Negro spiritual, "Free at last! free at last! thank God Almighty, we are free at last!" [28]

---

3. King is quoting a famous passage from the book of Isaiah (40:4–5).

4. The figures of three leaders of the Confederacy are carved onto the face of Stone Mountain, near Atlanta.

5. Site of a major battle during the Civil War in 1863.

## UNDERSTANDING THE SPEECH

1. Speaking in 1963, a hundred years after slavery was abolished by President Lincoln's Emancipation Proclamation, Martin Luther King Jr. tells his **AUDIENCE** that African Americans still are "not free" (2). Why not? How and where does he **DESCRIBE** this "appalling condition" (2)?

2. King uses his description of segregation as the basis for an **ARGUMENT**. What is the central **CLAIM** of that argument? What does King ask his audience to do about the situation he describes?

3. What does King mean by "the tranquilizing drug of gradualism"(4)? Why does he warn his audience to resist it?

4. King does not describe his "dream" until almost midway through his speech (11). Why? How does the first half of King's address help to prepare his audience for the vision of the future he presents in the second half?

5. In King's vision, the oppressed do not rise up and crush their oppressors. Why not? How do the details by which he **DEFINES** his dream fit in with what King tells his audience in paragraphs 6–7 and with his general philosophy of nonviolence?

6. King relies heavily on **FIGURES OF SPEECH** throughout his address, particularly **METAPHOR**: the nation has given its black citizens a "bad check" (4); racial injustice is "quicksands" (4); brotherhood is a "table" (13); freedom is a bell that rings from the "hilltops" (22). Choose several of these figures that you find effective, and explain how they help King to **COMPARE AND CONTRAST** the "appalling condition" of the past and present with his brighter vision for the future.

# APPENDIX
# USING SOURCES IN YOUR WRITING

•———————————————————————•

Whatever your purpose, academic research requires finding sources of information that go well beyond your own immediate knowledge of a subject. If you're examining an issue discussed in one of the selections that appear in this book—the role war memorials play in learning about history or the way technology influences our relationships—it's likely that you will need to consult additional sources. This appendix shows how to find reliable sources, use what you learn in your own writing, and document your sources accurately.

## FINDING AND EVALUATING SOURCES

As you do your research, you will encounter a wide range of potential sources—print and online, general and specialized, published and firsthand. You'll need to evaluate these sources carefully, choose the ones that best support your thesis, and decide how to incorporate each source into your own paper.

### Finding Appropriate Sources

The kinds of sources you turn to will depend on your topic. If you're doing research on a literary or historical topic, you might consult scholarly books and articles and standard reference works such as *The Dictionary of American Biography* or the *Literary History of the United States*. If your research is aimed at a current issue, you would likely consult newspapers and other periodicals, websites, and recent books.

Check your assignment to see if you are required to use primary or secondary sources—or both. PRIMARY SOURCES* are original works, such as

*Words printed in SMALL CAPITALS are defined in the Glossary/Index.

historical documents, literary works, eyewitness accounts, diaries, letters, and lab studies, as well as any original field research you do. SECONDARY SOURCES include books and articles, reviews, biographies, and other works that interpret or discuss primary sources. For example, novels and poems are primary sources; articles interpreting them are secondary sources.

Whether a work is considered primary or secondary often depends on your topic and purpose. If you're analyzing a poem, a critic's article analyzing the poem is a secondary source—but if you're investigating the critic's work, the article would be a primary source.

## LIBRARY SOURCES

When you conduct academic research, it is often better to start with your library's website rather than with a commercial search engine such as *Google*. Library websites provide access to a range of well-organized resources, including scholarly databases through which you can access authoritative articles that have been screened by librarians or specialists in a particular field. In general, there are three kinds of sources you'll want to consult: reference works, books, and periodicals.

- *Reference works.* The reference section of your school's library is the place to find encyclopedias, dictionaries, atlases, almanacs, bibliographies, and other reference works. Remember, though, that reference works are only a starting point, a place where you can get an overview of your topic or basic facts about it. Some reference works are *general,* such as *The New Encyclopaedia Britannica* or the *Statistical Abstract of the United States.* Others are *specialized,* providing in-depth information on a single field or topic.

- *Books.* The library catalog is your main source for finding books. Most catalogs are computerized and can be accessed through the library's website. You can search by author, title, subject, or keyword. When you click on a specific source, you'll find more bibliographic data about author, title, and publication; the call number (which identifies the book's location on the library's shelves); related subject headings (which may lead to other useful materials in the library)—and more.

- **Periodicals.** To find journal and magazine articles, you will need to search periodical indexes and databases. Indexes (such as the *New York Times Index*) provide listings of articles organized by topics; databases (such as LexisNexis) provide the full texts. Although some databases are available for free, many can be accessed by subscription through your library.

## ONLINE SOURCES

The web offers countless sites sponsored by governments, educational institutions, organizations, businesses, and individuals. Because it is so vast and dynamic, however, finding useful information can be a challenge. There are several ways to search the web:

- **Keyword searches.** *Google, Bing,* and other search sites scan the web looking for the keywords you specify.

- **Metasearches.** *Yippy, SurfWax,* and *Dogpile* let you use several search engines simultaneously.

- **Academic searches.** For peer-reviewed academic writing in many disciplines, try *Google Scholar*; or use *Scirus* for scientific, technical, and medical documents.

Although many websites provide authoritative information, keep in mind that web content varies greatly in its stability and reliability: what you see on a site today may be different (or gone) tomorrow. So save or make copies of pages you plan to use, and carefully evaluate what you find. Here are just a few of the many resources available on the web.

- **Indexes, databases, and directories.** Information put together by specialists and grouped by topics can be especially helpful. You may want to consult *The World Wide Web Virtual Library* (a catalog of websites on numerous subjects, compiled by experts); or in subject directories such as those provided by *Google* and *Yahoo!*

- **News sites.** Many newspapers, magazines, and radio and TV stations have websites that provide both up-to-the-minute information and also archives of older news articles. Through *Google News* and *NewsLink,* for example, you can access current news worldwide, whereas *Google News Archive Search* has files going back to the 1700s.

- *Government sites.* Many government agencies and departments maintain websites where you can find government reports, statistics, legislative information, and other resources. *USA.gov* offers information, services, and other resources from the U.S. government.

- *Digital archives.* These sites collect and organize materials from the past—including drawings, maps, recordings, speeches, and historic documents—often focusing on a particular subject or country. For example, the National Archives and Records Administration and the Library of Congress both archive items relevant to the culture and history of the United States.

- *Discussion lists and forums.* Online mailing lists, newsgroups, discussion groups, and forums let members post and receive messages from other members. To join a discussion with people who are knowledgeable about your topic, try searching for your topic—for example, for "E. B. White discussion forum." Or consult a site such as *Google Groups.*

### SEARCHING ELECTRONICALLY

When you search for subjects on the web or in library catalogs, indexes, or databases, you'll want to come up with keywords that will lead to the information you need. Specific commands vary among search engines and databases, but most search engines now offer "Advanced Search" options that allow you to narrow your search by typing keywords into text boxes labeled as follows:

- All of these words
- The exact phrase
- Any of these words
- None of these words

In addition, you may filter the results to include only full-text articles (articles that are available in full online); only certain domains (such as *.edu*, for educational sites; *.gov*, for government sites; or *.org*, for nonprofit sites); and, in library databases, only scholarly, peer-reviewed sites. Type quotation marks around words to search for an exact phrase: "Twitter revolution" or "Neil Gaiman."

Some databases may require you to limit searches through the use of various symbols or Boolean operators (AND, OR, NOT). See the Advanced Search instructions for help with such symbols, which may be called *field tags*.

If a search turns up too many sources, be more specific (*homeopathy* instead of *medicine*). If your original keywords don't generate good results, try synonyms (*home remedy* instead of *folk medicine*). Keep in mind that searching requires flexibility, both in the words you use and the methods you try.

## Evaluating Sources

Searching the *Health Source* database for information on the incidence of meningitis among college students, you find seventeen articles. An "exact words" *Google* search yields thirty-seven. How do you decide which sources to read? The following questions can help you select reliable and useful sources.

- *Is the source relevant?* Look at the title and at any introductory material to see what it covers. Does the source appear to relate directly to your purpose? What will it add to your work?

- *What are the author's credentials?* Has the author written other works on this subject? Is he or she known for taking a particular position on it? If the author's credentials are not stated, you might do a web search to see what else you can learn about him or her.

- *What is the stance?* Does the source cover various points of view or advocate only one perspective? Does its title suggest a certain slant? If you're evaluating a website, check to see whether it includes links to sites expressing other perspectives.

- *Who is the publisher?* Books published by university presses and articles in scholarly journals are peer-reviewed by experts in the field before they are published. Those produced for a general audience do not always undergo such rigorous review and factchecking. At well-established publishing houses, however, submissions are usually vetted by experienced editors or even editorial boards.

- *If the source is a website, who is the sponsor?* Is the site maintained by an organization, interest group, government agency, or individual? If the site doesn't give this information on its homepage, look for clues in the URL domain: *.edu* is used mostly by colleges and universities, *.gov* by government agencies, *.org* by nonprofit organizations, *.mil* by the military, and

*.com* by commercial organizations. Be aware that the sponsor may have an agenda—to argue a position, present biased information, or sell a product—and that text on the site does not necessarily undergo rigorous review or factchecking.

- *What is the level of the material?* Texts written for a general audience might be easier to understand but may not be authoritative enough for academic work. Scholarly texts will be more authoritative but may be harder to comprehend.

- *How current is the source?* Check to see when books and articles were published and when websites were last updated. (If a site lists no date, see if links to other sites still work; if not, the site is probably too dated to use.) A recent publication date or updating, however, does not necessarily mean the source is better—some topics require current information whereas others call for older sources.

- *Does the source include other useful information?* Is there a bibliography that might lead you to additional materials? How current or authoritative are the sources it cites?

## Taking Notes

When you find material that will be useful to your argument, take careful notes.

- *Use index cards, a computer file, or a notebook,* labeling each entry with information that will allow you to keep track of where it comes from—author, title, the pages or the URL, and (for online sources) the date of access.

- *Take notes in your own words and use your own sentence patterns.* If you make a note that is a detailed paraphrase, label it as such so that you'll know to provide appropriate documentation if you use it.

- *If you find wording that you'd like to quote,* enclose the exact words in quotation marks to distinguish the source's words from your own.

- *Label each note with a subject heading* so you can organize your notes easily when constructing an outline for your paper.

# INCORPORATING SOURCE MATERIALS INTO YOUR TEXT

There are many ways to incorporate source materials into your own text. Three of the most common are quoting, paraphrasing, or summarizing. Let's look at the differences among these three forms of reference, and then consider when to use each one and how to work these references into your text.

## Quoting

When you quote someone else's words, you reproduce their language exactly, in quotation marks—though you can add your own words in brackets or omit unnecessary words in the original by using ellipsis marks ( . . . ). This example from Mary Roach's "How to Know If You Are Dead" uses all of these conventions:

> In her analysis of the life-saving role of human cadavers, Mary Roach notes that "a gurney with a [newly deceased] cadaver commands no urgency. It is wheeled by a single person, . . . like a shopping cart" (167).

## Paraphrasing

When you paraphrase, you restate information from a source in your own words, using your own sentence structures. Because a paraphrase includes all the main points of the source, it is usually about the same length as the original.

Here is a paragraph from Diane Ackerman's essay "Why Leaves Turn Color in the Fall," followed by two sample paraphrases. The first demonstrates some of the challenges of paraphrasing.

ORIGINAL SOURCE

Where do the colors come from? Sunlight rules most living things with its golden edicts. When the days begin to shorten, soon after the summer solstice on June 21, a tree reconsiders its leaves. All summer it feeds them so they can process sunlight, but in the dog days of summer the tree begins pulling nutrients back into its trunk and roots, pares down, and gradually chokes off its leaves. A corky layer of cells forms at the leaves' slender petioles, then scars over. Undernourished, the leaves stop producing the pigment chlorophyll, and photosynthesis ceases. Animals can migrate, hibernate, or store food to prepare for winter. But where can a tree go? It survives by dropping its leaves, and by the end of autumn only a few fragile threads of fluid-carrying xylem hold leaves to their stems.

### UNACCEPTABLE PARAPHRASE

Ackerman tells us where the colors of leaves come from. The amount of sunlight is the trigger, as is true for most living things. At the end of June, as daylight lessens, a tree begins to treat its leaves differently. It feeds them all summer so they can turn sunlight into food, but in August a tree begins to redirect its food into its trunk and roots, gradually choking the leaves. A corky group of cells develops at the petioles, and a scar forms. By autumn, the leaves don't have enough food, so they stop producing chlorophyll, and photosynthesis also stops. Although animals are able to migrate, hibernate, or stow food for the winter, a tree cannot go anywhere. It survives only by dropping its leaves, and by the time winter comes only a few leaves remain on their stems (257).

This first paraphrase borrows too much of the language of the original or changes it only slightly. It also follows the original sentence structure too closely. The following paraphrase avoids both of these pitfalls.

### ACCEPTABLE PARAPHRASE

Ackerman explains why leaves change color. Diminishing sunlight is the main instigator. A tree nourishes its leaves—and encourages photosynthesis—for most of the summer. By August, however, as daylight continues to lessen, a tree starts to reroute its food to the roots and trunk, a process that saves the tree but eventually kills the leaves. In autumn, because the leaves are almost starving, they can neither manufacture chlorophyll to stay green nor carry out photosynthesis. By this time, the base of the petiole, or leaf's stem, has hardened, in preparation for the final drop. Unlike animals, who have many ways to get ready for winter—hiding food ahead of time, moving to a warm climate, sleeping through winter—a tree is immobile. It can make it through the winter only by losing its leaves (257).

## Summarizing

Unlike a paraphrase, a SUMMARY does not present all the details in the original source, so it is generally as brief as possible. Summaries may boil down an entire book or essay into a single sentence, or they may take a paragraph or more to present the main ideas. Here, for example, is a summary of the Ackerman paragraph:

> In late summer and fall, Ackerman explains, trees put most of their food into their roots and trunk, which causes leaves to change color and die but enables trees to live through the winter (257).

## Deciding Whether to Quote, Paraphrase, or Summarize

Follow these rules of thumb to determine whether you should quote a source directly, paraphrase it in detail, or merely summarize the main points.

- *Quote* a text when the exact wording is critical to making your point (or that of an authority you wish to cite), or when the wording itself is part of what you're analyzing.

- *Paraphrase* when the meaning of a text is important to your argument but the original language is not essential, or when you're clarifying or interpreting the ideas (not the words) in the text.

- *Summarize* when the main points of the text are important to your argument but the details can be left out in the interest of conciseness.

## Using Signal Phrases

When you quote, paraphrase, or summarize a source, identify your source clearly and use a signal phrase ("she says," "he thinks") to distinguish the words and ideas of your source from your own. Consider this example:

> Professor and textbook author Elaine Tyler May claims that many high-school history textbooks are too bland to interest young readers (531).

This sentence summarizes a general position about the effectiveness of certain textbooks ("too bland"), and it attributes that view to a particular authority (Elaine

Tyler May), citing her credentials (professor, textbook author) for speaking as an authority on the subject. By using the signal phrase "claims that," the sentence also distinguishes the words and ideas of the source from those of the writers.

The verb you use in a signal phrase can be neutral (*says* or *thinks*), or it can indicate your (or your source's) stance toward the subject. In this case, the use of the verb *claims* suggests that what the source says is arguable (or that the writer of the sentence believes it is). The signal verb you choose can influence your reader's understanding of the sentence and of your attitude toward what it says.

# ACKNOWLEDGING SOURCES AND AVOIDING PLAGIARISM

As a writer, you must acknowledge any words and ideas that come from others. There are numerous reasons for doing so: to give credit where credit is due, to recognize the various authorities and many perspectives you have considered, to show readers where they can find your sources, and to situate your own arguments in the ongoing academic conversation. Using other people's words and ideas without acknowledgment is plagiarism, a serious academic and ethical offense.

## MATERIAL THAT DOESN'T HAVE TO BE ACKNOWLEDGED

- Facts that are common knowledge, such as the name of the current president of the United States
- Well-known statements accompanied by a signal phrase: "As John F. Kennedy said, 'Ask not what your country can do for you; ask what you can do for your country.' "

## MATERIAL THAT REQUIRES ACKNOWLEDGMENT

- Direct quotations, paraphrases, and summaries
- Arguable statements and any information that is not commonly known (statistics and other data)

- Personal or professional opinions and assertions of others
- Visuals that you did not create yourself (charts, photographs, and so on)
- Collaborative help you received from others

Plagiarism is (1) using another writer's exact words without quotation marks, (2) using another writer's words or ideas without in-text citation or other documentation, (3) paraphrasing or summarizing someone else's ideas using language or sentence structure that is close to the original. The following practices will help you avoid plagiarizing:

- *Take careful notes,* clearly labeling quotations and using your own phrasing and sentence structure in paraphrases and summaries.

- *Check all paraphrases and summaries* to be sure they are stated in *your* words and sentence structures—and that you put quotation marks around any of the source's original phrasing.

- *Know what sources you must document,* and identify them both in the text and in a works-cited list.

- *Check to see that all quotations are documented;* it is not enough just to include quotation marks or indent a block quotation.

- *Be especially careful with online material*—copying source material directly into a document you are writing invites plagiarism. Like other sources, information from the web must be acknowledged.

- *Recognize that plagiarism has consequences.* A scholar's work will be discredited if it too closely resembles the work of another scholar. Journalists who plagiarize lose their jobs, and students routinely fail courses or are dismissed from school when they are caught cheating—all too often by submitting essays that they have purchased from online "research" sites.

So, don't take the chance. If you're having trouble with an assignment, ask your instructor for assistance. Or visit your school's writing center. Writing centers can help with advice on all aspects of your writing, including acknowledging sources and avoiding plagiarism.

# DOCUMENTATION

Taken collectively, all the information you provide about sources is your *documentation.* Many organizations and publishers—for example, the American Psychological Association (APA), the University of Chicago Press, and the Council of Science Editors (CSE)—have their own documentation styles. The focus here is on the documentation system of the Modern Language Association (MLA) because it is one of the most common systems used in college courses, especially in the liberal arts.

MLA style has two basic parts (1) brief in-text documentation for quotations, paraphrases, or summaries and (2) more detailed information for each in-text reference in a list of works cited at the end of the text.

See p. 607 for a sample paper with MLA-style citations.

MLA style requires that each item in your works-cited list include the following "core elements" when they are available: author, title of the source, title of any "container" (MLA's term for a larger work in which the source is found—an anthology, a website, a journal or magazine, a database, even a streaming service like Netflix), other contributors, version, volume and issue numbers, publisher, date of publication, and location of source (page numbers, URL, permalink, DOI, etc.). Here is an example of how the two parts work together. Note that you can identify the author either in a signal phrase or in parentheses:

### IN-TEXT DOCUMENTATION (WITH AND WITHOUT SIGNAL PHRASE)

As Lester Faigley puts it, "The world has become a bazaar from which to shop for an individual 'lifestyle' " (12).

As one observer suggests, "The world has become a bazaar from which to shop for an individual 'lifestyle' " (Faigley 12).

### CORRESPONDING WORKS-CITED REFERENCE

Faigley, Lester. *Fragments of Rationality: Postmodernity and the Subject of Composition.* U of Pittsburgh P, 1992.

# MLA IN-TEXT DOCUMENTATION

Brief documentation in your text makes clear to your reader what you took from a source and where within the source you found the information. As you cite each source, you will need to decide whether or not to name the author in a signal phrase—"as Toni Morrison writes"—or in parentheses—"(Morrison 24)." For either style of reference, try to put the parenthetical citation at the end of the sentence or as close as possible to the material you've cited without awkwardly interrupting the sentence. When citing a direct quotation (as in no. 1), note that the parenthetical reference comes after the closing quotation marks but before the period at the end of the sentence.

## 1. AUTHOR NAMED IN A SIGNAL PHRASE

If you mention the author in a signal phrase, put only the page number(s) in parentheses. Do not write *page* or *p*.

> McCullough describes John Adams's hands as those of someone used to manual labor (18).

## 2. AUTHOR NAMED IN PARENTHESES

If you do not mention the author in a signal phrase, put his or her last name in parentheses along with the page number(s). Do not use punctuation between the name and the page number(s).

> Adams is said to have had "the hands of a man accustomed to pruning his own trees, cutting his own hay, and splitting his own firewood" (McCullough 18).

## 3. AFTER A BLOCK QUOTATION

When quoting more than three lines of poetry, more than four lines of prose, or dialogue between two or more characters from a drama, set off the quotation from the rest of your text, indenting it half an inch (or five spaces) from the left margin. Do not use quotation marks, and place any parenthetical documentation *after* the final punctuation.

> In *Eastward to Tartary*, Kaplan captures ancient and contemporary Antioch:
>
> At the height of its glory in the Roman-Byzantine age, when it had an amphitheater, public baths, aqueducts, and sewage pipes, half a million people lived in Antioch. Today the population is only 125,000. With sour relations between Turkey and Syria, and unstable politics throughout the Middle East, Antioch is now a backwater—seedy and tumbledown, with relatively few tourists. I found it altogether charming. (123)

## 4. TWO OR MORE AUTHORS

For a work with two authors, name both, either in a signal phrase or in parentheses.

> Carlson and Ventura's stated goal is to introduce Julio Cortázar, Marjorie Agosín, and other Latin American writers to an audience of English-speaking adolescents (5).

For a work by three or more authors, name the first author followed by *et al.*, which means "and others."

> One popular survey of American literature breaks the contents into sixteen thematic groupings (Anderson et al. A19–24).

## 5. ORGANIZATION OR GOVERNMENT AS AUTHOR

Acknowledge the organization either in a signal phrase or in parentheses. It's acceptable to shorten long names.

> The U.S. government can be direct when it wants to be. For example, it sternly warns, "If you are overpaid, we will recover any payments not due you" (Social Security Administration 12).

## 6. AUTHOR UNKNOWN

If you can't determine an author, use the work's title or a shortened version of the title in the parentheses.

> A powerful editorial in last week's paper asserts that healthy liver
> donor Mike Hurewitz died because of "frightening" faulty postopera-
> tive care ("Every Patient's Nightmare").

## 7. LITERARY WORKS

When referring to literary works that are available in many different editions, give the page numbers from the edition you are using, followed by information that will let readers of any edition locate the text you are citing.

*Novels*: Give the page and chapter number, separated by a semicolon.

> In *Pride and Prejudice*, Mrs. Bennett shows no warmth toward Jane when
> she returns from Netherfield (105; ch. 12).

*Verse plays*: Give the act, scene, and line numbers; separate them with periods.

> Macbeth continues the vision theme when he says "Thou hast no
> speculation in those eyes / Which thou dost glare with" (3.3.96−97).

*Poems*: Give the part and line numbers (separated by periods). If a poem has only line numbers, use the word *line(s)* in the first reference.

> The mere in *Beowulf* is described as "not a pleasant place!" (line 1372).
> Later, it is called "the awful place" (1378).

## 8. WORKS CITED TOGETHER

If you cite two or more works in the same parentheses, separate the references with a semicolon.

> Critics have looked at both *Pride and Prejudice* and *Frankenstein* from a
> cultural perspective (Tanner 7; Smith viii).

## 9. SOURCE IN ANOTHER SOURCE

When you are quoting text that you found quoted in another source, use the abbreviation *qtd. in* in the parenthetical reference.

Charlotte Brontë wrote to G. H. Lewes: "Why do you like Miss Austen so very much? I am puzzled on that point" (qtd. in Tanner 7).

## 10. WORK WITHOUT PAGE NUMBERS

For works without page numbers, including many online sources, identify the source using the author or other information either in a signal phrase or in parentheses. If the source has chapter, paragraph, or section numbers, use them with the abbreviations *ch., par.,* or *sec.*

Studies show that music training helps children to be better at multitasking later in life ("Hearing the Music," par. 2).

## 11. AN ENTIRE WORK

If you cite an entire work rather than a part of it, or if you cite a single-page article, there's no need to include page numbers.

Throughout life, John Adams strove to succeed (McCullough).

# MLA LIST OF WORKS CITED

A works-cited list provides full bibliographic information for every source cited in your text. Here's some general advice to help you format your list:

- Start the list on a new page.
- Center the title (Works Cited) one inch from the top of the page.
- Double-space the whole list.
- Begin each entry flush with the left-hand margin and indent subsequent lines one-half inch or five spaces.
- Alphabetize entries by the author's last name. If a work has no identifiable author, use the first major word of the title (disregard *A, An, The*).
- If you cite more than one work by a single author, list them all alphabetically by title, and use three hyphens in place of the author's name after the first entry (see no. 4 for an example).
- *Authors:* List the primary author last name first, and include any middle name or initial after the first name.
- *Titles:* Capitalize all principal words in titles and subtitles, including short verbs such as *is* and *are*. Do not capitalize *a, an, the, to,* or any preposition or conjunction unless they begin a title or subtitle. Italicize book titles, periodical titles, and titles of other long works, but place quotation marks around a chapter of a book, a selection from an anthology, or an article title.
- *Versions:* If you cite a source that's available in more than one version, specify the one you consulted in your works cited entry. Write ordinal numbers with numerals, and abbreviate *edition*: 2nd ed.
- *Numbers:* If you cite a book that's published in multiple volumes, indicate the volume number. Abbreviate *volume*, and write the number as a numeral: vol. 2. Indicate any volume and issue numbers of journals, abbreviating both *volume* and *number*: vol. 123, no. 4
- *Publishers:* Write publishers' names in full, but omit business words like *Inc.* or *Company.* For university presses, use *U* for "University" and *P* for "Press"—Princeton UP, U of California P.
- *Dates:* Whether to give just the year or to include the month and day (or even the time stamp) depends on the source. Give the full date that you find there. If the date is unknown, simply omit it.

  Abbreviate months except for May, June, and July: Jan., Feb., Mar., Apr., Aug., Sept., Oct., Nov., Dec.—9 Sept. 2016.

For books, give the year of publication: 1948. If a book lists more than one date, use the most recent one.

Periodicals may be published annually, monthly, seasonally, weekly, or daily. Give the full date that you find in the periodical: 2011, Apr. 2011, Spring 2011, 16 Apr. 2011.

For online sources, use the copyright date or the most recent update, giving the full date that you find in the source. If the source does not give a date, use the date of access: Accessed 6 June 2016. And if the source includes the time when it was posted or updated, give the time along with the date: 18 Oct. 2016, 9:20 a.m.

Because online sources may change or even disappear, the date of access can be important for indicating the exact version you've cited. Some instructors may require this information, so we've included access dates in this chapter's guidelines for specific kinds of sources, but check with your instructor to see if you're required to include this information.

- **Location:** For most print articles and other short works, give a page number or range of pages: p. 24, pp. 24-35. For articles that are not on consecutive pages, give the first page number with a plus sign: pp. 24+.

Indicate the location of online sources by giving the URL, omitting *http://* or *https://*. If a source has a permalink (a stable version of its URL) or a DOI (a digital object identifier, a stable number identifying the location of a source accessed through a database), give that instead.

- **Punctuation:** Some URLs will not fit on one line. MLA does not specify where to break a URL, but we recommend breaking it before a punctuation mark. Do *not* add a hyphen.

Sometimes you'll need to provide information about more than one work for a single source—for instance, when you cite an article from a periodical that you access through a database. MLA refers to the periodical and database (or any other entity that holds a source) as "containers." Use commas between elements within each container and put a period at the end of each container.

> Semuels, Alana. "The Future Will Be Quiet." *The Atlantic*, Apr. 2016, pp. 19-20. *ProQuest*, search.proquest.com/docview /1777443553?accountid+42654. Accessed 5 Apr. 2016.

# Authors and Other Contributors

The following guidelines for citing authors and other contributors apply to all sources you cite: in print, online, or in some other media.

## 1. ONE AUTHOR

> Anderson, Curtis. *The Long Tail: Why the Future of Business Is Selling Less of More.* Hyperion, 2006.

## 2. TWO AUTHORS

Follow the order of names on the book's title page. List the second author first-name-first.

> Lunsford, Andrea, and Lisa Ede. *Singular Texts/Plural Authors: Perspectives on Collaborative Writing.* Southern Illinois UP, 1990.

## 3. THREE OR MORE AUTHORS

Provide the first author's name, followed by et al. (Latin for "and others").

> Sebranek, Patrick, et al. *Writers INC: A Guide to Writing, Thinking, and Learning.* Write Source, 1990.

## 4. MULTIPLE WORKS BY AN AUTHOR

Give the author's name in the first entry, and then use three hyphens in the author slot for each of the subsequent works, listing them alphabetically by the first important word of each title.

> Kaplan, Robert D. *The Coming Anarchy: Shattering the Dreams of the Post Cold War.* Random House, 2000.
> - - -. *Eastward to Tartary: Travels in the Balkans, the Middle East, and the Caucasus.* Random House, 2000.

## 5. AUTHOR AND EDITOR OR TRANSLATOR

> Austen, Jane. *Emma.* Edited by Stephen M. Parrish, W. W. Norton, 2000.
> Dostoevsky, Fyodor. *Crime and Punishment.* Translated by Richard Pevear and Larissa Volokhonsky, Vintage Books, 1993.

Start with the editor or translator if you are focusing on that contribution rather than the author's.

> Pevear, Richard, and Larissa Volokhonsky, translators. *Crime and Punishment.* By Fyodor Dostoevsky, Vintage Books, 1993.

6. ORGANIZATION OR GOVERNMENT

> Diagram Group. *The Macmillan Visual Desk Reference.* Macmillan, 1993.

For a government publication, give the name of the government first, followed by the names of any department and agency.

> United States, Department of Health and Human Services, National
> Institute of Mental Health. *Autism Spectrum Disorders.*
> Government Printing Office, 2004.

## Articles and Other Short Works

Articles, essays, reviews, and other shorts works are found in journals, magazines, newspapers, other periodicals, and books—all of which you may find in print, online, or in a database. For most short works, you'll need to provide information about the author, the titles of both the short work and the longer work, any page numbers, and various kinds of publication information.

7. ARTICLE IN A JOURNAL

PRINT

> Cooney, Brian C. "Considering *Robinson Crusoe's* 'Liberty of Conscience'
> in an Age of Terror." *College English,* vol. 69, no. 3, Jan. 2007,
> pp. 197–215.

ONLINE

> Gleckman, Jason. "Shakespeare as Poet or Playwright? The Player's Speech
> in Hamlet." *Early Modern Literary Studies,* vol. 11, no. 3, Jan. 2006,
> purl.oclc.org/emls/11-3/glechaml.htm. Accessed 31 Mar. 2015.

8. ARTICLE IN A MAGAZINE

PRINT

> Neyfakh, Leon. "The Future of Getting Arrested." *The Atlantic,*
> Jan.-Feb. 2015, pp. 26+.

ONLINE

> Khazan, Olga. "Forgetting and Remembering Your First Language." *The*
> *Atlantic,* 24 July 2014, www.theatlantic.com/international
> /archive/2014/07/learning-forgetting-and-remembering-your-first
> -language/374906/. Accessed 2 Apr. 2015.

## 9. ARTICLE IN A NEWSPAPER

### PRINT

> Saulny, Susan, and Jacques Steinberg. "On College Forms, a Question of
>     Race Can Perplex." *The New York Times,* 14 June 2011, p. A1.

To document a particular edition of a newspaper, list the edition (*late ed., natl. ed.,* and so on) after the date. If a section of the newspaper is numbered, put that detail after the edition information.

> Burns, John F., and Miguel Helft. "Under Pressure, YouTube Withdraws
>     Muslim Cleric's Videos." *The New York Times,* 4 Nov. 2010, late
>     ed., sec. 1, p. 13.

### ONLINE

> Banerjee, Neela. "Proposed Religion-Based Program for Federal Inmates
>     Is Canceled." *The New York Times,* 28 Oct. 2006, www.nytimes
>     .com/2006/10/28/us/28prison.html?_r=0. Accessed 4 Apr. 2015.

## 10. ARTICLE IN A DATABASE

> Stalter, Sunny. "Subway Ride and Subway System in Hart Crane's 'The
>     Tunnel.'" *Journal of Modern Literature,* vol. 33, no. 2, Jan. 2010, pp.
>     70-91. *JSTOR,* doi: 10.2979/jml.2010.33.2.70. Accessed 30 Mar. 2015.

## 11. ENTRY IN A REFERENCE WORK

### PRINT

Provide the author's name if the entry has one. If there's no author given, start with the title of the entry.

> "California." *The New Columbia Encyclopedia,* edited by William H. Harris
>     and Judith S. Levey, 4th ed., Columbia UP, 1975, pp. 423-24.
> "Feminism." *Longman Dictionary of American English,* Longman, 1983,
>     p. 252.

### ONLINE

Document online reference works the same as print ones, adding the URL and access date after the date of publication.

> "Baseball." *The Columbia Electronic Encyclopedia,* edited by Paul Lagassé,
>     6th ed., Columbia UP, 2012, www.infoplease.com/encyclopedia.
>     Accessed 25 May 2016.

## 12. EDITORIAL

### PRINT

"Gas, Cigarettes Are Safe to Tax." Editorial. *The Lakeville Journal,* 17
Feb. 2005, p. A10.

### ONLINE

"Keep the Drinking Age at 21." Editorial. *Chicago Tribune,* 28 Aug. 2008,
articles.chicagotribune.com/2008-08-26/news/0808250487_1
_binge-drinking-drinking-age-alcohol-related crashes. Accessed
26 Apr. 2015.

## 13. LETTER TO THE EDITOR

Pinker, Steven. "Language Arts." Letter. *The New Yorker,* 4 June 2012,
www.newyorker.com/magazine/2012/06/04/language-arts-2.
Accessed 6 Apr. 2015.

## 14. REVIEW

### PRINT

Frank, Jeffrey. "Body Count." Review of *The Exception,* by Christian
Jungersen. *The New Yorker,* 30 July 2007, pp. 86-87.

If a review has no author or title, start with what's being reviewed:

Review of *Ways to Disappear,* by Idra Novey. *The New Yorker,* 28 Mar.
2016, p. 79.

### ONLINE

Donadio, Rachel. "Italy's Great, Mysterious Storyteller." Review of
*My Brilliant Friend,* by Elena Ferrante. *The New York Review of
Books,* 18 Dec. 2014, www.nybooks.com/articles/2014/12/18
/italys-great-mysterious-storyteller. Accessed 28 Sept. 2015.

## 15. ONLINE COMMENT

Nick. Comment on "The Case for Reparations." *The Atlantic,* 22
May 2014, 3:04 p.m., www.theatlantic.com/business
/archive/2014/05/how-to-comment-on-reparations
/371422/#article-comments. Accessed 8 May 2015.

# Books and Parts of Books

For most books, you'll need to provide information about the author, the title, the publisher, and the year of publication. If you found the book inside a larger volume, a database, or some other work, be sure to specify that as well.

## 16. BASIC ENTRIES FOR A BOOK

### PRINT

> Watson, Brad. *Miss Jane*. W. W. Norton, 2016.

### EBOOK

Document an ebook as you would a print book, but add information about the ebook—or the type of ebook if you know it.

> Watson, Brad. *Miss Jane*. Ebook, W. W. Norton, 2016.
> Watson, Brad. *Miss Jane*. Kindle ed., W. W. Norton, 2016.

### IN A DATABASE

> Anderson, Sherwood. *Winesburg, Ohio*. B. W. Huebsch, 1919. *Bartleby
> .com*, www.bartleby.com/156/. Accessed 8 Apr. 2015.

## 17. ANTHOLOGY

> Hall, Donald, editor. *The Oxford Book of Children's Verse in America*.
> Oxford UP, 1985.

## 18. WORK IN AN ANTHOLOGY

> Achebe, Chinua. "Uncle Ben's Choice." *The Seagull Reader: Literature*,
> edited by Joseph Kelly, W. W. Norton, 2005, pp. 23-27.

### TWO OR MORE WORKS FROM ONE ANTHOLOGY

Prepare an entry for each selection by author and title, followed by the anthology editors' last names and the pages of the selection. Then include an entry for the anthology itself (see no. 17).

> Hiestand, Emily. "Afternoon Tea." Kitchen and Jones, pp. 65-67.
> Ozick, Cynthia. "The Shock of Teapots." Kitchen and Jones, pp. 68-71.

## 19. MULTIVOLUME WORK

If you cite all the volumes, give the number of volumes after the year of publication.

**ALL VOLUMES**

> Churchill, Winston. *The Second World War*. Houghton Mifflin, 1948-53.
> 6 vols.

If you cite only one volume, give the number after the title and the total number of volumes after the year of publication.

**SINGLE VOLUME**

> Sandburg, Carl. *Abraham Lincoln: The War Years*. Vol. 2, Harcourt,
> Brace & World, 1939. 4 vols.

## 20. GRAPHIC NARRATIVE

> Bechdel, Alison. *Fun Home: A Family Tragicomedy*. Houghton Mifflin,
> 2006.

If the work has both an author and an illustrator, start with the one whose work is more relevant to your research, and label the role of anyone who's not an author.

> Pekar, Harvey. *Bob & Harv's Comics*. Illustrated by R. Crumb, Running
> Press, 1996.
> Crumb, R., illustrator. *Bob & Harv's Comics*. By Harvey Pekar, Running
> Press, 1996.

## 21. EDITION OTHER THAN THE FIRST

> Fowler, H. W. *A Dictionary of Modern English*. 2nd ed., Oxford UP, 1965.

## 22. REPUBLISHED WORK

Provide the year of original publication after the title, followed by the current publisher, and year of republication.

> Bierce, Ambrose. *Civil War Stories*. 1909. Dover, 1994.

## 23. FOREWORD, INTRODUCTION, PREFACE, OR AFTERWORD

> Tanner, Tony. Introduction. *Pride and Prejudice,* by Jane Austen,
> Penguin, 1972, pp. 7-46.

## 24. PUBLISHED LETTER

> White, E. B. Letter to Carol Angell. 28 May 1970. *Letters of E. B. White,*
> edited by Dorothy Lobarno Guth, Harper & Row, 1976, p. 600.

# Websites

Many sources are available in multiple media—for example, a print periodical that is also on the web and contained in digital databases—but some are published only on websites. This section covers the latter.

### 25. ENTIRE WEBSITE

Provide the author's name followed by the author's role.

> Zalta, Edward N., principal editor. *Stanford Encyclopedia of Philosophy.* Metaphysics Research Lab, Center for the Study of Language, Stanford U, 1995-2015, plato.stanford.edu/index.html. Accessed 21 Apr. 2015.

#### PERSONAL WEBSITE

> Heath, Shirley Brice. *Shirley Brice Heath.* 2015, shirleybriceheath.net. Accessed 6 June 2015.

### 26. WORK ON A WEBSITE

Provide the author's name, if any. If there is no author, begin with the title of the work.

> "Global Minnesota: Immigrants Past and Present." *Immigration History Research Center*, U of Minnesota, 2015, cla.umn.edu.ihrc. Accessed 25 May 2016.

### 27. BLOG ENTRY

> Hollmichel, Stefanie. "Bringing Up the Bodies." *So Many Books,* 10 Feb. 2014, somanybooksblog.com/2014/02/10/bring-up-the-bodies/. Accessed 12 Feb. 2014.

If the entry has no title, use "Blog entry" (without quotations marks). Document a whole blog as you would an entire website (no. 25) and a comment on a blog as you would a comment on an online article (no. 15).

### 28. WIKI

> "Pi." *Wikipedia,* Wikimedia Foundation, 28 Aug. 2013, en.wikipedia.org /wiki/Pi. Accessed 25 Oct. 2013.

# Personal Communication, Social Media, and Other Sources

### 29. EMAIL

Smith, William. "Teaching Grammar—Some Thoughts." Received by Richard Bullock, 19 Nov. 2013.

### 30. POST TO AN ONLINE FORUM

@somekiryu. "What's the hardest part about writing for you?" *Reddit,* 22 Apr. 2016, redd.it/4fynio.

### 31. POST ON SOCIAL MEDIA

@POTUS (Barack Obama). "I'm proud of the @NBA for taking a stand against gun violence. Sympathy for victims isn't enough—change requires all of us speaking up." *Twitter,* 23 Dec. 2015, 1:21 p.m., twitter.com/POTUS/status/679773729749078016.

Black Lives Matter. "Rise and Grind! Did you sign this petition yet? We now have a sign on for ORGANIZATIONS to lend their support." *Facebook,* 23 Oct. 2015, 11:30 a.m., www.facebook.com /BlackLivesMatter/photos/a.294807204023865.1073741829 .180212755483311/504711973033386/?type=3&theater.

@quarterlifepoetry. Illustrated poem about girl at Target. *Instagram,* 22 Jan. 2015, www.instagram.com/p/yLO6fSurRH/.

# Audio, Visual, and Other Sources

### 32. ADVERTISEMENT

#### PRINT

Cal Alumni Association. Sports Merchandise ad. *California,* Spring 2016, p. 3.

#### AUDIO OR VIDEO

Chrysler. Super Bowl commercial. 6 Feb. 2011. *YouTube,* www.youtube .com/watch?v=SKLZ254Y_jtc. Accessed 1 May 2015.

### 33. ART

#### ORIGINAL

Van Gogh, Vincent. *The Potato Eaters.* 1885, Van Gogh Museum, Amsterdam.

### REPRODUCTION

Van Gogh, Vincent. *The Potato Eaters*. 1885. *History of Art: A Survey of the Major Visual Arts from the Dawn of History to the Present Day*, by H. W. Janson, Prentice-Hall/Harry N. Abrams, 1969, p. 508.

### ONLINE

Warhol, Andy. *Self-portrait*. 1979. *J. Paul Getty Museum*, www.getty .edu/art/collection/objects/106971/andy-warhol-self -portrait-american-1979/. Accessed 20 Jan. 2015.

## 34. CARTOON

### PRINT

Chast, Roz. "The Three Wise Men of Thanksgiving." *The New Yorker*, 1 Dec. 2003, p. 174. Cartoon.

### ONLINE

Munroe, Randall. "Up Goer Five." *xkcd*, 12 Nov. 2012, xkcd.com/1133/. Accessed 22 Apr. 2015. Cartoon.

## 35. FILM

Name individuals based on the focus of your project—the director, the screen-writer, the cinematographer, or someone else. If your essay focuses on one or more contributors, you may put their names before the title.

*Breakfast at Tiffany's*. Directed by Blake Edwards, Paramount, 1961.

### STREAMING

*Interstellar*. Directed by Christopher Nolan, Paramount, 2014. *Amazon Prime Video*, www.amazon.com/Interstellar-Matthew-McConaughey/dp /B00TU9UFTS. Accessed 2 May 2015.

## 36. INTERVIEW

If the interviewer's name is known and relevant to your argument, include it after the word "Interview" or the title: Interview by Stephen Colbert.

### BROADCAST

Gates, Henry Louis, Jr. Interview. *Fresh Air*, NPR, 9 Apr. 2002.

PUBLISHED

> Stone, Oliver. Interview. *Esquire,* Nov. 2004, pp. 170–71.

PERSONAL

> Roddick, Andy. Personal interview. 17 Aug. 2013.

## 37. MAP

If the title doesn't make clear it's a map, add a label at the end.

> "National Highway System." US Department of Transportation Federal Highway Administration, www.fhwa.dot.gov/planning/images/nhs .pdf. Accessed 10 May 2015. Map.

## 38. MUSICAL SCORE

> Stravinsky, Igor. *Petrushka.* 1911. W. W. Norton, 1967.

## 39. PODCAST

If you accessed a podcast online, give the URL and date of access; if you accessed it through a service such as *iTunes* or *Spotify,* indicate that instead.

> Koenig, Sarah, host. "DUSTWUN." *Serial,* season 2, episode 1, WBEZ, 10 Dec. 2015, serialpodcast.org/season-two/1/dustwun. Accessed 23 Apr. 2016.
>
> Foss, Gilad, author and performer. "Aquaman's Brother-in-Law." *Superhero Temp Agency,* season 1, episode 1, 16 Apr. 2015. *iTunes.*

## 40. RADIO PROGRAM

> Glass, Ira, host. "In Defense of Ignorance." *This American Life,* WBEZ, 22 Apr. 2016, thisamericanlife.org/radio-archives/episode/585 /in-defense-of-ignorance. Accessed 2 May 2016.

## 41. SOUND RECORDING

ONLINE

> Simone, Nina. "To Be Young, Gifted and Black." *Black Gold,* RCA Records, 1969. *Spotify.*

CD

> Brown, Greg. "Canned Goods." *The Live One,* Red House, 1995.

## 42. TV SHOW

Name contributors based on the focus of your project—director, writers, actors, or others. And if there's a key contributor, you might include his or her name and role before the title of the episode.

> "The Silencer." *Criminal Minds,* written by Erica Messer, season 8,
>     episode 1, NBC, 26 Sept. 2012.

### DVD

> "The Pants Tent." 2003. *Curb Your Enthusiasm: Season One,* performance
>     by Larry David, season 1, episode 1, HBO Video, 2006, disc 1.

### ONLINE

> "Shadows in the Glass." *Marvel's Daredevil,* season 1, episode 8, Netflix,
>     10 Apr. 2015. *Netflix,* www.netflix.com/watch/80018198.
>     Accessed 3 Nov. 2015.

## 43. VIDEO GAME

> Metzen, Chris, and James Waugh, writers. *StarCraft II: Legacy of the
>     Void.* Blizzard Entertainment, 2015. OS X.

# SOURCES NOT COVERED BY MLA

To document a source that isn't covered by the MLA guidelines, look for models similar to the source you're citing. Give any information readers will need in order to find the sources themselves—author, title, subtitle; publisher; dates; and any other pertinent information. You might want to try out the citation yourself, to be sure it will lead others to your source.

# SAMPLE RESEARCH PAPER

The following report was written by Dylan Borchers for a first-year writing course. It's formatted according to the guidelines of the MLA (style.mla.org).

Dylan Borchers
Professor Bullock
English 102, Section 4
4 May 2012

Against the Odds:
Harry S. Truman and the Election of 1948

Just over a week before Election Day in 1948, a *New York Times* article noted "[t]he popular view that Gov. Thomas E. Dewey's election as President is a foregone conclusion" (Egan). This assessment of the race between incumbent Democrat Harry S. Truman and Dewey, his Republican challenger, was echoed a week later when *Life* magazine published a photograph whose caption labeled Dewey "The Next President" (Photo of Truman 37). In a *Newsweek* survey of fifty prominent political writers, each one predicted Truman's defeat, and *Time* correspondents declared that Dewey would carry 39 of the 48 states (Donaldson 210). Nearly every major media outlet across the United States endorsed Dewey and lambasted Truman. As historian Robert H. Ferrell observes, even Truman's wife, Bess, thought he would be beaten (270).

The results of an election are not so easily predicted, as the famous photograph in fig. 1 shows. Not only did Truman win the election, but he won by a significant margin, with 303 electoral votes and 24,179,259 popular votes, compared to Dewey's 189 electoral votes and 21,991,291 popular votes (Donaldson 204-07). In fact, many historians and political analysts argue that Truman would have won by an even greater margin had third-party Progressive candidate Henry A. Wallace not split the Democratic vote in New York State and Dixiecrat Strom Thurmond not won

Fig. 1. President Harry S. Truman holds up an edition of the *Chicago Daily Tribune* that mistakenly announced "Dewey Defeats Truman" (Rollins).

four states in the South (McCullough 711). Although Truman's defeat was heavily predicted, those predictions themselves, Dewey's passiveness as a campaigner, and Truman's zeal turned the tide for a Truman victory.

In the months preceding the election, public opinion polls predicted that Dewey would win by a large margin. Pollster Elmo Roper stopped polling in September, believing there was no reason to continue, given a seemingly inevitable Dewey landslide. Although the margin narrowed as the election drew near, the other pollsters predicted a Dewey win by at least 5 percent (Donaldson 209). Many historians believe that these predictions aided the president in the long run. First, surveys showing Dewey in the lead may have prompted some of Dewey's supporters to feel overconfident about their candidate's chances and therefore to stay home from the polls on Election Day. Second, these same surveys may have energized Democrats to mount late get-out-the-vote efforts ("1948 Truman-Dewey Election"). Other analysts believe that the overwhelming predictions of a Truman loss also kept at home some Democrats who approved of Truman's policies but saw a Truman loss as inevitable. According to political analyst Samuel Lubell, those Democrats may have saved Dewey from an even greater defeat (Hamby, *Man* 465). Whatever the impact on the voters, the polling numbers had a decided effect on Dewey.

Historians and political analysts alike cite Dewey's overly cautious campaign as one of the main reasons Truman was able to achieve victory. Dewey firmly believed in public opinion polls. With all indications pointing to an easy victory, Dewey and his staff believed that all he had to do was bide his time and make no foolish mistakes. Dewey himself said, "When you're leading, don't talk" (Smith 30). Each of Dewey's speeches was well crafted and well rehearsed. As the leader in the race, he kept his remarks faultlessly positive, with the result that he failed to deliver a solid message or even mention Truman or any of Truman's policies. Eventually, Dewey began to be perceived as aloof and stuffy. One observer compared him to the plastic groom on top of a wedding cake (Hamby, "Harry S. Truman"), and others noted his stiff, cold demeanor (McCullough 671-74).

As his campaign continued, observers noted that Dewey seemed uncomfortable in crowds, unable to connect with ordinary people. And he made a number of blunders. One took place at a train stop when the candidate,

Paragraphs indent $\frac{1}{2}$ inch or 5 spaces.

Two works cited within the same sentence.

commenting on the number of children in the crowd, said he was glad they had been let out of school for his arrival. Unfortunately for Dewey, it was a Saturday ("1948: The Great Truman Surprise"). Such gaffes gave voters the feeling that Dewey was out of touch with the public.

Again and again through the autumn of 1948, Dewey's campaign speeches failed to address the issues, with the candidate declaring that he did not want to "get down in the gutter" (Smith 515). When told by fellow Republicans that he was losing ground, Dewey insisted that his campaign not alter its course. Even *Time* magazine, though it endorsed and praised him, conceded that his speeches were dull (McCullough 696). According to historian Zachary Karabell, they were "notable only for taking place, not for any specific message" (244). Dewey's numbers in the polls slipped in the weeks before the election, but he still held a comfortable lead over Truman. It would take Truman's famous whistle-stop campaign to make the difference.

Few candidates in US history have campaigned for the presidency with more passion and faith than Harry Truman. In the autumn of 1948, he wrote to his sister, "It will be the greatest campaign any President ever made. Win, lose, or draw, people will know where I stand" (91). For thirty-three days, Truman traveled the nation, giving hundreds of speeches from the back of the *Ferdinand Magellan* railroad car. In the same letter, he described the pace: "We made about 140 stops and I spoke over 147 times, shook hands with at least 30,000 and am in good condition to start out again tomorrow for Wilmington, Philadelphia,

Title used when there's no known author.

Jersey City, Newark, Albany and Buffalo" (91). McCullough writes of Truman's campaign:

> No President in history had ever gone so far in quest
> of support from the people, or with less cause for the
> effort, to judge by informed opinion. . . . As a test of
> his skills and judgment as a professional politician,
> not to say his stamina and disposition at age sixty-
> four, it would be like no other experience in his long,
> often difficult career, as he himself understood per-
> fectly. More than any other event in his public life, or
> in his presidency thus far, it would reveal the  kind of
> man he was. (655)

He spoke in large cities and small towns, defending his policies and attacking Republicans. As a former farmer and relatively late bloomer, Truman was able to connect with the public. He developed an energetic style, usually speaking from notes rather than from a prepared speech, and often mingled with the crowds that met his train. These crowds grew larger as the campaign progressed. In Chicago, over half a million people lined the streets as he passed, and in St. Paul the crowd numbered over 25,000. When Dewey entered St. Paul two days later, he was greeted by only 7,000 supporters ("1948 Truman-Dewey Election"). Reporters brushed off the large crowds as mere curiosity seekers wanting to see a president (McCullough 682). Yet Truman persisted, even if he often seemed to be the only one who thought he could win. By going directly to the American people and connecting with them, Truman built the momentum needed to surpass Dewey and win the election.

The legacy and lessons of Truman's whistle-stop campaign continue to be studied by political analysts, and

Quotations of more than 4 lines indented one-half an inch (5 spaces) and double-spaced.

Parenthetical reference after final punctuation.

politicians today often mimic his campaign methods by scheduling multiple visits to key states, as Truman did. He visited California, Illinois, and Ohio 48 times, compared with 6 visits to those states by Dewey. Political scientist Thomas M. Holbrook concludes that his strategic campaigning in those states and others gave Truman the electoral votes he needed to win (61, 65).

The 1948 election also had an effect on pollsters, who, as Elmo Roper admitted, "couldn't have been more wrong." *Life* magazine's editors concluded that pollsters as well as reporters and commentators were too convinced of a Dewey victory to analyze the polls seriously, especially the opinions of undecided voters (Karabell 256). Pollsters assumed that undecided voters would vote in the same proportion as decided voters—and that turned out to be a false assumption (Karabell 257). In fact, the lopsidedness of the polls might have led voters who supported Truman to call themselves undecided out of an unwillingness to associate themselves with the losing side, further skewing the polls' results (McDonald et al. 152). Such errors led pollsters to change their methods significantly after the 1948 election.

Work by 3 or more authors is shortened using et al.

After the election, many political analysts, journalists, and historians concluded that the Truman upset was in fact a victory for the American people, who, the *New Republic* noted, "couldn't be ticketed by the polls, knew its own mind and had picked the rather unlikely but courageous figure of Truman to carry its banner" (T.R.B. 3). How "unlikely" is unclear, however; Truman biographer Alonzo Hamby notes that "polls of scholars consistently rank Truman among the top eight presidents in American history"

(*Man* 641). But despite Truman's high standing, and despite the fact that the whistle-stop campaign is now part of our political landscape, politicians have increasingly imitated the style of the Dewey campaign, with its "packaged candidate who ran so as not to lose, who steered clear of controversy, and who made a good show of appearing presidential" (Karabell 266). The election of 1948 shows that voters are not necessarily swayed by polls, but it may have presaged the packaging of candidates by public relations experts, to the detriment of public debate on the issues in future presidential elections.

Works Cited

Donaldson, Gary A. *Truman Defeats Dewey*. UP of Kentucky, 1999.

Egan, Leo. "Talk Is Now Turning to the Dewey Cabinet." *The New York Times*, 20 Oct. 1948, p. 8E, www.nytimes.com/timesmachine/1948/10/26/issue.html. Accessed 18 Apr. 2012.

Ferrell, Robert H. *Harry S. Truman: A Life*. U of Missouri P, 1994.

Hamby, Alonzo L., editor. "Harry S. Truman: Campaigns and Elections." *American President*, Miller Center, U of Virginia, 11 Jan. 2012, millercenter.org/president/biography/truman-campaigns-and-elections. Accessed 17 Mar. 2012.

- - -. *Man of the People: A Life of Harry S. Truman*. Oxford UP, 1995.

Holbrook, Thomas M. "Did the Whistle-Stop Campaign Matter?" *PS: Political Science and Politics,* vol. 35, no. 1, Mar. 2002, pp. 59–66.

Karabell, Zachary. *The Last Campaign: How Harry Truman Won the 1948 Election*. Alfred A. Knopf, 2000.

McCullough, David. *Truman*. Simon and Schuster, 1992.

McDonald, Daniel G., et al. "The Spiral of Silence in the 1948 Presidential Election." *Communication Research,* vol. 28, no. 2, Apr. 2001, pp. 139–55.

"1948: The Great Truman Surprise." *The Press and the Presidency*, Dept. of Political Science and International Affairs, Kennesaw State U, 29 Oct. 2003, kennesaw.edu/pols.3380/pres/1984.html. Accessed 10 Apr. 2012.

"1948 Truman-Dewey Election." *American Political History,* Eagleton Institute of Politics, Rutgers, State U of New

Jersey, 1995-2012, www.eagleton.rutgers.edu/research
/americanhistory/ap_trumandewey.php. Accessed 18
Apr. 2012.

Photo of Truman is San Francisco. "The Next President Travels
by Ferry Boat over the Broad Waters of San Francisco Bay."
*Life*, 1 Nov. 1948, p. 37. *Google Books*, books.google.com
/books?id=ekoEAAAAMBAJ&printsec=frontcover#v
=onepage&q&f=false. Accessed 20 Apr. 2012.

Rollins, Byron. "President Truman with *Chicago Daily Tribune*
Headline of 'Dewey Defeats Truman.' " Associated Press,
4 Nov. 1948. *Harry S. Truman Library & Museum,* www
.trumanlibrary.org/photographs/view.php?id=25248.
Accessed 20 Apr. 2012.

Roper, Elmo. "Roper Eats Crow; Seeks Reason for Vote Upset."
*Evening Independent,* 6 Nov. 1948, p. 10. *Google News,* news
.google.com/newspapers?nid=PZE8UkGerEcC&dat
=19481106&printsec=frontpage&hl=en. Accessed 13
Apr. 2012.

Smith, Richard Norton. *Thomas E. Dewey and His Times*. Simon
and Schuster, 1982.

T.R.B. "Washington Wire." *The New Republic,* 15 Nov. 1948,
pp.3-4. *EBSCOhost,* search.ebscohost.com/login.aspx?direct
=true&db=tsh&AN=14779640&site=ehost-live.
Accessed 20 Apr. 2012

Truman, Harry S. "Campaigning, Letter, October 5, 1948."
*Harry S. Truman,* edited by Robert H. Ferrell, CQ P,
2003, p. 91.

A range of dates is given for web projects developed over a period of time.

Every source used is in the list of works cited.

# PERMISSIONS ACKNOWLEDGMENTS

## IMAGES

p. 486: Evan Agostini/Invision/AP Photo; p. 490: Julia Xanthos/New York Daily News; p. 492: Aaron M. Sprecher via AP; p. 496: photo by Kiyash Monsef; p. 498: Sandy Huffaker/Zuma Press; p. 499: Joshua Lott/Getty Image; p. 502: Blake Fitch Photographs; p. 508: W.W. Norton video; p. 516: Carlos M. Saavedra/Sports Illustrated/Getty Images; p. 517: Shelby Daniel/ Icon SMI/ Newscom; p. 521: Photo by Jeff Siner; p. 523: ZUMA Press, Inc. / Alamy Stock Photo; p. 528: © Judy Sirota Rosenthal; p. 542: Granger Collection; p. 553: Granger Collection; p. 558: Photo Researchers/Alamy Stock Photo; p. 561: Alexander Helser/FPG/Archive Photos/Getty Images; p. 565: Everett Collection Historical/Alamy Stock Photo; p. 571: Lee Lockwood//Time Life Pictures/Getty Images; p. 607: Bettmann/Getty Images.

# GLOSSARY/INDEX

—•⟩————————————⟨•—

## A

**Abstract, 47, 67, 72, 76, 174, 180** Generally, having to do with essences and ideas: Liberty, truth, and beauty are abstract concepts. Most writers depend upon abstractions to some degree; however, abstractions that are not fleshed out with vivid particulars are unlikely to hold a reader's interest. See also **CONCRETE**.

**Addison, Liz 476**

*Ain't I a Woman?* (Truth), 558

*All Seven Deadly Sins Committed at Church Bake Sale* (*The Onion*), 190

**Allusion** A passing reference to a work, person, place, or event. Allusions are an efficient means of enlarging the scope and implications of a statement. They work best, of course, when they refer to works most readers are likely to know.

**Analogy, 471, 484** A **COMPARISON** that explains aspects of something unfamiliar by likening it to something that is more familiar. In **EXPOSITORY** writing, analogies are used as aids to explanation and as organizing devices. In a **PERSUASIVE** essay, a writer may argue that what is true in one case is also true in the similar case that he or she is advancing.

---

This Glossary/Index defines key terms and concepts and directs you to pages in the book where they are used or discussed. Terms set in **SMALL CAPITALS** are defined elsewhere in the glossary/index.

An **ARGUMENT** "by analogy" is only as strong as the terms of the analogy are close.

**Anecdote, 125, 176** A brief **NARRATIVE** or humorous story, often told for the purpose of **EXEMPLIFYING** or explaining a larger point. Anecdotal evidence is proof based on such stories rather than on statistical or scientific inquiry.

**Argument, 6, 27, 41, 420, 461–74, 541** An argument makes a case or proves a point. It seeks to convince someone to act in a certain way or to believe in the truth or validity of a statement or **CLAIM**. According to traditional definitions of argumentation and persuasion, a writer can convince a reader in one of three ways: by appealing to reason, by appealing to the reader's emotions, or by appealing to the reader's sense of ethics.

**Arp, Robert, 481**

**Audience, 18, 28, 33–34, 72, 125, 177–78, 222, 277–78, 321, 369, 420, 421–22, 461, 465** The people to whom a piece of writing is addressed. Writers are more likely to achieve their purpose in writing if they keep the needs and expectations of their audience in mind throughout the writing process when making choices about topics, **DICTION**, support, and so on. For example, an essay written for athletes that attacks the use of performance-enhancing drugs in sports might emphasize the hazards of taking steroids. On the other hand, an essay with the same **PURPOSE** but written for an audience of sports fans might focus more on the value of fair play and of having heroes who are drug-free.

**Definition, 6, 41, 61–62, 125, 365–73** A basic strategy of **EXPOSITORY** writing. Definitions give the essential meaning of something. *Extended* definitions enlarge on that basic meaning by analyzing the qualities, recalling the history, explaining the purpose, or giving **SYNONYMS** of whatever is being defined. See the introduction to Chapter 11 for further discussion of this strategy.

**Description, 6, 16, 25, 40, 57, 67–76, 540** One of four **PATTERNS**. Description appeals to the senses: it tells how something looks, feels, sounds, smells, or tastes. An *objective* description focuses on verifiable facts and the observable physical details of a subject, whereas a *subjective* description conveys the writer's thoughts and feelings about a subject, in addition to its physical characteristics. See Chapter 5 for further discussion of the descriptive mode.

**Desmond, Matthew, 206**

**Dialogue, 123, 128–29** Direct speech, especially between two or more speakers in a **NARRATIVE**, quoted word for word.

**Díaz, Junot, 146**

**Diction** Word choice. Mark Twain was talking about diction when he said that the difference between the almost right word and the right word is the difference "between the lightning bug and the lightning." *Standard* diction is defined by dictionaries and other authorities as the language taught in schools and used in the national media. *Nonstandard* diction includes words like *ain't* that are generally not used in formal writing. *Slang* includes informal language such as *bonkers* and *weirdo*, or *dough* for money, and *garbage* for nonsense. Slang words often pass quickly into the standard language or just as quickly fade away. *Colloquial diction* is the language of informal speech or writing: *I'm crazy about you, Virginia*. *Regional* language is that spoken in certain geographic areas—for example, *remuda*, a word for a herd of riding horses, is used in the Southwest. *Obsolete* language includes terms like *pantaloons* and *palfrey* (saddle horse) that were once standard but are no longer used.

*Dollar-Store Economy, The* (Hitt), 242

**Dominant impression, 16, 69–74** In **DESCRIPTIVE** writing, the main impression of a subject that a writer creates through the use of carefully selected details.

*Dreamland* (Quinones), 85

# E

*English Is a Crazy Language* (Lederer), 200

**Etymology, 367–68, 372** A word's history or the practice of tracing such histories. The modern English word *march*, for example, is derived from the French *marcher* ("to walk"), which in turn is derived from the Latin word *marcus* ("a hammer"). The etymological definition of *march* is thus "to walk with a measured tread, like the rhythmic pounding of a hammer." In most dictionaries, the derivation, or etymology, of a word is explained in parentheses or brackets before the first definition is given.

**Evidence, 34, 38, 43–44, 461, 465–66, 541** Proof; the facts and figures, examples, expert testimony, personal experience, and other support that a writer provides in order to make a point.

**Example, 6, 27, 40, 58–59, 173–82, 420** A specific instance of a general group or idea. Among "things that have given males a bad name," for example, humorist Dave Barry cites "violent crime, war, spitting, and ice hockey." See the introduction to Chapter 7 for more on using examples in writing.

**Exposition, 6** One of the four **PATTERNS OF WRITING**. Expository writing is informative writing. It explains or gives directions. All the items in this glossary are written in the expository mode; and most of the practical prose that you write in the coming years will be—e.g., papers and examinations, job applications, business reports, insurance claims, your last will and testament.

*Extraordinary Characteristics of Dyslexia, The* (Horner), 401

# F

*F-16 Pilot Was Ready to Give Her Life on Sept. 11* (Hendrix), 138

reduced his native Ireland to extreme poverty. His intent was to point out the greed of many of his countrymen and thereby shame them all into looking out for the public welfare. This desire to correct vices and follies distinguishes *satire* from *sarcasm*, which is intended primarily to wound. See also **IRONY**.

*Se Habla Español* (Barrientos), 388
*Second Inaugural Address* (Lincoln), 561

**Second person, 272, 280–81** See **POINT OF VIEW**.

**Secondary source, 578** Sources such as books and articles, reviews, biographies, and other works that interpret or discuss primary sources. For example, novels and poems are primary sources; articles interpreting them are secondary sources.

**Setting, 121** The physical place or scene in which an action or event occurs, especially important in **NARRATIVE** and **DESCRIPTIVE** writing.

*She* (Treacy), 375
*Should Batman Kill the Joker?* (White and Arp), 481

**Simile, 17, 69, 74** A **COMPARISON** that likens one thing to another, usually with *like* or *as*. See **FIGURES OF SPEECH**.

*So, You Want to Be a Writer? Here's How.* (Goodman), 300
Soto, Gary, 350
Sotomayor, Sonia, 454
*Splitting Hairs* (Moradi), 284
Steinbach, Alice, 98
*Stop Coddling the Super-Rich* (Buffett), 253

**Style, 18, 27–31** The kind of language you use and the way you arrange words, sentences, and punctuation to achieve a desired effect, whether it's coming across as formal or informal, personal or impersonal, or something else.

**Subject, 20, 34** A broad field of inquiry. A subject is narrowed down by choosing a **TOPIC**, a specific area within a subject that can be the focus of the composition you are writing.

**Subjective, 68, 72** A **DESCRIPTION** that presents the writer's personal response to the subject.

**Summary, 5, 43, 541** A restatement, in your own words, of the most important point(s) of a text.

Sussman, Robert Wald, 264
Swift, Jonathan, 542

**Syllogism, 468** The basic form of **DEDUCTIVE** reasoning, in which a conclusion is drawn from a major (or wider) premise or assumption and a minor (or narrower) premise. For example, *Major premise*: All men are mortal. *Minor premise*: Socrates is a man. *Conclusion:* Socrates is mortal.

**Synonym, 367, 371** A word or phrase that has essentially the same meaning as that of another word or phrase: for example, *make do* or *get by* for *cope*.

# T

*Taking My Parents to College* (Crucet), 336
Tan, Amy, 234
Tannen, Deborah, 356

**Thesis, 20–24, 38–39, 73, 127, 179, 225, 280, 324, 371, 423** The main point that a paragraph or an essay is intended to make or prove. A *thesis statement* is a direct statement of that point.

**Third person, 123, 128** See **POINT OF VIEW**.

**Tone, 27–28, 369, 472** An author's attitude toward his or her subject or audience: sympathy, longing, amusement, shock, sarcasm—the range is endless. When analyzing the tone of a passage, consider what quality of voice you would use in reading it aloud.

**Topic, 20, 34** A specific area within a **SUBJECT** that is written about in a text.

**Topic sentence, 53–55** A sentence, often at the beginning of a paragraph, that states the paragraph's main point. The details in the rest of the paragraph should support the topic sentence.

**Transitions, 55–57, 128, 181, 280** Connecting words or phrases—such as *next, by contrast, nevertheless, therefore, on the other hand*—that link sentences, paragraphs, and ideas in a piece of writing.